Register Now for
to Your E

SPRINGER PUBLISHING COMPANY
CONNECT™

Your print purchase of *Global Aging, Second Edition* **includes online access to the contents of your book**—increasing accessibility, portability, and searchability!

Access today at:
http://connect.springerpub.com/content/book/978-0-8261-6254-0
or scan the QR code at the right with your smartphone and enter the access code below.

B5NC0CLM

Scan here for quick access.

SPRINGER PUBLISHING COMPANY

View all our products at springerpub.com

Frank J. Whittington, PhD, is professor emeritus of gerontology, Department of Social Work, at George Mason University, and professor emeritus of sociology at Georgia State University (GSU), where he was both a faculty member (1973–1995) and director (1995–2008) of the Gerontology Institute. His research interests focus on the social dimensions of health and health care of older persons, especially African Americans. His publications include 11 books and more than 60 articles and chapters on health behavior, medication use, long-term care, and global aging. Based on research funded by the National Institute on Aging, he coauthored, with five colleagues at the GSU Gerontology Institute, *Communities of Care: Assisted Living for African Americans* (2005). More recent projects include *The International Handbook on Aging*, coedited with Erdman Palmore of Duke University and Suzanne Kunkel of Miami University, and the first edition of *Global Aging: Comparative Perspectives on Aging and the Life Course*, coauthored with Suzanne Kunkel and Scott Brown of Miami University. Dr. Whittington has served as the president of the Southern Gerontological Society, from which he received the Gordon Streib Academic Gerontologist Award in 2009; he also received the 2010 Clark Tibbitts Award for outstanding contributions to academic gerontology from the Association for Gerontology in Higher Education.

Suzanne R. Kunkel, PhD, is University Distinguished Professor of Gerontology and executive director of the Scripps Gerontology Center at Miami University. Her research is broadly focused on the social determinants of health, including the system of programs and services designed to support older adults in their goals to remain healthy, active, and engaged in their communities for as long as they choose. Dr. Kunkel has been involved in large-scale projects to assess the implementation and effectiveness of these programs, including innovations such as consumer self-direction and dementia-friendly communities, and the role of cross-sectoral organizational partnerships in enhancing population health. She has served as the principal investigator or the coprincipal investigator on grant-funded projects totaling more than $7 million; she has published more than 45 articles, books, and book chapters and more than 30 research monographs on the Aging Network, innovations in the delivery of home care, population projections, global aging, and gerontology education. Dr. Kunkel is a coauthor (with Leslie Morgan) of *Aging, Society, and the Life Course*, a gerontology textbook in its fifth edition and currently being revised for a sixth edition with Rick Settersten. With Frank Whittington and Erdman Palmore, she coedited the most recent edition of the *International Handbook on Aging*. She is a fellow of both the Gerontological Society of America and the Association for Gerontology in Higher Education (AGHE); she has served as the president of AGHE, and she is currently the treasurer of the Gerontological Society of America.

Kate de Medeiros, PhD, is the O'Toole Family Professor of Gerontology in the Department of Sociology and Gerontology and a Scripps Research Fellow at Miami University. Dr. de Medeiros's research is broadly focused on understanding the experience of later life using narratives and other qualitative and mixed-methods approaches. Research topics include storying later life, the meaning of home, suffering in old age, generativity, moral development in later life, and friendships and social connectivity among people living with dementia. She has authored or coauthored more than 45 research articles and book chapters and is the author of two books on aging—*The Short Guide to Aging and Gerontology* (2017) and *Narrative Gerontology in Research and Practice* (Springer Publishing Company, 2013)—and is the series editor for the series, *The Humanities and Later Life: Exploring Contexts and Meanings of Growing Old*. Working with The Hastings Center for bioethics, she recently coedited a special volume, *What Makes a Good Life in Late Life: Citizenship and Justice in Aging Societies*. Her research has been funded by the National Institutes of Health, the Alzheimer's Association, and the Brookdale Foundation.

GLOBAL AGING

Comparative Perspectives on Aging and the Life Course

Second Edition

Frank J. Whittington, PhD
Suzanne R. Kunkel, PhD
Kate de Medeiros, PhD

SPRINGER PUBLISHING COMPANY

Springer Publishing Company, LLC
11 West 42nd Street
New York, NY 10036
www.springerpub.com
http://connect.springerpub.com/home

Acquisitions Editor: Kate Dimock
Compositor: Exeter Premedia Services Private Ltd.

ISBN: 978-0-8261-6253-3
ebook ISBN: 978-0-8261-6254-0
DOI: 10.1891/9780826162540

Qualified instructors may request supplements by emailing textbook@springerpub.com
Instructor's Manual ISBN: 978-0-8261-6247-2
Instructor's PowerPoints ISBN: 978-0-8261-6248-9

19 20 21 22 / 5 4 3 2 1

The author and the publisher of this Work have made every effort to use sources believed to be reliable to
provide information that is accurate and compatible with the standards generally accepted at the time of publication. The author and publisher shall not be liable for any special, consequential, or exemplary damages
resulting, in whole or in part, from the readers' use of, or reliance on, the information contained in this book.
The publisher has no responsibility for the persistence or accuracy of URLs for external or third-party Internet
websites referred to in this publication and does not guarantee that any content on such websites is, or will
remain, accurate or appropriate.

Cataloging-in-Publication Data is available from the Library of Congress.
LCCN: 2019043578

Contact us to receive discount rates on bulk purchases.
We can also customize our books to meet your needs.
For more information please contact: sales@springerpub.com

Publisher's Note: **New and used products purchased from third-party sellers are not guaranteed for quality,
authenticity, or access to any included digital components.**

Printed in the United States of America.

CONTENTS

CONTRIBUTORS

Fauzia Erfan Ahmed, PhD, Associate Professor, Department of Sociology and Gerontology, Miami University, Oxford, Ohio

Robert Applebaum, PhD, Professor, Scripps Gerontology Center and Department of Sociology and Gerontology, Miami University, Oxford, Ohio

Jaye Atkinson, PhD, Associate Professor and Associate Chair, Department of Communication, Georgia State University, Atlanta, Georgia

Anthony Bardo, PhD, Assistant Professor, Department of Sociology, University of Kentucky, Lexington, Kentucky

Barbra J. Brottman, BA, Graduate Research Assistant, Department of Sociology and Gerontology, Miami University, Oxford, Ohio

Paulo Renato Canineu, Laboratory of Neuroscience, Department and Institute of Psychiatry, Faculty of Medicine, Sao Paulo, SP, Brazil

Jasleen K. Chahal, MSG, Grants Program Manager, UK Health Care CECentral, University of Kentucky, Lexington, Kentucky; Doctoral Candidate, Department of Sociology and Gerontology, Miami University, Oxford, Ohio

Adrienne Chang, MA, Graduate Student, Department of Sociology and Gerontology, Miami University, Oxford, Ohio

Habib Chaudhury, PhD, Professor, Department of Gerontology, Simon Fraser University, Vancouver, Canada

Tatiana Cojocari, Faculty of Sociology and Social Work, University of Bucharest, Bucharest, Romania

Phyllis Cummins, PhD, Senior Research Scholar, Scripps Gerontology Center, Miami University, Oxford, Ohio

Stephen J. Cutler, PhD, Professor of Sociology, University of Vermont, Burlington, Vermont; and Faculty of Sociology and Social Work, University of Bucharest, Bucharest, Romania

Jouce Gabriela de Almeida, Laboratory of Neuroscience, Department and Institute of Psychiatry, Faculty of Medicine, Sao Paulo, SP, Brazil

Oksana Dikhtyar, MBA, Graduate Research Assistant, Department of Sociology and Gerontology, Miami University, Oxford, Ohio

Marvin Formosa, PhD, Associate Professor, Department of Gerontology and Dementia Studies, Faculty for Social Wellbeing, University of Malta, Msida, Malta

Emily Hautz, PhD, Adjunct Instructor, Department of Sociology and Gerontology, Miami University, Oxford, Ohio

Oliver Hautz, PhD, CEO, Grafschafter Diakonie gGmbH – Diakonisches Werk Kirchenreis Moers, Moers, Germany

Kathryn Hyer, PhD, Professor, School of Aging Studies, Florida Policy Exchange Center on Aging, University of South Florida, Tampa, Florida

Jennifer M. Kinney, PhD, Professor, Department of Sociology and Gerontology, and Research Fellow, Scripps Gerontology Center, Miami University, Oxford, Ohio

Kathrin Komp-Leukkunen, PhD, Associate Professor, Faculty of Social Sciences, University of Helsinki, Finland

Mahmood Messkoub, PhD (Econs.), Senior Lecturer, International Institute of Social Studies, Erasmus University of Rotterdam, The Hague, The Netherlands

Nader Mehri, MA, PhD Student, Department of Sociology and Gerontology, Miami University, Oxford, Ohio

Roberto Millar, MA, Gerontology Doctoral Candidate, University of Maryland, Baltimore County, Baltimore, Maryland

Samuel M. Mwangi, PhD, Lecturer, Department of Sociology, Gender and Development Studies, Kenyatta University, Nairobi, Kenya

Holly Nelson-Becker, PhD, LCSW, Professor of Social Work and Division Lead, College of Health and Life Sciences, Department of Clinical Sciences, Brunel University London, Uxbridge, United Kingdom

Candidus Nwakasi, MS, Graduate Research Assistant, Department of Sociology and Gerontology, Miami University, Oxford, Ohio

Lindsay J. Peterson, PhD, Assistant Professor, School of Aging Studies, University of South Florida, Tampa, Florida

Senjooti Roy, PhD, Postdoctoral Research Fellow, Louis and Gabi Weisfeld School of Social Work, Bar-Ilan University, Ramat Gan, Israel

Rachael M. Scicluna, PhD, Visiting Lecturer, Department of Anthropological Sciences, Faculty of Arts, University of Malta, Msida, Malta

Kishore Seetharaman, MS, Doctoral Student, Department of Gerontology, Simon Fraser University, Vancouver, Canada

Florindo Stella, MD, Laboratory of Neuroscience, Department and Institute of Psychiatry, Faculty of Medicine, Sao Paulo, SP, Brazil

Janardan Subedi, PhD, Professor, Department of Sociology and Gerontology, Miami University, Oxford, Ohio

Mark Tausig, PhD, Emeritus Professor, Department of Sociology and Gerontology, Miami University, Oxford, Ohio

Noriko Tsukada, PhD, Professor, College of Commerce, Nihon University, Tokyo, Japan

Eleanor van den Heuvel, MSC, DTPs, Research Fellow, Member – Institute of Environment, Health and Societies – Ageing Theme, College of Health and Life Sciences, Brunel University London, Uxbridge, United Kingdom

Elizabeth Wilson, PhD, Professor, Department of Comparative Religion, Miami University, Oxford, Ohio

Takashi Yamashita, PhD, MPH, MA, Associate Professor, Department of Sociology, Anthropology, and Health Administration and Policy, University of Maryland, Baltimore County, Baltimore, Maryland

PREFACE

Since the publication of the first edition of this textbook in 2014, much has happened in the world to change the way people live and age. As we approach a revision, we cannot, of course, catalogue all those changes and their effects, or even most of them. We will leave it to you, the reader, to recall the massive waves of desperate people immigrating from Africa and the Middle East to Europe and from Latin America to the United States; the U.S. presidential election of 2016; the United Kingdom's vote to exit the European Union; the typhoons, hurricanes, and tsunami that devastated Japan, the Philippines, South Asia, Puerto Rico, Haiti, and Mexico; and the political, social, and human effects on all nations of terrorism, war, and famine, wherever in the world they occurred.

One thing that has not changed in the past 6 years is population aging; it is still a universal and consequential phenomenon. In fact, as reported in 2014, for the first time in human history, people aged 60 and older outnumbered children younger than age 5, and we still can foresee a day when those older adults will be more numerous than children younger than age 15. This truly revolutionary situation—expected to occur within the next four decades—will demand a completely different political, economic, and social response from all national governments.

As a result, the field of gerontology continues to expand in every corner of the world and is becoming increasingly internationalized. The inclusion of cross-national content in gerontology curricula and major journals and the development of gerontology education programs in many countries are indicative of a still-growing worldwide interest in aging. This interest is driven, in part, by the undeniable demands an aging population places on a society—for policies and programs designed to meet the unique needs and utilize the potential contributions of an older population, for a workforce trained to fulfill those needs, and for citizens educated about their own aging and the issues of an aging world.

The major change in the book's content was done consciously: We decided to seek greater balance between the two overarching concepts in social science—structure and culture. We love demography and believe population aging remains a hugely powerful global force, so it is not slighted in this second edition. We have reduced its overall weight within the book, however, as we have paid more heed to cultural forces, such as values, norms, beliefs, and emotions. The result, we believe, is a more accurate picture of the everyday lives of older people around the world, even as their existence is being altered in major ways by structural and demographic forces they cannot see or understand.

Flowing from this shift is another that involves the book's authorship. As you may have noted, our colleague, Scott Brown, who contributed so much to the first edition, is no longer involved with this edition. In his place, we asked another Miami colleague, Kate de Medeiros, to join us. Kate is a gerontologist trained in anthropological and qualitative methods who has devoted her career to the study and teaching of a variety of gerontological topics, including assessment of and care for people living with dementia in multicultural settings, the development of gerontology as an independent discipline, and various perspectives from older persons on the experience of growing old. Kate brings to this project a keen understanding of social science methods and data and a perceptive skill and creativity in explaining complex data to students. Her deep appreciation of the importance and power of culture infuses this book to the benefit of us all.

As for the first edition, the intended audiences for this text remain students in undergraduate and graduate courses in global aging and their faculty. In addition, many of the topics addressed herein will also be of interest to faculty and students in undergraduate and graduate courses in the demography of aging and sociology of aging, as well as courses in gerontology taught with a comparative, international focus. We hope also that it will serve to focus the attention of all gerontologists on the growth and value of the research and teaching going on in countries outside the United States and Europe. The importance and value of cross-national research is another key theme of the book. Until we incorporate findings from research on non-Western, non-White samples of aging people living in less developed areas of the world, we will not have a deep or accurate understanding of how all people and societies age.

This edition of the book, like the first, provides an overview of major issues associated with societal and global aging, paralleling the structure of many introductory social gerontology textbooks. Unlike most existing textbooks in the field, however, the discussion of each topic in this work is explicitly comparative, focusing on similarities and variations in the aging experience across nations, regions, and levels of economic and social development. The text is organized thematically, with examples from around the world embedded throughout the narrative where they are available and appropriate. The comparative perspective is enhanced further by topical essays and country-specific descriptions of aging policies, programs, and experiences, about which more will be said in the following.

We also introduce in this edition several important innovations not found in the previous version. First, we have dropped two chapters ("The Welfare State" and "Disability and Active Life Expectancy"), incorporating their content elsewhere. In addition, we split three earlier chapters ("Health and Health Care Systems"; "Work and Retirement"; and "Families, Caregiving, and Community Support Systems") into two new chapters each, so now we include six separate chapters: (a) "Health Patterns and Behavior", (b) "Health Care Systems," (c) "Older Workers," (d) "Retirement and Pensions," (e) "Families," and (f) "Caregiving." Finally, because the first edition neglected two topics crucial to the lives of older people—physical environments and religion—we have added an entirely new chapter devoted to each. All chapters have been rethought, reorganized, and updated with as much new data and findings as we could manage.

This new volume opens, as did the first, with an overview of aging in global perspective (Chapter 1, Our Aging World), introducing and explaining the crucial concept of culture and its effect on the status and role of older people in a given society. Chapter 2, The Study of Global Aging, follows with a description of what comparative research is and how it is done. Chapter 3, Demographic Perspectives on an Aging World, explains how demographic forces behind population aging are affecting the welfare state in both developed and developing nations and is followed by the new chapter, Chapter 4, Aging Environments, on how aging unfolds in, and is affected by, specific environments. The environment is seen as both a physical place—buildings and cities with a particular climate—and the social constructs of families and communities. We devote three chapters to the substantial issue of aging and health. Chapter 5, Health Patterns and Behavior, focuses on health and disability as an individual status and on the individual's experience of illness, showing how the older person behaves when sick and whether help is sought and medical advice is followed. Chapter 6, Health Care Systems, features an in-depth discussion of different models of providing health care and the major public health issues in both the more developed and less developed countries, whereas Chapter 7, Long-Term Services and Supports, presents a typology of the different national policies and programs that provide long-term services and supports for older adults with significant chronic health conditions. In Chapter 8, Older Workers, we turn to another vital concern of older people in every country—the issue of work and its relationship to the income needed to live. Following that is a chapter (Chapter 9, Retirement and Pensions) devoted to the topic of retirement from work and the different pension policies enacted by countries to provide for people after their work lives end. Chapter 10, Families, discusses another universal topic: how families address the aging of their members and how older family members can continue to play an active, productive role in the lives of their families. As promised, an entirely new chapter (Chapter 11, Caregiving), is aimed at explaining the struggles of both families and societies with the issues surrounding caregiving for disabled and chronically ill elders. Chapter 12, World Religions and Aging, the new chapter on religion, describes how the five major world religions—Christianity, Judaism, Islam, Buddhism, and Hinduism—view age and aging and how their older believers are treated. Finally, in Chapter 13, Global Aging and Global Leadership, we identify 13 major themes of the book and describe how the world community—through the United Nations and nongovernmental organizations—is responding to the burdens that economic and demographic changes are placing on older people and their families. We conclude the chapter with a call to readers for global leadership—on both aging concerns and beyond.

We undertook the first edition of this text with considerable experience as gerontological researchers and educators and with confidence that we were up to the task. However, we quickly learned that the content of an adequate book on this subject was already far beyond our expectations. We realized that the scope of work would be much broader—and take longer—than we had first imagined, and that scope has only become more broad and challenging to capture over the intervening 6 years. The pace of international research and publication has, if anything, quickened during that recent period to the point where we can truly say a global science of gerontology is quickly emerging.

Another lesson learned from the first edition, especially as reported by instructors who have used the book as a text, is that few of today's students are as aware of the names and locations of the nations of the world as we might like or the political histories that have shaped current policies and perspectives. In fact, we must admit that none of the authors could locate on a map every country mentioned in the book. Therefore, as an aid to the reader (and to us, the writers), we are following this preface with a table listing all countries, grouped by continent and with the latest population count of each. We encourage each of you to use the following link to access a current map of the world: https://www.mapsofworld.com/world-map-image.html.

As with the first edition, we gratefully acknowledge that, without the able assistance of many, many people, we could not have completed this revision. Chief among these are several wonderful colleagues who undertook leading or sharing authorship with us as we revised some of the chapters. For their contributions, we offer our most sincere appreciation. In the first edition, we scattered nine short essays throughout the book, one in almost every chapter, each illustrating interesting issues in a specific country. The invited essay authors were colleagues and former students who were able to provide distinctive perspectives on specific topics, each of which was related to the chapter in which it was embedded. As we reimagined this new edition, we decided to expand on these unique perspectives by increasing their overall number in the book, so now we include 21 such essays, with most chapters including two. Six of the original nine essays have been retained and updated for the second edition, and 15 new ones have been commissioned and added. Again, we have called upon some of our colleagues, former colleagues, students, and former students to contribute an essay on a topic they have studied, written about, taught, and know well; most are native to the country about which they write, and many currently live there. We sincerely appreciate our essay authors' cultural insight, their deep knowledge of their topic, and their eloquence. The book would not have been as good without their contributions.

The work of all these contributors has made this a much better book, but the assistance of several other people who have supported our efforts along the way has also made this possible. We acknowledge and thank Amanda Baer at George Mason University and a long list of graduate assistants, support staff, and colleagues at Miami University for their valuable help with this project. We wish also to express our heartfelt gratitude to Sheri W. Sussman, our first-edition editor at Springer, for helping us bring that volume to press and this one to life. Our appreciation for Sheri's faith in us and in our project is as unstinting as she herself was in her encouragement and support. We will never forget her contributions to these two books. Sheri's editorial role has been ably and beautifully assumed by Kate

Dimock, who, with the team at Springer—Mindy Chen, Mehak Massand, Rachel Haines, Haydee Hidalgo, Joseph Stubenrauch, Joanne Jay, and Cindy Yoo—has been unfailingly helpful and encouraging. To each of them we owe a huge debt for both their technical expertise and patient understanding.

To the rest of you who have known of our work, adopted it as a textbook in your courses or simply used it as one of the few reference sources on global gerontology, and waited patiently for this updated installment, we again offer apologies for taking so long. As we did 6 years ago in the preface to the first edition, we paraphrase Penny Wharvey McGill (a character in one of our favorite Homeric classics, the American movie, *O Brother, Where Art Thou?*): people (and books) should be, must be, *bona fide*. We agree and have done all we can to ensure this one, like the other one, is bona fide, authentic, certified, *pukka* (Hindi), *echt* (German and Yiddish), and *dinkum* (Australian and New Zealander). We hope it again meets your expectations, but especially those of your students. We recognize that, as U.S. authors, we are undoubtedly presenting a clearly American perspective despite our best efforts to be broad in our thinking and approach. If we have fallen short in any way, we sincerely apologize and remain anxious to hear about our book's shortcomings, with the aim of improving our effort if there may someday be a third iteration. Of course, if you do think we have done justice to your region or country and have captured the essence of aging around the world, and if your students are as captivated as we are by the amazing diversity of the ageways of the peoples of the world and wish to know more, then we will be even more grateful to know it—and far more satisfied.

Frank J. Whittington, PhD
Suzanne R. Kunkel, PhD
Kate de Medeiros, PhD

Qualified instructors may obtain access to supplementary material (Instructor's Manual and PowerPoints) by emailing textbook@springerpub.com.

LIST OF COUNTRIES

Countries of the World: Their Continents and Populations*

Country	Continent/Area	Population (in Millions)
Afghanistan	Asia	34.9
Albania	Europe	3.1
Algeria	Africa	41.7
Angola	Africa	30.4
Antigua and Barbuda	Caribbean	0.096 (96,000)
Argentina	South America	44.7
Armenia	Asia	3.0
Australia	Australia	23.5
Austria	Europe	8.8
Azerbaijan	Asia	10.0
Bahamas	Caribbean	0.3
Bahrain	Asia	1.4
Bangladesh	Asia	159.5
Barbados	Caribbean	0.3
Belarus	Asia	9.5
Belgium	Europe	11.6
Belize	Central America	0.4
Benin	Africa	11.3
Bhutan	Asia	0.8
Bolivia	South America	11.3
Bosnia/Herzegovina	Europe	3.8
Botswana	Africa	2.2
Brazil	South America	208.8

(continued)

Country	Continent/Area	Population (in Millions)
Brunei/Darussalam	Asia	0.5
Bulgaria	Europe	7.1
Burkina Faso	Africa	19.7
Burma (Myanmar)	Asia	55.6
Burundi	Africa	11.8
Cambodia	Asia	16.4
Cameroon	Africa	25.6
Canada	North America	35.9
Central African Republic	Africa	5.7
Chad	Africa	15.8
Chile	South America	17.9
China	Asia	1,384.7 (1.38 billion)
Colombia	South America	48.2
Congo	Africa	5.1
Costa Rica	Central America	5.0
Cote d'Ivoire (Ivory Coast)	Africa	26.3
Croatia	Europe	4.3
Cuba	Caribbean	11.1
Cyprus	Europe	1.2
Czechia (Czech Republic)	Europe	10.7
Democratic Republic of the Congo	Africa	85.3
Denmark	Europe	5.8
Djibouti	Africa	0.9
Dominica	Caribbean	0.074 (74,000)
Dominican Republic	Caribbean	10.3
Ecuador	South America	16.5
Egypt	Africa	99.4
El Salvador	Central America	6.2
Equatorial Guinea	Africa	0.8

(*continued*)

Country	Continent/Area	Population (in Millions)
Eritrea	Africa	6.0
Estonia	Europe	1.2
Ethiopia	Africa	108.4
Fiji	Pacific	0.9
Finland	Europe	5.5
France	Europe	67.4
Gabon	Africa	2.1
Gambia	Africa	2.1
Gaza Strip	Middle East	1.8
Georgia	Europe	4.0
Germany	Europe	80.5
Ghana	Africa	28.1
Greece	Europe	10.8
Greenland	Europe	0.06 (57,000)
Grenada	Caribbean	0.1
Guatemala	Central America	16.6
Guinea	Africa	11.9
Guinea-Bissau	Africa	1.8
Guyana	South America	0.7
Haiti	Caribbean	10.8
Honduras	Central America	9.2
Hungary	Europe	9.8
Hong Kong	Asia	7.2
Iceland	Europe	0.3
India	Asia	1,296.8 (1.29 billion)
Indonesia	Asia	262.8
Iran	Asia	83.0
Iraq	Asia	40.2
Ireland	Europe	5.1
Israel	Asia	8.4
Italy	Europe	62.2

(continued)

Country	Continent/Area	Population (in Millions)
Jamaica	Caribbean	2.8
Japan	Asia	126.2
Jordan	Asia	10.5
Kazakhstan	Europe	18.7
Kenya	Africa	48.4
Korea, North	Asia	25.4
Korea, South	Asia	51.4
Kuwait	Asia	2.9
Kyrgyzstan	Europe	5.8
Laos	Asia	7.2
Latvia	Europe	1.9
Lebanon	Asia	6.1
Lesotho	Africa	2.0
Liberia	Africa	4.8
Libya	Africa	6.8
Lithuania	Europe	2.8
Luxembourg	Europe	0.6
Macau	Asia	0.6
Macedonia	Europe	2.1
Madagascar	Africa	25.7
Malawi	Africa	19.8
Malaysia	Asia	31.8
Maldives	Asia	0.4
Mali	Africa	18.4
Malta	Europe	0.4
Mauritania	Africa	3.8
Mauritius	Africa	1.4
Mexico	North America	126.0
Moldova	Europe	3.4
Monaco	Europe	0.03
Mongolia	Asia	3.1
Montenegro	Europe	0.6

(continued)

Country	Continent/Area	Population (in Millions)
Morocco	Africa	34.3
Mozambique	Africa	27.2
Myanmar (see Burma)	Asia	55.6
Namibia	Africa	2.5
Nepal	Asia	29.7
Netherlands	Europe	17.2
New Zealand	Pacific	4.5
Nicaragua	Central America	6.1
Niger	Africa	19.9
Nigeria	Africa	203.5
Norway	Europe	5.4
Oman	Asia	4.6
Pakistan	Asia	207.9
Panama	Central America	3.8
Papua New Guinea	Pacific	7.0
Paraguay	South America	7.0
Peru	South America	31.3
Philippines	Pacific	105.9
Poland	Europe	38.4
Portugal	Europe	10.4
Qatar	Asia	2.4
Romania	Europe	21.5
Russia	Europe	142.5
Rwanda	Africa	12.2
Saint Kitts and Nevis	Caribbean	0.05
Saint Lucia	Caribbean	0.2
Saint Vincent and the Grenadines	Caribbean	0.1
Samoa	Pacific	0.2

(*continued*)

Country	Continent/Area	Population (in Millions)
Saudi Arabia	Asia	33.1
Senegal	Africa	15.0
Serbia	Europe	7.1
Seychelles	Africa	0.1
Sierra Leone	Africa	6.3
Singapore	Asia	6.0
Slovakia	Europe	5.4
Slovenia	Europe	2.1
Somalia	Africa	11.3
South Africa	Africa	55.4
Spain	Europe	49.3
Sri Lanka	Asia	22.6
Sudan	Africa	43.9
South Sudan	Africa	10.2
Suriname	South America	0.6
Swaziland	Africa	1.4
Sweden	Europe	10.0
Switzerland	Europe	8.3
Syria	Asia	19.5
Taiwan	Asia	23.5
Tanzania	Africa	55.5
Tajikistan	Europe	8.6
Thailand	Asia	68.6
Tibet	Asia	3.2
Timor-Leste (East Timor)	Asia	1.3
Togo	Africa	8.2
Tonga	Pacific	0.1
Trinidad and Tobago	Caribbean	1.2
Tunisia	Africa	11.5
Turkey	Europe	81.3
Turkmenistan	Europe	5.4
Uganda	Africa	40.9
Ukraine	Europe	43.9

(continued)

Country	Continent/Area	Population (in Millions)
United Arab Emirates	Asia	9.7
United Kingdom	Europe	65.1
United States	North America	329.0
Uruguay	South America	3.4
Uzbekistan	Europe	30.0
Venezuela	South America	31.7
Vietnam	Asia	97.0
West Bank	Middle East	2.8
Western Sahara	Africa	0.6
Yemen	Asia	28.7
Zambia	Africa	16.4
Zimbabwe	Africa	14.0

*Adapted from list of world countries in the U.S. Central Intelligence Agency (CIA) *World Factbook: 2019*. Population figures are estimates as of July 2018.

World Countries
Grouped by Continent and Region

SUB-SAHARAN AFRICA
(N = 46)

Angola	Mali
Benin	Mauritania
Botswana	Mauritius
Burkina Faso	Mozambique
Burundi	Namibia
Cameroon	Niger
Central African Republic	Nigeria
Chad	Republic of the Congo
Democratic Republic of Congo	Rwanda
Djibouti	Senegal
Equatorial Guinea	Seychelles
Eritrea	Sierra Leone
Ethiopia	Somalia

Gabon
Gambia
Ghana
Guinea
Guinea Bissau
Ivory Coast
Kenya
Lesotho
Liberia
Madagascar

South Africa
South Sudan
Sudan
Swaziland
Tanzania
Togo
Uganda
Western Sahara
Zambia
Zimbabwe

ASIA
(N = 37)

Afghanistan
American Samoa
Australia
Azerbaijan
Bangladesh
Bhutan
Brunei
Burma (Myanmar)
Cambodia
China
Hong Kong
India
Indonesia
Japan
Kazakhstan
Kyrgyzstan
Laos
Macau
Malaysia

Maldives
Mongolia
Nepal
New Zealand
North Korea
Pakistan
Philippines
South Korea
Singapore
Sri Lanka
Taiwan
Tajikistan
Thailand
Tibet
Timor-Leste (East Timor)
Turkmenistan
Uzbekistan
Vietnam

CARIBBEAN
(N = 13)

Antigua and Barbuda
Bahamas
Barbados
Cuba

CENTRAL AMERICA
(N = 8)

Belize
Costa Rica
El Salvador
Guatemala

CARIBBEAN (*continued*)

Dominica
Dominican Republic
Grenada
Haiti
Jamaica
Saint Kitts and Nevis
Saint Lucia
Saint Vincent and the Grenadines
Trinidad and Tobago

CENTRAL AMERICA (*continued*)

Honduras
Nicaragua
Panama

EUROPE
(N = 47)

Albania
Austria
Azerbaijan
Belarus
Belgium
Bosnia/Herzegovina
Bulgaria
Cyprus
Czechia (Czech Republic)
Denmark
Estonia
Finland
France
Georgia
Germany
Greece
Greenland
Hungary
Iceland
Ireland
Italy
Kazakhstan
Kyrgyzstan
Latvia
Lithuania
Luxembourg
Macedonia
Malta
Moldova
Monaco
Montenegro
Netherlands
Norway
Poland
Portugal
Romania
Russia
Serbia
Slovakia
Slovenia
Spain
Sweden
Switzerland
Turkmenistan
Ukraine
United Kingdom
Uzbekistan

MIDDLE EAST/NORTH AFRICA
(N = 22)

Algeria	Oman
Bahrain	Palestine
Egypt	Qatar
Gaza Strip	Saudi Arabia
Iran	Sudan
Iraq	Syria
Israel	Tunisia
Jordan	Turkey
Lebanon	United Arab Emirates
Libya	West Bank
Morocco	Yemen

SOUTH AMERICA
(N = 13)

PACIFIC
(N = 7)

Argentina	Fiji
Bolivia	New Zealand
Brazil	Papua/New Guinea
Chile	Philippines
Colombia	Samoa
Ecuador	Solomon Islands
French Guyana	Tonga
Guyana	
Peru	
Paraguay	
Uruguay	
Venezuela	
Suriname	

Link to map: https://www.mapsofworld.com/world-map-image.html

OUR AGING WORLD

INTRODUCTION

For the first time in human history, there are more people in the world who are 60 years of age and older than below 5 years of age, and the world's older population (65+ years) is growing more than twice as fast as the world's total population (U.N. Department of Economic and Social Affairs, Population Division, 2017). In 2017, one in eight people in the world was aged 60 or above. This is predicted to increase to one in six people in 2030 (U.N. Department of Economic and Social Affairs, Population Division, 2017). Some countries already have seen a drastic change in their population's age structure. Japan, for example, has experienced incredible growth in the percentage of its people aged 65 and above, exploding from just 10% in 1985 to 26.5% in 2015 (Kojima et al., 2017). Small, less developed countries, too, like Kenya, have seen a threefold increase in people aged 65 and above in the past 50 years (U.N. Department of Economic and Social Affairs, Population Division, 2017), although Kenya's total percentage of older persons is still comparatively low (5% of the total population). In this opening chapter, we consider several aspects of aging as a global phenomenon, starting with the role of culture in shaping how we view old age and then turning to the far-reaching social and economic impacts of an aging world within countries and across regions.

CULTURE, "OLD AGE," AND AGING

It is important to pause a moment to think about what it means to be "old." "Old age" as a label describing a particular time in one's life may seem familiar at first. After all, each of us knows someone we consider to be "old." However, when we stop to think about how, when, and why we apply the label of "old" to a person or group, old age becomes something much more complex than the number of years a person has lived or his or her physical appearance. "Old" becomes an identity, a judgment, a category, or a right, depending on a variety of social and cultural circumstances. To consider this larger question of "old" in the context of global aging, it is worthwhile to first consider the ways that culture influences stages of life and how those definitions influence one's place in a given society. The cultural framing of old age also includes examining stereotypes and myths associated with later life, terms used to describe older persons, ageism (or the systematic discrimination and devaluation of someone based on age or the appearance of age), and criteria used to define the concept of "old."

Culture and Old Age

Although **culture** is often used to describe the fine and performing arts (e.g., opera, literature, paintings), this book relies on the social science perspective on culture—the unwritten rules one must know to function in a given social group. The anthropologist Clifford Geertz (1973) defined culture as "an historically transmitted pattern of meanings embodied in symbols, a system of inherited conceptions expressed in symbolic forms by means of which [people] communicate, perpetuate, and develop their knowledge about and attitudes toward life" (p. 89). For Geertz and other scholars who study culture, the "rules" of a culture are transmitted and reinforced through the actions of others within the culture. Think, for example, of how you learned to shop for groceries. Most likely, you were not given a formal set of rules or lessons on how to shop for items, pay for them, and package them to take with you. In the United States, shopping generally involves visiting a large grocery store; taking a shopping cart; selecting items based on a preestablished, nonnegotiable price; placing items (sometimes enough to last several days or weeks) in the cart; waiting in line at a cashier to pay; and having a store employee place purchased items in paper or plastic disposable bags. In other countries, people might visit individual food sellers every day for fresh items such as vegetables, eggs, bread, fish, and so on, bringing with them their own bags to take the items home. The buyer and seller may negotiate (sometimes called "haggling") about the price. There may be no lines to wait in (i.e., the most aggressive and determined person wins). As this example illustrates, it may be only when we have an experience outside our cultural expectation that we realize something is "different." The "right" way to do something, like shop for groceries, is so culturally ingrained that we never have bothered to think that other people do it differently.

The same can be said for aging. Cultural definitions of who is "old" are transmitted in very subtle ways, so most people do not give much thought to it. In fact, one way that "aging" has been described is as a cultural interpretation of a biological phenomenon. In other words, biological changes that a person undergoes over time, such as graying hair, wrinkles, and changing vision, are given a cultural meaning. Consider gray hair. Advertising in the United States reinforces the idea that gray hair for women is unattractive. In contrast, advertisements encourage men to keep a "touch of gray" as a sign of distinction and power. In Bangladesh, though, women who have gray hair are associated with power and status, since advancing age is how women assume positions of authority within households (Ahmed, 2014). In short, while gray hair is a product of biological change, the *meaning* of gray hair is culturally determined.

"Old" can be also defined through one's role in society or relationship to others. In the Bangladesh example, higher status may be conferred on people of advancing age not just because of appearance, but because of their position within the household. A woman in Bangladesh builds a family through marriage, children, and grandchildren. Her change in role from daughter-in-law to parent to grandparent further establishes her as "old" (in a positive way), regardless of chronological age.

Chronological Age

Of course, another way that "old" is defined is through chronological age. While the number of birthdays a person has had might seem like a straightforward way of defining the boundaries of "old," chronological age has its challenges. We all have had the experience of meeting someone, making a mental estimate of their age based on appearance or other observable traits, and then being surprised to learn that their chronological age differed from what we thought. This is because chronological age is a poor marker for many things. A person's physical environment (e.g., climate, exposure to harsh conditions), lifestyle choices (e.g., alcohol and tobacco use), and genetics all can influence how a person ages biologically; physical manifestations that may appear to be a reflection of chronological age may, in fact, be determined to a greater degree by things other than the passage of time.

Chronological age became important in the late 19th century during the development of social programs called the "welfare state." For citizens of the United States, the term "welfare" typically connotes a particular kind of government-funded program for people who are poor. However, the "welfare state" is a much broader concept. It describes the collection of social-assistance policies and programs provided by a government that takes the place of support traditionally provided by the family or by religious institutions. Such policies emerged as a result of industrialization and often included public old-age pensions, health care programs, family allowances, sickness and maternity/birth benefits, and unemployment compensation. Eligibility for programs such as when one can start earning a retirement pension (or must mandatorily retire) or the age at which someone is considered an adult is determined by chronological age. Some countries, such as Thailand, have a relatively low mandatory retirement age of 60 (see Social Security Administration, 2014). Many African countries use age 50 as the point when one is officially considered "old" (Naidoo et al., 2010). In the United States and several Western European countries, pension eligibility ages are being raised to reflect increasing life expectancy of retirees. For example, eligibility for Social Security in the United States has recently increased from 65 to 67 and will continue to increase incrementally over the next several years. The same can be said for Germany, where, in 2017, the retirement age was 65, although that age also gradually will be raised over the next several years (Organization for Economic Co-operation and Development [OECD], 2019).

Ageism

Defining "old" is more difficult than one would think. While many people might associate later life with positive qualities such as wisdom or gained experience, more negative views of age—ageism—are present in many cultures. Ageism describes the systematic discrimination of people because of their age or the appearance of age (Cruikshank, 2013). Ageism can be intentional, whereby a person is openly ridiculed or devalued because of his or her age; or unintentional, as when someone thinks they are being kind to an older person by using terms such as "elderly," "senior citizen," or "cute," or calling a person "young lady" when she is clearly not a young lady. In the latter example, making a point of pretending someone is "young" underscores the idea that being "old" is bad or undesirable. Ageism can also be either external, which describes an outsider's behaviors toward someone else, or internal, which occurs when an older or even a middle-aged person uses self-deprecating words as a way of apologizing for being older, such as when a person who forgets a name says they are having a "senior moment." (Cruikshank, 2013). Ageism is problematic because ageist attitudes and portrayals in the media and other forms of popular culture ascribe negative attributes to older people, positioning them as weak, dependent, incompetent, and as somehow "less" than younger people. It is important to keep in mind that ageist portrayals can have negative consequences for older persons. Ageism positions older people as burdens, nullifies positive contributions that people make throughout their life course, and sets up a young/old dichotomy that separates people rather than bringing them together. Because of the pervasiveness and harmful effects of ageism worldwide, the World Health Organization (WHO) has launched a global campaign to combat it (Ayalon & Tesch-Römer, 2018).

Myths About Old Age in Different Cultures

Along with ageism, it is also important to be aware of myths—both positive and negative—about aging in various cultures across historical time. Many students new to gerontology and aging believe there was a time in the past when older people were revered and held in high respect within the community. However, rather than age alone being an indicator of respect, many scholars have suggested that social class, status, and value to society were stronger indicators of respect (Thane, 2000). For example, an older person who had mastered a unique skill (e.g., calligraphy) might be held in high esteem, whereas an older person who held a common skill (e.g., rice farming) might not. Since the poor comprised the majority in many cultures, people with wealth and social position, regardless of age, held much higher levels of respect than older persons from lower social classes.

Another common myth is that older persons are still revered in some parts of the world, especially East Asia. For example, in 1966 Japan officially established Respect for the Aged Day, celebrated on the third Monday in September. Although this day recognizes the importance of respecting older persons, to be respected is not the same as to be revered. In addition, while older persons may receive a formalized form of respect that includes honorific titles such as "aunt" or "father," many countries struggle with combatting mistreatment of older persons, including elder abuse. The WHO estimates that 15.7% of people aged 60 and above worldwide are victims of elder abuse. It believes this percentage is much lower than the actual occurrence, since many people may be unwilling to report such abuse (WHO, 2019a). Of the types of elder abuse (physical, sexual, psychological, or financial, and neglect) included in the WHO's research study database, neglect was most common; countries cited as having the highest median levels of elder neglect were Egypt, Israel, Spain, and China.

The high prevalence of neglect speaks to similar myths regarding the revered status of older persons, specifically in countries that practice **filial piety** versus countries where older people are not cared for by family in the same way. Filial piety (literally, "the devoted child") describes a Confucian and Buddhist value of respect for one's ancestors, elders, and parents. According to Charlotte Ikels (1993), China's traditional, precommunist culture of the early 20th century was based on Confucianism, "an ethic of familism that not only served as the standard to guide proper family organization for many centuries but was also codified into law" (p. 124). This system emphasized vertical family ties—those between the generations—as more important than horizontal ties, such as those between spouses, which were viewed primarily as a means by which to continue the lineage (or vertical line) through offspring. Confucian filial piety requires that each person respect his or her place in the family and show proper levels of respect to others according to their place (e.g., child to parent, adult to elder; Canda, 2013). While filial piety continues to be part of the cultural framework of many countries, this does not mean that older persons who live in these countries are without challenges or that all children are willing and able to provide care for older parents. China, for example, enacted legislation requiring children to be involved with their aging parents and to visit parents at least once a year (Cheung & Kwan, 2009). This raises a question: If legislation is necessary to ensure that children are looking after their parents, is filial piety as powerful a norm as we have assumed?

In contrast, families in Western countries often are viewed as having abandoned their older family members, since multigenerational households are not the norm in many of those countries. However, living arrangements of family members in developed countries are more a reflection of Western cultural values by both older and younger family members than of their views toward care for older family members. For example, people in the United States place great value on independence in family relationships across the life cycle, which translates into a preference for patterns such as **"intimacy at a distance"** (living near family members but not together) and older adults not wanting to "be a burden" on their children.

This value is reflected in contemporary living arrangements in many developed countries, such as retirement communities or "in-law suites" (freestanding apartments within a larger house), and has a long history. Historian and gerontologist Thomas Cole (1992), in his cultural history of aging in Western Europe, points out that older Europeans have long preferred to live near but not with their adult children. In addition to citing historical European records of parents signing formal contracts with their primary heir to guarantee future care should the parent require assistance, Cole points to Shakespeare's *King Lear* as an example of a cautionary tale about living with one's children. In the play, Lear divides his kingdom between two daughters (Regan and Goneril) who profess (albeit insincerely) the magnitude of their love for him. Later, they take away Lear's land and money, which leads to several tragic outcomes.

What to Call Older Persons

Finally, it is important to consider terms used to refer to older persons. Although the term "the elderly" is frequently used to describe older persons, often in a well-intentioned way, it could be considered offensive for several reasons. "Elderly" implies dependence, weakness, and frailty. It is a term generally used by people who do not consider themselves to be "elderly" to emphasize need, to garner sympathy, or to underscore helplessness. In effect, what the term "elderly" does is to stereotype a large group of people, generally those aged 65 and above. Although one easily can still find the word in print in various publications, several academic journals in the aging field prohibit its use (de Medeiros, 2018). The American Medical Association *Manual of Style* and the *Journal of the American Geriatrics Society* have taken a strong stand against ageist and ablest language. Authors are asked to avoid use of "elderly," "aged," "elders," or "seniors," and to use specific age ranges instead. While such a strong stance might initially seem like "political correctness" gone awry, it is important to remember that several studies report that people aged 65 and above overwhelmingly reject the terms "elderly" and "old," preferring the term "older persons" (Falconer & O'Neill, 2007).

USEFUL ECONOMIC AND POPULATION CONCEPTS

The previous section provided a framework for thinking about how culture influences aging. This section examines some basic economic concepts as a way to help understand how systems and supports for older persons function within countries. This section therefore provides a very basic overview of some population wide economic terms that are helpful in looking at global aging across countries and regions. The first, **gross domestic product** (GDP), is an indicator of a country's total economic activity. It is the monetary value of the goods and services produced by a country within a given time period (e.g., a year, a quarter). **GDP per capita** is the GDP for a given country divided by its total population. GDP and GDP per capita can provide a snapshot of a country's wealth and standard of living. According to the U.S. Central Intelligence Agency (CIA) *World Factbook* (2019), the countries with the 10 highest GDP per capita in 2017 were Liechtenstein ($139,100), Qatar ($124,500), Monaco ($115,700), Macau ($111,600), Luxembourg ($106,300), Bermuda ($99,400), Singapore ($93,900), Isle of Man ($84,600), Brunei ($78,200), and Ireland ($75,000). The United States was 19th on this list, with a GDP per capita of $59,500. It is important to note that while GDP per capita provides information about the relative prosperity of a country, it does not account for differences in social class that might lead to unequal distributions of wealth or financial resources.

Inflation is another important economic term for global aging. Inflation describes the rate at which general prices for goods and services increase, which in turn decreases purchasing power. An inflation rate of 5% means that prices are 5% higher this year than they were last year. If a person's earnings did not rise by 5% or more, his or her earnings would pay for less, making them lower in purchasing power. Inflation is important to global aging since the value of funds in retirement savings and pension plans is affected by inflation, as is people's ability to purchase necessary goods and services. People living in countries with high inflation rates may find it difficult to cover their living expenses in later life, either through retirement funds for people in wealthier countries or through familial or other forms of aid for those in more socioeconomically disadvantaged regions. Governments also may find it difficult to support pension programs or other social programs if the value of currency and spending power is reduced through inflation. For example, in 2017, Argentina's inflation rate was estimated at 25.7%, compared to Japan, which had an inflation rate of 0.5% that same year (Central Intelligence Agency World Factbook, 2019). Although Japan struggles with increasing numbers of people drawing pensions, the small change in the price of goods means pension income holds its value. On the other hand, with such a high inflation rate, Argentina must worry about the devaluation of currency and its ability to help people meet their basic food and housing needs.

Another useful economic statistic is **health care spending**, which is the total expenditure on health care goods and services, including public health services, long-term care, rehabilitative care, and curative care (OECD, 2019). Spending on health per person is correlated with GDP and life expectancy. The WHO estimates that, although US$44 is needed per person in the world for basic health services, 26 WHO member countries spent less than that per person in 2011, and six spent less than US$20 (WHO, 2014). The country with the highest total per capita spending on health was Norway (US$9,908); the lowest was Eritrea (US$12). Norway also had the highest government spending on health per person (US$8,436) and Myanmar (also known as Burma) the lowest (US$3). Not surprisingly, Norway's **average life expectancy at birth** (the average number of years a person born at a given time and a given place can expect to live) in 2018 was 82 years, quite good compared to Eritrea (65.6 years) or Myanmar (68.6 years).

GEOGRAPHY AND GLOBAL AGING

In addition to economics, geography also plays an important role in global aging. This includes shifts in populations from rural to urban areas as well as movement among the general regions of the world.

Urban and Rural

Whether one lives in an urban or rural area likely will affect many aspects of aging. Tony Champion and Graeme Hugo (2017) point to the following differences between urban and rural areas. Urban areas are characterized by manufacturing, construction, and administrative and service occupations, while agriculture is the focus of rural areas. People in urban areas tend to have higher levels of education, access to services and information, and in-migration than rural areas. In contrast, rural areas tend to have higher fertility and mortality rates than do urban areas. In 2018, 55% of the world's population lived in an urban area. This is expected increase to 68% by 2050 (U.N. Department of Economic and Social Affairs, 2018). In addition, the United Nations reports that, with 37 million people, Tokyo is the world's largest city, followed by New Delhi, India (29 million); Shanghai, China (26 million); Mexico City, Mexico (22 million); Sao Paulo, Brazil (22 million); and 20 million each for Cairo, Egypt; Mumbai, India; Beijing, China; and Dhaka, Bangladesh.

The move from rural to urban areas is rooted in industrialization. One of the most important social changes influencing the need for, and development of, a welfare state is industrialization, which requires large concentrations of workers for factories and thus often induces a substantial migration from poorer rural farmlands to urban areas. This migration introduces a new way of life: Individuals are separated from the land and, frequently, from their extended families. Whereas rural farmers often have kin for neighbors, ensuring others nearby who can provide social and economic assistance when necessary, urban dwellers typically find themselves among strangers, separated from their traditional social-support networks. This new social living condition requires some mechanism to replace that lost family support, and this mechanism became the welfare state. The process that unfolded for Western Europe and the United States in the late 19th and early 20th centuries is similar to what is happening in the developing nations of the world today. In many countries, the migration of young people to cities in search of better jobs and a higher standard of living has resulted in isolation of older people in rural areas, which in turn has led to changes in family care. Sometimes, working-age parents need to leave their children to be raised by their grandparents. Other times, children who traditionally may have provided care for their parents (filial piety) are no longer close by and therefore unable to assist with care needs. This has resulted in millions of the rural older population, the so-called "left behind," being without reliable family support or care. (While this term appears to have originated in China, it is a common phenomenon in a growing number of developing countries.)

Country Classifications

Although classifying countries or regions is complicated, the categorization is based generally on the area's level of economic development. The U.N. Statistics Division (2019) cautions that such designations should be understood as a "statistical convenience" rather than a judgment and that no single, established standard exists for economic classification of nations. For our purposes, think of the designations as the result of a two-step process. First, the World Bank calculates a gross national income per person for each country, and then places each into one of four categories: low income, lower-middle income, upper-middle income, and high income. In the next step, high-income countries are defined as developed countries, and all remaining (low- and middle-income) countries are classified as developing countries. As a point of reference, the threshold for high-income (developed) countries in 2018 was a gross national income per person of greater than US$12,055; at the other end of the continuum, low-income countries were at or below US$995 per person, with the other groups in between (lower-middle income from US$996–$3,895 and upper-middle income from US$3,896–$12,055); see World Bank (2018). Even though these categorizations are only statistical conveniences, they do provide a general sense of the level of resources available in a country to address important needs, including those related to having an aging population.

A commonly used alternative to the World Bank categorization comes from the United Nations, which currently designates all of Europe and North America (Canada and the United States) plus Australia, New Zealand, and Japan as **more developed countries**; all others are **less developed** (or sometimes referred to in shorthand as "developed" and "developing"). Within the group of less developed countries is a special designation for **least developed countries** (LDCs). Several criteria are used to distinguish the nations in that category: (a) very low income per person, (b) economic vulnerability, and (c) poor human development indicators (population nutritional status, mortality, literacy, and education). LDCs currently include 34 African nations, 14 Asian countries, and Haiti (U.N. Department of Economic and Social Affairs, Population Division, 2017). For our exploration of global aging, these designations help to differentiate countries and regions of the world on a number of dimensions, including the current age of the country.

MORE DEVELOPED COUNTRIES

More developed countries currently have a much higher proportion of older people than do less or least developed countries. However, the populations of the less developed nations are aging much faster than did the populations of the developed nations during their modernization and population aging process in the latter half of the 19th and early 20th centuries. Consequently, the nations in these categories differ in the types of challenges they face related to population aging. For example, as the proportions of older people continue to grow, the relative size of the available labor force shrinks, which has implications for the sustainability of pension programs and for the ability of a country to fill the jobs it needs to keep the economy vibrant. **Age dependency ratios** compare the size of the working-age population to that of the older population; this measure is called a dependency ratio because of the assumption that the working-age population will, to some degree and in some way, have to support the older population (usually through taxes to pay for programs and public pensions for older people). Japan, Italy, Finland, Portugal, and Germany currently have the most challenging age dependency ratios in the world—three working-age people for every one person aged 65 and older (World Bank, 2017). The viability of Germany's well-established (since 1889) and generous public pension program already is threatened by increasing percentages of older people and decreasing fertility rates. At present, Germany spends about 13% of its GDP on the pension system, one of the highest percentages in the world (He, Goodkind, & Kowal, 2016). The proposed solutions to the public pension problem in Germany include increasing the tax rate or the age at which a person is eligible to receive the pension and expanding immigration from other countries to admit more workers (to pay more taxes). The political viability and economic wisdom of any of these solutions is under heated debate in Germany (Haub, 2007), just as in other nations.

In addition to a long-standing public pension program, Germany has a well-developed system of services and programs for older people, including formal long-term services offered in institutions and in the community. Even so, the significant size of the older population poses challenges for the future. Germany's response to, and planning for, these challenges reflects basic cultural values, as illustrated in a recent national report on aging policies. These values include a shared responsibility and solidarity, generational equity, lifelong learning, and disease prevention (Kruse & Schmitt, 2009). In its focus on promoting healthy, active aging and lifelong opportunities for learning and civic engagement, Germany is very similar to the United States. Developed nations in general have the luxury of such a focus as long as their economies permit sufficient funding, but they may find themselves challenged as the percentage of older people increases.

LESS AND LEAST DEVELOPED COUNTRIES

At the risk of oversimplifying a complex situation, the general pattern is that nations in the less developed regions of the world are faced with the dilemmas of devising new programs, policies, and services for aging populations, whereas more developed regions are dealing with the problems of funding, adapting, or expanding existing policies and programs. It has been said that today's developed nations got rich before they got old, while developing nations are getting old before they get rich (National Institute on Aging & WHO, 2011). Given what we know about both economic development and aging, it also may be true that poor countries beginning to age may never get rich.

Today, more than 60% of all people 65 and older live in less or least developed countries (often described as "developing"); that proportion is expected to exceed 75% by 2040 (He et al., 2016). These numbers may seem surprising, given the relatively low proportions who are old today in many of these countries as well as their lower life expectancies and median ages. Take India as an example: Although only 5% of India's 1.28 billion people currently are aged 65 or older, that 5% represents more than 64 million older people. Because so much of the world's population is concentrated in these developing nations, and because the regions in which they are located are beginning to experience rapid population aging, it is easy to see how three fourths of the world's older people will be living in these areas in only a few decades.

Population aging in developing nations (such as India, Thailand, Kenya, Chile, and Guatemala) poses unique challenges to the governments, families, and individuals in those countries. Their populations are aging quickly, but they are less likely to have in place programs, policies, or health care systems prepared to meet the needs of older people. This structural lag in the development of options to deal with coming older populations can be explained by a combination of factors, including relatively poor economies with little revenue to invest in new programs or services; pressing concerns about general nutrition and maternal and child health; traditional value systems that emphasize norms of family care; and the very rapid pace of demographic and health transitions (mentioned earlier)—giving countries little time to adjust to the new realities of an aging society. Many nations in the developing regions of the world are simultaneously dealing with relatively high fertility, problems of poverty and hunger, population aging, and new demands for chronic health care.

In many African countries, the HIV/AIDS epidemic has had a profound effect on life expectancy at birth, resulting in changes in life expectancy in countries like South Africa from 62.2 years in 1991 to only 52.6 years in 2005 (World Bank, 2019). More recently, the WHO African Region saw an increase in life expectancy to 61.2 years, attributed to antiretrovirals for treatment of HIV and improved child survival rates (WHO, 2019b). For many older people, the HIV/AIDS epidemic translates into loss of their adult children and results in the necessity to care for their orphaned grandchildren. The HIV/AIDS epidemic in Africa is broad-based, involving both women and men. This means that both marital partners may contract the disease and, without expensive (and sometimes unavailable) medications, both may die. Whereas the majority of older people in Kenya live with family, some are now living in **skipped-generation households,** with the middle generation missing and grandparents acting as surrogate parents. Of course, many countries (including the United States) face this problem, created by a number of factors that include parental addiction, incarceration, and serious illnesses. In the United States in 2014, 10% of children lived in a household headed by a grandparent (U.S. Census Bureau, 2014). For more than one half of these children (numbering 2.7 million), the grandparents were the primary care provider (U.S. Census Bureau, 2014). Africa, however, has the highest proportion of older people living in such a situation (around 20%), which is most often related to HIV/AIDS mortality of the middle generation (U.N. Department of Economic and Social Affairs, 2018).

In addition to the vast implications of HIV/AIDS mortality, older persons in many African countries face problems with poverty, illiteracy, poor nutrition, limited housing options, lack of income security, and few social service programs (Mwangi, 2014). In many nations across Africa, legal systems have not specifically recognized the rights of the older population and do not provide them with equal access to health care, social services, and income security or much protection from age discrimination, especially in matters of inheritance and property rights (HelpAge International, 2012).

THE STUDY OF GLOBAL AGING

While the previous sections have provided a context for issues and concepts related to global aging, this final section addresses why it is worthwhile to study global aging, regardless of one's career plans or academic major. As Whittington and Kunkel (2013) have argued elsewhere, studying global aging is important to everyone for three main reasons.

To Get Educated

Aging is a new, powerful social force—never seen before in human history—that already is changing the way Western societies are structured and how their citizens will live out their lives. For the first time in history, large numbers of the human species are living beyond their working years and confronting the personal and family issue of what to do with their time. Retirement is a concept that was unknown to most of our ancestors living during the first 70 centuries that civilized societies have been on Earth; now it must be designed and adapted to by more and more people. Part of being an educated person is having knowledge about this revolution in longevity.

Self-Interest

The world is globalizing—becoming, in the words of Marshall McLuhan (1962), a "global village." The twin revolutions in technology and communication that allow people in one part of the world to know what is happening in all other parts—and to go there quickly, as tourists, as temporary workers, or as permanent migrants—mean that we are not only connected but also *collected* with each other in important ways. If the economic and political well-being of the United States (or any other nation) is heavily dependent on the work and consumer behavior of 1.4 billion Chinese, the technical knowledge of 1.3 billion Indians, the religious tolerance of 260 million Indonesians, or even the political aspirations of 82 million Iranians, attention must be paid to what is going on in their countries. In the 2012 campaign for the Republican nomination for U.S. president, one of the candidates, Herman Cain, famously denied that it was of any importance that he should know the name of the president of Uzbekistan (he did not). But Uzbekistan is an important part of the connected world, and what happens among its 30 million residents may not remain isolated there. It can be quickly communicated, transmitted, or migrated to a neighborhood near you.

As aging transforms developing nations demographically and socially, it will create profound economic and developmental changes in these emerging world powers, along with exciting opportunities for the realization of human potential. Whatever is happening to the smallest, least-visible countries will affect the developed world in ways we can hardly imagine today. It is in the interest of all people that such far-reaching and fundamental changes be understood sooner rather than later.

The Smart Move

Each of us has a perspective on life and the world that is limited and shaped by our experience. Such limited perspectives can have unpleasant (even destructive) consequences when the nature, motives, and intents of others are misinterpreted by some—leading to prejudice, discrimination, racism, war, and even genocide. It is an article of faith of most educated people that expanding one's experience and broadening one's perspective can reduce such misunderstanding and destructive behavior. Learning about global aging will not, by itself, lead to world peace. However, it could contribute to a fuller, more accurate picture of how other people live, raise their families, care for their parents, and live out their lives. If that knowledge impresses us with the realization that aging is a universal experience, that all families, communities, and societies—no matter how different they may seem from our own—struggle as we do to cope with its results, and that many older people find it a productive, fulfilling time of life, we may begin to perceive our commonalities as greater than our differences. That would be the beginning of wisdom at least.

SUMMARY

The demographic reality of global aging is undeniable; clearly, the aging of a society is accompanied by, and is a catalyst for, enormous social reform. Global trends in longevity and population aging are heralded as a success story, but the challenges posed also are widely acknowledged (He et al., 2016). How these issues play out in specific countries or major regions of the world will vary, depending on a host of factors including demographics, economics, and cultural values.

Each region and each nation face both the challenge and the promise of aging societies. There has never been a clearer mandate for gerontology education and research. In response to this mandate, gerontology programs are beginning to appear in countries worldwide. In some places, such as the United States, Germany, and the United Kingdom, gerontology is a well-developed discipline (de Medeiros, 2017), with credentials offered at several levels of higher education. In other places, such as China, Israel, and Mexico, gerontology is a specialty within other professional programs such as medicine, nursing, and social work (Carmel & Lowenstein, 2007; Kunkel, 2008). In still other countries, such as Kenya, gerontology education is offered primarily as training for direct-care workers. In recognition of the need for data about aging populations, many national and cross-national efforts are underway. Examples of such research initiatives include a survey of aging, health, and well-being conducted in Argentina, Mexico, Barbados, Uruguay, Chile, and Brazil; a longitudinal study of aging in India; the Survey of Health, Ageing and Retirement in Europe (SHARE); a massive study of the oldest old in China; and the WHO longitudinal study of global aging and adult health. These are but a few illustrations of the educational and research efforts underway to meet the challenge and the promise of global aging. The remainder of this book is devoted to its implications.

DISCUSSION QUESTIONS

1. Describe an ageist character or ageist portrayal in a commercial, show, or film. What, do you think, is the intended result of ageism in your example?
2. Name a cultural practice that you find to be silly or oppressive. How do you think this practice came into being? Do you think it should be challenged?
3. Why is it important to understand global aging?
4. Do you live in a developed or developing country? How can you tell?
5. What are the worst and best things about living where you do?
6. What is so important about population aging?
7. Why is it said that poor nations may never get rich?
8. Which part of the world do you think is likely to have the best environment for its older citizens 50 years from now?
9. Look up the GDP and life expectancy at birth for a least developed, less developed, and developed country. What can you say about the relationship between the country's classification, economic activity, and life expectancy?
10. How will global aging affect your major or your chosen career path?

KEY WORDS

Ageism	Culture
Biological age	Filial piety
Chronological age	Functional age

GDP
Health care spending
Inflation
Least developed countries
Left-behind generation
Less developed countries

Life expectancy
More developed countries
Rural
Skipped-generation household
Welfare state
Urban

REFERENCES

Ahmed, F. E. (2014). Gender, aging and power in rural Bangladesh: Getting older as the priming of women. In S. R. Kunkel, J. S. Brown, & F. J. Whittington (Eds.), *Global aging: Comparative perspectives on aging and the life course* (pp. 23–26). New York, NY: Springer Publishing Company.

Ayalon, L., & Tesch-Römer, C. (Eds.). (2018). *Contemporary perspectives on ageism.* Gewerbestrasse, Switzerland: Springer International Publishing.

Canda, E. R. (2013). Filial piety and care for elders: A contested Confucian virtue reexamined. *Journal of Ethnic and Cultural Diversity in Social Work, 22*(3–4), 213–234. doi:10.1080/15313204.2013.843134

Carmel, S., & Lowenstein, A. (2007). Addressing a nation's challenge: Graduate programs in gerontology in Israel. *Gerontology & Geriatrics Education, 27*(3), 49–63. doi:10.1300/J021v27n03_04

Central Intelligence Agency World Factbook. (2019). Retrieved from https://www.cia.gov/library/publications/the-world-factbook/rankorder/2004rank.html

Champion, T., & Hugo, G. (2017). Introduction: Moving beyond the urban-rural dichotomy. In G. Hugo (Ed.), *New forms of urbanization: Beyond the urban-rural dichotomy* (pp. 3–24.) London: Routledge.

Cheung, C.-K., & Kwan, A. Y.-H. (2009). The erosion of filial piety by modernisation in Chinese cities. *Ageing and Society, 29*(2), 179–198. doi:10.1017/S0144686X08007836

Cole, T. R. (1992). *The journey of life: A cultural history of aging in America.* Cambridge, UK: Cambridge University Press.

Cruikshank, M. (2013). *Learning to be old: Gender, culture, and aging.* Lanham, MD: Rowman & Littlefield Publishers.

de Medeiros, K. (2017). *The short guide to aging and gerontology.* Bristol, UK: Policy Press.

de Medeiros, K. (2018). What can thinking like a gerontologist bring to bioethics? In N. Berlinger, K. de Medeiros, & M. Z. Solomon (Eds.), *What makes a good life in late life? Citizenship and justice in aging societies* (Vol. 48, pp. S10–S14). Garrison, NY: The Hastings Center. doi:10.1002/hast.906

Falconer, M., & O'Neill, D. (2007). Personal views: Out with "the old," elderly and aged. *BMJ: British Medical Journal, 334*(7588), 316. doi:10.1136/bmj.39111.694884.94

Geertz, C. (1973). *The interpretation of cultures.* New York, NY: Basic Books.

Haub, C. (2007). Global aging and the demographic divide. *Public Policy & Aging Report. 17*(4), 1–6. doi:10.1093/ppar/17.4.1a

He, W., Goodkind, D., & Kowal, P. (2016). *An aging world: 2015.* U.S. Census Bureau, International Population Reports, P95/16-1. Retrieved from https://www.census.gov/content/dam/Census/library/publications/2016/demo/p95-16-1.pdf

HelpAge International. (2012). *Aging in Africa.* Nairobi, Kenya: HelpAge Africa.

Ikels, C. (1993). Chinese kinship and the state: Shaping of policy for the elderly. In G. L. Maddox & M. P. Lawton (Eds.), *Annual Review of Gerontology and Geriatrics: Focus on kinship, aging and social change* (Vol 13, pp. 123–146). New York, NY: Springer Publishing Company.

Kojima, G., Iliffe, S., Taniguchi, Y., Shimada, H., Rakugi, H., & Walters, K. (2017). Prevalence of frailty in Japan: A systematic review and meta-analysis. *Journal of Epidemiology, 27*(8), 347–353. doi:10.1016/j.je.2016.09.008

Kruse, A., & Schmitt, E. (2009). Germany. In E. Palmore, F. Whittington, & S. Kunkel (Eds.), *International handbook on aging: Current research and developments I* (3rd ed., pp. 221–237). Santa Barbara, CA: Praeger.

Kunkel, S. R. (2008). Global aging and gerontology education: The international mandate. *Annual Review of Gerontology and Geriatrics, 28*, 45–58. doi:10.1891/0198-8794.28.45

McLuhan, M. (1962). *The Gutenberg galaxy.* Toronto: University of Toronto Press.

Mwangi, S. M. (2014). Social support systems for rural adults in Kenya. In S. R. Kunkel, J. S. Brown & F. J. Whittington (Eds.), *Global aging: Comparative perspectives on aging and the life course* (pp. 250–254). New York, NY: Springer Publishing Company.

Naidoo, N., Abdullah, S., Bawah, A., Binka, F., Chuc, N. T., Debpuur, C., . . . Van Minh, H. (2010). Ageing and adult health status in eight lower-income countries: The INDEPTH WHO-SAGE collaboration. *Global Health Action,* Global Health Action Supplement 2, 11–22.

National Institute on Aging and the WHO. (2011). Global health and aging. NIH Publication no. 11-7737. Washington, DC: National Institutes of Health. Retrieved from https://www.who.int/ageing/publications/global_health.pdf?ua=1

Organization for Economic Co-operation and Development. (2019), Health spending (indicator). Retrieved from http://www.oecd.org/els/health-systems/health-data.htm

Social Security Administration. (2014). Social Security programs throughout the world, 2016. Retrieved from https://www.ssa.gov/policy/docs/progdesc/ssptw/

Thane, P. (2000). *Old age in English history: Past experiences, present issues.* Oxford, Oxford University Press.

U.N. Department of Economic and Social Affairs, Population Division. (2017). World Population Ageing 2017 (ST/ESA/SER.A/408). Retrieved from http://www.un.org/en/development/desa/population/publications/pdf/ageing/WPA2017_Report.pdf

U.N. Department of Economic and Social Affairs. (2018). 68% of the world population projected to live in urban areas by 2050. Retrieved from https://www.un.org/development/desa/en/news/population/2018-revision-of-world-urbanization-prospects.html

U.N. Statistics Division. (2019). *China.* Retrieved from http://data.un.org/en/iso/cn.html

U.S. Census Bureau. (2014). 10 percent of grandparents live with grandchild. Retrieved from https://www.census.gov/newsroom/press-releases/2014/cb14-194.html

Whittington, F. J., & Kunkel, S. R. (2013). Think globally, act locally: The maturing of a worldwide science and practice of aging. *Generations, 37,* 6–11.

World Bank. (2017). Age dependency ratio, old (% of working-age population.) Retrieved from https://data.worldbank.org/indicator/SP.POP.DPND.OL?view=chart&year_high_desc=true

World Bank. (2018). World Bank classifications. Retrieved from https://datahelpdesk.worldbank.org/knowledgebase/articles/906519

World Bank. (2019). Life expectancy at birth, total (years.). Retrieved from https://data.worldbank.org/indicator/SP.DYN.LE00.IN?locations=ZG-ZA&name_desc=false

World Health Organization. (2014). *Global health expenditure atlas: September, 2014.* Geneva, Switzerland, The World Health Organisation Press.

World Health Organization. (2019a). Elder abuse. Retrieved from https://www.who.int/ageing/projects/elder_abuse/en

World Health Organization. (2019b). Life expectancy. Retrieved from https://www.who.int/gho/ortality_burden_disease/life_tables/situation_trends_text/en

A GLOBAL PERSPECTIVE ON OLDER ADULTS IN ADVERTISING

JAYE ATKINSON

"He may be 73, but you wouldn't want to spill his Chianti."

"A seventy-year-old couple demonstrating the benefits of a Mediterranean diet."

(Williams, Ylanne, & Wadleigh, 2007, pp. 11–12)

Those quotations are captions in a United Kingdom advertising campaign for Olivio, a margarine made from olive oil (Williams et al., 2007). The first caption accompanies a picture of an older man with thinning, graying hair; not smiling, he is scantily clad in a tank-top shirt that reveals a physically fit body. The text underneath further emphasizes his strength: "Even at this ripe old age he's still as tough as old boots" (p. 11). The second caption accompanies a close-up picture of a window with closed shutters. The text explains that eating Olivio "has got to be good for your family's health, not to mention the . . .*ahem*. . . active part you and your partner will take in later life" (p. 12). These are just two of Olivio's 16 advertisements employing older adults as the main characters. According to the company responsible, Unilever, using older adults in their campaign increased their sales by approximately 150%!

People often are used in advertising campaigns to sell products and services to others; this is not new! The people in advertisements, however, are not often older than 50 years of age. This chapter explores the portrayals of older adults in advertising in the United Kingdom, the United States, and India with modest references to preliminary research in China and Germany. As many scholars have argued, the lack of intergenerational contact outside the family emphasizes the role media portrayals will play in developing attitudes and beliefs about age and the aging process (Williams et al., 2007).

Williams and her colleagues used a case study approach to examine Olivio's seven-year advertising campaign. Detailed qualitative analysis of 11 of the 16 advertisements enabled them to identify four phases of the campaign and their connection to stereotypes of older adults. They argue that phase one was focused on educating the public about the health benefits of a Mediterranean diet and how their product fit into that lifestyle. This education focus required longer text with references to doctors, saturated fats, cholesterol, and other health-related information, but the main taglines describing the older adults pictured include:

> "She's never seen a JANE FONDA workout video, but she'll probably live longer than you."
>
> "It's not fame, glamour, and money that keeps them going."
>
> "They also hand down the secret of long life."
>
> (Williams et al., 2007, pp. 7–9)

Older adults pictured in these advertisements, therefore, were examples of longevity and the positive versions of what consumers could become if they eat properly.

The opening quotations were from phase two of the campaign, a phase that these scholars argue focuses on the elders questioning our expectations; that is, negative "stereotypes are invoked (and by their invocation arguably reinforced) but mediated" (Williams et al., 2007, p. 19). In this phase, older adults are strong (as in the 73-year-old with Chianti), sexual (as in the closed shutters), and active (as in an older adult male standing by his bicycle with a race number pinned to his chest). The tagline says, "He's never won a race in his life. It's the early days though" (p. 10). Not only is he active, but that activity is expected to continue, and he is expected to become more successful.

Phase three focuses on older adults enjoying their lives, showing one older woman in a challenging yoga position (lifted lotus, for yogi readers) and another happily driving a fancy convertible. Accompanying texts play on the word "oil" as something that helps one remain flexible or keep running smoothly. Phase four employs pictures of older adults who are happy, attractive, and in love. Although most of the text focuses on Olivio's name change to Bertolli, it also describes the older adult models as "arm candy" and "babe magnet," contrasting with negative expectations of beauty and age.

Williams et al. (2007) identified an extremely interesting, provocative, and positive campaign employing older adults, one that apparently was quite successful in the United Kingdom. The images, however, pictured 19 older males and only five females. Those numbers are similar to findings of the quantitative gender portrayal research conducted in the United States and India by Raman, Harwood, Weis, Anderson, and Miller (2008). These researchers examined older adult portrayals in U.S. and Indian magazine advertisements. From 40 randomly selected magazines across genres, they found 1,464 advertisements that included 1,445 people. They coded the ads for the presence of older people, type of product, and health and gender of the people. Older adults, those 50 years of age and older, were underrepresented in the ads in both cultures. In the U.S. sample, 145 of the 903 people depicted in the ads (16%) were 50 years of age or older, while in the Indian sample, 34 of 445 people (7.6%) were in that age group. According to the authors, those observed proportions significantly underrepresent the actual size of the 50-plus populations of both the United States (28%) and India (13%). Additionally, age and gender interacted such that older men appeared in ads more often than older women in both cultures, though this effect was stronger in the Indian sample. Men outnumbered women in the U.S. sample at age 50 and above, but men outnumbered women in the Indian sample at age 30 and above. This lower visibility of older people in marketing in both India and the United States reinforces the generation's lack of cultural importance and distorts the reality of gender ratios.

In both countries, older models were employed in ads focused on health products, but in India financial products also were sold by older adults. The authors also examined ad text and found that age references and associations between ill health and older adulthood were more common in the U.S. sample. Older adults were portrayed as unhealthy more often in the United States, especially for people above 60 years of age. This connection perpetuates a negative view of aging as inevitably unhealthy.

Unlike the Olivio campaign, these advertising images of older adults are less positive and yet very similar to those found by general age portrayal research (most of which focuses on U.S. media; see Atkinson & Plew, 2017 for a recent review). In China, too, advertising research has found that cultural values, such as filial piety (respect for older adults), are salient in television advertising (Zhang & Harwood, 2004). Zhang et al. (2006) summarize age portrayal research in Germany by stating that "analyses show that the predominantly negative images from the 1980s and 1990s (Bosch, 1990) have been modified by a tendency for positive, age-complimentary images, especially in television advertising" (p. 275).

Essentially, media portrayal research across the globe "is in its infancy" (Zhang et al., 2006, p. 278) and deserves further scholarly attention. Although particular images found in the Olivio campaign provide a diverse, healthy possibility for aging, the other research cited here suggests that negative stereotypes of older adulthood as inactive, unattractive, asexual/nonsexual, and unhealthy are alive and well. Earlier advertisements have more negative portrayals than more recent ones, but further research must be conducted to confirm or negate these findings. In fact, some of the aforementioned research, though the latest published, is already more than 10 years old, so final conclusions must await more current studies. Was the Olivio campaign unique and an aberration within particular cultural contexts (such as the United Kingdom or Germany), or is this truly a current, global trend? Other advertising research agendas could include examining multiple types of advertisements (print and video) and comparing these across media types and within/between countries of origin. Portrayal research also should be expanded to include television and movies (e.g., Atkinson & Plew, 2017) and should focus on how shows are adapted across countries. We can assume those adaptations are influenced by cultural values, but it would be instructive to know if any of these cultural adaptations are age-related? If so, what messages about aging and older adulthood are being reinforced or contradicted?

Media portrayals of older adults have been studied extensively within the United States across a wide variety of genres. Similar research is just beginning in other countries. Williams et al. (2007) state, "We would like to think that people of all ages who view these [age-positive] ads are presented with the idea that older age has many varied possibilities above and beyond the rather tired and traditional stereotypes that we usually encounter" (p. 19). It is time to examine media portrayals of elders worldwide! Knowing what portrayals exist is the first step in advancing a diverse view of the possibilities of old age.

REFERENCES

Atkinson, J. L., & Plew, M. S. (2017). Present, perceived as old, but not memorable: Analysis and perceptions of older characters in animated Disney films. *International Journal of Humanities and Social Sciences, 7*(6), 1–12.

Raman, P., Harwood, J., Weis, D., Anderson, J. L., & Miller, G. (2008). Portrayals of older adults in U.S. and Indian magazine advertisements: A cross-cultural comparison. *The Howard Journal of Communications, 19*, 221–240. doi:10.1080/10646170802218214

Williams, A., Ylanne, V., & Wadleigh, P. M. (2007). Selling the 'Elixir of Life': Images of the elderly in an *Olivio* advertising campaign. *Journal of Aging Studies, 21*, 1–21. doi:10.1016/j.jaging.2006.09.001

Zhang, Y. B., & Harwood, J. (2004). Modernization of tradition in an age of globalization: Cultural values in Chinese television commercials. *Journal of Communication, 54*, 156–172. doi:10.1177/0261927X06289479

Zhang, Y. B., Harwood, J., Williams, A., Ylanne-McEwen, V., Wadleigh, P. M., & Thimm, C. (2006). The portrayal of older adults in advertising: A cross-national review. *Journal of Language and Social Psychology, 25*, 264–282. doi:10.1111/j.1460-2466.2004.tb02619.x

GENDER, AGING, AND POWER IN RURAL BANGLADESH: GETTING OLDER AS THE PRIMING OF WOMEN

FAUZIA ERFAN AHMED

> I am running [for public office] because I see the injustice. And I saw that things could get even worse. We [women] have been repeatedly pushed and shoved [by society]; let us see what happens if we push back just once.
>
> —Alveerah, Muslim woman

Illiterate and with a low income, Alveerah is a middle-aged Muslim women in rural Bangladesh who is running for public office in local-level elections. Like many older women whom I interviewed during my ethnographic study of gender, power, and aging in a sharecropper village community, she is considered a leader in her community and exercises considerable power. In a gerontocratic culture, aging for women is also priming for power. It is a process of getting ready to accept the mantle of leadership, which means to be a role model and to act as a spokeswoman for other women in the community. Alveera looks forward to the future with determination, courage, and hope; opportunities, hitherto denied, are just beginning to open up for her.

In most Western societies, aging, especially for women, is seen as a general decline; and getting older is synonymous with the shrinking of opportunities. Older women are seen as less employable, less attractive, and less deserving of respect. This is even more true if they are less educated and have lower income. Further, women in Western cultures who are running for public office need to look as young as they possibly can.

Why are things different in Bangladesh? I explore the various dimensions of the answers to this question through an analysis of the nexus of gender, aging, and power in both the village (meso) and the national (macro) contexts.

AGING IN THE VILLAGE (MESO) LEVEL CONTEXT: TRADITIONAL PATHWAYS TO POWER

Rural society in Bangladesh is gerontocratic. What this means is that it is organized around a hierarchy based on age. Villages comprise *paras* (neighborhoods), and each *para* consists of several households (*baris*). A *bari* (household) constitutes several dwellings built around a courtyard. Though the extended family occupies a *bari*, the entire neighborhood is considered kin. When a bride first enters the *bari* as a daughter-in-law, she occupies the lowest rung of the ladder. Her mobility is restricted by *purdah* (a custom that defines relationships between men and women through segregated boundaries). Her conduct is regulated and proscribed by the *shalish*, an indigenous village court system, which consists of an all-male jury. Young and inexperienced in the ways of her *shoshur bari* (in-laws' household), she knows that she has to please everyone in the entire neighborhood, especially her mother–in-law. But she also knows that as she ages, she will climb the ladder to one day gain a position of authority, just like her mother-in-law.

Though *purdah* is oppressive to women in many ways, restricting access to education and jobs, opportunities for gaining authority exist even in this traditional system. When she sets foot in her in-laws' household, the young bride is primed for leadership through two pathways, both of which widen as she ages. First, she can look forward to greater geographic mobility. *Purdah* restrictions decrease with age. This resulting physical freedom is linked to increased kin ties, considered a tangible source of social capital in rural society. As a woman ages, her network expands to go beyond the neighborhood. Where they entered as outsiders, older women become insiders and have increased kin ties: they not only may arrange marriages of their own children, they also may arrange marriages of other young people in the village.

Second, in gerontocratic culture, increased equity in gender relations is an inevitable result of getting older. If, as the young daughter-in-law, Alveera kept quiet when addressed by male relatives, as a middle-aged woman, she now has a number of younger men, including her son(s) and nephews, who occupy a lower status. Aging also means that older women are addressed with an honorific, which specifically signifies the status that can only come with age. When she talks, these men have to listen respectfully, even if they do not agree with her. If she was compelled as the young bride to be subservient to her elders, as an elder now herself, she can expect subservience and *seva* (service) from those who are younger. In return, she is in the privileged position of conferring her blessings on the next generation.

Third, some older women like Alveerah are also midwives, and bringing children into the world is viewed as holy in village society. This status that emanates from her is also conferred on her husband. Such men often willingly take on household responsibilities, a switch in gender roles, because they know that their wives are compelled to leave the household at short notice without any definite indication of when they will return. Linked to the greater physical mobility allowed for midwives is the increase in kin ties. As they deliver babies, midwives create a permanent relationship with the infant and its parents. A younger woman who serves as an apprentice can look forward to the day when she gets older and also can "do work that gains Allah's blessings."

In addition to being a midwife, Alveerah also manages her own grocery store. She earns income through her entrepreneurial activities, has savings in the bank, and serves as the treasurer in the women's collective, where she has been a member for the past 10 years. She argues with the male relatives in her village about gender wage equity and the need for women to run for public office—something that no woman, of any age, would have been able to do in the past. This transformation has taken place because of structural changes in the national (macro) arena.

THE NATIONAL (MACRO) LEVEL CONTEXT: MODERN ROUTES TO POWER

In the four and a half decades since Bangladesh, a Muslim-majority nation of over 160 million people, gained independence, gender and development programs at the national level have contested the gender order. The fertility rate has decreased from 6.9 births per woman of childbearing age in 1970 to 2.1 (replacement rate) in 2016 (Bangladesh Bureau of Statistics, 2016). In 2015, the primary school completion rate for girls was 79%, higher than that of boys, which was 69% (World Bank, 2016), and maternal mortality has decreased from 574 per 100,000 births in 1990 to 178 in 2016. The percentage of girls enrolled in secondary school in 2016 was 73.1, higher than that of boys (63.8%) (Bangladesh Education Report, 2016). Approximately 34 million women utilize microcredit (Microcredit Regulatory Authority, 2015); it extends to about 60% of all poor households (Nahar, 2013), which, as a programmatic ideal, challenges the structure of patriarchal gender relations. Women's entrepreneurial activities have increased female mobility and their household income (Pitt, Cartwright, & Khandker, 2006). Women now can obtain microcredit loans with no collateral. With loans as small as $40, they increase their entrepreneurial skills and improve their household welfare. Defying oppressive notions of *purdah*, women now leave the *bari* for entrepreneurial activities, work in the fields alongside men, and run for public office. At least 3.6 million Bangladeshi women are employed in the garment industry, now the second largest in the world. Women's labor force participation increased from 4% in 1974 (Heintz, Kabeer, & Mahmud, 2018) to 33.1% in 2017.

These dramatic improvements underscore an even more dramatic reality: A tenacious and visionary women's movement is effectively forging alliances with all sectors of civil society in Bangladesh (Ahmed, 2006). Few know that older women like Alveerah constitute its popular leadership base. The success of the national family planning program is a result of the continuing discourse that older women led all over Bangladesh about Islamic principles and reproductive health. The reach of the movement is best understood by the effervescence of the *adda* (public discussions) led by such older village women; their vitality continues to change a male-dominated society on a daily basis. For these leaders of a widespread movement for social change, their *adda* goes beyond reproductive health to gender wage equality; more profoundly, village women now want to define Allah in their own terms.

How does Alveerah express her authority when she argues with male elders in her village? The shape and form of this new women's leadership combines oral traditions of village culture with modern perspectives. These women challenge patriarchal beliefs and make men understand (*boojhano*) through sheer eloquence and wit. In fact, *boojhano* was repeatedly mentioned by men as an important mechanism in how they reframed masculinity and became more aware of gender injustice. Villagers respect and see these qualities as evidence of forensic ability and leadership. Discussion (or *adda)* is not only a traditional way of resolving disputes; it is a forum for reflection. Villagers learn through a dialogue in a town meeting format that is rich in metaphor.

The level of analysis that these women leaders use, however, is entirely modern. It is a systematic analysis of village patriarchy, or the male-dominated system, that leads them to challenge patriarchal Islam by reframing religion. In particular, these older women reframe traditional notions of sin. They refer to the "patriarchal definition of Islam" as "a long list of don'ts." Such women use their gerontocratic authority to castigate a husband who refuses to allow his wife to have property in her own name as "having sin in his heart." In fact, men who commit such infractions, along with those who are violent, can be tried in a reformed *village court* that now includes women jurors, yet another innovation of the traditional system.

To summarize, modern transformations at the national level have built on traditional village mechanisms to give older women power, thereby priming poor women, at the lowest rung of society, for leadership. Getting older still has its problems: After years of hard labor, Alveerah complains of back problems, and the fees of the nearest doctor who lives in the city are too high for her. Notwithstanding, fundamental improvements at the national level, combined with the traditional respect for age, have given poor women opportunities for leadership that they could not even have imagined 40 years ago. It is not surprising that, happy and proud to be considered old, Alveerah feels she is in the prime of her life.

REFERENCES

Ahmed, F. E. (2006). Women, gender, and reproductive health: South Asia. *Encyclopedia of women and Islamic cultures*, Vol. III, 3.041i. Netherlands: Brill Academic Publishers.

Bangladesh Bureau of Statistics. (2016). Report on Bangladesh Sample Statistics. Retrieved from http://bbs.portal.gov.bd/sites/default/files/files/bbs.portal.gov.bd/page/6a40a397_6ef7_48a 3_80b3_78b8d1223e3f/SVRS_REPORT_2016.pdf http://databank.worldbank.org/data/reports. aspx?source=2&series=SP.DYN.TFRT.IN&country=

Bangladesh Education Report. (2016). Retrieved from http://www.thedailystar.net/country/38-percent-secondary-students-drop-out-2016-bangladesh-education-banbeis-report-1408615

Heintz, J., Kabeer, N., & Mahmud, S. (2018). Cultural norms, economic incentives and women's labour market behaviour: Empirical insights from Bangladesh. *Oxford Development Studies*, *46*(2), 266–289. doi:10.1080/13600818.2017.1382464

Microcredit Regulatory Authority. (2015). Microcredit in Bangladesh. Microcredit Regulatory Authority. Retrieved from http://www.mra.gov.bd/index.php?option%BCcom_content&view%BCcategory& layout%BCblog&id%BC29&

Nahar, A. (2013). Rich-peasant resistance to development organizations. In M. Guhathakurta & W. Van Schendel (Eds.), *The Bangladesh reader: History, culture, politics*, (pp. 423–425). Durham, NC: Duke University Press.

Pitt, M., Cartwight, J., & Khandker, S. R. (2006). Empowering women with microfinance: Evidence from Bangladesh. *Economic Development and Cultural Change, 54*(4), 791–831. doi:10.1086/503580

World Bank. (2016). Retrieved from http://data.worldbank.org/indicator/SE.ENR.PRIM.FM.ZS. The enrollment of girls in secondary school has increased more than seven times since 1980 (UNESCO Country Programming Report for Bangladesh 2012-2016). (http://www.unesco.org/new/ fileadmin/MULTIMEDIA/FIELD/Dhaka/pdf/Publications/UNESCO_Country_Programming _Document_For_Bangladesh.pdf)

2

THE STUDY OF GLOBAL AGING

SUZANNE R. KUNKEL | OLIVER HAUTZ

INTRODUCTION

We are in the midst of an explosion of interest in global aging. Since every country in the world has a growing number of older adults, it is not surprising that the amount of research literature and the number of government reports are increasing exponentially. Try a quick Internet search for "global aging" or for "aging in ..."—pick any country from Afghanistan to Zimbabwe—to verify the extent of information available. As one sorts through the growing number of reports and research articles on this topic and considers what it really means to study aging around the world, it helps to remember that the study of global aging actually encompasses several types of investigation, depending on the type of knowledge to be gained.

TYPES OF GLOBAL AGING INVESTIGATION

Three general categories of research in global aging differ from each other based on the kind of question being asked and whether the information sought is about the experiences of aging individuals (e.g., aging within a country) or about characteristics of countries (e.g., descriptive global patterns). This typology is shown in Table 2.1. One kind of investigation asks broad questions about the aging of the world as a whole. **Descriptive global pattern** research **focuses on** macrolevel, aggregated depictions of major demographic, economic, and social trends in many countries. This kind of research provides answers to questions such as: Which countries rank in the top 10 in the number of older people? What is the rate of literacy among older women and older men in different regions of the world? How long do people live, on average, in various countries? What are the major causes of

TABLE 2.1 Types of Investigation in Global Aging

Type of Global Aging Investigation	Description	Sample Question
Descriptive global patterns	Compares nations, regions, or groups of countries on demographic, economic, health, and social trends	Which countries have the highest happiness ratings among older adults?
Single-nation studies	Seeks to understand aging experiences of individuals within one location; often compares subgroups of individuals within that location	What are the factors that influence the happiness of older men and women in Chile?
Cross-national comparisons	Compares aging experiences of individuals in more than one country or culture	What influences the happiness of older adults in Chile, China, and India?

death for people in different parts of the world? Two very good reports that exemplify this kind of research on global aging are *World Population Ageing* (United Nations [UN] Department of Economic and Social Affairs, 2017) and *An Aging World: 2015* (He, Goodkind, & Kowal, 2016). Both publications describe important trends related to population aging, such as increasing life expectancy, increasing burden of chronic rather than infectious diseases, work and retirement patterns, and living arrangements among older people in a wide range of countries.

This type of research relies on international data sets that include information on demographics, health, economic development, and characteristics of the population in a given country, such as labor-force participation, income, and educational levels. The Luxembourg Income Study is a good example of an international comparative data set; this resource provides standardized income, poverty, and inequality data from 50 countries, enabling researchers to easily draw comparisons. Some countries have participated for more than 30 years, also permitting comparisons over time for developing or developed nations (LIS Cross-National Data Center, 2018).

A second category of global aging research focuses on questions about aging *within* a country. This type of scholarship contributes to the literature on global aging by illuminating the policies, social structures, cultural practices, and experiences of older people *in one particular location*. The research questions are about the lives of older adults in that location. A recent example of a **single-nation global aging study** investigated the predictors of happiness among older Korean women living alone in the community. Living alone is less common in South Korea than it is in the United States, so the researchers were concerned that women in this situation were likely to have lower levels of happiness; they sought to identify factors that might positively influence their happiness, so that programs and services could be put in place to meet their needs. For the women in this study, unhappiness was associated with physical discomfort, economic insecurity, lack of self-esteem, and depressive symptoms (Kim, Song, Kim, & Park, 2019). Another study of the correlates of happiness compared older men and women in rural Chile on three food-related variables: (a) satisfaction with food-related life, (b) being the main person responsible for managing household income, and (c) quantity of food in the home. For both older men and women in Chile, satisfaction related to food (measured by having responders rank the importance of items such as "food and meals are positive elements in my life") was associated with overall happiness; for women, greater happiness was associated with having dinner with a companion on a daily basis and with being the main person responsible for managing household income (Lobos, Grunert, Bustamante, & Schnettler, 2016). These studies might make you curious about what "happiness" actually means, why researchers in two different countries would consider such an array of possible correlates (such as satisfaction with food life in Chile and depressive symptoms in South Korea), and how happiness can be measured and compared across cultures. Later in this chapter, you will read more about the challenge of measuring complicated ideas such as happiness across cultures where it might be defined and experienced differently. This type of single-nation inquiry is unique in its focus on what aging is like for *people within one particular place*. It is different from the first category because it does not compare countries or regions of the world and because it focuses on individuals rather than countries as the entity of interest (unit of analysis). These in-depth explorations of aging within a culture or within a nation are growing in number, as are the outlets for such publications, pointing to the increasing prominence of this category (single-nation studies) of global aging research. Research that focuses on aging within a particular culture or society relies on the same range of methods used by social scientists in general. The specific within-nation examples mentioned here used interviews and surveys and analyses of **secondary data** (data already collected for other purposes). Articles based on secondary data follow the same rules of conceptualization, measurement, sampling, and analysis already familiar to those who have learned about social science research methods. These social science methods take on a new dimension when **cross-national comparative research**, the third type of global aging research, is considered.

Comparative global aging studies in some ways combine characteristics of the first two categories (descriptive global patterns and single-nation, within-country aging research); this type of research looks at similarities and differences across two or more countries (as does **descriptive global pattern research**, mentioned earlier) but looks in depth at a particular topic related to aging such as pension plans, quality of life, happiness, or family caregiving (as does the within-country research already described). Comparative global aging research seeks to understand the nature of differences and degree of similarity in the experiences of aging across locations. A recent article on the link between trusting others and health of older adults in six different countries provides a good example of this kind of research. The authors of this study (Chan, Hamamura, Li, & Zhang, 2017) wanted to see if the relationship between trusting others and better health, something which had been consistently observed in Western countries, also held true in non-Western countries. They chose countries at lower levels of socioeconomic development than the Western countries that had been previously studied, making it possible to consider whether trust might have a stronger or weaker influence on health in countries with less developed health and social service systems due to lower economic resources for public services. Trust was measured by a single item about whether the respondent thought that others could generally be trusted. The countries (Ghana, China, India, Mexico, South Africa, and Russia) are quite different from each other culturally; they also vary in terms of human development indicators (such as life expectancy, average level of education, and standard of living), allowing a detailed look at whether the trust–health relationship varies by setting. Interestingly, the percentage of older adults in these countries who reported generalized trust in others ranged from a high of 89% in China to a low of 21% in South Africa. Even though the level of trusting others varied greatly among these countries, the relationship between trust and health was confirmed: in general, trust in others is positively associated with better health (Chan et al., 2017). This study illustrates the two important features of comparative global aging research. The authors looked in-depth **and** across countries to understand the experiences of aging. Comparative research presents extraordinary opportunities to get at the heart of what is universal and what is unique in our "**ageways**" (expectations in a particular culture for how one ages, views older people, and treats them). These opportunities, however, are accompanied by some challenges in attempting to sort out the complex interactions of policies, cultures, economic development, and other unique aspects of nations being compared.

USING A COMPARATIVE PERSPECTIVE

Like all good research, comparative research requires a clear statement of the problem, an explicitly stated research question with strong conceptual grounding, and rigorous methods. However, there is an additional and important consideration. To understand the distinctive goals, challenges, and value of comparative research, consider why it might be of interest to compare the happiness of older people in different countries, such as Finland, which ranked first in the most recent World Happiness Report (Helliwell, Layard, & Sachs, 2019), and Turkey, which ranked near the middle of the list of 156 countries. Even though the overall happiness ratings of these two places diverge, one might ask: Are the older people in these two countries as far apart in terms of happiness as the national numbers overall? If so, why is this the case? Do these two countries' systems of services and support for older adults differ, and what about the health of their older populations? Are there challenging economic or political situations that might be at play? That is the essence of comparative research on aging: to discover patterns of similarity and difference in the experiences of aging across settings or circumstances.

Writing specifically about comparisons of aging across cultures, Palmore succinctly states, "Cross-cultural research is essential for two purposes: separating universal processes of aging from culture-specific processes, and understanding how cultural factors influence aging" (1983, p. 46). Thus, comparative research is appropriate for answering questions such as: Is aging the same in different countries? Does any particular experience of growing older hold true across those settings? If not, what explains the differences? Answering any of these questions requires enough depth of understanding about the uniqueness of specific locations and a conviction that patterns in those unique locations do exist and can be identified.

The question about happiness in Finland and Turkey points to an interesting challenge in research across different cultures. To know how people in these two countries are similar or different regarding their life satisfaction first requires finding out whether the concept is shared by both cultural contexts, an idea which was briefly introduced earlier in the chapter, and if it can be measured in meaningful—and comparable—ways in both places. This unique facet of comparative research is one example of the ways in which good comparative research forces us to question our assumptions, confront our own cultural biases, and carefully consider the design and purpose of our study. These distinctive features of comparative research are more fully explained later in this chapter.

Scholars who specialize in studying the experiences of people in different places debate about whether there is greater value in first seeking an in-depth understanding of one place as in a case study, or whether a better understanding of human experiences can be attained by beginning with comparisons across settings. To continue with the happiness example, a case-study approach would require deep exploration into the definitions, meanings, and components of this complex and subjective concept in one country or the other. A comparative approach would lead a researcher to seek a measure of happiness that could be used in both locations, as is the case with the World Happiness Project. As with most such debates, there is common ground in the middle. There is value—and disadvantage—in both perspectives. The former **one-case approach** focuses on the uniqueness of one culture and the experiences of people living in that location, giving depth and richness of understanding. The latter **multicase perspective** calls for a comparative approach, sacrificing an in-depth focus on uniqueness for the ability to observe, and measure, similarities and differences.

The Importance of Comparison: From Description to Explanation

In many ways, comparative research (e.g., a multicase perspective) is the logical next step after an in-depth, one-case study of a single culture. Whereas a one-case study can provide insight into key aspects and values of a given culture and how the pieces of the puzzle seem to be connected, full explanation of similarities and differences between cultural groups requires comparisons. To move toward explanation after an initial descriptive case study, the researcher might conduct (or look at results from) another case study, organizing and categorizing descriptive information from the two. From that categorization of descriptive elements, the investigator would develop a set of variables that might help to explain similarities and differences between the two settings such as how each culture demonstrates trust and what a typical annual household income is. In this final step, the research is moving from descriptive questions about what things look like to relational questions about why things are the way they are; the latter type of research question "ask(s) how traits are related to other traits" (Ember & Ember, 2009, p. 37) (e.g., how is trust related to financial security?).

We can illustrate the path from a one-case description to categorization across cases to explanation with a hypothetical example about the social status of older people in society. Imagine studying a society where agriculture is the basis of the economy and life expectancy is low. Based on observations of daily life, conversations and reading about cultural traditions, and discussions with residents of this society, researchers can document the interactions, roles, and respect accorded to older people in this one place. With careful analysis, this information could yield a rich understanding of the ways in which traditional cultural values and economic realities coincide (if at all) with a reverence for age. Reasonable connections might be drawn among the facts that, in this fictional society, not many people live to be old, old age is believed to be a sign of favor from the gods, and older people hold valuable knowledge about planting cycles. It would make sense that older people have high status in this culture. However, we could not conclude that all societies with similar values and economies hold older people in high esteem nor could it be inferred that those values and economies are the sole explanation for the status of older persons. For a better understanding of the connection between economic development and social status of older people, it would be necessary to look at another, and then another, and then another case. The research design would require measurement of important aspects of culture that might be related logically to the position of older people and then analyses of the extent to which those connections hold true across different cultures. At this point, cross-national comparative research is being conducted.

The particular example of the link between economic development and status of older people is one of a much larger set of propositions put forth by **modernization theory**. This early theory in gerontology was rooted in cross-cultural foundations and cross-national comparisons. The authors (Cowgill & Holmes, 1972) argued that as societies "modernize," the shift from agricultural to industrial economies devalued the knowledge and skills held by older people; new jobs require new skills and tend to be concentrated in growing urban areas. As a result of their exclusion from the new economy, the migration of younger people to urban areas, and away from traditional living arrangements, the status of older people is hypothesized to decline. Modernization theory (highly simplified here) generated a great deal of literature and a great deal of controversy. Although it has received very little empirical support, it remains an important stimulus to the study of global aging and has generated significant comparative research over the past four decades.

The current social science literature is full of examples of research that compare two or more groups of people (e.g., age groups, income groups, people who participated in a program and those who did not), two or more countries, or two or more points in time. These studies seek to learn something about the similarities and differences among groups, locations, or time periods, and the causes of those patterns. The global aging literature is similarly replete with research on factors associated with similarities and differences in the experiences of aging. For example, Do and Malhotra (2012) were interested in the experiences of aging within South Korea, but the strength of their study came from making some comparisons across groups of older people within South Korean culture. The authors were interested in levels of depression among older South Korean widows who live with children. But they did not simply describe the level of depression among these women. They wanted to know whether depression is higher or lower, depending on living arrangements. And it was. Living with an adult child appeared to have a protective effect against depressive symptoms for the widowed women in this study. Because Korean culture places value on children caring for their aging parents, the widows living with an adult child were compared to those *not* living with an adult child. The participants in this study are presumed to share an important cultural value that living with adult children is preferred and expected. If such a study were done in the United States, the comparisons might be different, based on the cultural values or concerns held about aging. Perhaps widows living alone might be compared to those who live with relatives, assuming that the most important factor for depression is not whether the widow lives with children but whether or not she lives alone or lives in accordance with her expectations (e.g., living with a spouse versus being widowed).

This example illustrates the value of comparative research within one culture, but one of the great promises in comparative studies of aging is looking across countries or cultures. Another example of current global aging research does just that. Nguyen and Cihlar (2013) explored the differences between older adults in Vietnam and Germany with respect to physical fitness and self-rated health. The authors were interested in sorting out how much decline in physical health is due to aging and how much might be due to differences in lifestyle. Citing possible cultural differences such as labor-force participation of older adults in the two countries, the authors wondered whether the longer working life of Vietnamese compared to older Germans would have a positive or negative effect on health. They found that older Vietnamese in their study maintained higher levels of physical fitness than did the older Germans, which could be due to a variety of reasons (e.g., lack of available transportation, preference for exercise). It is not possible from this one study to isolate exactly which factors might be responsible for these differences, but the research makes a significant contribution to the global aging literature by identifying some variations across culture in the impact of aging on health. Interestingly, these authors also found no difference in the self-rated health of the two groups, even though the performance measures suggested that the older Vietnamese were healthier (Nguyen & Cihlar, 2013). The value of, and need for more, comparative research seems clear.

The Challenge and the Promise of Comparative Research

Comparative studies accomplish two important objectives: (a) distinguishing between culture-specific and universal behaviors and experiences (Ember & Ember, 2009) and (b) isolating the culture- or location-specific factors that explain differences. The underlying premise of comparative research is the possibility of universals, or, as Ember and Ember (2009) have suggested, "If you want to say something about [aging] in general, there is no substitute for a worldwide cross-cultural study" (p. 20). Obviously, a worldwide cross-cultural study is not feasible, given the resources and time it would take. But even if the goal is comparison across two or three cultures or locations, there are some significant challenges to keep in mind.

The search for similarities must allow for the possibility of differences and must consider why these differences might exist. Therein lies one of the most important assumptions of comparative research: Something about setting (geographic place, culture, subcultures within a larger culture, or historical time) might make a difference. Ideally, research questions should be explicit about why variations might be found. By identifying the features of a culture or place that might reasonably be expected to produce different experiences, a stronger case for universality can be built if we find similarities.

If we find differences, there can be some explanation for those variations. For example, the article discussed earlier by Nguyen and Cihlar (2013) offered some ideas about why a difference in physical health might be observed between older adults in Vietnam and those in Germany (sedentary lifestyle in Germany; longer working life in Vietnam). Too often, however, comparative research looks for similarities and then uses culture or location as a way to explain away observed differences (Chi, 2011) such as by simply stating that Western countries have different values than do Eastern countries without identifying what those different values might be. To avoid the use of culture or location as nothing more than the residual explanation for differences, it is much more desirable, and much more scientifically sound, to identify the particular aspect of culture or place that might make a difference. These features should, in fact, be treated as variables in a study.

In our earlier example of the relationship between age and happiness in Finland and Turkey, the focus would be on the extent to which age does or does not affect life satisfaction and whether those effects are the same in these two countries. To answer these questions (what is the same and what is different), the researchers could not simply look at a sample of people in Turkey and a sample in Finland and compare the correlation between age and happiness. That would tell only part of the story. Instead, they need to include other variables that might help to explain any differences between the two countries in their degree of life satisfaction–age correlation. If this study revealed that life satisfaction increases with age in both countries, there is no problem: Perhaps the pattern of improved happiness in later life is universal (at least in these two countries). However, if there is a decrease in happiness with age in Finland but no decrease in Turkey, we would want to know more. Had the research included some cultural or economic variables that might be important, there would be the possibility of accomplishing two objectives with this study: (a) illustrating the extent to which a change in life satisfaction universally occurs with age, and (b) isolating some of the reasons that this might be a culture- or place-specific experience rather than a universal experience.

But what are those variables, and are they features of a country, a culture, a group, or a sample? These questions illustrate some of the challenges inherent in comparative research.

CHALLENGE #1: UNIT OF ANALYSIS

In the Turkey/Finland comparison, the first task for a careful comparative researcher would be an attempt to clarify the "unit" of study. Are countries, cultures, or subgroups of individuals within a country being compared? The answer to this question immediately raises another: What are the boundaries of the units to be compared? For countries, recognized geographic boundaries are generally appropriate, but those boundaries are sometimes political and contested. Geographic boundaries may define a single cultural group, or they may include multiple cultural groups. For example, many readers of this book are accustomed to thinking about the United States as a geographically defined country. However, within this nation are numerous groups that are culturally distinct from each other despite sharing a national identity. Abundant literature in gerontology explores the differences in experiences of aging across racial and ethnic groups in the United States. Jackson (2002) draws linkages between the methodological and conceptual issues that underlie studies of racial and ethnic minorities in the United States to those that are important in cross-national research: considering how different groups "traverse the individual life course as they age" (p. 827) and "removing cultural blinders ... and focusing on what makes a difference and what does not" (p. 826).

So far, this chapter has referred often to country and sometimes to culture. This is one of the unique trials of comparative research—deciding, defending, and following through with the geographic or otherwise bounded aggregations intended for study. Hantrais (2009) offers a list of the units, beyond individuals, that might be the focus of comparative research in the social sciences and humanities: "societies, countries, cultures, systems, institutions, social structures, and change over time and space" (p. 2). Since each of these units could be a valuable focus for a comparative study of aging, it is essential to be clear which we have chosen (despite the fact that this chapter thus far has taken liberties with this rule).

Culture

Clarity about whether the unit of analysis is location or culture requires an understanding of what the term culture might refer to. There are many complex, sophisticated, and varied definitions of **culture**; however, for our purposes, it is adequate to define it as the values, practices, beliefs, and behaviors shared by a group of people in a particular place or time, exhibited in ways of life and everyday existence. **Filial piety,** the idea that the older generation is to be respected and cared for by younger generations, is an example of a cultural value. This belief, often associated with Asian cultures, is translated into expectations and behaviors related to living arrangements and long-term care for older adults. In contrast, in the United States and many Western European countries, independence is a dominant cultural value—reflected in the general preference among older adults to live close to, but not with, their children. There are certainly many more examples of cultural values and practices that help to create variability in the experiences of aging.

Culture is transmitted in many ways, including by family, religious institutions, and education systems. It is apparent how geographic proximity makes it easier for a culture to become shared. However, if we want to study culture, how do we determine who belongs to which culture? For countries, geographic boundaries are generally appropriate. Depending on the specific research question, a situation might arise where data are collected from people who live in the same area (possibly even neighbors) but who grew up in very different cultural contexts and thus might hold very different perspectives on the world. This is particularly true in a globalized world in which people relocate to other countries for better jobs or political reasons.

Location

It is common to use location as the unit of analysis in comparative research, sometimes as a shorthand for culture. Studies of global aging often make comparisons across countries, especially in demographic research. Geographic units are relatively easy to define and draw boundaries around. Depending on the research question, geographic units of analysis may be most appropriate. Some social indicators, such as proportion aged, literacy levels, and health status, are collected at the national level by most countries, making broad-scale comparisons possible.

Beyond the convenience and feasibility of national (or other geographic) comparisons, it is reasonable to think that geographic boundaries help to define, at least at a general level, shared values, norms, and behaviors. However, even if we decide that a geographic location is the unit of analysis for the study, this immediately raises another concern: What are the boundaries of the units to be compared? In addition to the mutability of political boundaries, border regions might be characterized by large populations of people from one country commuting to the other country or even living in the other country for economic, political, or security reasons.

The meaningfulness of geographic borders raises the question of whether, in fact, our ultimate interest might be in the role of culture, rather than location. Even when location is a more convenient (and often appropriate) unit of analysis, it is worthwhile to consider the extent to which location and culture intersect and to clarify whether location is being used as a proxy for some aspect of shared cultural experiences.

Nation

Given the complexity of defining and measuring culture, comparative researchers often use stand-ins to conduct meaningful studies involving multiple cultural contexts. As noted, geographic locations often are used as a proxy for culture. The proxy that is used most often is the nation-state (Miller-Loessi & Parker, 2003). The term "nation-state" is a bit more complicated that just "nation" or "country," because it connotes a combination of political, cultural, and geographic boundaries that contribute to a sense of national identity among its citizens. The countries we have been discussing thus far are examples of nation-states. Using the nation (or nation-state) as a proxy for culture seems to be recognized as feasible, although fraught with limitations—not the least of which is that cultural identities often vary within a nation. Indeed, this practice continues to stimulate academic debate about the difference between cross-cultural and cross-national research that goes far beyond the purposes of this book. Therefore, we use "nation" and cross-national research as the most convenient and generally understandable terms.

Kohn (1987) defines cross-national research as research that "is explicitly comparative ... using systematically comparable data from two or more nations" (p. 714). He further distinguishes four different kinds of cross-national research: (a) nation is the *object* of study; (b) nation is the *context* of study, and the focus is often on the experiences and circumstances of people who live in that nation; (c) sets of nations are the *unit of analysis*; and (d) *transnational* research. Table 2.2 summarizes the main characteristics of the four different approaches as described by Kohn.

In describing these categories of cross-national research, Kohn notes that the distinctions are not always clear, but he offers a convincing discussion about the differences in emphasis in each of these categories. Where nations are the objects of study, the focus is on the nations themselves, or on particular social institutions within those countries. A comparison of pension systems in two different countries

TABLE 2.2 Types of Cross-National Research

1. Nation is *object* of study	Investigator is primarily interested in comparisons across specific countries (i.e., How does country A compare to country B?).
2. Nation is *context* of study	Investigator is mainly interested in how culture and social and economic structures within a nation affect the individuals.
3. Groups of nations are *unit of analysis*	Investigator attempts to find similarities and differences between types of nations without reference to a specific nation. Nations are classified along certain characteristics and are compared on the basis of these characteristics.
4. *Transnational*	Nations are treated as part of larger systems (e.g., the financial system, regions, or the European Union).

Source: Data from Kohn, M. L. (1987). Cross-national research as an analytic strategy: American Sociological Association, 1987 presidential address. *American Sociological Review, 52*(6), 713–731. doi:10.2307/2095831

is a good example: Who is eligible to receive a pension? How generous are the benefits? How is the program funded? Answering these questions comparatively allows for observations about the similarities and differences across social and economic structures and policies that affect the lives of older adults. When nation is context, the research becomes a bit richer in its exploration of how particular social arrangements help to explain similarities or differences in the experiences of people in those countries. This category is analogous to what we described above as **single-nation** studies of aging. The last two categories in Kohn's list move to higher levels of abstraction about what characteristics of nations, or interrelated international systems of countries, make a difference in the topic of interest. When nations are the unit of analysis, researchers are interested in how categories of countries (e.g., developed and developing) compare to each other. Comparing the long-term care systems of developed nations to those of developing nations would be an example of this kind of research. **Transnational** is a term that is becoming increasingly common in the globalized world. In **transnational research**, countries are treated as components of larger international systems; there is presumed to be an observable connection among those nations. For example, in transnational families, family roles and relationships are affected by the fact that family members may live and work in different countries for part of the time. In the case of families whose lives are affected by workers who spend some time overseas, the connectedness of the sending and receiving nations can be measured in terms of migration patterns; the impact of such connectedness is the topic of transnational research. While Kohn's very sophisticated classification of types of cross-national research is beyond the scope of this chapter, it serves to illustrate how carefully these issues are considered within the field of comparative research.

For those who are most familiar and comfortable with research on individuals, the idea that nations might be the object of study may not be intuitive. An example may help. Mwangi (2012) was interested in why some countries have developed systems of palliative care and others have not. Palliative care is designed to provide care and comfort rather than cure for people living with terminal illnesses. Mwangi analyzed several national-level factors that might explain this variation. He considered the overall level of economic development, assuming that the resources for this specialized care might not be available in the poorest countries. His study also included the major causes of death in each country. He reasoned that countries where infectious diseases are predominant might not consider palliative care a priority since the period between onset and death is relatively short. In contrast, countries where chronic diseases such as cancer or HIV/AIDS are prevalent will typically see much longer dying processes and thus might be more focused on end-of-life care. He also researched the proportion of the population that was older and the level of government expenditures for health care. These variables (economic development, population aging, health care expenditures, and major causes of death) were features of the countries themselves, not of the individuals who live there. In general, he found that higher-income countries and those with high rates of complex medical conditions were more likely to have palliative care options. Some countries in southern Africa were in the less economically developed category, but they did have formal palliative care in place to deal with high rates of HIV/AIDS.

CHALLENGE #2: CONCEPTUALIZATION AND MEASUREMENT

At the core of every research project are the concepts that investigators seek to understand. In comparative research, as in all research, the first task is to clarify the research question and the variables that researchers want to include. In other words, what exactly is it that we want to know and what pieces of data will help us answer that question? The special challenge in comparative research is to find or devise concepts that are meaningful across cultures and across languages.

In the Turkey/Finland example, the possibility was raised that the very concept of happiness may not mean the same thing at all in those two countries. How do investigators handle this situation? If they really want to compare happiness among older adults in both of those countries, they need a measure that is standardized enough so that it can be compared. Asking entirely different questions in the two locations is not an option, but asking exactly the same questions might not work either since concepts can have very different meanings within a cultural context.

In an attempt to gather data on the functional health of older adults in Nepal and then to compare the rates of functional impairments across Nepal and the United States, two researchers (Kunkel & Subedi, 1996) set out to use the standard U.S. measures of functional ability with a sample of older adults in Nepal. These two scales, activities of daily living (ADLs) and instrumental activities of daily living (IADLs), ask about whether the person is able to independently accomplish the things necessary for everyday life: bathing, preparing food, shopping, dressing, eating, and the like. The researchers encountered two significant problems. The first was with the basic premise of the ADL/IADL scale. The questions center on whether the respondent is still able to do a particular task independently, without the help or supervision of another person. As it turned out, the very idea of *independence* in getting daily tasks accomplished was simply not meaningful, or even translatable, in Nepal. Especially in rural areas where this study was being conducted, life is organized around the ideal of **interdependence,** not independence. All do what they can, and they help each other. This is quite different from the U.S. cultural context, where the loss of independent functioning is an unwelcome marker of physical decline, frailty, and old age itself.

The second problem encountered by these researchers was related to the specific activities they asked about. Again, using the standard U.S.-based ADL/IADL scale, they wanted to know whether the participants still were able—on their own—to bathe, dress, prepare meals, shop for groceries, and so forth. In the United States, the ability to bathe without help is typically related to whether the individual can safely get in and out of a bathtub and stand or sit safely while bathing. In rural Nepal, bathing involves hauling water and heating it over a fire.

Clearly, "impairment in bathing" means entirely different things in the two countries. Similar challenges were encountered with understanding what is involved in shopping for food and, importantly, with activities that *were not* included but were meaningful to everyday living for rural Nepalese (such as getting to prayers and freshening up the walls with a new coat of specially prepared mud).

The essay by Tausig and Subedi at the end of this chapter, "The Challenges of Measuring Mental Illness: A Comparison of the United States and Nepal," addresses this fascinating challenge of conceptual comparability. Their research on mental health among adults produced results very different in the United States from results in Nepal (Tausig, Subedi, Broughton, Subedi, & Williams-Blangero, 2003). For example, nearly one half of the U.S. respondents reported that they had felt sad, empty, or depressed for several days in a row at some time in their life, but only 12% of the Nepal respondents said they had this experience. Tausig and Subedi suggest that perhaps the question was not understood in the same way in the two locations or that cultural values were at work in helping to shape the answers the respondents gave.

Comparative research in global aging has come a long way since that somewhat misguided early attempt to import a U.S.-based measure of health status to a very different location and culture. Numerous cross-national research projects on aging have been implemented, allowing scholars to address the very issues raised here regarding conceptualization and measurement. The Health and Retirement Study (conducted by the University of Michigan) has been gathering data from more than 20,000 Americans aged 50 and older every 2 years since 1992; the survey covers a wide range of topics, including health, finances, social support, families, and retirement planning. This very rich data set has become the model for longitudinal studies of aging and as of 2019 has been the basis for nearly 4,500 articles, reports, book chapters, and dissertations (Health and Retirement Study, n.d.). The U.S.-based study has grown into a family of studies with more than 15 versions adapted for specific countries and regions of the world, including China, Brazil, Costa Rica, Indonesia, Thailand, South Korea, Mexico, and Europe. The Survey of Health, Ageing and Retirement in Europe (SHARE) is an excellent illustration of these collaborative, coordinated, well-designed cross-national research initiatives. SHARE is a multidisciplinary and cross-national database of information on health, socioeconomic status, and social and family networks of more than 140,000 individuals aged 50 and over from 27 European countries and Israel (Survey of Health, Ageing and Retirement in Europe, n.d.). The SHARE is designed so that the measures, coding, and analyses can be directly compared with those in the Health and Retirement Survey (one of the most extensive ongoing studies of aging in the United States) and the English Longitudinal Study of Ageing, allowing for endless possibilities to compare and understand the experiences of aging in many different countries (Börsch-Supan et al., 2013). This rigorous process of standardizing measures, coding, analyses, and study design to maximize comparability across different locations is called **harmonization**.

Another illustration of remarkable progress in the design and implementation of culturally sensitive research about aging is the World Health Organization Quality of Life (WHOQOL) project. This initiative responded to two important needs in research on aging: (a) holistic measures of health that go beyond disease, mortality, and functional status, and (b) instruments that are truly cross-cultural, not merely translations of existing measures (often developed in Western nations). According to the WHO, "The WHOQOL is a quality-of-life assessment developed by the WHOQOL group with 15 international field centres, simultaneously, in an attempt to develop a quality-of-life assessment that would be applicable cross-culturally" (WHOQOL, n.d.). The measure has been used extensively to study the factors related to quality of life for older adults in a range of locations, including the positive impact of social support on quality of life among older men in Kenya (Campbell, Gray, & Radak, 2011), differences in the way quality of life is described by Nepalese women who live with family compared to those who live in an old-age home (Shrestha & Zarit, 2012), and higher quality of life for Dutch citizens aged 50 and older who possess a secret (Maas, Wismeijer, & Van Assen, 2019).

CHALLENGE #3: GETTING VALID DATA

As mentioned earlier, having a well-conceptualized and compelling research question with culturally appropriate measures is the first step in any project. Once the topic, the concepts, and the unit of analysis have been decided, the researchers must turn their attention to decisions about how to get the information they need. Secondary data (data that already has been collected) can be the most appropriate source of information for some questions related to global aging. Earlier in this chapter, the description of global pattern research gave some examples of secondary data. Researchers interested, for example, in comparing the level of literacy and proportion of older people with a decent standard of living across different countries could use data from the Human Development Index, constructed by the United Nations.

Very often, however, the topic of study will require the collection of new data. In this case, researchers must grapple with sampling—selecting and reaching the right people to interview, survey, or observe. Sampling strategies are key in every social science discipline, whether research is being done *across* or *within* societies or cultures. The two basic questions related to sampling are: Who should be talked to (or observed) in order to understand the topic being studied? How many and which people should be included in order to result in a good representation of an entire group and a valid understanding of the topic? The art and the science of sample design are far beyond the scope of this book, but the ideas behind them are not. Since social science researchers virtually never have the option of communicating with every member of a population, they must have a plan for choosing the appropriate subset of people to include. In some studies, this subset might be *key informants*—people who possess specialized and in-depth knowledge about the topic being studied. For example, if investigators want to learn about the every-day lives of grandmothers in Swaziland who are raising their grandchildren, it would be essential to talk to some of those women. After all, they are the experts on this topic; hearing directly from them will help build a rich understanding of the shared joys and challenges they face.

In other types of studies, the sample will not focus on a relatively small group of key informants who can give researchers a deep understanding of their experiences, but rather on a group of people who, taken together, can accurately represent a much larger group. This representative group would be selected through sampling techniques that ensure the right number and type of participants. If, for example, researchers were interested in the prevalence of certain health conditions among grandmothers raising grandchildren in Swaziland, it would *not* be sufficient to interview 10 or 12 women. Although the stories of those 10 women would be highly enlightening, investigators could not conclude that their experiences (or health conditions) were generalizable to the whole population of women in this situation. In order to generalize, researchers need larger samples of people who can, through careful selection techniques, represent the whole group.

CHALLENGE #4: RESPECTING PARTICIPANTS

Whether based on key informants or a representative sample (or some combination), comparative research adds interesting new twists to the strategies for selecting, and reaching, participants. The establishment of trusting relationships with research participants is a cornerstone of ethical and valid research no matter where it is being conducted. When differences in language and cultural values are in play, the responsibility for researchers to learn how to appropriately interact with participants is significantly heightened. The essay on dementia in Brazil at the end of this chapter, "Aging and Dementia in Brazil," mentions that stigma about the disease presents challenges to diagnosis and treatment. Researchers interested in understanding more about attitudes toward dementia in Brazil would need to be especially sensitive to the fact that people may be reluctant to discuss it.

Challenge #2 addressed another aspect of respecting participants—ensuring that concepts are translatable and that the translations capture meanings correctly. At one level, these may appear to be very pragmatic concerns that make cross-cultural research more challenging. But they are more than that: They speak to the profound opportunity afforded by such research—to deeply understand the experiences of aging in other cultures. They also speak to the ethical issues related to the fairness, justice, and respect due to all research participants. In the United States, as in many other nations, both professional associations and the government have formal processes and written standards for the ethical conduct of research. These standards include making sure that participation in research is voluntary and not coerced, that participants clearly understand what they are being asked to do as part of the research as demonstrated through a process of obtaining informed consent, that the risk of participating in research does not outweigh the benefit of the knowledge to be gained, and that data related to individuals be kept secure and confidential. In cross-cultural studies, researchers are obligated to think carefully about how the ethical principles apply in different settings. Marshall (2006) discusses the challenges in getting **informed consent** from participants. This universally accepted idea rests on two foundations—that potential participants must fully understand the research in which they are being asked to take part ("informed") and that they are free to say no ("consent"). A variety of factors can make informed consent difficult in cross-cultural research, including comprehension of information, understanding of risk, and perceptions about the authority and power held by the researcher (Marshall, 2006).

In the United States, **institutional review boards** (IRBs) are charged by federal law to oversee and approve researchers' plans to study human subjects. Many IRBs have shown great concern about—and, in fact, on occasion have blocked—investigators offering cash to potential participants as compensation and incentive for agreeing to be interviewed. They are especially concerned that—to people living in poverty in less developed countries—even a modest amount of money (sometimes as little as $5) might be coercive, practically forcing them to consent to be studied. This ethical dilemma represents a truly thorny problem for cross-cultural researchers.

The WHO offers a casebook with numerous illustrations of, and guidance for, ethical research in cross-cultural studies (Cash, Wikler, Saxena, & Capron, 2009). To highlight the issue of voluntary informed consent with older populations, the authors describe a situation in which researchers sought to understand traditional health practices among the older adults of the community. Respecting the local system in which the oldest adult son is recognized as the head of the household, the researchers first sought permission from the son before approaching the older adults in the household. However, the interviews were conducted only with the elders; no other family members were present. One of the older adults became agitated during the interview, and his son accused the researchers of making his father ill in order to force him into the hospital. The complicated situation described in this case example illustrates questions of trust, cultural misunderstanding, whose consent and comfort is in play, and even the voluntariness of the consent given by the older person once his son had agreed.

CONCLUSION

With all of these challenges to cross-cultural comparative research, why should we try? Each challenge is actually an essential feature of the enormous opportunity afforded by comparative research. For example, thinking through the principles of ethical research and how these principles must be applied in a culturally respectful way requires researchers to learn a great deal about the group or society they seek to study before they even begin; the knowledge gained in this way is apart from, but foundational to, truly understanding the specific topic of interest. It simply does not work for researchers to take their own assumptions, definitions, and research practices into a culturally unique setting. Doing so would inevitably result in mistakes, potentially create misunderstandings, and ultimately undermine attempts to gain the valid knowledge they seek.

Comparative research requires investigators to be better than they might otherwise be, taking nothing for granted and focusing on the underlying principles of good design and respect for participants, not just the pragmatics. In addition to the heightened awareness about the research enterprise that can be gained in comparative research, there are many other good reasons to conduct such studies. In an elegant summary, Baistow (2000) identifies four ways that we can learn from comparative research: learning about others, learning from others, learning about ourselves, and learning with others.

Perhaps there is no more compelling statement of the value of comparative research than American political scientist Seymour Martin Lipset's succinct claim that, "[A person] who knows only one country, knows none" (quoted in Lipset, 1996). This is an era of unprecedented opportunity to expand the depth of knowledge about *ageways*, thanks to the perspective that may be gained from learning about many other countries. It is the obligation of researchers—and readers—to apply the highest standards of rigorous and culturally respectful comparative research to ensure the validity and utility of that new knowledge.

DISCUSSION QUESTIONS

1. Find an article on some aspect of aging of interest to you (caregiving, grandparenthood, health, happiness, living arrangements, nursing homes, etc.) in a country of interest to you. What question(s) is the article addressing? What is the unit of analysis? What kinds of comparisons are being made? How are the key concepts defined? Given what you have read in this chapter, what data are being used? What do you feel are the strengths and weaknesses of the article?

2. What are some of the benefits and barriers of cross-national research?

3. Why is getting valid data so important? What are some ways to ensure that information is valid?

4. Is it always a good idea to compensate research subjects with money? Think of an example that illustrates a pro and a con for research compensation.

5. Pick two countries and an outcome that you would like to compare. What type of information would you need to make your comparison? What might be some of the barriers in getting your data? Where might you look for data sources?

KEY WORDS

Ageways
Cross-national comparative research
Culture
Descriptive global pattern research
Filial piety
Harmonization
Informed consent
Institutional review boards

Interdependence
Key informants
Modernization theory
Secondary data
Single-nation research
Transnational research
Unit of analysis

REFERENCES

Baistow, K. (2000). Cross-national research: What can we learn from inter-country comparisons? *Social Work in Europe, 7*(3), 8–13.

Börsch-Supan, A., Brandt, M., Hunkler, C., Kneip, T., Korbmacher, J., Malter, F., & Zuber, S. (2013). Data resource profile: The survey of health, aging, and retirement in Europe (SHARE). *International Journal of Epidemiology, 42*(4), 1–10.

Campbell, B. C., Gray, P. B., & Radak, J. (2011). In the company of men: Quality of life and social support among the Ariaal of Northern Kenya. *Journal of Cross-Cultural Gerontology, 26*(3), 221–237. doi:10.1007/s10823-011-9146-x

Cash, R., Wikler, D., Saxena, A., & Capron, A. (2009). *Casebook on ethical issues in international health research.* Geneva, Switzerland: World Health Organization.

Chan, D., Hamamura, T., Li, L., & Zhang, S. (2017). Is trusting others related to better health? An investigation of older adults across six non-Western countries. *Journal of Cross-Cultural Psychology, 48*(8), 1288–1301. doi:10.1177%2F0022022117722632

Chi, I. (2011). Cross-cultural gerontology research methods: Challenges and solutions. *Ageing and Society, 31*(3), 371. doi:10.1017/S0144686X10000942

Cowgill, D. O., & Holmes, L. D. (1972). Summary and conclusions: The theory in review. In D. O. Cowgill & L. D. Holmes (Eds.), *Aging and modernization* (pp. 305–323). New York, NY: Appleton-Century-Crofts.

Do, Y. K., & Malhotra, C. (2012). The effect of co-residence with an adult child on depressive symptoms among older widowed women in South Korea: An instrumental variables estimation. *The Journals of Gerontology Series B: Psychological Sciences and Social Sciences, 67*(3), 384–391. doi:10.1093/geronb/gbs033

Ember, C. R., & Ember, M. (2009). *Cross-cultural research methods* (2nd ed.). Lanham, MD: AltaMira Press.

Hantrais, L. (2009). *International comparative research: Theory, methods and practice.* Basingstoke, England: Palgrave Macmillan.

He, W., Goodkind, D., & Kowal, P. (2016). An Aging World: 2015. *U. S. Census Bureau International Population Reports, P95/16-1.* Retrieved from https://www.census.gov/content/dam/Census/library/publications/2016/demo/p95-16-1.pdf

Health and Retirement Study. (n.d.). Publications. Retrieved from https://hrs.isr.umich.edu/publications

Helliwell, J., Layard, R., & Sachs, J. (2019). *World Happiness Report 2019.* New York, NY: Sustainable Development Solutions Network.

Jackson, J. S. (2002). Conceptual and methodological linkages in cross–cultural groups and cross–national aging research. *Journal of Social Issues, 58*(4), 825–835. doi:10.1111/1540-4560.00292

Kim, J., Song, Y., Kim, T., & Park, K. (2019). Predictors of happiness among older Korean women living alone. *Geriatrics and Gerontology International, 19*(4), 352–356. doi:10.1111/ggi.13615

Kohn, M. L. (1987). Cross-national research as an analytic strategy: American Sociological Association, 1987 presidential address. *American Sociological Review, 52*(6), 713–731. doi:10.2307/2095831

Kunkel, S., & Subedi, J. (1996). Aging in south Asia: How "imperative" is the demographic imperative? In V. Minichiello, N. Chappell, H. Kendig, & A. Walker (Eds.), *Sociology of aging* (pp. 459–466). Melbourne, Australia: International Sociological Association; Toth.

Lipset, S. M. (1996). *American exceptionalism: A double-edged sword.* New York, NY: W.W. Norton and Company.

LIS Cross-National Data Center. (2018). *LIS Database.* Retrieved from http://www.lisdatacenter.org/our-data/lis-database

Lobos, G., Grunert, K., Bustamante, M., & Schnettler, B. (2016). With health and good food, great life! Gender differences and happiness in Chilean rural older adults. *Social Indicators Research, 127*(2), 865–885. doi:10.1007/s11205-015-0971-0

Maas, J., Wismeijer, A., & Van Assen, M. (2019). Associations between secret-keeping and quality of life in older adults. *International Journal of Aging and Human Development, 88*(3), 250–265. doi:10.1177/0091415018758447

Marshall, P. S. (2006). Informed consent in international health research. *Journal of Empirical Research on Human Research Ethics, 1*(1), 25–41. doi:10.1525/jer.2006.1.1.25

Miller-Loessi, K., & Parker, J. N. (2003). Cross-cultural social psychology. In J. Delamater (Ed.), *Handbook of social psychology* (pp. 529–553). New York, NY: Kluwer Academic Plenum.

Mwangi, S. M. (2012). Salient factors associated with growth of palliative care around the world. Presented at first IAGG African Regional Conference on Ageing, Cape Town, South Africa.

Nguyen, H. M., & Cihlar, V. (2013). Differences in physical fitness and subjectively rated physical health in Vietnamese and German older adults. *Journal of Cross-Cultural Gerontology, 28*(2), 181–194. doi:10.1007/s10823-013-9195-4

Palmore, E. B. (1983). Cross-cultural research: State of the art. *Research on Aging, 5*(1), 45–57. doi:10.1177/0164027583005001003

Shrestha, S., & Zarit, S. H. (2012). Cultural and contextual analysis of quality of life among older Nepali women. *Journal of Cross-Cultural Gerontology, 27*(2), 163–182. doi:10.1007/s10823-012-9167-0

Survey of Health, Ageing and Retirement in Europe. (n.d.). Retrieved from http://www.share-project.org/home0.html

Tausig, M., Subedi, S., Broughton, C., Subedi, J., & Williams-Blangero, S. (2003). Measuring community mental health in developing societies: Evaluation of a checklist format in Nepal. *International Journal of Social Psychiatry, 49*(4), 269–286. doi:10.1177/0020764003494005

United Nations Department of Economic and Social Affairs. (2017). *World population ageing 2017.* Retrieved from https://www.un.org/en/development/desa/population/publications/pdf/ageing/WPA2017_Highlights.pdf

World Health Organization Quality of Life. (n.d.). Retrieved from https://www.who.int/mental_health/publications/whoqol/en

THE CHALLENGES OF MEASURING MENTAL ILLNESS: A COMPARISON OF THE UNITED STATES AND NEPAL

MARK TAUSIG | JANARDAN SUBEDI

In order to understand any social phenomenon in a cross-national comparative context—be it aspects of aging, elder care, or mental illness—it would seem obvious that we need to measure the same phenomenon in each national context. This is simple: just ask the identical questions in each country and compare the answers. Alas, the reality is far from simple. In order to make the needed comparisons, it is important that (a) the same questions are being asked, (b) the questions are understood in the same way, and (c) respondents' answers are unbiased by the context of the survey. Only after each of these problems has been addressed do researchers have confidence that the information can be compared across different countries and cultures. These concerns are technical aspects of the method used to collect data, but they are also crucial to understanding cross-national differences and similarities.

Cultural, linguistic, material, geographic, and social differences among countries may make it difficult to know if the same questions are being asked in different societies. This type of difficulty refers to the validity of the construct the investigators are trying to measure and compare. As an example, related to aging, consider the concept of IADL skills that are measured by assessing the following (among other skills): ability to use the telephone, use transportation, and ability to manage medication. Whereas these questions are perfectly sensible in the United States, they are not as appropriate in a country like Nepal. Residents in Nepal very often have no telephones, no motorized vehicles may exist in a rural village, and modern medicine is not available. How can we compare the answers given by U.S. citizens to those given by Nepalese citizens? Indeed, we simply cannot ask the same questions to assess IADL skills in the United States and in Nepal. And if we change the questions we ask in Nepal to fit the circumstances, can we compare the answers we get from a modified list of IADL skills ("Can you carry water from the village well to your house?") with the list used in the United States?

The measurement of psychiatric symptoms using a survey format can be similarly difficult. Even if we suppose it is possible to ask the same questions about an individual's feelings and emotions in the United States and Nepal, we must assess the extent to which survey respondents in both countries understand the questions being asked and the extent to which they will answer accurately. Notice that the problem is true for data collected both in the United States and in Nepal. This is because the challenges are related to the method for collecting the information, and they occur *because* of the method—in this case, a survey.

From 2002 to 2003, identical large-scale surveys of psychiatric disorders in adults in the United States and in Nepal were conducted using a survey called the World Health Organization Composite International Diagnostic Interview (WHO CIDI). This survey is designed to diagnose up to 23 psychiatric disorders using standard diagnostic criteria and has been shown to agree with diagnoses done by clinical interviews conducted by trained psychiatric personnel. The objectives of the studies included the ability to compare rates of disorder between countries.

Of course, the U.S.-designed interview had to be translated into Nepali, and interviewers needed to be trained. The translation was done using standard procedures, and the quality of the translation was extensively checked to make sure it was accurate. Similarly, the interviewers were trained for several weeks to ensure the quality of their work. Because of all this work, we thought we had asked the same questions in the United States as in Nepal.

The results, however, raised some concerns about whether the questions were understood in the same way and whether the recorded answers were accurate. In the United States, for example, looking at a series of 16 questions that were designed to screen respondents for possible disorders, the average respondent reported 3.7 symptoms; in Nepal the average respondent reported 1.2 symptoms. There were also big differences in the percentages of respondents who reported specific symptoms. In the United States, for example, 49% of respondents reported having felt sad, empty, or depressed for a period of several days sometime in their lives; in Nepal, only 12% said they had ever felt this way.

Possibly the questions were misunderstood by respondents in either the United States or Nepal. Or, maybe respondents did not give accurate answers. Indeed, these are common concerns when conducting surveys, and ways have been devised for checking on them and for estimating their effects on observed answers. To see if respondents understand the questions being asked, surveys often ask the interviewer to evaluate the respondents' comprehension of the survey questions. Overall, respondents in the United States were rated as having poor understanding of the survey 7% of the time; in Nepal, this figure was 13%. We also found that when respondents have a good understanding of the question, they tend to report fewer of the symptoms being asked about. In both the United States and Nepal, respondents reported a statistically significantly lower likelihood of having ever felt sad, empty, or depressed during their lives when they understood the question.

What about accuracy? Again, this is a common concern when using surveys to collect information. We do not think respondents will lie to survey interviewers (although they probably do sometimes). Rather, it is not unusual for respondents in any country to worry if they give answers that might cast some shame or embarrassment or disapproval on themselves or their family members. Hence, they are more likely to give the socially desirable answer, the answer they think the interviewer expects and that will seem "normal." The survey had a series of questions that measure social desirability, which we can use to compare the type of answer we get from respondents who may be giving socially desirable answers that do not reflect their true feelings versus respondents who do give us true answers. In this instance, we found that U.S. respondents were answering from the social desirability perspective 15% of the time; in Nepal, the figure was 36%! In both the United States and Nepal, persons answering from this perspective reported much fewer symptoms. Since symptoms of mental illness are socially undesirable, respondents who are sensitive to that idea were less likely to report feelings of sadness, emptiness, or depression.

Another factor that affects the accuracy of reports is whether someone else in the household is present when the interview occurs. Particularly when the interviewer asks questions about feelings and emotions, we might expect that having someone else in the room would cause the respondent to withhold information. As it turns out, it was the opposite. Respondents reported more symptoms when someone else was present during the interview. This was true in both the United States and Nepal, but the effect on symptom reports was larger in the United States. That is, U.S. respondents rather than Nepalese were more likely to report symptoms when someone else was present at the interview.

So, what are the overall conclusions? When we adjust the survey responses in the United States and in Nepal to account for these common sources of misreporting, misunderstanding, and social desirability, we find that the rates of psychiatric symptoms reported are still much higher in the United States than in Nepal. The adjustments made in both surveys give us a more precise count of symptoms that now can be compared across these two countries. They show far more psychiatric disorders in the United States than in Nepal. But how true is this conclusion? We do not think the differences are as dramatic as the adjusted data suggest. We think that the cultural differences between the United States and Nepal are such that the Nepalese respondents vastly underreported their feelings. Nepalese are not accustomed to thinking about how they feel emotionally and, when they do, may not think in the same terms as people living in the United States. In addition, people in Nepal are almost never surveyed, and they are very suspicious of revealing information to strangers (our interviewers). We also found that Nepalese are sensitive to the stigma associated with mental illness and also are very likely to ignore or self-deny symptoms when they occur. In this instance, asking the same questions in two different countries (even after adjusting for the methodological biases that can affect survey results) may not give us a good basis for comparing the levels of psychiatric disorder in these two countries. Not so simple!

FURTHER READING

Angel, R., & Thoits, P. (1987). The impact of culture on the cognitive structure of illness. *Culture, Medicine and Psychiatry, 11*, 465–494.doi:10.1007/BF00048494

Chang, J. M., Hahn, B-J., Lee, J-Y., Shin, M. S., Jeon, H. J., Hong, J-P., . . . Cho, M. J. (2008). Cross-national difference in the prevalence of depression caused by the diagnostic threshold. *Journal of Affective Disorders, 106*, 159–167. doi:10.1016/j.jad.2007.07.023

Jang, Y., Small, J., & Haley, W. E. (2010). Cross-cultural comparability of the Geriatric Depression Scale: Comparison between older Koreans and older Americans. *Aging and Mental Health, 5*, 31–37. doi:10.1080/13607860020020618

Kleinman, A. (1987). Anthropology and psychiatry: The role of culture in cross-cultural research on illness. *British Journal of Psychiatry, 151*, 447–454. doi:10.1192/bjp.151.4.447

AGING AND DEMENTIA IN BRAZIL

FLORINDO STELLA | JOUCE GABRIELA DE ALMEIDA |
PAULO RENATO CANINEU

Brazil is the fifth largest country in the world in terms of both population size and landmass (Schneider, 2018). In fact, Brazil accounts for nearly half of the land (47%) of South America and has an area equal to about 90% of the United States. Brazil has three levels of government: federal, state (there are 26 states in five geographic regions), and municipal (5,563 municipalities); see Paim, Travassos, Almeida, Bahia, and Macinko (2011). It is also multiethnic, with half of the population self-classified as Brown (43.8%) or Black (6.8%); see Paim et al. (2011). In 2018, people aged 65 years or older in Brazil comprised 9.2% (19.2 million people) of the general population (208 million people). Women continue to be a significant majority of this group, representing about 56% of elders (Brazilian Institute of Geography and Statistics [IBGE], 2018). Certainly, rapid population aging is a worldwide phenomenon, occurring in Brazil as well as most countries of the world.

Two conditions have contributed to the growth of older persons in Brazil over the past few years: increasing life expectancy due to improvement of health conditions and a decreasing fertility rate, currently 1.77 children per woman. Life expectancy at birth in Brazil also has increased since 1940, from 45 years to an average of 76 years in 2018 (73 years for men; 79 years for women). Interestingly, life expectancy is higher in the south and southeast regions of the country, which typically have a high standard of living, compared to the north region, which is almost entirely covered by the Amazon rainforest and is consequently the most isolated region in the country. The states of Rio Grande do Sul in the south and Rio de Janeiro in the southeast have the highest percentages of older people, around 18.6% of their populations, while the state of Amapá, in the north, has the lowest percentage, around 7.2%. Another important consideration for the north region is that few studies have been conducted of elders living in small villages in the Amazon Basin. In these villages, people essentially maintain a subsistence economy with very low incomes. Fishing, cultivation of roots for flour, and hunting by some groups are important activities. Access to external information by radio, TV, newspapers, and telephone is limited due to the region's geographic isolation.

Of special concern in this essay are two closely linked major challenges affecting elders in Brazil: dementia and caregiving. While the majority of the essay discusses some of the challenges surrounding dementia diagnosis and treatment, it concludes with some considerations for improving the quality of life of both the person with dementia and his or her caregivers. Special attention is given to efforts to reduce the violence against older persons in Brazil.

DEMENTIA AND COGNITIVE IMPAIRMENT IN BRAZIL

Dementia is a broad term, describing a variety of chronic cognitive conditions that feature problems with memory, learning, behaviors, and orientation to time and place to a point where it interferes with a person's ability to perform tasks needed in everyday life (e.g., bathing, dressing, eating). While there are several types of dementia (e.g., vascular dementia, Lewy body dementia), the most common type is Alzheimer's disease (AD). The prevalence of global dementia among people aged 65 years and older is estimated to be around 7%; more than 60% of dementia cases in older people are of Alzheimer's type. Although no definitive test for AD exists (it can only be confirmed through an autopsy), this particular dementia features the presence in the brain of beta-amyloid plaques and neurofibrillary tangles from tau protein, which are hallmarks of the disease.

Cerebrovascular Risk Factors

Cerebrovascular disease is a very frequent condition in older people, even in individuals without dementia, and has been associated with other risk factors that are not adequately controlled. In Brazil, additional risk factors include diabetes mellitus, hypertension, dyslipidemia (an abnormal amount of lipids [fats] in the blood), heart disease, smoking, alcoholism, obesity, and sedentary lifestyle, especially among elders with low educational levels and those economically disadvantaged.

These risk factors can cause a deleterious impact on the structure and functioning of the brain, subsequently causing vascular dementia, which is a dementia caused by reductions in blood flow to the brain. In deprived areas with minimal support for primary health care, cerebrovascular risk factors are poorly controlled. In addition, the occurrence of mixed dementia—AD and vascular dementia—is quite frequent.

Different than dementia is cognitive impairment, which describes some loss in memory, language ability, thinking, or judgment that is greater than is common for one's age but not significant enough to prevent a person from completing ADLs, as in dementia. Cognitive impairment rates in Brazil are estimated at 7.7% among people aged 65 or older and nearly 20% in the general population.

General Challenges in Dementia Diagnosis and Treatment

In Brazil, specifically, a considerable challenge to diagnosing and treating dementia is a general lack of understanding about the condition and its complexities. Misunderstandings about the differences between age-associated cognitive changes and early dementia are common, even among health professionals. In addition, the delayed detection of clinically relevant cognitive changes reflects the stigma regarding mental health conditions that still is common in Brazil, thereby preventing many people from being appropriately diagnosed and treated. In Brazil, few large-scale studies of the general population have been carried out of public stigma about dementia. An investigation enrolling adults in São Paulo, the largest city in Brazil, found that just under half of participants agreed with notions of domains that make up the concept of stigma, which is composed of stereotypes (41.6%), prejudice (43.4%), and discrimination (35.5%) against people with AD. Interestingly, stigma associated with AD was less than for depression (56% for stereotypes about people with depression) and schizophrenia (74.2% for stereotypes about people with depression); see Blay and Peluso (2010). Such data suggest less intolerance toward AD compared with other mental disorders. However, by using the composite criterion of stigma, which simultaneously encompasses all domains of the concept (stereotypes, prejudice, and discrimination), 14.8% of the responders revealed holding some stigma associated with AD.

In Latin America, including Brazil, the diagnosis of dementia is primarily a clinical procedure. In general, routine laboratory investigations, such as blood tests, may be available. As mentioned earlier, there are different types of dementia with differing etiologies and symptoms; so appropriate diagnosis is important for treatment. However, clinicians have great difficulty in obtaining a detailed neuropsychological evaluation, as well as a brain MRI, in order to support their diagnostic hypothesis.

It is important to note that the health care system in Brazil is a public–private mix whereby a person's ability to pay plays a major role in determining what care is accessible to them. Since 1988 when it was created, the Brazilian National Health System (SUS), a public system, aims to provide individual and collective health care. In the past few decades, this public system saw a substantial growth in the population's use. Nowadays, the SUS has been suffering a critical deterioration. Over the years, basic health care has been progressively migrated to private medical insurance plans, which do not always cover clinical demands. The costs for elders who participate in these private plans are very high and are becoming increasingly unaffordable. Therefore, expensive complex medical procedures are restricted to the minority of individuals who have the financial means to cover the cost themselves or through their families.

Subsequently, according to characteristics of the services accessible to the patient, there are substantial differences in the outcome of clinical evaluations. For instance, in public health institutions, evaluation of dementia patients is a major challenge because the small number of trained health professionals is insufficient for the growing number of patients who require clinical attention. Persons from developed regions of the country with high economic incomes are far more likely to receive careful clinical attention than patients from poor areas.

More specifically, people who live in high-income areas have a better chance of receiving an in-depth evaluation based on a detailed clinical interview. This involves a clinical examination, performance of a neuropsychological assessment, as well as collecting information from caregivers. A neurological assessment includes administering tests to determine functional activity, identification of neuropsychiatric symptoms (e.g., depression, apathy, agitation, and others), and obtaining brain scans or other laboratory tests if necessary.

Clinicians from public services and private clinics in general use some tests tailored to measure the cognition of the person with dementia, which can be highly influenced by education level and literacy. A person's inability to answer questions of basic knowledge or skills may have more to do with literacy level and educational attainment rather than with cognitive trouble. Therefore, a brief test of cognitive ability designed for people with lower educational attainment has been successfully applied to people with medium levels of schooling. However, neuropsychological assessment with more extensive investigation of cognition is still restricted to research centers and specialized clinics.

In addition to cognitive assessments of the patient, the caregiver is interviewed to determine his or her level of burden and emotional distress, which is taken into account in the patient diagnosis. Measurement of biomarkers in the brain (concentrations of the beta-amyloid peptide, total tau protein, and phosphorylated tau protein) to confirm the diagnosis of AD is restricted to patients with access to selected private insurance or with sufficient capacity to pay for these analyses.

In Brazil, the drugs available to treat AD are cholinesterase inhibitors (drugs used to increase the brain concentration of cholinesterase, an important neurotransmitter thought to improve cognition). The Brazilian government had supported prescriptions of cholinesterase inhibitors for AD (by paying for them) during the past decade. Despite the government's effort to reach a goal of furnishing pharmacological treatment to at least 50% of patients with AD, only a small proportion of them to date have received cholinesterase inhibitors. However, an increase of 34% in the number of cholinesterase inhibitor prescriptions supported by the public health system was reported during the 6 years from 2008 to 2014.

Undertreatment rates have been attributed to several conditions: the delay of diagnosis of AD, the distance of small cities from centers with available resources to diagnose and treat patients (north and central-west), and lower income (north and northeast). The small number of specialized centers and experts on dementia also has been recognized in these regions. Bureaucratic obstacles and time-consuming administrative procedures represent other barriers to obtaining medicines. Regarding nonpharmacological interventions, some sites, mainly from the south and southeast, have developed cognitive stimulation for patients with mild dementia as well as occupational therapy for moderate and severe dementia.

However, comparisons of these procedures among different Brazilian geographical regions have not been done.

Impact of Low Literacy and Low Educational Attainment

As mentioned in the previous section, another important issue concerns the assessment of dementia in poor people in Brazil who have low education attainment and limited literacy skills. Although literacy among older adults has risen from 51.9% in 1983 to 77.2% in 2014, the average number of years in school has remained low (5.1 years of school for men, 4.9 years for women); see Neumann and Albert (2018).

Low education and illiteracy affect about 10% of the Brazilian adult population, and some misconceptions about aging and cognition still remain among these people. For instance, memory loss and depression even now have been considered as normal features among some groups from this population, especially older persons. Therefore, the cognitive and functional evaluation of patients with low education or literacy levels who also have dementia requires special care. Illiterate persons and individuals with low education tend to use distinct strategies during clinician visits that differ from those with higher literacy and educational attainment and consequently require more time to complete assessments. Tests and scales used to diagnose and measure the cognitive and functional profiles of people with dementia were designed for use in developed countries where people have attained substantially higher levels of formal education than in Brazil. Consequently, dementia diagnosis and treatment in Brazil is likely to be compromised by low levels of formal schooling and literacy.

Digit cancellation tests (tests where a person has to correctly identify a pattern of numbers and cross out or cancel numbers that do not belong) are also influenced by educational levels. Literate people use "conventional" patterns to perform such tests. For example, people with high educational attainment and literacy levels who read Western languages follow a left-to-right pattern, the manner in which the tests were designed to be completed. However, illiterate people who live far from urban cultures, such as river dwellers in the Amazon region, do not use a conventional pattern to complete the tasks since they have never been formally taught how to complete such tests. They show extensive "disorganization" in searching and identifying the patterns and need more time to perform tests that require formal education, thereby complicating a correct diagnosis.

CARE AND CAREGIVER CONSIDERATIONS

As is the case in many countries, women in Brazil live longer on average than men and commonly become caregivers for their spouses with dementia. Daughters or daughters-in-law also often assume this role, giving up personal interests such as study, professional jobs, and leisure. In Brazil, people have significant resistance to institutionalizing people with dementia in places such as nursing homes. Culturally, many families prefer to keep the patient at home because of their strong emotional ties. Even so, the remarkably high cost of keeping a patient in well-qualified long-term care facilities makes such care inaccessible to many families.

Caregiver Burden

Emotional stress affects the majority of people responsible for the daily care of patients with dementia. In the south and southeast regions of the country, emotional distress affects 60% to 70% of the caregivers for dependent patients with dementia or other illnesses. Neuropsychiatric symptoms such as agitation, nocturnal wandering, delusions, and hallucinations in the dementia patient are predictors of emotional exhaustion and chronic depression in family caregivers. In Brazil, many middle-aged women, like daughters, take on the role of caring for dementia patients. Often, poor ability to manage neuropsychiatric symptoms, challenges with attending to the constant demands of caregiving, lack of technical training or knowledge about health problems, and the absence of a minimal framework for caring within a home context (e.g., lack of home modifications) are factors that generate emotional distress for the family caregiver. Caregivers exposed to prolonged emotional distress have a significant reduction in their quality of life; as a result, a significant proportion of them consume alcohol at harmful levels.

Caregivers' Cognitive Status

Another important concern is the cognitive level of the dementia patient's caregiver. It is not uncommon for the person responsible for the dementia patient to be the patient's spouse or partner. The caregiver therefore is likely to be an older person himself or herself and have some degree of cognitive impairment. In turn, this caregiver may not be able to provide accurate reports to the clinician about the dementia patient's symptoms because of his or her own cognitive challenges and lack of sufficient knowledge about the disease.

Economic Costs

In Brazil, the direct economic cost of caring for patients with dementia represents more than 60% of the family income. When patients with dementia have comorbidities such as diabetes, heart disease, or hypertension, the cost can account for more than 80% of the family income. In addition, a substantial proportion of the direct and indirect cost of dementia is associated with the long time spent by family members in caregiving and patient support, which affects their own occupation opportunities and, in turn, reduces family income.

Violence Against Older People

It is important to note that in addition to dementia, violence against older people presents a big challenge. Since the establishment of a national law to protect older people from abuse, a progressive effort to prevent such violence has been noticeable. This statute compels all health professionals attending older people to report suspicion of or observed violence against them, including neglect of care, which was included as a type of mistreatment. Even so, this population segment is still vulnerable to ill-treatment. In 80% of violence cases against older people, the perpetrator is a member of their own family and lives with the elder. Women are the most affected, especially those with low levels of schooling, living in areas of poverty, or with some physical or mental handicap. Female gender, physical proximity to the aggressor, the domestic place, and the family's financial precariousness are all factors associated with the practice of violence against older persons. Yet, elders often fail to report abuse because of shame, intimidation, fear of revenge, or forced institutionalization in inappropriate places.

FINAL CONSIDERATIONS

Aging in Brazil has led to increases in the number of both healthy and frail, dependent elders. Several groups have been dedicated to integrating autonomous elders into psychosocial and cultural activities to maintain their healthy status and their quality of life. Despite the efforts by these groups, public policies to preserve the health for this population are still scarce.

Furthermore, a gap exists between the growing older population and the availability of social, economic, and health resources required for their well-being. It is also crucial to implement strategies designed to prevent diseases in late life and to establish mechanisms for attenuating or caring for incapacities, especially the early diagnosis and treatment of dementia. In Brazil, there is an urgent need to build respect for elders among the general population and to discourage any kind of violence against them. Also necessary are educational programs to improve the ability of both professional caregivers and family members in order to appropriately manage older dependent patients with dementia and to help them cope with the burdens and strains of their important role.

REFERENCES

Blay, S. L. & Peluso, E. T. P. (2010). Public Stigma: The Community's Tolerance of Alzheimer Disease. *The American Journal of Geriatric Psychiatry, 18*(2), 163–171. doi:10.1097/JGP.0b013e3181bea900

IBGE. (2018). Retrieved from https://www.ibge.gov.br/apps/populacao/projecao//index.html. Consulted 9/25/19.

Paim, J., Travassos, C., Almeida, C., Bahia, L., & Macinko, J. (2011). The Brazilian health system: history, advances, and challenges. *The Lancet, 377*(9779), 1778–1797. doi:10.1016/S0140-6736(11)60054-8

Schneider, R. M. (2018). *Brazil: culture and politics in a new industrial powerhouse.* New York, NY: Routledge.

Neumann, L. T. V., & Albert, S. M. (2018). Aging in Brazil. *The Gerontologist, 58*(4), 611–617. doi:10.1093/geront/gny019

3

DEMOGRAPHIC PERSPECTIVES ON AN AGING WORLD

INTRODUCTION

For the first time in human history older people (65 and older) now outnumber children under the age of 5, due to increasing longevity and declining fertility worldwide. The momentous point at which the number of older people surpassed the number of children happened in 2018, and it was heralded by many news stories, articles, and reports. Why was this moment so newsworthy? Beyond its historical significance, this demographic moment dramatically illustrates the reality of **population aging**—the social and demographic processes that result in the transition to an age structure with increasing numbers and proportions of older people and decreasing proportions at the youngest ages. This shifting age structure is important because it changes many aspects of the social arrangements that affect daily lives. Work, housing, retirement, transportation, technology, health care, and intergenerational relationships are being transformed by population aging. You can see signs of these changes all around you, in your own country. For example, a recent U.S.-based Internet search for "aging baby boomers" yielded about 7 million websites covering demographic information, health tips, adult living communities, skin care products, the job market, and thousands more topics of interest to older people. The breadth and the scope of implications of population aging are worldwide and societywide. An aging workforce, a short supply of younger workers, and strained pension systems are causing citizens of the United States, Canada, and Europe to rethink attitudes and policies about older workers and retirement. In China, the one-child policy, which was in effect from 1979 through 2015, continues to have an impact on traditional family caregiving practices and the lack of formal care alternatives. The nature of the changes facing any particular aging society depends on several different factors. A brief example will help to illustrate this point.

Consider these differences between India and the United States in 2018. India is a relatively young society: Only 6% of its population is aged 65 or older, and average life expectancy at birth is 70 for women and 67 for men (Population Reference Bureau, 2018). The United States is considered to be an *aging* society, with 15% of its population aged 65 or older and an average life expectancy at birth of 81 for women and 76 for men. As we see in our following discussion about population pyramids, young societies have high birth rates (fertility) and high death rates (mortality), whereas aging societies have low fertility and low mortality. Many aspects of social life (such as the kind of health care available, the number of generations in a family who live together, the availability of pensions, and the status of women) are related to these patterns of birth and death that produce population aging. For example, health care in India is focused largely on maternal and child health, family planning, and immunization. In contrast, the United States spends its health care dollars very differently: Medicare, the government-sponsored health insurance for older people, is the nation's largest health insurer (U.S. Centers for Medicare and Medicaid Services, 2019).

The availability of public education, access to safe water and sufficient food, and the demands that compete for limited government resources are very different in the two countries. In the United States, we take clean water for granted (though there is increasing evidence that perhaps we should not), education through age 18 is guaranteed as a basic right of all citizens, and nearly 90% of the older population are eligible for a public pension (Social Security). In India, older people depend heavily on their families, about two thirds are fully or partly dependent on their children for financial support, and older people who need long-term services and supports have few options other than family care (Panruti, Liebig, & Duvvuru, 2015). The lack of public policies and programs for older adults in India should not be interpreted as criticism. India is still a relatively "young" society, facing the dual challenges of providing for a large number of children and planning for a rapidly growing older population. The causes and consequences of population aging are far-reaching, and every nation in the world is facing the challenges and opportunities of growing numbers of older adults.

Given the importance of population aging, it is logical to ask how populations grow old. The simple answer is that societies grow older when both the fertility and mortality rates remain low for a sustained period of time. In short, population aging occurs when large numbers of people survive into old age and relatively few children are born. In such societies, life expectancies are high and the proportion of the population aged 65 and older is high. But how does mortality decline? Under what circumstances does a whole society of people decide to have fewer children, lowering the fertility rate? An important framework for understanding these changes is the demographic transition theory.

DEMOGRAPHIC TRANSITION THEORY

The **demographic transition** is a set of interrelated social and demographic changes that result in both rapid growth and aging of a population. The prototypical transition pattern occurred throughout Western Europe in the 19th and early 20th centuries. The first stage of the transition is related to mortality (the rate of death in a society). During the European transition, the economies of these countries went through enormous shifts, changing from an agricultural base to an industrial mode of production, requiring and enticing large numbers of rural farm workers to migrate to the cities to work in factories. At the same time, as a by-product of economic and scientific development, these countries experienced significant mortality decline. They gained control over infectious diseases, improved the availability of clean water, and saw the emergence of more advanced medical technology. This shift from high and somewhat variable mortality (variable because of epidemics) to lower mortality is shown in Figure 3.1.

As you also can see in this graph, fertility remained high longer than did mortality as these societal changes unfolded; but fertility then began to decline when people realized that large families were no longer necessary for agricultural labor

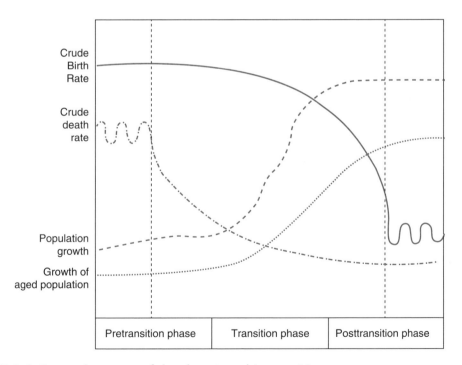

FIGURE 3.1 General pattern of the demographic transition.

Sources: Data from Myers, G. C. (1990). Demography of aging. In R. H. Binstock & L. K. George (Eds.), *Handbook of aging and the social sciences* (3rd ed., pp. 19–44). New York, NY: Academic Press; Yaukey, D. (1985). *Demography: The study of human population.* Prospect Heights, IL: Waveland Press.

and in fact were a financial drain in a wage economy, and women were increasingly educated on topics related to reproductive health. This second transition phase, the lag between mortality decline and fertility decline, sets the stage for rapid population growth. Mortality was not removing nearly as many people from the population as before, and continued high fertility was adding many additional people. Finally, with sustained low mortality and low fertility, population aging occurs. Figure 3.1 shows the curves for population growth and for growth in the aged population that result from the demographic transition.

Thus far, the demographic transition has been discussed as a pattern of change in mortality and fertility that accompanied industrialization. But the *theory* behind these patterns has not been mentioned. A theory goes beyond description to search for explanations and ultimately to make predictions. We need to ask: (a) How well does this theory explain what happened in the past in Western Europe? and (b) How well did it predict patterns of change in other countries? To answer the first question, we can acknowledge that the connections between the demographic trends and social changes related to industrialization are logical. An industrial economy created, for the first time, an economic surplus; all members of a society could be supported by a smaller number of workers. For this reason, it was not necessary for families to have large numbers of children as workers or to ensure that at least some survived. It may seem unusual to imagine that people decide how many children to have based on such a rational calculation. There is an extensive literature in demography about the many factors, including the "economic" cost and benefits of having children, that go into such a personal and emotional decision. Even if we accept the logic of the original formulation of the demographic transition theory, data on the consistency of the prototypical pattern suggest that even in Western Europe there were variations in the timing of fertility and mortality declines.

We can appreciate the underlying logic and general value of the transition model in explaining patterns in Western Europe, even if it did not perfectly predict the timing of changes for each country. The second test of the theory is how well the pattern and predictions are holding for the developing regions of the world that are still relatively young and in earlier stages of economic development. The story gets interesting, and the theory has to account for some unexpected changes. Quite a few countries have experienced fertility declines much more precipitous than those experienced in Western Europe. For example, the fertility rate (the average number of children born per woman) in Iran dropped from 6.2 in 1970–1975 to 1.7 in 2010–2015. During that same time period, China's birth rate dropped from 4.9 to 1.6; and for Mexico, the drop was from 6.7 to 2.3 (United Nations, Department of Economic and Social Affairs [UN, DESA], Population Division, 2015). Those are very rapid and steep fertility declines. Across that same time period, these countries experienced a significant increase in life expectancy (to about 75 years in 2018, from 50 in the case of Iran, 60 for China, and 62 for Mexico in 1970). In these countries, and many others, rapid fertility decline occurred at the same time as significant improvements in life expectancy. While the demographic changes that took place in Western Europe occurred at the same time as economic development, in developing nations today, partly because of the rapid importation of technology to limit fertility and to control mortality, population aging can occur ahead of economic development. This combination has led to the observation that today many countries are becoming old before they become rich, while Western Europe and the United States became rich before they became old.

In addition to the rapidity with which medical advances and options for fertility control are shared across geographic boundaries, there are other factors that were not explicitly addressed by the original demographic transition model. Most notable is the role of public policy. Several of the countries that went through steep fertility declines had enacted policies to limit fertility; these policies included incentives for having fewer children and penalties for having more than the prescribed number. China's one-child policy is probably the most well-known. The essay on Iran at the end of this chapter, "Population Aging in Iran and Its Implications," shows the dramatic effect of their fertility policy on the speed of population aging and discusses some of the effects of that rapid change on families, individuals, and public policy pressures.

Like any good theory, the demographic transition theory has evolved to accommodate emerging patterns and new knowledge. Scholars today are writing about a **second demographic transition**; it is similar to the first in that it seeks to identify the mutual influences among demographic forces (fertility, mortality, and migration) and social changes. It is different because the second transition (Lesthaeghe, 2014) identifies new trends in fertility and migration, and mortality plays much less of a role in the second transition because of the relatively high degree of stability in control over mortality (with notable exceptions in some parts of the world and for particular diseases). For readers of this book from the United States and Europe who are in their late teens and early 20s or who have friends and family members in that age range, the changes marking the second demographic transition may seem familiar: delayed family formation (late marriage and late parenting), a multitude of living arrangements other than marriage, a disconnection between marriage and procreation, increasing proportions pursuing higher education, increasingly selective migration between countries, and within-country geographic mobility. These social and cultural shifts that have direct effects on future fertility and geographic distribution of population are related to past fertility, mortality, and migration: the dramatic changes of the first demographic transition that produced unprecedented population growth and population aging.

DEMOGRAPHIC DIVIDE

The nature, scope, and importance of global aging far exceed simple descriptions of economic or demographic patterns. However, such information sets the stage for—and is an integral part of—a deeper discussion of social and cultural changes associated with global aging. For example, the concept of the demographic divide captures some significant patterns in population aging and social change. The **demographic divide** refers to the distinction between countries with low birth rates and high life expectancies (aging populations with slow or no growth) and those with high birth rates, significant growth, and comparatively young populations. This divide is defined by demographic patterns, but it coincides with the more/less/least-developed designations.

The less developed nations, characterized by high fertility and young populations, will contribute virtually all of the population growth that will take place in the world over the next four decades (Haub, 2007). They will also contribute the vast majority of new older people to be added to the world since life expectancy is increasing, in some cases rapidly, in most of the less developed countries. Some of these societies will be addressing the challenges of nearly simultaneous population growth and population aging. The countries already on the old side of the demographic divide are, in contrast, facing labor-force pressures that arise from low birth rates and low fertility, resulting in little or no population growth. These countries may not have enough workers to sustain economic productivity or to nurture the support programs necessary for an older population. The demographic divide is one of many ways to think about global patterns of aging and how those patterns relate to the economic and social challenges of population aging.

Table 3.1 provides some information about the three major regions of the world (developed, less developed, and least developed) on the indicators related to the demographic divide: life expectancy, fertility, and proportion aged 65 and older. The information on fertility helps to illustrate how countries on the young side of the demographic divide—those in less developed regions—will contribute virtually all of the coming growth in the world's population. It is easy to see that, with an average fertility rate of 2.6 children per woman and a 2018 population of more than 6.3 billion people, the less developed region of the world will be contributing a much higher proportion of new global citizens. In contrast, the more developed

TABLE 3.1 Population Data for Regions of the World, 2018

Region	Midyear Population in 2018 (in millions)	Total Fertility Rate	Percentage of Population Aged 65 and Older	Life Expectancy at Birth	
				Males	Females
World	7,621	2.4	9	70	74
More developed	1,266	1.6	18	76	82
Less developed	6,355	2.6	7	69	73
Less developed (excluding China)	4,953	2.8	6	67	71
Least developed	1,284	4.2	4	63	66

Source: From Population Reference Bureau. (2018). *2018 World population data sheet with focus on changing age structures.* Retrieved from https://www.prb.org/2018-world-population-data-sheet -with-focus-on-changing-age-structures

region already has low fertility, longer life expectancy, and an older population. Although today there are a wide array of age profiles across the two sides of the demographic divide, that gap will be closing very quickly—making aging a world-wide challenge, not simply an issue for the richer countries of the world.

SPEED OF POPULATION AGING

Aging is occurring much more rapidly in less developed regions than it did in the United States and other already aging countries. This pattern may seem counterintuitive, since developing regions have much higher fertility and younger populations than the developed nations. How is it possible that they can grow older so much faster? The primary explanation is that the improvements in mortality (i.e., the extension of life expectancy that is part of the demographic transition) happened more slowly in the developed nations and typically followed a decline in fertility. In developing nations today, fertility rates are declining at different paces (some very rapidly, others more slowly), but control over mortality is, in general, happening faster than was the case in Europe and the United States. The medical and public health advancements necessary to reduce mortality, such as immunizations and cleaner food and water, became more rapidly and widely available to the developing world than they had been in today's developed nations. For example, it took France 115 years for the proportion of its population aged 65 and older to increase from 7% to 14%; Sweden took 85 years for this change; and, in the United States, this increase will be completed in 59 years. For Thailand, this same doubling of the proportion of older population will take place in a little more than 20 years, and in South Korea, it will take a mere 18 years (He, Goodkind, & Kowal, 2016).

Figure 3.2 illustrates the length of time it will take various countries to double and triple their older populations, going from 7% to 14% to 21%. France completed its 115-year transition by 1980; the United States reached the 14% mark in 2013. South Korea only began its aging transformation in 2000 but will have completed the change by 2018, only 5 years after the United States! It is easy to imagine the magnitude of the challenges facing countries within which populations will age so rapidly. Systems to serve the unique health, housing, social, and economic needs of older people continue to be at issue in countries such as the United States, which have had a considerably longer time to prepare for this change. The less developed countries are having or will have significantly less time and fewer resources to face these challenges, making the development of culturally appropriate adaptations even more difficult.

DEMOGRAPHIC DIVIDENDS

While population aging is proceeding at varying speeds in different countries, all countries are experiencing, or are on the cusp of, significant demographic shifts as part of population aging. In contrast to the challenges of the demographic divide, the

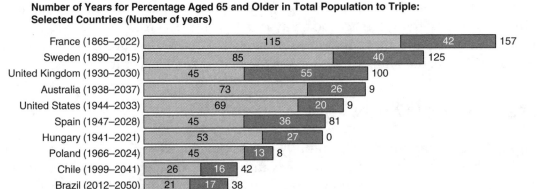

Number of Years for Percentage Aged 65 and Older in Total Population to Triple: Selected Countries (Number of years)

FIGURE 3.2 Speed of population aging for selected countries.

Source: From He, W., Goodkind, D., & Kowal, P. (2016). An aging world: 2015. *International Population Reports*, P95/16-1. Washington, DC: U.S. Government Printing Office.

demographic dividend is a different and interesting perspective on these changes. As the name implies, this term refers to the positive economic impacts and potential benefits a nation might experience during the demographic transition. Fertility rates decline, and the young people already born are very likely to survive to become part of the adult labor force—a change that may enhance progress toward economic development. At this stage, the older population remains relatively small because changes in fertility and mortality have not yet produced their long-term result—an increasing older population. A demographic dividend can be realized because the labor force is larger than the younger and older populations that depend on it, thus "freeing up resources for investment in economic development and family welfare" (Lee & Mason, 2006, p. 1). Thailand and China are examples of countries currently in the midst of this phase in their transitions. They have large populations in the prime working ages due to past high fertility, smaller-size groups under age 15 because of current lower fertility, and relatively small older populations because improved longevity has only recently allowed large numbers of people to live long enough to become old. Whether the shifting age structure, which results in a large labor force and small non–working-age groups, will produce a positive impact on economic development in any particular country depends on a host of factors, including policies about the larger economy (e.g., wages and taxation rates) as well as social norms about consumer spending and saving (Kinsella & He, 2009).

Some scholars postulate a second demographic dividend as countries move into later stages of the demographic transition. As a society ages, the population becomes concentrated in the older working ages, as is the case today in the United States and many European countries. Since these older workers (people in their 50s and 60s) can look forward to a long life after retirement, they have strong incentives to save and invest for their later years. These savings, in turn, contribute to individual economic well-being (which can encourage both midlife investment and later-life spending, both of which benefit the economy) and to total national income. As with the first demographic dividend, whether the shifting age structure will result in the full potential gains depends on complex economic and policy factors, including tax incentives and disincentives for work and for investment, policies about mandatory retirement, and patterns of consumption across the life cycle (Lee & Mason, 2006; Mason, Lee, & Jiang, 2016). The potential for demographic dividends illustrates the importance of connecting changes in fertility and mortality and shifting population age structures with their consequences for all aspects of social life, including the vigor of a nation's economy.

The third—and perhaps most important—dividend of more years for individuals is an extended opportunity for personal experience, growth, wisdom, and productivity. The societal benefit of this potential third dividend is continued contribution of older adults to the social, cultural, and economic lives of their communities through volunteering, civic and social engagement, and perhaps continued employment. The possibility of a third demographic dividend, however, depends on investments in good health across the life course and on construction of social roles and responsibilities for older adults that allow them to contribute their accumulated social capital (Fried, 2016).

MEASURES OF POPULATION AGING

How can we show whether a population is aging? The six commonly used indicators of population aging are *population pyramids, proportion aged, median age, life expectancy, dependency ratios,* and *prospective age.* Although using six different tools or measures to describe the same phenomenon may seem excessive and somewhat confusing, each is actually a simple, elegant piece of arithmetic that tells an important part of the story of a society's "age"; together they form a powerful national narrative. Each is described and compared in the following sections.

Population Pyramids

A **population pyramid** is a graphic illustration of the age and gender structure of a population. The bars on a population pyramid show the number (or sometimes percentage) of people who are in a particular age and sex category. In Figure 3.3A, the bar on the bottom left-hand side shows that there were around 10.5 million boys aged 0 to 4 in the United States in 2019; the bar on the right for ages 25 to 29 shows about 12 million women in that category. While the exact numbers in a given category are often important (and are readily available), the value of a population pyramid is in the overall story it tells. Population pyramids are truly pictures worth a thousand words. In showing the shape of a population's age and sex structure in a given year, the pyramid for that year also tells us about past, present, and future demographic trends. Comparing population pyramids for one country over time, or for different countries, will help to illustrate these ideas further. Keep in mind that *only three demographic forces directly determine the shape of a pyramid: fertility, mortality, and migration.* The numbers of people being born, dying, and moving into or out of a location will affect the relative size of all the age and gender groupings for that population, whether it is a town or a country. The impact of fertility, mortality, and migration in shaping a population structure is discussed in the following examples of population pyramids.

Figure 3.3A shows the population pyramid for the United States in 2019. The bulge of people in the 45- to 65-year-old range is the baby boom generation (the large number of people born after World War II, between 1946 and 1964). Thus we can see the powerful impact of a past fertility trend reflected in the shape of today's pyramid. The slightly lopsided top of the pyramid shows the greater number of older women than men. This imbalance is a manifestation of past and current trends in mortality: Women live longer than men. This phenomenon is covered in greater detail later in this chapter.

Based on the age/gender structure illustrated in the 2019 pyramid, we can make some predictions about the shape of the U.S. population pyramid in the future. The most significant feature of that shape will be the movement upward of the baby boom generation. Demographers sometimes refer to this as the "pig in a python," conjuring up the earthy image of watching a whole pig move slowly through the digestive tract of a large snake. So, too, the baby boom bulge moves slowly upward through the population pyramid of the United States. The midlife baby boomers of today (in 2019, they are aged 55–73) are the older generations of tomorrow, and young adults today are the middle-aged of the near future! Figure 3.3B shows this very phenomenon, with projections for the population in 2050.

In contrast to the U.S. pyramids, the population pyramid for the United Arab Emirates (UAE) (Figure 3.4) has a very unusual shape. Working-age men far outnumber women of the same age. Why would this be so? As noted earlier, there are only three possible influences on the shape of a pyramid: fertility, mortality, and migration. In this case, the imbalance in the numbers of working-age men and women is due to the immigration of thousands of people from Asia and other parts of the Middle East to work in the oil fields. These workers are nearly always men who migrate into the UAE without their families, skewing the gender distribution in these age ranges. In 2010, about 43% of the population of the UAE was foreign-born (Malit & Youha, 2013).

For most countries, migration does not currently play such a big role in the age and gender structure; fertility and mortality are by far the more powerful influences. However, for smaller geographic units, such as states and counties within the United States, migration can be an important factor. Think about what the population pyramid would look like for a small county that builds a 500-unit, state-of-the-art, low-cost retirement community that can accommodate 1,000 older people. This desirable location would attract people from all around the area, including neighboring counties; the relative size of the older population for the receiving county would be affected immediately and significantly. If the

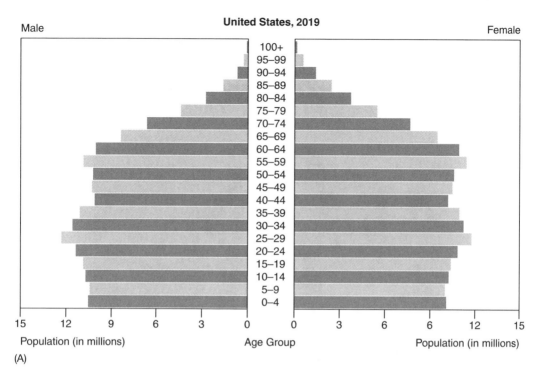

(A)

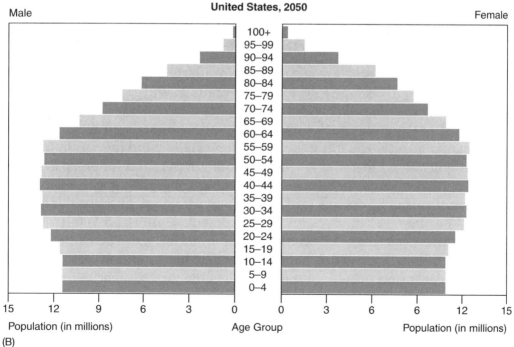

(B)

FIGURE 3.3 (A) Population pyramid for the United States, 2019; (B) population pyramid for the United States, 2050.

Source: From U.S. Census Bureau International Data Base. (n.d.). Retrieved from https://www.census .gov/data-tools/demo/idb/informationGateway.php

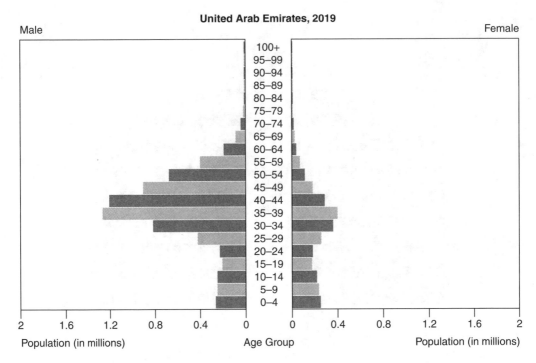

FIGURE 3.4 Population pyramid for the UAE, 2019. UAE, United Arab Emirates.

Source: From U.S. Census Bureau International Data Base. (n.d.). Retrieved from https://www.census
.gov/data-tools/demo/idb/informationGateway.php

receiving county had a small rural population, a large number of new older residents could create a T-shaped population pyramid, with a concentration at the top age ranges.

The shape of a population pyramid tells us something about the past, present, and future of a society—not only the fertility, mortality, and migration trends but also something about life in that society. Population pyramids often take on one of three basic stylized shapes, each of which distinguishes, in a general way, demographic patterns and other aspects of social life, such as a stage in the demographic transition and the level of economic development. Figures 3.5A and 3.5B show two of the three basic shapes. The true pyramid, or fast-growth shape, is characteristic of young countries with high fertility and high mortality such as Kenya. The rectangular, or no-growth, pyramid shows the effects of sustained very low fertility and very low mortality, as is projected for Germany.

The third classic pyramid shape is a slow-growth, beehive-shaped pyramid; it represents a transition stage between the true pyramid and a rectangular pyramid. This shape was seen for the United States in Figure 3.3B, reflecting a pattern of low mortality and fertility. Some demographers have suggested a fourth pattern: the collapsing or inverted pyramid, which is narrowest at the base. The bottom half of the pyramid for Germany (in Figure 3.5B) has this shape, and it is possible that Germany will eventually have an inverted pyramid, if current levels of extremely low fertility continue.

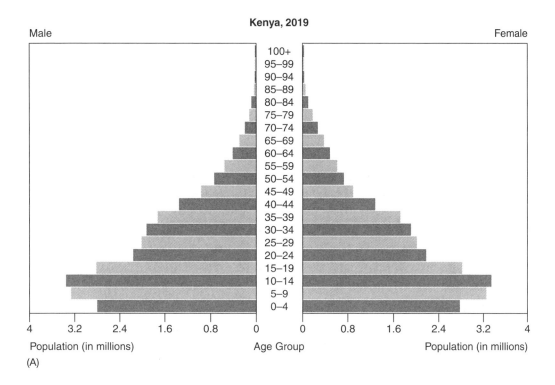

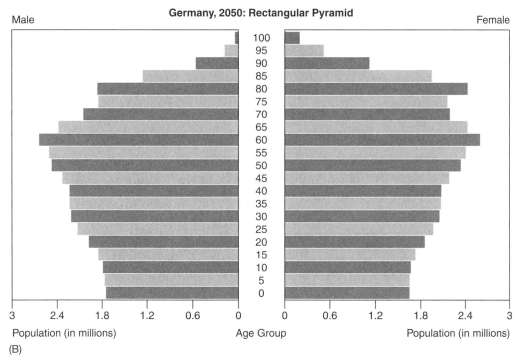

FIGURE 3.5 (A) Traditional pyramid shape: Kenya, 2019; (B) rectangular pyramid shape: Germany, 2050.

Source: From U.S. Census Bureau International Data Base. (n.d.). Retrieved from https://www.census.gov/data-tools/demo/idb/informationGateway.php

Students often are curious about which pyramid is most desirable for a society. That question has no simple answer: Each pyramid shape represents a different set of challenges. For example, a pyramid with a wide base and narrow apex describes a society with many children, large families, and high rates of mortality. In such a society, the major focus of public policy probably will be on maternal and child health, schools, and family planning—as in India today. In a society with a rectangular pyramid, the relative size of the older population is large and in many ways likely to dominate public attention and concern. It is fairly certain that significant public policy and tax resources will be devoted to caring for this society's older members. The society in between—transitioning from a child-centered to an older adult–focused society—may have the most difficult challenges: recognizing and tracking the trends and gearing national policies and spending accordingly. So, no population pyramid shape is considered best; views on the most acceptable set of challenges are determined by economic development, cultural and social values, political will and adaptability, and, perhaps, age of individuals.

Population pyramids are elegant, informative, intuitively useful representations of the age and gender structure of a society. They give information about how old or young a society is and provide an indication of the level of economic development, the state of advancement in medical technology, and the nature of the resource allocation dilemmas faced by a society.

Proportion Aged

A very straightforward measure of population aging that does allow for easy comparisons is the proportion of a society that is older. "Older than what?" is a good question to ask. Most reports of *proportion aged* use age 65 as the marker, but some, especially those comparing countries around the world, use age 60 as a cutoff point. The use of age 60 allows for the fact that the age marker for later life is affected by life expectancy; in countries with shorter life expectancy, the age threshold for being considered "older" might be lower. So it is wise to be attentive to the precise definition of proportion aged and the implication of using different age boundaries. The first two columns in Table 3.2 show the proportion of population that is aged 65 and older for several countries, as of 2018 and as projected for 2050. These proportions for 2018 range from lows of 1% for the UAE and 3% for Swaziland to a high of 28% for Japan. The average proportion of the population aged 65 and older for the more developed countries is 18%; for less developed nations, it is 7% (Population Reference Bureau, 2018).

As noted, the proportion or share of population that is 65 and older is easily used to make comparisons among nations or across historical time periods within a country, state, or city. Proportions are both less complicated and less informative than population pyramids, which give a more detailed picture of the age structure of the population. Nonetheless, trends in the proportion aged in a society are a very important, widely used indicator of population aging. For example, the second column in Table 3.2 projects dramatic growth in the proportion aged 65 and

TABLE 3.2 Measures of Population Aging for Selected Countries

	Population Aged 65 and Older		Median Age	Life Expectancy at Birth	
	2018 (%)	2050 (projected %)		Men	Women
Swaziland	3	6	21.7	54	61
Thailand	12	29	37.7	72	79
China	11	26	37.4	75	78
United Arab Emirates	1	14	30.3	77	79
United States	15	22	38.1	76	81
Germany	21	31	47.1	78	83
Japan	28	36	47.3	81	87

Source: From Population Reference Bureau. (2018). *2018 World population data sheet with focus on changing age structures.* Retrieved from https://www.prb.org/2018-world-population-data-sheet -with-focus-on-changing-age-structures

older in selected countries. Although Swaziland will still have a relatively small proportion of older adults, in the next few decades that proportion will double. By 2050, it is predicted that over one third of Japan's population will be older people.

Median Age

Like the proportion aged, median ages are single numbers that often are used in conjunction with other measures of population aging. The **median** (from the Latin word for middle) is the midpoint of a range of numbers—the point at which one half of cases fall above and one half fall below. The third column of Table 3.2 shows quite a range of median ages. Japan, by many measures the oldest country in the world, has a median age of 47.3; Germany is not far behind at 47.1. That means that half of the people in Germany and Japan are over the age of 47. Swaziland, among the youngest countries in the world, has a much lower median age of 21.7. There are some countries with an even lower median age, including Afghanistan (18.8 years) and Niger, with an amazingly low median age of 15.4 (World Population Review, 2018); one half of the people in this landlocked African nation just north of Nigeria are children! Curiosity about these patterns would lead to an investigation of the recent history, fertility patterns, political turmoil, natural disasters, and food shortages that might have befallen a country with such unusual demographic patterns.

Life Expectancy

Another measure of population aging included in Table 3.2 is **life expectancy**, which is defined as the average length of time the members of a population can expect to live. It is not the same as **life span**, which is the theoretical maximum length of life that humans (or any other species) could achieve biologically under ideal conditions. There are calculations for the life span of different animal species that can be raised in those optimal conditions, but for humans it is neither ethical nor practical to control the environment. For humans, the maximum possible life span is gauged by using the most recent reliable data on how long a single individual has actually lived. Currently, the life span for humans is estimated to be about 120 years. The oldest living person as of March 2019 is Kane Tanaka from Japan; her age was verified by Guinness World Records. Such verification is necessary since birth records from more than 100 years ago are not always readily available in every country.

Life expectancy, then, is the *average* experience of a population. It is calculated from actual mortality data from a single year and describes what would happen to a hypothetical group of people if they moved through their lives experiencing the mortality rates observed for the country as a whole during the year in question. It is important to know that life expectancy at birth is different from life expectancy at any other specific age. In fact, life expectancy goes up with every year of life. For example, Table 3.2 shows that life expectancy at birth for females in Swaziland was 61 in 2018, while Swazi women who made it to age 60 had an additional life expectancy of approximately 18 more years—living on to age 78.

It is probably not surprising that among the countries in Table 3.2, those with the lowest percentages of aged persons and lowest median ages are also those with the lowest life expectancies at birth. These various measures of societal aging are all related; Germany and Japan have the highest median ages and highest life expectancies. However, because of the many factors that shape the health and age structure of a population, there is not a perfect correlation between life expectancy and other measures of population aging. For example, Swaziland and Thailand have relatively low median ages; however, Thailand's life expectancy is considerably higher than that for Swaziland (age 79 for women in Thailand but only age 61 for women in Swaziland). Swaziland is one of the world's nations hardest hit by the HIV/AIDS epidemic, along with many other countries in sub-Saharan Africa.

A gender difference in life expectancy is readily apparent in Table 3.2. In every country, women have higher life expectancy than men. Why do women live longer than men in most countries? The general pattern of higher life expectancy for women comes from the fact that, in general, at every age, men are more likely to die than women. How can this "excess male mortality" be explained? Readers probably have some ideas on the subject. Whenever this question is presented in classes, in talks, or in casual conversation, there is never a long wait for responses. Explanations for the gender differential fall into two major categories: biological and social/behavioral. Biological explanations are based on the premise that women have a physiological advantage that results in greater longevity, whereas social/behavioral explanations focus on lifestyle choices, socialization, risk-taking, stress, and occupational hazards. Evidence exists to support both types of explanations. For example, women have lower mortality than men *at every age*, even *in utero* and during early infancy before cultural and environmental influences have had a chance to affect the genders differently. However, by the childhood years, boys rather than girls in nearly all cultures are being socialized to seek more dangerous lifestyles and assume more life-threatening occupations—producing a further negative impact on masculine longevity.

The same pattern of "excess male mortality" holds true for most countries, but the size of the gap is different. In more developed nations, the gender gap has been about 7 years but is decreasing. In less developed nations, the gap is currently smaller (about 3.5 years) but is expected to widen with increased education and economic growth (UN, DESA, 2009). In a few places, men outlived women until recently. For example, in Southern Africa (the region that includes the countries of Botswana, Lesotho, Namibia, South Africa, and Swaziland), life expectancy for men in 2011 was age 55 compared to age 54 for women (Population Reference Bureau, 2012). The smaller or reversed gender difference in longevity in the developing nations is due primarily to maternal mortality—deaths among women during pregnancy and childbearing. This same pattern in the United States was seen in the late 19th century when knowledge of infection, sterile practices, and medical care during childbirth was less widely available.

Dependency Ratios

Dependency ratios are, as the term suggests, measures of the proportion of a population that falls within age categories traditionally thought to be economically dependent: traditionally, those under age 15 (the child dependency ratio) and over age 64 (the old-age dependency ratio). We can take issue with the definition of anyone under age 15 or over age 64 as automatically being economically dependent, especially in countries where people enter the labor force long before age 15 and sometimes stay long after age 65. In some calculations of dependency ratios in Western nations, age 18 or 19 is used instead of age 15, but international comparisons still use age 15. Other scholars have challenged the dependency assumption by pointing out that some older people fuel economic growth through their taxes and income and that some working-age people may be unemployed (Kinsella & Phillips, 2005; Martin, 2011). Despite this limitation, however, dependency ratios are useful as comparative indicators of the relative proportions of working-age versus non–working-age people. They point to different patterns of demand on economic and social resources across states or nations for such social needs as health care, tax dollars, and the educational system. In the earlier section on the **demographic dividend**, dependency ratios are an important part of the story. The capacity for economic growth during the demographic shift from high to low fertility and high to low mortality depends on the size of the working-age population relative to the proportion of people in the two groups not typically in the labor force (those under age 15 and those 65 and older).

The old-age dependency ratio is similar to proportion aged but is calculated and interpreted in a different way. The proportion aged in a society is simply the number of older people divided by the total population (including those aged

65+). The old-age dependency ratio is the number of older people divided by the number of people aged 15 to 64. It is interpreted as the number of older people for every working-age person (sometimes stated as the number of older people per 100 working-age people). Most often, it is translated into the number of workers in a society it takes to support each older person.

Figure 3.6 shows the child, old-age, and total dependency ratios for the same selection of countries as in Table 3.2. The country with the highest total dependency ratio in the list is Swaziland, which has almost 70 younger and older citizens for every 100 working-age citizens. Countries such as the United States and Germany have roughly two working-age people for every dependent person. If you look at the two components (old age and child) of the total dependency ratio for countries with very high total dependency ratios and those with relatively low ones, you see that most often the child dependency ratio contributes disproportionately to high overall ratios. This pattern would be predicted by the demographic transition theory. As you will recall, high fertility and high mortality are typical of a country in the pretransition or early transition phase. Many children are being born and many people are dying, producing a low proportion of older people and a high proportion of children relative to the working-age population. The relative sizes of the child and old-age dependency ratios are also reflected in the shape of a country's population pyramid and in their capacity for a demographic dividend.

One final point about dependency ratios is important to keep in mind. Although the numbers and patterns may be interesting in and of themselves, they are based

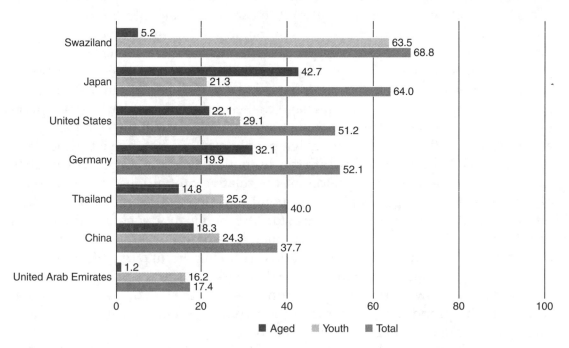

FIGURE 3.6 Dependency ratios for selected countries, 2015: child, old age, and total.

Source: From U.S. Central Intelligence Agency. (2015). CIA World Fact Book: 2015. Retrieved from https://www.cia.gov/library/publications/resources/the-world-factbook/fields/342.html

on some assumptions that bear careful inspection. First, the ages used to categorize people as dependent (or not) must be standardized so that countries can be compared to each other over time. However, just considering the United States, it is clear that not everyone aged 65 and older or aged 15 and younger is out of the workforce. It is not difficult to find cultures where many children and older adults are working; even if it is informal unpaid labor such as work in the family fields, these efforts contribute to the economic well-being of the household and the nation. Compared to more developed countries, older people in the developing regions of the world remain economically active longer, partly because pensions are less likely to be available and, if available, they provide relatively little income (UN, DESA, 2009). Hence the idea of dependency is problematic, as are the ages that define the category.

The second problem with dependency ratios, despite all their usefulness and value, is that they sometimes are used to make an argument, defend a position, or influence public policy. In the United States and in some other older developed societies, the increasing proportion of older persons and the accompanying increase in the old-age dependency ratio has "prompted concern and even alarm about society's capacity to pay for pensions, to finance health care, and to provide the personal assistance that disabled older adults need in their daily lives" (Treas, 1995, p. 6). However, the ability of a society to meet the needs of its aging population—indeed, its entire population—depends not simply on numbers of old people in relation to working-age people, but also on the productivity of the economy, the continued contributions of older adults, and the conscious, value-driven decision-making by politicians and voters (Friedland & Summer, 2005).

Prospective Age

As a final note in this section on measures of population aging, consider the expression that "50 is the new 40." This statement makes some intuitive sense—the average 50-year-old today often seems as young as a 40-year-old of earlier times. We are likely thinking of overall health and vitality when we make such an observation. Some very innovative demographers (Sanderson & Scherbov, 2008) are shedding scientific light on the notion that 50 is the new 40 by analyzing prospective age rather than chronological age. **Prospective age**, based on life expectancy, is the average number of remaining years of life for a person. These researchers suggest that this measure can be more meaningful than chronological age (how many years a person has already lived) for understanding population aging. Sanderson and Scherbov illustrate this idea by comparing data on French women born in 1922 and those born in 1975. The 1922 cohort had a life expectancy at birth of 74.7 years, whereas the younger group, born more than half a century later, had a life expectancy of 84.4 years. If the focus becomes how many years of life each cohort has left, it is seen that the older group had 44.7 years left by the time they reached age 30; however, the younger group would be age 40 (in 2015) before their remaining life expectancy is 44.7 years. For this younger group, their prospective age can be used to say that 40 is the new 30. These scholars go on to show the significant implications of using prospective age instead of some of the measures of population age that have been discussed in this chapter. Their work offers a scientific and provocative look at new ways to measure, think about, and respond to population aging.

INTERPRETING AND USING DEMOGRAPHIC DATA

Demographic data provide an important foundation from which to visualize, illustrate, and compare (across time and across nations) important features of the age structure and composition of a society. In using such data about the older population, it is extremely important not to overgeneralize—not to make blanket statements about all older people or about the typical older person. This caution takes on even more weight when comparing major regions of the world encompassing countries that may be quite different from each other. So, although the use of demographic data is encouraged as a valuable tool to summarize and illustrate the aging experiences of a country or a group of older people, we caution you to use these data ultimately as a way to uncover the complexities and varieties of aging.

One common trap is to assume that the demography of aging, as compelling as it might be, will attract popular attention and spur policies and planning for aging populations. This is known as the **fallacy of the demographic imperative**. One key to avoid this fallacy is to keep in mind that "demography is not destiny." Larger numbers of older people do not compel a particular course of action. In fact, those numbers can be used to promote very different courses of action. Friedland and Summer (2005) illustrate various interpretations of even commonly accepted demographic wisdom. The general public has probably heard and read a great deal about the baby boomers and what their aging will mean to individuals and to society. Friedland and Summer point out that everyone can get a different sense of the magnitude of the "baby boom problem" if they consider not just the total number of people in that birth cohort but also the additional people born solely because of the higher birth rate. During the 18 years of the baby boom era, the higher birth rate added about 12 million additional children beyond the number that would have been born if the pre–World War II birth rates had continued. In 1957—the peak year of the American baby boom—4.3 million babies were born; in 2008, 4.25 million babies were born in the United States, very nearly the same number (Hamilton, Martin, & Ventura, 2010). If we think about it in this way, the baby boom does not seem as large. These authors reiterate what has been emphasized throughout this chapter: Although they may seem compelling, numbers are only part of the picture. What any society decides to do about the aging of its population depends not simply on how many older people it has, but also on the political, social, and moral values of the society. Demography contributes to, but is not, by itself, destiny.

The warning against invoking the demographic imperative certainly applies to those who use the dependency ratio to foretell an impending economic disaster. The implication of the numbers describing a coming "age wave" is a matter of interpretation. Choices about which numbers to present are critical and often very ideologically based. Some critics have suggested that language such as the "silver tsunami" should be avoided because of the destructive, negative image it portrays. So, whereas demographic information should be considered as a useful resource, it is important to be aware of the social and political contexts (and organizations) that generate the numbers and direct their uses.

Although demographic information provides an essential framework from which to understand the aging of societies, it is equally important to remain aware of the powerful influence of culture and the overarching impact of other social institutions (the economy, politics, family systems) when considering how best to deal with the challenges of aging. "We need not believe ourselves to be at the mercy of blind forces such as demographic and economic imperatives, as if these existed outside the realm of public discussion and debate" (Robertson, 1991, p. 147).

SUMMARY

This chapter illustrates that the increase in the size and proportion of the older population has an impact on every aspect of social life. In the United States, the number of older people is projected to exceed 70 million by the year 2030, at which time all the baby boomers will have reached age 65; older people will represent about 20% of our population by then—one in every five people on the sidewalks and in the grocery store will be old! Even more dramatic is the extent to which population aging is changing the world. All of the countries in Table 3.2 will have significant growth of the older population by 2050. More than one third of the people in Japan in 2050 are projected to be 65 and older. In the United States, the proportion aged will rise from 15% in 2018 to 22%. Other countries will have significantly higher growth. Swaziland's proportion of older people will double; Thailand's proportion aged will more than double; and the UAE will go through a profound shift from virtually no older adults to a population that is 14% older adults. Germany and Japan will have median ages of 54 and 53, respectively. The demographic patterns of global aging and the specific ways in which population aging is affecting life in every society around the world have never been of greater importance.

The causes, consequences, and measurement of population aging are large-scale issues. Powerful forces such as fertility and mortality, alarmist warnings about the consequences of global aging, and assumption-laden measures of dependency ratios may seem far distant from your life. However, we hope that you have begun to see that population aging affects each of us, as individuals and our families. On a more macro level, it is influencing the government, public policy, health care systems, and the economy of every nation. As seen earlier in this chapter, a large proportion of all older people will live in developing nations by the year 2020. Enormous challenges are facing the nations where rapid population aging will compete with maternal and child health concerns. Of equal magnitude are the challenges for the global community to plan for their aging societies and to propose and implement culturally relevant solutions to the challenges of health care and economic security.

DISCUSSION QUESTIONS

1. How has population aging affected your country?
2. How do you think the population in your country will age in the future? For example, do you expect changes in fertility rates? In immigration? Other demographic variables?
3. Do you think Bangladesh and Cambodia will experience the same demographic transition as Canada and France? Provide a brief explanation to support your position.
4. Japan is currently the world's oldest country. What does that mean? How does it affect Japan's families, economy, and health care system?
5. Do you think aging will be good or bad for your country? Why?
6. What are some of the demographic dividends of an aging population?
7. Which of the various measures of a population's age seems most useful to you?
8. Is there any basis for the claim that "50 is the new 40?"
9. What is the fallacy of the demographic imperative?
10. How do you react to the statement that "demography is destiny?" Do you agree or disagree? Why?

KEY WORDS

Demographic divide
Demographic dividend
Demographic transition theory
Dependency ratio
Fallacy of the demographic imperative
Life expectancy

Life span
Median age
Population aging
Population pyramid
Prospective age
Second demographic transition

REFERENCES

Fried, L. (2016). Investing in health to create a third demogrhic dividend. *The Gerontologist 56*(2), S167–S177. doi:10.1093/geront/gnw035

Friedland, R. B., & Summer, L. (2005). *Demography is not destiny, revisited.* Washington, DC: Center on an Aging Society, Georgetown University Commonwealth (Pub. No. 789).

Hamilton, B., Martin, J., & Ventura, S. (2010). Births: Preliminary data for 2008. *National Vital Statistics Reports, 58*(16), 1–6.

Haub, C. (2007). Global aging and the demographic divide. *Public Policy & Aging Report, 17*(4), 1–6. doi:10.1093/ppar/17.4.1a

He, W., Goodkind, D., & Kowal, P. (2016). An aging world: 2015. *International Population Reports*, P95/16-1. Washington, DC: U.S. Government Printing Office.

Kinsella, K., & He, W. (2009). An aging world: 2008. In U.S. Bureau of the Census (Ed.), *International population reports P95/09-1.* Washington, DC: U.S. Government Printing Office. Retrieved from https://www.census.gov/prod/2009pubs/p95-09-1.pdf

Kinsella, K., & Phillips, D. R. (2005). Global aging: The challenge of success. *Population Bulletin, 60*(1), 3–42.

Lee, R., & Mason, A. (2006). What is the demographic dividend? *Finance and Development, 43*(3), 1–9.

Lesthaeghe, R. (2014). The second demographic transition: A concise overview of its development. *PNAS, 11*(51), 18112–18115. doi:10.1073./pnas.1420441111

Malit, F., & Youha, A. (2013). *Labor migration in the United Arab Emirates: Challenges and responses.* Washington, DC: Migration Policy Institute. Retrieved from http://www.migrationpolicy.org/article/labor-migration-united-arab-emirates-challenges-and-responses

Martin, L. (2011). Demography and aging. In R. H. Binstock and L. K. George (Eds.), *Handbook of aging and social sciences* (7th ed., pp. 33–46). Cambridge, MA: Academic Press.

Mason, A., Lee, R., & Jiang, J. X. (2016). Demographic dividends, human capital, and saving. *The Journal of the Economics of Ageing, 7*, 106–122. doi:10.1016/j.jeoa.2016.02.004

Panruti, R., Liebig, P., & Duvvuru, J. (2015). Gerontology in India. *The Gerontologist, 55*(6), 894–900. doi:10.1093/geront/gnv022

Population Reference Bureau. (2012). World Population Data Sheet 2012. Retrieved from https://www.prb.org/wp-content/uploads/2012/07/2012-population-data-sheet_eng.pdf

Population Reference Bureau. (2018). *2018 World population data sheet with focus on changing age structures.* Retrieved from https://www.prb.org/2018-world-population-data-sheet-with-focus-on-changing-age-structures

Robertson, A. (1991). The politics of Alzheimer's disease: A case study in apocalyptic demography. In M. Minkler & C. Estes (Eds.), *Critical perspectives on aging: The political and moral economy of growing old* (pp. 135–152). Amityville, NY: Baywood.

Sanderson, W., & Scherbov, S. (2008). Rethinking age and aging. *Population Bulletin, 63*(4), 3–16. doi:10.4054/DemRes.2007.16.2

Treas, J. (1995). Older Americans in the 1990s and beyond. *Population Bulletin, 50*(2), 2–46.

United Nations, Department of Economic and Social Affairs, Population Division. (2015). *World fertility patterns 2015 – Data booklet* (ST/ESA/ SER.A/370). Retrieved from https://www.un.org/en/development/desa/population/publications/pdf/fertility/world-fertility-patterns-2015.pdf

United Nations, Department of Economic and Social Affairs. (2009). *World population ageing: 2009.* New York, NY: United Nations Publications.

U.S. Centers for Medicare and Medicaid Services. (2019). *National health expenditure fact sheet: 2017.* Retrieved from https://www.cms.gov/research-statistics-data-and-systems/statistics-trends-and-reports/nationalhealthexpenddata/nhe-fact-sheet.html

World Population Review. (2018). Countries by median age 2018. Retrieved from http://worldpopulationreview.com/countries/median-age

POPULATION AGING IN IRAN AND ITS IMPLICATIONS

MAHMOOD MESSKOUB | NADER MEHRI[1]

Iran[2] has one of the fastest rates of population aging in the world. This is due mainly to reduced fertility that was produced by family planning policies, increased education of women, rising age of marriage, and urbanization. Infant and child mortality declined through the widespread introduction of public health measures such as vaccination, improved sanitation, and better nutrition, thus increasing average life expectancy (Abbasi-Shavazi & Hosseini-Chavoshi, 2011; Mirzaie, 2005; Saadat, Chowdhury, & Mehryar, 2010). This essay provides a summary of the determinants of population aging in Iran as well as the social and economic consequences of this rapid shift to an aging population.

---

[1] The authors wish to thank the editors for their valuable and insightful comments. The remaining errors, alas, are ours!

[2] Iran, a country of about 80 million people and with an over 3,000-year history, lies between the Caspian Sea in the north and the Persian Gulf in the south in Western Asia, covering an area of 1.6 million square kilometers (6.3 million square miles). It is a multiethnic and multilingual country with Farsi (Persian) as its official language. Since the mid-1950s, rural–urban migration and natural population growth have made Iran a highly urbanized country; in 2018, about three quarters of its population lived in urban areas. According to the World Bank, Iran had a per capita income of about US$5,000 and is considered an upper-middle-income country. Iran has high literacy rates: 91% for males and 84% for females. Its economy is dominated by the hydrocarbon industry (oil and natural gas) and has substantial industrial and manufacturing sectors. In 2018, industry comprised 35% of the gross domestic product, services 54%, and agriculture 9%. (For further information, see Encyclopaedia Iranica, 2019; Encyclopaedia Britannica, 2019; and World Bank, 2019.)

DETERMINANTS OF POPULATION AGING IN IRAN

Population aging—the rise in the proportion of people aged 60 and above in the total population—is a direct consequence of decline in fertility and decline in infant and child mortality, leading to an overall increase in average life expectancy at birth. Over the past four decades, Iran has experienced a substantial decrease in its total fertility rate (TFR), which is the average number of children per woman during her reproductive years (15–49). Iran's TFR declined from a high of 6.9 children per woman in 1960 to 1.9 children per woman in 2005 (UN, DESA, Population Division, 2014), the largest percentage decline in the world as noted by the UN Population Division (UN, DESA, Population Division, 2009). The TFR decreased by 72% from 1960 to the mid-2000s, while life expectancy at birth has been consistently on the increase, from 40 years in the 1950–1955 period to 57 years in the 1975–1980 period. After a drop during the Iran–Iraq war (1980–1988), life expectancy continued its rise, reaching 75 years in 2010–2015, and is projected to reach 80 years by 2050 (UN, DESA, Population Division, 2015a); see Figure 3.7.

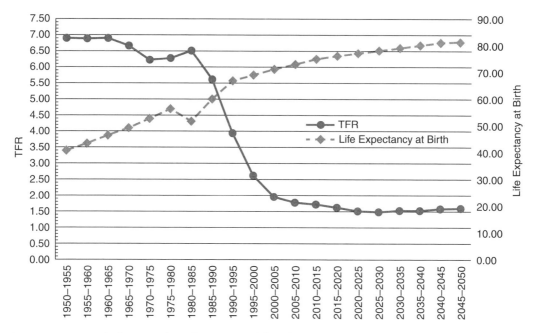

FIGURE 3.7 Total observed and projected fertility rates and life rxpectancy, Iran, 1950–2050 (medium fertility variant). TFR, total fertility rate.

Source: Authors' compilation based on United Nations, Department of Economic and Social Affairs, Population Division. (2015a). *World Population Prospects: The 2015 Revision, DVD Edition.*

POPULATION AGING TRENDS IN IRAN

As Figure 3.8 illustrates, the percentage of older adults in the total population in Iran has closely followed fertility trends since 1950. The upward trend in the proportion of older people will gather pace well into the 21st century. An important feature of population aging in Iran is its speed, including a rapid increase in the number of older people in the next 30 years. The share of 60-and-older in the population nearly doubled over a 40-year period, from 4.8% in 1980 to 8.8% in 2015; but this 40-year doubling time is expected to be cut in half as the 60-and-older proportion is projected to reach 20% by 2040 (see Figure 3.8). By 2050, the number of older people aged 60 and older is projected to be around 30 million, representing nearly a third of Iran's total projected population of 92 million.

In addition, the gender composition of Iran's older population has gone through some changes. In 1950, the male-to-female ratio among people aged 60 and older was 109 (109 males for every 100 females), but that declined to 93.7 in 2000. The ratio is projected to decrease to 93.2 and 89 in 2025 and 2050, respectively (UN, DESA, Population Division, 2015b). With the improvement in health care, female mortality declined, resulting in higher life expectancy in favor of women and a shifting sex ratio among older people. Life expectancy at age 80 for males and females in 2000–2005 was 5.4 and 5.5, respectively. Those figures are projected

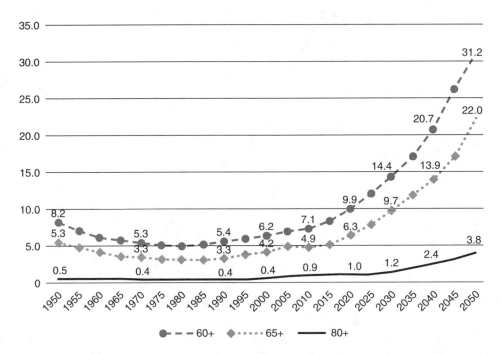

FIGURE 3.8 The percentage of aged (60 years and older, 65 years and older, and 80 years and older) in Iran, 1950–2050 (medium fertility variant).

Source: Authors' compilation based on United Nations, Department of Economic and Social Affairs, Population Division. (2015a). *World Population Prospects: The 2015 Revision, DVD Edition.*

to increase to 5.9 and 6.8 for males and females in 2025–2030 and to 6.7 and 8.5 in 2045–2050, respectively (UN, DESA, Population Division, 2015b).

This change is also reflected in the male to female sex ratio of the cohort of oldest people (those 80+) that changed from 104.6 in 1950 to 83.7 in 2015. This sex ratio is projected to decrease to 76.1 in 2025 and 63.9 in 2050 (UN, DESA, Population Division, 2015b), indicating that a large majority of the 80-and-older population of 3.5 million in 2050 will be women.

ECONOMIC AND SOCIAL SUPPORT FOR OLDER ADULTS IN IRAN

The population aging of Iran has occurred during the rapid urbanization of the country. In the mid-1950s, about one third of the older population was living in urban areas; that number had increased to two thirds by 2006. This change closely follows the trend in urbanization of the total population. Unlike some other countries, such as China, where younger people move to urban areas but older people stay put in their rural homes (Messkoub & Davin, 2000), urbanization in Iran generally involves the move, over time, of entire multigenerational families (including older family members) from rural to urban areas. This is important because the high concentration of health and other services in urban areas would help to cater for the needs of the old.

Kunkel, Brown, and Whittington (2014) noted that when people aged 60 and older outnumber children younger than age 15, there is a revolutionary situation from a demographic point of view, with social, cultural, economic, and political consequences. This point will be reached in Iran in 2035. An important implication of this tipping point is the changing balance between young and old dependency on the population of working-age adults.

The old-age dependency ratio (65+ population relative to working-age adults, aged 15–64) has steadily been increasing since the 1970s, while the child dependency ratio has been declining since 2000. These shifting dependency ratios closely track the fall in mortality and fertility in Iran. There were 6.3 older persons for every 100 working-age people in 1970; that number had increased to 7.1 in 2015 but is expected to rise dramatically by 2050 to 34.9 (UN, DESA, Population Division, 2015a).[3]

To prepare for this challenge, Iran has a 30-year window to design and develop the social and economic policies as well as institutions to accommodate an aging population. An important asset for this endeavor is the current young age structure of Iran that will ensure a stable working-age population of around 70% of the population for the next 25 years.

This is not to imply that older people are passive recipients of care or entirely dependent on younger people. However, health changes and problems of economic

---

[3]For a critical discussion of economic and social "dependency" of older people, see Messkoub, 1999.

security among older adults in Iran do suggest that policies and programs to support elders will be necessary. This situation calls for more state resources not only to help older adults directly but also to help families who still are the main source of care for older adults.

The great majority of older adults in Iran live on their own or with their children. Less than 1% live in an institutional setting (old-age home); see Islamic Republic News Agency (IRNA, 2019). According to the 2006 census, 92% of older men and 59% of older women lived with their unmarried children and spouse (Aghajanian & Thompson, 2016). It is quite a common practice in Iran for children to live in their parental home until they marry. This practice indicates the important supporting role that the older generation plays as their children find their way in life. In this context, common living arrangements should not be viewed as the dependency of the old on the young but as an institution for mutual support that the young and the old provide for each other. However, this mutual support has to be further qualified by considering differences in living arrangements by gender.

Older men are more than twice as likely as older women to live with their single children, despite the higher life expectancy of women. A plausible explanation lies in the Islamic inheritance law in Iran, according to which widowed wives lose their right to reside in the family home. All assets of a deceased husband have to be distributed among his surviving family members. Death of a partner could bring great uncertainty and vulnerability to a wife in a patriarchal society where housewives have limited rights to work and accumulate assets. In general, women are at a higher risk of living on their own in old age. In 2006, 21% of older women lived on their own, compared with only 4% of older men (Aghajanian & Thompson, 2016). These authors also found that since the mid-1970s, marked differences have emerged between living arrangements of old men and women—men live with a spouse either through marriage or remarriage and continue to be the head of the household, while women either live alone or with their children, mainly sons.

SOCIOECONOMIC SECURITY

Socioeconomic security in old age is based on a combination of accumulated resources: income from labor, assets including own pension savings, family support (in-kind or cash), and institutional support from the state and employers in the form of state and work-based pensions, health coverage, and other benefits. The relative contribution of the aforementioned sources to the economic well-being of older people in Iran varies greatly across different socioeconomic groups. In general, richer households rely on their own resources while the middle and lower socioeconomic groups have to rely on family and state-funded institutional support.

Iran does not have a universal age-related or citizen-based pension scheme comparable to state pensions in Europe or Social Security in the United States. But it has a range of employment-related pension plans that are managed either by the Social Security Organization for private-sector employees or various state pension-fund schemes for civil servants, the armed forces, and other government employees. These formal pension schemes covered 4.3 million pensioners in 2016 (Ebrahimi & Hemmati, 2018), or about half of the 7.2 million 60-and-older population of Iran. Two other major state-financed agencies—Emam Khomeini Assistance Committee (Komiteh Emdad Emam) and Behzisti Organization—also provide some support to the older population. Their support is means-tested, with the former covering 1.5 million retirees and the latter 0.5 million in 2016. The formal pension schemes cover mainly men, given the male-dominated structure of formal employment in Iran, but women do inherit the pension of their deceased partners.

There is a great deal of variation in the adequacy of pensions, which depend largely on the final salary/income. For example, the high-ranking civil servants, military, and police officers who retire on high final salaries do have a reasonably adequate pension, but the majority of pensioners struggle to cover their basic living expenses. In recent years, there have been widespread demonstrations by pensioners protesting against inadequate pensions due to high inflation.

Finally, Iran has a near-universal cash transfer program that currently pays 450,000 rials (R) a month (about US$3.75 at the black market exchange rate of R120,000 per dollar in July 2019) to every Iranian citizen, as long as they register to receive it. By default, older Iranians do benefit from this system, although a cash transfer of this amount is totally inadequate to cover the basic needs of food, clothing, health care, and housing of an older person.

Overall, social policy measures to supplement family resources and advance the broad national agenda to ensure societal and macrolevel intergenerational support will be essential in the coming decades. A hands-off position about the role of government effectively increases the burden on the family, and particularly the women within it. In the context of intergenerational support, the state intervention could have the objective of improving family budgets through subsidies and decommodifying (through regulation and intervention in the market) the basic necessities of life. Decommodification does not necessarily mean free provision of goods and services. It could take different forms, such as rent control, subsidized medicine and staple food, and subsidized education. It is of note that some of these subsidies, such as that for education, are not directed at older people; however, freeing resources at the family level can indirectly contribute to the family budget and thus improve its capacity to provide support to older members. Moreover, old age could be set as a target for direct subsidies to older adults; the most obvious example is state-sponsored health insurance and subsidies to medicine for chronic diseases that usually are associated with age. For example, out-of-pocket expenses comprised 54% of household health expenditures over the 1998–2012 period (World Health Organization, Global Health Expenditure database, quoted in Ghiasvand, Naghdi, Abolhassani, Shaarbafchizadeh, & Moghri, 2015). In 2014, the Health Evolution Plan of Iran was introduced with the main objective of reducing out-of-pocket expenses and reducing the burden of health care expenditures on low-income families (Moradi-Lakeh & Vosoogh-Moghaddam, 2015). This program has had some success in meeting its objectives, but its sustainability is in question, given its financing costs.

CONCLUSION

The speed of aging in Iran is truly remarkable. The proportion of its population that is aged 60 years and above will triple in 30 years; this transition took 157 years in France, 100 years in the United Kingdom, and 89 years in the United States. The speed of this transition would be challenging under any conditions, but Iran faces additional risk since it has neither the national income and economic resources nor the financial and institutional infrastructure that these countries had time to put in place as their populations were aging over many decades.

Providing care for a growing aging population will be one of the most significant challenges faced by Iranian families, the great majority of whom do not have sufficient resources to care for their elders but are motivated to do so out of familial and humanitarian solidarity. Family caregiving comes at a cost, particularly to women. Care is a very gender-based activity all over the world. Family support also should be put in the context of the declining average household size in Iran, which decreased from 5.1 persons in 1986 to 4 in 2006 (Aghajanian & Thompson, 2013). Moreover, nuclear families, which increased from 79.2% of total households in 1986 to 83.8% in 2006, have replaced multifamily/generational households, further reducing the capacity of the family to provide old-age care.

In summary, although Iran's rapid fertility decline and population aging have important social and economic implications, they should not be seen as demographic catastrophes. Such views could hinder positive public and policy responses, as witnessed by the pronatalist policies promoted by the most powerful conservative political leaders in Iran, who have called for the downgrading and even withdrawal of family planning services. Demographic transition and population aging, instead, should be understood as a genuinely new situation that will significantly affect the economy, pension system, public policies, labor force, and the health care system in Iran.

REFERENCES

Abbasi-Shavazi, M. J., & Hosseini-Chavoshi, M. (2011). Family planning, fertility, and evolution of population policies in Iran. *Journal of Knowledge in Islamic [Persian] University [Maarefat dar Daneshgah-e Islami]*, 15(3), 8–26.

Aghajanian, A., & Thompson, V. (2013). Household size and structure in Iran: 1976–2006. *The Open Family Studies Journal*, 5, 1–9. doi:10.2174/1874922401305010001

Aghajanian, A., & Thompson, V. (2016). Gender and living arrangements of the elderly in Iran. *Asian Population Studies*, 12(2), 177–186. doi:10.1080/17441730.2016.1150697

Ebrahimi, E., & Hemmati, M., (2018). *The role in and influence of pension funds on the financial stability of Iranian economy*. Paper presented in 28th Annual Conference on Iran's Fiscal and Monetary Policies. Tehran, Iran.

Encyclopaedia Britannica. (2019). Retrieved from https://www.britannica.com/place/Iran/Settlement-patterns3ref230050

Encyclopaedia Iranica. (2019). Retrieved from http://www.iranicaonline.org/articles/encyclopaedia-iranica

Ghiasvand, H., Naghdi, S., Abolhassani, N., Shaarbafchizadeh, N., & Moghri, J. (2015). Iranian households' payments on food and health out-of-pocket expenditures: Evidence of inequality. *Iran Journal of Public Health.* 44(8), 1103–1113.

Islamic Republic News Agency. (2019). About 15000 old people live in the old people's home [run by Behzisti organisation]. News code: 82705188. Retrieved from https://www.irna.ir/news/82705188

Kunkel, S. R., Brown, J. S., & Whittington, F. J. (2014). *Global aging: Comparative perspectives on aging and the life course.* New York, NY: Springer Publishing Company.

Messkoub, M. (1999). Crisis of ageing in less developed countries: Too much consumption or too little production? *Development and Change, 30,* 217–235. doi:10.1111/1467-7660.00115

Messkoub, M., & Davin, D. (2000). Patterns of migration under the reforms. In T. C. Cannon (Ed.), *China: Economic growth, population and environment.* London: Macmillan.

Mirzaie, M. (2005). Swings in fertility limitation in Iran. *Middle East Critique, 14*(1), 25–33. doi:10.1080/10669920500056973

Moradi-Lakeh, M., & Vosoogh-Moghaddam, A. (2015). Health sector evolution plan in Iran; Equity and sustainability concerns. *International Journal of Health Policy and Management, 4*(10), 637–640. doi:10.15171/ijhpm.2015.160

Saadat, S., Chowdhury, S. A., & Mehryar, A. (2010). Fertility decline in the Islamic Republic of Iran 1980-2006: A case study. Washington, DC: World Bank. Retrieved from http://documents.worldbank.org/curated/en/316231468340135221/Fertility-decline-in-the-Islamic-Republic-of-Iran-1980-2006-a-case-study

United Nations, Department of Economic and Social Affairs, Population Division. (2009). World Population Prospects: The 2008 Revision, Highlights. Retrieved from https://population.un.org/wpp/

United Nations, Department of Economic and Social Affairs, Population Division. (2014). World Fertility Report 2013: Fertility at the Extremes, New York, United Nations. Retrieved from http://www.un.org/en/development/desa/population/publications/pdf/fertility/worldFertilityReport2013.pdf

United Nations, Department of Economic and Social Affairs, Population Division. (2015a). *World Population Prospects: The 2015 Revision, DVD Edition.*

United Nations, Department of Economic and Social Affairs, Population Division. (2015b). World Population Ageing 2015 Report. Retrieved from http://www.un.org/en/development/desa/population/publications/pdf/ageing/WPA2015_Report.pdf

World Bank. (2019). Retrieved from https://www.worldbank.org/en/country/iran/overview

4

AGING ENVIRONMENTS

INTRODUCTION

According to the World Health Organization (WHO, 2019), one's health and well-being are determined as much by physical and social environments as they are by genetic makeup and personal life choices. Older persons throughout the world spend the majority of their time where they are housed (Gitlin, 2003; Golant, 2011). But does that mean that people are spending their time in a home of their choice? Does the place where they are being housed come with security, privacy, and opportunities to exert control? These are some issues that we consider in this chapter.

Whether people live alone or with family members or friends, home is an important consideration throughout their lives. In this chapter, we first explore what is meant by *home*, including similarities and differences between private homes and institutions. We also consider *place* and *housing* in the context of dwelling types and recent social movements. Environmental theory in gerontology and *aging in place* provide a framework to explore ways in which home environments can help or hinder people as they age. Finally, the chapter looks at ways in which environments can enable or disable people by their physical features (e.g., accessible entryways) and explores concepts related to age-friendly communities. The brief vignette in Exhibit 4.1 introduces some of the themes surrounding home, place, and housing for older persons.

HOME AND PLACE AS BUILDING BLOCKS OF ENVIRONMENT

It is difficult to talk about environments and aging without considering basic terms such as *home*, *place*, and *housing*. We begin this section by looking at definitions and examples of each within the context of global aging.

EXHIBIT 4.1

When Children Move Away From the Family Home

Maria Cabral, aged 82, lives alone in Achadinha, a small town (population 535) on the northeast part of São Miguel, one of the nine islands of the Azores, located in the Atlantic Ocean 950 miles (1,525 km) off the cost of Portugal. Maria has lived in the small home that her husband built since the 1950s, long before electricity came to her part of the island in the 1970s. Maria's three children left for Canada in the 1980s to find jobs. It is where they met their spouses, started families, and built new lives. Like most of her neighbors, many of whom are also widows, Maria does not get to see her children much. Many younger people leave the islands to find better jobs abroad.

When Maria's husband died 10 years ago, her children tried to persuade her to move to Canada. They worry that the uneven cobblestone streets make walking difficult and even dangerous, and the isolated village (there is only one grocery market, which doubles as the only restaurant) does not provide adequate services. They are afraid that if Maria twists an ankle—or worse, falls and breaks her hip—she will have only limited access to emergency medical services. Ponta Delgada, where the hospital and airport are located, is at least 40 minutes away by car. Despite what her children say, Maria wants to stay in the town where she was born; where her husband, parents, and siblings are buried; and where she remains an active part of the local Catholic church. She knows that as her neighbors move away or pass on, the village will gradually disappear, and the houses will be torn down and replaced by something new. She wishes that her children lived nearby and could help her, as she helped her parents when they got older. But times have changed. She knows she must accept this because, despite the challenges, she never wants to leave the place she calls home.

Home

Home is an idea that everyone can relate to, even though our definitions and thoughts about what makes a home might differ. **Home** can mean many different things, depending on one's cultural context; home has physical, personal, and social characteristics (Grenier, Barken, & McGrath, 2016; Tipple & Speak, 2009). For example, for some, home might evoke emotional memories attached to a place where one lived. Home might also invoke the notion of belonging and comfort, such as "feeling at home." It may also describe a physical structure, such as a house or apartment. Regardless of definition, home can be a place of security, familiarity, comfort, and privacy. Home can also be a place where cultural rules determine power and place. For some, home can be a source of oppression and violence. When we consider environments and aging, it is important to consider cultural understandings and expectations of what is meant by home as well as power dynamics that exist within homes of all types.

In the vignette in Exhibit 4.1, Maria Cabral's home is at one level a structure, a house with rooms, windows, and other features that Maria identifies with. It also has personal characteristics for her. Maria has memories associated with the home, it is familiar to her, and she feels safe there. It has a style expressed through décor or the display of personal objects such as family photos, making it a place that mirrors many things important in her life (Rubinstein, 1987). Her home also serves a social function. It is embedded within a village and gives her access to friends, church, and shopping. For Maria, home is linked with her identity and concept of self (Rubinstein & de Medeiros, 2005). As Stones and Gullifer (2016) observe:

> Home provides more than just a physical shelter for older people. Home nourishes their sense of self, provides continuity of history and support in times of change, and connects older people with their younger selves to their current physical and psychological status. (p. 454)

Along with identity, home also implies a sense of choice or control, although status within the household (e.g., child) likely determines how much control a person has. For example, in patriarchal cultures, women may have prescribed roles within the home that can make them powerful in some parts of the home (e.g., the kitchen, places where children are raised) but not in others (e.g., the bedroom.) In other cultures, power may rest with whoever owns the home (e.g., an adult daughter, a grandmother, a government agency), regardless of gender.

Control broadly refers to the ability of a person to achieve a desired outcome. Control can be something that one perceives or believes is possible. For example, a person may perceive himself or herself as having control over his or her health when many aspects of health are beyond a person's control. Perceived control, not demonstrated control, is the important part (Rodin, 2014). If a person lacks a feeling of control, he or she may feel helpless or unable to cope with events. With regard to control in the home environment, Tipple and Speak (2009) write:

> "Home" should be a place where a person is able to define the space as their own, where they are able to control its form and shape. This may be through control of activities and of defining their privacy in terms of access to their space. When this is done, they have made a home with a sense of their identity. (p. 4)

As we see later in this chapter, control becomes an important consideration in living environments, especially as one ages; creating a "home-like" environment for people who do not own their homes (e.g., apartments, institutions) is a goal for many housing providers and policy makers throughout the world (Grenier et al., 2016).

Place

While home can be both physical and emotional, **place** describes a location. This could be a physical place where one lives (e.g., one's own house), a particular neighborhood, a city or town, and so on. Like home, place also carries emotional attachment and significance and is deeply rooted in culture (Becker, 1997; Tilley, 1994). It is the cultural inferences and interpretations that we apply to a given space that inform our thoughts about it (de Medeiros, 2016; Rubinstein & de Medeiros, 2003). **Place attachment** describes "the (re)production of affective, cognitive and behavioral ties to a physical location as a result of the meanings and daily functions positioned within it" (Coleman & Kearns, 2015, p. 207). For example, we may identify with and have strong attachment to the place where we grew up. In later life, we may therefore try to either recreate meaningful aspects of that place (e.g., similar views, pictures that evoke a sense of place) or even physically return to that place. **Aging in place**, which is discussed in more detail later in this chapter, describes a person's desire to continue living in his or her privately owned or rented home rather than moving into an institution or care home (Abramsson & Andersson, 2016). As illustrated in the vignette in Exhibit 4.1, Maria has a strong attachment to place as well as a clear desire to age in that place.

Although home and housing have received a substantial amount of attention in the research literature, place often is overlooked, especially when thinking about environments for older persons. In the United States, for example, it is common for retirement communities to be located in either very remote areas or in dense but not necessarily socially desirable areas of larger communities. The underlying message of such locations is that place plays a secondary role to housing. Such a view overlooks meaning that people can derive from place.

An interesting example of the relationship of place and meaning comes from Coleman and Kearns's (2015) investigation of the importance of **blue space** (or ocean views) for older people from Waiheke Island, New Zealand, where the majority of residents are aged 65 or above. Given that place attachment includes the cognitive, behavioral, and affective ties and the subsequent meaning that a place has to a person, it is not surprising to find that people who lived in the coastline region and who had daily views of the ocean felt inextricably linked to the water and its blue scape. To think of a person's living environment as only a dwelling (e.g., house, apartment) without considering the dwelling within the context of place would be to overlook a large part of a person's identity. Consequently, moving a person to a dwelling that lacks place attachment (e.g., an inland house that lacks an ocean view) could have negative consequences for the person. Place, therefore, is a significant consideration of aging environments.

HOUSING FOR OLDER PEOPLE

Housing

Related to yet distinct from home is *housing*. **Housing** refers to the physical structures and services and the symbolic characteristics associated with where one lives. At its most basic, housing describes where a person sleeps. He or she might also prepare meals there, although there are certainly a variety of housing types where meal preparation is done by others, away from the living area. What is important to keep in mind is that housing and home do not necessitate one another. A person can live in a house that he or she does not consider to be a home, such as in an institution or within someone else's (e.g., an adult child's) home.

The broad category of "housing" for older people includes living arrangements, which will be addressed briefly, and types of housing, such as independent living, assisted living, and nursing homes.

Living arrangements describe household composition or with whom one lives, such as with a spouse, alone, with a family member, or in a home with others who are not family members. Most older adults in Western countries prefer to live independently, although what comprises *independent living* may differ such as living in one's home or moving into an age-segregated or retirement community (Kramer & Pfaffenbach, 2016; Peace, Wahl, Mollenkopf, & Oswald, 2007). For example, in Spain, more than 80% of people over age 65 own their homes, since home ownership is a primary way that Spaniards save for their retirement. In addition, most (88%) live alone or with a spouse. Very few (less than 12%) live with children or in institutions such as nursing homes (Costa-Font, Elvira, & Mascarilla-Miró, 2009). Researchers in Sweden found a few key characteristics that determined housing choice. In larger cities where people lived in rented apartments, the preference of older persons was to continue staying in those apartments. Divorced persons preferred renting to home ownership in later life. Older persons who started new romantic relationships in later life preferred to live apart from their romantic partner rather than cohabitate (Abramsson & Andersson, 2016). The authors of the Swedish study emphasized that age cohort likely played a role in housing preferences, with older cohorts who had lived in their private home for many years preferring to remain in that home.

In contrast to the independent living preferences in most Western countries, intergenerational coresidence is preferred in many Eastern countries, such as China, Japan, Vietnam, Thailand, and South Korea, and in many African countries. **Intergenerational coresidence** refers to multiple generations of one family living in the same residence. For example, in countries in sub-Saharan Africa, intergenerational coresidence households, often composed of three generations, are more common than living alone. This structure allows financial and caregiving resources to be easily shared among family members (Zimmer & Dayton, 2005).

In some respects, many countries in South America resemble Eastern countries in preferences for intergenerational cohabitation. For example, in Brazil, which has one of the fastest growing populations of people aged 65 and above, most older people live with family (Andrade & DeVos, 2016). Less than 25% of unmarried (i.e., widowed or never married) older women lived alone in Brazil, compared to around 70% of unmarried older women in the United States (Andrade & DeVos, 2016). Given the cultural expectation that children live at home until married, unmarried adult children in Brazil are far more likely to live in their older mother's home than the other way around.

It is important to note, however, that despite older persons' preferences, societal changes brought on by globalization are changing where older people live

(Yamada & Teerawichitchainan, 2015). For examples, adult children who have relocated for work may not be able to have their older parents live with them. Older parents who expected to live with an adult son or daughter may not be emotionally or financially prepared to live on their own. Research suggests that people who expected to live in an intergenerational coresidence but are not able to because of changes in family circumstances are at much greater risk for adverse psychological outcomes such as depression, sleep disorders, and poor appetite (Yamada & Teerawichitchainan, 2015). Other studies, however, have found that it may not be the lack of coresidential housing leading to poorer psychological outcomes, but rather the lack of social interaction. For example, Sun, Lucas, Meng, and Zhang (2011) found that even in a country like, China where intergeneration coresidential housing is an expectation, older persons who lived alone and had frequent and meaningful social interactions with others had similar depression rates to those who cohabitated with family members (Sun et al., 2011), suggesting that opportunities to socialize, which may be more likely in co-residential situations, might be important.

HOUSING TYPES

Several types of housing fall within the broad category of aging environments. Here we look at *independent housing, assisted living*, and *nursing homes*. **Independent housing**, as the name implies, describes housing where a person lives on his or her own (U.S. Centers for Medicare and Medicaid Services [CMS], 2019). Most older people in the world live in independent housing, whether with family, in a house they outwardly own, in rented housing, or in government-provided housing. In many places, older persons have lived in the same dwelling for decades. Unlike care homes or assisted living (described later), independent housing generally does not feature built-in care features such as those found in hospitals or nursing homes, although the line between living independently and living with in-home assistance is continuing to be blurred. Because of increases in in-home care and service options and new technology that makes it possible to monitor a person's medical status remotely, many independently living persons no longer need to relocate to a care facility to receive care assistance. We note again that while there are many important considerations regarding delivery of long-term care services and housing, the primary focus of this chapter is on housing itself. Consequently, care services are only addressed briefly relative to housing type rather than discussed in depth.

Age-segregated housing describes housing built specifically for older adults living independently. In the United States, this includes government-subsidized congregate housing, such as Section 202 Supportive Housing for the Elderly programs provided through the U.S. Department of Housing and Urban Development (HUD); private-pay congregate housing, such as retirement villages; independent living apartments in continuing care retirement communities (CCRCs); and veterans retirement communities (Sheehan & Oakes, 2003). Early studies suggested that older persons preferred age segregation to age integration. Advantages attributed to age-segregated housing include the benefits of age-peer relations and the residue of similar life-course experiences. For example, in the 1980s, Golant (1985) argued that criticism of age-segregated housing was based on the ideal of inclusion that did not take into account the preferences of the older person or the benefits of living in age-segregated housing, such as feeling less stigmatized by others and the greater ability to form new age-peer friendships. However, later research suggested that people's self-esteem suffered when they resided with people who were more frail than they were (Percival, 2001). Debate still continues on whether there are more potential positive or negative outcomes associated with age-segregated housing.

Assisted living (in the United States) describes a living environment where a person receives assistance with services such as meal preparation, personal care, or housekeeping (U.S. CMS, 2019). In many countries, the term **care home** is used instead of assisted living and also describes residential settings where personal care (nonmedical) services are provided (Elderly Accommodation Counsel, 2019). The focus of assisted living and care homes that do not provide nursing services is not on providing extensive medical support such as skilled nursing, which is part of what is provided by nursing homes (discussed in the next section). In theory, assisted living and care homes are places where people live semi-independently, with some personal care provided, although not in their own private home. Such facilities often resemble apartment complexes, much like independent living units.

Nursing homes (also called **skilled nursing facilities** in the United States or **care homes with nursing** in other countries) are a type of institutional environment that provides temporary, rehabilitative, or permanent nursing care for people who are injured, disabled, or ill to a point where they cannot be cared for at home (U.S. CMS, 2019). As with many definitions, there is slight variation depending on the country although most definitions for nursing homes and care homes with nursing have a medical component in the care provided in addition to nonmedical care, such as help with meal preparation or bathing.

Nursing homes are a much feared part of growing older, mainly because of the institutional nature of nursing home care. In contrast to homes that are private spaces, institutions have been described as a "public place that expresses itself with monumental architecture, high ceilings, grand spaces and landscaping similar to parks" (Caouette, 2005, p. 255). Institutions typically are designed for safety for both the inhabitants and the surrounding community and may include surveillance zones or places where staff can monitor the comings and goings of other staff, visitors, and residents, thereby creating potential barriers between residents and the institution. Hospitals, college dormitories, prisons, and even some retirement communities can fit this description. Most feature a surveillance area (e.g., a reception desk) and rules (e.g., visiting hours) about who may be present and during what hours. Residents typically have limited control within institutional settings. For older persons with no available family caregiver, having a home that is poorly adapted to meet their needs can be a major reason for moving into more institution-like settings.

In 2014, there were approximately 3.4 nursing home beds for every 100 older people in the United States (Harris-Kojetin et al., 2019). Even among high-income countries that belong to the Organisation for Economic Co-operation and Development (OECD), there is great variation in the number of nursing home beds available. For example, although there has been a slight increase in the number of long-term care beds since 2000 in OECD countries, some countries, such as the Netherlands, Denmark, and Norway, significantly reduced their number of beds by around 1 per 1,000 in 2015, with Sweden reducing beds by 2.4 between 2000 and 2013 (OECD, 2015). In contrast, South Korea saw an increase of 4.5 beds, the largest increase of any of the OECD countries (OECD, 2015). There are several possible explanations for these changes. In many high-income countries, new programs are being implemented to enable care at home rather than within an institution. Not only is living at home preferred by most, but such care can also be less expensive than nursing home care. For a country like South Korea, one of the most rapidly aging countries in the world without a lot of formal services or institutions for long-term care, the supply is likely increasing to meet a baseline level of demand.

Housing and Environmental Theories of Aging

To further understand the bigger picture of environments and aging, it is helpful to turn to ecological theories in gerontology that explore how physical, social, and emotional factors shape how and where people age and their effects on people's overall well-being (Rowles & Chaudhury, 2005; Rowles & Teaster, 2015). The sub-specialty of **environmental gerontology** grew from Kurt Lewin's (1951) *field theory* idea that described behavior as a function of person and environment. From these beginnings, researchers became more interested in how older people "fit" in their environments or, more specifically, how a person's behavior (e.g., apathy, satisfaction) was affected by qualities within the environment: Is an environment challenging enough to be stimulating? Is an environment too challenging for a person to live there independently?

A well-known and still applicable environmental theory in gerontology is Lawton and Nahemow's (1973) **ecological theory of aging**. Here, Lawton and Nahemow argue that one's ability to adapt in an environment is the "outcome of a relationship between changing individual competence (needs) and the changing constraints of the environmental context (referred to as 'press')" (p. 6). In this model, a misalignment between a person's capabilities and needs and the degree of environmental press could lead to maladaptive behavior or a negative outcome. In a residential care facility, for example, staff members may want to do everything they can to make a resident's life easier. In doing so, staff may inadvertently cause the environment to be without any challenge at all, thereby becoming boring and unstimulating for the resident. A more ideal situation would be an environment where a person was challenged, but not challenged beyond his or her capacity.

For example, preparing a meal might be beyond a person's capacity at a certain point in his or her life, but setting a table might be a way for the person to interact with the environment in a way that is better aligned with his or her current abilities. In this theory, Lawton and Nahemow recognized that many housing types and living environments should be considered in light of one's abilities, needs, and preferences combined, rather than, for example, choosing where to live just on preference alone (Vasunilashorn, Steinman, Liebig, & Pynoos, 2012).

Aging in Place and "Appropriate" Housing

Although researchers do not agree on a single definition, **aging in place** generally describes people's ability to live in the environment that they choose and to have access to the types of service they need if faced with declines in physical or cognitive competence. In this definition, aging in place could therefore refer to living with one's family or friends, if that is the environment of choice, or living alone. Although not explicitly included in the definition provided here, aging in place is assumed to be in a noninstitutional setting such as a home or apartment within the community. Others define aging in place as remaining in one's familiar home environment, which would imply remaining in a dwelling where one has been for a long time and has affective attachments (Wahl, Iwarsson, & Oswald, 2012), even if that happens to be an institutional setting such as an assisted living community (Ball et al., 2004).

Ecological theories are important when considering aging in place and other types of housing. A person's ability to successfully meet the multiple levels of challenges and demands that a given environment presents can determine what a successful environment for any individual might look like. For example, given what we know about Maria Cabral from the vignette in Exhibit 4.1, it appears she is able to adequately compensate for any "press" or challenge provided by her environment. If she were to twist her foot on the cobblestone road and sprain her ankle, she might be able to still meet her environment's demands as long as she had a crutch to help her walk or another mobility aid. If she were to experience a more serious event, such as a hip fracture or decline in cognitive abilities, it might be necessary for her to have outside help in order to continue to live alone. Without such help, she would be at increased risk for poor health outcomes such as malnutrition, complications from lack of treatment, or even social isolation if she is no longer able to get out to socialize with others. In this example, even though the home has a deeply important and personal meaning for Maria, her own health and access to services will heavily determine the house's appropriateness for her.

As mentioned earlier, in most OECD countries, older persons are more likely to live in the community rather than in institutions or with family (Costa-Font et al., 2009). Like Maria from the vignette in Exhibit 4.1, many older persons prefer to age in place, receiving any needed assistance with care within their home, even if the home poses challenges such as stairways or is in a high-crime neighborhood. Compared to institutions, which can be very costly for either the consumer or government payer, aging in place may be less expensive, especially if any needed services such as help with meal preparation or routine health therapies can be delivered at home (Abramsson & Andersson, 2016). However, despite being more preferred by many older people and policy makers, there are some added risks with aging in place. These can include financial strain for home maintenance, environmental barriers within the home (e.g., stairs), changes in the neighborhood (e.g., safety, access to goods and services), and social exclusion.

The ability to provide adequate housing for its citizens has been a major part of many countries' national policies. Some countries, such as the Netherlands and France, have viewed housing as a social issue, so the government plays an active role in making sure that all types of housing options are provided (Scanlon, Fernández Arrigoitia, & Whitehead, 2015). Other countries (e.g., the United Kingdom, Ireland, and Norway) focus instead on providing housing for low-income citizens. A third group of countries, to include Sweden, have focused on improving overall supplies of housing regardless of payer or income level of residents. **Social housing** broadly describes rent-controlled housing that is often managed by the government or an agent approved by the government (Gov.UK, 2012), although there are slight variations among countries regarding who is the owner and who sets the rent prices. Social housing is rooted in the idea that housing is not a commodity, but rather is one of the central pillars of a society along with health, education, and income maintenance (Harloe, 2008). In the Netherlands, for example, 32% of the entire housing stock in 2010 was classified as social rented housing, compared to 18% in Sweden, 9% in Ireland, and 2% in Spain (Scanlon et al., 2015).

Many countries are recognizing the need for more adequate and appropriate housing for older populations (Abramsson & Andersson, 2016; Addae-Dapaah & Juan, 2014). The term adequate housing implies two major considerations: affordability and appropriateness. For example, Singapore, with the world's third fastest-growing aging population, is struggling to find adequate housing for this burgeoning group, especially given its small size and densely populated territory (Addae-Dapaah & Juan, 2014). Although people who can afford condominiums or apartments in Singapore have housing options, there is a growing need for public rental blocks (called *social housing* or *subsidized housing* in other countries) that are government-owned and -controlled, specifically for people with low incomes. In the case of Singapore, although social housing was developed for all citizens in need, the majority (75%) of residents of such housing are aged 55 or above (Addae-Dapaah & Juan, 2014). Similar patterns have been reported in European countries such as Germany and Sweden, where the majority of occupants in government-subsidized social housing are older.

Housing Insecurity and Homelessness

Although homelessness has been recognized as a growing social problem in many countries, most programs and services are aimed at younger families with children rather than older persons specifically. Yet homelessness among older persons is increasing throughout the world, often as the result of increasing poverty and soaring housing prices (Grenier et al., 2016). Although homelessness creates many other vulnerabilities, including a greater risk of violence, malnutrition, and a lack of health or care services (Tipple & Speak, 2009), in this section we explore what is meant by homelessness, causes and prevalence of homelessness among older persons, and how homelessness figures into social policy about housing and care for people in later life.

Homelessness has been defined as "the situation of an individual or family without stable, permanent, appropriate housing, or the immediate prospect, means, and ability of acquiring it" (Grenier et al., 2016, p. 74). This definition includes people who are living in temporary shelter or in a dwelling with high insecurity, not just people who are living on the streets or outdoors (Culhane, Metraux, Byrne, Stino, & Bainbridge, 2013; Nooe & Patterson, 2010). In addition, the term homelessness includes people who have been homeless throughout their lives (chronically homeless) and those who have recently lost a secure dwelling place (new homeless) because of change in social, political, or environmental circumstances (e.g., war, natural disaster).

Unfortunately, little is reported about homeless older persons, partly because of the difficulties in identifying who is homeless and what classification is used to determine homelessness. Consequently, just how many older people are homeless is difficult to determine. The age at which a homeless person is considered "older" is also important. Grenier et al. (2016) point out that in Canada, homeless persons aged 50 and above are considered "older," in large part, since the homeless population in Canada has a disproportionate number of persons suffering from lifelong mental disabilities, causing them to experience vulnerabilities (e.g., increased risk of illness, cognitive impairment) associated with old age at a much earlier time of their lives. In addition, they report that in their study of homeless persons in Montreal, they found that the largest proportion of homeless people were those aged 50 and above (41%) with ages 31 to 49 comprising 39% and those under age 30 comprising 19%. In an attempt to estimate homelessness among older persons in Australia, Lipmann (2009) gathered data from patrons staying in night shelters for the homeless and found that on any given day, nearly half of the 100,000 people who used such shelters were aged 65 or above.

Displacement through situations such as forced relocation, immigration, or natural disasters causes homelessness through either high insecurity or actual loss of home. Major development projects, such as the construction of sports complexes for the 2016 Olympic Games in Rio de Janeiro and the upcoming 2020 Games in Tokyo, led to the mass relocation of low-income residents to make room for construction. Age-related data for people relocated from *favelas* (a term to describe extremely low-income slum areas in Brazil) are not readily available. However, Suzuki and colleagues (Suzuki, Ogawa, & Inaba, 2018) report that an undisclosed number of homeless people plus residents from 300 living units in the government-subsidized Kasumigaoka housing complex, the majority of whom were aged 65 and over, were relocated to accommodate reconstruction of the national stadium for the 2020 Tokyo Olympic games. Interestingly, the Kasumigaoka complex was built in 1964 to house people who were relocated to make room for the original national stadium constructed for that year's Olympics (Suzuki et al., 2018).

Another cause of homelessness is rising housing costs in the face of growing poverty, especially for those who never had access to enough wealth to purchase their own home or whose social position (e.g., being female, of a lower social caste) makes home ownership difficult if not impossible. In many countries, homelessness can also occur when one's situation changes due to circumstances such as divorce, widowhood, unemployment, or illness; these changes lead not only to a lower income but also to a loss of social standing. In some communities, such changes can lead to social labeling or accusations of immoral practice by family or community members, even to domestic violence or other stigmatizing events (Babafemi & Edoni, 2015). Women are especially vulnerable to homelessness in countries where they are afforded few rights or opportunities to own property or possess independent financial resources. In such countries, counting on family for help in the face of destitution can end in homelessness for the women in need.

Housing and Wealth

Housing also can be a means for accumulating wealth. In many countries in Western Europe, for example, older persons have been described as "income poor but housing rich" (Costa-Font et al., 2009, p. 301), meaning that older people who invested their savings earlier in life into purchasing their homes enjoy housing security in later life, but they do so at the expense of having cash savings.

Interestingly, research on poverty and home ownership in older persons has found a relationship between home ownership and lower poverty levels among older persons who receive pensions (Delfani, De Deken, & Dewilde, 2015). Since housing payments or rent are no longer needed, pension income can be spent on other items. In addition, in some countries, older persons can take a loan on their home equity through what is called a **reverse mortgage** (or *pensioning by housing*). In a reverse mortgage, a homeowner takes a loan based on the equity or value of the house they own. Repayment of the loan is not due until the homeowner dies or sells the house (Keene, Sarnak, & Coyle, 2018). However, people are charged a monthly service fee plus interest, which is deducted from the home's equity. Although the reverse mortgage can enable people to augment whatever retirement income they may have through their home's value, fees, high interest rates, taxes, and an accruing loan balance may ultimately offset the benefits for some.

LIVABLE CITIES/AGE-FRIENDLY CITIES

In this final section, we look at how communities *enable* or *disable* their members through policies of either inclusion or exclusion of older persons or persons with cognitive or functional limitations. First we consider environments within the rural and urban context, moving then to focus on so-called "friendliness" initiatives, such as age-friendly cities and age-friendly universities, which are part of a global movement to improve living environments for older persons. Whereas the previous section looked at individuals and groups in relation to various types of dwellings, now we describe much broader issues involving communities as a whole.

Urban and Rural Living Environments

In 2010, half of the world's population lived in cities (Buffel & Phillipson, 2012; Plouffe & Kalache, 2010), and it is projected that by 2030, three of every five persons in the world will do so (Plouffe & Kalache, 2010). Given that people aged 65 and above will outnumber those 14 and below, we can expect that a significant majority of city dwellers will be older persons. Thinking about how cities and communities throughout the world can better accommodate the changing needs of residents is at the heart of the age-friendly cities movement.

Age-Friendly Initiatives

It is first important to stress that age-friendly initiatives, which often are specifically focused on older persons, are actually designed to address varying needs of all people across their life spans, including persons with disabilities and parents of young children. Therefore, *age-friendly* could better be thought of as *all-inclusive* with **universal design** (i.e., designs that strive to provide access for the widest array of individuals, regardless of age or ability level); see Menec, Means, Keating, Parkhurst, and Eales (2011). As a formal movement, the age-friendly initiative began with the goal of bringing community design together with components from Lawton and Nahemow's (1973) ecological model of environments and aging mentioned earlier in this chapter. Specifically, the age-friendly movement incorporates the "dynamic interplay between individual adaptation and environmental alteration to maintain optimal functioning in older age" (Plouffe & Kalache, 2010, p. 734). Age-friendly communities address areas of the natural environment (e.g., the outdoors), the built environment (e.g., buildings, roadways), respect and social inclusion, the social environment (opportunities for and access to participation in community events and spaces), transportation, housing, communication, and community support and health services.

Areas of the natural environment include safe walking paths, frequent benches to allow people to sit and rest if needed, green spaces such as parks and gardens, and public restrooms. The built environment is concerned with architectural features that allow access, such as ramps, elevators, doors that are wide enough to accommodate wheelchairs, handrails, smooth transfer points at street crossings, and other physical features that can make the difference between being accessible or enabling to a person and being inaccessible or disabling (Menec et al., 2011).

In 2016, the WHO's global age-friendly community network included 33 countries and 287 communities (Jeste et al., 2016). Examples from the WHO age-friendly community network include Loncoche, Chile, a community located around 50 miles (82 km) from the regional capital Temuco (WHO, 2018). Particular challenges for Loncoche included the outward migration of younger people to more populated urban areas, leaving older persons behind; the coming together of over 120 different ethnic groups; and a local poverty rate of 69% for people above 65 years (compared to a regional rate of 16% and national rate 8.9% for the same age group); see WHO (2018). While Loncoche is still a work in progress, efforts to date have focused on socialization and removing isolating barriers such as transportation. Accomplishments include a center for older persons that includes restrooms, places to sit and have coffee, access to the Internet, and places to socialize; covered and lighted shelters for public transportation stops; and an intergenerational school program.

The city of Manchester, England, is another example of a community participating in the WHO age-friendly initiative. Slightly different than Loncoche's, Manchester's goals were to "develop age-friendly neighborhoods, develop age-friendly services, and promote age-equality" (WHO, 2018). To achieve these goals, the city started a culture program with museums, theaters, and other venues to increase attendance by older persons and accessibility to events and cultural spaces for people who may need special assistance such as ramps, elevators, or devices to enhance hearing. In 2004, the city established an Age-Friendly Older People's Board composed of 15 people from different neighborhoods and backgrounds to help the city with continual planning for inclusion of older members.

At first, the examples of Loncoche and Manchester might not seem all that impressive. Neither city tore down and rebuilt buildings, established new hospitals, or created special services such as housing for their older members, but they made significant changes to address the livability and inclusiveness of their communities for older adults. Both cities represent the challenges and successes of the age-friendly movement. One major challenge is funding. Widescale change, such as new construction, can be costly. Most communities do not start their participation in an age-friendly initiative with funding at their disposal and may never have sufficient resources to implement everything needed for a truly age-friendly city, such as health care centers or new affordable housing. However, the success in these examples and that of other cities has been in recognizing that the needs of all citizens—including older persons—must be addressed by the community. Social inclusion, connection, and contribution by older persons are an integral part of this movement. Communities' views of older persons have been linked to their quality of life. Not surprisingly, ageist, negative views toward older persons tend to lead to a poorer quality of life, compared to positive views, which have been linked to a positive quality of life (Ayalon & Tesch-Römer, 2017). An important first step, therefore, is implementing programs that demonstrate that older persons are valued and respected.

SUMMARY

Environment encompasses more than the home where an older person lives; it also includes emotional attachments to the broader community called *place*. The ecological theory of aging provides a helpful context for thinking about home environments, including the relationship between a dwelling, its physical challenges (environmental press), and the ability of the resident to successfully meet those challenges. In addition, the essence of home, which is deeply rooted in familiarity, privacy, and security, can be lacking in institutional settings such as nursing homes or government-controlled housing. In the latter, lack of control over space and threatened security (or risk of being relocated) can diminish one's ability to establish a home environment for themselves. While researchers and planners understand the characteristics of appropriate housing for older persons, there is also growing interest in making communities more age-friendly, including a heightened awareness of the importance of social inclusion. Although most countries are only beginning to seek and achieve a degree of age-friendliness, environments for older persons will continue to improve. Most hopeful is the fact that the livable cities/age-friendly communities movement is a powerful new and compelling idea that is being disseminated around the world and is already showing impact on older people's environments.

DISCUSSION QUESTIONS

1. What do you see as the biggest differences between *home* and *house*?

2. Some dwelling types have the word "home" in their title while others have the word "house." Think of examples of each type of dwelling. What are the key characteristics of each? Why do you think some use "home" while others use "house?"

3. What *place attachment* features are most important to you? Will these still be important to you as you grow older? Why or why not?

4. How do you think *home* is related to a person's sense of self and identity?

5. What do you think policy makers in Peru should be concerned with regarding housing for older people? What about policy makers in Vietnam? Do you see any major differences between the two? Why do you think that is?

6. Identify at least two pros and two cons of *aging in place*.

7. Give an example that you have seen or experienced of the *ecological theory of aging* in process. For example, maybe you or a friend struggled with "press" and competence in a particular environment.

8. What is your preference for housing when you age—*independent* or *coresidential*? Explain your choice.

9. What are the differences between a *nursing home* and an *assisted living facility* (or care home)?

10. Look up statistics regarding homelessness for people aged 50 and above in your city. What surprised you the most when doing this?
11. Do you think there should be *age-segregated housing*? Why or why not?
12. Should achieving *age-friendliness* be a priority for cities throughout the world? Why or why not?

KEY WORDS

Age-friendly initiative	Housing
Age-segregated housing	Independent housing
Aging in place	Intergenerational coresidence
Assisted living	Living arrangements
Blue space	Nursing home
Care home	Place
Control	Place attachment
Ecological theory of aging	Reverse mortgage
Environmental gerontology	Skilled nursing facility
Home	Social housing
Homelessness	Universal design

REFERENCES

Abramsson, M., & Andersson, E. (2016). Changing preferences with ageing–housing choices and housing plans of older people. *Housing, Theory, Society, 33*(2), 217–241. doi:10.1080/14036096.2015.1104385

Addae-Dapaah, K., & Juan, Q. (2014). Life satisfaction among elderly households in public rental housing in Singapore. *Health, 6*, 1057–1076. doi:10.4236/health.2014.610132

Andrade, F. C. D., & DeVos, S. (2016). An analysis of living arrangements among elderly women in Brazil. *Anais*, 1–29.

Ayalon, L., & Tesch-Römer, C. (2017). Taking a closer look at ageism: Self-and other-directed ageist attitudes and discrimination. *European Journal of Aging, 14*, 1–4. doi:10.1007/s10433-016-0409-9

Babafemi, A., & Edoni, O. A. (2015). Elderly widows destitution in Yenagoa, Nigeria. *Indian Journal of Gerontology, 29*(2), 216–230.

Ball, M. M., Perkins, M. M., Whittington, F. J., Connell, B. R., Hollingsworth, C., King, S. V., . . . Combs, B. L. (2004). Managing decline in assisted living: The key to aging in place. *Journal of Gerontology: Social Sciences, 59B*, S202–S212. doi:10.1093/geronb/59.4.S202

Becker, G. (1997). *Disrupted lives: How people create meaning in a chaotic world*. Berkeley, CA: Universotu of California Press.

Buffel, T., & Phillipson, C. (2012). Ageing in urban environments: Developing "age-friendly" cities. *Critical Social Policy, 32*(4), 597–617. doi:10.1177/0261018311430457

Caouette, E. (2005). The image of nursing homes and its impact on the meaning of home for elders. In G. D. Rowles & H. Chaudhury (Eds.), *Home and identity in late life: International perspectives* (pp. 251–275). New York, NY: Springer Publishing Company.

Coleman, T., & Kearns, R. (2015). The role of bluespaces in experiencing place, aging and wellbeing: Insights from Waiheke Island, New Zealand. *Health Place, 35*, 206–217. doi:10.1016/j.healthplace.2014.09.016

Costa-Font, J., Elvira, D., & Mascarilla-Miró, O. (2009). Ageing in place? Exploring elderly people's housing preferences in Spain. *Urban Studies, 46*(2), 295–316. doi:10.1177/0042098008099356

Culhane, D. P., Metraux, S., Byrne, T., Stino, M., & Bainbridge, J. J. C. (2013). Aging trends in homeless populations. *Contexts, 12*(2), 66–68. doi:10.1177/1536504213487702 de Medeiros, K. (2016). *The short guide to aging and gerontology.* Bristol, UK: Policy Press.

Delfani, N., De Deken, J., & Dewilde, C. (2015). Poor because of low pensions or expensive housing? The combined impact of pension and housing systems on poverty among the elderly. *International Journal of Housing Policy, 15*(3), 260–284. doi:10.1080/14616718.2015.1004880

Elderly Accommodation Counsel. (2019). *Housing care.org: Information for older people.* Retrieved from https://www.housingcare.org

Gitlin, L. N. (2003). Conducting research on home environments: Lessons learned and new directions. *The Gerontologist, 43*(5), 628–637. doi:10.1093/geront/43.5.628

Golant, S. M. (1985). In defense of age-segregated housing. *Aging, 348,* 22–26.

Golant, S. M. (2011). The quest for residential normalcy by older adults: Relocation but one pathway. *Journal of Aging Studies, 25*(3), 193–205. doi:10.1016/j.jaging.2011.03.003

Gov.UK. (2012). Definitions of general housing terms. Retrieved from https://www.gov.uk/guidance/definitions-of-general-housing-terms#social-and-affordable-housing

Grenier, A., Barken, R., & McGrath, C. (2016). Homelessness and aging: The contradictory ordering of 'house'and 'home.' *Journal of Aging Studies, 39,* 73–80. doi:10.1016/j.jaging.2016.11.002

Harloe, M. (2008). *The people's home? Social rented housing in Europe and America.* New York, NY: John Wiley & Sons.

Harris-Kojetin, L., Sengupta, M., Lendon, J. P., Rome, V., Valverde, R., & Caffrey, C. (2019). Long-term care providers and services users in the United States, 2015–2016. National Center for Health Statistics. *Vital Health and Statistics, 3*(43). Retrieved from https://www.cdc.gov/nchs/data/series/sr_03/sr03_43-508.pdf

Jeste, D. V., Blazer, D. G., II, Buckwalter, K. C., Cassidy, K. L. K., Fishman, L., Gwyther, L. P., . . . Feather, J. (2016). Age-friendly communities initiative: public health approach to promoting successful aging. *The American Journal of Geriatric Psychiatry, 24*(12), 1158–1170. doi:10.1016/j.jagp.2016.07.021

Keene, D. E., Sarnak, A., & Coyle, C. (2018). Maximizing home equity or preventing home loss: Reverse mortgage decision making and racial inequality. *The Gerontologist, 59*(2), 242–250. doi:10.1093/geront/gnx209

Kramer, C., & Pfaffenbach, C. (2016). Should I stay or should I go? Housing preferences upon retirement in Germany. *Journal of Housing and the Built Environment, 31*(2), 239–256. doi:10.1007/s10901-015-9454-5

Lawton, M. P., & Nahemow, L. (1973). Ecology and the aging process. In C. Eisdorfer & M. P. Lawton (Eds.), *The psychology of adult development and aging* (pp. 619–674). Washington, DC: American Psychological Association.

Lewin, K. (1951). *Field theory in social science.* New York, NY: Harper.

Lipmann, B. (2009). Elderly homeless men and women: Aged care's forgotten people. *Australian Social Work, 62*(2), 272–286. doi:10.1080/03124070902792454

Menec, V. H., Means, R., Keating, N., Parkhurst, G., & Eales, J. (2011). Conceptualizing age-friendly communities. *Canadian Journal on Aging/La Revue canadienne du vieillissement, 30*(3), 479–493. doi:10.1017/S0714980811000237

Nooe, R. M., & Patterson, D. A. (2010). The ecology of homelessness. *Journal of Human Behavior in the Social Environment, 20*(2), 105–152. doi:10.1080/10911350903269757

OECD. (2015). Long-term care beds in institutions and hospitals. *Health at a Glance 2015: OECD Indicators.* Paris: OECD Publishing.

Peace, S., Wahl, H., Mollenkopf, H., & Oswald, F. (2007). Environment and ageing. In J. Bond, S. Peace, & F. Dittmann-Kohli (Eds.), *Ageing in society: European perspectives on gerontology* (pp. 209–234). London, UK: SAGE Publications Ltd. doi:10.4135/9781446278918.n10

Percival, J. (2001). Self-esteem and social motivation in age-segregated settings. *Housing Studies, 16*(6), 827–840. doi:10.1080/02673030120090566

Plouffe, L., & Kalache, A. (2010). Towards global age-friendly cities: determining urban features that promote active aging. *Journal of Urban Health, 87*(5), 733–739. doi:10.1007/s11524-010-9466-0

Rodin, J. (2014). Health, control, and aging. *The Psychology of Control and Aging,* 139–165.

Rowles, G. D., & Chaudhury, H. (2005). *Home and identity in late life: International perspectives.* New York, NY: Springer Publishing Company.

Rowles, G. D., & Teaster, P. B. (2015). *Long-term care in an aging society: Theory and practice.* New York, NY: Springer Publishing Company.

Rubinstein, R. L. (1987). The significance of personal objects to older people. *Journal of Aging Studies, 1*(3), 225–238. doi:10.1016/0890-4065(87)90015-6

Rubinstein, R. L., & de Medeiros, K. (2003). Ecology and the aging self. In H.-W. Wahl, R. J. Schiedt, & P. G. Windely (Eds.), *Annual Review of Gerontology and Geriatrics* (Vol. 23., pp. 59–82). New York, NY: Springer Publishing Company.

Rubinstein, R. L., & de Medeiros, K. (2005). Home, self, and identity. In G. D. Rowles & H. Chaudhury (Eds.), *Home and identity in late life: International perspectives* (pp. 47–62). New York, NY: Springer Publishing Company.

Scanlon, K., Fernández Arrigoitia, M., & Whitehead, C. M. (2015). Social housing in Europe. *European Policy Analysis,* (17), 1–12.

Sheehan, N. W., & Oakes, C. E. (2003). Bringing assisted living services into congregate housing: residents' perspectives. *The Gerontologist, 43*(5), 766–770. doi:10.1093/geront/43.5.766

Stones, D., & Gullifer, J. (2016). 'At home it's just so much easier to be yourself': Older adults' perceptions of ageing in place. *Ageing & Society, 36*(3), 449–481. doi:10.1017/S0144686X14001214

Sun, X., Lucas, H., Meng, Q., & Zhang, Y. (2011). Associations between living arrangements and health-related quality of life of urban elderly people: A study from China. *Quality of Life Research, 20*(3), 359–369. doi:10.1007/s11136-010-9752-z

Suzuki, N., Ogawa, T., & Inaba, N. (2018). The right to adequate housing: Evictions of the homeless and the elderly caused by the 2020 Summer Olympics in Tokyo. *Leisure Studies, 37*(1), 89–96. doi:10.1080/02614367.2017.1355408

Tilley, C. Y. (1994). *A phenomenology of landscape: Places, paths, and monuments*: Oxford: Berg.

Tipple, G., & Speak, S. (2009). *The hidden millions: Homelessness in developing countries*. New York, NY: Routledge.

U.S. Centers for Medicare and Medicaid Services. (2019). Glossary. Retrieved from https://www.cms.gov/apps/glossary

Vasunilashorn, S., Steinman, B. A., Liebig, P. S., & Pynoos, J. (2012). Aging in place: Evolution of a research topic whose time has come. *Journal of Aging Research*, 1–6. doi:10.1155/2012/120952

Wahl, H.-W., Iwarsson, S., & Oswald, F. (2012). Aging well and the environment: Toward an integrative model and research agenda for the future. *The Gerontologist, 52*(3), 306–316. doi:10.1093/geront/gnr154

World Health Organization. (2018). *Global network for age-friendly cities and communities: Looking back over the last decade, looking forward to the next*. Geneva, Switzerland: Author.

World Health Organization. (2019). Age-friendly environments Retrieved from https://www.who.int/ageing/age-friendly-environments/en

Yamada, K., & Teerawichitchainan, B. (2015). Living arrangements and psychological well-being of the older adults after the economic transition in Vietnam. *Journals of Gerontology Series B: Psychological Sciences and Social Sciences, 70*(6), 957–968. doi:10.1093/geronb/gbv059

Zimmer, Z., & Dayton, J. (2005). Older adults in sub-Saharan Africa living with children and grandchildren. *Population Studies, 59*(3), 295–312. doi:10.1080/00324720500212255

TOWARD AN AGE-FRIENDLY URBAN AND HOUSING POLICY IN MALTA

MARVIN FORMOSA | RACHAEL M. SCICLUNA

INTRODUCTION

The United Nations (2015) *Sustainable Development Goals* demonstrates a clear global shift toward rethinking the urban fabric of cities and "spaces of well-being." Public policies on aging and later life are no exception, as witnessed by the WHO (2007) guide for age-friendly cities. This emergence of housing-friendly policy trends is largely due to a diverse mix of happenings, ranging from rapid urbanization, economic growth, aging population, low fertility rates, and climate change to conflicts that are putting unprecedented pressures on urban communities. However, to date, the emphasis has been on the importance of the built environment; not enough attention has been granted to social relations and the key role they hold in determining the well-being of urban communities (Baldwin & King, 2017).

Admittedly, housing a large and diverse population whose needs and realities are ever-changing is not an easy task for policy makers. In general, households tend to change over time and adapt in creative and sometimes unpredictable ways, especially when striving to meet the demands of market forces (Pilkey, Scicluna, & Gorman-Murray, 2015; Yotebieng & Forcone 2018). Changing households require a housing system that takes a broad, contextual, and longitudinal approach to understanding the household as a unit of analysis. Nevertheless, housing is also about homemaking and is the setting for domestic and community life, where important moral values and identities are learned from a very young age (Scicluna, 2017). Hence, the question is: How can policy makers attend to the "household in flux" and ensure that all citizens, regardless of their chronological age, dwell in good homes serviced by a range of facilities that meet their needs and realities?

CHANGING SOCIETY, CHANGING HOUSEHOLD: THE MALTESE CONTEXT

Over the past decade, Malta has experienced rapid social, economic, and legislative changes. The household was at the core of such shifts, mainly due to changes in family legislation, which included the amendments made to the Civil Code through the introduction of divorce in 2011 (which had been illegal in previous years), the Cohabitation Act in 2016 (which recognizes rights and responsibilities of various types of couples living together), and the Marriage Equality Bill in 2017 (which legalized same-sex marriages). It is important to understand that these changes in legislation were not solely the result of postmillennium increasing levels of marital breakdown, but also due to liberal shifts in sexual mores across all cohorts, mostly among youths.

Malta, as other postindustrial countries, is experiencing increasing low fertility and increasing life expectancy. In 2017, the Maltese population aged 60 and older reached 25.1% of the total population (National Statistics Office, 2018). A year previously, life expectancy reached 80.6 and 84.4 years for men and women, respectively. At the same time, the past decade witnessed significant economic shifts brought about by an increase in gross domestic product though the at-risk-of-poverty rate (number of persons earning below 60% of the median national equivalized income, which is calculated as median of total household income after tax and other deductions that is available for spending or saving and divided by the number of household members) reached 16.5% in 2016 (Formosa, 2017). Over one fifth of children (21%) under the age of 18 and one quarter (24.2%) of people aged 65 and above were found to be at risk of poverty in 2016 (males: 22.8%; females: 25.4%). As to be expected, such economic and social changes are leaving positive and negative impacts on the housing market. For the first time, Malta is experiencing a thriving, albeit unregulated, private rental sector, while research has uncovered an increase in intergenerational and shared households due to increasing housing costs that are becoming unaffordable for a widening sector of the Maltese population.

The preceding discussion suggests that it is best to move away from understanding the household as a static entity. Instead, policy makers and researchers should take household plasticity as a starting point and think of alternative domestic compositions such as postdivorce and intergenerational households, solo living, shared households with unrelated others, same-sex and interracial households, and cohabiting and living apart together (i.e., romantic couples who live in separate households) relationships.

Toward Spaces of Well-Being in Later Life: The Maltese Response

The understanding of that interface between well-being on one hand and the household as a dynamic spatial, emotional, and life-course landscape on the other has important implications for housing an aging population. Indeed, spatial dimensions of well-being change over the life course and are directly influenced by relations embedded in the environment, bodies, senses, and social connect-edness. The "spaces of well-being framework," as developed by Fleuret and Atkinson (2007), suggested that well-being of the household is always in constant production and reproduction with its surrounding environment. According to Atkinson (2013, p. 142), well-being "comprises complex assemblages of relations not only between people, but also between people and places, material objects and less material constituents of places including atmosphere, histories and values." Theoretical insights from environmental gerontology suggest that improving the environment where older people live has a positive impact on reducing disability and minimizing the loss of autonomy as people age (Buffel, Handler, & Phillipson, 2019). Studies, however, have reported that frail older people living in urban envi-ronments often experience neighborhood "erasure"—in other words, becoming invisible (Kelley-Moore, Dannefer, & Issa Al Masarweh, 2019).

With respect to Malta's social fabric, it is noteworthy that older persons in Malta change accommodation less frequently when compared to younger age groups, with only about 5% of movers being aged 60 and above. For those who change their accommodation, push factors driving community-dwelling older persons out of their accommodation included "having a large house," "living in a house in bad con-dition," when the "property was threatening their independence," stairs negotiation, and perhaps most important of all, not having easy access to shops, public trans-port, and other useful amenities. Many older persons in Malta live in relatively old houses, which are difficult to heat in the winter and characterized by relatively high levels of seasonal dampness and humidity, especially between December and March. Cognizant of the fact that older persons tend to encounter financial and logistical dif-ficulties in their attempts to make their houses more accessible and age-friendly, the Housing Authority in Malta offers, from time to time, a number of programs which, despite not being directly aimed at older persons, were very popular among older cohorts, including subsidies for the adaptation and repair work in leased privately owned properties to reach acceptable habitable standards, grants to tenants for the purchase of their leased privately owned properties and adaptation works in these properties, and tax rebates for installation of lifts for apartments (Formosa, 2017).

Such supportive housing policy can be momentarily helpful for the well-being of older persons and beyond. However, it does not address the existing gap in the housing scenario, where Malta does not offer any intermediate housing options between the possibility of living independently in the community and moving into residential long-term care.[1]

Possibly because Malta remains a patriarchal and kinship-based society, most informal care in later life is still provided by female family members, most notably daughters. Indeed, it is disquieting that Malta includes no sheltered housing accom-modation that would make it easier for older residents to live as independently as

---

[1] In general, Malta lacks a diverse housing market, where, for example, it does not have affordable housing, affordable rents, or housing associations. This is problematic for peo-ple falling out of the property market for any reason.

possible, while giving them unlimited access to visits on behalf of family relatives and friends. Sheltered housing provides an alternative to the situation where older persons are forced to live in a hospital or institutional ambience where they are literally waiting for death's call or to one where they feel that they are a burden to their caregivers. In brief, sheltered housing represents an ideal alternative to live in a secure domestic environment independently, which is not possible in institutions. Socially mixed affordable housing initiatives also could be an alternative solution to care homes and ought to be made available to seniors.

CONCLUDING REFLECTIONS

Considering that Malta has no national housing policy, we contend that this gap could be opportunistic, whereby the planning and design of the local housing market could benefit from an age-friendly approach while simultaneously taking into account the "household in flux" (Yotebieng & Forcone, 2018) and "alternative domesticities" (Pilkey et al., 2015) as inherent characteristics in policy making. Conducting research with this perspective in mind opens up a space for all those groups of people who may be sidelined by the dominant ideology of the normative and able-bodied household. Such an approach has the potential to address the range of exclusionary criteria attached to factors related to socioeconomic status, ethnicity, gender, sexuality, disability, and issues related to aging such as loneliness, isolation, and "erasure" within the urban environment.

The achievement of such a policy may become a real possibility if older persons are made central to the design and planning of urban spaces. Nevertheless, it is not enough to check the WHO (2007) macroinstitutional specifications since such items are ultimately an arbitrary checklist and represent a top-down approach to the "ideal city" designed by authorities (Liddle, Scharf, Bartlam, Bernard, & Sim, 2014). Rather, older persons should be full participants in defining the "actual opportunities and constraints in cities for maintaining quality of life as people age" (Buffel, Phillipson, & Scharf, 2012, p. 601). Furthermore, older people are a diverse group and a top-down approach fails to recognize the heterogeneity of their needs and the ongoing changes in urban environments. Standardization and conformity are exclusive rather than inclusive and may create spaces that are ill-suited for older persons because they diminish needs tied to ethnicity, sexuality, gender, socioeconomic status, and so on. An alternative way forward should incorporate the following list of recommendations that Malta, as well as other countries, could benefit from when designing urban policy (Baldwin, 2014):

- *Cities are diverse*. A life-course perspective may be beneficial for citizens of all ages through the active involvement of older persons in community planning.
- *Research-based policy*. Quantitative and ethnographic research should be key in developing an inclusive policy and should take into consideration the relationship between various categories such as aging, care, disability, gender, sexuality,

well-being, infrastructure, planning, climate change, migration, transport, and civic participation. What is important is that the methods used in macroeconomic studies ensure that people remain central.

- *Changing households*. Understanding household fluidity as a unit of analysis has great potential for policy makers, as they can design policies that meet grounded realities that modern patterns of living bring about.

- *Thinking socially from the start*. The social dimension is often a lower priority in urban development. Design choice, no matter how small-scale it is, can greatly influence individuals' interactions with one another and facilitate a positive sense of well-being. International research is demonstrating that significant economic benefits result when developers consider the social dimension in the planning phase, alongside the economic, environmental, and governance dimensions. This approach is a cost-saving measure because it eases the burden from other services by ensuring optimal quality and best value of resources.

REFERENCES

Atkinson, S. (2013). Beyond components of wellbeing: The effects of relational and situated assemblage. *Topoi, 32*(2), 137–144. doi:10.1007/s11245-013-9164-0

Baldwin, C. (2014). A new approach: Social factors in urban development. *TheCityFix.* Ross Center: World Resources Institute.

Baldwin, C., & King. R. (2017). What about the people? Unlocking the key to socially sustainable and resilient communities. *TheCityFix.* Retrieved from https://thecityfix.com/blog/what-about-the-people-unlocking-the-key-to-socially-sustainable-and-resilient-communities-cathy-baldwin-robin-king

Buffel, T., Phillipson, C., & Scharf, T. (2012). Ageing in urban environments: Developing "age-friendly" cities. *Critical Social Policy, 32*(4), 597–617. doi:10.1177/0261018311430457

Buffel, T., Handler, S., & Phillipson, C. (2019). *Age-friendly cities and communities: A global perspective.* UK and USA: Policy Press.

Fleuret, S., & Atkinson, S., (2007). Wellbeing, health and geography: A critical review and research agenda. *New Zealand Geographer, 63*(2), 106–118. doi:10.1111/j.1745-7939.2007.00093.x

Formosa, M. (2017). Responding to the Active Ageing Index: Innovations in active ageing policies in Malta. *Journal of Population Ageing, 10*(1), 87–99. doi:10.1007/s12062-016-9163-1

Kelley-Moore, J. A., Dannefer, D., & Issa Al Masarweh, L. (2019). Addressing erasure, microfication and social change: Age-friendly initiatives and environmental gerontology in the 21st Century. In T. Buffel, S. Handler, & C. Phillipson (Eds), *Age-friendly cities and communities: A global perspective* (pp. 51–72). UK and USA: Policy Press.

Liddle, J., Scharf, T., Bartlam, B., Bernard, M., & Sim, J. (2014). Exploring the age-friendliness of purpose-built retirement communities: Evidence from England. *Ageing & Society, 34*(9), 1601–1629. doi:10.1017/S0144686X13000366

National Statistics Office. (2018). *World population day: 11 July 2018*. Malta: Author.

Pilkey, B., Scicluna, R. M., & Gorman-Murray, A. (2015). Alternative domesticities: A cross-disciplinary approach to home and sexuality. *Home Cultures, 2*(2, Special Issue), 1–15.

Scicluna, R. M. (2017). *Home and sexuality: The "other" side of the kitchen*. UK/USA: Palgrave Macmillan.

United Nations. (2015). *Transforming our world: The 2030 agenda for sustainable development*. New York, NY: Author.

World Health Organization. (2007). *Global age-friendly cities: A guide*. Geneva: Author.

Yotebieng, K. A., & Forcone, T. (2018). The household in flux: Plasticity complicates the unit of analysis. *Anthropology in Action, 25*(3), 13–22. doi:10.3167/aia.2018.250302

DESIGNING DEMENTIA-FRIENDLY NEIGHBORHOODS TO IMPROVE MOBILITY AND WAYFINDING

KISHORE SEETHARAMAN | HABIB CHAUDHURY

Dementia has been identified as a key factor leading to disability and dependency in later life (WHO, 2015). The term "dementia" collectively refers to the cognitive and behavioral signs and symptoms that result from several different brain diseases, for example, Alzheimer's, Lewy body disease, Huntington's, and Parkinson's, which have a detrimental effect on "memory, thinking, behaviour, and emotion" (Alzheimer's Disease International, n.d.). Dementia tends to be chronic and progressive; that is, symptoms start developing slowly and eventually worsen (Alzheimer's Association, 2018b). It is often mistaken to be a part of the normal experience of aging, whereas only four to eight of every 100 older adults worldwide actually develop dementia (WHO, 2017). However, with the rapid increase in the global aging population, the number of people with dementia is also expected to nearly triple from the current estimated 47 million cases to 135 million by 2050 (Alzheimer's Association, 2018a; Alzheimer's Disease International, 2013). Given its prevalence and implications for various aspects of quality of life, including daily functioning, social life, and financial management, the WHO (2015) has framed dementia as a public health priority.

People with dementia can "live for many years after the onset of dementia" and, with the appropriate level of support, can experience a high quality of life while staying meaningfully engaged in their community. Enabling older adults with dementia to age in place with the right supports is particularly important, since the majority of persons with dementia in many countries live in the community rather than in institutional settings (Alzheimer's Association, 2017). The Dementia Friendly Communities (DFCs) initiative offers a multipronged approach that combines top-down development and provision of supports through consultation with persons with dementia, along with a bottom-up grassroots mobilization of persons with dementia as engaged social citizens in their community (Alzheimer's Disease International, 2015). Improving the neighborhood physical environment has been identified as one of the priority action areas for creating DFCs, with an emphasis on using design strategies to resolve issues related to mobility (ability to move) and wayfinding (ability to find one's way between destinations); see Alzheimer Society of Canada (2016) and Alzheimer's Disease International (2015).

While being mobile is necessary for older adults with dementia to perform many daily activities and be engaged in the community, their impaired physical and/or cognitive capacities pose challenges for their mobility and wayfinding in the neighborhood (Clare et al., 2014; Passini, Pigot, Rainville, & Tétreault, 2000). Dementia causes reduced spatial abilities, such as distinguishing between left and right, identifying different shapes and sizes, and comprehending the relationship between different environmental details. As a result, spatial memory, planning, and decision-making are negatively affected (Sandberg, Rosenberg, Sandman, & Borell, 2017).

Additionally, dementia presents challenges of orientation in time and space, which may lead persons with dementia to misinterpret their surroundings and experience spatial disorientation (Brittain, Corner, Robinson, & Bond, 2010; Olsson, Lampic, Skovdahl, & Engström, 2013). For example, complex, high-traffic areas have been noted for imposing a high cognitive demand on persons with dementia, whose ability to process multiple sources of information simultaneously tends to be much lower than that of persons without dementia (Sandberg et al., 2017). For example, traffic intersections are known to result in persons with dementia getting lost, while associated traffic noise can make it very difficult for them to discern the sound of important information (e.g., audible pedestrian signal); see Brorsson, Öhman, Cutchin, and Nygård (2013). These cognitive barriers coupled, with physical barriers, such as insufficient street lighting, obstructions on footpaths, and lack of well-located public restrooms, exacerbate the difficulties faced by persons with dementia in relation to mobility and wayfinding (Blackman, Van Schaik, & Martyr, 2007; Brorsson, Öhman, Lundberg, & Nygård, 2011).

CHARACTERISTICS OF DFCs

Although the literature on dementia-friendly neighborhood design is sparse, it identifies a few key characteristics of the physical environment of DFCs, namely familiarity, legibility (or readability), distinctiveness, accessibility, comfort, and safety (Mitchell, Burton, & Raman, 2004). Previous research also recommends using environmental cues, such as landmarks and signs, which are structures or objects that act as points of reference by marking the locality they are in or indicate where a place, person, or thing may be found. Studies have identified certain key characteristics of environmental cues that can help guide design and planning solutions to improve the physical environment of neighborhoods for mobility and wayfinding. These key characteristics include (a) placement, (b) noticeability, (c) readability, (d) familiarity and engagement, and (e) stability.

Placement

Visual cues, such as landmarks and signage, placed along short and narrow streets are more visible than those on long and wide streets. Landmarks placed at key decision points, such as junctions of streets, tend to be more effective as wayfinding cues, as they can positively influence spatial decision-making. For optimal visibility at a distance and from all angles, research suggests placing signs perpendicular to walls at eye-level height (Blackman et al., 2007; Mitchell et al., 2004).

Noticeability

We have long known that the saliency of a landmark is determined by how well it contrasts with its context. Recent research suggests that incorporating distinctive architectural features and details (e.g., uniquely designed building facades and frontages, public art) into the street form can be useful for wayfinding, in contrast to streets that have a repetitive form and look similar to each other (Mitchell et al., 2004). Since older people tend to experience color agnosia (difficulty in recognizing and distinguishing between colors), research suggests using certain bright colors such as red and orange rather than those on the blue and green spectrum (Mitchell et al., 2004). Ensuring clear sight lines to the landmark or signage, without any visible obstructions, is critical for optimal visibility (Mitchell et al., 2004).

Readability

Signage should be simple and easily understood, containing only the most pertinent information for wayfinding (Mitchell et al., 2004). Research suggests that, for persons with dementia, signs containing text may be more useful for wayfinding than those with images (Blackman et al., 2003).

Familiarity and Engagement

Familiar cues such as signposts, crossroads, distinctive architectural landmarks, or familiar houses in the neighborhood reinforce people's spatial memory (Olsson et al., 2013). Landmarks linked to local history have been found to promote a sense of familiarity by triggering collective memories (Kelson, Phinney, & Lowry, 2017). Previous research has studied the interactive nature of public art and how sustained engagement can aid in developing a sense of familiarity (Kelson et al., 2017). Signage also may seem more familiar if it is frequently encountered, and it employs traditional insignia, certain colors, or known symbols (Alzheimer's Association, 2017; Brorsson et al., 2011).

Stability

Structures that have been in the same location for an extended period of time (e.g., historical buildings) also become easily imprinted in people's memories (Mitchell et al., 2004). On the other hand, changes in well-established landmarks used as wayfinding cues, such as repainting a familiar house in the neighborhood, may render the place unfamiliar to older adults with dementia (Brorsson et al., 2011).

FINAL THOUGHTS

As mentioned earlier, empirical evidence is lacking on the linkages between aspects of the neighborhood built environment and mobility and wayfinding of persons with dementia. Future research must fill the gaps in knowledge so that future planning and design recommendations for DFCs are based on scientific evidence. It is equally important for researchers interested and committed to this under-researched area of inquiry to realize the value and need to engage end users, that is, older adults living with dementia at critical junctures throughout the research process. Involving them as experts on lived experience with dementia, advisors, and coresearchers would increase the rigor of the research methods and the validity of findings, thus making them translatable for real-world application in policy and practice (Mann & Hung, 2018).

REFERENCES

Alzheimer Society of Canada. (2016). Dementia-Friendly Communities Local Government Kit. Retrieved from http://www.alzheimer.ca/sites/default/files/files/bc/municipal%20toolkit/dfctoolkitvjan2016.pdf

Alzheimer's Association. (2017). 2017 Alzheimer's disease facts and figures. *Alzheimer's & Dementia, 13*(4), 325–373. doi:10.1016/j.jalz.2017.02.001

Alzheimer's Association. (2018a). Alzheimer's & Dementia: Global Resources. Retrieved from www.alz .org/global/overview.asp

Alzheimer's Association. (2018b). Stages of Alzheimer's. Retrieved from https://alz.org/alzheimers -dementia/stages

Alzheimer's Disease International. (2013). Policy Brief for Heads of Government the Global Impact of Dementia 2013–2050. Retrieved from https://www.alz.co.uk/research/GlobalImpactDementia2013 .pdf

Alzheimer's Disease International. (2015). Dementia Friendly Communities (DFCs) New domains and global examples. Retrieved from https://www.alz.co.uk/adi/pdf/dementia-friendly-communities .pdf

Alzheimer's Disease International. (n.d.). About dementia. Retrieved from https://www.alz.co.uk/ about-dementia

Blackman, T., Mitchell, L., Burton, E., Jenks, M., Parsons, M., Raman, S., & Williams, K. (2003). The accessibility of public spaces for people with dementia: A new priority for the 'open city.' *Disability & Society, 18*(3), 357–371. doi:10.1080/0968759032000052914

Blackman, T., Van Schaik, P., & Martyr, A. (2007). Outdoor environments for people with dementia: an exploratory study using virtual reality. *Ageing & Society, 27*(6), 811–825. doi:10.1017/ S0144686X07006253

Brittain, K., Corner, L., Robinson, L., & Bond, J. (2010). Ageing in place and technologies of place: the lived experience of people with dementia in changing social, physical and technological environments. *Sociology of Health & Illness, 32*(2), 272–287. doi:10.1111/j.1467-9566.2009.01203.x

Brorsson, A., Öhman, A., Lundberg, S., & Nygård, L. (2011). Accessibility in public space as perceived by people with Alzheimer's disease. *Dementia*, *10*(4), 587–602. doi:10.1177/1471301211415314

Brorsson, A., Öhman, A., Cutchin, M., & Nygård, L. (2013). Managing critical incidents in grocery shopping by community-living people with Alzheimer's disease. *Scandinavian Journal of Occupational Therapy*, *20*(4), 292–301. doi:10.3109/11038128.2012.752031

Clare, L., Nelis, S. M., Quinn, C., Martyr, A., Henderson, C., Hindle, J. V., . . . Kopelman, M. D. (2014). Improving the experience of dementia and enhancing active life-living well with dementia: study protocol for the IDEAL study. *Health and Quality of Life Outcomes*, *12*(1), 164. doi:10.1186/s12955-014-0164-6

Kelson, E., Phinney, A., & Lowry, G. (2017). Social citizenship, public art and dementia: Walking the urban waterfront with Paul's Club. *Cogent Arts & Humanities*, *4*(1), 1354527. doi:10.1080/23311983.2017.1354527

Mann, J., & Hung, L. (2018). Co-research with people living with dementia for change. *Action Research*, *16*(2). Article published online, July 20, 2018. doi:10.1177/1476750318787005

Mitchell, L., Burton, E., & Raman, S. (2004). Dementia-friendly cities: Designing intelligible neighbourhoods for life. *Journal of Urban Design*, *9*(1), 89–101. doi:10.1080/1357480042000187721

Olsson, A., Lampic, C., Skovdahl, K., & Engström, M. (2013). Persons with early-stage dementia reflect on being outdoors: A repeated interview study. *Aging & Mental Health*, *17*(7), 793–800. doi:10.1080/13607863.2013.801065

Passini, R., Pigot, H., Rainville, C., & Tétreault, M.-H. (2000). Wayfinding in a nursing home for advanced dementia of the Alzheimer's type. *Environment and Behavior*, *32*(5), 684–710. doi:10.1177/00139160021972748

Sandberg, L., Rosenberg, L., Sandman, P.-O., & Borell, L. (2017). Risks in situations that are experienced as unfamiliar and confusing—the perspective of persons with dementia. *Dementia*, *16*(4), 471–485. doi:10.1177/1471301215603836

World Health Organization. (2015). Dementia: A public health priority. Retrieved from http://www.who.int/mental_health/neurology/dementia/dementia_thematicbrief_executivesummary.pdf

World Health Organization. (2017, December 12). Dementia. Retrieved from http://www.who.int/news-room/fact-sheets/detail/dementia

HEALTH PATTERNS AND BEHAVIOR

INTRODUCTION

This chapter explores the health of individual older people and how they behave when they feel ill. We should begin by mentioning the definition of health published by the United Nations (UN) World Health Organization (WHO) over 70 years ago: "Health is a state of complete physical, mental, and social well-being and not merely the absence of disease or infirmity" (1946). Yet, when we speak of health, we often use the opposite terms *disease* and *disability* because the negative state is easier to conceive, observe, and measure than the positive. It is ironic that we use the affirmative term *health* to refer to the generic state of physical and mental well-being, but can only think of it in concrete terms through its deviant states. To describe a person as *healthy* usually means we believe he or she is free of disease or disability. We must acknowledge, however, that relatively few adults are ever completely free of impairments (including vision problems, hearing loss, dental disease, hypertension, diabetes, respiratory infections, digestive upsets, headaches, arthritis and joint pain, mental illness, and obesity—and even social/cosmetic problems such as acne, dandruff, and skin rashes). Another irony is that none of the impairments listed earlier is likely to lead to death, but all can set serious limitations on both our functions and our feelings and hence represent an important human concern and area of research.

The health status of an older person is influenced by many social and behavioral factors, including lifelong health habits (such as diet and exercise), genetics, exposure to occupational and environmental hazards, and psychological stress. The quality and availability of health care throughout life also play a role in health in later life, though not as much as most of us might think. Most of the influences on individual health are, in large measure, socially and culturally shaped. Health behaviors are affected by societal values, cultural traditions, and beliefs and by the practices and habits of the people in one's immediate social world—their culture—such as family members and peers. For example, a person's food preferences and eating habits clearly are affected by family preferences and cultural traditions. Some people eat dogs, and others are repelled by the thought; some folks eat mainly fish, fruits, and vegetables, while others prefer beef hamburgers and fried potatoes. A growing number of people refuse to consume any animal, choosing to eat only plants. All food choices depend on the norms of the consumer's culture and what he or she has been taught to "like." The amount and type of physical activity a person has performed throughout life and that an older person continues to engage in are other examples of the impact of social and cultural factors on health behaviors.

Sorting out the puzzle of how the personal, behavioral, social, and cultural pieces fit together to produce a particular health outcome in an older individual is a compelling challenge but well beyond the scope of this book. Rather, we focus in this chapter on the cultural and social issues that influence the health status and disabilities of older adults and what they do when they feel ill. A broad view of three topics is provided: (a) patterns, causes, and results of disease across world regions; (b) global patterns, causes, and results of disabilities; and (c) an introduction to illness behavior, that is, what people do when they perceive themselves to be ill, and its importance for successful public health initiatives for aging populations. Our focus is on perhaps the most consequential illness behavior, patient nonadherence to a physician's advice.

DISEASE IN OLD AGE

The adage "When you have your health, you have everything" may be a Western overgeneralization that simply does not apply in all cultures. However, it certainly is true that health is a universal good and a lifelong concern for nearly all humans. Because aging is a marker for some physiological changes, the link between old age and health status is a topic of considerable research. In a few countries, such as Afghanistan (52 years), Zambia (53), Uganda (56), and Haiti (64), life expectancy is so low that only a relatively small proportion of people have the opportunity to experience later life and its health concerns (U.S. Central Intelligence Agency, 2019). For example, in sub-Saharan Africa, older people constitute only about 3% of the total population, while in Europe about 20% are aged 65 or above (World Bank, 2017). In least developed societies, infectious diseases (including HIV/AIDS) and childhood mortality are the greatest problems. On the other hand, in many places, such as the developed nations of North America, Western Europe, Australia, New Zealand, Asia, and South America, and increasingly in the fast-developing and modernizing countries of the world, the benefit of greater longevity brings with it the challenges of dealing with chronic diseases and burgeoning populations of frail and disabled older people in need of long-term services and supports.

From Acute to Chronic Diseases

Basic to any study of disease in populations are the two terms, **morbidity** (the rate of disease or illness in a population) and **mortality** (the rate of death in a population from whatever cause). Disease comes in two basic forms: **acute** (usually curable and of short duration) and **chronic** (not curable and therefore usually lifelong). Acute diseases are often caused by infectious microscopic organisms (either bacteria or viruses) and include such conditions as a cold, influenza, tuberculosis, dysentery, dengue fever, smallpox, and typhoid. Most also are communicable, either from person to person or from animal to person. To the extent the infectious agent can be killed by drugs or the person's immune system, the disease can be cured or prevented. Chronic diseases typically progress slowly, are degenerative, are so far incurable, and much more likely to affect people late in life. They include many of the most feared and deadly: coronary heart disease, hypertension (high blood pressure), cancer, diabetes, Alzheimer's disease, and HIV/AIDS. These are commonly referred to in the scientific literature as **chronic noncommunicable diseases** (CNCDs; WHO, 2018). Of course, some diseases formerly were incurable and now can, at least sometimes, be arrested, managed, or even cured. Each of the aforementioned examples would fall into this category. As recently as the early 1990s, anyone infected with the retrovirus HIV was almost certain to develop AIDS, a terminal disease. Now, with the availability of antiretroviral medications, HIV usually is controllable and can be prevented from progressing to AIDS; in fact, some persons with HIV (the former professional basketball star, Magic Johnson, for example) have survived for nearly three decades after a diagnosis.

As you may recall, the **demographic transition** is a set of interrelated social and demographic changes that result in both rapid growth and aging of a population (Cowgill, 1972). The prototypical transition pattern occurred throughout Western Europe in the 19th and early 20th centuries. The first stage of the transition is a shift from high mortality to lower mortality. During the European transition, the economies of these countries went through enormous shifts, changing from an agricultural base to an industrial mode of production, requiring and enticing large numbers of rural farm workers to migrate to the cities to work in factories. At the same time, as a by-product of economic and scientific development, these countries experienced significant mortality decline by gaining control over many infectious diseases, improving the availability of clean water and safe food, and creating more advanced medical technology. As these societal changes unfolded, fertility (the rate of birth in a population) remained high longer than did mortality, but it too began to decline when people realized that large families were no longer necessary for agricultural labor and in fact were a financial drain in a wage economy. This second transition phase, the lag between mortality decline and fertility decline, set the stage for rapid population growth. Mortality was not removing nearly as many people from the population as before, and continued high fertility was adding many more people. Finally, with sustained low mortality and low fertility, population aging occurred.

The **epidemiological transition** describes successive societal shifts in the major *causes* of mortality. As originally described by Omran (1971), in the early stages of the transition, when societies are relatively poor and undeveloped, mortality is high, life expectancy is short, and infectious diseases are responsible for the majority of deaths. As societies progress economically and scientifically, they develop strategies to improve public health, including greater availability of clean food and water, sanitation, immunizations against infectious disease, and advances in medical treatment. With these changes, many diseases are prevented, mortality is better controlled, death occurs later in life, and it is largely attributable to CNCDs.

Global Patterns of Disease

It is easy to see how all of these changes fit together to produce an overall picture of health, aging, and economic development. In 2016, all but one of the top 10 causes of death among people aged 70 and older were noncommunicable chronic diseases, whereas nearly all of the deaths among children under 5 were attributable to infectious disease (only one of the top 10 causes, congenital defects, was not); see WHO (2019). However, the higher prevalence of infectious diseases in developing nations and the higher chronic disease mortality in developed countries can lead to an incorrect assumption—that CNCDs are a problem of affluence. The reality is more complicated. Although infectious diseases do indeed take a heavy toll on developing nations, among the 15 million "premature deaths" due to CNCDs worldwide in 2014 (those of people between the ages of 30 and 69), 85% occurred in low- and middle-income countries (WHO, 2018).

The Burden of Disease

To compare health and disease more easily across nations and across time, the concept of **burden of disease** was introduced in 1990 by the WHO as part of an ongoing project to quantify and track the effects of various diseases in different regions of the world. This elegant concept measures the impact of specific diseases on years of life spent in poor health and years lost due to premature death. Figure 5.1 illustrates differences in the burden of diseases in high-, middle-, and low-income countries and across time. In 2008, noncommunicable diseases were responsible for virtually the entire burden of disease in high-income countries, about two thirds in middle-income countries, and about 40% of the health burden in low-income countries. By 2030, more than one half of the burden of disease in low-income countries will be attributable to chronic diseases; the remainder of the burden will come from infectious and parasitic diseases (Kinsella, Beard, & Suzman, 2013; U.S. National Institute on Aging, National Institutes of Health [NIH], & World Health Organization, 2011). These projected data clearly illustrate the positive impact of a globalizing economy on population health.

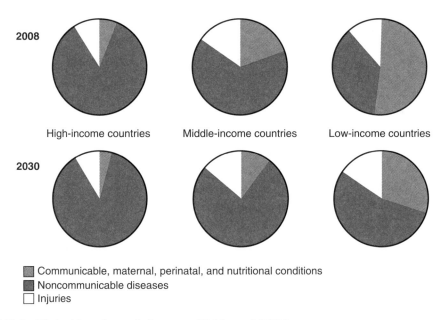

FIGURE 5.1 Global burden of disease, 2008 and 2030.

Source: From U.S. National Institute on Aging, NIH, & World Health Organization. (2011). World health and aging. Washington, DC: National Institutes of Health.

In rapidly aging nations, however, rising chronic disease prevalence combined with unresolved problems of child health and infectious diseases will present at least a double burden. If we add the fact that childhood health plays a strong role in later life well-being (the life-course perspective), the health prospects for aging adults who did not grow up with adequate nutrition or medical care suggest that the burden to come may be more than double what it is now (Lloyd, 2012, pp. 17–18). Illustrating the challenge facing rapidly aging developing countries, Duda et al. (2011) document the prevalence of obesity and hypertension among women aged 50 and older in Ghana—a country in which reproductive health remains a high priority. Compelling and perhaps competing priorities related to infectious disease, maternal and child health, and chronic diseases present significant challenges to the evolution of health care systems in developing nations with limited resources and infrastructure.

Differences Within Older Populations—Does Aging Cause Disease?

These disease burden patterns generally compare younger, less developed nations to older, more economically developed ones. Despite differences across these two types of countries, we now know that chronic diseases are of concern everywhere, partly because every country is seeing an increase in the size of its older population. But, does this mean that aging causes disease? Is old age inevitably accompanied by an increase in illness and poor health? Actually, the degree of diversity in health among older people suggests that age itself may not be a very strong predictor of health problems. Variations in health status across cultures, resulting probably from food and lifestyle choices, provide further evidence for the idea that age is not the most powerful influence and that environment can play a much larger role. For example, Americans experience a progressive age-related increase in blood pressure; in Japan and China, however, resting blood pressure changes very little well into old age (Alessio, 2001). We should remember that aging is accompanied by normal physical changes, such as a reduction in collagen, which results in wrinkling of the skin, and decreased elasticity of veins and arteries, which can reduce the ease and efficiency of blood flow through the body. The timing and extent of such changes, however, are highly variable among individuals, and they do not inevitably produce disease or disability.

Some diseases do become more common as people grow older, especially arthritis, heart disease, cancer, and Alzheimer's disease. So, it is true that age is highly correlated with the prevalence of chronic diseases, and age can be a marker for physiological declines, but its role as a *cause* is not entirely clear. Alzheimer's disease provides a good case in point. The risk of developing this condition increases with age. In the United States in 2015, 10% of people aged 65 and older had Alzheimer's disease, as did over one third (38%) of those aged 85 and older (Alzheimer's Association, 2019). Because the chance of having Alzheimer's disease increases so markedly with age, older countries (especially those with higher proportions of people in their 80s) have a higher prevalence rate than do younger countries. For example, an estimated 6.9% of the older population in Western Europe is affected by the disease, whereas only 3.9% of older adults in southern Africa are diagnosed (Alzheimer's Disease International, 2015). It is not yet clear whether people in developing nations will show the same patterns of prevalence of Alzheimer's disease in advanced old age as seen in developed nations, but current trends are pointing in that direction. By now you will recognize one of the major themes of this book: that is, variations in the prevalence of any disease (in fact, any impairment or social practice) are related less to age and more to a wide range of cultural factors, such as environmental or lifestyle risks and the availability of diagnostic technology and training.

The Role of Culture in Disease Patterns

To expand on the point just made, some older adults get chronic diseases; others do not. Age is therefore not a universal or inevitable cause, or almost everyone would get these diseases as they aged. Beyond this, the patterns of illness do not necessarily hold true across all cultures, as mentioned previously regarding high blood pressure. Compare, for example, the lower prevalence of breast cancer among Japanese women to its exponential increase with age among American women. In the United States in 2000, an average of 29.2 women per 100,000 died of breast cancer. The mortality rates of this type of cancer increase markedly with age, from 59 per 100,000 women aged 55 to 64 to 151 per 100,000 for the age 75 and older group (WHO, 2006). Based on these numbers, it might be concluded that something about the passage of time—simply living a certain number of years—increases the likelihood of breast cancer. However, in Japan in 2000, only 14 women per 100,000 (of all ages) died of breast cancer (WHO, 2006), less than half the rate for all American women. Although a noticeable difference in breast cancer rates still exists between the two countries, recent research (Jemal, Center, DeSantis, & Ward, 2010) suggests that breast cancer incidence is on the rise in Japan; observers speculate that this increase may be due to Westernization of lifestyles, including greater inactivity and consumption of more fat, calorie-dense foods, and alcohol. Such changes suggest that cultural factors—the context in which both aging and the passage of time are taking place—are at least as important as age. This conclusion could be further strengthened if ongoing research confirms the impact of Westernized lifestyles on breast cancer incidence in Japan.

The essays in this chapter, "Health Beliefs About Dementia in Nigeria" and "The Changing Nature of Health Care and Social Identity Among Older Adults in the Indian Himalayas," provide further excellent illustrations of how culture can affect the prevalence of health conditions of older people. In the case of Alzheimer's disease cited earlier, variations in prevalence rates across countries might be explained by a host of cultural differences—in levels of exposure to risk factors, in how the disease is understood by older people and their families, or in how and when the disease is diagnosed and treated by medical practitioners (see Nwasaki, 2019 on how dementia is viewed in Nigeria). As Roy (2019) points out in her essay on folk medicine in the Indian Himalayas, a society's health care system itself plays an important role in the patterns of disease of older people. Access to modern, scientifically based health care makes a difference in the number of diagnoses of any disease, as do cultural beliefs about disease and medical care and public awareness about health problems and solutions. Our global health statistics system is so far unable to compensate for such factors.

DISABILITY IN OLD AGE

Defining Disability

Disability sounds pretty bad. It conjures up images of wheelchairs, artificial legs, white canes, and guide dogs. Disabled people are often thought of as not being whole, as missing a crucial piece of anatomy (amputation), or having one that does not work (paralysis). Because of this, it is assumed people with disabilities (PWD) cannot participate completely in their own lives—or in ours. As we shall see, the situation usually is not that bleak. First, however, because *disability* is often used interchangeably with the terms *impairment* and *handicap*, we need some definitional clarity. One of the earliest attempts to distinguish among the three was made by the WHO (1980), which declared that **impairment** is any deviation from "normal" physiology, cognition, or emotion, while a **disability** is an inability to perform an activity in a normal way. That is, impairment is a problem with the body's structure, while disability is problem of functioning. To be sure, an impairment does not always produce a disability: in their early stages at least, this is true of hypertension, diabetes, and even cancer. But to consider two fairly common situations: the shape of the eye typically changes with age (impairment), causing vision to be blurred (disability); a soldier loses a leg in battle (impairment) and cannot walk (disability).

The third term associated with impairment and **disability** is **handicap**, which is the result of the interaction of impairment and disability with the physical and social environment, producing a restriction or preventing fulfillment of a normal social role. Very often the presence of an impairment and even a disability does not produce a handicap. In the two cases just cited, eyeglasses can compensate for the blurry vision, allowing the "impaired" and "disabled" person to see clearly in all situations, so we can say he or she is not *handicapped* in normal life. If the impaired soldier is fitted with a prosthetic limb and receives adequate physical and occupational therapy, he or she can resume a normal life with complete (or nearly complete) mobility. Some soldier/amputees even return to military duty after they recover; they certainly cannot be viewed as handicapped. A further example of how the terms have been confused and equated around the world is the signs, "Reserved for Handicapped and Elderly Persons," that dot public places throughout the world, including not only in Europe, North America, and Australia, but in the larger, more developed nations of Asia, South America, and (increasingly) Africa (Global Disability Rights Now, 2019). The fact that in many such circumstances, older people are grouped with the disabled or the handicapped should not be taken as an insult; the intent is to help, to support, and to provide compensation. But it certainly does reflect an unhelpful stereotype of older adults—that simply because of their age, they are disabled. In fact, age by itself often is seen as a handicap although of course it is not. Whereas many older people are disabled, it is the result of physical or mental impairment that causes a functional deficit for which the social and physical environment cannot compensate. We use a variety of terms to refer to a person thought to be *age-disabled*, including *frail, fragile, deteriorated, needing care, dependent,* and *incompetent*. Each term conveys a vivid image, but all lack specificity, and none is definitive. The vignette in Exhibit 5.1 provides an example of an older woman most of us would deem disabled at first glance, but is she?

Anyone seeing a close-up picture of Miriam would deem her disabled; however, a wider-angle view, encompassing her family, her neighbors, her community, and her culture, certainly would assess her situation differently. Miriam struggles to stand but maintains her role as matriarch of a large, needy family because she possesses both the personal will and the social supports to keep going. Clearly, her healthy, active life has ended. Yet in her larger community context, disabled she is not, because the functions of her central role continue to be performed, even if largely by others. Unsurprisingly, the WHO attempt to clarify how disability occurs has not been universally accepted, so we continue to see the three terms misapplied and used almost interchangeably, even in the scientific literature, with *disability* emerging as the default concept. In this section, we show how disability is central to an understanding of global aging and how social and

EXHIBIT 5.1

Miriam Hanging On—With Help of the Village

In a scrubby bush area of western Kenya, outside the city of Kisumu and not far from the shores of Lake Victoria, stands a smallish hut-type house belonging to an 83-year-old woman who we shall call Miriam. The house contains no more than 60 square meters of dirt floor but is home to Miriam and her 13 grandchildren, ranging in age from about 3 to 18. Each of the children is an AIDS orphan, left in Miriam's care by the death of her four sons and four daughters-in-law. Miriam's family receives a small amount of financial aid and social support from HelpAge Kenya, a Nairobi-based nongovernmental organization (NGO) affiliated with the parent organization, London's HelpAge International. Miriam appears to have a number of physical infirmities typical of old age, including muscle weakness and arthritis, and she is nearly blind. She has difficulty standing and requires assistance to rise from her chair and to remain upright. She appears completely unable to carry out normal household chores such as cooking, washing, cleaning, and child care, and her capacity for self-care seems very limited. By any measure, Miriam is physically impaired. Yet Miriam is the acknowledged head of the family, and each of her grandchildren shows her the filial respect and devotion due to one who is credited by the local authorities as "raising 13 grandchildren." Several female neighbors who live near, though not within sight of Miriam's house, function as her support system, making sure each of the children is fed, clothed, and able to get to school. As the children have become adolescents, each has taken on more family responsibilities. Miriam's impairments are real, and life in this isolated, rural Kenyan community is hard, but neither she nor her family is overwhelmed by it. If we can apply it to this aging context, the African proverb, popularized by Hillary Clinton's book of similar title (1996), "It takes a village to raise a child," is vividly illustrated by Miriam's family.

demographic forces have led to its rising importance. We also examine the current state of knowledge about disability and global aging in both the developed and the developing world.

Why Is Disability an Important Topic for Global Aging?

In order to understand the importance of disability for global aging, we must first understand the historical circumstances that have given rise to it. The WHO and World Bank (2011) estimate that about 1 billion of the world's people (15%) have a disability, which makes persons with a disability the largest minority group in the world. The WHO also estimates that between 140 million and 280 million (2%–4%) have significant problems functioning in their daily lives. The total group includes the roughly 5% of children under 14 with a disability and 20% of the world's poorest people.

In addition, one of the major contributors to the global rise in disability is the rapid growth of the older population. As we know, the result of the demographic and epidemiological transitions is that, unlike during any other period in history, most individuals born today can expect to live into later life—indeed the world's population today is estimated to include 573,000 centenarians (people aged 100 or older), about 78% of whom are women (UN Population Division, 2019)—and to experience chronic disease-related disability of some type before death. Just as we spoke earlier of the burden of disease on a country or region, we could also think of the burden of disability as its subset, composed largely of the societal responsibility for care of the chronically ill and dependent older members. By the way, the UN Population Division also projects the world will have 3.7 million centenarians by 2050, just over 30 years from now. Some of them will be today's "elderly" folks, perhaps some of your own grandparents.

We still have much to learn, however, about global trends in disability. For example, some have suggested that a second epidemiological transition occurred in the 1960s (Myers, Lamb, & Agree, 2003). This second transition, the result of increased attention to chronic illnesses by medical researchers and improved medical treatments, led to substantial drops in mortality rates from most late-life diseases, including the leading cause of death among all people—heart disease. This second transition could lead to lower disability rates if the interventions have a similar effect on morbidity; however, if they do not, nations that have experienced this second epidemiological transition would find themselves with an increasingly large disabled older population. The importance of comparative work on this matter is paramount, given that a global examination of disability would include nations that have experienced none, one, or both transitions. As a result, disability trends may be moving in different directions in developed and developing nations as well as in the more and less developed nations of the developing world.

These different directions for disability trends have tremendous potential policy ramifications for many nations in both the developed and developing world. If disability rates are indeed declining among the old, coupled with increasing **life expectancy**, this would result in an increasingly large segment of national populations that is older and relatively healthy. National policies in many countries, especially in the developed world, would need to be adjusted to reflect this new population distribution. For example, given the financial strains on public pension systems created by expanding older populations, understanding that they will become less disabled over time would be invaluable for planning changes in the retirement age for public programs or for targeting work-incentive programs to increase the pool of workers paying into such pension systems. On the other hand, if disability rates are *increasing*, along with rising life expectancy, this would increase the overall health care burden on individuals, families, and the state. In other words, if longer life is coupled with a larger portion of life lived with a disability, then policy makers need to plan for an increased burden on families and prepare for a rising tide of long-term care needs and costs, especially in the developing world, where family care for older kin is currently the norm and formalized public and private sector infrastructure for such care is sparse or nonexistent. Now we turn to measuring and comparing disability across nations.

Disability Measures for Global Comparisons

Although disability is clearly an important topic, defining and measuring it are not easy tasks. Indeed, researchers have been working on this problem for at least half a century. The focus of earlier work was on defining disability and developing measures to accurately capture those definitions. As definitions and measures became widely accepted and utilized in many nations, research has shifted to how to measure disability in a way that can be used in comparative work.

The earliest work on defining and measuring disability was done by Katz, Ford, Moskowitz, Jackson, & Jaffe (1963), who created what has become the most widely used set of disability measures to date—**activities of daily living** (ADLs). ADLs (as the measures are called) assess the abilities an individual needs to live independently on a day-to-day basis. That is, if individuals could not perform one of these tasks, they would need some form of assistance (e.g., special devices or the help of another person) to survive. Katz included six items in his original conceptualization of ADLs: the ability to (a) feed oneself, (b) dress oneself, (c) bathe oneself, (d) toilet oneself, (e) transfer from a bed or chair to a standing position, and (f) remain continent. Since that time, continence was removed from the list as it more accurately describes a symptom than a disability status and a within-the-home locomotion item (often referred to as the walking ADL) was added. Additionally, the ability to groom oneself (brush teeth, shave, comb hair, clip nails) has been included as an ADL in a significant minority of studies. Often researchers have referred to these as *basic activities of daily living*, given the relatively simple nature of each task. The inability to do any one of these tasks would necessitate the use of an assistive device, assistance from another person in one's home, or institutionalization in a care facility.

Following the development of ADLs as measures of basic disability, the desire for more nuanced measurement of differences in disability in the community setting led to the creation of a measure called the **instrumental activities of daily living** (IADL) scale, developed by Lawton and Brody (1969), which measures the ability to perform more socially complex tasks than the basic ADL, such as the ability to do laundry, use the phone, shop, manage money, and prepare meals. Such tasks make independent living easier, although they are not necessary to live independently. Unlike ADL, which usually is measured with the six fixed items noted, IADL measures are used by researchers in various combinations (often mixed with ADL items).

Verbrugge and Jette (1994) brought some clarity to this issue when they described disability as a ***process* of disablement**. Specifically, they described disablement as "impacts that chronic and acute conditions have on functioning of specific body systems and on people's abilities to act in necessary, usual, expected and personally desirable ways in their society" (p. 3). Verbrugge and Jette saw disablement as a process, moving from disease to disability, tracing a path beginning with disease diagnosis (pathology), followed by specific body system dysfunction (impairment), physical and mental restrictions (functional limitations), and ending in difficulty doing daily activities (disability). Importantly, though their terminology does not always match that of the WHO, Verbrugge and Jette's model clarified the relationships among the several concepts and clearly placed disability within the social context.

Measuring Disability Comparatively

Life expectancy is a relatively straightforward demographic concept: simply put, it is the number of years that an average individual of a certain age in a given population can expect to live. Historically, life expectancies have been used to examine gender and race/ethnic differences as well as differences in life expectancy for persons with specific diseases. It was a fairly natural extension of such analyses to focus on transitions into and out of disability and other health states. In disability research, overall life expectancy is referred to as **total life expectancy** (TLE), which is divided into a life expectancy for the disabled state and a separate life expectancy for the nondisabled state, which necessarily sum to the TLE (as shown in Table 5.1). The disabled state expectancy is referred to as **disabled life expectancy** (DLE), measured by the number of years a person lives with any one or more of the six ADL limitations, while the nondisabled state expectancy usually is called **active life expectancy** (ALE). Thus, TLE can be divided into the average number of years lived active (ALE) and the average number of years lived disabled (DLE). ALE is one of several ways by which disability in a population can be represented and, importantly, is the most common measure of disability in comparative and global research.[1]

TABLE 5.1 The Relationship Between Total, Disabled, and Active Life Expectancies

TLE	=	DLE	+	ALE
The number of years that an average individual of a certain age in a given population can expect to live		The number of years that an average individual of a certain age in a given population can expect to live disabled		The number of years that an average individual of a certain age in a given population can expect to live free of disability

ALE, active life expectancy; DLE, disabled life expectancy; TLE, total life expectancy.

---

[1] It should be noted that some analysts prefer the term disability-free life expectancy (DFLE), and European researchers tend to use a variant called healthy life expectancy (HLE) or healthy life years (HLY), based on self-rated health, while the WHO uses a measure adjusted for condition severity called health-adjusted life expectancy (HALE). These different measures tend to produce similar results, and we will use them almost interchangeably.

Data Comparability

Whereas the focus of most researchers has been, understandably, on the lack of detailed data for all countries (especially developing ones), less attention has been given to the validity and comparability of the disability measures themselves across national contexts. For example, one of the commonly used ADL items refers to an individual's ability to get out of (transfer from) a bed. Within the context of the United States and many countries in Western Europe, this ADL involves the underlying functional ability of being able to move oneself from a prone position on top of a soft, springy platform about 2 feet (or two thirds of a meter) above the floor to a standing position. In Japan, however, where many people sleep on futons (padded mats that are laid directly on the floor), and in parts of many other developing countries where the mats may not be padded, the functional limitation underlying the bed-transfer ADL involves a different process of elevating oneself to standing from an initial position of lying on the floor. Yet, the inability to get oneself out of bed in each context may have very similar social ramifications. Whether and how such cultural differences operate has not been fully examined in the disability literature.

Global Patterns of Disability

Given the challenges regarding disability data in the developing countries of the world, the amount and detail of knowledge varies considerably from nation to nation. Therefore, an examination of what disability looks like globally is done best by discussing the developed and developing world separately.

THE DEVELOPED WORLD

Considerable work has been done examining disability across the developed world. In particular, comparisons among European nations on ALE have been examined extensively by researchers of the Joint Action European Health & Life Expectancy Information System who have assembled an online database called "Eurostat," which includes health expectancy information on 31 European nations since 2000. From such extensive data collection and analysis, questions regarding disability in developed nations have moved well beyond basic documentation of ALE across nations. Instead, given that substantial differences have been noted in *healthy life years* (*HLYs*; roughly similar to ALE), attention has turned toward understanding these gaps and the policy initiatives that can reduce them. For example, as shown in Table 5.2, Sweden, Norway, Iceland, and Malta lead all other European countries in HLY for men, with an average number of HLYs at birth of 71 to 73 years. On the other hand, the Baltic states of Latvia, Estonia, and Lithuania have average HLY for men at birth of only about 52 to 56 years (Eurostat, 2019). What makes this 20-year gap even more remarkable is the fact that the differences in average TLE for men at birth are only about 10 years, ranging from the mid- to upper-60s for the Baltic states to the mid- to upper-70s for Sweden and Norway. These trends are

TABLE 5.2 **HLYs At Birth and Age 65 for Females and Males in Selected European Countries, 2016**

Country	At Birth		At Age 65	
	Females	Males	Females	Males
Sweden	73.3	73.0	16.6	15.1
Norway	67.8	72.0	15.2	15.4
Iceland	66.2	71.5	15.1	15.5
Malta	72.4	71.1	12.9	12.8
Italy	67.2	67.6	10.1	10.4
Ireland	69.8	67.3	13.2	12.0
Spain	66.5	65.9	10.4	10.4
Germany	67.3	65.3	12.4	11.5
Bulgaria	67.5	64.0	10.1	9.2
Greece	64.7	63.8	7.8	8.0
Belgium	63.8	63.7	11.4	10.3
European Union	64.2	63.5	10.1	9.8
United Kingdom	63.1	63.0	11.1	10.4
Netherlands	57.8	62.8	9.9	10.3
Czechia	64.0	62.7	8.9	8.4
France	64.1	62.6	10.6	9.5
Luxembourg	58.9	61.4	8.0	9.5
Poland	64.6	61.3	8.9	8.2
Switzerland	57.7	61.0	9.8	10.1
Denmark	60.3	60.3	11.9	11.5
Portugal	57.4	59.9	6.4	7.7
Romania	59.0	59.8	5.6	6.2
Hungary	60.2	59.5	6.4	6.7
Finland	57.0	59.1	8.9	9.4
Slovenia	57.9	58.7	8.2	8.4
Croatia	58.7	57.1	4.9	5.2
Austria	57.1	57.0	7.4	8.2
Slovakia	57.0	56.4	4.2	4.5
Lithuania	59.4	56.2	5.6	5.6
Estonia	59.0	54.4	7.0	5.5
Latvia	54.9	52.3	4.5	4.4

HLYs, healthy life years.
Source: From Eurostat. (2019). *Statistics explained: Healthy life years statistics*. Retrieved from ec.europa.eu/eurostat/statistics-explained/index.php/Healthy_life_years_statistics

mirrored in data on European women, although values for both TLE and HLY are slightly greater for women than for men.

These data also show the heterogeneity among the European nations in later-life health and function and suggest more complex relationships between health and longevity. For example, both Switzerland and France have longer TLEs for women at birth compared to Denmark (by about 3 years) although living standards in these nations are nearly identical. Yet, women of both nations experience fewer years (1.3–2.0) of healthy life at age 65 than women in Denmark. The patterns for European men are also quite heterogeneous. Thus, extra years of life do not directly translate into additional years of health, even in the relatively similar social and economic contexts of the European countries. Whereas socioeconomic measures may have some utility in explaining this heterogeneity (e.g., nations with higher gross national income per capita also tend to have higher TLE and HLY), more investigation is needed to understand the surprisingly substantial differences in healthy life observed in the developed world.

THE DEVELOPING WORLD

Our knowledge and understanding of disability and ALE in the developing world are even more limited. Indeed, it is only within the past decade that *estimates* of health expectancies have been available for many developing nations, and in many cases, these values are estimated from combinations of data and simulation techniques rather than through direct observations via vital-statistics records. Nevertheless, several insights have come from the limited data in developing countries. It is generally known, for example, that more economically advantaged nations have longer average healthy life expectancies than their less economically fortunate peers. This relationship, however, is not perfectly linear. For example, some less economically advantaged nations, like the Philippines and Malaysia, have greater ALE at age 60 than some more economically advantaged nations such as Russia and the Ukraine. Such differences, which are similar to those noted in developed nations, show clearly that socioeconomic status, although an important predictor of comparative differences in disability, is not the only driving force behind disability and health heterogeneity among nations.

ALE values at age 60 are the highest and relatively similar in Western Europe, the United States and Canada, Australia, New Zealand, and Japan, with healthy life exceeding 17 years at age 60 in these locations. Unsurprisingly, the worst ALE at age 60 can be found in sub-Saharan African nations and war-ravaged areas like Afghanistan, where average healthy life at age 60 is less than 8 years. Other less developed nations fall in between these extremes, with countries such as Argentina, China, and Thailand approaching the age-60 ALE values of the developed world, while others, such as Bolivia, India, and Ukraine, are faring only marginally better than the sub-Saharan African nations. Despite the usefulness of these patterns in comparing developing nations with each other and with the developed world, more reliable and detailed data are needed to truly understand the tremendous heterogeneity of health and disability across the developing world.

Finally, it is important to note that our discussion has been focused almost exclusively on issues of *physical impairment*. This focus is not accidental, since the large majority of comparative global research studies have ignored other types of disability. This is unfortunate, since evidence from developed nations suggests that cognitive impairments such as Alzheimer's disease and stroke-related dementia are a growing area of disability within these countries due, at least in part, to the aging of their populations. How such *cognitive impairment* compares across nations is largely unknown and even less so regarding how these impairments translate into disabilities. Given the apparently rapidly growing rates of cognitive impairment in nations like the United States, more comparative work, especially in developing countries, is urgently needed. Similarly, mental health problems can be equally disabling and even more difficult to measure comparatively. Likewise, other non–ADL-type disabilities are often ignored in comparative disability research. Vision and hearing impairment can lead to significant disability, especially in a developing nation where assistive devices are rarer and often cost-prohibitive. Comparative work on levels and trends in sensory disability is also urgently needed. The past few decades have seen significant growth in our knowledge of disability globally, especially in the developed world (Singer, Green, Rowe, Ben-Shlomo, & Morrisey, 2019), but much remains to be understood about the disablement process internationally.

HEALTH/ILLNESS BEHAVIOR OF OLDER PEOPLE

Disease and disability are real events in our lives. They most often are objectively visible, whether to others, to physicians, or to their medical diagnostic devices, and they certainly usually are felt by the person affected. Disease presents through either **signs**, defined as overt changes in anatomy or bodily functioning that are objectively observable by a health practitioner, or **symptoms**, feeling states that only can be experienced subjectively by the sick person. Examples of signs include body temperature, heart rate, respiration, brain waves, a broken bone; symptoms include pain, dizziness, queasiness, sadness, anxiety, and confusion. Many diseases present with both signs and symptoms (a person with the flu will have a fever [measurable] and body aches [not measurable]), but others bring no outward, detectable signs (such as early Alzheimer's, producing only mild memory loss and emotional reactions), so an early diagnosis depends entirely on the sick person's description of his or her symptoms.

We can imagine that people in different cultures with different values and beliefs about health and disease and its causes and cures will view disease very differently and be likely to behave differently when they believe themselves to be sick. But however that person acts in regard to the reality, the perception, or even the fear of the disease is defined as **health/illness behavior**. That definition has assumed several different connotations over the years of scientific study. The most common and obvious involves what a sick person does when he or she feels (or knows) himself or herself to be sick. All of us have been confronted with either signs or symptoms of a disease (or more likely both) and had to decide what to do—that is, what illness behavior to engage in. A variation on that theme is called **health behavior**, the actions we may take to prevent disease or injury and to stay healthy (Cockerham, 2017). Those can include our dietary choices, physical activity, stopping smoking, using seat belts, getting a flu shot, or taking vitamins or other supplements.

Illness behavior, on the other hand, encompasses a wide array of possible actions, including (a) ignoring observed body changes and simply doing nothing; (b) self-medicating with a readily obtainable drug purchased over the counter; (c) seeking help from a health practitioner; and (d) purchasing a medication prescribed by a physician and either taking it as directed (adherence) or not (nonadherence). Sometimes a person engages all four behaviors in serial order: a typical case of influenza might in its early stages be ignored in favor of meeting normal role obligations, then, as the symptoms intensify, the person self-medicates with a painkiller or an antihistamine, and finally by the third or fourth day, in the grip of fever, body aches, and misery, the person breaks down and calls his or her physician for an appointment. Some illness behaviors have been the focus of theoretical elaboration and research, including the *sick role*, *help seeking*, and *adherence* to medical instructions. Each is defined and briefly discussed in turn. Following that discussion, we explore in greater depth how perhaps the key illness behavior—adherence—is manifested in various countries.

The Sick Role

Among the various terms denoting a departure from the general state of wellness are disease, illness, and sickness. Among social scientists who study the phenomenon, **disease** is usually taken to mean the physical manifestation expressed, as stated earlier, in measurable signs; while **illness** is the psychological or emotional state expressed as symptoms or feeling states. **Sickness**, on the other hand, is seen as a social role that a person with a disease, disability, or illness is expected to play. According to its original description by sociologist Talcott Parsons (1951), a person who is unwell is actually a social deviant unable to perform normal roles. Parsons postulated a useful and powerful social control mechanism, which he called the **sick role,** that society uses to manage the deviant behavior.[2] The sick person, he said, may adopt the sick role, which, like any other social role, has privileges and obligations. The privileges are important for society's continuing routine functioning:

---

[2] Since Parsons lived and worked in the United States, he described this role as part of the modern biomedical system viewed it; little has been written about its direct applicability in other countries with very different health care systems, though it probably works very well in Europe, Canada, Australia, or any country with a physician-centered system.

because the sick person is presumed not to be responsible for being sick, he or she is excused from all other social roles (though he or she may, of course, choose to continue performing them if possible) and is not responsible for his or her own cure. To activate these role privileges, however, the sick person must behave according to each of four role expectations. He or she must: (a) admit he or she is sick and want to get well; (b) must accept forgiveness from their usual role obligations; (c) must seek competent medical help; and (d) must cooperate with that practitioner by following medical instructions.

As an example of how the sick role typically operates in the United States and other countries where such a culture of medical care is found, we can look to a person who contracts the influenza virus. The early experience probably is felt rather than observed: either body aches or headache or sore throat or just a general feeling of fatigue and not being "well." This will be followed closely by a worsening condition with such signs as a measurable fever, nasal discharge, and cough. Of course, each collection of symptoms and signs may be unique to the specific strain of the virus contracted, but a typical reaction is likely to be the person's admission of feeling badly, immediately taking a nonprescription medication intended to reduce the symptoms and signs and, in some cases, even shorten the course of the disease. Self-medication usually is accompanied by "going to bed," resting, or sleeping as required by the interruption of normal activities, such as work, child care, cooking, cleaning, or spending time with other family members. This is evidence of both an admission of sickness and showing a desire to get well. Should these actions not help the person feel better, the sick person is expected to visit a physician for a more precise diagnosis and, perhaps, a more powerful prescribed medication. Each different disease will have its own typical course of signs, symptoms, and sick-role behaviors, but, at least in developed countries where modern medicine dominates, the social role of the sick person will appear at some point in the process of being sick and getting well. Of course, the role was developed for and fits acute conditions best, while chronic diseases, for which no cure is possible, require significant adaptation (Nuttbrock, 1986).

Help Seeking

The third obligation of the sick role is to seek competent medical help. Of course, one's definition of "competent" is socially and culturally bound, though in Parsons' day, he clearly was thinking only of the modern medical context and considering a medical doctor as the default dispenser of diagnoses, prescriptions, and cures. Taking the global view, if the sick role is to be of use in understanding illness behavior in many different types of societies, we must include the possibility of traditional healers (or even folk healers) as competent to advise and treat their cultural compatriots.

Many studies of help seeking in Western societies have used a behavioral model developed by Andersen and Newman (1973) that conceived of three categories of factors leading a person to utilize health services: *predisposing, enabling,* and *need* characteristics. Predisposing factors include social and demographic characteristics of the person and beliefs and attitudes about health and health care. Enabling factors are such variables as income, health insurance coverage, and access to a care provider. These components together set the general conditions, but they must be triggered by some health need, such as signs or symptoms. Some researchers seek to determine the patient's perceptions of the need, such as the severity and persistence of pain or a lump, and how disruptive of normal role performance they are. In the United States, cost of care is very often a significant consideration in seeking care because so many people must pay all or a part of the fees out of pocket. In many other countries with a national health system where care is free, patients may not see cost as a barrier, but in most developing countries, especially those with large numbers of people living in rural or remote areas, transport to a care provider may be a major barrier (Umubyeyi, Mogren, Ntaganira, & Krantz, 2016). In addition, complementary and alternative therapies have proliferated in Western countries, while modern medicine has become more available globally, even in the poorest nations. The choice of care provider in all countries depends on who is most trusted and who is felt to give the best chance of recovery.

Adherence

As medical consumerism has grown over the past half-century and patients have become more health literate, they increasingly prefer to be partners in the clinical process, rather than merely receivers of a physician's orders. Potter and McKinley (2005) have written perceptively about the evolving doctor–patient relationship in Western medicine, but their observations may have increasing application to the emerging relationships between patients and doctors in developing countries as well. Potter and McKinley document the swift demise of the classic relationship between doctor and patient with its wide power differential and implied class distinction. In the past when most patients had much less education than their physician, especially in scientific matters, they were very hesitant to question the old dictum, "Doctor knows best." But as education levels have risen and, especially, with the increasingly intrusive role of third-party payers (government, private health insurance companies, and managed care organizations), the clinical freedom that doctors have enjoyed in the past and their legal protections against mistakes have eroded, encouraging patients to take a more active role in their own care. Also undermining the relationship, Potter and McKinley (2005) argue, is the government's increasing role as regulator of costs, protecting the interests of the payers (their own, the insurance companies', and, to a lesser extent, the patient's) at the expense of the medical profession's needs. A second cause of this shift of power between doctor and patient has been the explosion of new health products available without medical approval and the marketing through mass media of prescription medications directly to consumers, rather than through physicians. Finally, Potter and McKinley suggest the rise of chronic disease—and, necessarily, the increasing number of older patients who are bringing those ailments with them to see the doctor—is a trend that ought to improve the doctor–patient relationship since it argues for clinical management over a longer term and greater commitment by both parties to the effort. However, they also believe the other sociopolitical forces are simply too powerful for the rise of chronic care to make much difference. Doubtless, the continued penetration of the Internet and social media into the daily lives of billions living in developing countries will improve health literacy and feed the consumerist impulse (Alhuwail & Abdulsalam, 2019; Tan & Goonawardene, 2017; Xie, 2009). Since traditional medicine already is known, trusted, and available in many of these societies, we may see increasing pluralism in these new health battlegrounds.

The crux of the doctor–patient relationship is the point at which the doctor offers an opinion about the nature of the patient's underlying ailment and, in many cases, writes an order for a pharmacy to dispense a particular medication to the patient. That is the culmination of the medical encounter, but it is just the beginning of what, for someone with a chronic condition, could be a very long—possibly lifelong—course of treatment. The final normative obligation of the sick role is for the patient to cooperate with the doctor in order to get well. Traditionally, this behavior was termed *compliance* and was defined primarily as taking medications as a physician prescribed (i.e., "following the doctor's orders"). In recent years, the definition has been expanded to include all medical and health recommendations, and the phenomenon has been renamed **adherence** because that term carries no note of blame, as compliance was felt to do (Whittington, 2001; WHO, 2003, p. 3). The widely accepted definition now is: "The extent to which a person's behavior—taking medications, following a diet, and/or executing lifestyle changes—corresponds with agreed recommendations from a health care provider" (WHO, 2003).

For several very good reasons, medical adherence—more accurately, nonadherence—has become one of the most researched clinical phenomena in the world. The WHO (2003) has called poor adherence among patients with chronic diseases "a worldwide problem of striking magnitude" (p. 7). For example, the WHO (2003) estimates the nonadherence rate in developed countries, where health literacy is highest, averages 50% (i.e., half of all patients do not take their medications as instructed) and estimates the rate in developing nations (and among poor people generally) is even higher. Most studies of adherence are done on older patients taking multiple drugs for multiple conditions, a recognized problem in itself of poor prescribing or drug monitoring that creates billions of adverse drug reactions annually, with its own set of costs. But researchers usually measure adherence to only one particular medication at a time, and it is clear that adherence rates vary with the class of drug—and probably with the underlying condition. Measurement methods vary, but results consistently show very poor adherence. The WHO (2003) summarizes:

> . . . in China, the Gambia, and the Seychelles, only 43%, 27%, and 26%, respectively, of patients with hypertension adhere to their

antihypertensive medication regimen. . . . Data on patients with depression reveal that between 40% and 70% adhere to anti-depressant therapies. In Australia, only 43% of patients with asthma take their medications as prescribed all the time and only 28% use prescribed preventive medication. In the treatment of HIV and AIDS, adherence to antiretroviral agents varies between 37% and 83% depending on the drug under study and the demographic characteristics of patient populations.

More recent studies confirm that nonadherence generally ranges between 40% and 60% in the wide range of countries studied: South Korea (Jin, Kim, & Rhie, 2016); India (Shruthi, Jyothi, Pundarikaksha, Nagesh, & Tushar, 2016); the Netherlands (de Vries et al., 2014); Ireland, Spain, and Italy (Menditto et al., 2018); Singapore (Yap, Thiramoorthy, & Kwan, 2016); Palestine (Al-Ramahi, 2015); Zimbabwe (Wariva, January, & Maradzika, 2014); Bolivia, Peru, and Chile (Caqueo-Urizar, Urzua, Fond, & Boyer, 2017); and the United States (Patel, Chang, Shenolikar, & Balkrishnan, 2010). Many more studies could be cited, almost certainly with similar results, but we begin to see the massive scope of the problem.

The main consequences of nonadherence are poor health outcomes and increased health care costs (Whittington, 1983a). The risk of poor outcomes is seen in (a) the possible spread of an uncontrolled communicable disease; (b) the chronically ill patient not getting better, getting worse, becoming disabled, or possibly dying; and (c) the patient eventually needing more health care or family care resources. Each of these outcomes brings an increased overall health care bill for the patient, the family, the community, and third-party payers. The health care costs of such behavior were estimated by Iuga and McGuire (2014) to be at least $300 billion a year in the United States alone, accounting for about 30% of wasteful spending on health care. We can scarcely imagine the worldwide cost of this behavior, but it would be seen in unnecessary hospital stays, additional medications to do the work of the unconsumed pills, and steeper long-term care costs as uncontrolled chronic diseases such as diabetes, arthritis, and hypertension work their mischief. Perhaps the greatest uncounted cost, in the form of lost time, emotional stress, and caregiver burden, falls directly on the patient's family who, in all countries, rich and poor, bear the brunt of caring for the disabilities and frailties of older family members.

The good news is that many efforts are beginning to identify the causes of nonadherence, and others are designing interventions to reduce it (Meyer, 2019; Verloo, Chiolero, Kiszio, Kampel, & Santschi, 2017). The WHO (2003) has grouped causes (they prefer the phrase "barriers to adherence") into five broad categories: (a) *social and economic barriers*: such things as health literacy, communication skills, health insurance, and access to care; (b) *health care system barriers*: these include anything associated with the physician or the prescription itself. It has become trite to observe that too many drugs are prescribed for older patients by too many physicians who have received too little training in their pharmacological properties and dangers. Trite but true. For all their medical and scientific knowledge, most physicians are not well educated in caring for older patients, and there are simply too few geriatricians to handle the job, even in developed countries. Other health system barriers include the cost of medications, poor patient education effort, and poor continuity of care; (c) *condition-related barriers*: these are created by conditions such as depression, psychosis, or developmental disability that can interfere with the patient's ability to understand or follow directions; (d) *therapy-related barriers*: those that stem from **polypharmacy**, the overprescription of drugs to treat both the signs and symptoms of the patient's disease and the signs and symptoms of multiple drug interactions and side effects. The resulting regimens are just too complex for most older people to manage (see Rochon, 2019 for an excellent summary of the prescribing dilemma); and, finally, (e) *patient-related barriers* (both unintentional and intentional nonadherence): the litany of patient problems not under their control is long: they are too poor to afford the drug (an interaction with the cost); they are unable to travel to the pharmacy to obtain the medication; they are cognitively impaired and unable to remember to take their meds on time; they have sensory deficits, swallowing problems, impaired mobility or dexterity, fear of drug dependence, negative feelings toward the prescriber, the disease, or even the pill itself.

These categories would appear comprehensive, but they overlook patients who are nonadherent on purpose, deciding to alter the dose, taking more or—most times—less than the doctor directed (Haynes, McDonald, Garg, & Montague, 2002). Few analyses of nonadherence even mention the possibility of the patient taking charge of making decisions about his or her drug intake, but many report doing so, most often, as they say, "Because I didn't like the way it [the drug] made me feel." They know they need the drug, though perhaps not how crucially, but they simply will not put up with therapy that makes them dizzy, or drowsy, or nauseous, or forgetful, especially when the health threat, as in diabetes or hypertension, is silent and hard to imagine. The immediate "illness" problem created by the drug often supersedes the possibly more serious one down the road (Whittington, 1983b).

Again, how applicable these categories may be in the various countries of the world, with their vastly different cultures and health care systems, is unknown. However, we note that the WHO report was produced by at least 40 experts and scientists from 15 widely diverse countries, including the United States, Canada, Venezuela, the Netherlands, Mexico, Switzerland, Costa Rica, Italy, England, Ireland, Haiti, China, South Africa, Turkey, and Spain. On the face of it, we might conclude these 40, at least, thought their joint statement on adherence was at least relevant to their home country. We can be sure, however, that, as Meyer (2019, p. 13) comments on the five WHO categories of barriers: "Non-adherence involves interplay of all five dimensions, and each non-adherent patient has a unique set of influencing factors. A one-size-fits-all approach cannot apply to adherence because of the many independent variables that combine differently in each patient." And yet, as Haynes (2001) has argued, "Increasing the effectiveness of adherence interventions may have a far greater impact on the health of the population than any improvement in the specific medical treatments."

CONCLUSION

Health is important to all of us. Because it is so problematic in old age and is ultimately an existential question, the health of older people is a central concern to all societies. While acute diseases are more common at younger ages, older people tend to contract more chronic (incurable) diseases that accumulate and limit a person's ability to function in everyday life. The epidemiological transition describes a population's shift from predominantly acute to chronic diseases as that population ages and needs a different sort of health care system that provides special care for older people with chronic diseases and disabilities. We know that, through their public health efforts, societies are crucial actors in preventing disease and promoting health, and they have an important economic stake in increasing both the life expectancy of their population and their healthy life expectancy. While the developed countries are still far ahead of their developing sister nations in extending life and active life, developing countries are making strong progress on both fronts as they modernize and their economic well-being increases.

However, disease is ultimately an individual phenomenon. It usually manifests as an objective personal reality with measurable signs and symptoms, but it also operates on a social and psychological level, expressed in the subjective perception of patients, family members, and health providers. Illness behavior—what a person does when he/she feels ill—must be understood to create sound health policy. Illness behavior, such as the sick role, patterns of help-seeking, and patient adherence—whether individuals follow practitioners' advice and directions—is a key factor in our overall knowledge of health and our ability to achieve it for a national population.

DISCUSSION QUESTIONS

1. Why is health is a universal value?

2. Why do we say that chronic (noncommunicable) diseases are the major challenge for health care in the future?

3. What disease (or diseases) place(s) the greatest burden on the country you are from and on the families in your society?

4. How would Miriam be treated in your country? Would she be better or worse off than she is in rural Kenya?

5. Are there any things you can do now to increase your ALE?

6. Have you used WebMD or another health information site online? Was it helpful?

The authors gratefully acknowledge the contributions of Scott Brown and Jasleen Chahal to this chapter.

7. Have you ever questioned your doctor's treatment plan? How did he or she respond?

8. How do you feel about patients deciding for themselves what medicine they will take or whether they will refuse certain treatments?

KEY WORDS

Active life expectancy
Activities of daily living (ADLs)
Acute disease
Burden of disease
Chronic noncommunicable diseases
Demographic transition
Disability
Disabled life expectancy
Disease
Epidemiological transition
Handicap
Health behavior
Health beliefs
Help seeking
Illness

Illness behavior
Impairment
Instrumental activities of daily living (IADLs)
Life expectancy
Morbidity
Mortality
Polypharmacy
Process of disablement
Self-directed care
Sickness
Sick role
Signs
Symptoms
Total life expectancy

REFERENCES

Alessio, H. (2001). The physiology of human aging. In L. A. Morgan & S. Kunkel (Eds.), *Aging: The social context* (2nd ed., pp. 107–137). Thousand Oaks, CA: Pine Forge Press.

Alhuwail, D., & Abdulsalam, Y. (2019). Assessing electronic health literacy in the state of Kuwait: Survey of internet users from an Arab state. *Journal of Medical Internet Research, 21*(5), e11174. doi:10.2196/11174

Al-Ramahi, R. (2015). Adherence to medications and associated factors: A cross-sectional study among Palestinian hypertensive patients. *Journal of Epidemiology and Global Health, 5,* 125–132. doi:10.1016/j.jegh.2014.05.005

Alzheimer's Association. (2019). *2019 Alzheimer's disease facts and figures.* Chicago, IL: Author.

Alzheimer's Disease International. (2015). *World Alzheimer report 2015: The global impact of dementia.* London, England: Author.

Andersen, R., & Newman, J. F. (1973). Societal and individual determinants of medical care utilization in the United States. *Milbank Memorial Quarterly, 51,* 95–124. doi:10.2307/3349613

Caqueo-Urizar, A., Urzua, A., Fond, G., & Boyer, L. (2017). Medication nonadherence among South American patients with schizophrenia. *Patient Preference and Adherence, 11,* 1737–1744. doi:10.2147/PPA.S144961

Clinton, H. (1996). *It takes a village to raise a child.* New York, NY: Simon & Schuster.

Cockerham, W. C. (2017). *Medical sociology* (13th ed.). Upper Saddle River, NJ: Prentice-Hall.

Cowgill, D. O. (1972). A theory of aging in cross-cultural perspective. In D. O. Cowgill & L. D. Holmes (Eds.), *Aging and modernization* (pp. 1–14). New York, NY: Appleton-Century-Crofts.

de Vries, S. T., Keers, J. C., Visser, R., de Zeeuw, D., Haaijer-Ruskamp, F. M., Voorham, J., & Denig, P. (2014). Medication beliefs, treatment complexity, and non-adherence to different drug classes in patients with type 2 diabetes. *Journal of Psychosomatic Research, 76*, 134–138. doi:10.1016/j.jpsychores.2013.11.003

Duda, R., Anarfi, J., Adanu, R., Seffah, J., Darko, R., & Hill, A. (2011). The health of the "older women" in Accra, Ghana: Results of the women's health study of Accra. *Journal of Cross Cultural Gerontology, 26*, 299–314. doi:10.1007/s10823-011-9148-8

Eurostat. (2019). *Statistics explained: Healthy life years statistics.* Retrieved from ec.europa.eu/eurostat/statistics-explained/index.php/Healthy_life_years_statistics

Global Disability Rights Now. (2019). *The 10 principles of disability rights.* Retrieved from https://www.globaldisabilityrightsnow.org/principles

Haynes, R. B. (2001). Interventions for helping patients to follow prescription for medications. *Cochrane Database of Systematic Reviews,* (1). doi:10.1002/14651858.CD000011

Haynes, R. B., McDonald, H., Garg, A. X., & Montague, P. (2002). Interventions for helping patients to follow prescriptions for medications. *Cochrane Database of Systematic Reviews,* (2). doi:10.1002/14651858.CD000011

Iuga, A. O., & McGuire, M. J. (2014). Adherence and health care costs. *Risk Management and Healthcare Policy, 7*, 35–44. doi:10.2147/RMHP.S19801

Jemal, A., Center, M., DeSantis, C., & Ward, M. (2010). Global patterns of cancer incidence and mortality rates and trends. *Cancer Epidemiology, Biomarkers, and Prevention, 19*, 1893–1907. doi:10.1158/1055-9965.EPI-10-0437

Jin, H., Kim, Y., & Rhie, S. J. (2016). Factors affecting medication adherence in elderly people. *Patient Preference and Adherence, 10*, 2117–2125. doi:10.2147/PPA.S118121

Katz, S., Ford, A. B., Moskowitz, R. W., Jackson, B. A., & Jaffe, M. W. (1963). Studies of illness in the aged. The index of the ADL: A standardized measure of biological and psychosocial function. *Journal of the American Medical Association, 185*, 914–919. doi:10.1001/jama.1963.03060120024016

Kinsella, K., Beard, J., & Suzman, R. (2013). Can populations age better, not just live longer? *Generations, 37*(1), 19–26.

Lawton, M. P., & Brody, E. (1969). Assessment of older people: Self-maintaining and instrumental activities of daily living. *The Gerontologist, 9*, 179–186. doi:10.1093/geront/9.3_Part_1.179

Lloyd, L. (2012). *Health and care in ageing societies: A new international approach.* Bristol, England: The Policy Press.

Menditto, E., Cahir, C., Aza-Pascual-Salcedo, M., Bruzzese, D., Poblador-Plou, B., Malo, S., . . . Prados-Torres, A. (2018). Adherence to chronic medication in older populations: Application of a common protocol among three European cohorts. *Patient Preference and Adherence, 12*, 1975–1987. doi:10.2147/PPA.S164819

Meyer, L. (2019). Improving medication adherence. *Today's Geriatric Medicine, 8*(1), 12. Retrieved from https://www.todaysgeriatricmedicine.com

Myers, G. C., Lamb, V. L., & Agree, E. M. (2003). Patterns of disability change associated with the epidemiologic transition. In J. M. Robine, C. Jagger, C. Mathers, E. Crimmins, & R. Suzman (Eds.), *Determining health expectancies* (pp. 59–74). Chichester, England: John Wiley & Sons.

Nuttbrock, L. (1986). Socialization to the chronic sick role in later life: An interactionist view. *Research on Aging, 8*(3), 368–387. doi:10.1177/0164027586008003002

Nwasaki, C. (2019). Cultural views of dementia in Nigeria. In F. J. Whittington, S. R. Kunkel, & K. de Medeiros (Eds.), *Global aging: Comparative perspectives on aging and the life course* (2nd ed.). New York, NY: Springer Publishing Company.

Omran, A. (1971). The epidemiological transition: A theory of the epidemiology of population change. *Milbank Memorial Fund Quarterly, 49*, 509–538. doi:10.2307/3349375

Parsons, T. (1951). *The social system.* New York, NY: The Free Press.

Patel, I., Chang, J., Shenolikar, R. A., & Balkrishnan, R. (2010). Medication adherence in low income elderly type-2 diabetes patients: A retrospective cohort study. *International Journal of Diabetes Mellitus, 2*, 122–124. doi:10.1016/j.ijdm.2010.05.003

Potter, S. J., & McKinley, J. B. (2005). From a relationship to encounter: An examination of longitudinal and lateral dimension of the doctor-patient relationship. *Social Science and Medicine, 61*, 465–479. doi:10.1016/j.socscimed.2004.11.067

Rochon, P. A. (2019). Drug prescribing for older adults. Retrieved from www.uptodate.com

Roy, S. (2019). The changing nature of health care and social identity among older adults in the Indian Himalayas. In F. J. Whittington, S. R. Kunkel, & K. de Medeiros (Eds.), *Global aging: Comparative perspectives on aging and the life course* (2nd ed.). New York, NY: Springer Publishing Company.

Shruthi, R., Jyothi, R., Pundarikaksha, H. P., Nagesh, G. N., & Tushar, T. J. (2016). A study of medication compliance in geriatric patients with chronic illnesses at a tertiary care hospital. *Journal of Clinical and Diagnostic Research, 10*(12), 40–43. doi:10.7860/JCDR/2016/21908.9088

Singer, L., Green, M., Rowe, F., Ben-Shlomo, Y., & Morrisey, K. (2019). Social determinants of multimorbidity and multiple functional limitations among the ageing population of England, 2002-2015. *SSM Population Health, 38*(8), 100413. doi:10.1016/j.ssmph.2019.100413

Tan, S. S-N., & Goonawardene, N. (2017). Internet health information seeking and patient-physician relationship: A systematic review. *Journal of Medical Internet Research, 19*(1), e9. doi:10.2196/jmir.5729

Umubyeyi, A., Mogren, I., Ntaganira, J., & Krantz, G. (2016). Help-seeking behaviours, barriers to care and self-efficacy for seeking mental health care: A population-based study in Rwanda. *Social Psychiatry and Psychiatric Epidemiology, 51*, 81–92. doi:10.1007/s00127-015-1130-2

United Nations Population Division. (2019). *World population prospects, 2019.* Retrieved https://www.un.org/en/development/desa/population

U.S. Central Intelligence Agency. (2019). Fact book: 2019. Retrieved from https://www.cia.gov/library/publications/the-world-factbook

U.S. National Institute on Aging, NIH, & World Health Organization. (2011). *World health and aging.* Washington, DC: National Institutes of Health.

Verbrugge, L. M., & Jette, A. M. (1994). The disablement process. *Social Science & Medicine, 38*(1), 1–14. doi:10.1016/0277-9536(94)90294-1

Verloo, H., Chiolero, A., Kiszio, B., Kampel, T., & Santschi, V. (2017). Nurse interventions to improve medication adherence among discharged older adults: A systematic review. *Age and Ageing, 46*, 747–754. doi:10.1093/ageing/afx076

Wariva, E., January, J., & Maradzika, J. (2014). Medication adherence among elderly patients with high blood pressure in Gweru, Zimbabwe. *Journal of Public Health in Africa, 5*(304), 28–31. doi:10.4081/jphia.2014.304

Whittington, F. J. (1983a). Consequences of drug use, misuse, and abuse. In M. Glantz, D. M. Petersen, & F. J. Whittington (Eds.), *Drugs and the elderly adult* (pp. 203–225). Washington, DC: National Institute on Drug Abuse.

Whittington, F. J. (1983b). Misuse of prescription drugs and compliance with prescription directions. In M. Glantz, D. M. Petersen, & F. J. Whittington (Eds.), *Drugs and the elderly adult* (pp. 63–120). Washington, DC: National Institute on Drug Abuse.

Whittington, F. J. (2001). Adherence. In George L. Maddox (Ed.), *Encyclopedia of aging* (3rd ed., pp. 17–19). New York, NY: Springer Publishing Company.

World Bank. (2017). Population ages 65 and above. Retrieved from https://data.worldbank.org/indicator/SP.POP.65UP.TO.ZS

World Health Organization. (1946). Constitution of the World Health Organization. Adopted by the International Health Conference, New York, 19–22 June 1946.

World Health Organization. (1980). *International classification of impairments, disabilities, and handicaps.* Geneva, Switzerland: Author.

World Health Organization. (2003). Adherence to long-term therapies: Evidence for action. Geneva, Switzerland: Author.

World Health Organization. (2006). *The top ten causes of death.* Retrieved from www.who/int/mediacentre/factsheets/fs310/en/index2.html

World Health Organization. (2018). *Noncommunicable diseases.* Retrieved from https://www.who.int/news-room/fact-sheets/detail/noncommunicable-diseases

World Health Organization. (2019). *Top 10 causes of death: 2016.* Retrieved from http://origin.who.int/gho/mortality_burden_disease/causes_death/top_10/en

World Health Organization and World Bank. (2011). *World report on disability.* Retrieved from https://www.who.int/disabilities

Xie, B. (2009). Older adults' health information wants in the internet age: Implications for patient-provider relationships. *Journal of Health Communication, 14*, 510–524. doi:10.1080/10810730903089614

Yap, A. F., Thiramoorthy, T., & Kwan, Y. H. (2016). Medication adherence in the elderly. *Journal of Clinical Gerontology & Geriatrics, 7*, 64–67. doi:10.1016/j.jcgg.2015.05.001

CULTURAL VIEWS OF DEMENTIA IN NIGERIA

CANDIDUS NWAKASI

Sometimes, he seems completely off, like when cell service abruptly leaves your mobile phone and doesn't return for a while. … [T]here are also times when he talks about his dead friends in a way that makes you wonder if they are calling out for him to come join them. I mean, he is an old man and unfortunately, this also means he is getting closer and closer to his grave.

Anonymous

It is not uncommon to hear people in Nigeria describe dementia symptoms in a way that is similar to the preceding quote. It is important to note that dementia is not a disease; it is a collective word used to describe symptoms of cognitive decline. A person with dementia may have difficulties with remembering, communicating, reasoning, problem-solving, and handling complicated tasks. The older a person gets, the higher the risk of this progressive, cognitive condition, but because Nigeria is a young population with a life expectancy at birth of about 55 years, issues of older adults such as geriatrics and long-term care are not given much attention. In addition, the country's health care system is very weak, and with the burden of diseases it carries, most health care costs are paid by patients and their families.

Although the country is categorized as a young population, the total number of its older adults (65 years and above) is over 5 million (about 2.7% of the total population), and the number is rapidly increasing due to medical advances and better public health policies in the country. Thus, given that increasing age is a primary risk factor for dementia, there are likely an increasing number of people with dementia in Nigeria. In the absence of a robust health system that can cater to the needs of this growing older adult population, there is an increased dependence on informal practices like family caregiving for older adults living with dementia. Most informal practices are grounded in the culture of the people. Therefore, to better understand dementia in the Nigerian context, this essay explores some of the beliefs related to dementia to include the meanings attributed to dementia symptoms, views on caregiving, and formal long-term care for older people with dementia.

DEMENTIA IN THE NIGERIAN CONTEXT

Apart from English, a language widely spoken by Nigerians, the country has over 500 indigenous languages. Although none of the indigenous languages has a word for dementia, derogatory words like *ara* (*mad*) and *nzuzu* (*unintelligent/stupid*) are used to describe dementia symptoms that are mistakenly attributed to aging in general. Since few Nigerians live to 65 years and reaching age 75 is worthy of celebration, most ailments that affect older people are thought to be a normal part of aging. Therefore, when older persons exhibit dementia symptoms, their friends and family are likely to dismiss it as part of being old. It is important to note that aging is not a cause of disease or health conditions, and it is certainly not a cause of dementia. There are several types of dementia, including Alzheimer's disease, with different causes and symptoms. Again, although one's risk for experiencing a form of dementia increases with age, dementia is not part of normal aging.

In addition to seeing dementia and aging as intertwined, some Nigerians describe people living with dementia as witches or wizards, or they may believe dementia symptoms are some sort of punishment from a supernatural being. There is a belief in Nigeria that if a person is known for doing evil things, such as being abusive to their children, stealing, or murdering someone, while they were younger, the person may be punished for his or her wrongdoing by the gods of the land or by God. The term *ife onye metalu* (*you reap what you sow*) often is applied to a person with dementia and is even more convincing to others if the older adult with dementia has been abandoned by his or her relatives. Some family members may prevent their relatives with dementia from being out in public because they think their actions will be embarrassing to the family.

These views about dementia may increase the risk of stigmatization (labeling people in a way that make them seem inferior). Stigma is a mark associated with disgrace or bad reputation, and it also can mean an unfair feeling of disapproval people have toward a thing or another person. Those with dementia in Nigeria are at risk of being perceived as inferior, an attitude similar to one applied to people with other mental health conditions like depression, schizophrenia, and bipolar disorder.

In addition, stigmatizing dementia attitudes can be strong enough to affect other cultural practices in a Nigerian community. For example, people may avoid marrying into a family with dementia in fear of becoming associated with a family known to include a member with mental disorder. Some also may fear that their future children may be at risk of having dementia, which, in turn, reduces the number of potential suitors for daughters who are old enough to marry.

DEMENTIA CAREGIVING

Nigerians are quite religious: About 50% of the population are Muslims, while the other 50% are Christians. Some Nigerians believe that praying for persons with dementia will be helpful in making them feel or become better. Some believe that in addition to the care provided for the persons with dementia, prayers and spiritual support from their religious leaders (e.g., pastors, priests) are important parts of caring for a person with dementia. Sometimes, because of how strong cultural influences can be, it is difficult to convince those with incorrect beliefs about dementia and its symptoms that they are wrong. Some Nigerians with better education and dementia awareness may think that trying to tell others that their perceptions of dementia are wrong is like fighting a losing battle. According to an RN and public health practitioner who is aware of the issue of dementia awareness in Nigeria, "If you can't beat them, join them." Therefore, if someone asks that a pastor be called when his or her relative is showing symptoms of dementia, this nurse feels it is better not to argue with the person, but instead to simply call the pastor. As much as she might want to tell them otherwise, she has decided it is just be easier to go with the flow and speak in the language and tone they understand, which in this case are attributing incorrect meanings to dementia.

Not all Nigerian views about dementia result in stigmatization, but some of these views may limit the quality of care persons with dementia receive from relatives who are their caregivers. Informal caregiving is the main type of care available for people with dementia in the country. The lack of formal long-term care (e.g., nursing homes) also means that informal caregiving is the only option for most families caring for someone with dementia. Similar to practices in developed and other developing countries, Nigerian women are more likely than men to become caregivers for their parents or relatives with dementia. They assume the role of caregivers for their parents, and if they are married, in the absence of sisters-in-law, they may also become caregivers for their husbands' parents with or without dementia. Most Nigerian women believe caring for their older relatives is the right thing to do; those who do not play the role of caregiver often report feeling a deep sense of guilt.

Additionally, the idea of having nursing homes in Nigeria or putting one's parents in a nursing home is culturally frowned upon by and unacceptable to many Nigerian families. Largely due to their general respect for elders, Nigerians believe strongly that putting one's parents in a nursing home is disrespectful. Families also do not want to be negatively viewed by the community as the adult children who abandoned their parents in their time of greatest need. In some Nigerian communities, these beliefs are so strongly ingrained that family members may fear that relocating their parents into nursing homes will result in something bad happening to the family members. Unless such views and reservations change in the country, there will be continuing reliance on informal caregiving for people with dementia as the older population increases. Overall, cultural beliefs surrounding dementia and caregiving may be helpful in some ways and limiting in others, but understanding the way beliefs impact any group's health and well-being can only help in designing better health promotion programs for them.

CONCLUSION

This brief essay is an attempt to provide an informative snapshot of dementia and caregiving in Nigeria and how health beliefs play a huge role in the way families deal with older members with dementia. Despite the immense burden dementia can create, it may be viewed as less important due to some of the meanings attributed to it, such as dismissing it as a natural part of old age. Other meanings, such as madness, a lack of intelligence, wizardry, witchcraft, and karma, have the potential to stigmatize those with dementia and their families. To address some of the issues relating to dementia and caregiving, it is recommended that policy makers in Nigeria pay closer attention to aging issues and increasing dementia awareness in the country. While Nigerians need to establish formal long-term care, they must also support informal dementia caregivers who are currently the main source of long-term care for older adults with dementia.

THE CHANGING NATURE OF HEALTH CARE AND SOCIAL IDENTITY AMONG OLDER ADULTS IN THE INDIAN HIMALAYAS

SENJOOTI ROY

Everybody says that this [herbal medicine] is old-fashioned; that these are modern times. They say, "You don't go to doctors, you are ganwar *[backward] people"..., but older adults remember that it [herbal medicine] works. It always works.*

—*Rani Devi, 65 years*

It [folk medicine] is our advisor ... our healer ... and astrologer. It tells us everything. That is what we believe.

—*Bhuvan Singh, 73 years*

Perched atop the stone steps leading to the carved wooden door of her home in a village at 8,400 feet in the Indian Himalayas, Rani Devi reminisced about the bygone days when people experienced minor illnesses that were easily cured through traditional means. Medicinal plants, many of which are endemic to the Himalayan region, were abundantly available; they were natural, free of cost, and had few if any known side effects. The result: a largely healthy village population whose residents possessed, at the very least, basic understanding and knowledge of indigenous herbal health care that they had inherited from older family members and village residents. For persistent illnesses that herbal medicine could not cure, folk medicine, with its presumed supernatural powers, came to the rescue.

Rani Devi was part of an intensive study of herbal and folk medicine in the Himalayan region of India. She is one of the more knowledgeable custodians of herbal health care in her village. She can treat not only minor ailments, such as fever, cold, stomach ache, cuts, and burns, but also knows how to join broken bones. She learned about medicinal plants and their various uses from her father and, later, her mother-in-law. She still prefers to use herbal health care, if available, as she does not trust modern medicine. Like some of her peers, she is skeptical of the quick-curing abilities of modern medicine and considers it to be "poisonous" because it can lead to severe side effects. She is also a staunch believer in folk medicine. In her village, supernatural powers are invoked through various means such as prayers, chants, meditation, and religious rituals; spirits, gods, and ruling planets are pacified; and the resultant effects on people's health are almost always positive. She values the relationships that the village residents have established with their natural and supernatural environment over generations and rues the disinterest and skepticism of the younger generations surrounding the herbal and folk health care systems. She hopes that they will learn to cherish and value their heritage before it is too late.

Although Rani Devi would greatly appreciate the revival of herbal health care and an increased respect for folk medicine, she understands that the nature of illnesses has undergone a drastic change from the past due to increased pollution, changing food habits, and sedentary lifestyles, among other factors. She acknowledges the need for modern medicine to treat illnesses such as heart disease, cancer, and hypertension that were unheard of until very recently in her rural village. She is also able to accept the fact that the younger generation, with increased access to technology, communication, and links to urban cities, favors modern medicine over other forms of health care for its relatively easy accessibility and quick cures. Although she is gradually making peace with changing attitudes and health behaviors, she is deeply disappointed with the negative effects of the changing nature of health care on the status of older adults in her village. In her community, as with most of Indian society, older adults are usually accorded higher status than other members of a family. They are traditionally considered the heads of household, they exert significant influence over family finances, they make or guide important decisions on behalf of younger family members, and they are believed to possess considerable wisdom due to their long life experience. Consequently, they are also trusted to be the most knowledgeable about indigenous herbal and folk health care. This status, however, is being challenged in recent times with the proliferation of modern health care in rural India, of which older adults in villages have very little knowledge and understanding.

Medical pluralism—the coexistence of multiple, competing health care systems in a country or society—has been the cornerstone of health care delivery in India for thousands of years. Some traditions originated there, including (a) Ayurveda, a highly individualized system aimed at balancing the body's five elements—air, water, fire, earth, and ether—with a combination of natural medicine, diet, exercise, and lifestyle practices; (b) yoga, a holistic physical, mental, and spiritual practice that focuses on breath regulation, physical discipline, meditation, and contemplation to improve physical and mental health; and (c) Siddha, similar to Ayurveda in its basic principles, with a focus on the analysis of pulse, urine, stool, eye color, voice, color of tongue, color and feel of skin, and status of digestive system. Others found their way into the country over time. One of these is Unani, a system that originated in Greece and was brought into India by Persians and Arabs. It is based on the seven components that make up the human body: the four elements, the four humors, temperament, organs, spirits, faculties, and functions. Another is homoeopathy, a medical treatment established by Samuel Hahnemann in Germany in the early 19th century based on the "law of similars" or "like cures like"—treating diseases with small doses of remedies which, when taken by healthy people, are capable of producing symptoms similar to the disease. Herbal health care, especially indigenous home remedies, are ingrained in the daily lives and cuisines of people; the use of common herbs and spices to treat minor ailments is an ordinary occurrence in most Indian households. Such medical traditions, however, vary according to the climate and geographical region that people inhabit, and rural India is highly dependent on these forms of health care.

Modern medicine is the most recent addition to India's health care system, having been introduced in the 19th century by the British. It enjoys wide acceptance in urban India, being delivered through both government-funded and private facilities. India currently has a government-funded, decentralized modern health care system with provision for referrals from primary care centers in villages to progressively larger and better equipped facilities at district headquarters, state capitals, and, finally, large research and teaching hospitals in metropolitan cities. Additionally, a plethora of private health care options are available. Although the country provides universal health care to its citizens, government-funded hospitals often are overcrowded and understaffed and lack resources. Consequently, anyone who can afford to pay for health care services prefers to visit private care facilities. India currently spends just over 1% of its gross domestic product on health care and records very high out-of-pocket spending.

Health insurance is expensive for most of the country's population, and awareness of insurance is very low. In such circumstances, herbal, traditional, and folk medical systems are the best (and, often, the only) health care option available to millions of people. In order to expand accessibility to traditional medical systems, the government of India established the Ministry of AYUSH in 2014 to promote education, research, and use of Ayurveda, yoga, naturopathy, Unani, Siddha, homoeopathy, and Sowa-Rigpa (traditional Tibetan medicine) by setting up additional hospitals and medical schools around the country. Outside of established medical facilities, older adults like Rani Devi (quoted in the introduction of this essay) are integral to the survival and perpetuation of herbal and folk systems. However, the lack of interest among younger generations, who are often the first or second generation to live in cities and engage closely with modern technologies and conveniences, is hastening the decline of herbal and folk systems of medicine as well as the status of older adults as the custodians of traditions and customs.

The impact of this declining status can be profound because some older adults internalize the negative messages to which they are exposed. Several participants in a study of herbal medicine show how these changes are occurring. For example,

67-year-old Usha believes that the younger generation is more intelligent than the older generation, as they have enjoyed the privilege of receiving formal education at school rather than "just life skills" handed down from one generation to another. Similarly, 72-year-old Ramlal believes that the younger generation is much smarter and better informed, so much so that the older generation now needs to look to them for advice about modern illnesses and associated medicines. He has often been told that he and his peers possess "outdated" ideas of medicines, medical treatments, and techniques. Sukhwan, an 82-year-old shopkeeper, feels that the rapid growth and establishment of modern medical facilities has made it "fashionable to take tablets" for the smallest of inconveniences. And Lilavati, a 73-year-old weaver, has tried and failed to convince her children and grandchildren about the benefits of herbal medicine. They argue that to treat a case of fever they would rather spend a little money on paracetamol (a fever and pain reliever similar to acetaminophen) that will provide relief in 15 minutes than make a trip to the jungle, look for herbs, boil them in water, and drink the bitter concoction over the next few days. All these older men and women have been told time and again that their knowledge, accumulated over centuries and handed down through many generations, is now irrelevant. Moreover, they are told they now must switch to modern medicine and be dependent on the younger generations to navigate its vast and complicated web. In the process, they gradually lose their relevance in society.

Although it may seem surprising that the social status of older adults could be so closely tied to the type of medicine they (and others) prefer, it is important to recognize the role that older adults have traditionally performed in society—that of inheriting orally and experientially transmitted medical and nonmedical knowledge; preserving this undocumented knowledge accurately; enriching the inherited knowledge over their own lifetimes; and, finally, handing it over to the next generation to repeat the process. Today, in light of new illnesses and medicines, this knowledge is becoming redundant and older Indians committed to their folk healing traditions are losing an important part of their social role and identity. India is now trying to revive and repopularize traditional medicines alongside modern health care. The outcome of these efforts, however, remains to be seen in light of the evolving nature of illnesses, a rapidly aging population, and a large youth population with more faith in modern medicine than traditional and folk systems.

6

HEALTH CARE SYSTEMS

JASLEEN K. CHAHAL | FRANK J. WHITTINGTON |
JANARDAN SUBEDI

INTRODUCTION

According to most Western conceptions, the medical/health care system comprises a single, institutionalized, bureaucratic system of hospitals, clinics, and agencies providing health care services—the Western biomedical model or, as it is generically called, the modern medical system. The reality is that although the modern medical system is the dominant form of health care around the world, other approaches to health care coexist and, in some cases, are preferred by those who know them best. This phenomenon is called **medical pluralism**, which is the coexistence of two or more institutionalized forms of health care delivery that are available to, and can be utilized by, a population. Research in societies with medical pluralism indicates that these competing systems may be used simultaneously, such as the use of conventional or modern medicine and complementary and alternative medicine (CAM; to be discussed later in this chapter), or alternatively, a particular system is used exclusively (Subedi, 1989; Subedi & Subedi, 1993; Wade, Chao, Kronenberg, Cushman, & Kalmuss, 2008). However, in many societies, modern medicine is promoted above the other forms of medicine, and its practice is upheld by the law (Helman, 2007).

TYPES OF HEALTH CARE SYSTEMS

Various classification schemes have been used to describe health systems around the world, but F.L. Dunn's (1976) classification scheme is well referenced. He describes three types of health care services or systems: (a) the local system of informal folk practitioners and health care services, which he calls folk medicine;

(b) the regional system, involving codified, traditional health care services—for example, Ayurvedic, acupuncture, chiropractic, Unani, and Chinese medicines delivered by trained professionals in their practice, which is called traditional medicine; and (c) the professional, bureaucratic, or modern system of health care services, the so-called modern medicine. Health care systems in different parts of the world can be categorized into one of these three broad types: folk, traditional, and modern medicine.

Folk Medicine

This type of medicine has existed since the earliest times. Limited knowledge and control over what exists beyond the present, visible world appear to be the basis of folk beliefs. **Folk medicine** comprises a belief-based system that is informal and passed down through families from one generation to the other by word of mouth, observation, and experience. Since this system is belief-based, the explanations for illness causation and its subsequent treatment do not fit within the framework of scientific medicine, but instead are shaped by the social and cultural realities of the indigenous groups from which they are derived. Therefore, this body of beliefs and practices usually involves cultural, religious, and often supernatural explanations for illnesses and treatment options designed for individuals but often targeted at, and intended for, the health of the entire family or even the community.

Folk medicine practitioners are recognized by many names: *shaman* (originally used in Russia but also applied to many other cultures), *curandero* (Mexico), spirit medium, native healers, *kahuna* (Hawaii), *dhami-jhankri* (Nepal), and so forth. As with modern medical practitioners, each folk practitioner has a different and specific treatment approach based on the etiology and explanation for each illness. Thus, folk treatment may involve prayer, healing and cleansing ceremonies, religious rituals, cultural rites, medicinal herbs, hot and cold foods, and other belief-based practices. Animals (such as snakes, toads, eels, and earthworms) and animal parts or by-products are often believed to have healing properties and are used to treat certain illnesses and conditions (Huff, 2002). Traditional medicine involves some of these practices as well.

Traditional Medicine

The term traditional medicine has been used differently by writers and researchers. Many have used this term incorrectly to discuss all medicine other than or prior to modern medicine. The use of traditional medicine in this chapter refers to what Dunn's (1976) classification calls regional or scholarly traditional (folk medicine being nonscholarly traditional). This form of medicine also dates back centuries and to the earliest societies (such as Ayurveda in India and Chinese herbal practices, both of which originated well over 2,000 years ago or BCE [Before the Common Era]), whereas others (e.g., homeopathy, chiropractic, osteopathy) are much more recent developments, originating in the West in the 18th and 19th centuries. In fact, the founders of homeopathy and osteopathy were doctors trained in modern medicine.

According to the World Health Organization (WHO, 2013), **traditional medicine** refers to health knowledge, skills, and practices based on explanations indigenous to a culture (whether explicable or not) that are used to prevent, diagnose, and treat a wide variety of illnesses. Traditional medicine covers a diverse range of practices and therapies that vary not only from country to country but within countries (Table 6.1). These may include special diet, plants and herbs, minerals, animal-based medicines, lotions, ointments, and a wide array of other therapies (including music and massage).

Traditional medicine is developed around a body of beliefs and explanations in which illness and disease are seen as natural products of bodily imbalances (system-based). Therefore, treatment involves restoring the body's system to its natural equilibrium or balance and, in doing so, preventing future occurrences of the same illness and other illnesses as well.

Unlike folk medical practitioners who learn their skills through informal sources or claim special powers by birth or religion, most (though not all) practitioners of traditional medicine are educated and trained in specialized educational institutions offering degrees in the particular type of traditional medicine. In these institutions, although the instruction does not follow the framework of scientific medicine per se, it does have its own understanding and rationale about the body and the elements that help maintain balance and health (e.g., "humors," magnetic fields, dislocation of bones and viscera, loss or lack of adequate naturally occurring chemicals and water to maintain the body's optimal system).

Although traditional medicine is not based on belief alone, it can be closely related to the local culture from which it emerges and may often include elements of belief derived from religion and the host culture. Unlike folk medicine, however, traditional methods of treatment are considered by their advocates and practitioners to have a scientific (broadly defined) basis (Dunn, 1976). For example, acupuncture has an ancient history, dating back thousands of years to the use of sharpened stones and bones and officially documented as early as 100 BCE (White & Ernst, 2004). The continued refinement and codification of the philosophy and practice of acupuncture has resulted in increasingly precise understanding of the acupuncture points. This more formalized and clinical approach to medicine differentiates it from folk medicine; the focus of acupuncture on balance and flow of energy within the body, rather than on germs, clearly distinguishes it from modern medicine.

Modern Medicine

According to Weiss and Lonnquist (2012), one of the most significant events in the development of modern, scientific biomedicine was the discovery of Louis Pasteur's **germ theory of disease** in the late 1800s. This theory postulated that diseases could be traced to specific causal agents, such as bacteria, viruses,

TABLE 6.1 Characteristics of Several Important Traditional Medicine Systems

Name	Origin and Developing Nation	Characteristics of Theory or Application	Current Role or Status
TCM	China	Based on yinyang and wuxing concepts	Both TCM and conventional medicine exist at every gradation of the health care system, and both are covered under public and private insurance.
	Thousands of years ago	A TCM formula includes a group of various drugs that function together congenially to achieve a synergistic effect.	
		A classic formula is composed of four elements—monarch, minister, assistant, and servant—according to their roles in the formula.	There is a TCM division in most ordinary hospitals, and TCM services are supplied for both inpatients and outpatients.
			TCM is attracting increasing attention, interest, and acceptance around the world.
Ayurveda	India	Ayurveda uses natural elements to eradicate the main cause of the disease by reinstating balance.	More than 400,000 Ayurveda practitioners are registered.
	Pre-Vedic epochs (4000 BCE–1500 BCE)	The Ayurvedic philosophy is to live a healthy life to avoid the appearance of imbalance and unnecessary pain.	The Indian government has an official body to ensure Ayurveda's educational efforts, quality, and practice.
		In many Ayurvedic treatments, multiple herbs are united in a special quotient to create an ideal therapeutic effect and lessen the toxicity.	

(continued)

TABLE 6.1 Characteristics of Several Important Traditional Medicine Systems (continued)

Name	Origin and Developing Nation	Characteristics of Theory or Application	Current Role or Status
Unani medicine	India Derived from Greco-Arabic medicine dating back 2,500 years and developed during the Arab civilization	It treats a person's body, mind, and soul as a whole. Unani looks upon the human body as a single unit, which consists of four basic elements that have four disparate temperaments, respectively. A person's temperament reflects his or her physical characteristics and natural disposition. Disproportion in temperament makes the human body susceptible to many illnesses.	Unani is accepted by India as meeting the health care needs of people and has gained formal status. Unani has been acknowledged by the WHO as an alternative health care system. Unani is one of the most important traditional medicine systems.
Kampo (traditional Japanese medicine)	Japan Introduced from China via the Korean peninsula in the fifth or sixth century	Developed over the past 1,400 years and has been organically unified with Japanese original therapies Treats every human being as a complete and self-controlled whole in which body and mind impact mutually Diseases are thought to originate from the disorders of psyche and soma, and herbals are trusted to affect the soul and the body equally. Therapy places emphasis on the sufferer as a whole instead of on the illness.	Incorporated into the health care system in Japan All citizens can use Kampo herbal formulas approved by the government.

(continued)

TABLE 6.1 Characteristics of Several Important Traditional Medicine Systems (continued)

Name	Origin and Developing Nation	Characteristics of Theory or Application	Current Role or Status
TKM, SCM	SCM is a division of Korean traditional medicine First introduced in the mid-19th century	SCM classifies persons into four Sasang types—tae-yang, so-yang, tae-eum, and so-eum—according to his or her inborn features. SCM is holistic and theoretically similar to personalized medicine. Supplies individualized and constitution-specific treatments for various problems	Although the conventional health care organization is quite good in Korea, 86% of people still employ SCM. Traditional medicine doctors can supply Korean SCM both in private and public hospitals. Both national medical insurance and private insurance cover Korean SCM services.
Traditional aboriginal medicine	Australia	Indigenous peoples of Australia believe that health problems have three types of causes: natural bodily causes, harmful spirits, and witchcraft.	Currently, there is only one national folk organization in operation. During 2010–2011, 32.1% of the chief indigenous health care organizations in Australia provided some kind of traditional medicine services. Because of colonization, traditional aboriginal medicine is in danger of becoming extinct.

(continued)

TABLE 6.1 Characteristics of Several Important Traditional Medicine Systems (continued)

Name	Origin and Developing Nation	Characteristics of Theory or Application	Current Role or Status
Traditional medicine in Africa	Africa	Traditional medicine doctors treat patients holistically.

They generally seek to recombine the mental and social equipoise of sufferers according to social relationships and rules.

The accessibility of traditional medicine is one of the most important reasons for its popularity across Africa.

Traditional medicine exemplifies respect for the cultural heritage. | Eighty percent of African people use traditional medicine, either by itself or with conventional medicine.

Up to 80% of Ghanaians and Ethiopians depend on traditional medicine for their main health care demands.

Ghana's traditional medical system has been integrated into the national health care system and, therefore, it is comparatively well organized. |
| Russian herbal medicine | Russia

10th century | Due to the special geographical environment of Russia, Russian herbal therapy has collected and adopted traditional medicine methods that were introduced from Europe and Asia.

The Russian Federation follows the State Pharmacopoeia of the USSR; 32 of 83 individual plant monographs are found only in this pharmacopoeia. | Herbal therapy is a formal and independent department of medicine in Russia; thus, herbal medicinal products are regarded as official remedies.

A recent survey shows that 14% of the Russian people frequently use herbal remedies and 44% use them occasionally. |

BCE, Before the Common Era; SCM, Sasang constitutional medicine; TCM, traditional Chinese medicine; TKM, traditional Korean medicine; WHO, World Health Organization.

Source: Adapted from Yuan, H., Ma, Q., Ye, L., & Piao, G. (2016). The traditional medicine and modern medicine from natural products. *Molecules, 21*(5), 559. doi:10.3390/molecules21050559

parasites, and so forth (collectively, germs). Prior to this understanding, lay and professional treatments evolved through a multitude of approaches that were not necessarily scientific and included cultural and often supernatural explanations. One of the earliest attempts to formulate principles of medical treatment based on rational ideas, natural causes, and rejection of supernatural explanations was made by the Greek physician Hippocrates (400 BCE), who is known today for the **Hippocratic Oath** (the foundation of contemporary medical ethics), which physicians and other health professionals take before entering practice (Weiss & Lonnquist, 2012).

By 1881, the wide acceptance of germ theory was opening a new era in modern medicine (Cockerham, 2017). Attention became focused on recognizing a particular disease based on the recurrent symptoms it produced, identifying the agent that caused the conditions, and discovering ways to eradicate the disease-causing agent and thereby cure the person of the illness. Thus, **modern medicine** evolved into a symptom-based, curative model of health care.

As emphasis on natural causes of disease grew, the human body became an object of observation and analysis. Hospitals, clinics, and schools were established to train physicians and treat patients. According to Cockerham (2017, p. 9), "Disease was no longer considered an entity outside of the existing boundaries of knowledge, but an object to be studied, confronted scientifically, and controlled." The discovery of natural causes of disease led to improvements in public health measures that emphasized unhealthy social conditions and lifestyles that also could lead to a host of negative health outcomes. These advances were furthered by the discovery in 1928 of penicillin, the first antibiotic. Although many modern pharmacological treatments had their origins in herbology (the use of plants for medicinal purposes), during the mid-20th century drugs to treat a variety of conditions became mass-produced as the primary method to control or cure diseases. By the late 20th century, as chronic diseases replaced infectious diseases as major threats to health, modern medical practitioners were called upon to deal with health problems that extended beyond germs to include additional causal factors—environment, diet, lifestyle, demographic conditions, and genetic predispositions (Cockerham, 2017). These factors represent **social determinants of health**, which are individual and social conditions that people experience across their life course, resulting in varying health outcomes due to inequities in economic, social, and health-related resources (Baker et al., 2017).

Although modern medicine remains the world's dominant system of health care, the type of system found in a particular country is shaped by its social and political culture, history, availability of economic and other resources, and degree of governmental involvement in the organization and financing of health services. Together, these factors determine how health services are implemented and financed (Sanders, 2012). In some countries, health care is believed to be a fundamental right (at least for its citizens), whereas in other countries, health care is seen as a service to be purchased, just as any other service (Ogden, 2012). Four very different approaches to organizing and financing health care are now described.

MODELS OF ORGANIZING AND FINANCING MODERN MEDICINE

In his ambitious and influential study of global systems of health care, journalist T. R. Reid (2009) describes four main models of organizing and financing modern health care: (a) the Bismarck model; (b) the Beveridge model; (c) the national health insurance (NHI) model; and (d) the out-of-pocket model. Sorting out the specific differences among these four models and understanding the unique ways they have been modified and combined in different countries is a huge task that is not possible in this chapter. It is helpful, however, to keep in mind several major policy decisions that underlie the design of any particular health care system.

First is the issue of universal or targeted coverage. Will all citizens be covered by a particular health system, or will only certain groups be ensured access? The United States does not have universal health care, but it does have health insurance coverage for eligible people who are aged 65 and older (a program called **Medicare**) or who meet certain health criteria (e.g., have end-stage renal disease). Medicare currently provides a fairly new publicly mandated system of private insurance that is available for purchase by nearly all citizens. This scheme, created in 2009 through the **Affordable Care Act**, is more popularly known as *Obamacare* after its chief sponsor and advocate. However, in the decade since its passage, critics have challenged the program in court and have attempted to weaken or abolish it through legislative action, with mixed success.

A second fundamental issue is how the health care system is financed. In some countries, taxes paid by everyone help to pay for health care; in other places, individuals pay out of pocket or make contributions through their employers, and some health care models utilize a combination of all of these. Whether a system is publicly financed or not depends a great deal on whether health care is considered a right or a privilege as well as the overall economic wealth of the country. In places where health care is considered a privilege, individuals are expected to take responsibility for their own health care costs; where health care is considered a right, some level of public funding guarantees that all citizens have some access to basic health care.

A third feature that distinguishes different approaches to health care is whether there is a single payer. In a **single-payer system**, one entity (government-run) administers the health care system, collecting all fees and paying all health care costs, such as in the United Kingdom. In contrast to a single-payer system, in the United States, thousands of entities are involved in the administration of health care, including insurance companies, government agencies (e.g., the Department of Veterans Affairs), individual and corporate health care providers, and billing agencies.

The fourth distinction among health care systems is the role of private ownership and the possibility of profit. In some countries, health care providers are employed by the government; in other countries, it is possible for individual physicians and for health care organizations like hospitals to compete for customers, set their own prices, and make a profit. Although it is possible to differentiate health care systems along all of these dimensions, several features are often found in combination. For example, the term national health insurance typically refers to a health system in which health care is considered a right of citizenship, some level of access is guaranteed for everyone, and public funds (gathered through taxation) help to support the system. More fully developed national health care systems often use a single payer.

Reid's (2009) discussion of the four primary models of modern health care gives a more historic picture of the different ways in which health care systems are organized. As we can see in the following sections, whereas many countries have adopted one of these models, the United States is unique in that all four of these models are represented within the American health care system. American military veterans receive care organized similar to the Beveridge model; older people covered by Medicare have a plan that is similar to the NHI model; Americans with health insurance through their employers or Obamacare are familiar with a form of the Bismarck model; and the rest of the American population—often referred to as *the uninsured*—is operating on the out-of-pocket system (Reid, 2009). Subsequent sections serve as a brief introduction to each model and how it relates to existing health care systems around the world.

The Bismarck Model

The **Bismarck model** is the oldest health care model. Created and implemented in 1881 by Prussian Chancellor Otto von Bismarck (at the time Prussia was a powerful Germanic state that became a dominant force in the creation of modern Germany), this model was intended as a social insurance plan that would be used to protect all citizens when they became sick, were injured or disabled, or experienced health problems in old age (Cichon & Normand, 1994). Although it was a universal health plan, the model required joint contributions from both employers and employees to create a large pool of money (the **sickness fund**) that was used to pay expenses of individuals who needed medical attention. These contributions were deducted from employees' payroll checks and matched by their employers.

This may sound a lot like the currently most common health care financing system in the United States, where a good job might come with health insurance benefits, but it is drastically different. A fundamental difference between the U.S. system and the Bismarck model is that the money allocated to the sickness fund in the latter model is redistributed to cover the health of everyone in the country, not just the worker (and the worker's family members) who paid into the system. This model is consistent with some of the ideas behind a NHI approach in that every person has the right to health care, funded not by individuals but through a taxation and redistribution system.

Which countries have health care systems based on this model? Germany, the Netherlands, Switzerland, Japan, and even some countries in South America have adopted the Bismarck model as their own (Lameire, Joffe, & Wiedemann, 1999; Reid, 2009). This approach provides everyone with health care, but the overall health care system and health insurance plans do not profit, even though a majority of the hospitals and physicians' offices tend to be private. For example, Japan has more hospitals that are viewed as private than does the United States, even though Japan has a strong collective component to its Bismarck-based model for financing health care (Reid, 2009).

The Beveridge Model

Unlike the employer-/employee-financed Bismarck model, the **Beveridge model** offers an alternative to paying for health care (Reid, 2009). Proposed by the British social reformer Lord William Beveridge and implemented shortly after World War II, the U.K. National Health Service (NHS) capitalized on the general postwar collective feeling in Great Britain (composed of England, Scotland, and Wales) that helping each other, including providing health care for every citizen, was a political and moral duty. This notion appears to have had its roots in the deep collective commitment to national, rather than individual, survival and well-being the war had required of the British. Enacted in the United Kingdom (Great Britain plus Northern Ireland) in 1948, this model of financing and providing health care might be thought of as a fully developed public (or national) health care system (as opposed to NHI, in which some level of public funding is mandated but the system might be run by private or public entities) since the government employs most of the care providers and is the only payer. In countries utilizing the Beveridge model, payment for health care is very different from that in systems where patients pay bills upon receiving approved services and are later reimbursed for a percentage set by the government or by an insurance company. For example, in the United States, some must initially pay for care or medications and later file for reimbursement by their insurance companies. The British NHS has an integrated care model that is implemented across primary, acute, and community-based care where many types of care (including physician visits, surgical procedures, and diagnostic tests) are free to eligible patients (all citizens and permanent residents); some specialized services, such as eye tests and dental care; for most people, prescription drugs; and most personal care, carry an additional charge. For services that are free of charge, the patient never receives or even sees a bill. However, the patient might have to wait days, weeks, or months for nonemergency services.

Since the government pays for the national health care system, it only makes sense that they would also be responsible for deciding what services are offered, who can perform them, and how much they should cost. As a result of the lack of provider competition under this model (in contrast to capitalist, market-based systems where providers compete for clients and set their own prices), the NHS in the United Kingdom and the Beveridge model have been associated with lower costs and are thought by some to be the "epitome of tax-financed public health insurance" plans (Musgrove, 2000, p. 846).

Giving so much control to the government may be unappealing to some whose political beliefs and values lead them to oppose collective solutions to social needs.

Government-run NHI is also sometimes criticized as providing poor-quality care and no choice for consumers. Proponents of this position suggest that the competition among providers in a capitalist system (where they can benefit financially) leads to better quality and faster technological advances. This debate cannot be resolved here, but it is worthwhile to note that citizens of the United Kingdom report relatively high levels of satisfaction with the care they receive and the system that provides it. According to researchers using data from the British Social Survey of 2017, the British people remain strongly committed to the principles underlying the NHS, and, following a decade (1999–2009) of steadily increasing satisfaction with the way it is operating (from around 40% support in 1999 to 70% in 2009), the past several years (2009–2017) have shown a slight decline to around 60% (Robertson, Appleby, & Evans, 2018).

Although it might be counterintuitive, it is also worth noting that some private clinics and hospitals do exist in the United Kingdom, where consumers may receive private care at generally higher prices and with somewhat shorter waits. Such physicians and hospitals can collect partial reimbursements from the government for selected procedures that meet the service and cost criteria set by the NHS. Otherwise, private patients must pay out of pocket. Even in a country with a universal-coverage system, some degree of medical pluralism is a reality.

If the Beveridge model sounds familiar, it is probably from listening to news about the British royal family, including royal births and general health problems. Although the Beveridge model originally was developed for Great Britain, several other countries, including Italy, Sweden, Spain, Norway, Finland, Denmark, New Zealand, Hong Kong, and Cuba, have adopted varying versions of this health care model (Lameire et al., 1999).

The National Health Insurance Model

Aspects of both the Bismarck and the Beveridge models can be found in the third health care model, known as the **national health insurance (NHI) model**. Canada, Taiwan, and South Korea are excellent examples of countries with existing NHI models of care (Reid, 2009). NHI is similar to the Bismarck model in that health providers are private and funding is provided through private, nonprofit insurers, but they differ because the government is the single payer, as in the Beveridge model. Health care professionals do not have to work for the government, although the government does determine what it will pay for care, exercising excellent control over costs. A major advantage of this approach is that it utilizes both the private and public sectors to provide health care to individuals. A major disadvantage, at least in the Canadian system, is unusually long waiting times for some procedures. So cost is controlled, but at the expense of access. However, the NHI system in Taiwan shows high patient satisfaction with affordable and modern medicine, without wait times similar to the single-payer systems of the United Kingdom and Canada (Cheng, 2015). This suggests that the country-specific differences in customizing their health system based on the overarching framework of the health care models may provide improved outcomes in terms of patient satisfaction, access, affordability, and quality of patient care.

The Out-of-Pocket Model

The final form of health care, the **out-of-pocket model**, can be found in developing nations with no formal health care system as well as in most developed countries as an alternative or supplement to the dominant system of payment. This particular model provides care to individuals who can afford to pay for needed health services and procedures, and, of course, it often denies care to those who cannot pay and are not otherwise eligible for the available payment programs.

Paying out of your own pocket can have several meanings depending on the country and culture. In some countries, like the United States, the patient will be billed after receiving care or must pay immediately after the service has been rendered. In other countries, such as India, an individual who is unable to pay in advance and in cash for the cost of an anticipated length of stay in a hospital, plus potential supplies, medicine, and deposits for expected procedures is refused admission to the hospital. In some parts of the world, most often in rural regions of Africa, Asia, and South America, trained medical professionals are not readily available, and economic resources are often scarce, so paying in cash may seem unreasonable. In such regions, people often seek care from shamans, healers, or other folk practitioners or they use homemade treatments that have been passed down from one generation to another. These forms of health care fit the folk and traditional models discussed earlier in this chapter, but they also must be purchased in some manner with personal resources. Some families in rural areas who do not have money are forced to trade goods, such as animals, textiles, and produce, or to provide labor, such as farming or child care, in order to repay their debt (Reid, 2009). If one does not have the money and has no goods to trade, then the only alternative is to go without the needed care.

Some would argue that an out-of-pocket model of financing care is unfair to the poor and that individuals should not be turned away from receiving care based solely on the fact that they are unable to pay. Others might say that paying taxes into a general health fund for all citizens is not fair to those who work hard to make sure that they can afford care if they or their family members need it in the future. Regardless of which argument is favored, the important question is what type of health care model offers the best care to the most people at the most reasonable cost. But underneath this question is a set of very challenging decisions: Who defines best care? Who decides which citizens should be covered by the health care system? Who should pay for the cost of care? Cultural values (which vary within and among nations) have helped to fuel ongoing and heated debates about all these questions.

HEALTH SYSTEMS AND OLDER PEOPLE

It is not obvious how Dunn's scheme for classifying health care into folk, traditional, and modern medicine—or even Reid's four organizational models of modern, biomedical health care—relates to older people. An easy assumption is that older people, especially in developing regions, are drawn to the practice of folk or traditional medicine more than modern medicine. This might be based on the stereotyped connection between old age and old ways, between age and traditional values and practices. Since we learn and use culture throughout our lives, we often develop strong traditions as we age. Therefore, the type of health care that is preferred and sought can depend far more on what is dominant in our society or tribe, especially as we mature into adulthood (Haug, Wykle, & Namazi, 1989). That is, our birth cohort is far more likely to influence our choice of medical provider than our age. If a trip to the doctor, a referral to a medical specialist, and a stay in the hospital for surgical removal of a diseased body part (i.e., the modern medical model of care) is what our parents did and what we have done all our lives, we will not be inclined to seek or accept folk practitioners in later life. An Italian who has benefitted from tonsillectomy and appendectomy in early life is likely to accept hip replacement and cancer chemotherapy in old age. Conversely, an older Mexican farmer who has frequented the local *curandero* (folk healer) all his life is likely to continue to do so and shun trips to town to see a medical doctor. These choices are culture- and nation-specific and also have little to do with age.

It also must be kept in mind that the nature of health problems changes with age, from mostly acute (curable) to mostly chronic (incurable), so the type of care provided may need to change as well. One might assume, given their highly advanced medical capacity, that European nations, Australia, and the United States all have solved issues related to caring for older adults with chronic conditions. However, even among these nations we can see a variation in the aging experience and related health outcomes based on the health care model adopted by that nation. For example, 36% of older adults in the United States are reported to have three or more chronic conditions, compared to only 13% in New Zealand; 55% of Americans aged 65 and older report taking four or more prescriptions daily, compared to 22% of older adults in France; and a higher proportion of older U.S. citizens have experienced economic vulnerability (25%), compared to those residing in Norway (3%); see Osborn, Doty, Moulds, Sarnak, and Shah (2017). Trends related to cost and timeliness of access to care issues for older adults also vary based on medical expenses, length of waiting time for a doctor's appointment, and avoidable ED visits. The 2017 Commonwealth Fund International Health Policy Survey of Older Adults found that 23% of older adults in the United States had cost-related access to care issues, compared to only 5% or less in France, Norway, Sweden, and the United Kingdom. Only 7% of individuals 65 and older in New Zealand waited longer than 6 days for an appointment when sick, compared to 34% in Germany, 29% in Canada, and 18% in the United States; and although older adults in the United States waited fewer days for a sick visit, 15% experienced an avoidable ED visit, compared to 11% in Canada and less than 8% in Australia, France, Germany, the Netherlands, New Zealand, Norway, Sweden, Switzerland, and the United Kingdom (Osborn et al., 2017). These data show that, even though developed nations have had a longer time to adjust to the health needs of an aging population, both developed and developing nations have unique challenges to shift the focus from curative treatment to another form of health care that will improve health outcomes, quality of life with chronic conditions, and the overall aging and health care experience.

One illustration of how the curative model is no longer adequate for a growing population of older people is provided by Chahal's essay at the end of Chapter 7, "Palliative Care: Quality of Life at Its End," describing the expansion of **palliative care**, which focuses on relieving pain, preventing suffering, and a holistic approach to the medical, social, psychological, and spiritual needs of the patient. Whereas palliative care can be appropriate for any stage of dealing with disease, it often is offered during the last stages of life and helps to support the patient and the patient's family in their decisions about how to live fully until the very end of life. This is quite a different approach from one focused on treatment and cure. An example of this can be seen with the growing opioid epidemic. The field of medicine has implemented a change in recognizing pain as an acute to a chronic condition. This change has resulted in a shift from curative treatment toward palliative and alternative methods of pain and symptom management that engage patients and caregivers in a shared decision-making model of patient care. **Shared decision-making** is "a collaborative process that allows patients, or their surrogates, and clinicians to make health care decisions together, taking into account the best scientific evidence available, as well as the patient's values, goals, and preferences" (Kon, Davidson, Morrison, Danis, & White, 2016, p. 191). The idea of each patient sharing responsibility with the practitioner for his or her own care is antecedent of the notion that patients actually should take charge of and direct that care.

THE PATIENT IN CHARGE OF CARE

Our focus on patients and the role they play in their care will begin with an overview of medical consumerism, move to a brief discussion of health literacy, and conclude with an explanation of how the consumerist trend in Western societies has fueled a growing number of patients who are highly educated, well-informed on scientific and especially medical issues, and not only demanding partners in the health care process but seeking to become directors of their own care.

Medical Consumerism

As education levels in developed countries have risen over the past century and mass communication has grown into a daily part of the information flow in these (and now most) societies, health information is increasingly available. As part of the so-called consumer revolution, average buyers of all services (including health care) are seeking to become more informed about the personal risks and social impacts of their purchases (Potter & McKinley, 2005). In addition, the traditional power differential between doctor and patient and its resulting asymmetrical relationship, according to Shorter (1991), had largely ended by the 1960s. Today that relationship is being questioned even more closely by patients in developed societies: before office visits, patients do their own research online (e.g., with health education websites such as WebMD or MedlinePlus) and ask their doctors probing questions about the relative effectiveness of alternative procedures, the likely prognosis, and, of course, in those societies without state-provided care, the cost (Barker, 2008). Studies of the impact of Internet use by patients on their relationship with their physician in a variety of countries (United Kingdom, United States, Austria, and Australia) show patients reporting feeling more empowered in the management of their own health, less dependent on their provider, and, if their physician was receptive to discussing the Internet information, more satisfied with the doctor–patient relationship (Tan & Goonawardene, 2017). Although these trends began with educated, middle-class patients in developed countries, we may hypothesize that as more educated age cohorts grow old and Internet access becomes almost universal, the power of medical consumerism will grow.

Such questioning of medical authority has a reciprocal relationship with four major trends: (a) a dramatic increase in the health literacy of most people of developed nations and many in the developing world; (b) a rise in alternative health practices and practitioners (so-called **complementary and alternative medicine or CAM**); (c) greater emphasis on *health promotion and disease prevention*; and (d) a heightened role for educated and empowered consumers to have more responsibility for their health care decisions and actions and for the management and consequences of those actions. So, first we explore health literacy and how medical pluralism (discussed earlier) is becoming a much more common health care strategy, even among older people.

Health Literacy

Health literacy has been defined as "the degree to which individuals have the capacity to obtain, communicate, process, and understand basic health information and services needed to make appropriate health decisions" (Parnell, McCulloch, Mieres, & Edwards, 2014).

In the modern medical model, at least, these abilities play an essential role in a person utilizing health services, adhering to medical advice, and achieving good health-related outcomes. The concept of health literacy is embedded in the culture and clinical and public health settings in Europe and North America. Yet, it has been estimated that about 100 million people in *developed* nations are considered to be "functionally illiterate," indicating that this is still a relevant concern for both developed and developing nations (Kickbusch, 2001, p. 290).

In countries in the earlier stages of the demographic transition, where infections and mortality rates are extremely high, it is more effective to provide information that improves functional health literacy (the ability to follow basic instructions) than to explain the scientific basis of the disease or treatment. However, people who cannot read or write their native language may be fully knowledgeable about the local medical system (folk or traditional), including the causes and cures of disease and the best local practitioner to visit when sick. That is, they can be said to be "locally health literate," even if not in the Western sense.

In all countries where older adults have high rates of chronic conditions, the ability to understand medical advice, answer providers' questions, take the appropriate dosage of medications, and make decisions about different types of treatment all take on heightened importance. Improving health literacy for older adults would allow them to take a more active role in managing their own chronic conditions, preventing disease-related complications, and decreasing their risk of comorbidities (i.e., multiple chronic conditions).

Despite the apparent contradiction, both patient adherence (following doctors' orders) and autonomy (asserting personal control) are useful adjuncts to care. Given physicians' limited ability to treat and even manage many of the interrelated problems of old age and the difficulty and cost of being seen by a doctor in the first place, personal responsibility for managing illnesses and for directing care may be an important component of a healthier, longer life.

Complementary and Alternative Medicine

As mentioned at the beginning of this chapter, a clear trend in Western developed societies is toward medical pluralism. With the rise of health consumerism and ready availability of health-related information (both accurate and inaccurate), people have become more skeptical, even of modern medicine, its practitioners, and pharmaceutical companies. In this pluralistic atmosphere, scientific discoveries are considered by many people as no more likely true than nonscientific claims. Under a constant assault of marketing puffery and misleading claims, consumers often do not know whom to believe or what to think. Therefore, many feel free to choose from the marketplace any nostrum, diet, or therapy that appeals to them, even if offered by nonmedical or folk practitioners. Of course, some of these alternative treatments or approaches do have value—although many do not—and the medical establishment (in the United States, that is the National Center for Complementary and Alternative Medicine of the National Institutes of Health) is increasingly studying and testing the efficacy and safety of a variety of therapies. These therapies fall into two general categories: natural products such as dietary supplements and mind/body practices such as massage therapy, acupuncture (a traditional medical practice described earlier), aromatherapy, and tai chi (Barnes, Bloom, & Nahin, 2008).

CAM use has also grown more popular among older people. One study of an American Medicare population (Astin, Pelletier, Marie, & Haskell, 2000) found more than four in 10 seniors used at least one of the 10 types of CAM the researchers asked about. Some of the conditions for which older people are most likely to use CAM are arthritis, cancer, mental health, and sleep disorders (Arcury et al., 2013).It is interesting to note that consumers who use CAM therapies do not always subscribe to the classical model of patient compliance with doctors' orders. In one study of medication use by older people in Finland (Lumme-Sandt, Hervonen, & Jylha, 2000), the authors reported that "the respondents who talked about the natural products they used seemed to be more active than others with respect to their medication. They said explicitly that they did not obey doctors' orders" (p. 1847). In other words, a segment of older adults in Finland are choosing to go to the doctor for their medical problems but then are deciding for themselves whether to follow a doctor's advice or perhaps self-medicate with some other therapy that was not prescribed. Similarly, CAM users in the United States do not always report their use of alternative therapies to their physicians due to concerns about physicians' potentially negative attitudes toward CAM, the fact that physicians do not ask, and the conviction that physicians do not need to know (Arcury et al., 2013).

Cochran (2002, p. 74) suggests that older people, like younger adults, use CAM to assert their beliefs about the ineffectiveness of biomedicine. In his study of two age cohorts of older adults in Georgia (the United States), Cochran found that CAM users were quite similar to people who used biomedicine in that both held a range of views about the nature of health and how to achieve it. He asserts, "The CAM user cannot be characterized as some aberrant lay consumer with beliefs that are divergent from the mainstream; rather, the CAM user is squarely in the mainstream of belief about health" (p. 284). Cochran demonstrates that not only do older people differ in their definitions of health, but they also simultaneously subscribe to alternative means of achieving it, lending further support for our contention that medical pluralism is becoming more common in most Western nations. It may be that population aging is presenting all practitioners—biomedical and traditional—with chronic disease challenges that neither so far has been able to solve, or even to manage with only its own tool kit.

Health Promotion and Self-Care

As noted earlier in this chapter, the major health challenge that accompanies global aging is the increased burden of chronic noncommunicable diseases (CNCDs). Recently, an expert panel identified the 20 most critical steps that should be taken to address CNCDs (Daar et al., 2007). These include: (a) promoting healthy lifestyles and choices through education and public engagement; (b) promoting lifelong physical activity; (c) better understanding of environmental and cultural factors that affect health behaviors; and (d) developing strategies to integrate management of CNCDs into health care systems. The ambitious goals and specific recommendations put forth by this group of experts call for changes at the level of public health, public policy, and health care systems; however, many have implications for individual health behaviors and actions, with a clear focus on helping people *help themselves* live better and healthier, not just longer.

The self-care theme is echoed in several international health care initiatives for older adults. Within the United States, a heightened emphasis on health promotion and disease prevention is evidenced in a host of new programs seeking to maximize health by preventing falls, promoting good mental health, and enhancing older people's ability to manage chronic disease (National Alliance on Mental Illness [NAMI], 2019; Stevens, Smith, Parker, Jiang, & Floyd, 2017). For example, the Stanford Chronic Disease Self-Management Program (CDSMP) is a 6-week program, developed at Stanford University under the direction of Kate Lorig in the 1990s, to benefit individuals with one or more chronic conditions. The program is based on **self-efficacy theory** (Bandura, 1997), which states that "one's confidence in achieving a desired behavior predicts their level of success" (Lorig, 2014, p. 260). The program is designed to help participants learn how to gain (or regain) a sense of perceived control over their health and chronic conditions, which can be a challenge for people dealing with a condition (such as arthritis or diabetes) that will affect the rest of their lives. This new sense of control is achieved by utilizing personal skills and resources to better manage their chronic condition(s) through (a) understanding their condition, (b) making needed lifestyle changes, (c) setting and achieving personal goals for improving their health, (d) self-mastery of chronic disease self-management skills, and (e) improving communication with health care professionals (Lorig, 2014). The program has repeatedly demonstrated its effectiveness at (a) increasing patients' physical exercise; (b) reducing symptoms such as pain, depression, and fatigue; (c) reducing hospital ED visits and length of hospital stays; and (d) perhaps most importantly, increasing participants' own **self-efficacy** or sense of personal control over their own health (Lorig et al., 1999; Ory et al., 2013).

Two components of this program have implications for the health of older adults in all countries: the ability to understand and act on health information (health literacy) and a sense of empowerment and involvement in one's own health care (**self-care** or self-management). Not only has this program proven its effectiveness in the United States, but in a recent year (2013) it was used in at least 36 other countries to train between 50 and 100,000 people (Lorig, 2014). While use does not demonstrate effectiveness, many published evaluations over the past 20 years report that it produces measurable positive effects on patient/participant health outcomes in such diverse locations as the United Kingdom, China, Mexico, Australia, and, to a lesser extent, Switzerland and Germany (Fu, Ding, McGowan, & Fu, 2006; Haslbeck et al., 2015; Peñarrieta de Córdova et al., 2017).

Self-Directed Care

Clearly, one of the goals of health literacy is to provide individuals with the tools to be involved in, and to some extent take charge of, their own health care and outcomes. Access to health information can assist both individuals and family members, especially in patriarchal cultures and those who rely on an older family member to make needed health care decisions. This philosophy and practice can play out in all types of interactions between older adults and the health care system, including learning how to manage a chronic disease such as diabetes, asking more questions of health care providers, using CAM, or even seeking the advice of a traditional healer. The CDSMP mentioned earlier helps people gain information about their conditions (become more health literate) and empowers them to take charge of their own care. Perhaps one of the clearest examples of self-care comes from the **consumer direction movement** in long-term care. In this model, older adults who need assistance with activities of daily living (ADLs) are able to select, train, and manage the people who provide their care. For older adults who have adequate economic resources, hiring people to provide needed assistance, whether with housework or with ADLs, is a common strategy. For those without resources, the option to choose their own workers and tell them how the work should be done is not as readily available (Ball & Whittington, 1995).

What is unique about consumer direction in long-term care is its placement within publicly funded long-term care systems. In the United States, United Kingdom, and many European nations, some older adults are able to use funding from public programs to hire the workers of their choice, including family members. This movement represents an important step in respecting the rights and expertise of older people needing services. Interestingly, although it might seem quite reasonable to expect that older adults would be able to talk about what services they need and express preferences about how and when those services should be offered, the early days of the consumer-directed movement were fraught with controversies and concerns. Critics worried about whether older adults could effectively manage their own care, whether consumer-employed workers would take advantage of them, whether fraud and abuse would increase, and whether health outcomes would be better or worse. Careful research has revealed that self-directed consumers fare quite well: Rates of fraud and abuse are lower, health outcomes are as good or better than those in traditional care, and participants are more satisfied (Carlson, Foster, Dale, & Brown, 2007; Dale & Brown, 2006; Schore, Foster, & Phillips, 2007).

The fact that consumer-directed care was at first contested within the United States reflects the dominance of the medical model, the passivity that has been expected from older consumers, some degree of ageism, including negative opinions about the ability of older adults to understand complex medical issues or to be actively involved in their own care, and paternalism in publicly funded programs that invests rights and responsibilities with the care providers rather than with the receivers. Consumer-directed care along with disease self-management programs slowly but successfully is challenging each of these assumptions. Of course, in less developed nations where access to paid assistance for long-term care needs from professionals may not be readily available, consumer responsibility and involvement in self-care, supplemented by family care, have always been the norm.

CONCLUSION

Throughout history, humans have used many means, organized in a variety of social systems, to cure their ills and improve their health, but just as modern biomedicine seems to be gaining the upper hand on a broad range of communicable diseases, many of the world's populations are aging and in need of a different sort of health care model and intervention, which are just now beginning to be understood. The chronic diseases of late life remain incurable, but we are learning how to manage them, and we know that, through their public health efforts, societies are crucial actors in preventing disease and promoting health. Just as importantly, patients can play a significant role in improving their own quality of care and quality of life (not to mention its quantity) if they will assert their right to do so. In many countries, both developed and developing, we see the growth of health literacy, medical consumerism, medical pluralism, and an acceptance of self-directed care. Evidence also is mounting that personal autonomy is a key element of health and well-being in later life and, indeed, in all of life.

DISCUSSION QUESTIONS

1. How did historical events shape (a) the Bismarck model and (b) the Beveridge model? What recent events do you think will shape the future health care system where you live?

2. Do you think medical pluralism is a good thing? What are its advantages and disadvantages?

3. Can you think of examples of folk and traditional medicine in your own community?

4. What do you see as the biggest challenges and biggest successes of modern medicine? What do you think will be the next big discovery? How will that discovery shape the lives of people in the future?

5. Think of the current health care system in your home country. What works best? What needs improvement?

6. Have you ever used a CAM therapy? What influenced your decision to do so? Would you do it again? Why or why not?

7. Look up information on the type of health care system, gross domestic product, life expectancy at birth, and physicians per 1,000 people for a more developed, less developed, and least developed country. What observations can you make from the information you found?

KEY WORDS

Affordable Care Act
Beveridge model
Bismarck model
Complementary and alternative
  medicine
Consumer-directed care
Folk medicine
Germ theory
Health literacy
Hippocratic Oath
Medical consumerism
Medical pluralism

Medicare
Modern medicine
National health insurance model
Out-of-pocket model
Palliative care
Self-directed care
Self-efficacy theory
Shared decision-making process
Sickness fund
Single-payer system
Social determinants of health
Traditional medicine

REFERENCES

Arcury, T. A., Bell, R. A., Altizer, K. P., Grzywacz, J. G., Sandberg, J. C., & Quandt, S. A. (2013). Attitudes of older adults regarding disclosure of complementary therapy use to physicians. *Journal of Applied Gerontology, 32*(5), 627–645. doi:10.1177/0733464812443084

Astin, J. A., Pelletier, K. R., Marie, A., & Haskell, W. L. (2000). Complementary and alternative medicine use among elderly persons: one-year analysis. *Journal of Gerontology: Medical Science, 55*, M4–M9. doi:10.1093/gerona/55.1.M4

Baker, P., Friel, S., Kay, A., Baum, F., Strazdins, L., & Mackean, T. (2017). What enables and constrains the inclusion of the social determinants of health inequities in government policy agendas? A narrative review. *International Journal of Health Policy and Management, 7*(2), 101–111. doi:10.15171/ijhpm.2017.130

Ball, M. M., & Whittington, F. J. (1995). *Surviving dependence: Voices of African American elders.* Amityville, NY: Baywood Publishing Company.

Bandura, A. (1997). *Self-efficacy: The exercise of control.* New York, NY: W. H. Freeman.

Barker, K. K. (2008). Electronic support groups, patient-consumers, and medicalization: The case of contested illness. *Journal of Health and Social Behavior, 49*, 20–38. doi:10.1177/002214650804900103

Barnes, P. M., Bloom, B., & Nahin, R. L. (2008). *Complementary and alternative medicine use among adults and children; United States, 2007.* National Health Statistics Reports No. 12. Hyattsville, MD: National Center for Health Statistics.

Carlson, B. L., Foster, L., Dale, S. B., & Brown, R. (2007). Effects of cash and counseling on personal care and well-being. *Health Services Research, 42*, 467–487. doi:10.1111/j.1475-6773.2006.00673.x

Cheng, T. M. (2015). Reflections on the 20th anniversary of Taiwan's single-payer National Health Insurance System. *Health Affairs, 34*(3), 502–510. doi:10.1377/hlthaff.2014.1332

Cichon, M., & Normand, C. (1994). Between Beveridge and Bismarck: Options for health care financing in Central and Eastern Europe. *World Health Forum, 15*, 323–328.

Cochran, R. A. (2002). *The meaning of health: Differences between cohorts and between users of biomedicine and complementary/alternative medicine.* Ph.D. Dissertation, Georgia State University, Atlanta, Georgia.

Cockerham, W. C. (2017). *Medical sociology* (13th ed.). Upper Saddle River, NJ: Prentice-Hall.

Daar, A. S., Singer, P. A., Persad, D. L., Pramming, S. K., Matthews, D. R., Beaglehole, R., . . . Bell, J. (2007). Grand challenges in chronic non-communicable diseases. *Nature, 450*(7169), 494–496. doi:10.1038/450494a

Dale, S., & Brown, R. (2006). Reducing nursing home use through consumer-directed personal care services. *Medical Care, 44*, 760–767. doi:10.1097/01.mlr.0000218849.32512.3f

Dunn, F. L. (1976). Traditional Asian medicine and cosmopolitan medicine as adaptive systems. In C. M. Leslie (Ed.), *Asian medical systems: A comparative study* (pp. 133–158). Berkeley, CA: University of California Press.

Fu, D., Ding, Y., McGowan, P., & Fu, H. (2006). Evaluation of chronic disease self management program (CDSMP) in Shanghai. *Patient Education and Counseling, 64*, 389–396. doi:10.1016/j.pec.2005.05.002

Haslbeck, J., Zanon, S., Hartung, U., Klein, M., Gabriel, E., Eicher, M., & Schulz, P. (2015). Introducing the chronic disease self-management program in Switzerland and other German-speaking countries: Findings of a cross-border adaptation using a multiple-methods approach. *BMC Health Services Research, 15*, 576–594. doi:10.1186/s12913-015-1251-z

Haug, M. R., Wykle, M. L., & Namazi, K. H. (1989). Self-care among older adults. *Social Science and Medicine, 29*, 171–183. doi:10.1016/0277-9536(89)90165-2

Helman, C. G. (2007). *Culture, health and illness: An introduction for health professionals* (5th ed.). London: Hodder Arnold Publishers.

Huff, R. M. (2002). Folk medicine. In L. Breslow (Ed.), *Encyclopedia of public health*. New York, NY: Macmillan Reference.

Kickbusch, I. S. (2001). Health literacy: Addressing the health and educational divide. *Health Promotion International, 16*(3), 289–297. doi:10.1093/heapro/16.3.289

Kon, A. A., Davidson, J. E., Morrison, W., Danis, M., & White, D. B. (2016). Shared decision making in intensive care units: An American College of Critical Care Medicine and American Thoracic Society policy statement. *Critical Care Medicine, 44*(1), 188–201. doi:10.1097/CCM.0000000000001396

Lameire, N., Joffe, P., & Wiedemann, M. (1999). Healthcare systems—An international review: An overview. *Nephrology Dialysis Transplantation, 14*(suppl 6), 3–9. doi:10.1093/ndt/14.suppl_6.3

Lorig, K. (2014). Chronic disease self-management program: Insights from the eye of the storm. *Frontiers of Public Health, 2*, 253. doi:10.3389/fpubh.2014.00253

Lorig, K. R., Sobel, D. S., Stewart, A. L., Brown, B. W., Bandura, A., Ritter, P., ... Holman, H. R. (1999). Evidence suggesting that chronic disease self-management program can improve health status while reducing hospitalization: A randomized trial. *Medical Care, 37*(1), 5–14. doi:10.1097/00005650-199901000-00003

Lumme-Sandt, K., Hervonen, A., & Jylhä, M. (2000). Interpretative repertoires of medication among the oldest-old. *Social Science & Medicine, 50*(12), 1843–1850. doi:10.1016/S0277-9536(99)00421-9

Musgrove, P. (2000). Health insurance: The influence of the Beveridge report. *Bulletin of the World Health Organization, 78*(6), 845–846.

National Alliance on Mental Illness. (2019). NAMI Programs. Retrieved from https://www.nami.org/find-support/nami-programs

Ogden, L. L. (2012). Financing and organization of national healthcare systems. In B. J. Fried & L. M. Gaydos (Eds.), *World health systems: Challenges and perspectives* (3rd ed., pp. 49–70). Chicago, IL: Health Administration Press.

Ory, M. G., Smith, M. L., Patton, K., Lorig, K., Zenker, W., & Whitelaw, N. (2013). Self-management at the tipping point: Reaching 100,000 Americans with evidence-based programs. *Journal of the American Geriatrics Society, 61*(5), 821. doi:10.1111/jgs.12239

Osborn, R., Doty, M. M., Moulds, D., Sarnak, D. O., & Shah, A. (2017). Older Americans were sicker and faced more financial barriers to health care than counterparts in other countries. *Health Affairs, 36*(12), 2123–2132. doi:10.1377/hlthaff.2017.1048

Parnell, T. A., McCulloch, E. C., Mieres, J. H., & Edwards, F. (2014). *Health literacy as an essential component to achieving excellent patient outcomes*. Institute of Medicine of the National Academies.

Peñarrieta de Córdova, M. I., Leon, R., Gutierrez, T., Mier, N., Banda, O., & Delabra, M. (2017). Effectiveness of a chronic disease self-management program in Mexico: A randomized controlled study. *Journal of Nursing Education and Practice, 7*(7), 87–94. doi:10.5430/jnep.v7n7p87

Potter, S. J., & McKinley, J. B. (2005). From a relationship to encounter: An examination of longitudinal and lateral dimension in the doctor-patient relationship. *Social Science and Medicine, 61*, 465–479. doi:10.1016/j.socscimed.2004.11.067

Reid, T. R. (2009). *The healing of America: A global quest for better, cheaper, and fairer health care*. New York, NY: Penguin Press.

Robertson, R., Appleby, J., & Evans, H. (2018). Public satisfaction with the NHS and social care in 2017. Retrieved from kingsfund.org.uk/publications

Sanders, J. (2012). Financing and organization of national health systems. In B. J. Fried & L. M. Gaydos (Eds.), *World health systems: Challenges and perspectives* (3rd ed., pp. 25–38). Chicago, IL: Health Administration Press.

Schore, J., Foster, L., & Phillips, B. (2007). Consumer enrollment and experiences in the cash and counseling program. *Health Services Research, 42*, 446–466. doi:10.1111/j.1475-6773.2006.00679.x

Shorter, E. (1991). *Doctors and their patients*. New Brunswick, NJ: Transaction Books.

Stevens, J. A., Smith, M. L., Parker, E. M., Jiang, L., & Floyd, F. D. (2017). Implementing a clinically based fall prevention program. *American Journal of Lifestyle Medicine*, 1559827617716085. Published online, July 5, 2017.

Subedi, J. (1989). Modern health services and health care behavior: A survey of Kathmandu, Nepal. *Journal of Health and Social Behavior, 30,* 412–420. doi:10.2307/2136989

Subedi, J., & Subedi, S. (1993). The contribution of modern medicine in a traditional system: The case of Nepal. In P. Conrad & E. B. Gallagher (Eds.), *Health and health care in developing countries: Sociological perspectives*. Philadelphia, PA: Temple University Press.

Tan, S. S.-L., & Goonawardene, N. (2017). Internet health information seeking and the patient-physician relationship: A systematic review. *Journal of Medical Internet Research, 19*(1), e9. doi:10.2196/jmir.5729

Wade, C., Chao, M., Kronenberg, F., Cushman, L., & Kalmuss, D. (2008). Medical pluralism among American women: Results of a national survey. *Journal of Women's Health, 17*(5), 829–840. doi:10.1089/jwh.2007.0579

Weiss, G. L., & Lonnquist, L. E. (2012). *The sociology of health, healing, and illness*. Upper Saddle River, NJ: Prentice-Hall.

White, A., & Ernst, E. (2004). A brief history of acupuncture. *Rheumatology, 43,* 662–663. doi:10.1093/rheumatology/keg005

World Health Organization. (2013). *WHO traditional medicine strategy: 2014-2023*. Retrieved from https://www.who.int

Yuan, H., Ma, Q., Ye, L., & Piao, G. (2016). The traditional medicine and modern medicine from natural products. *Molecules, 21*(5), 559. doi:10.3390/molecules21050559

RUSSIA'S HEALTH AND HEALTH CARE SYSTEM

OKSANA DIKHTYAR

The modern health care system in Russia is based on a system that originated in the Soviet Union in the 1930s and was the world's first model of universal health care. The Semashko system (named for one of its organizers) guaranteed all citizens the right to free medical care provided by the state through the network of public medical facilities staffed by government-employed medical personnel. During the first few decades since its establishment, the system was successful in combating infectious diseases such as tuberculosis, smallpox, and typhus and decreasing child mortality through comprehensive vaccination programs and health screenings. By 1965, life expectancy and health of the population approached those in the United States and Europe (Eberstadt & Groth, 2010). However, the effectiveness and quality of care had declined by the early 1980s even though the number of hospital beds and doctors per capita doubled between 1950 and 1980. Government bureaucracy and inadequate financing led to shortages of medical equipment, drugs, and diagnostic chemicals, outdated medical technologies, and poor training of health care personnel. These factors contributed to the deterioration of the health status of the Russian population, which dramatically declined during the 1990s after the collapse of the Soviet Union in 1991. Average life expectancy declined for both males and females, and infant and maternal deaths increased. Between 1990 and 1995, life expectancy decreased from 74.3 to 71.6 years for women and from 63.7 to 58.1 years for men. During the same period, maternal deaths (per 100,000 live births) went up from 47.4 to 53.3 and infant deaths (per 1,000 live births) increased from 17.4 to 18.1 (Popovich et al., 2011).

In 1993, the newly emerged independent state now called the Russian Federation declared a constitutional right to free health care and medical assistance for its citizens, thus confirming continuity of the underlying principles of the Soviet model. However, to compensate for the shortage of state funding due to economic decline, private outpatient practices were legalized, and public medical facilities were allowed to charge for some of their services. In addition, production and distribution of pharmaceuticals and medical equipment became private (Cook, 2015; Marten et al., 2014). In 1993, the Federal Mandatory Medical Insurance Fund was established under the Ministry of Health to provide universal health insurance to the Russian people. In addition to the Federal Fund in Moscow, 86 regional funds of Mandatory Medical Insurance oversee the provision of health coverage in the regions of the country; these organizations collect a mandatory 5.1% payroll tax from employers to cover health insurance for the working population. Financing of coverage for the nonworking population—for example, children, people with disabilities who cannot work, and pensioners (people who have retired)—comes from regional and local budgets. Since regions with diverse economies finance the majority of health care costs, the quality and availability of care, and the health status of residents, vary substantially across Russia's many regions. For example, in 2011, per capita health spending of urban regions with booming economies was nine to 10 times that of provincial, less developed regions (Cook, 2015).

While the health status of the Russian population improved significantly during the economic growth of 2005–2013, making up for some of the decline of the 1990s, some worrisome trends have developed recently. According to the World Health Organization, cardiovascular diseases remain the leading cause of death in Russia and accounted for more than half of deaths in 2017 (World Health Rankings, 2018). This group of diseases is followed by influenza and pneumonia, and then lung cancer. These are somewhat similar to the leading causes of death in the United States and other developed countries, although the percentage of cardiovascular diseases is not as high in those countries (Murphy, Xu, Kochanek, & Arias, 2018). However, multidrug-resistant tuberculosis (MDR-TB) has been increasing in absolute and proportional numbers, and so has TB/HIV coinfection. Additionally, there has been a 10% annual increase in new HIV cases. These trends are unique to Russia and pose a challenge for its health care system.

Major causes of poor health in Russia are alcohol abuse (especially among men), tobacco consumption, unhealthy diets, and physical inactivity. Inadequate health promotion and prevention measures also play a role. Average life expectancy remains significantly low compared to other industrialized nations, currently 78 years for females and 68 for males (Population Reference Bureau [PRB], 2018), one of the largest gender gaps in the world. Lower male life expectancy can be attributed to high-risk behaviors, especially alcohol consumption and reckless driving. For example, in 2016, 34.4% of deaths among men aged 16 to 49 were alcohol-related, compared with 20.1% of their female age peers (Starodubov et al., 2018).

Although both the number of hospitals and the number of doctors in Russia have been steadily decreasing, they remain quite high compared to the rest of Europe and the United States. In 2016, Russia had 5,357 hospitals and 680,900 doctors, down from 9,479 hospitals and 690,300 doctors in 2005 (Russian Federal State

Statistics Service [Rosstat], 2018). In 2016, there were 46.4 doctors per 10,000 people in Russia, compared to 29.5 doctors in the United States (Rosstat, 2018; Young et al., 2017). Considering that Russia has one of the highest numbers of doctors and hospital beds, it is surprising that its population has such low life expectancy. Apparently, the abundance of doctors does not translate into accessible, high-quality medical care. This is the legacy of the Soviet system, where low salaries of health care professionals and underfinancing of health care were compensated for by an excess of doctors and hospital beds. Nevertheless, Russia today suffers from an estimated 13% shortage of primary care doctors and a troubling lack of skilled personnel and incentives for professional development (Shishkin, 2017). Although the government has steadily increased the average salary of medical workers, it attained only 81% of the average national salary in 2016, according to Rosstat (2018). This situation is conducive to continuation of the pervasive practice of informal payments to medical professionals by patients (payments for services/procedures they are entitled to receive free of charge), which existed during the Soviet era, proliferated in the early 1990s, and now has become widespread. In 2011, among patients who paid for services out of pocket, 34% made informal payments for outpatient services and 67% paid for inpatient services (Marten et al., 2014).

Low efficiency always has been one of the main issues for Russia's health care system. Russia was ranked 53rd among 56 countries based on date from 2015 on the Bloomberg Healthcare Efficiency Index, which was uses three metrics: (a) life expectancy, (b) absolute health expenditures, and (c) relative health expenditures (Miller & Lu, 2018). Top-ranked countries were Hong Kong, Singapore, and Spain. Outdated norms at medical institutions are partially responsible for the system's inefficiency. For example, the required hospital stay in Russia after giving birth is 5 days, while appendicitis surgery requires a 7-day stay, both far greater than current medical norms in the West.

The most vulnerable sector of the Russian health care system is polyclinics—medical centers where specialty doctors provide primary outpatient care, and which are a legacy of the Semashko model—since these clinics are most affected by budget cuts. Due to limited financial resources, these centers have been eliminating some of the specialty doctors from their staffs, resulting in longer waiting times and patients being forced to pay for services or go to private doctors. In addition to the lack of adequate skilled personnel, the majority of local public medical centers and hospitals have outdated medical equipment. The high-tech medical clinics are located in larger regional cities, requiring extra time and resources to visit them. Persons with disability are especially disadvantaged in Russia, since facilities for them are scarce and far below Western standards. Wheelchairs and artificial limbs are very expensive and in limited supply; Russia has virtually no wheelchair-accessible public bathrooms, building entrances, or sidewalks.

After the collapse of the Soviet Union, the health care system was decentralized and private practice was permitted; however, the private health sector remains small, is largely centered in urban areas, and is more common in certain fields such as dental care. Russia had 205 private hospitals in 2016, compared to 5,357 public hospitals (Rosstat, 2018). Also in 2016, among patients who applied for out-patient care, only 11% opted for private providers; among those who applied for inpatient care, only 2% did so (Shishkin, 2017) mostly because these services are not covered by public health insurance, requiring patients to pay out of pocket. An optional private health insurance plan can be purchased or received through the employer, but only 5% of the population living in major cities has this coverage, mainly through their employers (Cook, 2015). This insurance provides access to private, modern medical clinics where care is comparable to that of developed countries and clients are predominantly wealthy Russians and foreign expatriates. Nevertheless, the majority of wealthy Russians usually travel abroad to countries like Germany, Israel, Switzerland, Finland, and others for high-quality health care (Cook, 2015). Such "health tourism" is promoted at various trade shows in Moscow and even through newspaper advertisements.

Under universal health care coverage, all Russian citizens also have the right to medications during inpatient care. Certain groups also have the right to purchase medications at a 50% discount for outpatient care. Most medications are widely available for purchase without prescription except for narcotics, antidepressants, and some painkillers. For example, one can buy antibiotics without a prescription. This leads to a situation where people self-diagnose and self-medicate, often resulting in poor health outcomes. Adding to the pharmaceutical challenges, counterfeit medications are a lucrative business in Russia, so the medications people buy are sometimes not exactly what they paid for.

Even though Russia's health care system is unique, it contains elements of all three major health care models, with employers financing health care for their employees, public health care spending, and most medical personnel being government employees. While Russia's health care system is based on the principles of universal health care and guarantees all citizens the right to free medical care, it still has many challenges, such as system inefficiency, low quality of care, the practice of informal payments, and unequal access to care. According to the 2014 survey by the Levada Center, a Moscow-based polling agency, only 2% of Russians were proud of their health care system (Bruk, 2014). Increasing public financing, although unlikely in the near future, would solve only part of the problem. More efforts should be aimed at prevention and health promotion, particularly to educate people about benefits of a healthy lifestyle and to curb alcohol and tobacco consumption.

REFERENCES

Bruk, B. (2014). Has patriotism in Russia been hijacked? Institute of Modern Russia (2018). Retrieved from https://imrussia.org/en/nation/735-has-patriotism-in-russia-been-hijacked

Cook, L. (2015). *Constraints on universal health care in the Russian Federation: Inequality, informality and the failures of mandatory health insurance reforms* (UNRISD Working Paper No. 2015-5). Geneva, Switzerland: United Nations Research Institute for Social Development. Retrieved from http://hdl.handle.net/10419/148760

Eberstadt, N., & Groth, H. (2010). The Russian Federation: Confronting the special challenges of ageing and social security policy in an era of demographic crisis. *International Social Security Review*, *63*(3–4), 23–58. Retrieved from http://www.infekt.ch/content/uploads/2013/11/Nikolaus_Eberstadt.pdf

Marten, R., McIntyre, D., Travassos, C., Shishkin, S., Longde, W., Reddy, S., & Vega, J. (2014). An assessment of progress towards universal health coverage in Brazil, Russia, India, China, and South Africa (BRICS). *The Lancet*, *384*(9960), 2164–2171. Retrieved from https://www.sciencedirect.com/science/article/pii/S0140673614600751

Miller, L. J., & Lu, W. (2018, September). These are the economies with the most (and least) efficient health care. *Bloomberg*. Retrieved from https://www.bloomberg.com/news/articles/2018-09-19/u-s-near-bottom-of-health-index-hong-kong-and-singapore-at-top

Murphy, S. L., Xu, J., Kochanek, K. D., & Arias, E. (2018). Mortality in the United States, 2017. Retrieved from https://www.cdc.gov/nchs/data/databriefs/db328-h.pdf

Popovich, L., Potapchik, E., Shishkin, S., Richardson, E., Vacroux, A., & Mathivet, B. (2011). Russian Federation: Health system review. *Health Systems in Transitions*, *13*(7). Retrieved from https://www.ecoi.net/en/file/local/1302492/1930_1421317372_hit-russia-en-web-with-links.pdf

Population Reference Bureau. (2018). International Data, Russia 2017. Retrieved from https://www.prb.org/international/geography/russia

Russian Federal State Statistics Service. (2018). Public health. Health services. Retrieved from https://www.gks.ru/folder/13721

Shishkin, S. (2017). How history shaped the health system in Russia. *The Lancet*, *390*(10102), 1612–1613. Retrieved from https://journals-ohiolink-edu.proxy.lib.miamioh.edu/pg_200?::NO:200:P200_ARTICLEID:349399460

Starodubov, V. I., Marczak, L. B., Varavikova, E., Bikbov, B., Ermakov, S. P., Gall, J., . . . Naghavi, M. (2018). The burden of disease in Russia from 1980 to 2016: A systematic analysis for the Global Burden of Disease Study 2016. *The Lancet*, *392*(10153), 1138–1146. doi:10.1016/s0140-6736(18)31485-5

World Health Rankings. (2018). *Health profile: Russia*. Retrieved from https://www.worldlifeexpectancy.com/country-health-profile/russia

Young, A., Chaudhry, H. J., Pei, X., Arnhart, K., Dugan, M., & Snyder, G. B. (2017). A census of actively licensed physicians in the United States, 2016. *Journal of Medical Regulation*, *103*(2), 7–21. Retrieved from https://www.fsmb.org/siteassets/advocacy/publications/2016census.pdf

AN AMERICAN IN HAVANA: OBSERVATIONS ABOUT AGING IN CUBA

FRANK J. WHITTINGTON

Cuba represents an interesting case for aging and the older population. As Jim Sykes and Enrique Vega (2009) point out in their chapter on Cuba in the *International Handbook on Aging* (Palmore, Whittington, & Kunkel, 2009), Cuba has a less developed economy but an age structure that resembles a developed nation. In fact, Cuban life expectancy in 2018 (latest data available) stood at 80.1 years, slightly higher than that of the United States (age 79.7) and also very close to many of the nations of Western Europe (Pan American Health Organization, 2018). The proportion of the population older than age 65 is only slightly less than that of the United States (15.2% vs. 16.0%), due mainly to Cuba's lower infant mortality rate (4.4/100,000 live births, compared with 5.7 in the United States).

CUBAN–UNITED STATES HISTORY

Understanding how a very poor nation could achieve such a good result for its people probably requires some historical and political background. In the 1950s, Fidel Castro led a guerilla-style war against the dictator Fulgencio Batista, overthrowing him on New Year's Eve 1959, dramatically and memorably depicted in the movie *Godfather II*. Initially, most of the people in the United States and even the U.S. government were supportive of Castro's revolution—until it was learned that he and most of his *compadres* were Communists and were supported by the Soviet Union.

As Castro took over the country, he nationalized all land holdings and most businesses, causing many of the wealthy and middle class—those who were not killed or imprisoned—to leave Cuba for the United States. The large Cuban

American population in Florida today—descended from those immigrants—wields a disproportionate amount of political power, especially where the U.S. government's policy toward Cuba is concerned.

Several other events, including the Bay of Pigs invasion (1961), the Cuban Missile Crisis (1962), and the hypothesized role of Castro in the assassination of President John F. Kennedy (1963), created a relationship among the United States, Cuba, and the Cuban people that was actively hostile, tense, and difficult in the days following the revolution. Then the political relationship settled into an uneasy, passive hostility that gradually faded from public consciousness except among the Cubans in Florida and Havana. Because they were connected by blood and by history, these communities worked daily to keep the issue—and the hostility—alive. The Cuban Missile Crisis was resolved ultimately by a naval blockade of the island, pitting American warships against Soviet warships in the waters around Cuba; that crisis brought our nation closer to catastrophic nuclear war than any other time in our history. The naval blockade evolved into a permanent, full-scale economic embargo and a political shunning that we have not used against any other country—not even against Vietnam following that war, or against North Korea in the 66 years since the Korean War.

THE VISIT

It was against this backdrop that I was invited in 2010 to join a delegation of American gerontologists who traveled to Cuba to learn about aging and health care in that country. The trip was sponsored by the National Council on Aging (NCOA). The people in our group were all either members of NCOA or friends of members; they included local service providers, college professors, advocates, a senior center director, a health care administrator, an entrepreneur, a geriatrician, and an attorney. The delegation was led by Jim Sykes, a retired gerontologist from the University of Wisconsin who has traveled and studied extensively in Latin America and had visited Cuba more than 20 times.

One of the constant themes of our trip was the American economic boycott of Cuba. We learned that the impact of the boycott has produced significant hardship for Cubans. Their country remains one of the poorest in the Western Hemisphere. Its communications infrastructure is at least 20 years behind that of the United States, consumer goods for the average Cuban are in very short supply, and their housing stock and commercial buildings are inadequate, shabby, and in some places crumbling.

The country's economy is not vibrant, and development is slow. Yet Cuba has an antique feel and patina that are attractive and even charming to an American tourist. Some would attribute this stagnant economy to the Communist system, whereas others would blame the boycott for keeping Cuba out of the economic mainstream. It is probably due to a little of both.

Despite the boycott, Cubans enjoy two advantages that Americans do not: free education (from kindergarten through college) and free health care. Cubans pay nothing for a visit to a health clinic, nothing for delivery of their children, nothing for dental care, and nothing for hospital or nursing-home stays. One might assume that such free health care must take a huge chunk out of the country's gross domestic product (GDP), impoverishing every other sector of the economy. To the contrary, whereas the United States spends about 17% of its GDP on health care, Cuba spends only 11%.

My preconceived notion about the Cuban system was that the combination of free care and smaller expenditures must produce overuse and low quality. I cannot speak to overuse, since such data are not collected by the Cuban government and not deemed worthy of concern. However, I can testify that the clinic buildings, examination rooms, waiting rooms, and medical offices we saw were, by American standards, all of low quality: old, small, poorly furnished, and poorly maintained. None of us would want to work or be treated there. However, the results—in very low infant mortality and length of life—are hard to argue with. Cuba is an outlier in the relationship of economic well-being and health status of its population—one of the poorest nations in the Western Hemisphere is enjoying one of the highest levels of health and longevity.

A VISITOR'S OBSERVATIONS

I learned several things from my observations and discussions with Cuban health care and aging professionals during our visit to Cuba in late 2010.

1. Population aging is a well-understood reality for those in both government and academe, and most policy makers are at least thinking about how Cuba is changing as the age structure shifts away from youth toward maturity. It is understandable that countries with a higher proportion of older citizens would have the most advanced gerontology programs and research. Yet the increase in proportion aged has slowed recently in the highly developed countries, and it is the less developed nations like Cuba that are facing the most rapid growth—in both size and proportion—of their older populations, with all of the accompanying challenges. Perhaps the less developed nations have the greatest need to develop gerontological capacity and to rapidly create programs for their older people so that they can anticipate and minimize some of the problems of aging experienced by industrialized countries.

2. Geriatric medicine is now recognized and supported in Cuba, although no formal connections exist with professional geriatricians in North America or Europe. Gerontological researchers and educators, though still few in number, are engaging their nation's aging issues as best they can with insight and scientific rigor. I was especially impressed that an epidemiologist was located and engaged in applied research in a local health center (referred to as a polyclinic

because of its multidisciplinary team approach). Whereas his physical tools and technical support were limited, his methods were classic and effective. He could show how the clustering of rural immigrants living in his catchment area correlated closely with the reported cases of dengue fever in the community. He, like all the staff of the clinic, wore a white lab coat, conveying to all—patients and visitors alike—the sense of serious, scientific medicine being practiced there. Most members of our group were quite impressed with both the strong commitment and the sophistication of the staff in practicing community medicine. Prevention appeared to be their default mode and daily operating principle.

3. A third obvious lesson from my visit is that many of the phenomena we would label as problems of aging and that we struggle with in the United States are also found in Cuba. In fact, Cuba appears not to be very different in this regard from many other nations of the world, developed or not. In Palmore and his colleagues' handbook (2009), the authors of each nation's chapter describe their own aging populations and policies in terms that could pass for those of an American observer—and very similar to my observations in Cuba. Our hosts at the geriatric medicine program of the University of Havana gave a stimulating (if familiar) lecture on the ravages of physical decline with age and the shortage of good medical care and long-term care arrangements; a weakening of the family and social network of support for older adults; the serious negative effects of old-age poverty in Cuba; exploitation or outright abuse of vulnerable older people; and the psychological and mental health problems besetting older Cubans. Does that list sound vaguely familiar?

I was quite impressed with these geriatricians' descriptions of their decades of study, clinical experience, and research with older patients. Because government support of their work is quite limited by the poor national economy and other spending priorities, they do not have easy access to the books, journals, and conferences available to scientists in developed nations. They nevertheless have managed to keep up with most modern geriatric knowledge and understanding, and their clear grasp of the needs of their patients and an informed approach to care suggest that any of us would be as well treated in Havana as in Atlanta. Of course, we would receive fewer tests, shorter stays in the hospital, and fewer medications, but, because of the free care system, we would also receive no bill.

During our visit, we witnessed an amazing performance by a senior drama group of an original play highlighting aging and intergenerational themes. The group's director did not refer to it as *drama therapy*, as we might have done 20 years ago in the United States. Such experiences in the United States often teach us that older people are capable of far more than most lay persons suspect. Many Americans still expect an older person to be sick, weak, and disengaged; when we see evidence that for many, the opposite is true, we are struck by the contrast between our age stereotype and the reality before our eyes. Similarly, these Cuban older adults said they were especially gratified by their grandchildren's reactions to seeing them in the play: Grandma and Grandpa were suddenly *cool*, and the seniors knew that the kids' ageist biases would never be the same.

4. Differences do exist. We in the United States differ from Cuba and many other less developed countries of the world, mainly in the widespread challenges of an aging population and the well-developed support programs designed to ameliorate them. For all the surface similarities between the United States and Cuba's aging populations and issues, I did notice some jarring differences in where we are and where they are. In some cases, it appears that where they are is where we have been. Because we are a much richer nation, U.S. poverty is less widespread and probably less an actual burden on aging lifestyles here than it is in Cuba, at least in absolute terms. However, because Cuba is a socialist country and the wealth (or lack of it) is much more equally distributed, relative deprivation is likely felt more acutely here than there.

Although we saw one large and amazingly vibrant senior center with day health services and treatments on-site, we could not verify how common these are. The therapy equipment proudly displayed consisted of electromagnetic field devices attached to cots, where seniors could rest while receiving a low dose of magnetism. Because magnet therapy is scientifically unproven and actively rejected by most Western physicians, such treatments likely delivered only a placebo benefit that, of course, is not to be completely discounted. Center participants were lively, welcoming, and apparently healthy; however, the director also gratefully accepted our small gifts of soap, shampoo, and toothpaste, commodities not readily available or affordable to many Cuban seniors.

CONCLUSIONS

I am aware my observations are limited, having visited Cuba for only a short time. Nevertheless, Americans visiting Cuba for the first time bring many years of "distance education" about this island nation, its people and culture, and its political and economic system. I was not surprised, therefore, to conclude that Cuba is not totally free, totally open, or totally modern.

Despite Fidel Castro's relinquishing power in 2008 in favor of his younger brother, Raul, and Raul's retirement in 2018, the embargo, as it is often referred to, continues, keeping most U.S. goods away from Cuba. Cuban products out of U.S. markets. and, more importantly, the Cuban and U.S. governments from exchanging views directly or engaging each other for mutual benefit. Although some of these restrictions were loosened somewhat during the Obama administration, which also reestablished U.S. diplomatic relations with Cuba in 2014, some of the Obama-era changes (sometimes referred to as "the Cuban thaw") have been reversed by the Trump administration. Tight restrictions continue on Americans traveling to Cuba and Cubans coming to the United States, so the flow of visitors between the two countries is still meager.

Likewise on the Cuban side, at the time of my visit (2010) it was reported that then- Pesident Raul Castro was seeking to introduce capitalist-like incentives for entrepreneurs and eliminate the tight government control of all economic activity. Moreover, many observers thought Fidel's death in 2017 and Raul stepping down a year later "would bring about dramatic changes to the island's 59-year-old Communist regime." Yet, it has been reported that "Cuba stayed as oppressive as ever: arbitrary arrests soared, promised economic liberalization policies have yet to be seen, and the media remains heavily censored" (Hall, 2018).

However, during our visit, I was struck by the facts that Cuba seemed also freer and more open than I thought it would be and more advanced than I thought, especially in medical care and the promotion of health among people at the community level; and its population is older than I thought, owing to its low infant mortality rate and relatively high life expectancy. Most importantly, its national policy on aging appears to value age and older people in authentic and meaningful ways.

Despite six decades of political and economic boycott by the United States and its allies, Cuba is far less isolated than I had imagined. I met professionals who had studied and worked in Africa, China, Russia, and Western Europe. I met Cuban citizens who had traveled to Europe, the United States, and Asia; and I met and saw hundreds of people from the United States, Canada, Europe, and Asia who were visiting Cuba while we were there. Since the loosening of travel restrictions under President Obama, and despite their subsequent retightening under Trump, even more American visitors are traveling to Cuba. While there, I even heard several Cubans describe their favorite contemporary American television shows (in 2010, they were *House* and *Grey's Anatomy*) and movies (*The Godfather* and *Spiderman*). Clearly, a significant volume of cultural and economic exchange has been going on in Cuba for a number of years that undermines all external attempts to impose economic and political isolation on the country.

We hope our visit and new understanding have contributed to the growth of a truly international science and professional practice in gerontology. In this way, the study of global aging—in all of its forms—can provide the foundation for improved quantity and quality of life for the hundreds of millions of people already older in the world and those soon to be.

REFERENCES

Hall, K. (2018). Why Cuba's regime will survive the Castros. *RealClear World.com.* Published online March 16, 2018. Retrieved from realclearworld.com on July 16, 2019.

Palmore, E. B., Whittington, F., & Kunkel, S. (Eds.). (2009). *The International handbook on aging: Current research and developments* (3rd ed.). Santa Barbara, CA: Praeger Publishers, Inc.

Pan American Health Organization. (2018). *Health situation in the Americas: Core indicators, 2018.* Retrieved from http:paho.org

Sykes, J. T., & Vega, E. (2009). Cuba. In E. B. Palmore, F. Whittington, & S. Kunkel (Eds.), *The International handbook on aging: Current research and developments* (3rd ed., pp. 171–180). Santa Barbara, CA: Praeger Publishers, Inc.

7

LONG-TERM SERVICES AND SUPPORTS

ROBERT APPLEBAUM | EMILY HAUTZ | ANTHONY BARDO

INTRODUCTION

Most of us go through our day-to-day tasks—from taking a shower, to getting dressed, to making breakfast—without a second thought about the effort required to accomplish them. However, for older adults who may experience significant disability due to injury or disease, these daily activities present challenges that may require ongoing assistance from family members, friends, or a formal care service provider. **Long-term services and supports** (LTSS; a term that generally has replaced the older phrase **long-term care** [LTC]) enable those who need continual help because of physical, cognitive, or developmental disabilities to accomplish the necessary tasks of daily living. This support can be provided in one's home or the home of a friend or relative, in a congregate housing complex, in an assisted living residence, or in a skilled nursing facility. The array of options available to elders with disability vary across the globe, as do the size and proportion of a nation's older population experiencing a long-term disability, due to a number of factors including life expectancy, socioeconomic status, environment, cultural norms and lifestyle, and the availability of health care. Despite these differences, virtually every nation in the world has older individuals with disabilities who need assistance with the basic tasks of daily living. A report by the U.S. Census Bureau (Kinsella & He, 2009) estimated that worldwide, the number of people over age 80—those most likely to need long-term services—will increase by 233% between 2008 and 2040. A recent study by the World Health Organization (WHO, 2018) reported that worldwide, the number of adults with significant difficulties in functioning is estimated to be between 110 million and 190 million and that disability rates are increasing because of population aging and an increase in chronic health conditions.

Disability rates vary widely among countries, as do the long-term services designed to support the needs of individuals who require assistance. The need for long-term services is typically determined by a person's ability to carry out the common activities of daily living (ADLs). These activities include daily tasks such as dressing, bathing, transferring from bed, getting to the bathroom, and eating independently. Individuals who need help with these tasks are generally assumed to need long-term services. Definitions and level of support are dependent on a number of factors, such as governmental action and the culture of informal care. In attempting to understand the differences and similarities that exist among nations regarding LTSS, this chapter examines how countries are responding to the new and growing challenges of assisting older people with LTSS.

DEFINING LTSS

Prior to examining the different approaches used to deliver and finance long-term services, it is important to have a common understanding of what is meant by LTSS. As noted, individuals who require LTSS primarily need ongoing assistance with the basic daily tasks of living. In some instances, individuals may also have acute medical needs, but it is the personal tasks of life that define one's level of care needs each day. A typical case might involve an older person who experiences challenges in physical and/or mental abilities to the point where the individual can no longer function independently.

As an example, we look at Ruby, who is 88 years old and as a result of severe arthritis is now experiencing limitations in her ability to shop and cook, clean her apartment, and even to shower and dress independently. Ruby has three adult children, although only one of them, Dedree, lives nearby. Dedree tries to help as much as she can, but works full time at a large grocery store. Her days off vary, but she often works on the weekend. Her husband, Max, sells cars and typically works weekends and evenings. Dedree has two adult children who also have full-time jobs, though they do not work on the weekends. While Dedree's children can provide some support for Grandma Ruby, one of them just had a child and the other one is about to get married. Dedree provides as much support as she can, given her demanding job, but weekends are presenting a growing problem for the family. Ruby needs almost daily help to remain in her own apartment. A plan of care developed by Ruby's community social worker, who is often called a care manager, includes a personal care aide to assist with dressing, showering, and shopping; a daily home-delivered meal; a visit from a senior companion; and help from family members, which allows her to remain at home rather than move to a care facility. The big challenge is weekend care, because neither the personal care aide nor the home-delivered meal is available on weekends. Although it is a challenge, Dedree has worked out a schedule so that she, Max, or one of the children can stop by on each weekend day to provide assistance and a meal. This mixture of family support and formal services delivered at home is quite common in the

United States and other developed countries. In many communities throughout the world, however, LTSS typically are provided only informally, by family members or volunteers.

The type and amount of long-term assistance available to an elder with chronic care needs is the result of many factors, such as one's social and family environment, available technology, geographic locale, and level of care needs. Under some circumstances, because of the severity of disability or limited family or other informal supports, an older person with severe disability is unable to remain in his or her own home. In these instances, a person may need an apartment with supportive services, a residence with support and personal care services, or a facility that provides support, personal care, and skilled nursing services. The names of these facilities vary from country to country, although the institutions providing skilled long-term services typically are called **nursing homes**. Residential facilities' names vary widely by nation. An individual's circumstances can exacerbate or mitigate challenges of accomplishing the tasks of everyday living, but the need to provide ongoing LTSS is universal.

Since it is difficult in a brief discussion to capture their full variation across the globe, a typology of such LTSS is developed in this chapter to serve as a framework for categorizing national LTSS systems. Specific examples of how different countries handle LTSS tasks are presented to illustrate the range of approaches. These examples are used to help explain some of the complexities that arise when attempting to compare and contrast LTSS services on a global scale. Some of the LTSS policy issues common to many nations are described in the concluding discussion section of this chapter.

Typologies of LTSS

In order to better understand country approaches to long-term services, we have developed a model to categorize the nations of the world. As you can imagine, countries vary widely in their approaches to financing and providing long-term services. Our classification system builds on the work of earlier studies. Kraus et al. (2010) categorized 21 of the European Union (EU) LTSS systems using two distinct clustering strategies: One approach focused on service system characteristics, and the other focused on system use and financing. First, they examined the extent to which a nation's long-term services are *means-tested*—whether they are provided only to individuals without the money (means) to pay the cost themselves or to all equally as an **entitlement**. They also examined the availability of cash benefits, whether individuals had a choice of provider, the use of a quality assurance system, the amount of public expenditures for LTSS as a share of gross domestic product (GDP), and the amount of cost sharing required of service users. In this model, access to publicly funded long-term services can be viewed on a spectrum, from global entitlement to heavily means-tested. Based on these factors, the 22 EU countries were categorized into four groups (see Box 7.1 for listing of countries). The first cluster, including Denmark, Belgium, the Netherlands,

BOX 7.1

Countries Included in the Kraus et al. (2010) Typology

The following is an alphabetical list of the 22 European countries included in the Kraus et al. (2010) typology:

- Austria
- Belgium
- Bulgaria
- Czech Republic
- Denmark
- England
- Estonia
- Finland
- France
- Germany
- Hungary

- Italy
- Latvia
- Lithuania
- Netherlands
- Poland
- Portugal
- Romania
- Slovak Republic
- Slovenia
- Spain
- Sweden

Sweden, and France, was characterized as financially generous and having a well-developed LTSS system. Cluster 2 included such nations as Italy, England, and Spain, and was classified as having medium financial generosity and a moderately developed LTSS system. The countries placed in Clusters 3 (Bulgaria, Estonia, and the Czech Republic) and 4 (Hungary, Poland, and Romania) were classified as having a low amount of resources allocated to LTSS.

A second study, conducted by the Organisation for Economic Co-operation and Development (OECD), expanded on the Kraus typology (Colombo, Llena-Nozal, Mercier, & Tjadens, 2011; see Box 7.2 for listing of OECD member countries included in their analysis). Their classification is based on the funding structure (universal, means-tested, or mixed) and provision of care provided by each nation's LTSS system. **Universal systems** provide publicly funded nursing and personal care to all eligible individuals (defined by their level of disability) regardless of income or assets. Within the universal category are three different funding structures: (a) **tax-based**, (b) **social long-term care insurance** (LTCI), and (c) **long-term services included as part of overall health coverage**. Under a means-tested financing structure, income and/or asset tests are used to determine eligibility for publicly funded LTSS. Means-tested systems are the least accessible and provide services and benefits only to those whose income falls below a defined threshold (sometimes called the poverty level). The third OECD category is a mix of the universal system and the means-tested system. These systems tend to vary greatly in eligibility criteria, individual cost, and services provided. In countries with limited formal service delivery, benefits often are limited to nursing-home care.

BOX 7.2

OECD Member Countries

The following is an alphabetical list of OECD member countries as of July 12, 2012 (OECD, n.d.):

- Australia
- Austria
- Belgium
- Canada
- Chile
- Czech Republic
- Denmark
- Estonia
- Finland
- France
- Germany
- Greece
- Hungary
- Iceland
- Ireland
- Israel
- Italy
- Japan
- South Korea
- Luxembourg
- Mexico
- The Netherlands
- New Zealand
- Norway
- Poland
- Portugal
- Slovak Republic
- Slovenia
- Spain
- Sweden
- Switzerland
- Turkey
- United Kingdom
- United States

OECD, Organisation for Economic Co-operation and Development.

A New Typology

Building on the previous work, a five-category typology has been created to classify national approaches to LTSS. As noted, a range of criteria can be considered when assessing and comparing LTSS systems at a global level. In addition to the previously identified factors of funding and definition of disability, the supply of LTSS and people's access to them are included. It is critical to combine the issues of financial and functional disability requirements with the supply, balance, and array of long-term services available. The factors from the two major earlier studies have been combined with additional delivery system indicators, such as the availability of residential care and the balance of formal and informal services. A description of the categories established and a list of selected countries that have been classified in each group are presented in Table 7.1.

GROUP 1

Nations in this grouping have publicly funded systems that provide universal LTSS coverage for older individuals. Using a range of funding sources, including a

TABLE 7.1 Typology of National Long-Term Care Services and Supports Systems

Group 1	Group 2	Group 3	Group 4	Group 5
Public insurance funding available for long-term care services	Mixture of public insurance and means-tested funding available	All funding for long-term services is means-tested	Funds are means-tested, but quite limited in availability	No public funds are available for long-term care services
HCBS widely available	HCBS widely available	HCBS commonly available	HCBS limited availability	HCBS not available
Institutional care widely available	Institutional care widely available	Institutional care widely available	Institutional care somewhat available	Institutional care rarely available
Housing with services widely available	Housing with services widely available	Housing with services available	Housing with services limited availability	Housing with services not available
Cash payments often available for long-term services	Cash payments generally available	Cash payments available on a limited basis	Cash payments not available	Cash payments not available
Informal care is one component of the system	Informal care is an important part of the system	Informal care is a critical element of the system	Very heavy reliance on informal care	Exclusive reliance on informal care
Examples: Germany, Japan, South Korea, the Netherlands	Examples: France, Ireland, Spain, Switzerland, Australia	Examples: United States, Estonia, Italy, Poland, Romania	Examples: China, Thailand, South Africa, India, Egypt, Mexico, Argentina, Brazil	Examples: Kenya, Nepal, Ghana, Bangladesh

HCBS, home and community-based services.

payroll tax, personal income tax, and general revenues (national, regional, and/or municipal), these countries have in common a long-term benefit covering both in-home and institutional services for their older populations. These countries have systematic approaches to identifying and determining levels of long-term disability and an array of service options. Their LTSS systems typically include a supportive service option linked to housing and self-directed and cash options for recipients. Although informal caregivers are involved as both unpaid and sometimes paid caregivers, the overall LTSS system of nations in this category is designed to balance the help provided by informal and formal providers. Examples of countries in this group include Germany, Japan, South Korea, and the Netherlands.

Germany

In 1995, Germany established a universal, non–means-tested, contribution-based system for funding LTC (*Pflegeversicherung*); benefits vary based on whether an individual chooses cash or care reimbursement and whether care is received at home or in an institutional setting. Due in part to an increase in the number of persons needing care and heavy criticism of the lack of support for those with cognitive impairments, from 2015 to 2017 the German LTCI system underwent a series of comprehensive reforms (*Pflegestärkungsgesetze [PSG]*). The system remains funded through employee payroll contributions with matching employer contributions (contributions for unemployed persons are paid by unemployment insurance) with pensioners paying the entire contribution out of pocket; however, the percentage of contribution has changed. Beginning January 1, 2017, the contribution rate is 2.55% (up from 1.95%) of an individual's gross income; for those aged 23 and older without children, there is an additional 0.25% contribution charge (Bäcker, 2016). Those who opt out of the public system can do so if they have higher incomes that meet a strict eligibility standard. However, individuals who opt out of the public system are mandated to purchase private LTCI that guarantees at least as much coverage and benefits as the public system. With the introduction of the "Pflege-Bahr" program in 2013, the government aims to increase participation in the private system (Nadash, Doty, & von Schwanenflügel, 2018).

The LTCI fund in Germany provides for home care (family members or nonprofessional private persons), home help service (professional staff or ambulatory help), and institutional care. Individuals who have a physical illness/disability, or a mental illness or other mental incapacity, who regularly need help with ADLs or household tasks for a period of at least 6 months are eligible for benefits. The amount of benefits received is determined by the care grade into which individuals are designated. Determination of care grade is done via an examination by a medical review board (*Medizinischer Dienst der Krankenversicherung [MDK]*) designated by the insurance fund. Based on the assessment of the review board, individuals are placed into one of five care grades (previously three care levels).

Prior to the comprehensive reforms, there was little or no acknowledgment of care needs for those with cognitive impairments, and the level of care received was based on the number of minutes of care a person required. For instance, under the previous system, to receive the basic level of care (care level I), an individual would require help with basic activities (e.g., personal hygiene, feeding, mobility) at least once a day and need help with household tasks several times per week (90 minutes of care per day, of which at least 45 minutes was dedicated to basic activities).

The reform of the LTCI system saw a fundamental change in the definition of "need of care." The previous focus on estimating the length of care need was replaced by a focus on determining an individual's degree of independence (their ability to *still* perform certain tasks); assessment orientation is now focused on resources instead of deficits; there is now a comprehensive consideration of care needs (including cognitive and psychiatric) instead of an emphasis on ADLs; the idea of being dependent on assistance in order to perform specific activities was replaced by the idea that it is irrelevant whether the activity actually occurs (e.g., climbing stairs: the ability to do so is assessed even if no stairs are present in the person's environment); and the change from three care levels to five care grades (Link, 2018). Those receiving care prior to the reform were recategorized under the new care levels, so currently the German LTCI fund provides benefits for approximately 3.3 million people (Federal Ministry of Health, 2017).

Under the new evaluation criteria and expanded definition of care, assignment of care grades is based on six modules consisting of various items, which are weighted and combined for an overall care score (Link, 2018). The six modules (and their weights) are:

- Mobility (10%): for example, the ability to climb stairs or move around within the living area
- Cognitive and communicative abilities (15%): for example, temporal and spatial orientation and participating in a conversation
- Behavior patterns and psychiatric problems (15%): for example, night restlessness
- Self-care (40%): for example, washing, eating, and using the toilet
- Mastery of and dealing independently with illness or therapy-related requirements and burdens (20%): for example, taking medication or visiting the doctor
- Organization of everyday life and social contacts (15%): for example, occupying oneself and maintaining relations outside the immediate environment

Caregivers are also entitled to 6 months of leave and up to 24 months of part-time leave. The LTCI fund also contributes to pension insurance for family caregivers, defined as anyone providing care (at grade 2 or above) for at least 10 hours/week, 2 days/week and who is employed less than 30 hours (Nadash et al., 2018).

Although the LTCI system in Germany encourages care at home, nearly 27% of all individuals needing care reside in a care facility (Federal Ministry of Health, 2017). The fund covers nursing-related and medical care expenses and provides in-kind benefits for those receiving care in an institutional setting. As of May 2017, the average monthly copay for an individual receiving institutionalized care was 587€ (Federal Ministry of Health, 2017). Finally, to strengthen institutional care and improve quality, the comprehensive reforms provide for an increase in funding to support around 60,000 new professional caregivers.

Due to the relative newness of the program reforms, as of yet it is difficult to assess the success of the German LTCI system. However, it is clear that, despite political and financial challenges, the German system has been able to create and implement reforms in order to be able to provide some long-term service coverage for nearly all its citizens. Yet, with over 20% of the population aged 65 or older, a number projected to reach nearly 32% by 2050, it is unclear what new demands await the system and how Germany will face the challenges (Statistisches Bundesamt, 2015).

Japan

In April 2000, Japan implemented its national long-term insurance policy (*Kaigo Hoken Ho*), which provided a universal benefit for individuals aged 65 and older with severe disability (Yong & Saito, 2011). Since more than 23% of Japan's population was aged 65 and over in 2010 and projected to be as high as one-third by 2025 (Muramatsu & Akiyama, 2011), efforts to address the challenges of LTSS have attracted national support. The *Kaigo Hoken Ho* law relies on funds from general tax revenues, plan premiums, and copayments. Half of the program funds come from the government, either national, prefectural (prefectures are similar to states in the United States, provinces in Canada, shires in England, and departments in France), or local. The other half of funding comes from individuals, including: (a) Japanese adults between the ages of 40 and 64 who contribute through a payroll tax of 0.9%; (b) those older than age 65 who pay an income-based premium; and (c) copayment contributions by users who can afford them, equivalent to 10% of the total costs (Yong & Saito, 2011).

The LTCI covers all Japanese people aged 65 and older without regard to income. Individuals between the ages of 40 and 64 with severe disability also can qualify for LTCI benefits, but their disabilities must be caused by aging-related health conditions (e.g., early-onset dementia and cerebrovascular strokes) and require assistance with ADLs. Recipients can receive assistance at home through an array of in-home and community-based supports, including basic personal care assistance, rehabilitation and nursing services, and medical day care. The LTCI provides funding for medical equipment, such as an adjustable bed, and minor home renovation, such as a ramp (Yong & Saito, 2011). Institutional care also is covered under the LTCI fund. Nursing homes are placed into three major categories: those serving frail older people, those serving older people with high medical needs, and those focused on dementia care.

To determine eligibility for an LTCI benefit, the program relies on a structured assessment and eligibility determination process. After a person applies for or is referred to the program, a nurse or social worker employed by the municipality completes an in-home assessment of the individual's physical and mental functioning that also includes a report from the applicant's physician. The assessment information is electronically submitted, and the applicant is then placed into one of six levels of care. The assessment is then reviewed by a care needs certification board of health professionals who review the physician's report and the assessor's notes to make a final decision regarding the level of care. Eligible applicants are assigned a case manager, and service dollars are allocated based on the determined level of care. Although for planning purposes a dollar amount is associated with each specific level of care, the LTCI program does not allow a cash benefit to be paid directly to participants or their families. The case manager assists in developing, implementing, and monitoring the plan of care. The program has grown considerably since it was first introduced in 2000, when about 1.49 million users were covered. By 2010, the program was serving more than 4 million participants (about 14% of the age 65+ population;

Yong & Saito, 2011) and by 2016, the program was serving 5.11 million (Ministry of Health, Labour, and Welfare, 2016).

Reviewers of the implementation have identified a series of issues surrounding the LTCI experience (Yong & Saito, 2011). Utilization rates are higher than anticipated, with the proportion of individuals supported by the LTCI through in-home care increasing from 65% in 2000 to 75% in 2015 (Ministry of Health, Labour, and Welfare, 2016). Questions also have been raised about whether the age criterion of 65 and older is the optimum approach. In addition, the care-management component of the program in regard to the adequacy of the reimbursement rate and the independence of care managers is also an issue of concern. Finally, despite efforts to develop a national benefit, service and use patterns vary considerably across the country (Tsutsui & Muramatsu, 2005). In response to these concerns, additional revisions were made to the program in 2014. The revisions focus on two major areas; establishing a more effective community-based integrative system and making contributions to the plan more equitable. The program expanded its efforts to enhance coordination between in-home medical care and in-home long-term services and promoted efforts to serve those with dementia. The program also reinforced preventive services and attempted to more actively promote in-home services. Finally, the program worked on reducing premiums for low-income people and increased copayments for higher-income care recipients. As other countries develop efforts to respond to the LTSS needs of their citizenry, the experiences of Japan will be quite instructive in efforts to balance a comprehensive benefit with affordability.

GROUP 2

Nations included in this category have systems that rely on a mixture of public insurance and means-tested funding strategies, with a range of financing approaches. For example, some countries provide a universal benefit for certain long-term services, such as nursing-home care, but not for others, like assisted-living or in-home services. The nations in Group 2 typically have a wide array of institutional care options, community-based services, and specialized housing and supportive services. These countries typically have self-directed services available, and informal care is an important part of the system. Examples of countries in this group are Switzerland, Australia, Canada, Spain, Ireland, and France.

France

France's LTSS system includes a mix of universal and means-tested funding for a wide array of home and community-based services and institutional care. Until the 1990s, LTSS were traditionally a family or informal responsibility (Gannon & Davin, 2010). In 1997, France launched its first national LTSS program targeted at the age 60-and-older population (Le Bihan & Martin, 2013). The initial program was a care allowance to support frail older persons in need of ADL and instrumental activities of daily living (IADLs) assistance. After much criticism, this initial system was replaced by the Allocation Personnalisée d'Autonomie (APA), which is still in place today (Kraus et al., 2010). The new system is based primarily on a cash benefit. The French system is overseen by the federal government (the main funding source), but divides further fiscal and organizational responsibilities among regional or local departments (subnational governments; Colombo et al., 2011). Eligibility for APA assistance is nationally based and requires that beneficiaries be age 60 or older and meet a high level of dependency for ADLs and IADLs (Kraus et al., 2010).

The **dependency assessment** consists of three steps: (a) a request from the older person in need, (b) an evaluation by an assessment team (medical doctor, nurse, and social worker) that defines the care package, and (c) a final agreement on the care package by the departmental (state) authorities (Kraus et al., 2010). France is one of only a few countries that require a medical doctor to be involved in the assessment and care-package development process (Colombo et al., 2011). The local departmental authorities are responsible for coordinating and partially financing the APA, and they grant final approval for the care package (Kraus et al., 2010).

The APA covers both home and community-based services and institution-based care, but at a progressively reduced rate (Kraus et al., 2010). Every disabled person aged 60 and older is eligible for APA benefits, but beneficiaries are compensated based on their income. Recipients at the highest income level (about 3.5% of participants) pay 90% of their LTSS costs out of pocket, while those at the lowest income level (23%) have no cost-sharing requirements (Doty, Nadash, & Racco, 2015). Recipients receive a cash benefit that is strictly designated to support expenses that fall under an approved care package. In the case of home and community-based services, as in Japan, beneficiaries are prohibited from hiring their spouses or partners and may engage only accredited and approved providers to deliver care (Colombo et al., 2011). For institutional care, the APA covers only personal and nursing costs and requires users or their families to pay for board and lodging themselves. If the nursing-home residents and their immediate families are destitute, they can apply for housing subsidies (that is separate from the APA LTC system) to cover their nursing-home meals and lodging. The average out-of-pocket expense is about 20% of income for home and community-based services and 35% for institutional care (Colombo et al., 2011).

A unique element of the French system is that it includes one of the largest private LTCI markets in Europe. As an example, there were 5.7 million policy holders in 2012, accounting for 11% of the adult population (Doty et al., 2015). Less than 2.5% of the U.S. adult population has private LTCI. The typical policy in France provides a lower benefit amount but is less costly than the typical policy in the United States. The French system also includes caregiver support programs and increased attention to dementia-related problems. The APA provides a variety of caregiver programs such as education, training, and respite care. However, France also provides caregivers with a relatively long (3 months) unpaid leave from work that employers cannot decline, although leave is only available for caregivers of a relative with at least an 80% autonomy loss (OECD, 2011a).

Ireland

Ireland's LTSS system also combines a universal and means-tested approach. The development of a formal LTSS system is relatively new for Ireland, which launched its first national Office for Older People in 2008 (Colombo et al., 2011). Ireland's LTSS system is organized and financed by the national government, through the health service executive (HSE). Historically, Ireland's LTSS expenditure had been one of the lowest among OECD nations (OECD, 2011b), though after LTSS were prioritized through a 10-year strategy that began in 2006, Ireland's LTSS expenditure is now closer to the OECD mean (OECD, 2017). However, the use of formal LTSS remains low, with only about 0.5% of older individuals living in institutions, compared, for example, with about 5% in the United States. This low utilization rate reflects the importance placed on informal and community-based care as well as the newness of the formal LTSS system in Ireland.

In 2009, Ireland initiated the **Fair Deal legislation,** which states everyone with care needs is eligible for personal care in institutions (this plan, unlike France's, covers room and board; Colombo et al., 2011). This plan was revised in 2013 and now requires that all participants contribute 80% of their incomes and 7.5% (5% prior to 2013) of their assets' value toward the cost of their care. However, because the formal LTSS system is relatively new, access is limited by resources and has resulted in targeting those most in need. There is a 3-year cap on asset-based contributions (for a total of 22%; prior to 2013, the cap was 15%), and in the case of a couple when only one of the individuals is residing in an institution, the personal contribution is based on only half of their assets (HSE, 2017).

Despite Ireland's relatively clear-cut LTSS plan, several issues surround eligibility and asset protection. Until 2006, there was no national standard for needs assessment, but Ireland is currently using a common assessment report. This report takes into account ADLs, currently provided medical, health, and personal social services, available family and community support, and personal wishes and preferences and is carried out by an HSE-appointed health care professional (HSE, 2017). A system similar to the U.S. public reverse mortgage program, called the Nursing Home Loan, has been developed. Despite a 3-year cap on asset testing, this program allows individuals to borrow on the equity in their homes to pay for institutional care. This type of program demonstrates the role that the government can play in converting nonmonetary assets into cash to pay for nursing-home care (Colombo et al., 2011).

According to an OECD (2011b) report, an informal care provision in most countries is highly dependent on the health status of the care recipient. Those who have greater ADL limitations are more likely to receive care in an institutional setting. This is not the case in Ireland, however, where no correlation is found between the health status of care recipients and their care setting. This is likely related to the strong traditional informal support system in Ireland as well as the many caregiver support programs. For example, Ireland's Home Care Package Scheme is not means-tested and was recently expanded to target high-risk patients awaiting discharge from the hospital (Noonan, 2014). In addition, an array of public training, education, and counseling programs is available for caregivers. Ireland is one of a few nations that allow a long leave from work for caregivers (up to 1 year or more), but employers can refuse this on certain grounds (Courtin, Jemiai, & Mossialos, 2014). The Carer's Allowance (a means-tested government program) provides cash benefits to caregivers and acts like an income support program, replacing lost wages or caring expenses (Colombo et al., 2011). The Constant Attendance Allowance (a government program based on compulsory social insurance for employees) is considered more of an income support program than a formal caregiver payment and covers such expenses as travel and utilities (gas and electricity; Colombo et al., 2011). Beyond allowances, Ireland provides a respite-care grant that is tax-supported, non–means-tested, and available to all resident caregivers who provide full-time care (OECD, 2011b).

GROUP 3

Countries in this grouping offer a wide array of long-term services, including supportive housing, institutional care, and home and community-based services. Under this model, no public insurance is available to fund LTSS. Typically, a range of services is available to low-income persons meeting a high-disability and low-income threshold. Under the approach used in these countries, all LTSS are means-tested, and public financing does not begin until individuals have depleted their own resources. Self-directed care is available on a limited basis for some services for certain populations. Informal care is an integral part of this system, with an expectation that family will provide primary assistance prior to using governmental services. Examples of Group 3 countries include the United States, Italy, Poland, Romania, and Estonia.

United States

Because the United States continues to have policy debates and controversy about its overall approach to health care, it is not surprising that it has never designed an LTSS system. In fact, the major program for LTSS in the United States—Medicaid, adopted in 1965 as a health care program for the poor—did not even include most of the LTSS funded today. Neither the intermediate care nursing-home benefit (added in 1967) nor the home and community-based care benefit (added in 1981) was included in the original legislation. Medicaid accounts for almost 43% of all LTSS expenditures in the United States. It has very strict income and asset criteria and requires recipients to have severe disability. Under no exceptions can individuals receive Medicaid assistance for LTSS unless they meet the strict income and disability criteria.

Other sources of revenue for LTSS include Medicare, which now accounts for 22% of all expenditures; out-of-pocket payments by individuals (17%); individual private LTCI policies (6%); other private health insurance (5%); and other public entities (7%), such as the U.S. Department of Veterans Affairs (VA) and state-funded programs (Nguyen, 2017). The social insurance program covering health care for older people, Medicare, provides a 100% nursing-home rehabilitation benefit for 20 days following a 3-day or longer stay in the hospital, and 80 additional days with a significant copay. Medicare also provides home health care coverage, but again, it is only delivered in conjunction with an acute care illness and not as a chronic care benefit.

The United States has an extensive array of formal services available to the approximately 6 million older adults with disability, including more than 16,000 nursing homes serving more than 1.5 million individuals. The income-tested Medicaid program supports approximately two-thirds of all nursing-home residents, although when residing in the community fewer than 8% of these individuals were eligible for the program (Stone, 2011). In the United States, the majority of nursing homes are for-profit (70%; Harris-Kojetin et al., 2016). Additionally, about 800,000 individuals receive home and community-based services provided through Medicaid-waiver programs operated at the state level (Eiken, Sredl, Burwell, & Amos, 2018). The so-called "waiver" programs were initiated in 1981, when the U.S. Congress passed legislation allowing states to waive Medicaid requirements that required Medicaid LTSS funds to be spent in institutional settings. A sizable private home-care market, estimated to be similar in scope to publicly supported services, also exists for individuals who do not meet the strict Medicaid eligibility criteria for income and severity of disability. Private-pay individuals, and in some states publicly funded participants, can self-direct their services, determining both the nature of assistance received and who will provide the necessary assistance. Tested in a research demonstration called the National Cash and Counseling Demonstration and Evaluation (Benjamin & Fennell, 2007), self-direction for Medicaid recipients is now being expanded across the United States (Sciegaj et al., 2016).

Housing with supportive services is also an important component of the U.S. LTSS system. In particular, the assisted-living option has expanded rapidly in recent years. Under this model, an individual with severe disability resides in a small apartment with a bathroom and a basic food-preparation area. Residents receive personal care, meals, and housekeeping services directly from the facility; however, home health care generally is provided through an agency as though the individuals were living in the community. More than 800,000 individuals now reside in assisted-living facilities across the United States. Although typically funded privately, in recent years, the means-tested Medicaid home and community-based waiver program has allowed public funds to be used for assisted living.

In many states a not-for-profit network of organizations, termed area agencies on aging, provide case management and coordination for in-home service networks. These agencies often complete eligibility assessments for LTSS settings and help ensure that the needed services are provided. Information provided by these agencies is available to all older persons, although most of the programs and services are earmarked for low-income individuals.

As a large country with a well-developed services system, annually the United States spends more than $339 billion on LTSS (Nguyen, 2017). The majority of the nursing homes, assisted-living facilities, and home care agencies are proprietary in nature, and the U.S. delivery system is consistent with the market values of the nation. One of the major challenges faced by the U.S. LTSS system is the very high costs that are increasingly being shifted to the public Medicaid program, which is jointly funded by the federal and state governments. In many U.S. states, the costs of LTSS are becoming one of the highest expenditure categories in state government—rivaling the cost of education—and projections suggest that the current system will continue to represent a challenge to state budgets across the nation.

Estonia

Unlike many countries, due to out-migration, Estonia's population is actually decreasing. This makes LTSS for older adults (19% of the total population) even more of a challenge. The goal of LTSS in Estonia is to help individuals achieve the best possible quality of life, based on their needs and abilities—remaining at home for as long as possible (Paat & Merilain, 2010). LTSS in Estonia are mandated by the Social Welfare Act and are divided between local governments and the individuals needing care. Public health insurance pays for a significant portion of nursing care (financed via a payroll tax). Although LTSS are provided regardless of age, the amount of financial support or welfare services received is means-tested. Preference for funding is given to those who remain at home, with allowances for family caregivers provided by local municipalities (Colombo et al., 2011). Assurance of quality of care in institutional settings has been left to the local governments, which until recently have been criticized for not holding facilities to high standards. In many LTC institutions, there is a shortage of both beds and space and a lack of quality care (Paat & Merilain, 2010). Additional funds have been allocated to address this shortage, and in an attempt to identify effective methods by which to increase access to and coordination of LTSS, a preliminary case-management model was piloted in conjunction with the World Bank (Paat & Masson, 2018).

An interdisciplinary team of professionals conducts an assessment for LTSS eligibility. Specially trained case managers assess an individual's health and need for personal assistance, guidance, or supervision. Doctors assess an individual's need for nursing care and a local social worker examines an individual's need for welfare services. Estonia's health insurance fund pays for the initial assessment for care need and for nursing care. Service users can expect to pay a portion of institutional care, and home health care costs are divided between local governments and the service users (Paat & Merilain, 2010). However, there is no common nationally standardized needs assessment instrument. Thus, eligibility for publicly funded LTSS varies widely across municipalities (Paat & Masson, 2018).

Under the current Estonian system, service users can receive benefits from the state (in cash) or from the local government (either in cash or in-kind). In general, the state outlines the minimum requirements for service provisions. Local governments plan, implement, and supervise care services. Several different types of care are recognized by the state, but all are provided by local governments unless otherwise noted. Allowances are provided for care by relatives or informal nonfamily caregivers. Home services (e.g., household chores) are provided either by the local government or by a private company (Colombo et al., 2011). Additional types of care include housing services (providing 24-hour accommodations), a personal assistant, adult day care, institutional care, strengthened support care (which has a goal of improving independence), and strengthened supervision care services (with a goal of maintaining quality of life in an institution; Paat & Merilain, 2010).

A number of challenges are recognized throughout the Estonian LTSS system. With little national oversight, quality of care remains a significant issue. Additionally, the current system is rather fragmented, with some funds and services provided by the state and some by local governments or private companies. Finally, although the goal of the LTSS system is to promote domiciliary care (housing and care combined), financial support is insufficient (€62 per month, on average; Paat & Masson, 2018). To address these concerns, a special task force was assembled with the aim of identifying long-term service policy solutions. The changes have two significant goals: (a) to integrate state and local services and (b) to reduce the care burden of informal caregivers. With a fragmented system providing less than ideal care, it is clear that the Estonian LTSS system will need to see substantial changes in the coming years in order to meet the needs of an aging population.

GROUP 4

Nations included in Group 4 have very limited public funds to support individuals in need of LTSS, but they have begun to see the development of some private service providers, particularly in the areas of nursing-home and in-home care. Older people in Group 4 countries who need such care must rely on family and friends for the majority of assistance received. Examples of countries in this group include Thailand, India, Mexico, Brazil, South Africa, and China. The demarcation of Groups 4 and 5 (discussed later) is not always easily discerned, because nations with extremely limited LTSS funds may appear to be more similar to nations in Group 5 than others in Group 4.

Brazil

To prepare for population aging and LTSS issues, in the 1990s Brazil created the National Policy for the Elderly (Política Nacional do Idoso [PNI]), which includes a list of actions to ensure social rights, autonomy, integration, and effective participation in society among the older population (Neumann & Albert, 2018). However, with a lack of resources and formal structure to enforce these directives, implementation is largely the responsibility of municipalities and families. One of the most noteworthy outcomes of the National Policy for the Elderly was to ensure that anyone aged 65 and older who cannot provide their own livelihood is eligible for a noncontributory pension equal to the monthly minimum wage of R$954 (Brazilian real, or US$300). The Brazilian pension system also includes a mandatory pay-as-you-go system for private-sector workers and a series of separate mandatory systems for public workers—approximately 75% of the older adult population receives some social security benefit (Neumann & Albert, 2018). While often recognized as a leader among South American countries in pension reform, Brazil lacks a formal LTSS policy.

Established in 2006, the National Health Policy for the Elderly (Política Nacional de Saúde da Pessoa Idosa [PNSI]) provided national guidelines for active aging and the management of frailty, but failed to address a growing need for LTSS policy. Nursing homes are not common in Brazil; they provide care for only about 1% of the older population and mainly exist in large cities (Neumann & Albert, 2018). A few public nursing homes exist to serve older disabled individuals who have no family left and no means to pay for care (Garcez-Leme & Leme, 2014). Home and community-based supports are also limited. The Family Health Program (Programa Saúde da Família), which was originally designed to address maternal and child health, has expanded to incorporate chronic conditions. This program provides home visits to every household in 95% of municipalities and includes a multidisciplinary team of health workers (i.e., doctor, nurse, and community health workers), each of whom is responsible for 120 families in their defined area. However, the focus of this program is primary care, as training and resources for LTSS delivery are limited (Garcez-Leme & Leme, 2014).

China

With the largest older population in the world (more than 143 million people aged 65+), China faces monumental challenges as it addresses the LTSS needs of the nation. The aging population in China has increased from 3.6% of the total in 1964 to 10.5% in 2015; by 2050, the number of older people is expected to reach 349 million and account for one-quarter of China's population (He, Goodkind, & Kowal, 2016). Compounding China's challenges is the now well-known one-child policy that has contributed to China's fertility rate dropping from 2.9 in 1980 to 1.6 in 2012 (Das & N'Diaye, 2013).

Although it was not until the 1990s that institutional care became available in China, by 2006, the country had more than 39,500 institutions with about 1.5 million beds; by 2012, there were an estimated 45,000 nursing institutions; and by 2017, that number was estimated to be more than 144,000 (Flaherty et al., 2007; Xinhua, 2018; Zhan, Feng, Chen, & Feng, 2011). The definition of a nursing home in China is not the same as in the United States, with many of these facilities not providing any medical services; estimates vary, but probably about half provide no medical or nursing care. Further, about half of the "nursing-home" residents in China are reported to be able to take care of themselves, suggesting that for many residents this model of care is better described as "housing with supportive services." There are five types of institutions, varying by both the kind and level of disability and economic resources available (Chou, 2010). Institutions in rural areas tend to offer a lower level of care than urban facilities. These rural homes are also more likely than those in urban areas to be funded by the government (Wu, Mao, & Xu, 2008). These facilities appear to serve a range of residents, from those with minimal impairment to those with high levels of disability (Chou, 2010). In addition to government funding, these institutions are paid by medical insurance and through private (out-of-pocket) expenditures. Based on concerns about quality of care, legislation was passed in 2013 to establish new regulations requiring nursing-home inspections and better protections for residents.

China appears to have a strong commitment to family and community support. The overwhelming majority of older Chinese adults with severe disability receive assistance in their own homes, either from family caregivers or through a live-in maid system, termed *bao mu*. For example, a study in Shanghai found that more than 90% of individuals with dementia were cared by families at home (Hua & Di, 2002). In fact, the Chinese Constitution states that "children who come of age have the duty to support and assist their parents" (Chu & Chi, 2008). Although family care is the dominant mode of LTC, China's recent demographic changes in combination with the one-child policy present considerable future challenges.

Formal community services are now being developed across China, with estimates identifying more than 900,000 community service centers (Chu & Chi, 2008). A study of community service centers in Shanghai found that these government-funded entities provided such services as shopping, home maintenance, counseling, and meals (Wu, Carter, Goins, & Cheng, 2005). These centers also help to arrange the *bao mu* (housemaid service) that generally provides personal care services, household chores, shopping, and accompanying seniors to medical visits. The vast majority of the *bao mu* workers are paid out of pocket by older people and their families (Wu et al., 2005).

China certainly recognizes the tremendous challenges it faces in the future. As part of its national strategic plan, the government has set a goal of establishing a comprehensive social care system as the foundation of its LTSS system, to be supported by institutional care (Zhang, 2011). As a result of this plan, a large number of new institutional beds have been added in the past 5 to 7 years. China has made strides in its efforts to develop a more comprehensive system of LTSS, but the tremendous growth in the size of the older population and the reduced fertility rate suggest considerable challenges ahead.

GROUP 5

Nations falling into this final grouping are generally very poor and have a very limited array of formal services available. For the most part, nursing homes do not exist in these countries, and very few in-home services are available. Generally, public funding for support services for older individuals with severe disability does not exist. Families provide the majority of LTSS, and these nations expect families will continue to be responsible for such care. Countries included in this category are Nepal, Kenya, Ghana, and Bangladesh.

Kenya
Until now, the discussion of LTSS around the globe has focused on countries with at least some formal system for providing such services and supports to older

adults. Kenya, unlike the countries previously discussed in this chapter, stands in stark contrast, having essentially no formalized LTSS system. Moreover, the long-established informal network of social support via family caregivers has undergone significant changes in recent years, leaving many older adults impoverished and with little familial support.

Historically in Kenya, as in most of the less economically developed countries, parents provide care for their children until grown, and in return children have a duty to provide care for their parents when they reach old age. However, a number of social and economic factors have caused a change in this arrangement. On the economic side, in order to explore new job opportunities and advancements, a relatively recent shift toward urban migration for younger adults—rather than remaining in rural farming communities—has left many older adults alone in rural areas to tend the family homestead. This is also happening in many other nations, including China, Thailand, and Vietnam.

The most notable social factor remains the HIV/AIDS epidemic, which currently affects approximately 4.8% of the Kenyan population (U.S. Central Intelligence Agency *World Factbook*, 2017). Palliative care and LTSS in sub-Saharan Africa are primarily associated with HIV and AIDS, leaving the needs of older adults largely neglected (WHO, 2017). Due to the rise in the number of individuals who contract this often-fatal disease, caring roles have become less clear, as many parents are forced to provide care for their adult children who have AIDS. It has been noted that although older adults derive satisfaction from their caregiving roles, many still lack adequate knowledge, skills, and resources for patient care (WHO, 2017). Additionally, due to the AIDS epidemic, the number of grandparents providing care for grandchildren also is increasing (Small, Aldwin, Kowal, & Chatterji, 2017). Economic, emotional, and physical strain often are associated with becoming, as an older adult, a full-time caregiver for young children.

Although formal social support is still relatively sparse in Kenya, a few organizations, like HelpAge International (through its local affiliate, HelpAge Kenya), supply economic assistance in some parts of the country to impoverished older adults who provide care for orphaned children (HelpAge International, 2018a). On a national level, the Ministry of Gender, Children, and Social Development (MGCSD) coordinates programs for older adults. In an effort to ease the burden on older adults, beginning in 2004 the Older Persons Cash Transfer (OPCT) Program—targeting individuals over age 65—established a way to provide older adults with essential funds for obtaining necessary provisions such as food, clothes, and adequate shelter (Mwaisaji, 2015). In July 2009, Kenya launched a program targeting impoverished older adults with its new pension scheme (HelpAge International, 2009a). Traditionally, the old-age pension in Kenya was tied to employment, with employee contributions to the social security fund accounting for about 5% of their earnings (Social Security Administration, 2017). This pension program, which eliminates the contributory element, makes Kenya one of the few countries in the region to have a noncontributory pension. Beginning in December 2009, older citizens (aged 65+) in 750 "extremely poor households" in 44 districts received 1500Ksh (Kenyan shillings; approximately US$19.40) per month (HelpAge International, 2009b). Payments are made through mobile phones, post offices, or electronic cards. The Kenyan government plans to extend this program to all persons aged 70 and older (HelpAge International, 2018b).

Several policy plans have included provisions for the needs of older persons, although all were broad, general goal statements and took few direct actions (Mbithi & Mutuku, 2010). From 2002 to 2008, the ninth National Development Plan designed programs to sensitize the public to the needs and rights of older individuals. Another example of national-level policy proposals, the Kenya National Policy on Aging, aimed to integrate the needs and concerns of older adults into national policy by ensuring that older people were "reorganized, respected, and empowered to actively and fully participate in society and development" (Mbithi & Mutuku, 2010). Unfortunately, little progress has been made toward implementation of any national policies related to LTSS for older adults in Kenya.

An opportunity exists for the government of Kenya to begin implementing the policies that have been outlined to provide care and funds for older citizens in need. HIV and AIDS education, as well as teaching proper caregiving techniques, would benefit Kenya's older population, providing predictable, adequate levels of support to improve their living, working, and aging conditions.

Nepal

Family members, rather than governmental agencies or nonprofit government funded organizations (nongovernmental organizations [NGOs]), provide LTSS in Nepal. Institutional care is practically nonexistent, with fewer than a handful of old-age homes in the entire country. Nepal has approximately 28.5 million people, with 5.5% of the population aged 65 and older. Yet, life expectancy at birth has been improving for both men and women in Nepal, increasing from age 41 in 1971 to age 69 in 2016, when for the first time life expectancy for women surpassed that of men. Approximately 83% of the older population reside with their children in rural areas (Pienta, Barber, & Axinn, 2001). A 1995 study, the Disabled People of Nepal Survey, reported that the prevalence of disability across all age groups was 4.6% (Basnyat, 2010).

Nepal has a small number of old-age homes, called *Briddha Ashram*. Funded by the government of Nepal, *Pashupati Briddha Ashram* is one of the oldest old-age homes and is situated near a famous temple, since Nepali people share a religious and cultural belief that after-death cremation near this temple ensures entry to heaven (Basnyat, 2010). Although the capacity of this shelter home is only 150 individuals, approximately 200 older people reside there. Recently, several additional shelter homes for older adults have opened. The *Nishaya Sewa Sadan* (shelter home for the helpless) is partially funded by the government and has 56 residents. It also receives contributions from residents and/or their families, and some funds are provided by additional sources such as voluntary contributions. Siddhi Memorial Old Age Home, a private, nonprofit facility funded by residents' family and friends and a German nonprofit organization, also opened in 2008.

This institution targets those older people who can make private out-of-pocket payments for care and appears to be the only such facility in Nepal.

People aged 65 and older currently constitute almost 6% of Nepal's population, but by 2030 this proportion is projected to double (He, Goodkind, & Kowal, 2016). With no formal community-based services and an institutional capacity of fewer than 1,000 beds nationwide, older persons with disability rely exclusively on family and friends for LTC needs. Although the country has a long-standing cultural tradition of filial piety, economic and social changes are now presenting major challenges to this approach. As the nation shifts to a more urban economy, as are China, Kenya, Thailand, and other countries, many of the younger family members are migrating to the cities, resulting in higher levels of unmet need for the older population. Because of a weak economy, the country has been unable to develop even a basic infrastructure for old-age pensions, and the development of LTSS does not seem to be a high priority. A study of Nepali political officials found that the majority of respondents were unaware of problems associated with LTSS, and they did not believe that the development of such services was an important role of the government (Basnyat, 2010).

CROSS-CUTTING ISSUES FOR AN AGING PLANET

The examples provided in this chapter indicate tremendous variations in the ability of countries to address the LTC needs of their citizens. Despite the many differences that exist among nations, at least four LTSS policy issues unite them.

Financing

Although it is clear that nations with higher per capita incomes (typically those in Groups 1–3) have developed a much more extensive array of LTSS, it is also evident that literally every one of these nations is facing challenges of long-term financing. Even highly resourced nations such as the United States, Japan, and Germany face substantial funding issues as they address the potential needs of their boomer populations. Although the older population in need of long-term services in the developed world is projected to more than double in the next 30 years, none of these countries has programs ready for the demographic growth they will experience between now and 2050. Some of the countries in Group 4 that now are experiencing rapid economic growth and an evolving LTSS system, such as China, India, and Thailand, also will face huge future challenges. These nations are still in the process of developing their LTSS infrastructure, but they will experience a faster growth rate of their older populations than the nations in Groups 1–3. Thus, these nations will be under pressure to quickly create an adequately financed system for their elders. Finally, it is the Group 5 nations that may be in for the biggest challenge. With no formal long-term service funding on the horizon, but a recognition that their aging populations will grow substantially, these nations must develop both an infrastructure and financing mechanism quickly. However, many of these nations do not have basic pension plans in place, making it a remote likelihood that planning for long-term services will occur.

Support for Family

Regardless of a nation's resources, LTSS of older people are a family issue. Even for those nations with well-developed formal service systems, it is clear that informal supports are critical. However, a consistent theme heard in many countries is that demographic and social changes are placing more pressure on families. Whether it is the one-child policy of China, the migration patterns of rural Kenya and Nepal, or the dual-income worker structure in Europe and the United States, country after country is experiencing changes that are affecting the family's ability to provide assistance. Efforts to develop sound policies to support families in their role of assisting their elderly loved ones will be a universal challenge in years to come.

Need to Develop an Efficient and Effective LTSS System

No nation has yet figured out how to provide and pay for all types of LTSS in the most effective and efficient manner possible. Some countries have developed excellent supportive services in housing; others have created well-developed in-home care systems; still others have developed high-quality nursing homes or assisted-living communities. Certain nations are exploring the use of technology to improve service provision; others have developed effective and efficient systems to pay family members and friends for caregiving. Many interesting innovations are appearing, but countries have not done a good job of adopting the most successful approaches of other nations. The LTSS challenges that the world faces are monumental; in years to come, it will be necessary that countries share knowledge and take advantage of progress, similar to what has occurred in medical research and treatment.

Need for Prevention

A review of global demographic and social changes indicates that the number of older people with severe disability will more than double by 2040. Although such growth is a symbol of progress, suggesting many more people are surviving into old age and living longer with their disabilities, such changes will also place major financial pressures on all nations. Therefore, substantial efforts aimed at preventive actions will be necessary in four important areas. First, as mentioned in Chapter 1, Our Aging World, it must be recognized that aging occurs across a life course and that such issues as childhood obesity and malnutrition and access to adequate health care in early life will significantly affect rates of disability in later life. Second, we must continue to explore and encourage lifestyle changes, including exercise and social engagement, to help prevent or at least forestall disability in later life.

Small delays in disability will yield big economic and social benefits. Third, we must encourage environmental changes that can help older individuals optimize the livability of their home settings. Simply improving access to a toilet and the ease of use of a kitchen can make a significant difference in allowing a person to manage disability at home. Large-scale efforts such as the WHO Age Friendly Cities Project can have a large impact across the globe (WHO, 2007). Finally, technological development will be necessary. Whether it be more low-technology devices, such as water or door sensors (an electronic sensor that sounds an alarm when it detects running water or the opening of a door), or high-technology robots or floor sensors (actual devices built into the floor that monitor gait and assess fall risk), it is evident that technical innovation is needed to help meet the challenges of our aging populations.

CONCLUSION

Countries around the world have adopted a variety of fiscal and care system responses to their growing number of older adults who need assistance with the tasks of daily living. Based on the type of care provided and the financing structure, and in an effort to more clearly articulate the different approaches to LTSS, a typology of LTSS systems has been created, ranging from most to least comprehensive. For countries in Group 1, like Germany, care is widely available and publicly supported and funded. Group 2 countries, like France, have a mix of publicly funded and **means-tested LTSS**, and informal care is an important part of the system. For the United States, a country that falls into Group 3, most public funding is means-tested, and individuals are expected to be financially responsible for their own LTSS. In Group 4 countries like China, funding for care is means-tested and available only on a very limited basis, so Chinese elders rely heavily on informal family care. Finally, for countries like Kenya in Group 5, no public funds are available for LTSS; so very few care programs exist and older adults must rely almost exclusively on informal care and support networks. All nations must take steps to mitigate the challenges of an aging population by creating sustainable LTSS financing systems, finding better ways to support informal caregivers, sharing ideas for best-care practices, and focusing efforts on prevention.

DISCUSSION QUESTIONS

1. Who provides LTSS, and in what types of locations do individuals receive such assistance?

2. Is there a formal LTSS system in your country? How is it funded? Who is eligible to receive services?

3. What are the advantages and disadvantages of using means testing as a way for determining eligibility for publicly funded LTSS? How do these advantages and disadvantages compare to those for a universal system?

4. Should LTSS programs be designed specifically for, and only offered to, older people?

5. Can you see any overlap in the groupings included in the LTC typology? Are there countries that might fit in more than one category?

6. Of the countries you read about in this chapter, which two or three seem to have systems that make sense to you? Would their systems work in your country?

KEY WORDS

Activities of daily living
Dependency assessment
Entitlement
Fair Deal legislation
Home and community-based services
Housing with supportive services
Instrumental activities of daily living

Long-term care
Long-term services and supports
Means testing
Social long-term care insurance
Tax-based systems
Universal systems

REFERENCES

Bäcker, G. (2016). Reform of the long-term care insurance in Germany. *European Commission: ESPN Flash Report 2016/43.* Retrieved from https://ec.europa.eu/social/BlobServlet?docId=16074&langId=en

Basnyat, K. (2010). *Decision-makers' perception and knowledge about long-term care in Nepal: An exploratory study.* Master's Thesis, Miami University, Oxford, Ohio.

Benjamin, A. E., & Fennell, M. L. (2007). Putting the consumer first: An introduction and overview. *Health Services Research, 42*(1), 353–361.

Chou, R. J. (2010). Willingness to live in eldercare institutions among older adults in urban and rural China: A nationwide study. *Ageing & Society, 30,* 583–608. doi:10.1017/S0144686X09990596

Chu, L. W., & Chi, I. (2008). Nursing homes in China. *Journal of American Medical Directors Association, 9,* 237–243. doi:10.1016/j.jamda.2008.01.008

Colombo, F., Llena-Nozal, A., Mercier, J., & Tjadens, F. (2011). *Help wanted? Providing and paying for long-term care.* OECD Health Policy Studies, OECD Publishing. Retrieved from http://dx.doi.org/10.1787/9789264097759-en

Courtin, E., Jemiai, N., & Mossialos, E. (2014). Mapping support policies for informal carers across the European Union. *Health Policy, 118*(1), 84–94. doi:10.1016/j.healthpol.2014.07.013

Das, M., & N'Diaye, P. (2013). Chronicle of a Decline Foretold: Has China reached the Lewis Turning Point? IMF Working Paper 13/26, International Monetary Fund.

Doty, P., Nadash, P., & Racco, N. (2015). Long-term care financing: lessons from France. *The Milbank Quarterly, 93*(2), 359–391. doi:10.1111/1468-0009.12125

Eiken, S., Sredl, K., Burwell, B., & Amos, A. (2018). *Medicaid expenditures for long-term services and supports in FY 2016.* IAP: Medicaid Innovation Accelerator Program.

Federal Ministry of Health. (2017). Peer review on "Germany's latest reforms of the long-term care system" - Host Country Discussion Paper. *European Commission: DG Employment, Social Affairs and Inclusion.* Retrieved from http://ec.europa.eu/social/BlobServlet?docId=18962&langId=en

Flaherty, J. H., Liu, M. L., Ding, L., Dong, D., Ding, Q., Li, X., & Xiao, S. (2007). China: The aging giant. *Journal of the American Geriatrics Society, 55,* 1295–1300. doi:10.1111/j.1532-5415.2007.01273.x

Gannon, B., & Davin, B. (2010). Use of formal and informal care services among older people in Ireland and France. *European Journal of Health Economics, 11,* 499–511. doi:10.1007/s10198-010-0247-1

Garcez-Leme, E. L., & Leme, D. M. (2014). Costs of elderly health care in Brazil: Challenges and strategies. *Medical Express, 1*(1), 3–8. doi:10.5935/MedicalExpress.2014.01.02

Harris-Kojetin, L., Sengupta, M., Park-Lee, E., Valverde, R., Caffrey, C., Rome, V., & Lendon, J. (2016). Long-term care providers and services users in the United States: Data from the national study of long-term care providers, 2013-2014. *Vital & health statistics. Analytical and Epidemiological Studies, 38*, 1–105.

He, W., Goodkind, D., & Kowal, P. (2016). *An aging world: 2015*. U.S. Census Bureau, International Population Reports, P95-16-1. Washington, DC: U.S. Government Publishing Office. Retrieved from http://www.census.gov/library/publications/2016/demo/P95-16-1.html

HelpAge International. (2009a). Practical issues in ageing & development. *Ageing & Development, Issue 26*. Retrieved from https://www.helpage.org/silo/files/ageing-and-development-26.pdf

HelpAge International. (2009b). Practical issues in ageing & development. *Ageing & Development, Issue 27*.

HelpAge International. (2018a). Why we work in Kenya. Retrieved from http://www.helpage.org/where-we-work/africa/kenya

HelpAge International. (2018b). Kenya to launch universal pension scheme in January 2018. Retrieved from http://www.helpage.org/newsroom/latest-news/kenya-to-launch-universal -pension-scheme-in-january-2018

HSE. (2017). Nursing homes support scheme: Information booklet. Version No. 03/17. Retrieved from https://www.hse.ie/eng/fair-deal-scheme/applying-for-fair-deal/information-booklet.pdf

Hua, F., & Di, X. (2002). Case-study: China. In J. Brodsky, J. Habib, & M. Hirschfeld (Eds.), *The World Health Organization Collection on Long-Term Care: Long-Term Care in Developing Countries*. Geneva, Switzerland: World Health Organization.

Kinsella, K., & He, W. (2009). An aging world: 2008. In U.S. Census Bureau (Ed.), *International population reports P95/09-1*. Washington, DC: U.S. Government Printing Office. Retrieved from https://www .census.gov/prod/2009pubs/p95-09-1.pdf

Kraus, M., Riedel, M., Mot, E., Willeme, P., Rohrling, G., & Czypionka, T. (2010). *A typology of long-term care systems in Europe*. European Network of Economic Policy Research Institutes. Assessing Needs of Care in European Nations (ANCIEN).

Le Bihan, B., & Martin, C. (2013). Steps towards a long-term care policy in France: Specificities, process, and actors. In C. Ranci & E. Pavolini (Eds.), *Reforms in long-term care policies in Europe*. New York, NY: Springer Publishing Company.

Link, S. (2018). Long-term care reform in Germany—At long last. *Institute and Faculty of Actuaries*. Retrieved from https://www.actuaries.org.uk/documents/long-term-care-reform-germany-long-last

Mbithi, L. M., & Mutuku, M. (2010). *Social protection status in developing countries: The case of Kenya*. Draft paper prepared for ERD regional conference on promoting resilience through social protection in sub-Saharan Africa.

Ministry of Health, Labour and Welfare. (2016). Long-term care insurance system of Japan: Health and welfare Bureau for the elderly. Retrieved from https://www.mhlw.go.jp/english/policy/care -welfare/care-welfare-elderly/dl/ltcisj_e.pdf

Muramatsu, N., & Akiyama, H. (2011). Japan: Super-aging society preparing for the future. *The Gerontologist, 51*, 425–432. doi:10.1093/geront/gnr067

Mwaisaji. W., (2015). Scaling up cash transfer programs in Kenya. International Policy Center for Inclusive Growth, No. 286. ISSN: 2318-9118. Retrieved from https://www.ipc-undp.org/pub/eng/OP286 _Scaling_up_Cash_Transfer_Programmes_in_Kenya.pdf

Nadash, P., Doty, P., & von Schwanenflügel, M. (2018). The German long-term care insurance program: evolution and recent developments. *The Gerontologist, 8, 58*(3), 588–597. doi:10.1093/geront/gnx018

Neumann, L. T. V., & Albert, S. M. (2018). Aging in Brazil. *The Gerontologist, 58*(4), 611–617. doi:10.1093/ geront/gyn019

Nguyen, V., (2017). Long-term support and services. *AARP Public Policy Institute: Fact sheet*. Retrieved from https://www.aarp.org/content/dam/aarp/ppi/2017-01/Fact%20Sheet%20Long-Term%20 Support%20and%20Services.pdf

Noonan, B., (2014). Understanding the reasons why patients delay seeking treatment for oral cancer symptoms from a primary health care professional: An integrative literature review. *European Journal of Oncology Nursing, 18*(1), 118–124. doi:10.1016/j.ejon.2013.07.005

OECD. (n.d.). Country List. Retrieved from https://www.oecd.org/about/members-and-partners

OECD. (2011a). France long-term care. In *Help wanted? Providing and paying for long-term care*. Paris, France: OECD Publishing. Retrieved from https://www.oecd.org/els/health-systems/help-wanted-9789264097759-en.htm

OECD. (2011b). Ireland long-term care. In *Help wanted? Providing and paying for long-term care*. Paris, France: OECD Publishing. Retrieved from https://www.oecd.org/els/health-systems/help-wanted-9789264097759-en.htm

OECD. (2017). Long-term care expenditure. In *Health at a Glance 2017: OECD indicators*. Paris: OECD Publishing. doi:10.1787/health_glance-2017-81-en

Paat, G. & Masso, M. (2018). ESPN thematic report on challenges in long-term care: Estonia 2018. *European Commission, Brussels*.

Paat, G., & Merilain, M. (2010). *Long-term care in Estonia*. European Network of Economic Policy Research Institutes. ENEPRI Research Report No. 75.

Pienta, A. M., Barber, J. S., & Axinn, W. G. (2001). Social change and adult children's attitudes toward support of elderly parents: Evidence from Nepal. *Hallym International Journal of Aging, 3*, 211–235. doi:10.1092/D5T7-2BMY-YP4W-T2NU

Statistisches Bundesamt. (2015). Pflegestatistik 2013. Pflege im Rahmen der Pflegeversicherung. Deutschlandergebnisse. Retrieved from https://www.destatis.de/DE/Publikationen/Thematisch/Gesundheit/Pflege/PflegeDeutschlandergebnisse5224001159004.pdf?__blob=publicationFile

Stone, R. (2011). *Long-term care for the elderly*. Washington, DC: The Urban Institute Press.

Sciegaj, M., Mahoney, K. J., Schwartz, A. J., Simon-Rusinowitz, L., Selkow, I., & Loughlin, D. M. (2016). An inventory of publicly funded participant-directed long-term services and supports programs in the United States. *Journal of Disability Policy Studies, 26*(4), 245–251. doi:10.1177/1044207314555810

Small, J., Aldwin, C., Kowal, P., & Chatterji, S. (2017). Aging and HIV-related caregiving in Sub-Saharan Africa: A social ecological approach. *The Gerontologist, 59*(3), e223–e240. doi:10.1093/geront/gnx159

Social Security Administration. (2017). *Social Security programs throughout the world: Africa, 2017* (SSA Publication No. 13-11804). Washington, DC: U.S. Government Printing Office.

Tsutsui, T., & Muramatsu, N. (2005). Care-needs certification in the long-term care insurance system of Japan. *Journal of the American Geriatrics Society, 53*, S22–S27. doi:10.1111/j.1532-5415.2005.53175.x

U.S. Central Intelligence Agency World Factbook. (2017). Kenya. Retrieved from https://www.cia.gov/library/publications/the-world-factbook/geos/ke.html

World Health Organization. (2007). *Global age-friendly cities: A guide*. Geneva, Switzerland: Author.

World Health Organization. (2017). *Towards long-term care systems in Sub-Saharan Africa*. WHO series on long-term care. Geneva, Switzerland: Author. Retrieved from https://www.who.int/ageing/long-term-care/WHO-LTC-series-subsaharan-africa.pdf?ua=1

World Health Organization. (2018). Ageing and Health fact sheet. Retrieved from https://www.who.int

Wu, B., Carter, M. W., Goins, R. T., & Cheng, C. (2005). Emerging services for community-based long-term care in urban China: A systematic analysis of Shanghai's community-based agencies. *Journal of Aging & Social Policy, 17*, 37–60. doi:10.1300/J031v17n04_03

Wu, B., Mao, Z., & Xu, Q. (2008). Institutional care for elders in rural China. *Journal of Aging & Social Policy, 20*, 218–239. doi:10.1080/08959420801977632

Xinhua. (2018). China's nursing homes more than triples in past five years. *Xinhuanet*. Retrieved from www.Xinhuanet.com

Yong, V., & Saito, Y. (2011). National long-term care insurance policy in Japan a decade after implementation: Some lessons for aging countries. *Ageing International, 37*(3), 271–284. doi:10.1007/s12126-011-9109-0

Zhan, H. J., Feng, Z., Chen, Z., & Feng, X. (2011). The role of the family in institutional long-term care: Cultural management of filial piety in China. *International Journal of Social Welfare, 20*, S212–S134. doi:10.1111/j.1468-2397.2011.00808.x

Zhang, Y. (2011). *China's long-term care strategy for the elderly*. EAI Background Brief No. 668. Singapore: East Asian Institute, National University of Singapore.

THE NEED FOR FOREIGN LTC WORKERS IN JAPAN

NORIKO TSUKADA

Given the fact that foreign workers account for only 1.6% of the total workforce population in Japan, it is safe to say that Japanese people are not accustomed to working with, or being served by, foreign workers. Due to a shrinking workforce, however, the island nation has begun hiring foreign workers, especially in the LTC industry. How well can we manage and retain qualifying foreign LTC workers who arrive with a different cultural background? What kind of preparation do we need to establish a win-win relationship with foreign LTC workers? All of these are unanswered questions now and challenges that we will be facing for at least the next several decades.

It has been nearly two decades since Japan began a public LTC insurance program, in April 2000. The year was called *Kaigo gannen* (the first year of LTC), symbolizing a shift of caregiving responsibility from the family, especially women, to the society as a whole. In Japan, this shift is referred to as the "socialization of care." Given Japan's ever-increasing longevity, however (87.3 years for women and 81.1 for men in 2017), our proportion of older adults among the total population (28.1% in 2018), and unprecedentedly low birthrate (1.43 children per couple in 2017—far below a replacement rate), issues of the LTC workforce shortage have been a serious problem for some time. It is officially estimated that in the year 2025, the gap between supply of and demand for LTC workers will be 377,000.

During the past 10 years, the government of Japan has made four significant policy changes to encourage the hiring of foreign LTC workers. First, in August 2008, Japan for the first time in its history began hiring certified LTC worker candidates from Indonesia, followed by the Philippines (2009) and Vietnam (2014), based on Economic Partnership Agreements (EPAs) with each of these countries. The purpose of these agreements is to strengthen economic relationships, not to cope with shortages of LTC workers, and it allows only 300 worker candidates per year to enter Japan from each country. After 3 years of work experience in Japan, the candidates can take the national qualification examination (in Japanese) for certified care workers, and once they pass the examination, they can stay in Japan as long as they wish. These candidates are highly educated in their home countries, with at least nursing care qualifications, so that their pass rates for the national qualifying examination have been 37.9% in 2012, 44.8% in 2015, and 50.9% in 2018, rates that are generally comparable with those of all examinees, 63.9%, 61.0%, and 70.8%, respectively. So far, 2,106 EPA-certified care worker candidates have entered Japan since 2008, and about 250 EPA-certified care workers are still working in Japan.

Second, a new status of residence, *Kaigo* (LTC), was created in September 2017; it allows foreign students with a student visa to study LTC knowledge and skills at Japanese training schools for at least 2 years. After they graduate from these schools and meet certain criteria, they can work in Japan as certified care workers and stay indefinitely. For this status of residence, nationality does not matter.

Third, also in 2017, the government added a new job category, *Kaigo* (LTC), to an existing status of residence, *Ginou-jissyu* (technical intern training). This program allows foreigners with demonstrated basic Japanese language proficiency to learn Japanese LTC knowledge and skills for the purpose of technology transfer. By the second year of the training, trainees must have improved their language skills to continue their residence in Japan for an additional 2 years. If they have met additional criteria by the fourth year of their training, trainees can stay a further 2 years for a maximum length of stay of 5 years.

Since its implementation in 1993, however, this program has experienced unresolved issues in assurance of fundamental human rights of foreign trainees, including protection against exploitation and unsafe working conditions or unethical labor brokers (e.g., confiscation of passports). The Japanese Bar Association has been advocating for the abolition of this program. In response, the government of Japan in January 2017 established the Organization for Technical Intern Training (OTIT) to monitor the *Ginou-jissyu* program to protect its trainees. So, this program will be closely monitored in the future.

The fourth, and latest, policy change on hiring foreign LTC workers, effective in April 2019, created a new status of residence, *Tokutei Ginou* (Specified Skilled Workers). The purpose of this new policy is to cope with worker shortages in 14 work areas where shortages are serious, including the fishing industry, food service, construction building cleaning, the hotel industry, aviation, agriculture, and *Kaigo* (LTC), among others. This new status of residence allows foreigners with Japanese language proficiency to work as LTC workers and to stay up to 5 years if they meet certain criteria for specific LTC skills and knowledge. Currently, the plan is to hire up to 60,000 foreign LTC workers over the next 5 years.

Aside from the fundamental worker shortage in LTC, Japan faces several policy challenges in implementing these various policy solutions. The first is the language issue. We have learned that even EPA-certified care workers (who passed the national exam) are having difficulties in writing Japanese, so it is questionable if new foreign workers with even lower Japanese language proficiency levels than the EPA-certified care worker candidates can adequately fulfill their job responsibilities. Moreover, native Japanese LTC workers have had little contact with foreign LTC workers so far, and they may see cultural and religious diversity and different food habits and social norms as difficult to deal with. This is likely to be doubly true for clients of LTC institutions. In addition, once foreign LTC workers leave their working place, they will live in the same communities as Japanese people do. Japanese people living in the community may be required to adjust to living with foreigners. Unlike many other highly developed countries where immigration has been the norm for centuries, in Japan, foreigners account for only 1.9% of the total population, which is very low compared with other OECD countries (6.4% for France; 7% for the United States; 8.6% for the UK; and 11.1% for Germany). Japan remains one of the world's most culturally homogeneous societies.

The government of Japan clearly maintains that these policy changes are not related to immigration policies at all. In reality, however, enacting policy changes to continually broaden the qualifications for residence appears very similar to Germany's creation of their guest worker program in the 1960s. The German guest worker program envisioned that foreign workers eventually would return to their home countries, but most never did; instead, many not only stayed in Germany and made it their home but some even brought over other family members and relatives from their mother countries, raising major issues for social resources, social security, and so on. There is a proverb that grew out of the European experience with recruiting foreign workers: "We wanted workers, but we got human beings." It is time for Japan to learn lessons from other countries, which have a longer history of hiring foreign LTC workers. We must continuously seek better ways of (a) recruiting the workers needed to care for our burgeoning frail, older population; (b) establishing an ethical win-win relationship with these workers; and (c) learning how to live in an increasingly diverse (and possibly strange) society.

PALLIATIVE CARE: QUALITY OF LIFE AT ITS END

JASLEEN K. CHAHAL

Prior to the 1960s, medical and public health professionals rarely talked about ways to alleviate the suffering of dying patients. The sole focus of health care was on providing curative treatment. During that pivotal decade, the hospice movement, originating in the United Kingdom during a time of civil and consumer rights movements, was the first to place emphasis on relieving unnecessary end-of-life suffering (Beider, 2005). These movements gave people a new sense of empowerment to question medical authority and to fight for what they felt were basic human rights: to die humanely and to live their last days free from pain and suffering. Hospice appeared to be an answer to this call by developing a formal standard of care that helped to give patients more choice in treatment—alleviating pain and addressing end-of-life-care issues for both patients and their families.

Although hospice commonly has been referred to as a last resort to care when treatment fails, the basic principle of hospice is for health care professionals to act as a support system for patients and families throughout the entire dying process—immediately before, during, and after the death of a patient. Whereas it may seem that the hospice movement happened recently and quickly, it is important to acknowledge that the demographic transition and the epidemiological or health transition have both contributed to the emergence of hospice services. In the past, individuals did not have to worry about experiencing prolonged periods of suffering prior to death, since most deaths resulted from acute infectious diseases rather than chronic conditions and occurred rather quickly. However, as nations began to see improvements in sanitation and nutrition—and advancements in medical treatments and technology—rates of communicable diseases decreased, life expectancy improved, and the prevalence of chronic diseases increased. These transitions influenced medical practitioners to balance their focus on acute care with more interest in preventive and end-of-life care. Additionally, the health care field began considering the importance of utilizing medical treatments, such as palliative or comfort care, to improve both the quality and quantity of life.

Discussing death and dying has consistently been a taboo or negative topic within many societies. Even after Elisabeth Kübler-Ross developed a theoretical model for the five stages of coping with dying in her widely read 1969 book, *On Death and Dying*, the topic became slightly more acceptable for conversation and still is often avoided in most cultures. The dominant modern view seems to be that death is something that an individual can avoid through use of advanced medical care, public health interventions, and research (Meier, 2010, pp. 11–12).

Although this view is more commonly accepted in Western cultures, beliefs about death and dying differ among Asian nations. For example, whereas the commonly known Eastern faiths of Islam, Hinduism, and Buddhism have many differences, followers of each of these faiths believe in reincarnation and view death as a natural stage of life that acts as a transition from an individual's current life into a new life (Puchalski & O'Donnell, 2005). Similarly, in Sikhism, a religious group that arose from Hinduism in the 16th century, followers (or Sikhs) also believe in reincarnation in that those who have lived a life without "self-centeredness and spiritual blindness" will be greeted by God after death, whereas others will be reborn because of their karma or the fate determined by their previous actions (Firth, 2000, pp. 30–31). Additionally, beliefs and values related to dying also vary across cultures that are found within one nation. A good example of diversity within a national culture is that of India, where Christians, Buddhists, Hindus, Muslims, and many other religious cultures coexist to help create the values of a larger national culture. Therefore, a country's social and cultural values about death and dying may align with either Eastern or Western beliefs, or some combination of both, which in turn can heavily impact the understanding, importance, and delivery of end-of-life care.

People, including researchers and clinicians, tend to confuse palliative care with hospice care, leading ultimately to negative social views of death. Although palliative care originally emerged from the hospice movement, hospice and palliative care are significantly different, and it is important to distinguish between the two to help minimize the impact of social stigma attached to hospice care. To be eligible for hospice services in the United States, a patient must be diagnosed with a terminal illness, have less than 6 months to live, and be willing to forgo further lifesaving treatments. Whereas palliative care does require that an individual have a terminal or chronic condition, it does not put the same restrictions on treatment or life expectancy after the diagnosis or progression of an illness. Unlike hospice, palliative care can be initiated at any stage of a person's chronic disease continuum to improve the patient's quality of life. Therefore, the major difference between the two forms of end-of-life care lies in either restricting curative treatment (hospice) or providing a choice for its continuation (palliative care) as individuals and their families slowly face the inevitable.

It is important to note that even if patients decide to utilize palliative care, they still may use hospice services once they meet the eligibility requirements described. Many patients do not realize that by using palliative care they actually have control over whether or not to enter hospice or to stop medical treatments—simultaneously receiving treatments that help manage pain. In addition, complementary and alternative medicine (CAM)—much of which is based on Eastern medical principles and practices and includes such measures as acupuncture, self-hypnosis, group therapy, music therapy, nerve stimulation, and massage therapy—can be integrated into a palliative care initiative. It is seldom offered, however, or even considered for use within health care settings in developed countries, primarily due to the emphasis placed on Western (cure-oriented) medicine. CAM measures are intended to provide pain relief for patients without prescribing actual medications. The integration of both CAM and palliative care can provide a pain-management alternative for patients throughout the health continuum in a manner that supports both Western and Eastern medical practices. The combination of the two may provide an avenue to give patients more control over their end-of-life care based on their cultural, personal, and medical beliefs.

Although still not as widely accepted within Western medicine as it should be, palliative care slowly has come to be considered a humane approach to medicine, at least in North America and Europe, because, though it does not treat incurable diseases, it does help to comfort patients by alleviating symptoms and side effects of treatments.

In 2002, the WHO published a definition of palliative care, embodying nine principles that are centered on the view that dying is a normal part of life, that patients should be relieved from pain and suffering to the extent possible, and that patients and their families should receive emotional and social support through the process (see Box 7.3).

Despite the efforts of the WHO, several countries (e.g., Afghanistan, Chad, Somalia, and North Korea) show no sign of embracing palliative care. Among those that do, palliative care implementation and allocation of resources differ greatly based on available resources in the particular country (see Table 7.2).

Other examples include Kerala in India and Tanzania, which rely heavily on volunteers in the community and local churches to provide end-of-life care, in comparison to Vietnam where patients use a government program of the Ministry of Health (Connor & Sepulveda Bermedo, 2014). Both the WHO HIV/AIDS initiative in Africa and its cancer initiative in Europe focus on providing palliative care services to individuals of all ages, but, again, the nature and scope of the intervention depend greatly on a country's economic development and its ability to fund them. Some African countries simply are unable to afford the medical supplies and staff to provide pain relief, whereas some European nations lack the political will to spend so much money on people viewed as unproductive and a burden on society (Sepulveda, Marlin, Yoshida, & Ulrich, 2002). However, one

BOX 7.3

The WHO Definition of Palliative Care

- Provides relief from pain and other distressing symptoms
- Affirms life and regards dying as a normal process
- Intends neither to hasten nor postpone death
- Integrates the psychological and spiritual aspects of patient care
- Offers a support system to help patients live as actively as possible until death
- Offers a support system to help the family cope during the patient's illness and in their own bereavement
- Utilizes a team approach to address the needs of patients and their families, including bereavement counseling, if indicated
- Enhances quality of life, and may also positively influence the course of illness
- Is applicable early in the course of illness, in conjunction with other therapies that are intended to prolong life, such as chemotherapy or radiation therapy, and includes those investigations needed to better understand and manage distressing clinical complications

WHO, World Health Organization.

Source: From Connor, S. R., & Sepulveda Bermedo, M. C. (2014). Global atlas of palliative care at the end of life. Retrieved from https://www.who.int/nmh/Global_Atlas_of_Palliative_Care.pdf

---

TABLE 7.2 **Palliative Care Development and Funding in Nine Countries**

Country Examples	Summary
Norway DRGs	• Mixed payment system (vulnerable to budget cuts) • 60% from fixed grants, 40% from DRG fees • Provided across levels of care • Home care visits included since 1996
Hungary Average-based reimbursement system	• Palliative care now considered a DRG reimbursement • Physician incentives used to "engage and ensure care" • Covers one-third of Hungarians, 100% of home care visits, and 50%–80% of inpatient visits
Spain Cost-saving model	• Rapidly growing—combines cancer and geriatric care models • Led to reduced emergency admissions and hospital cost savings
United States Three levels of hospice care payments	• No integration between curative and palliative care • Most care in home (35% of all deaths, 40% of cancer deaths) • Payment based on three levels of care (routine, inpatient, and intensive), in which routine care covers 96% of all days and intensive care is the most expensive

(continued)

TABLE 7.2 Palliative Care Development and Funding in Nine Countries (*continued*)

Country Examples	Summary
Singapore Cost-sharing model	• Originates in voluntary sector • Rapidly growing, combined with geriatric or older care • Increasing number of older women shifted to this type of model because of user payment and families providing care for loved ones
Australia Needs-based approach	• Australian National Palliative Care Program organized funding to shift from charities to the national health system (1998) • Resources allocated based on need and size of population • Palliative Care Outcomes Collaboration established in 2005 to evaluate outcomes, later intended for benchmarking
Canada Prospective approach	• Covers 81% of palliative care for cancer patients • Publicly funded and prospective needs-based approach, with two-thirds of funding related to hospital costs • Costs increase in older versus younger people and at 6 months before death, with highest cost at 2 months before death
Ireland Publicly funded	• 85% government-funded (almost 100% reimbursement) • Geographical variations and highly related to cancer care
United Kingdom Generalist focus	• Covers about 60% of all cancer deaths • Two-thirds of palliative care specialist funding from charities and voluntary sector; one-third from government funding and increasing • 2008 initiative to allow people to die at home on their wishes, also looks to improve generalist and specialist palliative care for all, both cancer and noncancer, patients

DRG, diagnosis-related group.

Source: Adapted from Gomes, B., Harding, R., Foley, K. M., & Higginson, I. J. (2009). Optimal approaches to the health economics of palliative care: Report of an international think tank. *Journal of Pain and Symptom Management, 38*(1), 4–10. doi:10.1016/j.jpainsymman.2009.04.008

study of three relatively wealthy nations found that the United States (27%–30%), the Netherlands (26%), and Switzerland (18%–22%) had similar percentages of government spending for care during the last year of life for individuals aged 65 or older (Shugarman, Decker, & Bercovitz, 2009). Allotting such resources to end-of-life care is rare in such less wealthy nations as Iraq and Syria, where inpatient palliative care and cancer care units have not been established, mostly due to the continual shortage of trained medical professionals and acceptable forms of morphine to help alleviate pain and suffering (Zeinah, Al-Kindi, & Hassan, 2013).

In addition to facing economic issues (e.g., spending on end-of-life care), countries often face obstacles of political beliefs or governmental regulations regarding the availability of appropriate medication or interventions used to minimize pain and suffering. In developing countries like India, challenges arise with the accessibility of opioid medication, legislative issues regarding the use of pain-relieving medication, and a lack of both monetary and professional resources for palliative care training. Political issues are not limited to developing countries in Asia or Africa; similar restrictions have been found in countries in the EU, such as in Bulgaria where full payment for a palliative care consult is the patient's responsibility (Cherny, Catane, & Kosmidis, 2006; Woitha et al., 2015). In fact, programs such as Medicare (public health insurance for older adults in the United States) have limited the use of particular palliative care services. Although hospice benefits were initially provided to individuals in the United States in 1983, in 2009 the proposed reimbursement for advance care planning to initiate palliative care was excluded from the Affordable Care Act (popularly known as "Obamacare"). This congressional action was taken after the professional boards proposed to administer the advance care planning were labeled "death panels" by a national politician (Jones, Acevedo, Bull, & Kamal, 2016). Advance care planning was later covered by Medicare in 2016 as a separate billable service; however, other palliative care consult services are only covered if they meet Medicare Part B billing requirements for existing services such as evaluation and management (E/M) provider visits.

Differences in cultural beliefs about end-of-life care, based on racial, ethnic, religious, and personal values, also hinder utilization of palliative care. Such cultural beliefs tend to have a major impact on a patient's readiness, willingness, and ability to use such care. In some cases, even if patients meet the requirements to receive hospice or palliative care, some individuals choose to forgo treatments in accordance with their personal belief that it is essential to endure life's pain. One such example is that some African Americans believe that death is only a transition and that pain and suffering should not be avoided but tolerated because they represent a divine or spiritual obligation (Crawley et al., 2000). Both Latinos and African Americans tend to prefer more lifesaving measures toward the end of their life, likely due to their long-standing history of mistreatment and distrust of medical research and clinical practice (Cain, Surbone, Elk, & Kagawa-Singer, 2018). Studies also have suggested that cultural beliefs affect the way in which general health care decisions are made. Euro-Americans and African Americans tend to prefer making individual decisions about advance care planning; Mexican Americans and Latino Americans prefer making decisions as a family (Kelley, Wenger, & Sarkisian, 2010). A similar preference for depending on family members in decision-making and providing care is still present in many Asian countries. Families in India are considered a major care network since they are often large and willing to provide various forms of nursing care, ranging from changing dressings to administering injections (Shanmugasundaram, Chapman, & O'Conner, 2006). Meanwhile in Japan, prior to death, support for terminally ill patients usually is provided by children and siblings in addition to health care professionals (Matsushima, Akabayashi, & Nishitateno, 2002). Such support networks often aid patients in completing depressing tasks, while at the same time enhancing their quality of life. Thus, both social support and cultural beliefs play a major role in advance care planning and the end-of-life-care process; so sensitivity to such barriers would be one of the first steps in opening the door for palliative care in any cultural community.

One subculture that has a major effect on palliative care utilization is that of medicine. The impact of medical culture depends greatly on whether its practices are more aligned with Western or Eastern traditional beliefs about care. The use of medical interventions or pharmaceutical drugs for alleviating pain may not be equally accepted or available in all countries (Cherny et al., 2006). Global differences in the types of interventions and medications available to patients make it increasingly harder for international organizations such as the WHO to create an initiative to provide standardized palliative care measures worldwide. Without international standards, it will be hard to ensure the quality of life of older patients and their families if they choose to travel, move closer to loved ones at the end of their lives, or migrate back home to their country of origin.

Professionals are taught ideologically based terminology and beliefs about death that help create the medical culture as it is today, especially in Western countries. An essential component of the American health care culture is the need to obtain informed consent from the patient prior to initiating treatment. By obtaining such consent, physicians can provide or withdraw appropriate treatment to patients. In some cultures, however, such as in China, Bosnia, and even Italy, people prefer not to tell terminally ill family members about their diagnosis or treatment because it is viewed as being more humane and a sign of respect for that patient's emotional and physical well-being (Searight & Gafford, 2005). Sometimes the inability to provide information regarding the patient's condition can inhibit the amount of care or the appropriate care that physicians see fit to provide for a particular illness. In order to circumvent this dilemma, physicians in Western countries have been advised to ask patients if they would like to be medically informed regarding their condition and treatments or if they would like to designate a particular person to be responsible for all decisions (Crawley, Marshall, Lo, & Koenig, 2002). Another important complication is the fact that most physicians are trained to place great importance on saving lives. Therefore, if a patient needs to be referred to palliative care or hospice, physicians may view this as a negative outcome and a personal failure rather than the natural outcome of an illness. This sense of defeat among physicians may make them more prone to taking active, extravagant measures to forestall death and less likely to initiate end-of-life-care conversations and to use, or to refer patients to, palliative care.

The medical field should view the integration of CAM and palliative care as a service that presents suffering patients with a way to minimize pain, while still providing hope for curing their illness. Since end-of-life care has negative connotations in many cultures, there is still a need to differentiate palliative care from hospice in order to maximize utilization. Common misconceptions, economic and governmental constraints, and differing cultures will continue to provide challenges for the future of palliative care in both developed and developing nations. Reevaluation of both governmental drug regulations and health care benefit policies is necessary to furthering the accessibility of palliative care worldwide.

Additionally, more emphasis should be placed on continuing to educate both medical professionals and the general public about the benefits of earlier, culturally sensitive palliative care interventions as a way to promote quality of life and on allowing families to care for loved ones in the comfort of their own homes as they continue to age with a chronic, terminal condition.

REFERENCES

Beider, S. (2005). An ethical argument for integrated palliative care. *eCAM, 2*(2), 227–231. doi:10.1093/ecam/neh089

Cain, C. L., Surbone, A., Elk, R., & Kagawa-Singer, M. (2018). Culture and palliative care: Preferences, communication, meaning, and mutual decision making. *Journal of Pain and Symptom Management, 55*(5), 1408–1419. doi:10.1016/j.jpainsymman.2018.01.007

Cherny, N. I., Catane, R., & Kosmidis, P. A. (2006). Problems of opioid availability and accessibility across Europe: ESMO tackles the regulatory causes of intolerable and needless suffering. *Annals of Oncology, 17*(6), 885–887. doi:10.1093/annonc/mdl073

Connor, S. R., & Sepulveda Bermedo, M. C. (2014). Global atlas of palliative care at the end of life. Retrieved from https://www.who.int/nmh/Global_Atlas_of_Palliative_Care.pdf

Crawley, L., Payne, R., Bolden, J., Payne, T., Washington, P., & Williams, S. (2000). The initiative to improve palliative and end-of-life care in the African-American community. *Journal of the American Medical Association, 284*, 2518–2521.

Crawley, L. M., Marshall, P. A., Lo, B., & Koenig, B. A. (2002). Strategies for culturally effective end-of-life care. *Annals of Internal Medicine, 136*(9), 673–679. doi:10.1001/jama.284.19.2518

Firth, S. (2000). Approaches to death in Hindu and Sikh communities in Britain. In D. Dickenson, M. Johnson, & J. S. Katz (Eds.), *Death, dying, and bereavement*. London, England: Sage.

Gomes, B., Harding, R., Foley, K. M., & Higginson, I. J. (2009). Optimal approaches to the health economics of palliative care: Report of an international think tank. *Journal of Pain and Symptom Management, 38*(1), 4–10. doi:10.1016/j.jpainsymman.2009.04.008

Jones, C. A., Acevedo, J., Bull, J., & Kamal, A. H. (2016). Top 10 tips for using advance care planning codes in palliative medicine and beyond. *Journal of Palliative Medicine, 19*(12), 1249–1253. doi:10.1089/jpm.2016.0202

Kelley, A. S., Wenger, N. S., & Sarkisian, C. A. (2010). Opiniones: End-of-life care preferences and planning of older Latinos. *Journal of the American Geriatrics Society, 58*(6), 1109–1116. doi:10.1111/j.1532-5415.2010.02853.x

Kübler-Ross, E. (1969). *On death and dying*. New York, NY: Simon & Schuster.

Matsushima, T., Akabayashi, A., & Nishitateno, K. (2002). The current status of bereavement follow-up in hospice and palliative care in Japan. *Palliative Medicine, 16*, 151–158. doi:10.1191/0269216302pm522oa

Meier, D. E. (2010). The development, status, and future of palliative care. In D. E. Meier, S. L. Isaacs, & R. G. Hughes (Eds.), *Palliative care: Transforming the care of serious illness* (pp. 11–12). New York, NY: Jossey Bass.

Puchalski, C. M., & O'Donnell, E. (2005). Religious and spiritual beliefs in end of life care: How major religions view death and dying. *Techniques in Regional Anesthesia & Pain Management, 9*, 114–121. doi:10.1053/j.trap.2005.06.003

Searight, H. R., & Gafford, J. (2005). Cultural diversity at the end of life: Issues and guidelines for family physicians. *American Academy of Family Physicians, 71*(3), 515–522.

Sepulveda, C., Marlin, A., Yoshida, T., & Ulrich, A. (2002). Palliative care: The World Health Organization's global perspective. *Journal of Pain and Symptom Management, 24*(2), 91–96. doi:10.1016/S0885-3924(02)00440-2

Shanmugasundaram, S., Chapman, Y., & O'Connor, M. (2006). Development of palliative care in India: An overview. *International Journal of Nursing Practice, 12*, 241–246. doi:10.1111/j.1440-172X.2006.00576.x

Shugarman, L. R., Decker, S. L., & Bercovitz, A. (2009). Demographic and social characteristics and spending at the end of life. *Journal of Pain and Symptom Management, 38*(1), 15–26. doi:10.1016/j.jpainsymman.2009.04.004

Woitha, K., Carrasco, J. M., Clark, D., Lynch, T., Garralda, E., Martin-Moreno, J. M., & Centeno, C. (2015). Policy on palliative care in the WHO European region: An overview of progress since the Council of Europe's (2003) recommendation 24. *The European Journal of Public Health, 26*(2), 230–235. doi:10.1093/eurpub/ckv201

Zeinah, G. F., Al-Kindi, S. G., & Hassan, A. A. (2013). Middle East experience in palliative care. *American Journal of Hospice & Palliative Medicine, 30*, 94–99. doi:10.1177/1049909112439619

OLDER WORKERS

PHYLLIS CUMMINS | TAKASHI YAMASHITA | ROBERTO MILLAR |
SENJOOTI ROY

INTRODUCTION

In both developed and developing countries, older workers are increasingly important for economic growth. Adults worldwide are remaining in the labor force at older ages for various reasons, such as the desire to remain productive and, more often, for financial necessity. In this chapter, we discuss different types of work arrangements experienced by workers of all ages and include a discussion of employment arrangements that are common as older adults transition from career employment to retirement. We also discuss patterns in labor market participation in both developed and developing countries and illustrate examples of gender wage inequality.

Informal work arrangements are common throughout the world, especially in developing countries. We begin this chapter with a story about working in India. The story of Babulal and his family illustrates the precarious nature of work for much of the developing world. Reliance on family members to offer a support system is also a common occurrence. The story of work in India provides a framework for some of the issues that workers face throughout the world and for the discussion that follows.

WORKING IN INDIA

Babulal is a 58-year-old, low–wage-earning rickshaw puller. He owns a low-cost, eco-friendly, three-wheeled bicycle-like vehicle with seats for the puller in the front and two passengers at the back. He is among the thousands of rickshaw pullers in India and other Asian countries, where rickshaws are used for short-distance travel needs. Originally from a village in eastern India, Babulal moved to the nearest city decades ago to make a living. He works from 7 a.m. to 10 p.m. 6, sometimes 7, days a week with a 2-hour break in the early afternoon to eat and rest. He earns between INR250 and INR350 (Indian rupee; approximately US$3–US$5) a day. During festive seasons, his income may go up to INR500 (approximately US$7) per day. He takes a "holiday" to visit his village (and his wife, who lives there) twice a year for 2 weeks. Babulal lives alone in the city. He neither needs nor can afford to rent a whole room for accommodation, but, together with four other rickshaw pullers, he rents a room, where they each have a mat to sleep on, for INR6,500 (approximately US$90) per month, close to the rickshaw stand.

Babulal's wife, Lakshmi, 53, lives in their native village, where residents primarily engage in agricultural activities. She did not move to the city with him because she had to take care of her in-laws, children, and, now, her two grandchildren. She performs household work and looks after the family. She also grows a few vegetables on their small patch of land. She has recently opened a small tea shop in her village and is helped by her grandchildren, aged 9 and 11, who wash and clean tea glasses and utensils in the evenings. Sometimes, she sells her vegetables from her tea shop. Lakshmi's modest income of around INR150 (approximately US$2) a day is a welcome addition to the money that Babulal sends home each month to meet the needs of the family.

Babulal and Lakshmi have two children. Their daughter, Gita, 31, is married and lives in a neighboring village with her marital family. Their son, Ram, 33, is a *mazdoor*, or contract laborer, in the construction industry, carrying bricks, sand, cement, and concrete mixture on his head for INR350 (approximately US$5) a day. Due to the nature of his job, he and his wife, Chandni, frequently move from one location to another. They live in cramped tin shanties on construction sites for as long as Ram's job lasts, after which they move on to the next location of employment. Chandni currently works as a maid in three houses close to the construction site. She spends approximately 1.5 hours at each house every morning to wash utensils, sweep, and mop the floors; sometimes, she washes clothes. She earns between INR1,200 and INR1,600 (approximately US$16–US$22) per month at each house. In the evenings, Chandni works as a part-time seamstress in a small shop located on the construction site. Once Ram completes his current job and is required to move to the next location, Chandni also will have to look for new jobs. Ram and Chandni have left their two children in the village with Lakshmi, who looks after them. They also send home some money each month to help the family.

The entire family, comprising multiple generations, is engaged in the informal economy. They have no workers' rights and their occupational environments are not protected or regulated by labor laws. The family does not pay taxes, and none enjoy paid weekends, sick leave, maternity leave, or vacation. Both Ram and Chandni could lose their jobs at a moment's notice, and none of these six hard-working, yet still poor, Indians is insured against injury, disability, or death. Moreover, none of the family members can contemplate retirement—as workers in developed nations know it—since they are not eligible for an old-age pension from their respective occupations. For them, extremely poor health or disability, especially in advanced ages, likely will be the only reason to stop working. Even then, the older family members will have to perform household chores to the best of their abilities so that the younger generations are able to work outside the home and earn money. They are aware that the government provides some subsidies and old-age benefits to low-income seniors. They intend to apply when they become eligible, but the amounts are meager and application processes often complicated. They are fortunate not to belong to the 5% or 70.6 million-strong population of India that lives in extreme poverty (below the international poverty line of US$1.90 a day), but as a result, they are ineligible for certain government benefits. Therefore, they hope to remain capable of performing physical labor for as long as possible.

The family has few savings; most of their assets are in the form of gold jewelry that the women received during their respective weddings. The small piece of land on which they have built their mud and brick home and Babulal's rickshaw are their other assets. The family has neither the capital nor the financial acumen to invest in the market, nor can they afford to risk losing their hard-earned money to market fluctuations. Consequently, long-term financial stability is a constant concern for the family, as is common among low-income citizens of developing countries. The case of Babulal and his family is typical of modern rural India, where young men and women with low educational attainment migrate to cities in large numbers to work in occupations that offer little stability, opportunities for upward mobility, or long-term financial security. Many individuals and their families may be pushed to the brink of absolute poverty if even one person withdraws from the workforce due to injury or disability. Consequently, most adults expect to work for as long as their bodies are able to support them, after which they depend on the next generation to provide for the family.

Babulal and his family are hopeful that the two children will have better opportunities as they grow up. They currently attend a government school in the village where they receive some education and a midday meal. After school, they contribute to the household income by helping Lakshmi in her tea stall. They have dreams of studying and working in the city when they grow up. Their parents and grandparents, however, worry about tuition fees and the cost of living in the city. They try to save the extra income from Lakshmi's tea stall and Chandni's part-time housework for the children's future, and they hope that the children will provide for them in their old age just as they have done for their parents and grandparents before them.

THE MEANING OF WORK

Babulal and his family's work arrangements may be unfamiliar to those living in developed economies, but they are quite common in many parts of the world. From an economic standpoint, **work** can be defined as "activity for another party undertaken for compensation" (Cappelli & Keller, 2013, p. 576). Although work can have diverse meanings for different people, for most it is necessary for existence by providing funds for basic needs such as food and shelter. In most societies, work is also important in determining standing within a community and providing a source of identity—for many, it is the primary source of human interaction. In developed countries, work has been shifting from traditionally defined jobs (those that are full time and long term) to more flexible work arrangements such as contract work and part-time employment. In recent years, those living in developing countries have had access to new types of work, such as virtual employment with high-technology U.S.-based companies (Ardichvili & Kuchinke, 2009), but informal work arrangements, such as those experienced by Babulal and his family, are more common.

Formal and Informal Work

Defining formal and informal work is a challenging task, since their definitions vary from source to source (Stuart, Samman, & Hunt, 2018). Both formal and informal employments have two distinct components—self-employment and wage employment (Stuart et al., 2018). The **informal sector** is defined as "the production and employment that takes place in unincorporated small or unregistered enterprises" (Stuart et al., 2018, p. 9). Work in the formal sector must meet at least three criteria to be considered **formal work**. Specifically, one needs to contribute to an employer-sponsored social security program, to have paid annual leave, and to have paid sick leave. In case any of these three criteria is not met, it is considered employment in the informal sector or informal work (Stuart et al., 2018).

The reasons for engagement in informal work vary. In the global community, nearly two thirds of all employment can be considered informal work, and agriculture is the most common industry for informal employment (International Labour Organization [ILO], 2018). In developing nations, 30% to 40% of the gross domestic product (GDP) is produced by informal employment, whereas it accounts for only approximately 16% in developed nations (e.g., Organisation for Economic Co-operation and Development [OECD] nations; Schneider, Buehn, & Montenegro, 2010). It should be noted that the types and nature of informal work are large and extensive, and thus a full discussion is beyond the scope of this chapter.

In economically developed nations, the primary reason for engagement in informal employment, especially for younger workers, is to increase income that supplements the "day job" (Bracha & Burke, 2016). Sometimes, part-time workers use informal work to meet financial needs while looking for a full-time position. In addition, young workers occasionally see informal employment as an opportunity to improve their skills and gain work experience (Walther, 2011). In the United States in 2015, an estimated 37% of working-age adults engaged in some kind of informal work, and over half of adults engaged in informal work during a 2-year period (Bracha & Burke, 2016). Informal work has become increasingly common in the United States (Abraham & Amaya, 2018) and some European countries (ILO, 2018). For example, those who obtain temporary work from agencies, independent contractors, and freelancers are common informal workers, although some exceptions exist (e.g., a formal contract with benefits); see Katz and Krueger (2016). Interestingly, new types of informal work, such as with Uber, Lyft, Turo, Airbnb, and TaskRabbit have emerged in recent years. Each of these is a relatively new company in the United States (but expanding internationally) that employs independent contractors to perform needed services (taxis, rental cars, lodging, and small chores) using an Internet application to match customers with willing service providers. Earning supplemental income and having temporary jobs until obtaining a full-time position are the primary reasons adults in developed nations engage in informal work.

In economically developing nations, the main reason for informal employment is typically to make ends meet (Onokala & Banwo, 2015). Particularly, workers with low qualifications or other disadvantages (e.g., lack of professional networks, lack of full-time/formal job opportunities in the area) need informal employment to secure an income (Canning, Raja, & Yazbeck, 2015). Nonagricultural work in the informal sector is roughly 70% of all employment in South and Southeast Asia and sub-Saharan Africa (Charmes, 2016). When including both agricultural and nonagricultural work, informal employment makes up over 90% of the total employment in some of the sub-Saharan African and Southeast Asian nations in 2016 (ILO, 2018). While the origin of such high proportions of informal employment is unclear, it is possible the national economy has an impact on the distribution of informal work. For example, Latin America experienced an economic recession in the 1980s, which boosted the rates of informal employment during that time period (Biles, 2009). As a result, working in the informal sector has become normal and continued to grow even after the economic recovery. Across global communities, informal employment is most likely to remain in coming years (Chen, 2007).

Differences in Participation

Figure 8.1 shows the percentage of informal employment according to a country's economic development status and workers' gender and age. For example, over 85% of the youngest and oldest workers engage in informal employment in economically developing nations. On the other hand, in more developed countries, older workers have the highest percentage of informal employment participation (39%). Although the percentages are significantly lower in all age groups in developed compared to developing nations, workers in developed nations are appreciably more likely to be in informal employment in the late middle age (around 55 years old) to older ages than are younger workers. Higher proportions of informal work arrangements for individuals approaching retirement age are very likely to reduce employment and pension benefits associated with formal work. Informal work at older ages is sometimes a last resort. For example, if a 50-year-old career

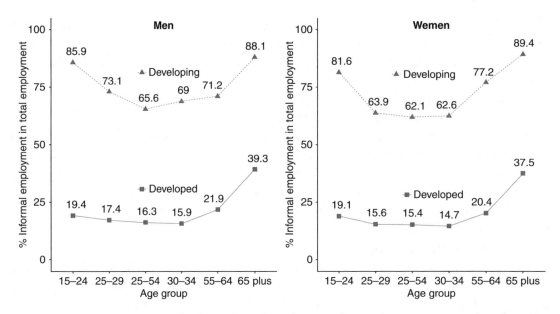

FIGURE 8.1 Percentages of informal workers by gender and age group in developed and developing nations.

Source: From International Labour Organization. (2018). *Women and men in the informal economy: A statistical picture, 3,* Geneva: Author. Retrieved from https://www.ilo.org/wcmsp5/groups/public/---dgreports/---dcomm/documents/publication/wcms_626831.pdf

employee working in the formal sector becomes unemployed due to a corporate downsizing, his or her only option might be to work in the informal sector. Men and women in all age groups show comparable patterns of informal work in both economic development stages.

Issues Related to Informal Work

In the context of global aging, understanding informal work is important because of (a) the collection of employment data, (b) economic impact, (c) ethnical/humanitarian issues, (d) health, and (e) education. Regardless of the economic development stage of a nation, informal work is often not included in the official labor statistics, mainly because it is very difficult to track. For example, in the United States, one of the primary data sources for national statistics, the Current Population Survey (CPS), does not sufficiently capture informal work participation, and therefore, the results are unlikely to reflect the effects of informal employment on the national economy (Abraham & Amaya, 2018; Bracha & Burke, 2016). Given a lack of informal employment data, the size, composition, and distribution of the informal employment in developed nations usually are unclear.

Higher rates of informal employment can have a negative impact on the local and national economy. Recent data suggest that the growing rates of informal employment are associated with lower or slower GDP growth (Stuart et al., 2018). Also, since informal employment often pays less to employees than formal employment, informal workers have less money to spend to support local and national economies. Lower wages in the informal sector appear to be a particularly salient factor in impeding economic growth in developing nations (Meghir, Narita, & Robin, 2015). Groups typically engaging in informal work tend to be the most vulnerable. For example, women, those with lower educational attainment, and residents in rural areas are more likely to be in informal sectors in many developing economies, with suboptimal work conditions and environments (Andrews, Sánchez, & Johansson, 2011; ILO, 2018).

Informal employment increases the risk of ethical abuses and poorer social protection programs for workers. Informal employment usually is not required to comply with existing labor laws and policies, and, in turn, safety nets such as minimum wages, paid sick leave, health insurance, and pensions typically are not provided (Andrews et al., 2011; Meghir et al., 2015). In other words, informal workers are less likely to be protected by the labor policies and other social welfare programs typically available to formal workers in modern welfare states. Additionally, child labor and forced labor are more likely to be prevalent in informal work than formal work (Muntaner et al., 2010). Furthermore, informal work may exploit disadvantaged populations including undocumented immigrants, their family members, as well as individuals with criminal records (Andrews et al., 2011).

Informal employment is linked to poorer health outcomes (Sivananthiran & Ratnam, 2005). Such health disadvantages in informal work may be due to a combination of poor work environment, lack of social protections (e.g., health insurance), and added stress (e.g., lower wages and the uncertainty of continued work). Individuals often experience worsening health as they age and might not be able to perform physically demanding work, making informal work especially challenging. Finally, informal employment may restrict social mobility and opportunities for continued education. Unlike formal work arrangements, informal employment is unlikely to provide education and training opportunities for workers (Andrews et al., 2011; Walther, 2011). Such a lack of opportunities may hinder the social mobility of employees in the informal sector. At the same time, it should be noted that informal work can function as an opportunity to gain work experience and hands-on training (Walther, 2011). Despite the issues related to it, informal work is likely to remain an important part of the future global economy and every nation that participates in it (Chen, 2007).

Implications for Older Workers

Several preliminary implications can be drawn from the earlier discussions on informal employment among older workers. To begin, retirement pensions and social security are more relevant to older workers than their younger counterparts. As noted earlier, informal work provides little, if any, opportunity to participate in retirement plans, social security, and/or similar programs for older adults (Stuart et al., 2018). A lack of retirement programs is particularly problematic in economically developing nations, where the majority (over 80%) of older workers may not have an income source from public or private pension programs at their statutory retirement age (ILO, 2018). Financial issues in retirement or unemployment among older adults not only add day-to-day stressors, but also burden their family members as well as the social assistance/welfare programs of a nation. Informal work, therefore, may contribute to reduced tax revenues and increase the need for expenditures for poor older adults.

Second, although we have witnessed a significant worldwide improvement in longevity in the 20th and 21st centuries, old age continues to be associated with chronic and disabling health conditions. Although most older workers are healthy, they still face a greater risk of absenteeism from work due to illness or injury than younger counterparts (U.S. Bureau of Labor Statistics [BLS], 2018). Whereas incidence rates of nonfatal occupational injuries and illness are lower for older workers, they do tend to miss more work days due to work-related health issues (U.S. BLS, 2013). Therefore, benefits such as health insurance, paid sick leave, and wellness programs, both from public and private sources, are more crucial for older workers in general. In this respect, informal work may put older adults in a disadvantageous position. In short, poorer social protections, such as lack of pensions, health-related issues, and fewer opportunities for personal growth, are especially impactful to older workers.

Improving Informal Employment

Given the distributions and disadvantages of informal employment, what could individual nations and the global community do to improve the existing situation and invest in the workforce regardless of their economic development stage? Considering the scope of the issues, policy-level interventions are indispensable to make tangible impacts. One overarching goal is to formalize existing informal work to protect the workforce, in general, and older workers, in particular (Stuart et al., 2018). However, eradicating informal employment altogether is an unrealistic goal (Chen, 2007), and, therefore, interventions must be more feasible for the greater good.

With regard to the management of informal employment, a lack of data on the frequency and types of informal work creates challenges to fully understand the extent of the issue (Abraham & Amaya, 2018; Katz & Krueger, 2016). Without more detailed data, policy interventions and resource allocation decisions are difficult to make. Economies also need to make efforts to formalize informal employment. Despite the fact that the majority of informal employment will likely continue in the future, even small changes would benefit future workers. For example, whenever a "new" type of informal employment emerges, new regulations and policies could be put in place (Chen, 2007). In addition, improving formal educational attainment at the population level would prevent informal employment at any stage of the life course. Specifically, individuals with greater educational attainment are more likely than those with fewer credentials to be formally employed (ILO, 2018).

With regard to the provision of social protections, a potentially effective approach is to tax informal employers. Taxing informal employment not only improves record keeping, but also provides a source of funds for workers' benefits (e.g., pensions, paid leave; Bastagli, 2015; ILO, 2014). At the same time, informal work can provide wage-earning as well as hands-on training opportunities for workers with lower qualifications (e.g., lower educational attainment) and the emerging workforce (e.g., young workers); see Canning et al. (2015) and Stuart et al. (2018). Stuart et al. suggest that, for countries without universal health care coverage, a social health insurance program is an effective strategy to indirectly protect both formal and informal workers.

HEALTH LIMITATIONS AND WORK

Evidence is accumulating that continued work at older ages may delay physical and cognitive health declines in middle-aged and older adults. International comparisons show steeper declines in cognitive functioning among older workers in countries with earlier retirement ages (World Health Organization [WHO], 2011). However, health changes associated with aging can affect work and retirement trends in middle and older adulthood. Health limitations are one of the leading risk factors for early retirement (Van Rijn, Robroek, Brouwer, & Burdorf, 2014). The increased risk of conditions such as arthritis, stroke, and declining physical health may lead older adults to experience difficulty completing their jobs and may result in involuntary exits from the workforce prior to retirement age. An aging society and an increase in the minimum retirement age across most developed nations mean that a greater proportion of workers will face health limitations and disability (Hasselhorn & Ebener, 2018).

The consequences of health declines for labor-force participation may be especially relevant for those in physically demanding occupations, such as manual laborers and blue-collar workers. While developed economies are increasingly dominated by service sector occupations that are less physically demanding and are implementing policies that accommodate aging workers, this is not the case in most developing economies. Workers in developing countries are more likely to engage in physically demanding informal work, with minimal, if any, labor law regulations or retirement benefits. Such is the case for Babulal, Ram, and Chandni, whose story we shared at the beginning of this chapter. This family's involvement in an informal labor market illustrates the risks associated with health limitations for older adults in developing economies. In the case of this family, poor health and disability are likely to be the reasons for retirement, rather than age. Once this occurs, they will have no social welfare programs to fall back on, such as disability insurance or pensions. Like billions of others in similar situations in less developed regions, Babulal, Ram, and Chandni strive to maintain the physical capability that their work requires in order to earn money and sustain their family for as long as possible.

FLEXIBLE WORK ARRANGEMENTS

The role of older adults in the workforce has transformed in recent decades. Due to the combination of population aging, lower fertility rates (e.g., smaller numbers of future workers), and public concerns about retirement programs' financial viability, older workers have been increasingly encouraged to continue working after the typical retirement age. For example, in the United States for many years, the typical and accepted retirement age was 65 (and still is in many other countries), but responding to an aging population and consequent greater burden on the public pension system known as Social Security, policy changes in the mid-1980s set a new age—67—for full benefits to be phased in over several years. Because retirement with reduced benefits was still available, however, many American workers have continued to retire at the traditional age of 65. Yet as the policy intended, the number of American workers over age 65 has been continuously increasing since the late 1990s (U.S. BLS, 2008; Lacey, Toossi, Dubina, & Gensler, 2017). The same pattern has occurred in other developed countries. Flexible work arrangements, through changes in labor market policies and appropriate employer supports, can help older workers remain in the workforce longer.

An increasing proportion of older workers require greater work flexibility, both in public policy terms and employer practices. Work flexibility often means **flextime** (arranging the working hours to suit the employee's needs rather than the employer's), alternative workday assignments (e.g., 4 days a week instead of 5), telecommuting (working from home through online platforms), shorter work hours, on-demand work (e.g., requested through an online application), and crowd work (e.g., work by a team of workers on one or more specific tasks online); see De Stefano (2016); Kelly and Kalev (2006). However, unless explicitly stated in local or national labor policies, workers must depend on the management of their companies or organizations to make flexible work arrangements available.

A number of developed nations have seen an increase in flexible work arrangements through policies that promote longer workforce participation and active aging of the workforce, while discouraging early retirement resulting from health declines. Countries like the Czech Republic and Hungary have implemented policies that merge health care, sickness, and disability pensions in order to prolong working years (European Commission [EC], 2012a). These policies have been in response to low employment rates and the high reliance on disability pensions among workers prior to the retirement age (EC, 2012a). In addition to policies related to the labor market, employers and older adults can take steps for longer working years for those with declining health who do not wish to retire or who do not yet qualify for a retirement pension. Changes in the workplace environment, reassignment of tasks, and the use of corrective eyeglasses or hearing aids may be some of the ways in which older adults can adapt to health declines and thus continue working (Hedge, Borman, & Lammlein, 2006). While policies and employer initiatives can help address issues associated with poor health and employment participation, there is variability across individuals, industries, and, most notably,

EXHIBIT 8.1

Accommodating an Aging Workforce at BMW

In 2007, an executive at BMW became concerned about the aging workforce at its 2,500-employee power train plant in Dingolfing, Germany. Over the next 10 years, the average age of workers at the plant was projected to rise from 39 to 47. Historically, the approach of many companies was to fire older workers or force them into an early retirement. Because of the age structure in Germany, this was not a viable option; there was not an adequate supply of younger workers to take the place of the older workers. In addition, firing a large number of older workers could be considered discriminatory. BMW chose to make changes in their production line to reduce physical strain for their workers. Examples of changes include:

- **Wooden flooring:** reduces knee strain
- **Barbershop chairs:** workers can sit or stand
- **Orthopedic footwear:** reduces strain on feet
- **Angled monitors and larger typeface on computer screens:** reduces eyestrain
- **Magnifying lenses:** reduces eyestrain and minimizes sorting errors
- **Adjustable tables:** eases physical strain
- **Large-handled gripping tools:** reduces strain on arms

The production line experienced a 7% productivity improvement in 1 year, equaling the productivity of lines staffed by younger workers. Similar changes in production lines have been implemented at other BMW plants.

BMW, Bavarian Motor Works.

Source: From Loch, C., Sting, F., Bauer, N., & Mauermann, H. (2010). How BMW is defusing the demographic time bomb. *Harvard Business Review 88*(3), 99–102.

between developed and developing labor market economies. Exhibit 8.1 describes efforts by Bavarian Motor Works (BMW) to accommodate older workers at one of their manufacturing plants.

AN AGING WORKFORCE

Because of population aging, both developed and developing countries face economic and social challenges in the coming decades. Increasing labor-force participation by older adults can play an important role in reducing the impact of population aging on economic growth and on costly social welfare programs. Countries show wide variations in the depth of their challenges; some countries have an older age structure (see Chapter 3, Demographic Perspectives on an Aging World), while others experience very low **labor-force participation rates** (LFPRs) by older adults. If participation rates remain at current levels in OECD countries, their ratio of retirees to workers is projected to increase from 38 retirees per 100 workers to 70 retirees per 100 workers by 2050. Countries that will be most impacted by the combination of an aging population and low labor-force participation by older adults include Greece, Italy, and Spain, while the Nordic countries, Iceland, and the United States will be less impacted (Keese, 2006). With low birth rates and a very high life expectancy, Japan has been especially affected by population aging. However, the Japanese have been able to avoid declines in labor-force participation by introducing robotics to allow work at older ages (Schlesinger & Martin, 2015) and by relaxing citizenship requirements for foreign workers. (See Noriko Tsukada's essay in Chapter 7, Long-Term Services and Supports, on "foreign workers" in long-term care.) As a result, since 2012, Japan's labor force has increased more than any other advanced economy (Ip, 2019).

Promoting work at older ages has been an important policy response to population aging. Policy reforms can be grouped into three broad categories: (a) reducing incentives to retire early and offering flexible retirement options; (b) changing employer attitudes and employment practices; and (c) improving employability (Keese, 2006; Sonnet, Olsen, & Manfredi, 2014). Reducing early retirement incentives and offering flexible retirement options are discussed in Chapter 9, Retirement and Pensions. In an effort to change employer attitudes about older workers, several countries, including Australia, Finland, Norway, the Netherlands, and the United Kingdom, have introduced large-scale, government-sponsored campaigns aimed at reducing ageism in the workplace (Keese, 2006). Examples of programs implemented to educate the public about age discrimination in the workplace include the "Age Positive Initiative" in the United Kingdom, "Solidarity Across Generations" in Poland, and "Concerted Action for the Employment of Older Workers" in France (Mosley, Scharle, & Stefanik, 2018). Improving employability includes providing job-related training opportunities for older workers, especially related to technology skills, and promoting better working conditions to accommodate an aging workforce.

WORKING LONGER

In the 1970s, early exit from the labor market was quite common in countries with developed economies. Employers implemented policies to encourage early retirement as a means of reducing labor costs and providing opportunities for the surge of younger "baby boom" workers just then beginning to enter the labor force. Between the 1970s and about 2000, the average labor market exit age in OECD member countries declined about 5 years for both females and males (OECD, 2017). As a result, pension spending dramatically increased, risking the financial stability of both public and private pension systems. Since then this trend has reversed, and reforms have been implemented in many countries throughout the world to encourage workers to remain in the labor force at older ages. Since about 2000, OECD member countries have experienced an average increase in labor market exit of about 2 years. Despite this increase, the average age of labor market exit is still lower now than it was 40 years ago, when life expectancy was much lower (OECD, 2017).

Pension reforms throughout the world since 2000 are the primary reason for increased LFPRs for older workers. Other reasons include the availability of less physically demanding jobs, improved health at older ages, the availability of flexible work arrangements, and financial incentives, such as lump-sum bonuses, to keep working. The majority of differences in LFPRs among older European workers are related to country-level factors, such as differences in pension and welfare programs combined with differences in employment and education systems and labor market policies, such as the availability of lifelong learning opportunities (Engelhardt, 2012).

The global economic crisis of 2008 had a great impact on older workers, both in the United States and throughout the world. Older workers with lower skills are especially vulnerable to unemployment in times of economic downturn. In most developed countries, long-term unemployment became a reality, especially for people with fewer skills, causing some to exit the labor market early. In some situations, the ability to find new employment was hindered by obsolete skills and employer attitudes toward older workers (EC, 2012b). Continual skill upgrades are increasingly important for adults of all ages to ensure employability. Unfortunately, older workers are less likely to be offered opportunities for skill upgrading than are their younger counterparts.

Between 2000 and 2016, both older males and females in most countries experienced substantial increases in LFPR. For example, in the United Kingdom, the LFPR for males aged 55 to 64 increased from 63% to 73% over that period, and the LFPR for females in the same age group increased from 43% to 60%. Australia, Chile, France, Germany, Greece, Italy, and the United States are among the countries with similar trends. China, South Africa, and Turkey did not experience the same trends, and in some cases saw declines in LFPR for both older males and females. The LFPRs for males and females aged 65 and older also grew for many countries between 2000 and 2016, with Australia, Norway, Chile, and the United States experiencing the largest increases. Interestingly, countries varied widely in LFPRs for this age group: In 2016, France's LFPR was 3%, Japan's was 23%, and Iceland's was 41% (OECD, 2018a). Detailed LFPR comparisons are shown in Figures 8.2, 8.3, and 8.4.

GENDER DISPARITIES

Over the past century and especially following World War II, participation in the labor force by women in developed countries, such as Australia, Canada, Japan, and the United States, increased dramatically. For example, LFPRs for women aged 55 to 64 increased by 17% in Australia, 15% in Canada, 7% in Japan, and 5% in the United States. Gender disparities in income, however, have been a persistent problem in developed countries for many years. Several factors contribute to

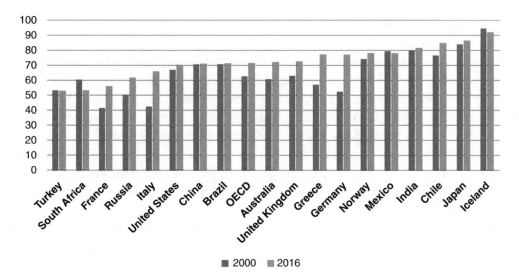

FIGURE 8.2 Labor-force participation rates in selected countries for men aged 55–64. 2000 and 2016.

OECD, Organisation for Economic Co-operation and Development.

Source: From Organisation for Economic Co-operation and Development. (2018a). *OECD.Stat.* Retrieved from https://stats.oecd.org

disparities for women, including lower LFPRs, fewer hours worked, and lower hourly wages. All of these, especially lower wages, are direct results of gender discrimination. While the differences in total before-tax annual income have declined by an average of 40% in OECD countries, the gap is still substantial. Nordic and Eastern European countries have experienced the greatest reductions, with

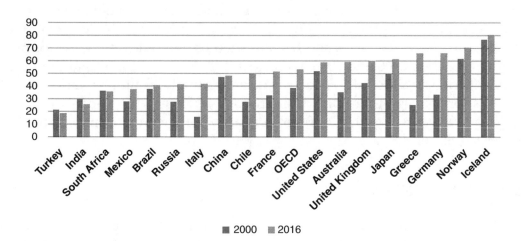

FIGURE 8.3 Labor-force participation rates in selected countries for women aged 55–64, 2000 and 2016.

OECD, Organisation for Economic Co-operation and Development.

Source: From Organisation for Economic Co-operation and Development. (2018a). *OECD.Stat.* Retrieved from https://stats.oecd.org

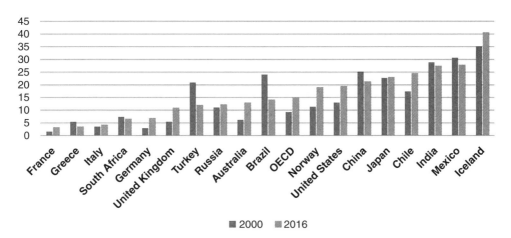

FIGURE 8.4 Labor-force participation rates in selected countries for men and women aged 65 and older, 2000 and 2016.

OECD, Organisation for Economic Co-operation and Development.

Source: From Organisation for Economic Co-operation and Development. (2018a). *OECD.Stat.* Retrieved from https://stats.oecd.org

women earning about 78% as much as men in Finland and Latvia. Greece, the Netherlands, and Eastern Asian countries experience much greater disparities, as high as 60%. Occupation and industry choices both contribute to wage disparities, as do differences in years of education and work experience (Kunze, 2017; Olivetti & Petrongolo, 2016). Unionization is also a factor in wage disparities, with heavily unionized countries, such as Germany and Sweden, experiencing lower gender wage gaps, and countries with lower levels of unionization, such as the United States, having wider gaps. Collective bargaining agreements negotiated by unions have resulted in this wage compression (Blau & Kahn, 2003). Disparities are lower when only the wage gap is considered, but it is important to consider all the components of income disparities because of their other implications, such as reduced retirement pensions and the increased risk of poverty at older ages (OECD, 2016).

Women are more likely to have responsibility for child care and household tasks, resulting in breaks in work careers and fewer hours worked. Women may be also disadvantaged by challenges of work–life balance when pursuing higher-paying occupations that often involve long hours and inflexible work schedules. Policy changes have been implemented in several countries to support labor market participation for women. Examples include tax benefits for child care, leave policies for both men and women, and flexible working arrangements (Mosley et al., 2018). Although more flexible work arrangements are available to women today than in prior decades, those opportunities often are outside the formal paid-work setting (Loretto & Vickerstaff, 2015).

Women are more likely than men to have informal, or nonstandard, work arrangements in some parts of the world, such as Latin America and sub-Saharan Africa. In addition, women in the informal economy are more likely to work in the most vulnerable and low-wage occupations, such as domestic workers (ILO, 2018). While informal work arrangements are more common in developing countries than in other parts of the world, nonstandard work is increasingly common in developed nations. For example, over the past decade, nonstandard work arrangements, which include part-time, temporary, self-employed, and freelance work arrangements, increased from 38% to 41% of total employment in European Union countries (Broughton et al., 2016). All types of work arrangements are at some risk for precariousness, but adults in nonstandard work arrangements are at greater risk than those with full-time work. Because precarious workers typically do not have benefits such as retirement savings plans or health insurance, precarious workers are also at increased risk for a precarious retirement and poverty in old age. Increases in pension ages, combined with shifts from defined-benefit to defined-contribution pension plans (see Chapter 9, Retirement and Pensions, for descriptions of pension plans), have amplified the risk of precarious work at older ages. Older workers, especially older women, often need to continue working for financial reasons and may have limited employment choices (Lain, Airey, Loretto, & Vickerstaff, 2019). Standing (2011) described different types of work-related insecurities related to precarious work (see Box 8.1).

POVERTY AT OLDER AGES

In both developing and developed nations, poverty at older ages is a significant issue. Poverty has no universal monetary boundary and is relative to the economic conditions in a specific country and even to a person's age and family situation. In a general sense, **poverty** can be understood as not having enough money to provide adequate housing, food, and clothing for oneself and one's family. Developed nations usually calculate a specific amount of money that they believe is necessary and adequate to

BOX 8.1

Precarious Work: Work-Related Insecurities

The "precariat," or those who experience precarious work, typically face one or more types of insecurity, including:

- **Labor market insecurity:** inadequate income earning opportunities at the country level
- **Employment insecurity:** lack of protection against arbitrary firing
- **Job insecurity:** lack of opportunities to advance in a career and skill obsolescence
- **Work insecurity:** lack of safety and health regulations at work
- **Income insecurity:** lack of adequate stable income

Source: From Standing, G. (2011). *The precariat: The new dangerous class* (p. 12). London, UK: Bloomsbury Academic.

live in their country, and they consider anyone whose income falls below that level to be *poor*. Poor citizens often are said to be "below the poverty line." In the United States, for example, in 2019, the poverty threshold is determined by the U.S. Census Bureau to be $12,490 for one person and $25,750 for a family of four (U.S. Department of Health and Human Services, 2019). These amounts are recalculated annually but are a source of continual debate among economists and advocates for poor people, who argue that the defining line is set too low in order to limit the number of people who can qualify for income-based programs; but at least they provide a standard against which data trends can be gauged and comparisons made.

Gender income disparities, informal work arrangements, and lack of savings for retirement each contribute to increases in poverty rates at older ages. Figure 8.5 compares poverty rates for working-age adults to those aged 66 and older in selected OECD countries. In this study, the poverty line is defined as half of the median income of the total population; people whose incomes are less than that are considered to be in poverty. Several countries, such as France, Norway, and Germany, have lower poverty rates at older ages, whereas poverty is more common among older adults compared to younger people in other countries, including the United States, United Kingdom, Australia, and Mexico. For example, the poverty rate for ages 18 to 65 in France is 8.5% compared to 3.4% for persons aged 66 and above. In the United States, the poverty rate is 15.5% for working-age adults, but is 22.9% for those aged 66 plus. Substantial gender differences also are evident. In 2014, the poverty rate for older men in Germany was 6.8%, while 11.5% of older German women were poor; in the United States, with its much less well-developed welfare state, the poverty rate was 17.2% for older men and 23.9% for older women (OECD, 2018a). Poverty data in less developed countries and

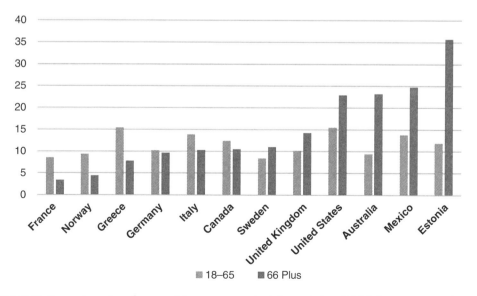

FIGURE 8.5 Poverty rates for working-age and older adults, 2016 (percentage).

Source: From Organisation for Economic Co-operation and Development. (2018b) Poverty rate. Retrieved from https://data.oecd.org/inequality/poverty-rate.htm#indicator-chart

those with large rural populations are much less reliable and often not available at all. However, economic security is recognized as a serious challenge for older adults in many countries, partly because of their lack of participation in the formal economy (as described at the beginning of this chapter) and the resulting lack of access to any kind of pension or income maintenance program.

FUTURE OF EMPLOYMENT IN THE CONTEXT OF GLOBAL AGING

As we have discussed in this chapter, informal employment is a significant and growing part of the global economy and is very relevant to all existing and future workers. Older workers are not an exception. Yet, significant uncertainties persist about how population aging will continue to affect the informal economy. An aging workforce is expected to continue its high rates of informal employment, particularly in developing nations (Chen, 2007). The issues related to participation in informal work have been discussed throughout this chapter. This concluding section highlights some of the critical issues to consider in the coming decades.

With an increasing polarization between high- and low-skilled employment opportunities, one topic that is universal, both in the economically developed and developing nations, is the role of adult education and training. In an era of rapid technological advancement and job automation, it is crucial for workers to constantly upgrade their work-related skills to maintain their employability (Cummins, Yamashita, Millar, & Sahoo, 2018). The promotion of education and training in informal work may improve individual workers' basic as well as job-related skills. Such human capital generally leads to better economic outcomes (e.g., greater earning potential, opportunities for promotion). Also, adult education and training are associated with the greater protection of workers in the informal sectors. Since government labor policies and social protections often are not applicable to informal workers, human capital investments (such as adult education) could promote employability and social mobility and reduce the risk of unemployment (Benjamin, Bergle, Recanatini, & Santini, 2014).

Flexible work arrangements may allow older adults to continue working longer and even beyond the conventional retirement age; however, that may change. We expect the need will continue for labor policies and employers to encourage longer working lives as well as education and training for older workers to stay competitive in the job market. Such attempts to expand the working years and enhance human capital of older workers are already evident in more economically developed nations (EC, 2012b). One of the main reasons for prolonging working lives is the need to finance social security, pension, and health care systems for older populations.

SUMMARY

In this chapter, we have discussed different types of work arrangements experienced by older adults as they approach and transition into retirement. In both developed and developing nations, individuals are remaining in the labor force at older ages, often due to financial necessity. Pension reforms in recent decades and the availability of less physically demanding jobs have contributed to increases in LFPRs at older ages. LFPRs for women have generally accelerated at a faster rate than men, but are still lower than those of men in most countries. Gender disparities in income are still a problem for women and increase the risk of financial insecurity at older ages.

Alternative work arrangements that are common at older ages, such as part-time work and informal work, often are precarious, offering few benefits and little employment security. Informal work arrangements, which are especially common in developing nations, are linked to poorer health outcomes, which can be exacerbated due to lack of health insurance. Insecurities experienced by those in precarious work situations require multifaceted attention by employers, researchers, policy makers, and governments to reduce the risk of economic insecurity and poverty in an aging population.

Declining health at older ages can result in early exit from the labor market, especially for those who work in physically demanding occupations. In developed nations, some employers have implemented policies to accommodate an aging workforce, but this is not common in developing nations. In both developed and developing nations, declining health, informal work arrangements, gender income disparities, and a lack of savings for retirement all contribute to poverty at older ages.

DISCUSSION QUESTIONS

1. What are some reasons for increases in informal work arrangements at older ages in both developed and developing nations?

2. What are the implications of informal work arrangement for adults as they approach retirement age?

3. Why are older people more likely to be poor than working people in some countries, while they are less likely to be so in others?

4. How might gender- and age-based income disparities be reduced?

5. What are your expectations for your own work arrangements over your life course?

KEY WORDS

Flextime	Labor-force participation rate
Formal work	Poverty
Freelancers	Precarious work
Gender gap	Telecommuting
Informal work	Work

REFERENCES

Abraham, K. G. & Amaya, A. (2018). *Probing for informal work activity*. National Bureau of Economic Research, Working Paper No. 24880. Retrieved from http://www.nber.org/papers/w24880

Andrews, D., Sánchez, A. C., & Johansson, Å. (2011). *Towards a better understanding of the informal economy*. OECD Economics Department, Working Paper No. 873. Retrieved from https://doi.org/10.1787/5kgb1mf88x28-en

Ardichvili, A., & Kuchinke, K. P. (2009). International perspectives on the meanings of work and working: Current research and theory. *Advances in Developing Human Resources, 11*(2), 155–167. doi:10.1177/1523422309333494

Bastagli, F. (2015). *Bringing taxation into social protection analysis and planning*. Overseas Development Institute, Working Paper No. 421. Retrieved from https://www.odi.org/sites/odi.org.uk/files/odi-assets/publications-opinion-files/9700.pdf

Benjamin, N., Bergle, K., Recanatini, F., & Santini, M. (2014). *Informal economy and the world bank*. Policy Research Working Paper, 6888. Retrieved from https://openknowledge.worldbank.org/bitstream/handle/10986/18799/WPS6888.pdf?sequence=1

Biles, J. J. (2009). Informal work in Latin America: competing perspectives and recent debates. *Geography Compass, 3*(1), 214–236. doi:10.1111/j.1749-8198.2008.00188.x

Blau, F. D., & Kahn, L. M. (2003). Understanding international differences in the gender pay gap. *Journal of Labor Economics, 21*(1), 106–144. doi:10.1086/344125

Bracha, A., & Burke, M. A. (2016). *Who counts as employed? Informal work, employment status, and labor market slack*. Working paper, No. 16-29, Federal Reserve Bank of Boston, MA. Retrieved from https://www.econstor.eu/bitstream/10419/171783/1/883107449.pdf

Broughton, A., Green, M., Rickard, C., Swift, S., Eichhorst, W., Tobsch, V., . . . Jonaviciene, D. (2016). *Precarious employment in Europe*. Retrieved from http://documents.worldbank.org/curated/en/416741468332060156/pdf/WPS6888.pdf

Canning, D., Raja, S., & Yazbeck, A. S. (Eds.). (2015). *Africa's demographic transition: dividend or disaster?* Washington DC: World Bank.

Cappelli, P., & Keller, J. R. (2013). Classifying work in the new economy. *Academy of Management Review, 38*(4), 575–596. doi:10.5465/amr.2011.0302

Charmes, J. (2016) 'The informal economy: Definitions, size, contribution and main characteristics.' In E. Kraemer-Mbula & S. Wunsch-Vincent (Eds.), *The informal economy in developing nations: Hidden engine of innovation?* Cambridge, UK: Cambridge University Press

Chen, M. A. (2007). *Rethinking the informal economy: Linkages with the formal economy and the formal regulatory environment*. DESA Working Paper No. 46. Retrieved from https://ideas.repec.org/p/une/wpaper/46.html

Cummins, P. A., Yamashita, T., Millar, R. J., & Sahoo, S. (2018). Problem-solving skills of the U.S. workforce and preparedness for job automation. *Adult Learning (in press)*.

De Stefano, V. (2016). *The rise of the just-in-time workforce: On-demand work, crowdwork and labour protection in the gig-economy*. Geneva: International Labour Organization. Retrieved from https://www.ilo.org/wcmsp5/groups/public/---ed_protect/---protrav/---travail/documents/publication/wcms_443267.pdf

Engelhardt, H. (2012). Late careers in Europe: Effects of individual and institutional factors. *European Sociological Review, 28*(4), 550–563. doi:10.1093/esr/jcr024

European Commission. (2012a). *EEO review: Employment policies to promote active ageing 2012*. Retrieved from https://www.ifa-fiv.org/wp-content/uploads/2015/03/6-EU-Active-Ageing-2012.pdf

European Commission. (2012b). *Rethinking education: Investing in skills for better socio-economic outcomes*. Strasbourg, France. Retrieved from https://eur-lex.europa.eu/legal-content/EN/TXT/PDF/?uri=CELEX:52012SC0375&from=EN

Hasselhorn, H. M., & Ebener, M. (2018). The differentiated role of health for employment participation among older workers—A discussion based on the "lidA conceptual framework on work, age, and employment." In E. Hohnerlein, S. Hennion, & O. Kaufmann (Eds.), *Erwerbsverlauf und sozialer Schutz in Europa*. Berlin: Springer.

Hedge, J. W., Borman, W. C., & Lammlein, S. E. (2006). Physical capabilities, cognitive abilities, and job performance. In *The aging workforce: Realities, myths, and implications for organizations* (pp. 49–62). Washington, DC: American Psychological Association.

International Labour Organization. (2014). *Transitioning from the informal to the formal economy.* Geneva: Author. Retrieved from https://www.ilo.org/wcmsp5/groups/public/---ed_norm/---relconf/documents/meetingdocument/wcms_218128.pdf

International Labour Organization. (2018). *Women and men in the informal economy: A statistical picture, 3,* Geneva: Author. Retrieved from https://www.ilo.org/wcmsp5/groups/public/---dgreports/---dcomm/documents/publication/wcms_626831.pdf

Ip, G. (2019, January 11). How aging Japan defied demographics and revived its economy. *The Wall Street Journal.* Retrieved from https://www.wsj.com/articles/how-aging-japan-defied-demographics-and-turned-around-its-economy-11547222490

Katz, L. F. & Krueger, A. B. (2016). *The rise and nature of alternative work arrangements in the United States, 1995-2015.* Working Papers, 2266. Retrieved from https://www.nber.org/papers/w22667

Keese, M. (2006). *Live longer, work longer.* Paris, France: OECD Publishing.

Kelly, E. P., & Kalev, A. (2006). Managing flexible work arrangements in us organizations: Formalized discretion or 'a right to ask'. *Socio-Economic Review, 4*(3), 379–416. doi:10.1093/ser/mwl001

Kunze, A. (2017). *The gender wage gap in developed countries.* (Working Paper No. 6529). Munich, Germany: Center for Economic Studies and Ifo Institute

Lacey, T. A., Toossi, M., Dubina, K. S., & Gensler, A. B. (2017). Projections overview and highlights, 2016–26. *Monthly Labor Review,* 1–25. Retrieved from https://www.bls.gov/opub/mlr/2017/article/pdf/projections-overview-and-highlights-2016-26.pdf

Lain, D., Airey, L., Loretto, W., & Vickerstaff, S. (2019). Understanding older worker precarity: The intersecting domains of jobs, households and the welfare state. *Ageing & Society, 39*(10), 2219–2241. doi:10.1017/S0144686X18001253

Loch, C., Sting, F., Bauer, N., & Mauermann, H. (2010). How BMW is defusing the demographic time bomb. *Harvard Business Review, 88*(3), 99–102.

Loretto, W., & Vickerstaff, S. (2015). Gender, age and flexible working in later life. *Work, Employment and Society, 29*(2), 233–249. doi:10.1017/S0144686X18001253

Meghir, C., Narita, R., & Robin, J. (2015). Wages and informality in developing countries. *The American Economic Review, 105*(4), 1509–1546. doi:10.3386/w18347

Mosley, H., Scharle, A., & Stefanik, M. (2018). *The role of PES in outreach to the inactive population.* Study report. Luxembourg: Publications Office of the European Union, 2017. Retrieved from https://publications.europa.eu/en/publication-detail/-/publication/ce86219d-2d84-11e8-b5fe-01aa75ed71a1/language-en

Muntaner, C., Solar, O., Vanroelen, C., Martínez, J. M., Vergara, M., Santana, V., . . . Benach, J. (2010). The role of employment relations in reducing health inequalities. unemployment, informal work, precarious employment, child labor, slavery, and health inequalities: Pathways and mechanisms. *International Journal of Health Services, 40*(2), 281–295. doi:10.2190/HS.40.2.h

Olivetti, C., & Petrongolo, B. (2016). The evolution of gender gaps in industrialized countries. *Annual Review of Economics, 8,* 405–434. doi:10.1146/annurev-economics-080614-115329

Onokala, U., & Banwo, A. (2015). Informal sector in Nigeria through the lens of apprenticeship, education and unemployment. *American Advanced Research in Management, 1*(1), 13–22.

Organisation for Economic Co-operation and Development. (2016). *OECD Employment Outlook 2016.* Paris: OECD Publishing. Retrieved from https://read.oecd-ilibrary.org/employment/oecd-employment-outlook-2016_empl_outlook-2016-en#page3

Organisation for Economic Co-operation and Development. (2017). *Pensions at a glance 2017: OECD and G20 indicators.* Paris: OECD Publishing.

Organisation for Economic Co-operation and Development. (2018a). *OECD.Stat.* Retrieved from https://stats.oecd.org

Organisation for Economic Co-operation and Development. (2018b). *Poverty rate.* Retrieved from https://data.oecd.org/inequality/poverty-rate.htm#indicator-chart

Schlesinger, J., M., & Martin, A. (2015, November 29). Graying Japan tried to embrace the golden years. *The Wall Street Journal.* Retrieved from https://www.wsj.com/articles/graying-japan-tries-to-embrace-the-golden-years-1448808028

Schneider, F., Buehn, A., & Montenegro, C. E. (2010). New estimates for the shadow economies all over the world. *International Economic Journal, 24*(4), 43–46. doi:10.1080/10168737.2010.525974

Sivananthiran, A., & Ratnam, V. (Eds.). (2005). *Informal economy: The growing challenge for labour administration.* Geneva: International Labour Organization.

Sonnet, A., Olsen, H., & Manfredi, T. (2014). Towards more inclusive ageing and employment policies: The lessons from France, The Netherlands, Norway and Switzerland. *De Economist, 162*(4), 315–339. doi:10.1007/s10645-014-9240-x

Standing, G. (2011). *The precariat: The new dangerous class.* London, UK: Bloomsbury Academic.

Stuart, E., Samman, E., & Hunt, A. (2018). *Informal is the new normal: Improving the lives of workers at risk of being left behind.* Working paper 530. London, UK: Oversees Development Institute.

U.S. Bureau of Labor Statistics. (2008). *Older workers: Are there more older people in the workplace?* Retrieved from https://www.bls.gov/spotlight/2008/older_workers

U.S. Bureau of Labor Statistics. (2013). *Older workers less likely to have severe work injuries, but they miss more work days to recover.* Retrieved from https://www.bls.gov/opub/ted/2013/ted_20131230.htm

U.S. Bureau of Labor Statistics. (2018). *Labor force statistics from the current population survey.* Retrieved from https://www.bls.gov/cps/cpsaat46.htm

U.S. Department of Health and Human Services. (2019). *2019 poverty guidelines.* Washington, DC: Office of the Assistant Secretary of Planning and Evaluation. Retrieved from www.aspe.hhs.gov

Van Rijn, R. M., Robroek, S. J. W., Brouwer, S., & Burdorf, A. (2014). Influence of poor health on exit from paid employment: systematic review. *Occupational and Environmental Medicine, 71*(4), 295–301. doi:10.1136/oemed-2013-101591

Walther, R. (2011). *Building skills in the informal sector.* Commissioned for the EFA Global Monitoring Report 2012. Retrieved from http://www.unesco.org/new/fileadmin/MULTIMEDIA/HQ/ED/pdf/gmr2012-ED-EFA-MRT-PI-08.pdf

World Health Organization. (2011). *Global health and aging.* Retrieved from http://www.who.int/ageing/publications/global_health.pdf

OLDER SWEDES: LIVING IN THE "ROLE MODEL OF WELFARE STATES"

KATHRIN KOMP-LEUKKUNEN

Populations around the globe are aging, and northern Europe is currently one of the oldest regions in the world (United Nations, 2015). Sweden is the largest country in this region, covering a surface of 450,000 square kilometers (about 174,000 square miles) and containing a population of about 10 million (U.S. Central Intelligence Agency, 2019). Sweden is well-known for its extensive forests, harsh winters, and vast population of elk. Among scholars, Sweden is also well-known for its welfare state. It is important to keep in mind that the idea of "welfare state" is not the same as the term "welfare" that is often used in the United States to refer to support for people who are poor. A welfare state refers to the system of social policies and programs designed by a government to protect and support the health and well-being of all of its citizens; in the United States, President Franklin D. Roosevelt's New Deal (which established jobs programs and Social Security) exemplifies the concept of welfare state, rather than a particular welfare program.

Sweden's welfare state is well-known for the wide range of support it offers its citizens and for its ability to even out social inequalities. Many scholars and policy makers look to Sweden for inspiration on how to design social policies. Some scholars even go so far as to refer to Sweden as the "role model of welfare states." Whether it can be maintained that one type of welfare state is better than another is debatable. After all, welfare policies reflect the culture, history, population, and geography of a country. However, Sweden's prominent position in debates about welfare states warrants taking a closer look. This essay (a) describes the state of population aging in Sweden; (b) outlines the key features of the Swedish welfare state; (c) portrays what the Swedish welfare state does for its older citizens; (d) shows how older Swedes participate in their welfare state; and, finally, (e) discusses challenges and opportunities for the welfare state in an aging Sweden.

HOW GRAY IS SWEDEN?

The Swedish population already has aged considerably, and this demographic shift is still continuing. In 2017, one in three Swedes was aged 60 and older and one in four Swedes was aged 65 and older. These numbers put Sweden in the group of the oldest countries in Europe, although not at the absolute top; that distinction belongs to Germany, Greece, and Italy (Eurostat, 2018). Sweden reached this stage of population aging through slow changes that took place over more than a century—a characteristic that sets Sweden apart from many other countries that have experienced a more recent and dramatic increase in the age of their populations. Chesnais (1992) argues that possible reasons might be that Sweden had a rather stable economy and did not suffer major losses in wars during that time. Expressed in numbers, the proportion of Swedes aged 65 and older doubled from 1960 until today, and it is expected to increase to almost one in three persons by 2050 (Eurostat, 2013). Interestingly, Sweden not only has a large number of older citizens, but its typical citizens reach the impressive age of almost 80 years. Once Swedes reach the age of 65, they can look forward to 14 more years of good health, followed by 5 years of poor health (Eurostat, 2011b). These numbers mean that Swedes can look forward to long lives and many years of health and activity after retirement.

WHAT IS THE SWEDISH WELFARE STATE LIKE?

If countries were compared according to the size of their welfare states, then Sweden would be a giant. In 2018, the Swedish government spent 26% of its GDP on social issues, ranking it seventh among both the OECD (the 36 most developed countries in the world) and European countries; this is 7% higher than the 19% spent by the United States (OECD, 2018). The reason for Sweden's high welfare expenditures is not only the range of welfare provisions there, but also the high level of state involvement in welfare provisions. Esping-Andersen (1999) explained that the Swedish government is active in many social areas that in other countries are left to families, companies, or welfare associations. Because of this engagement, the Swedish government manages to drastically reduce social inequalities. Moreover, it creates a densely knit safety net that effectively helps people faced with social risks, such as unemployment or poor health (Korpi & Palme, 1998). The bottom line is that the Swedish welfare state is very well developed, active, and supportive of its citizens.

WHAT DOES THE SWEDISH WELFARE STATE DO FOR ITS OLDER CITIZENS?

The Swedish welfare state supports its older citizens, but it does not favor them over younger ones. Lynch (2001) studied how much welfare states spend on older citizens compared to younger citizens and found that Sweden is much less biased in favor of its older citizens than, for example, Greece, the United States, or Italy. Instead of explicitly focusing on older citizens, the Swedish welfare state emphasizes programs that support young or middle-aged people, such as child care services and unemployment benefits, and it is very active in supporting programs that benefit all its citizens equally, such as universal health care that is accessible to anyone in need of help, regardless of their income (Trydegard & Thorslund, 2010).

Some governmental support programs that are particularly important to older Swedes are pension benefits (similar to Social Security in the United States), health services, and long-term care (LTC) services. The Swedish pension scheme sets age 65 as the mandatory retirement age. Swedes can transition into early retirement from the age of 55 on, but they have the legal right to continue working until the age of 67 if they wish (International Social Security Agency, 2010). If older Swedes experience health problems, they can call on the help of public health care services. These services are available to all Swedes, without the need to purchase supplementary health insurance (Paris, Devaux, & Wei, 2010). Finally, if health problems persist, older Swedes can use publicly funded LTC services. These services are provided both in the home of the frail person and in institutions (OECD, 2011).

HOW DO OLDER SWEDES PARTICIPATE IN THEIR WELFARE STATE?

Older Swedes generally are quite active, thanks to their good health. They use their time and capabilities to engage in various activities—several of which affect the welfare state. Older Swedes are politically active, voting in governmental elections more often than their younger counterparts (Komp, 2013), so they have a strong influence on what their government does. Additionally, older Swedes participate directly as members of parliament, having an immediate impact on their welfare state's policies. For example, in 2011 almost one half of the members of the Swedish Parliament were aged 55 or older (Eurostat, 2011a).

On the other hand, older Swedes also engage in activities that are important for welfare states, such as working for pay, volunteering, and helping their kin (Komp & Aartsen, 2013). The workforce participation among older citizens in Sweden is higher than in many other countries. In fact, in 2009 Sweden reached the highest workforce participation rate in Europe for people aged 55 to 64. In that year, 70% of the Swedes in this age group worked for pay (DeStatis [Federal Statistical Office of Germany], 2011). Similarly, Swedes aged 50 and older also are more likely to volunteer in organizations, provide care to kin, and help their kin and friends than are many other Europeans (Hank & Stuck, 2008). Only in their participation in religious organizations do we find older Swedes to be less active than most of their European peers (Sirven & Debrand, 2008).

CHALLENGES AND OPPORTUNITIES FOR THE WELFARE STATE IN AGING SWEDEN

The Swedish society changes as its population ages. This trend challenges the Swedish welfare state to cater more and more to the needs of older people. For this reason, the Swedish government has already begun to change some welfare provisions, such as pension schemes and LTC services (Trydegard & Thorslund, 2010). At the same time, a second type of change is occurring within Sweden: Due to the increasing healthy life expectancy, old age is more and more associated with an active lifestyle and social opportunities. This trend is particularly pronounced in Sweden because retirees experience a longer period of healthy postretirement life expectancy than in many other countries. This change opens up new opportunities for the Swedish welfare state. The Swedish government could, for example, try to prolong working lives even more, or it could try to increase social cohesion by encouraging older citizens to volunteer (Komp & Béland, 2012). The aging of the Swedish population is, therefore, more than a simple pressure point for the welfare state; it is a qualitative shift that requires policy makers to rethink what it means to be old. Consequently, it is also a shift that allows policy makers to develop a new type of old-age policy. The next few decades will show whether the Swedish government is able to seize this opportunity.

REFERENCES

Chesnais, J.-C. (1992). *The demographic transition. Stages, patterns, and economic implications.* Oxford, England: Oxford University Press.

DeStatis [Federal Statistical Office of Germany]. (2011). Retrieved from https://www.destatis.de/EN/FactsFigures/NationalEconomyEnvironment/LabourMarket/Employment/LabourForceSurvey/LabourForceSurvey.html

Esping-Andersen, G. (1999). *The social foundations of postindustrial economies.* Oxford, England: Oxford University Press.

Eurostat. (2011a). *Active ageing and solidarity between generations.* Luxembourg City, Luxembourg: Author.

Eurostat. (2011b). *Healthy life years and life expectancy at age 65, by gender* [Excel file]. Retrieved from https://ec.europa.eu/eurostat/databrowser/view/tepsr_sp320/default/table?lang=en

Eurostat. (2013). *Proportion of population aged 65 and over.* Retrieved from https://data.europa.eu/euodp/en/data/dataset/BwmbQtN3OBdlHE7HeYXSnQ

Eurostat. (2018). Your key to European statistics. European Commission. Retrieved from https://ec.europa.eu/eurostat/web/lucas/data/primary-data/2018

Hank, K., & Stuck, S. (2008). Volunteer work, informal help, and care among the 50+ in Europe: Further evidence for "linked" productive activities at older ages. *Social Science Research, 37*(4), 1280–1291. doi:10.1016/j.ssresearch.2008.03.001

International Social Security Agency. (2010). *Country profile: Sweden.* Retrieved from https://www.issa.int/en/country-details?countryId=SE&regionId=EUR&filtered=false

Komp, K. (2013). Political gerontology: Ageing populations and the state of the state. In K. Komp & M. Aartsen (Eds.), *Old age in Europe: A textbook of gerontology* (pp. 59–78). Dordrecht, The Netherlands: Springer.

Komp, K., & Aartsen, M. (2013). Introduction: Older people under the magnifying glass. In K. Komp & M. Aartsen (Eds.), *Old age in Europe. A textbook of gerontology* (pp. 1–14). Dordrecht, The Netherlands: Springer.

Komp, K., & Béland, D. (2012). Balancing protection and productivity: International perspectives on social policies for older people. *International Journal of Social Welfare, Supplement, 1*(21), S1–S7. doi:10.1111/j.1468-2397.2012.00888.x

Korpi, W., & Palme, J. (1998). The paradox of redistribution and strategies of equality: Welfare state institutions, inequality, and poverty in the Western countries. *American Sociological Review, 63*(5), 661–687. doi:10.2307/2657333

Lynch, J. (2001). The age-orientation of social policy regimes in OECD countries. *Journal of Social Policy, 30*(3), 411–436. doi:10.1017/S0047279401006365

OECD. (2011). Estonia long-term care. In *Help wanted? Providing and paying for long-term care*. Paris, France. Retrieved from http://www.oecd.org/estonia/47877618.pdf

OECD. (2018). *Social expenditures–aggregate data* [Excel file]. Retrieved from https://data.oecd.org/social exp/social-spending.htm

Paris, V., Devaux, M., & Wei, L. (2010). *Health systems institutional characteristics: A survey of 29 OECD countries* (OECD Health Working Papers No. 50). Paris, France: Organisation for Economic Cooperation and Development.

Sirven, N., & Debrand, T. (2008). Social participation and healthy ageing: An international comparison using SHARE data. *Social Science & Medicine, 67*, 2017–2026. doi:10.1016/j.socscimed.2008.09.056

Trydegard, G.-B., & Thorslund, M. (2010). One uniform welfare state or a multitude of welfare municipalities? The evolution of local variation in Swedish elder care. *Social Policy and Administration, 44*(4), 495–511. doi:10.1111/j.1467-9515.2010.00725.x

United Nations. (2015). *World population ageing*. New York, NY: Author. Retrieved from https://read.un-ilibrary.org/population-and-demography/world-population-ageing-2015_88fa44e7-en#page4

U.S. Central Intelligence Agency. (2019). *The world factbook*. Retrieved from https://www.cia.gov/library/publications/the-world-factbook/index.html

RETIREMENT AND PENSIONS

PHYLLIS CUMMINS | ROBERT APPLEBAUM

INTRODUCTION

Our chapter begins with a retirement planning story from Nigeria. While every country's economic and retirement system has unique features, this story about a married couple in Nigeria, Chuka and Rita, illustrates some issues that every nation needs to address. One such issue is the role of government versus the role of individuals in preparing for retirement. Another involves the age of retirement and whether leaving the workforce should be voluntary or mandatory. Finally, our story addresses the role of family responsibility in aging societies. The retirement situation for Chuka and Rita is in some ways an exception for those living in Nigeria, because many people do not have pensions; but it illustrates the precariousness of pensions for civil servants in developing nations and the reliance on family to provide supplemental income for those who may appear to be financially secure. These and other elements of the Nigerian experience will lay the groundwork for the issues that we discuss throughout this chapter.

RETIREMENT IN NIGERIA

Chuka and his wife, Rita, are both *career civil servants*—a term used in Nigeria to describe public employees. Chuka is 62 years old and works for one of the states in Nigeria, where he is an electrical engineer in the ministry of public utilities. He has worked for the government for over 30 years and will retire at age 65. In the absence of mortgage financing loan options in the country, he managed to build a medium-sized four-bedroom bungalow in his hometown, where he hopes to move when he retires. Rita is 57 years old and also works for the state government, as an elementary school science teacher. Because the statutory retirement age for teachers is 60 in Nigeria, she is expected to retire at that time, 5 years earlier than the mandatory retirement age for other workers in Nigeria. However, Rita is happy that she will be retiring almost at the same time as her husband because she would very much like to relocate with him to his hometown.

Government jobs, especially at the state level, do not pay as much as private or multinational companies (e.g., oil and gas, manufacturing, construction, and telecommunications companies) in the country. The job market in Nigeria is quite unstable, and people with nongovernmental employment tend to lose their jobs at a moment's notice. Therefore, Chuka and Rita's decision to work and remain in the public sector is likely from fear of finding themselves unemployed, as did some of their friends and relatives who worked in the private sector.

Chuka and Rita spent much of their earnings on postsecondary education for their four children in hopes of ensuring a better future for them. Therefore, they do not have a substantial amount of money saved, but do look forward to retirement. They both believe they have done enough to ensure they will not have to experience financial struggles as they age. Their pensions from the state are based on a **defined-benefit (DB) plan** in which they do not contribute a portion of their monthly income to the plan but will receive a pension at retirement based on their salary levels and number of years of service for the state. This type of pension is in contrast to the new **defined-contribution (DC) plan,** which was introduced by the federal government of Nigeria through the Pension Reform Act in 2004 and has been implemented in several states. In the DC plan, employees pay 7.5% of their salary and the employer pays 7.5% of the salary to a pension scheme toward retirement. Both types of pension plans are discussed more fully later in this chapter.

In a country where about 70% of workers are in the informal sector with no pension benefits, Chuka and Rita's situation is not typical; they are among the very few in Nigeria with a solid retirement plan. Only about 8% of Nigerians are covered by a pension plan, and those without a pension plan often have very little savings. High unemployment and poverty rates in the country result in many Nigerian workers barely having enough money to provide for their basic needs, such as food, potable water, clothing, and shelter. With such dire living conditions, there is little hope of saving for retirement.

Unfortunately, due to Nigeria's political and economic instabilities, even one's income from the state pension plan is not guaranteed. At times, older pensioners did not receive their income because the state government did not allocate adequate funds in the state budget. Sometimes pension funds were either mismanaged or misappropriated (stolen) by their government managers. Thus, even though Chuka and Rita expect to receive their retirement benefits when they retire, they are not very confident they will; they know that their monthly pension income could be delayed or come at irregular times. They have started receiving financial support from their children, especially from their sons, and they are confident that the family financial support will continue after retirement, perhaps until they die. Their two daughters are expected to provide other forms of support for them, like caregiving, when they become older and develop functional impairments. In a situation where they are unable to live independently, they will likely move into the homes of one of their daughters.

Aside from the civil service pension program, Nigeria has no federally funded or well-structured social assistance programs for the poor or older adults, so most retirees without pension benefits or other sources of income must depend entirely on their children for survival. Because of this cultural imperative for adult children to take care of their parents, older adults without pensions have a support system to fall back on. Nigerian culture expects adult children to provide support and care for their older parents regardless of their own socioeconomic situation. This increases the burden on the adult children if they are not economically well positioned to take on the extra responsibility and may result in unintentional abandonment of the older adults. This is what retirement in Nigeria looks like.

THE MANY FACES OF RETIREMENT

Today the vast majority of workers in the industrialized countries of North America, Western Europe, and East Asia believe that someday they will retire from the workforce. Despite economic variation within these nations, for even low-wage earners achieving retirement status is now part of the life course. However, for many workers across the globe, retirement remains an aspirational concept rather than a reality. For example, the proportion of older persons receiving a pension in South Asia and sub-Saharan Africa is below one in four. For the Arab states and Central Africa, the rate is less than 30%. In other parts of Asia, the Pacific, Latin America, and the Caribbean, about 70% of elders receive a retirement benefit (International Labour Organization [ILO], 2017). Even in a wealthy nation like the United States, the nature of retirement varies dramatically, with about 40% of retirees almost completely dependent on Social Security, receiving an average monthly benefit of less than US$1,400 per month. Thus, to understand retirement across the globe, it will be critical to recognize the context across and within individual nations and regions.

As we begin our discussion of retirement, it is also important to highlight that despite the growth in the number of retirees and growing interest in the institution, the concept of retirement is a modern phenomenon. Throughout history, the idea that a person could retire from his or her work has been relatively rare. While select examples of military pensions date as far back as the Roman Empire, for the most part individuals worked until death or incapacity. This was true even in the United States at the start of the 20th century, when two thirds of all men aged 65 and older were still employed (Coile, Milligan, & Wise, 2018). By the late 1990s, however, only 17% of American men aged 65 and older were in the workforce, though that number had increased by 2016 to 24%—still a far cry from the rate in 1900, when life expectancy was considerably lower. The labor force participation rate (LFPR) for women aged 65 and older in the United States in 2016 was

16% (U. S. Bureau of Labor Statistics, 2017). The nations of Western Europe have even lower rates of workforce involvement by older people and, despite some of the recent shifts to higher employment rates for older workers, retirement has become an institutionalized concept in some regions of the world. Even for countries with a smaller proportion of elders and developing economies, interest in retirement has become a major social policy issue. It is certainly the case that while many national differences exist in support and opportunity for retirement, efforts to develop retirement/pension programs now appear in most economies of the world. In this chapter, we explore the varying approaches and challenges to retirement and pensions across the globe.

Retirement Defined

Prior to looking at cross-national opportunities for retirement, it is critical to address the basic definition of retirement. Because of the significant economic, cultural, social, political, and demographic differences across nations, no single definition of retirement applies globally. "Retirement" has different connotations to people in different countries, and its meaning has become increasingly individualized. In some countries, such as India and Uganda, retirement does not exist, and only the most physically disabled and financially secure are able to leave the workforce. However, in other nations, age of eligibility for retirement can be as young as 55.

Coile (2015) suggests four different ways to describe retirement: (a) when an individual stops working for pay; (b) when an individual leaves his or her career job; (c) allowing individuals to define their retirement status; and (d) when an individual makes an initial claim for pension benefits, either public or private. These alternatives emphasize the complexity of retirement. For many, it is a process rather than a single event. **Unretirement** is another possible transition, when an individual shifts from full or partial retirement back to full-time employment (Maestas, 2010). Longer life expectancy has increased the probability for multiple transitions into and out of the labor force (Warner, Hayward, & Hardy, 2010).

As noted, at the beginning of the 20th century, most men worked until they were no longer physically able, and in many regions of the world this phenomenon continues. By the end of the 20th century, LFPRs in many economically developed nations had declined dramatically while life expectancy (and economic security) had increased, resulting in retirement becoming an important life phase. This decline in lLFPRs at older ages became possible as a result of the availability of public and private pension programs. In combination with mandatory retirement policies, leaving the workplace has become a normative phase of the life course in these economically developed countries. However, for many parts of the world, the concept of retirement that developed countries have routinized is not part of everyday life.

Types of Retirement

In regions where retirement has become institutionalized, there are variations in approaches to retirement both within and across countries. It is also important to note that trends in retirement fluctuate based on a host of factors, such as economic conditions, national policy, consumer confidence, and societal demographic changes.

EARLY RETIREMENT

Early retirement is characterized by exiting the labor force and collecting pension benefits earlier than the normal retirement age. Individuals who have more education, have had multiple jobs, have children at older ages, and have experienced later-life divorce are less likely to retire early. Those with less education, physically demanding work, and poor health are more likely to do so (Damman, Henkens, & Kalmijn, 2011). Early retirement can be either voluntary or involuntary. **Voluntary early retirement** is characterized by a preference for leisure activities as opposed to continued work. Alternatively, **involuntary retirement** is often unexpected and can result from events such as corporate downsizings or plant closures. Involuntary retirement also can result from poor health or family caregiving obligations. Although involuntary retirement increased as a result of the worldwide Great Recession (officially late 2007 through 2009, though recovery lasted several more years), it is still relatively uncommon in Canada, Denmark, Japan, Norway, and the United States as compared to France, the United Kingdom, and Germany; in Germany more than half of early retirements are involuntary (Dorn & Sousa-Poza, 2010; Ebbinghaus & Radl, 2015). Some European countries have age restrictions on new hires, making it quite difficult for older workers who become unemployed to find new jobs, thus forcing them to retire early (Dorn & Sousa-Poza, 2010).

DELAYED RETIREMENT

Individuals who decide to retire and receive their pension benefits later than their normal retirement age have delayed their retirement. While some of these persons have chosen to delay their retirement, **involuntary work** can result if an individual retires later than preferred. Involuntary work can result from financial necessity or from poor health that is not adequately debilitating for disability insurance eligibility (Steiber & Kohli, 2017). The Great Recession has resulted in involuntary work for some people to make up for losses in their retirement accounts.

PARTIAL RETIREMENT AND RETURN TO WORK

Partial retirement includes several different types of retirement transitions, including phased retirement, part-time work while collecting pension income, and bridge jobs. Only about one fourth of career employees leave their career jobs and the labor force simultaneously (Cahill, Giandrea, & Quinn, 2012). **Phased retirement** involves a gradual transition into retirement rather than an abrupt shift from full-time employment to full-time retirement. It does not necessarily involve a change of employers, but it can be simply a reduction of work hours with the same employer. Formal phased retirement policies are uncommon, but employers sometimes negotiate working arrangements on an informal basis, especially for employees who have specialized skills (Hutchens, 2010). In the United States, pension regulations can restrict access to pensions unless there is a change in employers. Thus, it may be necessary to change employers in order to receive pension benefits. Data suggest that most employers in the United States are unwilling to allow their employees to switch to part-time employment (Even & Macpherson, 2004). On the other hand, Germany and Italy have had work-sharing programs for several decades (Baker, 2011) that provide a mechanism for older workers to remain in the workforce on a part-time basis.

Pension System Components

As has been discussed throughout this book, individual and societal aging is a global reality. This unprecedented and massive demographic shift has resulted in growing older populations typically making up one eighth to one fifth of many nations' populations. Although life expectancy and the proportion of elders in a society continue to vary across nations, the global demographic story of today is the rapid rate of aging now experienced in both industrialized and economically developing countries. Global aging means that it is not just the industrialized societies that are thinking about retirement issues and challenges. However, nations that are still developing economically at the same time they are experiencing substantial population aging face even more critical challenges surrounding the implementation of retirement programs.

Global population aging has resulted in almost all nations thinking about or implementing retirement programs. In some nations, such as Nigeria and Mexico, retirement benefits are extremely limited, applying only to military, government political officials, or civil servants. In other nations, such as Germany and the United Kingdom, the opportunity to retire is supported by universal public programs and applied to all individuals. Some countries, such as Australia, Denmark, and Iceland, have relied heavily on employers to support workers through private pensions. Others, such as India and Uganda, essentially require individuals to be responsible for their own pensions, and some, such as the United Kingdom and the United States, employ a combination of approaches. The basic philosophy of any pension system is the assumption that at some point in life individuals may no longer be able to maintain full-time employment. Individuals and societies want to ensure that once a person can no longer work, they are able to have some degree of financial security for the remainder of their lives. Not surprisingly, opinions vary across countries about how best to design, fund, and operate a pension system. Debates surrounding the balance between individual and governmental responsibility for socioeconomic security in retirement and disability are commonplace. Country-specific approaches vary on critical elements such as age (and gender difference) of retirement; whether retirement is mandated by law; financing models and tax rates; benefit levels and redistribution; optional, compulsory, and supplemental participation; and public or private administration of the pension program. In this section, we provide country-specific examples to illustrate variation in pension program design.

AGE OF RETIREMENT

An important question faced by both public and private retirement programs is at what age one should be able to retire. Germany is credited with developing the first old-age insurance or retirement program, in 1889. The German chancellor, Otto von Bismarck, initially chose 70 as the retirement age, in part because there was an expectation that many would not reach that age, making the program more affordable. Germany subsequently lowered the age of retirement to 65, which caught on in many other countries as a common age for retirement. Age of retirement does vary throughout the world, and as life expectancy has increased, some nations have increased their established retirement ages.

The age of eligibility for pension benefits can include a normal retirement age, at which one receives a full benefit, and an early retirement age, with a reduced benefit. Retirement age also varies by gender in some nations (see Table 9.1). The most common eligibility age for full retirement is age 65; the most common age for early retirement is age 60. Several countries, including Iceland, Norway, and the United States, have changed their public pension full retirement to age 67, and more countries are expected to make similar adjustments. Several countries have lower eligibility ages for women: Turkey's early retirement age for women is age 58; for men it is age 60. China also has gender-specific retirement ages. Early retirement ages range from age 50 in Nigeria to age 65 in Iceland. Normal retirement ages vary from age 50 in India and Nigeria to age 67 in Iceland and Norway (Organisation for Economic Co-operation and Development [OECD], 2017; U.S. Social Security Administration, 2016, 2017a, 2017b).

As countries experience population aging, their full retirement age has been forced upward. Between 2013 and 2017, 18 nations, ranging from Belarus to Zambia and including both economically developed nations, such as Japan and Italy, and developing countries, such as Rwanda and Nigeria, have raised the normal retirement age (ILO, 2017). Since 1980, many developed countries have implemented reforms that encourage work at older ages in an effort to delay retirement (and pension payments). For example, between 1996 and 2015, Denmark, France, Germany, Italy, Japan, and Sweden all raised the early eligibility age for pensions. At the same time, France, Germany, Italy, Japan, and Spain reduced the benefit generosity (Börsch-Supan & Coile, 2018).

Social security programs that include financial incentives to continue to work at older ages have influenced labor-force participation at older ages and

TABLE 9.1 **Pension Systems and Eligibility Ages in Selected Countries**

| Country | Pension Scheme Types | | | Eligibility Age | | | |
| | Public | Mandatory Private | Voluntary DC | Early | | Normal | |
				M	F	M	F
Australia		X		55	55	67	67
Brazil	X			–	–	60	65
Chile	X	X		–	–	65	60
China	X			55	50	60	55
France	X			–	–	60	60
Germany	X		X	63	63	65	65
Greece	X			60	60	65	65
Iceland	X	X		65	65	67	67
India	X			50	50	58	58
Japan	X			–	–	65	65
Mexico	X	X		60	60	65	65
Nigeria	X			50	50	50	50
Norway	X	X	X	62	62	67	67
Russian Federation	X	X		–	–	65	60
Saudi Arabia	X			–	–	60	55
South Africa	X			–	–	60	60
Turkey	X			60	58	65	65
United Kingdom	X		X	–	–	65	60
United States	X		X	62	62	66	66

Notes: DC, defined contribution; F, female; M, male. Several countries have provided for increases in retirement ages in the coming years. For example, over the next several years, the age for early retirement in Australia will increase to 60, the age for normal retirement in Germany will increase to 67 for those born in 1964 or later, and the age for normal retirement in the United States will increase to 67 for those born in 1960 or later. Some countries vary retirement age depending on employment; in China, men who have physically demanding jobs can retire at age 55 and women with similar jobs can retire at age 50 while in Brazil, male rural workers can retire at age 60 and female rural workers can retire at age 55.

Sources: From Organisation for Economic Co-operation and Development. (2011). *Pensions at a glance 2011: Retirement-income systems in OECD and G20 countries*, Paris: OECD Publishing; Organisation for Economic Co-operation and Development. (2012). *OECD Pensions Outlook 2012*. Paris: OECD Publishing. doi:10.1787/9789264169401-en; U.S. Social Security Administration. (2016). *Social Security programs throughout the world: Asia and the Pacific, 2016*. Retrieved from https://www.ssa.gov/policy/docs/progdesc/ssptw/2016-2017/asia/ssptw16asia.pdf; U.S. Social Security Administration. (2017a). *Social Security programs throughout the world: Africa, 2017*. Retrieved from https://www.ssa.gov/policy/docs/progdesc/ssptw/2016-2017/africa/ssptw17africa.pdf; U.S. Social Security Administration. (2017b). *Social Security programs throughout the world: The Americas, 2017*. Retrieved from https://www.ssa.gov/policy/docs/progdesc/ssptw/2016-2017/americas/ssptw17americas.pdf

have impacted retirement decisions. Availability of pension income from private and/or public sources also affects the timing of retirement. A high replacement rate (i.e., pension income is not substantially less than income from employment) could result in an individual retiring sooner than a person with a low replacement rate. Personal savings or availability of income from family members also impacts retirement timing. The Great Recession caused a decline in the value of pension accounts and savings for many of those approaching retirement age in developed nations, resulting in retirement delays to allow time to rebuild assets.

Financial status varies by gender and impacts the timing of retirement. Women in general have lower retirement benefits than do men due to lower lifetime earnings. As a result, LFPRs for older women have increased over the past several decades. Women often hold lower-paying jobs, have a higher prevalence of part-time and informal work, and have intermittent careers due to family responsibilities; therefore, many need to remain in the workforce at older ages in order to avoid poverty in retirement. In some countries, such as China, Vietnam, and Indonesia, public pensions contribute little to retirement income and retirees, especially women, rely on family members for support (Song, Li, & Feldman, 2012). In addition, lower retirement ages in some countries, along with sex-specific mortality tables (reflecting the fact that women generally live longer than men) used to calculate pensions, also contribute to gender inequalities (ILO, 2017). A recent study estimates the gender gap in pensions for women aged 65 to 74 to be about 40%, whereas the gender pay gap for workers is *only* 16% (Lodovici, Drufuca, Patrizio, & Pesce, 2016). The large pension gap as compared to the pay gap results from pension design features that penalize women and from differences in LFPRs.

Historically, European labor markets were characterized by low labor-force participation at older ages, primarily because the structure of their pension systems provided monetary incentives to exit the labor force early. Over the past several decades, governments in several European countries implemented early retirement programs that allow workers to retire and receive pension benefits prior to the mandatory retirement age. Countries in Central and Southern Europe have high levels of wage replacement in their public pensions, encouraging early retirement; this is not the case in the United Kingdom or the United States. In recent years, European Union (EU) countries have increased their focus on keeping older workers in the labor force in order to maintain the financial viability of their pension systems. In 2001, the EU established the Stockholm and Barcelona targets for their 28 member countries. Their goals were to increase employment rates for those aged 55 to 64 (Stockholm target) and to increase average retirement age for each nation (Barcelona target). Although these programs have met with success in some countries, such as Germany and Sweden, the Great Recession resulted in most countries falling short of their targets (Rix, 2011).

Mandatory Retirement by Law

Some countries actually have **mandatory retirement** age policies, often developed in conjunction with their public pension eligibility rules (e.g., full benefits are made available from the public pension plan at the mandatory retirement age). In some nations, both public pension and company-level rules affect the age at which an individual can or must withdraw from the labor market. In 1986, the United States became one of the first countries to abolish mandatory retirement at any age (for most occupations) and a few other countries, such as Canada and New Zealand, soon implemented similar regulations. The United Kingdom, Denmark, and Poland have also abolished mandatory retirement ages. Mandatory retirement is permitted in Finland, Iceland, Japan, France, Norway, Portugal, and Sweden, but the minimum permitted retirement age varies among these countries. In Japan, the minimum permitted mandatory retirement age increased from age 60 to age 65 in 2013, but employers can extend employment through age 70 at their discretion. In Sweden, the minimum mandatory retirement is age 67, while in Iceland, France, and Portugal, it is age 70. Ireland permits mandatory retirement but allows employers to make retirement-age decisions; minimum retirement ages are not set by government policy (OECD, 2017; Wood, Robertson, & Wintersgill, 2010). Japan's retirement age is among the highest in the OECD countries: the average retirement age between 2012 and 2017 was age 70.6 for men and 69.3 for women (OECD, 2018a). Japan has also one of the highest life expectancy rates in the world, which partially explains the relatively high retirement ages. The Japanese government has encouraged firms to increase their mandatory retirement age or to eliminate mandatory retirement entirely. Although many Japanese workers retire at age 65, it is common for individuals to be rehired by the same firm or become employed by another firm through an introduction by their career employer (Shimizutani & Takashi, 2010).

PUBLIC AND PRIVATE PENSION SYSTEMS

In countries that support a retirement system, the ideal structure recommended is to incorporate three sources of retirement income: a public pension, a private pension, and personal savings. This often is referred to as a "three-legged stool" of retirement income. This idealized system is actually atypical and is most likely to exist in some of the western European countries. However, even in many economically developed nations, including the United States, this ideal system is not universally found in practice. For example, 40% of U.S. retirees receive almost all of their retirement income from one source—the public Social Security pension system—and only about 55% of workers have a private pension or company-supported retirement account. Thus, retirees, even in nations with a public retirement system, often rely on a "two-legged stool" of the public pension plus either their private savings or savings from an individual retirement account. Availability of private pension plans generally is limited to people living in industrialized nations;

people in developing countries typically do not have access to private pension plans, but instead must rely on informal support from their families and communities (Vlachantoni & Falkingham, 2011). Globally, about 68% of the working-age population is covered by mandatory public contributory and noncontributory pension plans. In addition to these plans, about 18% of the world's workers have the option of contributing to voluntary private pension plans, though many of these people choose not to participate (ILO, 2017).

Social Security Systems

Currently, 186 countries have public social security programs, which benefit more than 3 billion people (International Social Security Association [ISSA], 2018). A nation must make a number of decisions as it considers developing a social security retirement system. First, is it the role of government to help workers save for retirement? Some politicians do not recognize this as a responsibility of government, suggesting that such preparation is an individual responsibility. This was a topic fiercely debated in the United States before the passage of the Social Security Act in 1936; thus, the public system did not appear in the United States until almost 50 years after the first modern social security system was implemented in Germany, in 1889.

Once a nation decides on the development of a public system, a second decision involves whether such a system should be mandatory or voluntary and whether the system is mandatory for all workers at all income levels. The majority of national retirement systems are mandatory for all workers, although in a number of nations there is a ceiling on contributions required by high-income pensioners. Other policy considerations include such questions as (a) how such a public pension would be funded, including the type of tax, the rate, and the contribution balance between the employee, employer, and government; (b) whether the program is a social insurance (covering all or most of the population) or a welfare program (covering only the poor); (c) whether the program should provide the same percentage return (the replacement rate of the pension), regardless of income; and (d) whether the program includes incentives for remaining in the workforce longer or penalties for leaving the workforce earlier.

Pension systems most often are funded through a payroll tax (a tax on a worker's wages), typically applied to both the employee and employer. Nine in 10 nations fund at least part of their social security system through such a "contributory" tax, with 38% using only the contributory tax approach. In a small number of nations (6%), all of the retirement benefit is funded from general tax revenues. Table 9.2 reveals two noteworthy differences in country approaches to the payroll tax. One is the variation in the tax rate, and the second involves the balance between employee and employer. As an example, Italy has a combined payroll tax rate of 33% of earnings, compared to about 9% for Australia and Mexico and 12.4% for the United States. The share of the contribution also varies dramatically by country, with some nations, such as Russia, Australia, and Iceland, requiring

TABLE 9.2 Selected Countries' Social Security Contribution Tax Rates

Country	Employee	Employer	Total
Italy	9.2	23.8	33.0
Brazil	8.0	20.0	28.0
China	8.0	20.0	28.0
United Kingdom	12.0	13.8	25.8
France	10.3	15.1	25.3
Russia	0.0	22.0	22.0
Greece	6.7	13.3	20.0
Turkey	9.0	11.0	20.0
Iceland	4.0	15.4	19.4
Germany	9.3	9.3	18.7
Nigeria	8.0	10.0	18.0
Japan	8.9	8.9	17.8
Chile	11.4	1.4	12.8
United States	6.2	6.2	12.4
Kenya	5.0	5.0	10.0
Australia	0	9.5	9.5
Mexico	1.8	6.9	8.7

Sources: From U.S. Social Security Administration. (2016). *Social Security programs throughout the world: Asia and the Pacific, 2016.* Retrieved from https://www.ssa.gov/policy/docs/progdesc/ssptw/2016-2017/ asia/ssptw16asia.pdf; U.S. Social Security Administration. (2017a). *Social Security programs throughout the world: Africa, 2017.* Retrieved from https://www.ssa.gov/policy/docs/progdesc/ssptw/2016-2017/africa/ ssptw17africa.pdf; U.S. Social Security Administration. (2017b). *Social Security programs throughout the world: The Americas, 2017.* Retrieved from https://www.ssa.gov/policy/docs/progdesc/ssptw/2016-2017/ americas/ssptw17americas.pdf

most or all of the contributions to come from the employer, while others, such as Chile, requiring most of the contributions to come from the employee. In a number of countries, including Germany, Japan, Kenya, and the United States, the contribution rates are equal for employee and employer.

WORKER COVERAGE

One of the critical questions faced in the development of a public pension system involves the breadth of coverage. As an example, many of the social security programs in economically developed countries are both mandatory and cover the entire workforce. In these nations, all workers and employers must participate in contributing to the pension system. In some nations, however, universal participation does not occur. In these nations, such as Kenya and Nepal, eligibility for a public pension is limited to political officials, civil servants, and the military. The majority of the workforce in these nations does not participate in public pensions;

in these nations, this large group of individuals, typically comprising more than 80% of the workforce, are called **informal workers**. Data for 2015–2017 found 51 countries where less than 20% of older persons received a pension, down from 73 nations in 2000. Again, regional differences are pronounced. Looking at active pension contributors as a proportion of the labor force, we see a 98% rate in North America (Canada and the United States), 87% in Western Europe, 34% in eastern Asia, 31% in the Arab states, and less than 10% in sub-Saharan Africa (ILO, 2017). These rates illustrate the tremendous challenges facing countries who are experiencing population aging but whose economic development has not created enough wealth to support a large public pension program. In fact, recent research found that some of these countries that had been able to expand pension coverage during good economic times had to cut back on their expansions due to national and individual funding constraints (Wang, Williamson, & Cansoy, 2016).

In addition to coverage of the workforce, a public pension plan must also determine the **income replacement rate** for retirees. Data from the European Commission reported replacement rates ranging from a generous 80% in Spain to the marginal 35% in Hungary (ILO, 2017). Given population aging pressures being experienced across Europe, projections indicate that many of these nations may have to cut back benefits in the future. The United States reports an average replacement rate of 40%, but the actual rate for any individual is dependent on the income level of the retiree; Social Security replaces a higher percentage of preretirement wages for lower-income workers, who receive benefits that are between 69% and 77% (Khan, Rutledge, & Sanzenbacher, 2017; Poterba, 2014).

Functional and Health Limitations and Disability

Health can have a significant impact on the decision to retire. Indeed, employment in physically demanding jobs has been a cause of early retirement for many older workers. Over the past several decades, however—as industrialized economies have shifted to postindustrial employment dominated by service-sector occupations—jobs have become less physically demanding and have tended to rely more on cognitive ability and interpersonal skills. Lower-skilled and more physically demanding jobs are often occupied by those with less education and lower socioeconomic status. Men, manual laborers, and blue-collar workers are more likely than other groups to retire before their normal retirement age because of poor health or functional limitations. Poor health can result in the inability to perform work-related tasks, but it also may cause a person to value leisure time more. Employers will sometimes offer older workers with physical limitations the option of less physically demanding work or shorter hours or provide special equipment so that they can remain employed (Boockmann, Fries, & Göbel, 2011). Exiting the labor market due to health limitations can result from either physical deterioration, such as worsening arthritis, or from a health or disability shock, such as a stroke or automobile accident, though deteriorating health is more common than a health shock.

Variations in country-level policies on disability benefits affect continued employment and the timing of labor market exit. Countries with more liberal disability benefits are likely to experience higher levels of labor market exit for health reasons. European countries, Japan, the United States, and many other developed nations provide long-term disability benefits prior to eligibility for a public pension, but eligibility requirements and actual benefits vary considerably. In recent years, rules for obtaining disability insurance have been tightened in several countries (OECD, 2017). Depending on age and availability of early retirement benefits from either public or private pensions, an individual may choose retirement or participation in a disability insurance program rather than remain in a physically demanding job.

Economic conditions also can affect the timing of labor market exit for those with health limitations. In several countries, applications for disability insurance experienced a substantial increase during the Great Recession. Disability insurance claims increased as employment rates fell in Canada, Denmark, Italy, Sweden, the United Kingdom, and the United States. Those with lower levels of education, who are more likely to be in physically demanding jobs, are more likely to participate in disability insurance programs than those with a college degree (Coile, Milligan, & Wise, 2017). If individuals with physically demanding jobs become unemployed, their physical limitations may limit their reemployment options.

Private Pension Systems

Some nations have in place **private pensions** that are provided directly by employers and generally supplement the public system. The proportion of the labor force with access to a private pension varies widely: for example, 88% of workers in the Netherlands have an occupational pension, while 70% in Germany, 30% in France, and 20% in Italy have such a pension (OECD, 2017). Figure 9.1 provides data on coverage by private pension plans in a sample of OECD countries.

Private pension plans are mandatory in some countries, such as Chile, Australia, Mexico, and Sweden (OECD, 2012). Private pensions are typically categorized as either DB or DC plans. In traditional DB plans, pension payments are determined by a formula that considers salary and length of employment along with other factors. DB pension benefits result from retirement, disability, or survivorship (i.e., a spouse or dependent child receives benefits following the pensioner's death) and generally are paid out as a fixed monthly payment over the life of the pensioner (or beneficiary) rather than as a lump-sum distribution. In a DB plan, the employer bears the risk of investing funds in the retirement account to ensure that balances will be adequate to pay all future pension liabilities.

DC plans (typically known as 401(k) plans in the United States) are retirement accounts established by employers but owned and controlled by the employees. In the United States and most developed countries, contributions to these DC plans are voluntary (OECD, 2012). Employers often subsidize DC plans through matching a portion of the employees' contributions. To illustrate, if employees

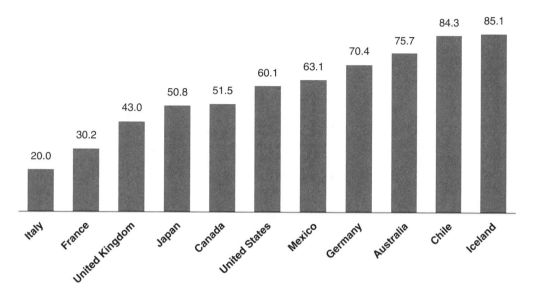

FIGURE 9.1 Proportion of working population with private pensions for OECD nations, 2016.

OECD, Organisation for Economic Co-operation and Development.

Source: From Organisation for Economic Co-operation and Development. (2017). *Pensions at a Glance 2017.* Paris: OECD Publishing. doi:10.1787/pension_glance-2017-en

contributed 5% of their income to their 401(k) account, the employer might match up to 3%, so the employees actually are saving 8% per year for retirement. In DC plans, however, all the risk lies with the employee. The employers make contributions, but their liability is limited to that current cost. In that sense, a DC plan is the same as a savings account that can grow in value—or decline over time—and can lose buying power due to inflation.

Over the past three decades, employers in industrialized countries have been shifting from DB plans to DC plans for three main reasons: (a) they were facing an increasing number of retirees; (b) those retirees were living longer and thus drawing more monthly checks; and (c) the benefit formulas that most DB plans had originally promised turned out to be overly generous. Each of these factors contributed to larger annual pension payouts and obligations than employers had planned for. Hence, many plans were beginning to run out of money, or they could project a shortfall in the foreseeable future. As noted earlier, the move to DC plans placed more of the risk on the employee than on the employer.

In the previous section, we showed data on the replacement rates for public pension systems. In this section, we combine the public pension replacement rates with benefits from the private pension systems when such programs exist and compare net replacement rates for average-wage earners with those of low-wage earners. Net replacement rates indicate the proportion of after-tax income that is paid through the combination of public and private pension plans. It is interesting to note that in several countries, replacements rates are higher for low-wage

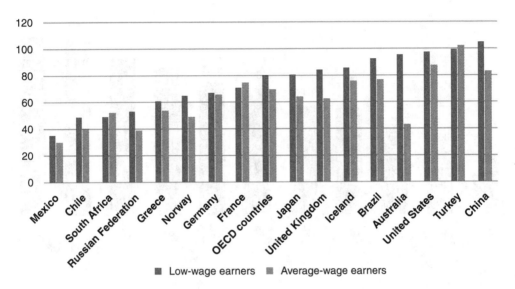

FIGURE 9.2 Net income replacement rates for public and private pensions combined, 2017.

OECD, Organisation for Economic Co-operation and Development.

Source: From Organisation for Economic Co-operation and Development. (2017). *Pensions at a Glance 2017*. Paris: OECD Publishing. doi:10.1787/pension_glance-2017-en

earners than for average-wage earners. For example, the replacement rate for low-wage earners in Australia is 95% as compared to 43% for average-wage earners (see Figure 9.2; OECD, 2017). Higher replacement rates for low-wage earners can result from income redistribution by public pension plans.

Retirement plans for public employees (civil servants) are sponsored by governmental entities, such as federal, state, or local governments. About half of the countries in the world—including some large developing countries, like Brazil, China, India, and Nigeria—have separate pension plans for civil service employees. In some more affluent OECD countries, spending on pensions for civil servants constitutes up to about 25% of total pension spending, whereas in developing countries the proportion is much higher, creating a substantial fiscal problem for some nations (Palacios & Whitehouse, 2006). The risk of irregular pension payments was illustrated in Chuka and Rita's story at the beginning of this chapter.

RETIREMENT IN DEVELOPING NATIONS

With most of the global population living in the developing world, where the notion of retirement ranges from an emerging social reality to a nearly nonexistent concept, the idea and experience of retirement varies dramatically. Significant progress, however, has been made in recent years in extending pension coverage in developing countries. Universal pensions have been implemented in Argentina, Botswana, China, Georgia, Uruguay, and Zanzibar (ILO, 2017). Several countries have sought to provide mechanisms for informal workers to receive pensions through **noncontributory plans**. These plans are funded through taxation, mineral resource revenue, or grants, although benefits from such noncontributory plans typically are very modest. For example, Thailand's noncontributory plan provides monthly benefits of US$18 to US$30, which is less than half of the poverty-level income. South Africa, Brazil, and Kyrgyzstan are among the countries that have implemented noncontributory pension plans that benefit informal workers along with farmers and rural workers (ILO, 2017).

Another strategy of providing pension benefits to informal workers is to simplify the process of contributing to a pension plan. Mexico implemented a strategy to encourage all types of workers, including informal workers, to save for retirement. Their strategy included a promotional campaign to inform people about the system and a network of more than 7,000 locations around the country where they could deposit their money. Thus far, the results are promising, with voluntary savings growing an average of 33% annually since 2014 (OECD, 2018b). Another strategy that has been used to improve savings is for banks to send reminders. Banks in Bolivia, Peru, and the Philippines implemented this strategy, which resulted in an increase in savings and also increased the likelihood of achieving savings goals (OECD, 2018b).

In wealthier developing nations, such as China, retirement from work in later life is a growing possibility for some portion of their populations. In the poorest of developing nations, like Haiti in the Caribbean or Sierra Leone in West Africa, retirement is a concept largely absent from the experiences of everyday people. Adulthood permits only three phases: work, dependency, and death. Life and retirement in developed—and, increasingly, developing—countries may not be easy or simple or even secure, but it is much more desirable than that in the poorest nations.

Where extreme poverty is common, and working often consists of laboring in subsistence agriculture, no surplus income is available to save for retirement; although some governments are beginning to provide small public assistance/pensions for their older citizens, these are typically far too small to live on without supplementing them with substantial time working. As Chuka and Rita's story illustrates, it is common for older adults in developing countries to rely on children to provide financial support when they are no longer able to work.

RETIREMENT POLICY ISSUES FOR AN AGING WORLD

An aging world certainly presents serious challenges as countries address retirement and pension planning. This chapter highlights the range of approaches used by nations to develop social security systems. As we have noted, country circumstances vary dramatically as have their strategies, but regardless of the nation, retirement and pension system obstacles exist. In this section, we discuss the major cross-cutting policy issues faced by all countries.

Can We Afford to Grow Old?

Another way to phrase the question asked in this section's heading is, "Can demographic changes and retirement adequacy coexist?" Despite tremendous variations in the wealth of nations, one common theme for all is the resources required to prepare for income security in old age. Whether we are talking about the wealthy nations of Western Europe, North America, and East Asia, or countries still developing economically, such as those in sub-Saharan Africa, South Asia, or Latin America, resource constraints are universal. In more well-developed nations today, the aging of the population often means that between 20% and 30% of the population has reached old age. In combination with relatively generous pension benefits and continued low fertility rates, financial pressures are placing considerable constraints on the overall economy in many of these nations. Although developing countries have a smaller proportion of their population who are old and continue to have higher, but declining, fertility rates, they are now aging rapidly. Workers in these countries are being squeezed by having to support their aging parents in retirement while also having to contribute to a formal retirement system to support their own retirement in the future. Funding retirement for two generations presents a financial challenge, causing some nations to cut back on current or future retirement benefits. Moving forward, both economically developed and developing nations will need to strike a balance between system affordability and income security for an ever-growing population of retirees. There is no magic answer and the response will vary by nation, but it remains a central question to all societies.

Should Mandatory Retirement Be Retired?

Another area of difference across the globe involves **mandatory retirement**. Although a few countries, including the United States, Canada, Spain, the Czech Republic, Poland, and the United Kingdom, have effectively eliminated mandatory retirement for most occupations, in most countries, including Japan, Russia, Iceland, and Australia, the policy still exists. The policy argument for mandatory retirement is that such a system allows younger people the opportunity to advance and have access to higher-level positions. The rationale is that each generation should have career opportunities, but with no mechanism (other than death) to end employment of more senior workers, those opportunities will not be available. Some have argued that at some age functional decline is bound to occur, and mandatory requirement is simply a proactive approach to reducing incompetence in the workforce. Others argue that aging and decline vary dramatically from person to person, and that a 60-year-old worker may no longer be able to function while a 90-year-old may still be highly productive. Probably everyone has seen evidence of this phenomenon in our own lives. This argument concludes that using chronological age is a bad approach to determining competency for an individual and suggests that one's ability actually to do the job should be the only criterion used, not age. Coupled with this argument are continued advances in life expectancy and an increasing retirement age based on longevity. These changes suggest that a mandatory retirement age would be in direct conflict with the longevity advances now being achieved. Others talk about this issue as a human rights concern as well. Should a person be told that because of his or her age they can no longer have the right or opportunity to work? Many argue that mandatory retirement is ageist—just as racially biased hiring practices are racist—and that if we would never use such personal characteristics as race, gender, or disability to deny a person a job, how could age possibly be an acceptable criterion?

What Happens When All Workers Are Not Included in the Retirement System?

We have discussed in this chapter that some nations do not have universal pension coverage. This is a particular challenge in some of the economically developing nations where the formal retirement system is still being designed and implemented. In some of these nations, a majority of workers (called informal) are not included in the formal social security system. In most of these nations, exclusion of workers from the formal system is based on economics, with low wages and business profits limiting the system's ability to generate retirement funds. However, in some countries, an ideological debate is being held about the role of government in mandatory pension participation. As an example, some politicians believe it is not the job of government to make individuals save for retirement. Should pension contributions be mandatory or should individuals have choice about participation? If saving for retirement is not mandatory, what happens to a person who has reached old age with inadequate savings? Does society simply say, "Too bad; you had your chance," or should it intervene to encourage, or even force, retirement saving? Other variants of the argument are that higher-income workers should be able to opt out or have other pension options. Finally, a number of nations do have supplemental or occupational add-on pensions to a core public pension based on occupation or income.

Should Public Pension Plans Redistribute Income?

As we have seen in this chapter, many countries use public pension systems as a form of **income redistribution**. This happens through a mechanism in which calculation of the retirement benefit provides a higher replacement rate for low-income workers. The rationale for that approach is that low-income workers would have a difficult time surviving on their pension if a universal replacement rate were used. As an example, many nations use a 40% replacement rate as a target. Looking at a low-wage worker in the United States with a $1,000 monthly income provides an example of the challenge. If that person's pension were based on a 40% replacement rate policy, he or she would receive only $400 a month to live on and, as a low-wage worker, likely would not have other income to draw upon. In the U.S. Social Security system, that person actually receives a replacement rate of 75% to 80%, bringing his or her monthly income to US$750–US$800. Similarly, a higher-income person, whose benefit also would be higher, might have a considerably lower replacement rate of 25% to 30%. Some other nations provide the same rate of replacement for all pensioners, regardless of income. Again, social values and political ideology drive every nation's approach to this question, but it also provides a lot of fuel for policy debates.

What Is the Best Way for a Nation to Design Its Retirement System?

Our review described the wide range of approaches used by countries to provide social security for their growing older populations. Systems ranged from a public social insurance with income redistribution to a completely private program with individual accounts; from systems with all or most of the contributions from the employee to those that are primarily from the employer; from major income redistribution to none; and often an array of retirement ages, governed in some cases by a mandatory retirement age policy and in others, none.

Although each of us as individuals might have our personal preferences, the systems that have developed have done so in their own national and cultural context. What works in one country may not work in another. The bottom line is, no retirement system is perfect, and each nation must develop the system that works best for its current political and economic conditions. However, evidence from around the world shows that including all workers in a public retirement pension system and mandating their participation appear to be two common characteristics of comprehensive, stable social security systems that provide adequate support for elderly and disabled persons who have retired from the workforce.

SUMMARY

In this chapter, we discussed different types of retirement, including early retirement, delayed retirement, and partial retirement and return to work. These retirement options are widely available in developed nations, but are less common in developing nations. In many countries, especially developing countries, global population aging has resulted in nations considering or actually implementing retirement programs, but in developing nations, retirement benefits are generally quite limited. Workers with informal work arrangements, which are quite common in developing nations, are typically excluded from public pension programs. In most countries, population aging has resulted in increases in the age for full retirement benefits.

Three sources of retirement income—a public pension, a private pension, and personal savings—are common in countries that support a retirement system.

There are wide variations in the availability of both private and public pension programs, especially in developing countries. The availability of pension income affects the timing of retirement, as does health status. Those working in physically demanding jobs, who often have less education and lower socioeconomic status, are more likely to retire before their normal retirement age. At the same time, the shift in private pension plans from DB to DC by employers in industrialized countries has resulted in workers remaining in the labor force at older ages for economic reasons.

DISCUSSION QUESTIONS

1. At what age should people retire? Why?
2. Why do people retire?
3. What is the difference between a defined-benefit (DB) and a defined-contribution (DC) pension plan?
4. Should the retirement age be increased in developed nations? Why?
5. What are the potential consequences of increasing a country's retirement age? What are the potential benefits?
6. How might a universal pension program affect the local economy of a given country?
7. What are the components of a "three-legged stool" of retirement income? Do most people in the world have access to all three sources?
8. What are potential funding sources for pensions for informal workers?
9. Should there be a mandatory age for retirement? Why?
10. If you were in charge of managing the retirement system for your country, what information (e.g., demographics, economic data) would you want to know about that country in order to help you plan?

KEY WORDS

Defined-benefit pension plan
Defined-contribution pension plan
Delayed retirement
Early retirement
Income redistribution policy
Income replacement rate
Informal workers
Involuntary work
Mandatory retirement

Partial retirement
Payroll tax
Pension eligibility age
Phased retirement
Retirement
Social Security system
Statutory retirement age
Three-legged stool of retirement income
Unretirement

REFERENCES

Baker, D. (2011). *Work sharing: The quick route back to full employment*. Washington, DC: Center for Economic and Policy Research. Retrieved from http://cepr.net/documents/publications/work-sharing-2011-06.pdf

Boockmann, B., Fries, J., & Göbel, C. (2011). *Specific measures for older employees and late career employment*. Retrieved from http://doku.iab.de/fdz/events/2011/Fries.pdf

Börsch-Supan, A. H., & Coile, C. (2018). *Social Security programs and retirement around the world: Reforms and retirement incentives–introduction and summary*. Retrieved from https://www.nber.org/papers/w25280.pdf

Cahill, K. E., Giandrea, M. D., & Quinn, J. F. (2012). Older workers and short-term jobs: Patterns and determinants. *Monthly Labor Review, 135*(5), 19–32.

Coile, C. C. (2015). Economic determinants of workers' retirement decisions. *Journal of Economic Surveys, 29*(4), 830–853. doi:10.1111/joes.12115

Coile, C., Milligan, K., & Wise, D. A. (2017). Introduction. In D. A. Wise (Ed.), *Social security programs and retirement around the world: The capacity to work at older ages* (pp. 1–31). Chicago, IL: University of Chicago Press.

Coile, C., Milligan, K. S., & Wise, D. A. (2018). *Social security programs and retirement around the world: Working longer–introduction and summary*. Retrieved from https://www.nber.org/papers/w24584

Damman, M., Henkens, K., & Kalmijn, M. (2011). The impact of midlife educational, work, health, and family experiences on men's early retirement. *The Journals of Gerontology, Series B: Psychological Sciences and Social Sciences, 66*(5), 617–627. doi:10.1093/geronb/gbr092

Dorn, D., & Sousa-Poza, A. (2010). 'Voluntary' and 'involuntary' early retirement: An international analysis. *Applied Economics, 42*(4), 427–438. doi:10.1080/00036840701663277

Ebbinghaus, B., & Radl, J. (2015). Pushed out prematurely? Comparing objectively forced exits and subjective assessments of involuntary retirement across Europe. *Research in Social Stratification and Mobility, 41*, 113–128. doi:10.1016/j.rssm.2015.04.001

Even, W. E., & Macpherson, D. A. (2004). *Do pensions impede phased retirement?* (IZA Discussion paper series, No. 1353). Bonn, Germany: Institute for the Study of Labor (IZA).

Hutchens, R. (2010). Worker characteristics, job characteristics, and opportunities for phased retirement. *Labour Economics, 17*, 1010–1021. doi:10.1016/j.labeco.2010.02.003

International Labour Organization. (2017). *World Social Protection Report 2017-2019: Universal social protection to achieve sustainable development goals*. Geneva: Author. Retrieved from https://www.ilo.org/wcmsp5/groups/public/---dgreports/---dcomm/---publ/documents/publication/wcms_604882.pdf

International Social Security Association. (2018). *Annual review 2017/2018*. Retrieved from https://www.issa.int/en/details?uuid=a549334f-e420-4c7c-bcf7-77852b7fd36c

Khan, M., Rutledge, M. S., & Sanzenbacher, G. (2017). *Social Security and total replacement rates in disability and retirement* (CRR WP 2017-6). Boston, MA: Center for Retirement Research at Boston College. Retrieved from https://crr.bc.edu/working-papers/social-security-and-total-replacement-rates-in-disability-and-retirement

Lodovici, M. S., Drufuca, S., Patrizio, M., & Pesce, F. (2016). *The gender pension gap: Differences between mothers and women without children*. Retrieved from http://www.europarl.europa.eu/RegData/etudes/STUD/2016/571363/IPOL_STU(2016)571363_EN.pdf

Maestas, N. (2010). Back to work: Expectations and realizations of work after retirement. *The Journal of Human Resources, 45*(3), 718–748.

Organisation for Economic Co-operation and Development. (2011). *Pensions at a glance 2011: Retirement-income systems in OECD and G20 countries*, Paris: OECD Publishing.

Organisation for Economic Co-operation and Development. (2012). *OECD Pensions Outlook 2012*. Paris: OECD Publishing. doi:10.1787/9789264169401-en

Organisation for Economic Co-operation and Development. (2017). *Pensions at a Glance 2017*. Paris: OECD Publishing. doi:10.1787/pension_glance-2017-en

Organisation for Economic Co-operation and Development. (2018a). *Ageing and employment policies: Statistics on average effective age of retirement*. Retrieved from http://www.oecd.org/els/emp/average-effective-age-of-retirement.htm

Organisation for Economic Co-operation and Development. (2018b). *OECD Pensions Outlook 2018*. Paris: OECD Publishing. doi:10.1787/pens_outlook-2018-en

Palacios, R., & Whitehouse, E. (2006). *Civil-service pension schemes around the world* (Social Policy Discussion Paper No. 0602). Washington, DC: World Bank. Retrieved from https://openknowledge.worldbank .org/bitstream/handle/10986/20205/903400NWP0P1320Box0385283B00PUBLIC0.pdf?sequence=1

Poterba, J. M. (2014). Retirement security in an aging population. *American Economic Review, 104*(5), 1–30. doi:10.1257/aer.104.5.1

Rix, S. E. (2011). Employment and aging. In R. H. Binstock & L. K. George (Eds.), *Handbook of aging and the social sciences* (7th ed., pp. 193–206). Burlington, MA: Academic Press.

Shimizutani, S., & Takashi, O. (2010). New evidence on initial transition from career job to retirement in Japan. *Industrial Relations: A Journal of Economy and Society, 49*(2), 248–274. doi:10.1111/j.1468-232X.2010.00598.x

Song, L., Li, S., & Feldman, M. W. (2012). Out-migration of young adults and gender division of intergenerational support in rural China. *Research on Aging, 34*(4), 399–424. doi:10.1177/0164027511436321

Steiber, N., & Kohli, M. (2017). You can't always get what you want: Actual and preferred ages of retirement in Europe. *Ageing and Society, 37*(2), 352–385. doi:10.1017/S0144686X15001130

U.S. Bureau of Labor Statistics. (2017). *Civilian labor force participation rate, by age, sex, race, and ethnicity*. Retrieved from https://www.bls.gov/emp/tables/civilian-labor-force-participation-rate.htm

U.S. Social Security Administration. (2016). *Social Security programs throughout the world: Asia and the Pacific, 2016*. Retrieved from https://www.ssa.gov/policy/docs/progdesc/ssptw/2016-2017/asia/ssptw16asia.pdf

U.S. Social Security Administration. (2017a). *Social Security programs throughout the world: Africa, 2017*. Retrieved from https://www.ssa.gov/policy/docs/progdesc/ssptw/2016-2017/africa/ssptw17africa.pdf

U.S. Social Security Administration. (2017b). *Social Security programs throughout the world: The Americas, 2017*. Retrieved from https://www.ssa.gov/policy/docs/progdesc/ssptw/2016-2017/americas/ssptw17americas.pdf

Vlachantoni, A., & Falkingham, J. (2011). *Exploring gender and pensions in Japan, Malaysia and Vietnam* (CRA Discussion Paper No. 1101). Southampton, UK: Centre for Research on Ageing, School of Social Science, University of Southampton.

Wang, X., Williamson, J. B., & Cansoy, M. (2016). Developing countries and systemic pension reforms: Reflections on some emerging problems. *International Social Security Review, 69*(2), 85–106.

Warner, D. F., Hayward, M. D., & Hardy, M. A. (2010). The retirement life course in America at the dawn of the twenty-first century. *Population Research and Policy Review, 29*, 893–919. doi:10.1007/s11113-009-9173-2.

Wood, A., Robertson, M., & Wintersgill, D. (2010). *A comparative view of international approaches to mandatory retirement* (Research Report No. 674). Norwich, UK: Department for Work and Pensions.

10

FAMILIES

JENNIFER M. KINNEY | BARBRA J. BROTTMAN

INTRODUCTION

The family is the most basic social institution throughout the world. Each of us is born into and spends our life in one kind of family or another. Families are studied in many disciplines, including anthropology, demography, economics, family studies, geography, gerontology, psychology, public health, social work, and sociology. Despite our personal experience with families and a great deal of academic research on families, we have no agreed-on definition of *family*. Part of the difficulty defining this universal social group comes from the fact that families are incredibly diverse—they are found throughout history, in all parts of the world, and they change over time. Based on data from 250 societies, sociologist Murdock (1949) famously defined a **family** as "a social group characterized by common residence, economic cooperation, and reproduction" and claimed that families include "adults of both sexes, at least two of whom maintain a socially approved sexual relationship, and one or more children, own or adopted, of the sexually cohabiting adults" (p. 1).

Think about your current family and the families you know. It is likely that you know families that do not fit within Murdock's definition. For example, do you consider yourself to be part of your family while you are away from home attending college? Do you include in your family anyone who does not live with you (maybe your grandparents)? Do all of the families you know share financial (and other) resources in the same way? Is it necessary for two people to have a child (reproduce) in order to be considered a family? Must a family include two adults—specifically, one adult male and one adult female? What exactly is an "approved sexual relationship?" And why must the adults in a family be "sexually cohabitating?" As you might expect, the concept of "family" has evolved since

Murdock's definition. It is also the case that families can look very different from one another—both across countries and within the same country—and the same family can look different over time.

The purpose of this chapter is to explore what contemporary families look like around the globe, with a special focus on older members. This is a challenge, because one of the major characteristics of families is their diversity. The chapter begins with a brief example of the variability in contemporary definitions of the family. The second section examines how population aging and global interconnections (specifically, economic and social factors) have changed the structure of families. The third section examines the living arrangements of older adults and their families, and the fourth section looks at relationships within families. The fifth section explores macro- and microlevel factors that influence family functioning, and the sixth section presents two important emerging roles of older adults in families.

CONTEMPORARY DEFINITIONS OF FAMILY

We have come a long way since Murdock's (1949) definition of a family. Because of changes in society during those seven decades, contemporary definitions are broader and more inclusive. For example, Leeder (2004) proposes this inclusive and efficient definition of family: "a group of people who have intimate social relationships and have a history together" (p. 25). This definition of family is based on the idea of kinship—that people can choose whom they feel related to.

Canada's Vanier Institute of the Family (2018), an organization that promotes the well-being of families, defined family as:

> ... any combination of two or more persons who are bound together
> over time by ties of mutual consent, birth and/or adoption or
> placement and who, together, assume responsibilities for variant
> combinations of some of the following: physical maintenance and care
> of group members; addition of new members through procreation
> or adoption; socialization of children; social control of members;
> production, consumption, distribution of goods and services; and
> affective nurturance—love.

These two definitions demonstrate that contemporary views of family are continuing to evolve. Leeder focuses on aspects of relationships among members, while the Vanier Institute of the Family takes a more comprehensive approach, incorporating structural (the kinds of formal or legal bonds that define a family) and functional characteristics (i.e., what members do for each other/what resources they exchange). Both structural and functional characteristics are important when we look at families throughout the world; the social/cultural context shapes these characteristics.

Because of the complexity and variability of families over time and across cultures, important key concepts will help you make sense of family life in a particular context. Two of these concepts are population aging and globalization.

POPULATION AGING, GLOBALIZATION, AND DIVERSITY IN THE STRUCTURE OF CONTEMPORARY FAMILIES

Population aging and globalization are useful concepts that help us understand the diversity in the structure of contemporary families. **Population aging** refers to the increase in the proportion of older adults in every country throughout the world. This is happening because of decreases in fertility and increasing life expectancies. In its broadest terms, **globalization** refers to the increasing interconnections and interdependencies of people, materials, products, and institutions throughout the world. Especially since the 1980s, the rates of economic and social change around the globe have been faster than ever before. According to Phillipson (2015), globalization presents both opportunities and challenges for older adults and their families. The effects of population aging and globalization on families are interrelated (i.e., it can be difficult to separate them).

The Impact of Population Aging and Economic and Social Changes on the Structure of Families: The United States as a Case Study

One factor that contributes to diverse family structures is average life expectancy at birth. In the United States in 1900, two-generation (parents and children) and three-generation families (grandparents, parents, and children) were common, but in many families, grandparents did not live long enough to see their grandchildren enter adulthood. Today it is not unusual for member(s) of four, and even five, generations of a family to be alive at the same time (i.e., great-great-grandparents, great-grandparents, grandparents, parents, and children). Also since 1900, more recent generations have fewer children. Together this results in a **vertical** or **beanpole family structure**, with more generations of a family alive at the same time, but with fewer people in each generation.

A second factor that contributes to diversity in family structure is the age at which women have children. Because of the civil rights and women's rights social movements during the 1960s and 1970s, many women who were part of the "baby boom" generation (i.e., born between 1946 and 1964) pursued educational and career opportunities. Many of the women who followed this path delayed getting married and having children until they had launched their careers. (In the United States, it was still legal to fire a woman because she became pregnant until the late 1970s.) For example, if a woman has her first child at age 35, and her daughter repeats that pattern, the woman will be 70 years old when her first grandchild is born. If her grandchild repeats the pattern, the woman would have to live to be 105 in order to meet her first great-grandchild. This has been referred to as an

age-gapped family structure (Bengtson, Rosenthal, & Burton, 1990). On the other hand, if women in a family have their children early in their lives, there can be an **age-condensed family structure** (Bengtson et al., 1990), in which there are fewer than 20 years between generations; such a structure could mean that an 80-year-old woman could be a great-great-great grandmother.

The aforementioned examples are extreme; most families are not entirely age-gapped or age-condensed. However, think about what it would be like to grow up in a very age-gapped or age-condensed family. There are potential advantages and disadvantages for each family structure. For example, in the United States, it has been suggested that age-gapped families typically are more economically stable, whereas age-condensed families have more members available to provide support.

Economic and social trends in the United States since the 1970s resulted in other changes to the structure of families. For example, with more women working outside the home and having children outside of marriage, and with increases in divorce rates, there has been a decrease in traditional **nuclear families** (i.e., a mother, father and child[ren] living together in the same household).

Typically, when we think about a traditional nuclear family a marriage is involved. But marriage has various meanings in different cultures, and definitions of marriage have changed over time. If we limit our thinking to traditional marriage (i.e., between a man and a woman and lasting "until death do us part"), we have seen changes in both the United States and other parts of the world. Marriage is still common, but increasingly diverse. For example, same-sex marriages became legal in the United States in 2015, and is now legal in at least 25 other countries (Pew Research Center, 2017).

Even when people do marry, divorce is increasingly common throughout the world. For example, it is estimated that in the past decade in the United States, between 40% and 50% of marriages end in divorce, often resulting in a single-parent family. Contemporary definitions of families have changed because of the rise in divorce. Many people who do divorce then choose to remarry, often resulting in blended or reconstituted families. Table 10.1 describes these and a diverse set of other emerging family structures.

The Impact of Population Aging and Economic and Social Changes on the Structure of Families Around the Globe

Table 10.1 is important, because these diverse family structures are found all over the world, not just in the United States. Countries in many regions of the world (e.g., Western Europe, North America, Central and Eastern Europe, the Middle East, South and Central Asia, East and Southeast Asia) have witnessed a decrease in fertility, fewer and later marriages, and more divorces. As a result, we are seeing more children born into, and raised outside, a traditional nuclear family. In addition to decreasing family sizes, there has been a decrease in the average household size (i.e.,

TABLE 10.1 Common Diverse Family Structures

Type of Family	Definition
Nuclear	A husband and wife couple and their children who live in the same household.
Extended	Typically used to refer to the people you are related to either through blood or marriage, although it is sometimes used to refer to three or more generations of a family who share a household.
Modified extended	Two or more generations of a family who live in the same community and provide support to each other even though they do not live in the same household.
Single-parent	A family that is headed by a parent who has never been married or is divorced or widowed.
Blended/ reconstituted	A family in which one or both parents have children from a previous relationship.
Cohabitating	An unmarried couple who live together with their children.
LGBTQ	A family in which the parents are lesbian, gay, bisexual, or transgender.
LAT	Two people in a long-term, committed relationship who choose to live in separate households.
Skipped-generation	A family in which grandparents are raising grandchildren because the parental generation is not able/available to do so.
Truncated	A family in which the members of the youngest generation do not have children.
Sibling-based	Sisters and/or their brothers who live together without their parent(s). This is becoming more common among older adults.

LAT, living apart together; LGBTQ, lesbian/gay/bisexual, transgender, queer.

the number of people living together in a single home) in many parts of the world. Among the alternative family forms that are increasing throughout the world are some of those listed in Table 10.1: single-parent; blended/reconstituted; cohabitating; lesbian, gay, bisexual, transgendered, queer (LGBTQ); living apart together (LAT); as well as skipped-generation (e.g., grandparents raising grandchildren), truncated (the youngest generation does not have children), and sibling-based.

Although family structures are becoming more diverse, this diversity is occurring at different rates and is influenced by multiple interrelated factors, including demography, economics, and social and cultural forces. The U.N. Department of Economic and Social Affairs (2003) identified five interrelated aspects of development that affected families around the globe at the beginning of the 21st century: (a) demographic changes, (b) changes in family structure, (c) migration, (d) globalization, and (e) the HIV/AIDS pandemic. The U.N. report examined how these five aspects of development "played out" in 10 regions (including 120 countries) of the world.

Of the five aspects of development that affect families described in the U.N. Department of Economic and Social Affairs (2003) report, we already have talked about demographic changes and changes in family structure. The third factor discussed in the U.N. report is migration. Migration refers to people relocating from one geographic point to another. This includes **internal migration** (i.e., migration within the same country) and **international migration** (i.e., migration to another country). Typically both internal and international migration involve moving from a rural area to a more urban area to pursue better educational or employment opportunities. This is important for families, because it is often young and working-age adults who migrate, leaving their elders and younger family members behind. If you do not have personal experience with migration within your own family, it is quite likely that you know students who have left home to take advantage of educational opportunities—whether this involved migrating from a different part of the state or country or migrating to a new country.

Table 10.2 provides a brief summary of the major migration trends that affect families, organized by the 10 U.N. world regions. As you can see in the table, migration is complicated and reflects increasing globalization (i.e., interdependencies among different parts of the world). Because the table contains a lot of information, it might help you to pay attention to when migration happened and the patterns of internal and international migration in each region. Factors that influence migration throughout the world include reasons for migration (education, employment, political unrest), who migrates (gender, skilled or unskilled workers), and the impact of the migration on the family members who are left behind.

In order to be a good consumer of summary information like the information in Table 10.2, keep in mind four key ideas. First, because the table summarizes data from many countries over more than 50 years, it includes only highlights and major trends and is not comprehensive. Second, the factors that contribute to worldwide trends toward smaller, more diverse family structures vary in when they started and how quickly they unfolded/are unfolding. Third, although the table mostly emphasizes similarities, remember the great amount of diversity among families within every community, country, and region of the world. Finally, the table captures a "snapshot" of time, roughly from the 1950s to the early 2000s. Demographic, economic, social, and cultural factors have continued to change and, because of globalization, a change in one part of the world often directly affects structures and patterns in other parts of the world.

THE LIVING ARRANGEMENTS OF OLDER ADULTS

Just as family structures vary across time and cultural context, so, too, do the living arrangements of older adults. Recent U.N. Department of Economic and Social Affairs reports (2017a, 2017b) identified important patterns and trends in older adults' living arrangements based on data from 67 countries, which they organized into five world regions (North America, Europe, Latin America and

TABLE 10.2 Major Migration Trends Affecting Families Throughout the World

World Region	Trends
Western Europe and North America (Cliquet, 2003)	• Economic development since the 1960s resulted in increased internal (within country) and international (to another country) migration • Western Europeans and North Americans who immigrate typically migrate to similarly developed locations • Migration can result in the development of formal systems to meet the needs that families traditionally filled • There is a lot of variability in how well countries welcomed and integrated immigrants
Central and Eastern Europe (Philipov, 2003)	• Early 1990s: increased migration occurred for political reasons (asylum seekers, refugees from civil wars) • Late 1990s: overall migration lessened, but migration for labor and family reunification increased • Internal migration was five–10 times higher than international migration
South and Central Asia (De Silva, 2003)	• 1960s: out-migration of professional and technical workers to North America, the United Kingdom, and Australia • 1970s–1990s: high migration of (mostly poor) women and men for skilled, semi-skilled, and unskilled jobs in the Middle East • 1980s: migration and tourism led to growth of HIV/AIDS in South Asia and India • 1990s: high rural to urban migration in South Asian countries (primarily for economic reasons—better education, health services) • By 1995, out-migration was mostly by contract workers, refugees, and asylum seekers, many of whom went to Canada, Australia, or New Zealand
East and Southeast Asia (Quah, 2003)	• 1980s–2000s: skilled and unskilled immigration was relatively stable • Singapore and Hong Kong experienced internal migration and the Philippines, international migration • 2000s: internal migration slowed due to economic downturn • International migration remained high in the 2000s and internal migration from rural to urban was common in the Philippines
South America (Jelin & Diaz-Munoz, 2003)	• 1950s–2000s: rapid urbanization and high internal rural to urban migration • 1980s–2000s: political violence and repression led to politically motivated international migration of urban (educated middle class, trade union and working class leaders) and economically motivated migration of rural (men, women, children, black and indigenous) citizens to neighboring countries • 2000s: migratory flow of men to unskilled construction and industrial work and women to domestic service in United States, Europe, and Japan • Workers sent remittances to family back home • Family members left behind rely on remittances

(continued)

TABLE 10.2 Major Migration Trends Affecting Families Throughout the World (*continued*)

World Region	Trends
Central America and the Caribbean (St. Bernard, 2003)	• From the 1950s to the 2000s, most countries had population loss due to unskilled laborers, asylum seekers, and refugees migrating to North Atlantic countries (United States, Canada, United Kingdom) for economic reasons • Heavy intraregional migration • 1990s: tourism attracted migrants from neighboring islands to the Bahamas, British Virgin Islands, St. Maarten, and the U.S. Virgin Islands
Sub-Saharan Africa (Bigombe & Khadiagala, 2003)	• Internal migration by educated young men and women (rural to urban) for job opportunities, social mobility, and income transfers • Men often kept wives in rural areas and other wives/partners in urban settings (a modern version of polygamy with female-headed households) • Family members who stay behind (mostly females) have a lot of responsibilities and rely on remittances from the migrants • 2000s: international migration more difficult because industrialized countries implemented more restrictive immigration policies, which leads to illegal migration and few employment opportunities
North Africa (Nosseir, 2003)	• Increasing feminization of the family due to urban relocation of males to Gulf or European countries, which left women in charge • 1960s: changing political, economic, and social conditions pushed people with higher socioeconomic status to emigrate to North America • 1970s: large majority of emigrants were unskilled or semiskilled laborers from rural areas • 2000s: negative net migration in all countries
El Mashrek and El Araby (Badran, 2003)	• 1970s: migration into Gulf oil countries to build infrastructure • Except for Iraq, these countries were labor exporting (reduced the country's unemployment rate, families benefited from income) • Early 1990s: over 1 million Egyptian workers returned home; returnees to Jordan lost their property and faced many problems • By 1995, many Egyptians were working on construction sites in Libya, Saudi Arabia, Kuwait, and the United Arab Emirates • 2000s: countries begin developing immigration policies; political and economic development in oil-rich countries changed economic employment opportunities, which caused many people to lose jobs
Gulf countries (El-Haddad, 2003)	• In the 1970s, radical changes began due in larger part to migration from rural to urban areas and exposure to global values of consumerism, materialism, and personal interest

Source: From U.N. Department of Economic Affairs. (2003). *Major trends affecting families.* Retrieved from https://www.un.org/development/desa/family/publications/major-trends-affecting-families.html

the Caribbean, Asia, and Africa). For example, the report found that globally, in 2010, 40% of older adults (i.e., those over age 60) lived independently, which they defined as either (a) living only with their spouse or (b) living alone. As you should expect, there was regional variation in these rates. Over 70% of older adults in North America and Europe lived independently, compared to 33% in Latin America and the Caribbean, 27% in Asia, and 21% in Africa.

Although worldwide 40% of older women and 41% of older men lived independently, an important gender difference is embedded here: more older women live alone. The UN. Department of Economic and Social Affairs (2017b) report found that worldwide, 17% of older women live alone, compared to only 9% of older men. And older women were twice as likely as older men to live alone both in Europe and Africa. The U.N. Department of Economic and Social Affairs (2017b) report also found that both 50% of older women and men in the world lived with at least one of their adult children. Rates of older adult/child(ren) coresidence were over 50% in Asia, Africa, and Latin America and the Caribbean, and approximately 20% in North America and Europe. Table 10.3 presents a summary of older women's and men's living arrangements by world region.

The percentages of older adults who live independently and those who coreside with their child(ren) also vary by region of the world. In terms of coresidence, slightly higher percentages of older women than men live with their children in most regions. The one exception is Africa, where the percentage of men living with their child(ren) is 66%, compared to 53% for older women. When the U.N. researchers compared these data from 2010 to data from 1990, they identified an important trend: over the 20-year period, the percentage of the world's older adults who lived independently increased from 24% to 37%, while the proportion who coresided with their children decreased from 65% to 53%. This trend began earlier in the more developed countries and regions, where today approximately four out of

TABLE 10.3 Older Adults' Living Arrangements by World Region

Region	Living Arrangement					
	% Living Alone		% Living With Spouse		% Residing With Child(ren)	
	Female	Male	Female	Male	Female	Male
North America	31	17	39	56	21	18
Europe	36	17	39	58	21	21
Latin America and the Caribbean	14	11	16	24	53	51
Asia	9	5	16	23	66	62
Africa	13	6	8	13	53	66

Source: From U.N. Department of Economic and Social Affairs, Population Division. (2017b). *World Population Ageing 2017 - Highlights (ST/ESA/SER.A/397)*. New York, NY: United Nations. Retrieved from https://www.un.org/en/development/desa/population/publications/pdf/ageing/WPA2017_Highlights.pdf

five (80%) of people aged 60 and over live independently, and the remaining 20% live with child(ren). In contrast, coresidence still dominates in developing countries and regions. Although the U.N. Department of Economic and Social Affairs (2017a, 2017b) expects the trend of older people living independently to increase in developing countries, they are not sure that it will ever match the levels found in North America and Europe.

One factor that contributes to variability in older adults' living arrangements is the income level of the country. In 2010 in more developed countries/regions, over 70% of older adults lived independently, and 20% coresided with their child(ren). In contrast, in the developing countries/regions, 27% of older adults lived independently, while 62% coresided with children (U.N. Department of Economic and Social Affairs, 2017a). These numbers clearly reflect the wealthier nations' greater ability to provide adequate pensions and employment opportunities, and thus economic independence, to their older citizens. And the trend continues. Today, in the most developed regions, approximately 80% of older adults live independently (U.N. Department of Economic and Social Affairs, 2017a). Other factors that contribute to whether older adults live independently are demographics (Are people living long enough to reside with their adult children? Do they have children with whom they can live?), social norms (What are the expectations about living with family among the religious and other communities in which someone is a member?), and personal preferences. It is these last three factors that lend variability to older adults' living arrangements, both within different regions of the world and within a given country.

RELATIONSHIPS WITHIN FAMILIES

How families function (how they think about and interact with one another, and the things they do for each other) are as complex and culturally variable as family structures and living arrangements. To help us understand and compare the key dimensions of relationships among family members, in 1971 Bengtson and his colleagues started a research project called the Longitudinal Study of Generations. For more than 35 years, the research team interviewed members of a group of families. Over time, this resulted in interviews with family members of four generations (i.e., children, parents, grandparents, great-grandparents). Based on their early findings, Bengtson and his colleagues developed the **intergenerational solidarity model** (Bengtson & Roberts, 1991; Bengtson, Giarrusso, Mabry, & Silverstein, 2002). The intergenerational solidarity model identified six key dimensions of the relationships between parents and their children and between grandparents and their adult children. The model says that the higher the rating for each dimension of solidarity, the more positive the family relationship. Over time, the model evolved to include ambivalence and conflict as important dimensions found in families. The six dimensions of solidarity, ambivalence, and conflict are presented in Table 10.4.

TABLE 10.4 Dimensions of Family Functioning: Intergenerational Solidarity, Conflict, and Ambivalence

Dimension of Solidarity*	Description
Affectual	Type and degree of positive sentiments/emotional closeness held about family members and the degree of reciprocity of these sentiments
Associational	Frequency and patterns of interactions among family members
Consensual	Degree of agreement on values, attitudes, and beliefs among family members
Functional	Degree of instrumental and emotional support given and received among family members
Normative	Strength of commitment to norms and expectations regarding the performance of familial obligations (e.g., filial and parental responsibilities)
Structural	Opportunities for intergenerational relationships based on the number, type, and geographic proximity of family members
Additional Dimensions[†]	**Description**
Conflict	Tension or disagreement among family members, even if not explicitly expressed
Ambivalence	Having competing and/or conflicting feelings about family member(s) at the same time

*Adapted from Bengtson, V. L., & Roberts, R. E. L. (1991). Intergenerational solidarity in aging families: An example of formal theory construction. *Journal of Marriage and the Family, 53*(4), 856–870. doi:10.2307/352993

[†]Adapted from Bengtson, V. L., Giarrusso, R., Mabry, J. B., & Silverstein, M. (2002). Solidarity, conflict and ambivalence: Complementary or competing perspectives on intergenerational relationships? *Journal of Marriage and the Family, 64*(3), 568–576. doi:10.1111/j.1741-3737.2002.00568.x

When you look at the dimensions of family solidarity, it might be helpful to think about your relationships with your own family members, or the relationships within another family with whom you are very familiar. If you are like most of us, as you apply each dimension to a specific family relationship, you begin to appreciate how complicated family relationships can be. For example, it is possible to love (and like) a family member (high affective solidarity) but still be frustrated by them if they do not live up to your expectations (low normative solidarity); you can have very different values from a family member (low consensual solidarity) yet feel obligated (high normative solidarity) to spend a lot of time with them (high associational solidarity) and/or provide them with emotional or financial support (high functional solidarity). On the other hand, you might be fortunate to have the opportunity (high structural solidarity) to spend a lot of time (high associational solidarity) with a family member you feel very close to (high associational solidarity). These are just a few examples, but we hope you can see how the different dimensions of solidarity, ambivalence, and conflict could be used to produce a wide variety of family relationship profiles.

It is also important to point out that most people have a distinct family relationship profile with each family member and that these profiles change over the course of the relationship, sometimes in response to changes in society. For example, with respect to functional solidarity, do your parents give you the same type of assistance today as they did 10 years ago? Do they get the same type of assistance from their parents as they did 10 years ago? As another example, think about the difference that globalization and technology have had on structural solidarity. Prior to the Internet, it was very difficult to stay in touch with family members who had migrated to another country. Today, it is possible for international students to have daily contact with family members back home, allowing them to maintain high structural solidarity despite vast geographic distance.

Family Solidarity in Western Europe and Israel

The intergenerational solidarity model has been used to identify specific types of families and explore whether they find different patterns of family types in different countries. For example, Dykstra and Fokkema (2011) studied the patterns of structural, associational, normative, and functional solidarity among late-life families in 11 countries in Western Europe (Sweden, Denmark, the Netherlands, Belgium, Germany, France, Austria, Switzerland, Italy, Spain, and Greece) using data from the Survey of Health, Ageing and Retirement in Europe (SHARE). They found four types of families.

In the first family type, **descending familialism**, family members lived in close geographic proximity (modified extended structure; see Table 10.1), had frequent contact with one another and a strong norm of family obligation, and parents primarily provided help to their adult children (35% of families). The second family type, **ascending familialism**, was the same as descending familialism, except adult children primarily provided help to their parents (25% of families). They called the third type **supportive-at-distance families**. In these families, members did not live close to one another, and they did not have a norm of family obligation, but they saw each other frequently and parents provided help to their adult children (7% of families). The fourth family type, **autonomous families**, did not live close to one another, they did not have a norm of family obligation, they did not see each other frequently, and they did not exchange resources (33% of families). Does it surprise you that one third of families were in this last family type?

Although descending and ascending familialism were most common, the researchers found all four family types in each of the 11 countries (although the proportions varied). Together, descending and ascending familialism were most common in Southern Europe (approximately 75% of families in Greece, Italy, and Spain were either descending or ascending). Although there were fewer supportive-at-distance families overall, they were most common in Northern Europe (12% in Denmark and Sweden). Autonomous families were most common in Western

Europe (approximately 45% in France and Switzerland). It is important to remember that family type can shift over time (e.g., from descending to ascending), that these findings are limited to specific countries in Western Europe, and that government policies can influence the support that family members provide to one another. We return to this last idea in upcoming paragraphs.

Based on these findings and their own research, Katz, Lowenstein, Halperin, and Tur-Sinai (2015) offered four conclusions: (a) each family type has different resources that its older and younger members can draw on; (b) cultural differences in intergenerational family support exist within and between countries; (c) each country has multiple family types; and (d) intergenerational family solidarity is strong in European countries and Israel. It is unfortunate that we do not know more about patterns of intergenerational family solidarity in other parts of the world, and we hope such research is underway.

Intergenerational Family Transfers

One aspect of **functional solidarity** (i.e., the degree of instrumental and emotional support given and received) is the exchange of money between generations of a family. In the National Transfer Accounts (NTA) Project, research teams in more than 35 countries worked together to examine the transfer of economic resources from one age group to another at an aggregate level—either an entire country or a world region. A general finding from the NTA Project is that, across the globe, older adults typically give more financial resources to younger generations of their families than they receive from them. For example, older adults in Brazil, Mexico, the United States, and Uruguay, among other countries, give far more to their younger family members than they receive from them (Lee & Mason, 2011).

Kahn (2014) was interested in the types of transfers that adults exchange with their family members and close friends. He looked at three types of transfers (financial assistance, practical assistance, providing care) that adults between the ages of 40 and 79 exchange with their family and friends. He did this using the Global Ageing Survey, which included more than 20,000 participants from 24 countries and territories that Kahn categorized into five world regions (North America, Europe, Latin America, Asia, and the Middle East/Africa). Across the world regions, females received more financial assistance and gave more practical assistance, and they provided more care to others than did men; also, people with more education were more likely to provide financial and practical assistance. Several interesting regional differences emerged: old people in North America and Europe did not frequently receive financial assistance, but it was very common in Latin America, Asia, and the Middle East/Africa; and in developing countries, older people who lived in larger households were more likely to receive social support.

Intergenerational transfers clearly are influenced by sociodemographic and cultural factors. Thus, patterns of intergenerational transfers will vary across geographic locations and over time, especially with globalization and as developing countries become more developed. Some researchers have predicted that decreasing family sizes, increasing number of older adults who live alone, and changing attitudes toward older adults are trends likely to result in decreases in within-family transfers to older adults (Lee & Mason, 2011). Supporting this idea, family transfers to older adults in Japan, the Republic of Korea, and Taiwan have declined in the past several decades (Vos, Ocampo, & Cortez, 2008).

FACTORS THAT INFLUENCE FAMILY FUNCTIONING

So far, we have seen ways in which families throughout the world are similar and ways in which they are different. The next step is to consider explanations for these similarities and differences. To do this, it is important that you understand that each family is embedded in a set of social structures/institutions, each one more complicated than the one before.

Think of your own family as a small circle in the middle of a piece of paper (this represents the smallest, or most microlevel social structure/institution). Next, draw a larger circle around your family circle. This second circle can represent your extended family or your neighborhood; it is what you identify as the next larger social structure/institution outside the people you consider to be your family. Around these two, you might draw a third circle, representing your community. Both the second and third circles are examples of micro–macrolevel social structures, because they are in between the micro- and macrostructure/institution. You can keep drawing circles, indicating larger social systems/institutions, until you get to the country you live in with its typical political and economic systems (for this discussion, the macrolevel social structure).

Now that you understand the idea that families are embedded in increasingly complex social contexts, we will examine two aspects of social contexts that influence family functioning: (a) government policies and programs in the country in which a family lives (macrolevel) and (b) values about families (micro–macrolevel).

Government Policies and Programs
CHINA'S ONE-CHILD POLICY

Even though intergenerational relationships within families are personal and occur at the microlevel, they are influenced by both micro- and macrolevel factors. A good example of how a government policy can affect families is China's family planning policy. Because of rapid population growth, starting in the 1960s, the Chinese government introduced limitations on family sizes. Despite these efforts, the government was concerned that they would not have enough resources to support their burgeoning population. So, in 1979 they implemented the **one-child policy**, which mandated that a couple could have only one child. The one-child policy was not consistently enforced, and it was modified over the years. For example, it was more heavily enforced in urban than in rural areas.

An urban couple could have a second child after 5 years if their first child had a physical or developmental disability, if the husband and wife had been divorced, or if the husband and wife were both only-children. In rural areas, parents were allowed to have a second child after 5 years if the first child was a girl (Phillips & Feng, 2015).

Over the years, the one-child policy had some unintended consequences. First, because sons are preferred in China, abortions of female fetuses increased, and many young girls were abandoned by their families. Second, families who did not follow the policy did not register their other children with the government, so these children were not able to obtain formal education. Third, because of the gender imbalance, many young men have had (and still have) a hard time finding a woman to marry. Fourth, as the children became adults, they found themselves responsible for older parents and grandparents, without siblings to help them. This has been called the 4-2-1 family structure—an adult couple can be responsible for four grandparents (and possibly a great-grandparent or two) and their own child (Phillips & Feng, 2015). Because of these (and other) unintended consequences, in 2013 the Chinese government began to relax the one-child policy, so, as of January 1, 2016, all couples in China may have two children (Wang, Gu, & Cai, 2016). This example shows the impact that a policy can have on families and that policies can change over time.

GOVERNMENTS AND THE WELFARE STATE

The most important macrolevel factor that influences families is their governments' policies and programs. A government that has policies and programs to protect and promote the economic security, health, and well-being of its citizens is called a **welfare state**. This is different from welfare programs that provide subsidies to the poor, such as Supplemental Security Income, Medicaid, and other programs in the United States. Welfare states are found in developed (and some developing) countries. Welfare states are designed to provide equal opportunities for, and to distribute resources to, all citizens. This can be done by providing free or low-cost services (e.g., education, paid maternity and paternity leave from jobs, child care, health care, retirement pensions, care for old people) and by providing cash benefits directly to people who need them. But because countries have limited economic resources, they must decide how to invest these resources. Such decisions often are based on need and/or age.

With respect to age-based decisions, each welfare state has a particular **intergenerational social contract**. An intergenerational social contract is the basic understanding a country (and its citizens) has about whether the government or productive individuals (usually the middle-generation family members who are most likely to be employed) are responsible for those who are dependent or vulnerable (most typically, children and old people). Table 10.5 provides examples of different types of welfare states, several countries that have each type of welfare state, and some of the key characteristics of each type.

TABLE 10.5 **Types of Welfare States, Sample Countries, and Key Characteristics**

Type of Welfare State Sample Countries	Key Characteristics
Liberal Australia, Canada, United Kingdom, New Zealand, Northern Ireland, United States	Relatively low social spending, with few universal benefits and limited means-tested welfare programs Policies do not interfere with the free market Family is largely responsible for caring for children and old people Does not advocate for gender equality, so there is little public child care High degree of individualism and personal responsibility Not particularly strong public support for children or old people
Conservative Austria, France, West Germany, Israel (Arabs and Jews), Japan, Switzerland	High level of social spending based on occupation and status, which promotes inequalities Encourages traditional family forms and gender roles, so there is little public support for child care Long-standing government support for old people
Social Democratic Denmark, Finland, Norway	Generous social welfare programs with universal entitlements Many social programs for children and old people Child care enables mothers to work outside the home The government pays for services that are usually the responsibility of individual families Very strong intergenerational social contract welfare state
Postsocialist Cyprus, Italy, Spain	Transitioning from communism, which provided many social programs "from the cradle to the grave" (e.g., child care, guaranteed employment, universal health care, old age pensions) and promoted gender equality (many women are employed outside the home) Because economies are struggling, there has been a decrease in public spending/services offered by the welfare state With the move toward capitalism, there is more expectation of individual responsibility rather than a strong welfare state
Southern European Czech Republic, East Germany, Hungary, Latvia, Poland, Russia, Slovenia	Traditionally there was a high degree of intergenerational dependence within families (very familistic) Social welfare policies and formal services are relatively new The system is fragmented and benefits are tied to occupation The social contract includes children and old people
New/Emerging Brazil, Chile, Philippines, South Africa	Initial efforts focus on building infrastructure (sewage treatment, clean water supplies), providing health care and education to children and income supplements/social security for the poor Expanding on current intergenerational social contracts

Source: Adapted from Marcum, C. S., & Treas, J. (2013). The intergenerational social contract revisited: Cross-national perspectives. In M. Silverstein & R. Giarrusso (Eds.), *Kinship and cohort in an aging society: From generation to generation* (pp. 293–313). Baltimore, MD: Johns Hopkins University Press.

Marcum and Treas (2013) surveyed citizens in the 29 countries listed in Table 10.5 to find out if families thought their country's intergenerational social contract should (a) emphasize children, (b) favor old people, (c) treat old people and children equally, or (d) make both children and old people the responsibility of individual families. Across the different welfare states, between 55% (liberal welfare states) and 89% (postsocialist welfare states) thought that the welfare state should emphasize both children and old people. When asked whether children or old people should be provided for, far more people in all these countries indicated that old people (rather than children) should be provided for (the percentages for old people ranged from 8.5% to 38.2%, compared with a spread for children of 0.2%–2.8%). Across the types of welfare states, very few people thought that the social contract should put responsibilities on individual families (percentages ranged from 0.8% to 6.3%). These findings show that, in all types of welfare states, the intergenerational social contracts include old people. Nonetheless, at the same time some developing countries are just beginning to implement a welfare state, many developed countries are adjusting their welfare state to shift responsibilities from the state to the individual and the family.

Dykstra (2017) wanted to know how different welfare states affect intergenerational transfers, such as providing financial assistance, practical help, and physical care within families. To answer this question, she reviewed findings from studies based on two international data sets: (a) SHARE, which included data from 26 European countries and Israel; and (b) the Generations and Gender Survey, which included data from 19 European countries and four non-European countries. In general, generous welfare states complement the support that family members provide one another. Generous welfare states also create a shared responsibility between the government and the family, such that family members do not feel as obligated to exchange resources with family members and can do so voluntarily because they want to/for a sense of enjoyment, or out of a sense of reciprocity.

For example, with respect to financial transfers, when a family member receives financial assistance, he or she often redistributes the money within his or her family, giving it to the person who needs it the most. Looking at data from 13 European countries, Mudrazija (2016) found that this redistribution most often involved older parents sharing the assistance they received with their adult children until the older adults were in their mid-80s. Similarly, because of the well-developed Social Security system and public policies that promote savings for old age in the United States, on average, older parents are more likely to provide assistance to their adult children than to receive it until they reach their 80s (Frankenberg & Thomas, 2011; Lee & Mason, 2011).

The services provided by the welfare state also influence nonfinancial transfers. In countries with generous welfare states, families rely on the services provided by the government to meet their children's and older relatives' needs for physical care and on family members for practical help (Brandt, Haberkern, &

Szydlik, 2009). For example, in European countries that have more nursing-home beds, fewer adult children care for their parents (Van den Broek & Dykstra, 2017), and in a comparison of family members in the United States and the Netherlands, family members in the United States, where there are not as many services, felt more obligated to care for an older relative (Cooney & Dykstra, 2011). These are just a few examples that show how generational interdependency is influenced by the welfare state.

In general, welfare states are far more generous in European countries than in the United Sates, and some countries are just beginning to develop their welfare state. In countries without welfare states, private transfers from family or social network members constitute the main source of support for older adults (U.N. Population Fund, 2012). Types of support include financial payments (money or transfers of assets) and/or in-kind transfers such as food, clothing, shelter, or care-giving. Familial transfers are especially important to the very old in Asia, Latin America, and many countries in sub-Saharan Africa.

Values About Family Relationships

If a country's welfare state/policies and programs were the only factors that influenced kinship ties, living arrangements, and intergenerational relationships within families, we would see great diversity across countries, but within a particular country all families would function about the same. But we know that is not true; there is a lot of diversity among families within the same country. Value differences form a second reason for diversity among families. Values are complicated. They are considered micro–macrolevel factors because they are influenced by your family, the social structures and institutions that surround your family (e.g., educational and religious institutions), and past experiences—your own and those of the people to whom you are close.

It is quite possible that you have heard at least one older adult say "Families just aren't what they used to be. When I was young ..."; and then they tell you about "the good old days" before families "broke down." But as you learned earlier in this chapter, despite their increasing diversity, families throughout the world interact with and exchange resources among their younger and older members. So, the statement about modern family breakdown is a stereotype. You might also have heard someone (in fact, it could even be the same person) say that families in Western countries (especially the United States) do not respect their elders the way that families in Asian countries do. This is another stereotype. It is a mistake to dichotomize parts of the world as having "good" and "bad" family values. Instead, as is the case with all aspects of families, it is important to be aware of and appreciate that values about families differ within and between different parts of the world. In the following sections, we look at four important family values: (a) filial piety; (b) filial responsibility; (c) an individualistic versus a collectivistic family orientation; and (d) family interdependence.

FILIAL PIETY

Filial piety is "the practice of respecting and caring for one's parents in old age, based on a moral obligation that children owe their parents" (Hashimoto & Ikels, 2005, p. 437). This reverence for parents is said to be the foundation for all human relationships in East Asian cultures. Filial piety is based in Confucianism. Although Confucianism often is thought of as a religion, it is more accurate to think of it as a set of values that tells individuals how to live in harmony with one another. Traditional filial piety in East Asia has reinforced hierarchies based on gender (males are dominant) and age (elders dominate). For decades, the Confucian principles of filial piety were used to maintain social order, provide a moral and spiritual foundation for societies, and ensure social control. In recent decades, globalization and migration, demographic changes, and social and legal mandates have lessened the practice of filial piety in many East Asian countries (including China, Japan, and South Korea). The future of filial piety in these countries is uncertain due also to global concerns with individual rights and autonomy.

Although people tend to associate filial piety with Asian culture and assume the value is found only in Asian countries, this is not true. Virtually all religions (including Buddhism, Christianity, Islam, and Judaism) teach some degree of filial responsibility. As such, filial piety is a value observed and practiced to some extent in both Eastern and Western countries and in developing and developed nations.

FILIAL RESPONSIBILITY

The norm of filial responsibility differs from the norm of filial piety in two ways: (a) it does not have the philosophical underpinnings associated with Confucianism, and (b) it is not associated with a particular part of the world (e.g., Asia). **Filial responsibility** is "the extent to which adult children feel obligated to meet the basic needs of their aging parents" (Katz et al., 2003, p. 308). A large body of contemporary research conducted in many parts of the globe documents that, in general, the norm of filial responsibility is strong, although it differs according to sociodemographic characteristics such as age, gender, ethnicity, socioeconomic status, and whether families live in urban or rural areas. As you learned earlier, it is also associated with the services that are provided by the welfare state (government) in a particular country. You have seen evidence of filial responsibility in the earlier sections on family solidarity and intergenerational family transfers, and you will see more evidence of filial responsibility in discussions of family caregiving, when younger family members care for their old relatives who need assistance.

INDIVIDUALISTIC VERSUS COLLECTIVIST FAMILY ORIENTATION

Researchers have identified two general orientations that characterize families: individualist and collectivist. **Individualistic families** (and their members) are characterized by independence, self-reliance, autonomy, self-fulfillment, and personal achievement. In individualistic families, loose kinship ties predominate among members, relationships tend to be voluntary and egalitarian, and the emphasis is on individual self-sufficiency rather than duty and obligation to other family members. In contrast, **collectivistic families** are characterized by feelings of continuity, belongingness, and identity. In collectivistic families, kinship ties and family responsibility are strong, and members tend to meet each other's emotional needs. You might wonder about the relationship between family orientation and the intergenerational solidarity, conflict, and ambivalence model described earlier. You can think about family orientation as a general classification, and the intergenerational solidarity, conflict, and ambivalence model as a tool to document the specific profile of emotions, attitudes, and behaviors that a family demonstrates.

If you think about countries and regions of the world as being made up of large numbers of families, it might not surprise you that some social scientists have characterized different regions of the world as either individualistic or collectivist. This characterization is based on the orientation of the majority of the families in that area. Typically, Western European countries, the United States, Canada, and Australia are characterized as individualistic, whereas countries in Africa, Asia (e.g., China, India, Japan, Pakistan), Latin America, and the Middle East (e.g., Egypt, Saudi Arabia, Iran, Iraq) are characterized as collectivistic (Triandis, 1993). But do not confuse family orientation with government policies/programs and the welfare state. Family orientation operates on a micro–macrolevel, and government policies and programs take place at the macrolevel, with both factors influencing family functioning.

INTERDEPENDENCE

Throughout the world (North America, Europe, the Middle East and Africa, Latin America, and Asia and the Pacific), support between younger and older family members is best characterized as a two-way *inter*dependency rather than a unidirectional dependency of the younger members on the older members, or the older members on the younger ones. This **interdependence**, defined as each generation needing, accepting, and giving support to other generations, acknowledges older adults' contributions earlier in life (e.g., raising children and/or caring for their own older kin) or more recent contributions within the family (e.g., intergenerational financial transfers) or community, both of which entitle them to receive care in later life.

Despite the interdependence within families throughout the world, interdependence looks different in different families and societies. For example, to respect their older members' autonomy and also meet their needs for care, contemporary families in the Italian region of Tuscany (a) monitored older adults who remained in their long-time homes; (b) created three-generational households; (c) had older family members stay with different family members for extended periods of time; (d) hired professional caregivers to assist in the home despite a value of family care for older relatives; and (e) developed community strategies for older adults who did not have family members who were able/willing to provide care to them

(Weibel-Orlando, 2009). If these strategies sound familiar, it may be because they are also used in some combination in many, possibly most, other Western societies.

TWO EMERGING PATTERNS IN FAMILIES: A TROUBLING CHALLENGE AND AN IMPORTANT OPPORTUNITY

Despite much diversity among families, two important commonalities also have been observed throughout the world. The first pattern—elder abuse—is very troubling and requires strategies to end it. In contrast, the second pattern—grandparents raising their grandchildren—should be supported and nurtured so that it can continue and flourish. Both national and international efforts are underway to accomplish both of these goals.

Elder Abuse: A Dark Side of Family Life

Beginning in 2012, the United Nations declared each June 15 as World Elder Abuse Awareness Day. It did this to let people know that many older adults throughout the world are mistreated by their family members. Elder abuse or mistreatment occurs in five different ways: (a) psychological abuse; (b) financial exploitation; (c) neglect (either by someone else or the older adult himself or herself, which is called self-neglect); (d) physical abuse; and (e) sexual abuse.

Worldwide, it is estimated that one of six (almost 16%) community-dwelling older adults (aged 60 or older) experienced some type of abuse in the past year (Yon, Mikton, Gassoumis, & Wilber, 2017). This statistic is based on a comprehensive study that summarized the findings from studies of elder abuse in 25 European countries, 15 countries in the Americas, five Southeast Asian countries, five Southwest Pacific Island nations, and two Eastern Mediterranean countries. Of these, 34 were high-income, 13 were upper-middle-income, and five were lower-income countries. Across the studies, the average percentage of older adults who had been abused in the past year was 20.2% in Asia, 15.4% in Europe, and 11.7% in the Americas. Although Yon and colleagues did not examine variation in elder abuse at the country level, in an earlier study Dong (2015) examined research from 30 countries on five continents (Asia, Africa, Europe, and the Americas). At this point in the chapter, it should come as no surprise to learn that rates of elder abuse varied from country to country. However, to understand fully why these rates vary, more research is needed on elder abuse in middle- and low-income countries and on cultural factors that predict abuse.

Older adults who experience elder abuse are more likely to experience psychological distress and physical health problems than are older adults who are not abused. They also are more likely to use health care services, especially hospital emergency departments (EDs); they are at greater risk of being hospitalized (and have more rehospitalizations); and they have higher mortality rates. Elder abuse is "prevalent, predictable, costly, and sometimes fatal" (Dong, 2015, p. 1214). It is for these reasons that elder abuse is considered both a public health and a human rights issue.

As serious as elder abuse is today, the United Nations (n.d.) is concerned that it will increase in the coming years due to rapid population aging around the world. We do know that elder abuse seems to be more common among social minority groups, adults with cognitive and physical limitations, and those who are socially isolated. But it is not enough to identify characteristics of victims. We need research on characteristics of the perpetrators who abuse older adults. We must also promote awareness of elder abuse and develop policies and community-based strategies that intervene to stop elder abuse when it happens and, ultimately, prevent it from occurring.

Grandparents: New Opportunities and Responsibilities

What you know about grandparents and your opinion of them probably is a result of how many you have known, how many you can claim within your own family, and the nature of your contact with them.

AVAILABILITY

Whether you grew up in an age-condensed or an age-gapped family (Table 10.1 describes different types of families), chances are good that you have (or had) a relationship with several of your grandparents—and possibly even one or more of your great-grandparents. You might be in the first generation of your family to have this opportunity. In 1900 in the United States, only 20% of 30-year-olds had a living grandparent; by 2000, this percentage had jumped to 80% (Chamie, 2018). Do you know how old your parent(s) were when their grandparents died, and whether your parent(s) knew any of their great-grandparents? Not only have you probably known more of your family elders than your parent(s) did, you probably will know them for a longer time.

Worldwide, grandparents make up approximately 20% of the population (Chamie, 2018). The proportion of grandparents ranges from approximately 15% in developing countries (e.g., Ethiopia, Kenya, Nigeria, Pakistan) to 25% in more developed/fully developed countries (e.g., Costa Rica, Japan, Russia, Ukraine). Several factors influence these percentages. First, grandparenthood is more common in developed countries, where life expectancies are higher and therefore the probability of living long enough to meet a grandchild is also higher. Second, it is not possible to have a grandchild if you (and at least one of your children) did not have children (unless you are part of a reconstituted family that includes grandchildren). Currently, in many developing countries (e.g., India, Indonesia, Pakistan, South Africa, Turkey), fewer than 5% of women in their late 40s do not have children, whereas in developed countries (e.g., Austria, Canada, Finland, Spain, United Kingdom, United States), 20% of women in their late 40s do not have children. This suggests that we could see changes in the percentages of grandparents throughout the world as more countries advance economically.

Obviously, if a person has children, the age at which his or her first child is born determines the age at which he or she will become a grandparent. For example, if you are part of an age-gapped family (i.e., you have your first child at age 30, and that child does the same), you will become a grandparent around age 60, which is the norm in developed countries (e.g., Canada, Germany, Italy, Japan, the Netherlands, Switzerland). In contrast, if you are part of an age-condensed family (i.e., you have your first child before age 20, and that child does the same), you will become a grandparent before age 40, which is the norm in developing countries (e.g., Bangladesh, Chad, Mali, Nigeria, Zambia) and in many poor communities in wealthier nations. Imagine the difference in becoming a grandparent at these different ages and how it might affect how you behave as a grandparent. And, of course, the longer you live and remain in the role of grandparent, the more likely it is that you will become a great-grandparent.

THE GRANDPARENT ROLE

Grandparents are found throughout the world, and they provide a variety of functions within the family. They can pass down family history and stories to later generations and provide emotional, social, financial, and/or instrumental support. Many grandparents provide most (or all) of these functions. Recent research from different countries (e.g., the United Kingdom, Israel, South Africa, and Malaysia) indicates that being a grandparent has positive consequences. Grandparents report better mental health, more resilience, and positive interactions with their grandchildren (Attar-Schwartz & Buchanan, 2018; Tan, 2018; Wild, 2018). Of course, not all grandparents are involved in their grandchildren's lives. Some grandparents choose not to be particularly involved, while a few parents serve as gatekeepers, keeping grandparents from seeing their grandchildren.

Although grandparents are found throughout the world, the roles they fill vary based on several factors. One important factor you are familiar with by now is the level of development of a country and its welfare state. In less developed countries and countries that do not have generous welfare states to provide support for children, grandparents often play an important role in helping to raise their grandchildren. For example, in Southern European countries (e.g., Italy, Greece, and Spain) and other countries that have less generous welfare states (e.g., Poland and South Africa), grandparents provide more direct care to their grandchildren than they do in Northern European countries, which have more generous welfare states. This is also the case in developing countries throughout the world, as economies change and more women are interested in working outside the home. For example, it is common for grandparents in Asia (e.g., Japan and Singapore) to watch their grandchildren so that their mothers can work outside the home. Despite differences in welfare states, 44% of grandmothers and 42% of grandfathers across Europe either occasionally or regularly help their grandchildren (Glaser, Price, Ribe, di Gess, & Tinker, 2013). Unfortunately, we do not have such systematic information from other regions of the world.

GRANDPARENTS RAISING GRANDCHILDREN

A special role that is becoming more common for grandparents (most typically, grandmothers) throughout the world is raising their grandchildren. Grandparents assume this role for three main reasons (Buchanan & Rotkirch, 2018). First, the increase in divorce rates and children born outside of marriage has resulted in more single- (usually female-) headed households in which one parent is both raising child(ren) and working outside the home. Combined with economic downturns in many regions of the world, this has resulted in more multigenerational households in which grandparents assume responsibility for raising their grandchildren.

Second, with globalization, to provide for their families, many parents, including mothers, have chosen to migrate internally (i.e., from rural areas to urban areas within their country) or externally (i.e., from their home country to another country that has more employment opportunities). In both types of migration, the parent(s) send money ("remittances") to their children and parents back home to help meet their financial needs. This is most common in developing regions of the world, including Eastern Europe, Central and South America, Asia, and Africa.

Third, a crisis can affect individual families, requiring grandparents to "step up" and assume responsibility for their grandchildren. Examples of a social crisis that can affect families in developing countries are illness and death due to HIV/AIDS, while in developed countries (including the United States), a more common cause of parental absence is drug addiction, especially the opioid epidemic (Buchanan & Rotkirch, 2018). Other examples of family crises include parental incarceration, mental and/or physical health conditions, or death, all of which prevent parents from being able to care for their children. In situations where the parent generation is "missing," whether due to migrant work, incarceration, illness, drug abuse, or death, these families are referred to as **skipped-generation families**.

Dolbin-MacNab and Yancura (2017) were interested in the experience of grandparents raising grandchildren (which they called "surrogate parenting") in four different social and cultural contexts: China, New Zealand, Romania, and South Africa. For each country, they identified relevant macrolevel (societal) factors, welfare state family policies that affected grandparents raising grandchildren, and characteristics of family situation (microlevel) factors. Table 10.6 summarizes their analysis. As you look at the table, you will see some overlap in the macrolevel factors in each country, but more important differences in the welfare state policies, which in turn shape the experience of surrogate parenting for grandparents in the four countries.

Grandparents are taking on more responsibility within the family, both in developing and developed countries, and countries differ in the support that they provide to grandparents. Many countries do not recognize grandparents as surrogate parents unless they go through time-consuming and expensive procedures. So, for example, a grandparent who is informally a surrogate parent for his or her

TABLE 10.6 Macro- and Microlevel Aspects of GPRGC in Four Countries

Country	Macro (Societal)-Level Factors	Family Welfare Policies	Micro (Family)-Level Factors
China	Economic problems Modernization Migration	Few policies support GPRGC Some older adults are eligible for small pensions	Parents' rural-to-urban migration for work leaves 20% of children behind (BBC, 2016a); most are raised by grandparents (norm of familism and generational reciprocity) Skipped generation (parents) sends remittances to GPRGC Rural GPRGC do not get much help and are stressed
New Zealand	Historical oppression and discrimination of indigenous people	Policies support keeping families together and GPRGC Complicated system provides social programs, financial assistance, housing supplements, hardship pay to grandparents, allowances to grandchildren Special benefits for age 65+ GPRGC	GPRGC due to a crisis (illness, drugs, incarceration) with the skipped generation (similar to Western countries) Norm of extended families is strong among indigenous people (due to separation of families during British rule in the 1800s)
Romania	Economic problems Migration Recent political turmoil (policies designed to improve economic conditions weakened families, for example, building the workforce by not providing sex education or birth control to women with fewer than four children)	Weak social policies Family (rather than government) responsibility for children Few cash benefits or support for mothers who do not work outside the home; few child care services; little support for GPRGC Policy requires migrating parents to record a guardian for their children, but few do	20% of children aged between 10 and 15 are raised by grandparents because parents migrated to Western Europe for work (BBC, 2016b) Despite strong family structures, many children are abandoned at orphanages High poverty; GPRGC struggle Little trust of the government Support for GPRGC comes from informal and family networks

(continued)

TABLE 10.6 Macro- and Microlevel Aspects of GPRGC in Four Countries (continued)

Country	Macro (Societal)-Level Factors	Family Welfare Policies	Micro (Family)-Level Factors
South Africa	Economic problems Migration Historical oppression and discrimination Disease (AIDS) epidemic	Multiple government social assistance programs (old-age pensions, child support grants, foster child grants, free education, school nutrition programs, free health care for children less than 6 years old, housing subsidies, public works projects, adult education grants) Not everyone is eligible for social assistance; those who receive it often redistribute the benefits within their family Lack of knowledge of benefits Nongovernmental and faith-based organizations work to fill unmet needs	70% of all South African children live with nonparent relations; 20% live with neither parent Often grandmothers raise grandchildren; some GPRGC situations are voluntary (access to education); others are crises (AIDS, migration of parents for work) 40%–60% of orphans live with grandmothers (Beegle et al., 2008) Multigenerational households are common Children are viewed as the community's responsibility; child care as an obligation Grandmothers are vulnerable and they struggle, but they are very resilient (spiritual, instrumental, emotional support from community)

GPRGC, grandparents raising grandchildren.

Source: Adapted from Dolbin-MacNab, M. L., & Yancura, L. A. (2017). International perspectives on grandparents raising grandchildren: Contextual considerations for advancing global discourse. *The International Journal of Aging and Human Development, 86*(1), 3–33. doi:10.1177/0091415016689565

grandchildren might not be able to enroll them in school. Moving forward, it is important for countries to develop more inclusive family policies that encourage and support grandparents' efforts.

To acknowledge the important (and growing) role that grandparents have within families, approximately 30 countries celebrate a national Grandparents Day. Although many countries, especially in Latin America, Asia, and Southeast Asia, have traditionally had holidays to honor elders, Grandparents Day was first celebrated in the United States in 1978. Although countries do not yet agree on a designated international date, once a year countries on every continent pay tribute to the unique contributions that grandparents make to both their families and their communities (Grandparently.com, 2019). And, in upcoming decades, as people live longer with greater economic security, it is anticipated that these contributions will increase.

CONCLUSIONS

In this chapter, we have provided a snapshot of what families look like throughout the world. This was not easy because, as you now know, families are complex, especially when viewed in their particular context. Our hope is that you now have the vocabulary and concepts necessary to think about families in a global context, to appreciate their similarities and differences, and to understand the major factors that contribute to these similarities and differences. It is important to remind you that, like any family photograph, this chapter represents a snapshot in time. When you look at family photographs from 10 (or more) years ago, you are probably surprised to see how your family has changed. We expect the same thing will happen when we look at families in the future. We will still recognize some aspects of families we see today, but we also can expect important changes.

Today most older adults live in more developed countries (U.N. Department of Economic and Social Affairs, 2017a). However, the most rapidly aging populations are in less-developed countries. It is estimated that by 2050, eight of 10 older adults will live in developing regions (U.N. Department of Economic and Social Affairs, 2017b). The U.N. Department of Economic and Social Affairs (2017b) also estimates that by 2050, older adults will account for 35% of the population in Europe, 28% in North America, 25% in Latin America and the Caribbean, 24% in Asia, 23% in Oceania (Australia, Melanesia, Micronesia, and Polynesia), and 9% in Africa. Thus, wherever in the world you live or travel to, as you continue to grow into adulthood, middle age, and beyond, there likely will be more older adults in your own family and in other people's families—and eventually, if you are lucky, you will be an elder in your own family. This means that the roles that older adults play in our families will change and probably become more important.

The African Union Plan of Ageing argued that countries should (a) "enact legal provisions that promote and strengthen the role of the family and the community in the care of its older members," (b) "ensure that legal instruments exist to protect the rights of older people within the family and community," (c) "develop and strengthen strategies that empower older people to contribute to their families," and (d) "implement policies and programmes that strengthen families and are inclusive of older people" (African Union and HelpAge International [AU/HelpAge], 2003, pp. 15–16). These recommendations were made over 15 years ago about older adults living in sub-Saharan Africa. But they are just as important today, and they apply to all older adults around the globe. Yet we know that countries are at different levels of development and that even in developed countries, not all welfare states provide these benefits for old people and their families.

Recently, Aboderin and Hoffman (2015) proposed an agenda to help accomplish the goals of the African Union Plan of Ageing in sub-Saharan Africa—but their agenda can be used to advance these goals for old people and their families throughout the world. They advocate (a) the importance of strengthening families, especially in the absence of government support, and (b) realizing that, even though old people can be vulnerable, in many situations they are essential to a family's success. Aboderin and Hoffman also make three recommendations to researchers and policy makers that constitute good advice for us all: (a) make no assumptions about what constitutes family, but look to families to see how they define themselves; (b) use theories and concepts to understand families better, with an emphasis on different family experiences; and (c) appreciate the importance of context in shaping what families look like and how they function.

DISCUSSION QUESTIONS

1. Use the terms in Table 10.1 and Table 10.4 to describe your extended family or another family with whom you are familiar. How many of the terms apply to this family? What did you learn about this family's structure by applying these terms?

2. As shown in Table 10.2, migration has happened throughout the world. Pick two of the world regions in Table 10.2 and describe how migration is both similar and different in these two world regions.

3. Table 10.2 describes migration around the globe until the early 2000s. Pick one region of the world and find out what the current trends in migration are.

4. Based on the descriptions in Table 10.5, pick the type of welfare state that you think is the most and least supportive of families. Identify one country in each category and find a current article about families in the two countries.

5. Find an example in a contemporary news source of a grandparent raising grandchildren. What micro- and macrolevel factors can you identify that contribute to that grandparent's situation?

KEY WORDS

Age-condensed family
Age-gapped family
Ascending familialism
Autonomous families
Collectivistic families
Descending familialism
Family
Filial piety
Filial responsibility
Functional solidarity
Globalization
Individualistic families

Interdependence
Intergenerational social contract
Intergenerational solidarity model
Internal migration
International migration
Nuclear families
One-child policy
Population aging
Skipped-generation families
Supportive-at-distance families
Vertical or beanpole family structure
Welfare state

REFERENCES

Aboderin, I., & Hoffman, J. (2015). Families, intergenerational bonds, and aging in Sub-Saharan Africa. *Canadian Journal on Aging, 34*(4), 282–289. doi:10.1017/S0714980815000239

African Union and HelpAge International (AU/HelpAge). (2003). *AU policy framework and plan of action on aging.* Nairobi, Kenya: HelpAge International Nairobi.

Attar-Schwartz, S., & Buchanan, A. (2018). Grandparenting and adolescent well-being: Evidence from the UK and Israel. *Contemporary Social Science, 13*(2), 219–231. doi:10.1080/21582041.2018.1465200

Badran, H. (2003). Major trends affecting families in El Mashrek El Araby. In United Nations Department of Economic and Social Affairs. *Major trends affecting families: A background document.* Retrieved from https://www.un.org/development/desa/family/publications/major-trends-affectingfamilies.html

BBC. (2016a). Counting the cost of China's left-behind children 12 April 2016. Retrieved from http://www.bbc.co.uk/news/world-asia-china-35994481

BBC. (2016b). Left behind children in Romania. Retrieved from http://www.bbc.co.uk/news/av/world-europe-36542014/romania-s-left-behind-children

Beegle, K., Filmer, D., Stokes, A., & Tiererova, L. (2010). *Orphanhood and the living arrangements of children in Sub-Saharan Africa.* Policy research working paper 4889. Washington, DC: The World Bank.

Bengtson, V. L., & Roberts, R. E. L. (1991). Intergenerational solidarity in aging families: An example of formal theory construction. *Journal of Marriage and the Family, 53*(4), 856–870. doi:10.2307/352993

Bengtson, V. L., Giarrusso, R., Mabry, J. B., & Silverstein, M. (2002). Solidarity, conflict and ambivalence: Complementary or competing perspectives on intergenerational relationships? *Journal of Marriage and the Family, 64*(3), 568–576. doi:10.1111/j.1741-3737.2002.00568.x

Bengtson, V. L., Rosenthal, C., & Burton, L. (1990). Families and aging: Diversity and heterogeneity. In R. H. Binstock & L. K. George (Eds.), *Handbook of aging and the social sciences* (3rd ed., pp. 263–287). San Diego, CA: Academic Press.

Bigombe, B., & Khadiagala, G. M. (2003). Major trends affecting families in sub-Saharan Africa. In United Nations Department of Economic and Social Affairs. *Major trends affecting families: A background document.* Retrieved from https://www.un.org/development/desa/family/publications/major-trends-affecting-families.html

Brandt, M., Haberkern, K., & Szydlik, M. (2009). Intergenerational help and care in Europe. *European Sociological Review, 25,* 585–601. doi:10.1093/esr/jcn076

Buchanan, A., & Rotkirch, A. (2018). Twenty-first century grandparents: Global perspectives on changing roles and consequences. *Contemporary Social Science, 13*(2), 131–144. doi:10.1080/21582041.2018.1467034

Chamie, J. (2018). Increasingly indispensable grandparents. Yale University: Yale Global online. Retrieved from https://yaleglobal.yale.edu/content/increasingly-indispensable-grandparents

Cliquet, R. (2003). Major trends affecting families in the new millennium: Western Europe and North America. In United Nations Department of Economic and Social Affairs. *Major trends affecting families: A background document.* Retrieved from https://www.un.org/development/desa/family/publications/major-trends-affecting-families.html

Cooney, T. M., & Dykstra, P. A. (2011). Family obligations and support behaviour: A United States–Netherlands comparison. *Ageing & Society, 31*, 1026–1050. doi:10.1017/S0144686X10001339

De Silva, I. (2003). Demographic and social trends affecting families in the South and Central Asian Region. In United Nations Department of Economic and Social Affairs. *Major trends affecting families: A background document.* Retrieved from https://www.un.org/development/desa/family/publications/major-trends-affecting-families.html

Dolbin-MacNab, M. L., & Yancura, L. A. (2017). International perspectives on grandparents raising grandchildren: Contextual considerations for advancing global discourse. *The International Journal of Aging and Human Development, 86*(1), 3–33. doi:10.1177/0091415016689565

Dong, X. Q. (2015). Elder abuse: Systematic review and implications for practice. *Journal of the American Geriatrics Society, 63*, 1214–1238. doi:10.1111/jgs.13454

Dykstra, P. A. (2017). Cross-national differences in intergenerational family relations: The influence of public policy arrangements. *The Gerontologist, 67*, 1–8. doi:10.1093/geroni/igx032

Dykstra, P. A., & Fokkema, T. (2011). Relationships between parents and their adult children: A West European typology of late-life families. *Ageing and Society, 31*(4), 545–569. doi:10.1017/S0144686X10001108

El-Haddad, Y. (2003). Major trends affecting families in the Gulf Countries. In United Nations Department of Economic and Social Affairs. *Major trends affecting families: A background document.* Retrieved from https://www.un.org/development/desa/family/publications/major-trends-affecting-families.html

Frankenberg, E., & Thomas, D. (2011). Global aging. In R. H. Binstock & L. K. George (Eds.), *Handbook of aging and the social sciences* (7th ed., pp. 73–89). San Diego, CA: Academic Press.

Glaser, K., Price, D., Ribe, E., di Gess, G., & Tinker, A. (2013). *Grandparenting in Europe.* London: Grandparents Plus (2018). Retrieved from https://www.grandparentsplus.org.uk/what-is-kinship-care

Grandparently.com (2019). Grandparents Day around the world. Retrieved from https://www.grandparently.com/grandparents/grandparents-day-around-the-world

Hashimoto, A., & Ikels, C. (2005). Filial piety in changing Asian societies. In M. L. Johnson (Ed.), *The Cambridge handbook of age and ageing* (pp. 437–442). New York, NY: Cambridge University Press.

Jelin, E., & Diaz-Munoz, A. R. (2003). Major trends affecting families: South America in perspective. In United Nations Department of Economic and Social Affairs. *Major trends affecting families: A background document.* Retrieved from https://www.un.org/development/desa/family/publications/major-trends-affecting-families.html

Kahn, H. T. A. (2014). Factors associated with intergenerational social support among older adults across the world. *Ageing International, 39*, 289–326. doi:10.1007/s12126-013-9191-6

Katz, R., Daatland, S. O., Lowenstein, A., Bazo, M. T., Ancizu, I., Herlofson, K., . . . Prilutzky, D. (2003). Family norms and preferences in intergenerational relations: A comparative perspective. In V. L. Bengtson & A. Lowenstein (Eds.), *Global aging and challenges to families* (pp. 305–326). New York, NY: Aldine De Gruyter.

Katz, R., Lowenstein, A., Halperin, D., & Tur-Sinai, A. (2015). Generational solidarity in Europe and Israel (2015). *Canadian Journal on Aging, 34*(3), 342–355. doi:10.1017/S0714980815000197

Lee, R., & Mason, A. (2011). Population aging and the generational economy: Key findings. In R. Lee & A. Mason (Eds.), *Population aging and the generational economy* (pp. 3–31). Northampton, MA: Edward Elgar Publishing Limited.

Leeder, E. (2004). *The family in global perspective: A gendered journey.* Thousand Oaks, CA: Sage Publications.

Marcum, C. S., & Treas, J. (2013). The intergenerational social contract revisited: Cross-national perspectives. In M. Silverstein & R. Giarrusso (Eds.), *Kinship and cohort in an aging society: From generation to generation* (pp. 293–313). Baltimore, MD: The Johns Hopkins University Press.

Mudrazija, S. (2016). Public transfers and the balance of intergenerational family support in Europe. *European Societies, 18*, 336–358. doi:10.1080/14616696.2016.1207792

Murdock, G. (1949). *Social structure.* New York, NY: Free Press.

Nosseir, N. (2003). Family in the millennium: Major trends affecting families in North Africa. In United Nations Department of Economic and Social Affairs. *Major trends affecting families: A background document.* Retrieved from https://www.un.org/development/desa/family/publications/major-trends -affecting-families.html

Pew Research Center. (2017). Gay marriage around the world. Retrieved from http://www.pewforum .org/2017/08/08/gay-marriage-around-the-world-2013

Philipov, D. (2003). Major trends affecting families in Central and Eastern Europe. In United Nations Department of Economic and Social Affairs. *Major trends affecting families: A background document.* Retrieved from https://www.un.org/development/desa/family/publications/major-trends -affecting-families.html

Phillips, D. R., & Feng, Z. (2015). Challenges for the aging family in the People's Republic of China. *Canadian Journal on Aging, 34*(3), 290–304. doi:10.1017/S0714980815000203

Phillipson, C. (2015). Global and local ties and the reconstruction of later life. In J. Twigg & W. Martin (Eds.), *Routledge handbook of cultural gerontology* (pp. 389–396). New York, NY: Routledge Taylor & Francis Group.

Quah, S. R. (2003). Major trends affecting families in East and Southeast Asia. In United Nations Department of Economic and Social Affairs. *Major trends affecting families: A background document.* Retrieved from https://www.un.org/development/desa/family/publications/majsor-trends -affecting-families.html

St. Bernard, G. (2003). Major trends affecting families in Central America and the Caribbean. In United Nations Department of Economic and Social Affairs. *Major trends affecting families: A background document.* Retrieved from https://www.un.org/development/desa/family/publications/major -trendsaffecting-families.html

Tan, J.-P. (2018). Do grandparents matter? Intergenerational relationships between closest grandparents and Malaysia adolescents. *Contemporary Social Science, 13*(2), 246–260. doi:10.1080/21582041.2018.14 24931

Triandis, H. C. (1993). Collectivism and individualism as cultural syndromes. *Cross-Cultural Research, 27*(3&4), 155–180.

United Nations. (n.d.). World Elder Abuse Awareness Day. Retrieved from http://www.un.org/en/ events/elderabuse

United Nations Department of Economic and Social Affairs. (2003). *Major trends affecting families.* Retrieved from https://www.un.org/development/desa/family/publications/major-trends -affecting-families.html

United Nations Department of Economic and Social Affairs, Population Division. (2017a). *World Population Ageing 2017 (ST/ESA/SER.A/408).* New York, NY: United Nations.

United Nations Department of Economic and Social Affairs, Population Division. (2017b). *World Population Ageing 2017 - Highlights (ST/ESA/SER.A/397).* New York, NY: United Nations.

United Nations Population Fund. (2012). *Ageing in the twenty-first century: A celebration and a challenge.* New York, NY: United Nations.

Van den Broek, T., & Dykstra, P. A. (2017). Residential care and care to community-dwelling parents: Out-selection, in-selection and diffusion of responsibility. *Ageing & Society, 37*, 1609–1631. doi:10.1017/ S0144686X16000519

Vanier Institute of the Family. (2018). Definition of family. Ottawa, Ontario: Author. Retrieved from https://vanierinstitute.ca/definition-family

Vos, R., Ocampo, J. A., & Cortez, A. L. (2008). *Aging and development.* New York, NY: United Nations Publications.

Wang, F., Gu, D., & Cai, Y. (2016). The end of China's one-child policy. *Studies in Family Planning, 47*(1), 83–86. doi:10.1111/j.1728-4465.2016.00052.x

Weibel-Orlando, J. (2009). La cura degli nostril cari anziani: Family and community elder care roles in contemporary Italy. In J. Sokolovsky (Ed.), *The cultural context of aging: Worldwide perspectives* (3rd ed., pp. 536–549). Westport, CT: Praeger Publishers/Greenwood Publishing Group.

Wild, L. (2018). Grandparental involvement and South African adolescents' emotional and behavioural health. *Contemporary Social Science, 13*(2), 232–245. doi:10.1080/21582041.2017.1422536

Yon, Y., Mikton, C. R., Gassoumis, Z. D., & Wilber, K. H. (2017). Elder abuse prevalence in community settings: A systematic review and meta-analysis. *Lancet Global Health, 5*, e147–e156.

WHAT DO YOU CALL YOUR GRANDMOTHER?

FRANK J. WHITTINGTON

If you are lucky enough to have a grandmother—or two—or knew her before she died, you probably know her real name, but you also probably use a more familiar name in speaking to her and referring to her in conversations with others.

In the United States, there is a limited supply of common words (both formal and informal) to apply to grandmothers, including "grandmother," "grandma," "granny," and "gran." Many families depart from these limited choices, however, and customize their own names. To my siblings and me, our grandmothers were called "grandmother" (maternal) and "mama" (paternal). Both were fine, hard-working women, raised on farms in the southern United States in the early 20th century. We knew this, but could not think of them each as a person with a real name and identity apart from their "grandmother name." When our own mother became a grandma, the child himself, in his garbled expression, created her name, "Meema," perhaps expressing his personal sense of ownership of this wonderful, fully available, giving, and nonjudgmental presence in his young life.

In every society, grandmothers and grandfathers assume a new status, identity, and name when they become grandparents. In most languages, grandparents have prescribed names that almost everyone uses (see Exhibit 10.1). In some cases, there are several choices, depending on whether it is the paternal or maternal grandparent or on whether the speaker wants to make a formal address or an informal one. The formality generally depends on the speaker's relationship to the grandparent or on the social situation.

In many modern and modernizing societies, the role and status of grandparents has changed or is now in transition. As views of old age and the life course are evolving, and grandparents are healthier than in previous generations, many

EXHIBIT 10.1

Grandmother in Any Language

Aborigine		French	
Australian Formal	Garrimaay	Formal	Grandmere
Australian Paternal	Mamaay	Informal	Gra-mere, Meme
Australian Maternal	Momu	Semiformal	Grandmaman
Africa		Germany	
Ambuya Swahili	Bibi	Formal	Grossmutter
Umakhulu Zulu	Ugogo	Informal	Oma
Afrikaans	Ouma	Greece	Yaya, Gigia
Arabic		Hawaiian	
Formal	Jaddah	Formal	Kapuna Wahine
Informal	Teta	Informal	Puna, TuTu, Kuku
Cajun	Mawmaw	Hungary	
Catalan	Avia, Iaia	Formal	Nagyanya
China		Informal	Yanya, Anya
Cantonese Maternal	PoPo	Iceland	Amma
Cantonese Paternal	Ngin	India	
Mandarin Maternal	Wai po, LaoLao	Bengali Paternal	Thakur-ma
Mandarin Paternal	Zumu, NaiNai	Bengali Maternal	Dida, Didima
Croatia	Baka	Hindi	Daadima
Denmark		Southwestern	Ajji
Formal	Bedstemoder	Urdu Paternal	Daadi
Paternal	Farmor	Urdu Maternal	Nanni
Maternal	MorMor	Indonesia	Nenek
Estonia	Va naema	Iran	Mader Bozog, Momon
Finland	Isoaiti, Mummo	Ireland	
Israel (Hebrew)	Savta, Safta	Formal	Seanmhair
Italy	Nonna	Informal	Maimeo, Morai
Japan		Swaziland	Gogo
Formal	Obaasan, Oba-Chan, Sobo	Sweden	
Informal	Obaba	Paternal	FarMor
Korea	Halmoni	Maternal	MorMor
Lithuania	Senele, Mociute	Switzerland	

(continued)

EXHIBIT 10.1 (*continued*)

Netherlands	Grootmoeder	Formal	Grossmami
Norway	Bestemor, Godmor	Thailand	
Paternal	Farmor	Maternal	Ya
Maternal	MorMor	Paternal	Yai
Philippines		Turkey	Buyuk Anne, Anneanne, Babanne
Formal	Apohang babae	Ukraine	
Informal	Lola	Formal	Babusia
Poland		Informal	Baba
Formal	Babka, Babcia	United Kingdom	
Informal	Jaja, Zsa-Zsa, Busha	Formal	Grandmother
Portugal	Avo	United States	
Romania	Bunica	Formal	Grandmother
Russia	Babushka	Informal	Grandma, Granny
Sanskrit		Vietnam	
Paternal	Pitaamahii	Formal	Danh ta
Maternal	Maataamahii	Informal	Ba, Be gia
Serbia	Baba, Mica	Wales	
Slovakia	Babicka	Southern	Mamgu
Slovenia	Stara, Mama	Northern	Naini, Nain
Spanish		Yiddish	Bubby, Bubbe
Formal	Abuela		
Informal	Abuelita, Uelita, Tita, Abby, Abbi, Lita		

Source: From Grandmother in Any Language. Retrieved from https://considerable.com/grandpa-grandma-different-languages

grandparents, especially those experiencing the role in middle age, are resisting the traditional, stereotyped vision of what a grandmother (or grandfather) is or does.

Part of this refusal to accept the traditional role, at least in the United States, seems to be a widespread rejection of the traditional names for grandparents, and this appears especially true for grandmothers. In some Western countries, grandmothers have publicly expressed their displeasure with being called "grandma," "granny," or "gran." They say, "I'm not old. I don't feel old. And I'm not going to accept an old-sounding name."

Rather, many have chosen names for themselves that, to them, reflect the youth, vitality, and "coolness" they still feel themselves to embody, despite the sudden onset of grandparenthood. Most are short, easy to say, and sound much like nicknames: Mimi, Gigi, Cici, Gogo, Gaga (no connection intended to the popular singer), Birdie, Foxy, G-ma, Pippy, Tammy, and hundreds of others. These trendy names often are chosen by the grandmother, but almost as often they are the result of the grandchild's garbled effort to say the name originally chosen (Bon Bon, BelBel, Grandee, Nema, and Mooma) or their random choice of a word for an object or behavior that was associated with the grandmother (Pebbles, Salsa, Vanna, Shugah). Often the "pet name" given by the first grandchild will "stick" to the grandparent, and all subsequent grandchildren will be taught that she is "Mimi," and everyone in the family will adopt that name for her. Before long, no one uses or even remembers what her real name is. In my own family, a new grandfather named Dannie announced his new identity by renaming himself, "Grand-Dannie." Not only did the grandchildren use it, but also the rest of the adults in the family have come to refer to him almost exclusively by that name.

These observations are based on an idiosyncratic observation of practices in the United States and do not reflect grandparent naming practices in other countries, though it will be interesting to see if other nations are already adopting the practice of "self-naming" or will begin to as the shape of the life course and the grandparent role are changed by social and economic modernization.

SOCIAL AND ECONOMIC SUPPORT FOR RURAL ELDERS IN KENYA

SAMUEL M. MWANGI

The family structure in contemporary Kenya has been changing rapidly and drastically as a result of modern economic, social, and political changes that have continued to weaken extended family systems (Kinsella, 1992; Nyambedha, Wandibba, & Aagaard-Hansen, 2001). This observed trend is explained in terms of two important processes: rural–urban migration of younger adults moving to the cities in pursuit of education and employment, leaving older adults isolated and poor in the rural areas; and a decline in the traditional kinship-based support of elders as a result of economic hardships experienced by people across all the age groups. The latter has been exacerbated by the effects of the recent global economic meltdown, leaving elders further impoverished and with significant unmet health care, social, and economic needs. The scenario is further complicated by the impacts of HIV/AIDS where older adults, despite meager resources, provide care for their ailing adult children as well as their orphaned grandchildren. These realities have psychological, economic, and social consequences (Menken & Cohen, 2006), further driving older adults into hopelessness and destitution in most rural villages of Kenya. Nevertheless, older people have remained resilient in hard times and seem to find ways of adapting and surviving.

This essay discusses the resources, structures, and systems that provide social and economic support to the older adults in rural parts of Kenya to meet their everyday needs against the backdrop of diminishing support from kin. The formal social support systems, most of which are donor-funded initiatives, reach a handful of older adults. For instance, HelpAge International has projects in several counties of Kenya that provide economic security in the form of cash handouts for impoverished older adults caring for orphaned children, while the national government has programs to provide monthly stipends equivalent to US$20 per month.

Informally, there are various ways in which older adults' needs are met despite the decline in kin support and social isolation in rural villages due to changes brought by the processes of modernization, rapid urbanization, formal education and employment, and Westernization that have so dramatically changed their social space. In this essay, three crucial sources of formal and informal support are discussed in their order of importance to Kenyan elders: subsistence farming, social networks within their rural communities, and the recently introduced government-sponsored and donor-funded cash transfer programs.

SUBSISTENCE FARMING

Traditionally, rural communities in Kenya and elsewhere in Africa have relied predominantly on subsistence farming (Nyambedha et al., 2001), with little or no external support from the government. Governments have perennially marginalized rural subsistence farming, which in turn has hindered economic and agricultural development of rural Africa, leading to low asset base and variable incomes (Omiti & Nyanamba, 2007). Thus, subsistence farming to some extent can be seen as perpetuation of a "hunting and gathering" way of life. This is because this type of farming has not lifted rural communities out of deprivation and chronic poverty. On the contrary, dependency on subsistence farming exposes rural communities to vulnerabilities and adversities, such as crop failure due to unreliable rainfall and the collapse of market prices due to surplus imported commodities or constrained purchasing capabilities (Omiti & Nyanamba, 2007).

Despite the shortcomings mentioned, subsistence farming remains the most common and significant way of providing basic necessities to the rural older adults in sub-Saharan Africa. This includes both food crops, such as corn/maize, beans, arrowroot, sweet potatoes, and vegetables, and a few cash crops, such as coffee, tea, pineapples, sugarcane, sisal, and pyrethrum; and rearing livestock (e.g., cattle, sheep, goats, poultry, pigs) to feed their families and sell the surplus in the local market. The money raised in selling such commodities is used in meeting other needs, such as sending children to school, improving homesteads, and buying medicines and nonperishable food items (e.g., cooking fat/oil, sugar, salt, flour, tea leaves), although in most cases the money is inadequate to meet all the needs for many rural households. In other cases, goods are used in informal barter trade, where commodities are exchanged for others in place of monetary resources as a medium of exchange. For instance, one would exchange cattle fodder (e.g., a stack of African "napier" grass) for a pint of milk (i.e., about half a liter). Therefore, subsistence farming is an important part of the fabric of social support systems in rural communities of Kenya. It is especially important for older adults who have no formal education or previous employment histories to entitle them to formal pensions and employment-based health insurance coverage.

SOCIAL NETWORKS IN THE RURAL COMMUNITIES

Closely related in importance to subsistence farming are social support networks within rural communities of Kenya. Prior to colonialization in Africa, communities held resources communally and created strong, ingrained networks. These networks were instrumental in buffering people from adversities associated with low economic resources, sickness, and death. In other words, the community provided a social safety net in times of hardship. However, colonialism disintegrated the existing community structures, and many young people and the economic elite adopted new ways and modern lifestyles and sought education. Colonialism further weakened the social support systems through the infamous "divide and rule" approach used by British colonial authorities to conquer African territories and impose their rule in the late 19th and early 20th centuries (Christopher, 1988).

In the rural parts of postindependence Kenya, however, social support networks have remained a significant resource because community members have a strong social fabric as opposed to individualistic culture that has emerged in the urban areas. A significant proportion of older adults live in the rural areas in Kenya, as elsewhere in Africa (Kinsella, 1992), where they benefit from community resources in the form of social support networks. But this support is strained by the responsibilities and burdens of grandparenting due to the effects of HIV/AIDS and the rising mortality of elders resulting from unmet medical/health needs.

GOVERNMENT SUPPORT THROUGH SOCIAL PENSIONS

Social protection is defined as the range of public actions carried out by the state and others (e.g., community-based organizations and nongovernmental organizations [NGOs]) in response to vulnerability, poverty, hunger, sickness, and risk (Mbithi & Mutuku, 2010; Omiti & Nyanamba, 2007). They seek to guarantee relief from destitution for vulnerable populations, who, for reasons beyond their control, are not able to meet their own basic needs. This approach is gaining importance as a tool for older people in developing nations burdened with social, economic, and health needs. Social protection has been successfully implemented in other developing regions of Asia and Latin America, and it is steadily taking root in Africa. According to HelpAge International, African governments and policy makers have recently been involved in the creation of social protection programs and strategies as part of their development agenda. These efforts have been responses to the two global plans of action on aging (Madrid and Vienna International Plan of Action on Aging) and the African Union's framework on aging policy in Africa (HelpAge International, 2006).

The Kenyan government, through various ministries, departments, and agencies, has instituted a process of putting in place policy and structures necessary for the development, coordination, and implementation of national social protection programs (Mbithi & Mutuku, 2010; Omiti & Nyanamba, 2007). Programs for older people are coordinated by the Ministry of Gender, Children and Social Development (MGCSD) in collaboration with HelpAge Kenya, a nonprofit organization (Mbithi & Mutuku, 2010). An interim National Social Protection Secretariat was established at the MGCSD to oversee these processes. The secretariat is headed by a social protection advisor to provide leadership and coordination to this system. One of the various cash transfer initiatives introduced by the government is the Older Persons Cash Transfer (OPCT) program, which targets older adults above age 65. The OPCT program was developed and implemented through partnership with development partners such as the U.K. Department for International Development (DFID) and the World Bank (Government of Kenya, 2008).

The program was started in 2004 on a pilot basis in three districts: Nyando, Busia, and Thika (HelpAge International, 2006). The MGCSD and its social protection partners (i.e., bilateral donors, NGOs, and other government ministries) have been expanding the program. Currently, there is coverage in 44 districts countrywide, especially those with high poverty levels in northern Kenya as well as in urban slums. Approximately 750 older persons in each covered district benefit from this program, which translates to 33,000 households nationally. In the fiscal year 2014–15, the government allocated KES950 million (Kenyan shillings; i.e., US$9.5 million) for this program. Each household received a total of KES2,000 (US$20) per month. By Kenyan living standards in rural areas, this amount is modest to meet the needs of older adults and is used mainly to supplement food gained from subsistence farming and to buy medications. However, in some rural areas, due to poor infrastructure and lack of basic services such as communication and banking, the OPCT program has not reached the targeted number of beneficiaries. Additionally, the administration of social protection programs is fragmented, thus marginalizing the needy and deserving individuals (Mbithi & Mutuku, 2010). Further, the Kenyan media have reported unsubstantiated cases of embezzlement of these public funds, although government sources and partners in these programs have not raised a "red flag" about the alleged malpractices.

The benefits of social protection programs for older adults in several countries in the southern part of Africa have been documented through evaluation projects. In Kenya, however, the evaluation of the impact of this program is just underway. In addition to the challenges cited earlier, barriers to effective implementation of the program include (a) lack of knowledge among the potential beneficiaries about the existence of such programs, (b) irregular and unpredictable support, and (c) inadequate data on utilization of the program (Omiti & Nyanamba, 2007).

CONCLUSION

Both formal and informal social support systems exist in rural Kenya. Subsistence farming and social support networks are the informal systems that traditionally have provided support to rural families, especially to uneducated and unemployed middle-aged and older adults. These two will continue playing very crucial roles.

Recently, formal government efforts through social safety nets have started taking shape. Social protection mechanisms have been implemented after the government's recognition of the need to provide assistance to vulnerable groups such as older adults, orphaned children, female-headed households, people with disabilities, and people living with HIV/AIDS. The importance of the formal social safety nets for elders is yet to be determined as the government rolls out this program. However, the three pillars of support—subsistence farming, social networks, and social protection—provide necessary and complementary sustenance for rural older Kenyans as the pressure of population aging is realized.

REFERENCES

Christopher, A. J. (1988). "Divide and rule": The impress of British separation policies. *Area, 20,* 233–240.

Government of Kenya. (2008). *National social protection policy.* Nairobi, Kenya: MGCSD.

HelpAge International. (2006). *Social cash transfers for Africa, A transformative agenda for the 21st century.* Intergovernmental Regional Conference report, Livingstone, Zambia, 20-23 March.

Kinsella, K. (1992). Aging trends in Kenya. *Journal of Cross-Cultural Gerontology, 7,* 259–268. doi:10.1007/BF00122512

Mbithi, L. M., & Mutuku, M. (2010). *Social protection status in developing countries: The case of Kenya.* Draft Paper prepared for ERD Regional Conference, on Promoting Resilience through Social Protection in Sub-Saharan Africa.

Menken, J., & Cohen, B. (2006). *Aging in sub-Saharan Africa: Recommendations for furthering research.* Washington, DC: The National Academies Press.

Nyambedha, E. O., Wandibba, S., & Aagaard-Hansen, J. (2001). Policy implications of the inadequate support systems for orphans in Western Kenya. *Health Policy, 58,* 83–96. doi:10.1016/S0168-8510(01)00145-2

Omiti, J., & Nyanamba, T. (2007). *Using social protection policies to reduce vulnerability and promote economic growth in Kenya.* Research Paper Series for Kenya Institute for Public Policy Research and Analysis (KIPPRA).

11

CAREGIVING

JASLEEN K. CHAHAL | JENNIFER M. KINNEY

INTRODUCTION

Older people are part of interdependent family systems, giving and receiving support of all kinds and performing important functions for their families. What any one of us needs and gives to our family support unit depends on many things, including stage of life. If and when poor health, frailties, or declining physical reserves interfere with individuals' regular activities, they may need assistance. Who provides this care and what kinds of systems of support are in place depend on a host of factors, including cultural values, economic development, and demographic change. Families are universally the bedrock of elder caregiving in developing countries; families are also an important source of economic security for older people. At the same time, in both developing and developed countries, some older adults provide economic support for younger family members. Nonetheless, family members are not always available, able, or willing to provide such care, especially for chronic conditions such as advanced dementia, which present particular caregiving challenges. The need for formal care support, such as government programs or for-profit industries, is something many countries currently are trying to address.

This chapter provides an overview of informal and formal systems of care, with a special emphasis on family caregiving. Understanding who provides what kinds of care, and why, in different cultures is a complicated task because ideas about who *should* provide a specific type of care are deeply embedded in each culture. How deeply those values are held and how powerfully they can be challenged by shifting economic and demographic change is a question that is considered implicitly throughout this chapter. We begin, however, by considering why caregiving is such a crucial issue for both families and societies—the stress and burden it places on the caregiver.

CAREGIVING STRESS AND BURDEN

Caregiving stress is the unequal exchange of assistance between an individual who is caring for someone and the care recipient that results in tension, fatigue, and emotional strain placed on the caregiver (Llanque, Savage, Rosenburg, & Caserta, 2016). It can occur across the life course and in a variety of circumstances. Although some aspects of caregiving can be rewarding and even enjoyable, for most people it is also very difficult.

Acute caregiving—providing care to another over a short and defined period of time, such as postsurgery—carries its own stresses, but providing care for an older adult with a chronic condition can last months or years, sometimes many years, and often ends only with the transition into formal care in an institution or, ultimately, the death of the person receiving care. Persons receiving care may need assistance with activities of daily living (ADLs)—basic self-care tasks such as bathing, dressing, and feeding—or instrumental activities of daily living (IADLs) such as money management, shopping, and providing transportation. Caregiving for a person with dementia has been shown to be extremely stressful because the caregiver must not only manage the individual's ADLs and IADLs, but also cope with their cognitive decline and resulting behavioral changes, in addition to the persistent memory loss of a personal relationship with the caregiver. One of the most wrenching testimonies from most caregivers for a loved one with dementia is the sorrowful cry: "He doesn't even know who I am anymore." In a Danish study, the spouse of a person with dementia explains the difficulties with caregiving:

> Suddenly I got a lot of responsibilities, things I had never tried and I
> just didn't know what to do. It's easy to make mistakes and nobody
> else was there. Everything was up to me and it was really a burden.
> (Ågård, Egerod, Tønnesen, & Lomborg, 2015, p. 1898)

Providing care for older adults with a chronic condition can be especially stressful and burdensome when the responsibility of caregiving falls on one person. Most older adults who need care have one primary caregiver, such as a spouse or an adult child. Extended family, such as siblings and cousins, often play little or no caregiving role, placing a greater amount of stress on the primary caregiver (Leopold, Raab, & Engelhardt, 2014). A survey conducted by the AARP Public Policy Institute (2015) found that 40% of American caregivers had modified their schedules by eliminating personal activities. For example, they canceled plans with friends and even doctors' appointments to make time for their caregiving responsibilities. The caregivers also reported poorer overall health since becoming a caregiver.

Caregiving stress is subjective. **Subjective stress** refers to one's perception that he or she is not able to manage a particular demand. That is, what is stressful for one caregiver is not necessarily stressful for another. For example, if caregivers believe they are unprepared to provide care, they may feel depressed or overwhelmed. The reaction to seeing one so beloved "slip away" from the normal relationship enjoyed by the spouses or parent and child over a lifetime is particularly painful. Caregivers for stroke survivors assume this new role with little or no warning or experience in providing care. Caregiving for someone after a stroke can vary from "physical (help walking, carrying from bed to toilet), to communication (verbal and nonverbal cues to other family members), nursing (feeding, personal hygiene), emotional support (handling disruptive behavior) along with an overwhelming financial responsibility" (Ain, Dar, Ahmad, Munzar, & Yousafzai, 2014, p. 50). Living arrangements also can play a role in perceived stress. The Survey of Health, Ageing and Retirement in Europe (SHARE) and English Longitudinal Study of Ageing (ELSA) found that caregivers in Europe experience greater subjective caregiver stress if they resided with the care recipient, resulting in a decline in mental health (Kaschowitz & Brandt, 2017).

Caregivers are likely to experience financial stress due to the amount of money it takes to care for an older adult and because changes in work probably will be required that could result in lost income. Although primary stressors of caregiving are more likely tied to financial and physical demands of caregiving, social events, such as attending a wedding or meeting with friends, also can be stressful in terms of planning, taking time away from caregiving, and even being a caregiver during a social event. As a result, many caregivers reduce their social interactions after becoming a caregiver. For example, some caregivers do not attend church or temple as often, no longer call or meet with friends and family, or give up hobbies and activities that they enjoyed before assuming the caregiver role. Many of these stressors can lead to caregiver burden.

Acute stress is usually not an issue for most individuals because a stressful life event occurs, such as taking an exam, where a person's body adjusts temporarily to the stressor and then readjusts back to "normal." However, long-term or chronic stress, such as that experienced by a caregiver, can result in what McEwen (2005) has termed **allostatic overload,** or the overresponse of the body's endocrine system to stress. Typically, these responses are "adaptive processes that maintain homeostasis [in the body] through the production of mediators such as adrenalin, cortisol and other chemical messengers" (McEwen, 2005, p. 315), but repeated and prolonged stress causes them to build to destructive levels. Allostatic overload, therefore, is defined as the total burden associated with multiple objective or subjective stressors (Bevans & Sternberg, 2012). If not properly managed, chronic caregiver stressors described earlier can turn into caregiver burden in various contexts. **Caregiver burden** is the experience of negative psychological, emotional, social, physical, and financial stress and associated consequences with providing care to another person. To reduce the chance of caregiver burden or for an individual reaching allostatic load, several coping skills and resources can be used to diminish the perceived burden of caregiving. **Coping skills** have been defined as skills or strategies that one implements to deal with "voluntary efforts to regulate one's cognitive, behavioral, emotional, or physiological responses to a stressor or toward the stressor itself" (Coiro, Bettis, & Compas, 2017, p. 177). Examples of coping skills for caregivers can be support groups or blogs, exercising, meditation, reading, or utilizing additional personal and public resources to assist with the demands of caregiving.

In developed and developing countries where caregiving is common, resources such as caregiver support groups, adult day programs for the person receiving care, and educational programs help caregivers manage their stress and reduce their burden. The financial burden for caregiving and obligation to provide care create a need for countries and individuals to evaluate how they can better use current resources to reduce caregiver burden and support caregivers for older adults. Six out of 10 American caregivers stated they had to make changes at work to accommodate caregiving. Such changes likely affect their financial ability to pay for associated caregiving costs (AARP Public Policy Institute, 2015). Because women are more likely to provide direct care than men, women in developed countries are more likely to make work accommodations, such as reducing hours, taking time off, shifting their work schedule, or choosing to leave the workforce in order to provide care, thereby reducing their earnings and disrupting their paid work trajectory (Haberkern, Schmid, & Szydlik, 2015).

WHO PROVIDES CARE?

Researchers have studied care arrangements for older adults in different cultural contexts. The OASIS study (Old Age and Autonomy: The Role of Intergenerational Solidarity and Service Systems; Katz et al., 2003) used the intergenerational solidarity model (Bengtson & Roberts, 1991) to study family norms and preferences regarding intergenerational relations in five countries—Spain, Israel, Germany, Norway, and the United Kingdom. **The intergenerational solidarity model** describes the relationships among members of a family using six characteristics: association (spending time together), affection, consensus (agreement), family functioning (providing help and emotional support), shared norms, and the structure of the family. The purpose of the research was to document norms and preferences regarding intergenerational relations and the balance of family and state responsibility for older adults.

The results revealed both commonalities and differences across the countries, which the researchers attributed to interactions between variations in family and cultural norms and behaviors at the individual level and in the social policies of each country (Katz et al., 2003). For example, in Spain the role of the family in caring for older adults is stronger than in the other four countries, and policy reform reinforces family care. The importance of family, combined with a well-developed welfare state, resulted in the interesting combination of strong filial obligation but a preference for formal services in Israel. A majority of older adults in Norway preferred help from formal services rather than their families, reflecting the expanding social democratic welfare regime that characterizes Norway and other Scandinavian countries. Families in Germany believed that families and the welfare state should share responsibility for older adults. The preferences of participants from the United Kingdom fell between those found among Germans and Norwegians.

The difference between Asian and Western countries with respect to who provides care for older adults is partially related to the speed of population aging. The very rapid population aging being experienced by developing nations means that the demands of economic growth might compete with traditional values to determine whether younger generations are available to provide care for older adults who need assistance. Western Europe and the United States have had decades to adapt to population aging by creating infrastructures for formal support services, but nations in the developing world must adapt much more quickly and at the same time their economies are being built. Although the United States, Japan, and countries in Europe were affluent before they experienced population aging, other countries, such as Nepal, Thailand, and those in Latin America, experienced population aging before they were wealthy. This "old before rich" circumstance magnifies the challenges of allocating family and government resources to a growing population of older people who need assistance at the same time governments need to invest in the infrastructures that support economic growth, including education and labor force development.

INFORMAL CAREGIVING

Many older people are part of interdependent family systems, giving and receiving support of all kinds and performing important functions for their families. What any one of us needs and gives to our family support unit depends on many things, including stage of life and functional abilities. **Informal support** is defined by the National Health Committee of New Zealand (NHC) as "caring for a friend, family member, or neighbor who … can't manage everyday living without help. … [It] is not usually based on any formal agreement or service specification. Informal caregiving is characterized by relationships and social expectations" (Goodhead & McDonald, 2007, p. 4).

Reciprocity is at the heart of most informal caregiving. The concept of reciprocity is an important component of social exchange theory, a social theory that describes how perceptions of power within a relationship are affected by social, emotional, or financial exchanges of tangible and intangible items (Cropanzano & Mitchell, 2005). To compensate for losses in resources in later life, older adults may begin to exchange goods or services for assistance with family members who live with them or close by. For example, a son may take time off from work and pay $100 to purchase and deliver his mother's medications; in exchange, his mother may regularly make him dinner and watch his children (her grandchildren). In this example, it is difficult to calculate the exact monetary value of the exchange between the two, but the relationship continues because there appears to be an equal and beneficial transfer of goods and services. If the exchange is perceived by the family members to be uneven for a lengthy period of time, the interactions likely would decrease until the arrangement ceased.

It is important to note that not all relationships or transfers are equally beneficial. If the exchange is felt to be unequal, or if the caregiver feels taken advantage of by another, the caregiver may neglect their caregiving duties or even express his or her anger toward the person receiving care, leading possibly to abuse. Elder abuse happens in both developed and developing countries, including the United States and European countries. In East Asia, a growing body of literature exists on the abuse of older persons by daughters-in-law in countries such as South Korea, Japan, and China. Daughters-in-law in these countries often are expected to care for their mothers-in-law, but daughters-in-law, who hold a lower status in the household, may feel disempowered by this arrangement and therefore neglect their duties or resort to physical or emotional abuse (Institute of Medicine, 2014).

Gendered Caregiving

Gender and a person's role within the family (e.g., son, wife) often determine the type of care one family member provides to another. For example, a son who cares for his older father might manage his father's land or finances, while a wife or daughter might be in charge of making her father's dinner or bathing him. A major form of informal care is related to responsibilities associated with filial piety. **Filial piety** derives from Confucianism and represents a sociocultural norm and moral principle for many Asian families to care for older adults (Yi, George, Sereny, Gu, & Vaupel, 2016). The obligation to care for, and usually live with, parents in later life continues to be practiced today, although there are signs of it diminishing with increased work migration in younger generations. Similar to the other aspects of caregiving, there are gender differences in filial piety. Patriarchal cultures (those in which men typically have more power and authority over women in many domains), such as those found in Asian countries, traditionally value sons more than daughters for their ability to provide for the family and to pass on the family name as well as transfer inheritance and land from generation to generation. However, a recent study using the Chinese Longitudinal Healthy Longevity Study (CLHLS) found that older adults in the oldest-old and young-old groups in rural areas of China were more satisfied with and preferred care from daughters because they were able to "enjoy greater filial piety from and better relationships with daughters than sons" (Yi et al., 2016, p. 244). The difference in relationships is not surprising, based on our previous discussion of women providing more emotional support and personal care for elder family members, which may lead to a more supportive caregiving relationship.

In patriarchal cultures around the world, including some countries in Asia and Latin America, the *responsibility* of caregiving for parents often falls on sons, while direct care is provided by the responsible son's wife, thereby eliminating or minimizing the son's direct role as a primary caregiver. In South Korea, for example, the moral expectation and cultural norm requires a daughter-in-law to assume caregiving responsibilities for the family she married into, while abandoning similar obligations for her own birth parents (Ogawa, Chan, Oishi, & Wang, 2018; Zuo, Li, Mao, & Chi, 2014). Therefore, parents of a family with multiple married daughters and no sons likely will be left to rely on extended social networks and government services to help coordinate care as they age, rather than on their children.

Similar to the gender differences for caregiving responsibilities, men and women tend to depend on different services and supports to help with caregiving tasks. Women usually provide a higher level of direct care for older adults to assist with ADLs and are less inclined to rely on services and support outside the family. In contrast, men are more likely to help with IADLs, such as money management and providing transportation (Morgan, Williams, Trussardi, & Gott, 2016; Sugiura, Ito, Kutsumi, & Mikami, 2009). Gendered expectations and cultural norms also shape how people expect to be cared for themselves later in life. Many men have an expectation that they will continue to be cared for by spouses, whereas many women anticipate that they will need to depend on additional services and care providers who are outside of their family or social network (Brazil, Thabane, Foster, & Bèdard, 2009; Morgan et al., 2016).

Regardless of preferences, availability is perhaps the crucial determinant of who provides care. The increasing migration of younger generations out of developing countries—or within those countries from rural to urban settings—in search of better opportunities for a more prosperous and financially secure life has significant implications for caregiving. In China, the elders who remain on their farms or villages after their child (or children) has migrated are called both "the stay-at-home elders" (Du & Yang, 2009) or "the left-behind generation," while other researchers (King, Cela, Fokkema, & Vullnetari, 2014) have labeled both those who stay and those who follow their children to a new place the "**zero generation**," meaning the generation who, at least initially, stayed home while their adult children moved away for better jobs (the first-generation migrants). Without adult children nearby, those "zero" elders have no reliable caregivers at hand, and we can expect those migrations, which are happening worldwide, to have hugely disruptive effects on family caregiving patterns in the future.

Older Adults as Caregivers

The preceding discussion has focused on older people as recipients of care. But another equally important part of the story is that older adults also *provide* care, both to their spouses and siblings and to younger family members. Spousal caregivers, who are more likely to reside with the care recipient, tend to become the primary caregiver and represent over 80% of caregivers who are 65 and older (Cash, Hodgkin, & Warburton, 2016). Compared to younger generations, such as caregiving children, spousal caregivers experience greater challenges with the physical demands of caregiving and any associated caregiver stress if they themselves also have age-related declines in health (Queen, Butner, Berg, & Smith, 2017). Spouses may have difficulty balancing their caregiving role with that of spouse as well as their other family roles as parent or grandparent, causing them additional burden and stress.

Throughout the world, families rely on their older members, especially older women, to assist with childcare. Grandmothers and, to a lesser extent, grandfathers provide care to their grandchildren for a variety of reasons. They care for their grandchildren while parents are at work locally and when work requires parents to migrate either within their home country (e.g., from a rural area to a city for more work opportunities) or beyond it. Even in countries that provide state-sponsored child care, grandparents often participate in raising their grandchildren. For example, in Denmark and the Netherlands, more than 60% of grandmothers and 40% of grandfathers between the ages of 60 and 65 provide care for their grandchildren (Croda & Gonzalez-Chapela, 2005). Grandparents in rural China care for almost two fifths of children under age 5 whose parents have migrated to work in urban areas (China Development Gateway, 2008), and 70% of Bolivians who migrated to Spain left their children at home, the majority with grandparents (Asociación de Cooperación Bolivia España, 2008).

Grandparents also provide care for grandchildren when parents are absent because of incarceration, serious illness, or death. Worldwide, the most common reason for these **skipped-generation family** situations is HIV/AIDS among the middle (i.e., parental) generation. Community members within a neighborhood or village come together as **fictive kin** (i.e., nonrelatives who are considered and treated like family members and often assume the responsibilities of family members) or **extended kin** (i.e., relatives who extend beyond the nuclear family such as uncles, nieces, or cousins) to help provide care. An example of this is seen in Botswana, where adults have assumed kin roles to provide care for those with AIDS (Klaits, 2010; Manderson & Block, 2016, p. 208). Over 14 million children in sub-Saharan Africa have become orphaned as a result of the HIV epidemic (Kuo, Cluver, Casale, & Lane, 2014). Older family members (primarily grandmothers) care for 40% to 60% of children in eastern and southern Africa whose parents no longer are able to care for them, either due to severe impairment or death (United Nations Children's Fund [UNICEF], 2006). A vast majority (81%) of orphans in Zimbabwe are cared for by older people (Beegle, Filmer, Stokes, & Tiererova, 2008).

Role of Technology in Caregiving

Technological advances and social media have provided an opportunity for new forms of caregiving across the world. These options allow those who have migrated to stay in touch with family members and even help to manage care while someone else on site might be directly providing it. Caring **for** a family member typically involves providing direct and personal care related to ADLs and IADLs, but it also involves caring **about** a family member, which "encompasses contact and emotional support and refers to emotional functions connected with sociability, advice, comfort, and self-validation" (Plaza & Below, 2014, p. 30). Although caring about a loved one and caring for them are not interchangeable, technology and social media can help to ease some of the burden of working abroad and leaving an older adult behind. Writing letters, sharing posts and pictures on Facebook and Instagram, and FaceTime conversations can reduce the feeling of distance. In a Caribbean study on caregiving, most Trinidadian participants felt Facebook was a unique platform for transnational caregiving because they were able to communicate with friends and family; others chose to follow family members on Facebook, but did not necessarily choose to "like" or post comments so that they might be able to avoid any obligations or responsibilities (Plaza & Below, 2014). Use of technology and social media can give caregivers and older adults in the zero generation more choice to share as much or as little personal information as they like. It provides transnational caregivers with the opportunity to fulfill some family caregiving responsibilities by engaging with older family members across the world.

FORMAL SUPPORTS FOR CAREGIVING

When societies go through the changes that typically accompany economic development (such as industrialization and urbanization), the traditional family institution becomes less able to address all the needs of its members. Out of this combination of demographic, economic, and social change, the welfare state arises—a system of public programs and policies that supplant, or at least complement, some of the roles fulfilled by families in earlier times. Formal policies and programs that are government-sponsored or -funded are definitely an important piece of the puzzle in providing support and protections for elders. Medicare (publicly financed health insurance for older people in the United States) is an excellent example of a government program that makes a significant difference in the lives of older adults.

Formal support is typically provided for pay by an organization or individual whose work is clearly specified and often governed by regulations about payment and standards about how care must be provided. In the United States, for example, most formal home health care services are provided by for-profit companies that are certified by state and federal agencies; the work itself and the training required for workers who provide the services are carefully spelled out in formal contracts between government agencies and the care providers.

Community organizations and nongovernmental organizations (NGOs)—defined and discussed in the following section—also may provide crucial scaffolding to the support network for older adults. An example of community organizations is the "old-age clubs" in India. Housed in centers run by voluntary organizations with some support from the government, these clubs provide opportunities for socialization, some limited access to health education and services, and "pleasure and mental peace" for older adults to help improve emotional health by reducing loneliness and depression (Kumari, 2015). HelpAge International is an example of an NGO that provides support for older persons in several developing countries. Its global network consists of more than 140 organizations in 80 countries, and its mission is to "promot[e] the right of all older people to live dignified, healthy and secure lives" (HelpAge International, n.d.).

Comparing the systems of support and protection available to older persons in different countries reveals unique blends of family, government, community, and NGO assistance. While it is the case that an old-age welfare state dominated by publicly sponsored programs is more common in developed Western nations than in developing countries, it is also the case that families, the state, communities, and NGOs are part of the support network for older adults in every aging society. You can think about services for vulnerable elders as a continuum anchored at one end by family support and at the other end by state support. In between these two support systems are community and neighborhood supports (either individual or organizational such as churches or voluntary organizations) that can supplement or substitute for family and state support systems.

Organizations can help caregivers determine eligibility and benefits for formal care. Payment for services and some sort of contractual arrangement are the two distinguishing features of formal care, while informal care typically involves unpaid family or friends, This distinction gives us some language with which to talk about who provides what kind of care for what reasons. However, even these distinctions are getting blurrier. Many Western nations are adopting models of publicly funded paid care directed by the recipient, who is permitted to hire a friend or family member as caregiver (Nadash & Crisp, 2005). This newer concept that some countries are referring to as **semiformalized care** provides a "gray" area that lets families choose a hybrid option between formal and informal care to meet the needs of the older adult, to acknowledge the demands of caregiving, and to best accommodate whatever physical, emotional, and financial resources the caregiver may have (Kodate & Timonen, 2017; Pfau-Effinger & Rostgaard, 2011). Semiformalized care often is a response to the need for formal care policies to evolve to compensate for a growing demand for care for older adults. In European and Asian countries, this hybrid form of care often occurs in three main ways: with the

> integration of informal care into the broader care system ...; reducing and modifying formal services so that the need for family inputs increases; or enabling extremely flexible forms of care labour that necessitate the constant active involvement of family members ....
> (Kodate & Timonen, 2017, p. 294)

NGOs AND CAREGIVING

Dispelling the myth that "families aren't what they used to be," we have seen examples of the many ways in which younger and older family members both ask for and provide assistance to each other. But families do not operate in isolation.

Just as each individual is embedded in a family, each family is embedded in a community. And communities organize themselves in many ways to provide elder care when it is needed. Such **community care** includes services and supports to supplement and fill the gap between family and governmental efforts; it is considered a type of formal support because it is organized and programmatic, though not connected with the government. Worldwide, one of the most important community resources that support older adults and their families is **NGOs**, defined as:

> any non-profit, voluntary citizens' group which is organized on a local, national or international level. Task-oriented and driven by people with a common interest, NGOs perform a variety of service and humanitarian functions, bring citizen concerns to Governments, advocate and monitor policies and encourage political participation through provision of information. Some are organized around specific issues, such as human rights, environment or health. They provide analysis and expertise, serve as early warning mechanisms and help monitor and implement international agreements. (United Nations, n.d.)

NGOs play an important role in the well-being of older adults. They educate elders about their human rights and entitlements and lobby policy makers and service providers for improvements. Working individually and with governmental agencies, these organizations provide education, counseling, and assistance to caregivers in countries with high rates of HIV/AIDS, fight against elder abuse and family violence, and develop disaster response strategies that address the specific vulnerabilities of older adults (United Nations Population Fund, 2012).

Several NGOs have been established around the world to provide additional caregiver resources. For example, the Coalition of Caregivers and Advocates for the Elderly in Liberia was established to improve the quality of life of older adults through advocacy and service delivery (United Nations Open-Ended Working Group on Ageing [OEWGA], 2016). In addition, the International Alliance of Carer Organizations (IACO), established in 2012, includes a coalition of 14 nations that collaborate to provide caregiver networks, facilitate conversations, and identify and initiate programs and research relevant to global caregivers. A U.S. member organization, the National Alliance for Caregiving, was founded in 1996 with a focus on advocacy, awareness, and improving quality of life for care recipients by developing evidence-based, best-practice caregiving programs. A recognizable accomplishment of this organization is that it collaborates with the AARP to publish a study on family caregiving in the United States every 5 years. Similar organizations are found in Canada, Australia, Denmark, India, Nepal, Japan, Sweden, New Zealand, the United Kingdom, Taiwan, Israel, Ireland, France, and Finland. Caregiving resources and organizations in countries in South America and Africa appear to be developing, though they are not yet as established as those previously mentioned. Each of these organizations focuses on improving the caregiving experience for both the care provider and recipient by offering resources for best practices in providing care for older adults, support for caregivers to alleviate stress, and access to information about local, state, and national services to reduce caregiver burden and improve care.

CONCLUSION

Caregiving is an essential component of all societies throughout the world. Much of the caregiving that occurs is within families: Older adults care for the younger members and younger members care for their elders. Yet it is also clear that families often cannot fulfill these functions without help from both their government and from NGOs. As economic development allows, nations are moving toward establishing public systems of economic and health support to supplement the efforts of family units.

Government support versus family support, or formal versus informal care, is not an "either/or" situation in which one type of care substitutes for the other; the reality is that the two types of care are complementary and both are supplemented by community care. How any country organizes its system of care is based on a combination of culture, history, demography, and economics. And these systems evolve over time: We are seeing a greater role for the state in Asian nations, a diminished role in Western nations, and across both Asia and the West an increase in shared responsibility between families and the state. As one example, the role of government in providing care for older adults has increased in China. A nation that once relied heavily on "filial piety," so much so that it is included in the nation's constitution, is now being forced to provide government-funded health services, such as nursing-home care, because the one-child policy resulted in smaller families, fewer younger individuals, and inadequate resources to provide elder care.

It is not yet clear whether societies in the developing world will tend to copy the Western, industrialized welfare states' social care and formal long-term care systems or whether they will adapt or invent their own culturally appropriate systems. At the same time developing nations are struggling to join a globalizing economy and increase their usable resources, both developing and developed nations face challenges in balancing the educational and health requirements of their citizens. A swiftly aging world challenges us to learn from each other and to work to develop comprehensive systems of care for older adults that integrate informal, semiformal, and formal care.

DISCUSSION QUESTIONS

1. Identify the patterns of caregiving among younger and older members of your family (e.g., who is providing and receiving care, what types of care are provided)?

2. What public policy changes should be made in your country to help or support older people and their families?

3. Choose a country in which you are interested and, based on credible Internet sources (e.g., governmental sites), summarize what formal services are available to help family/informal caregivers to an older adult.

4. Choose a country in which you are interested and, based on credible Internet sources, identify an NGO that operates in that country and the services they provide to older adults and/or their family/informal caregivers.

5. What do you think is your personal responsibility in caring for your grandparents and your parents?

6. React to the statement: "It takes a village to care for an older person."

KEY WORDS

Allostatic overload
Caregiver burden
Caregiver stress
Community care
Coping skills
Extended kin
Fictive kin
Filial piety
Formal support

Informal support
Intergenerational solidarity model
NGO
Reciprocity
Semiformalized care
Skipped-generation family
Subjective stress
Zero generation

REFERENCES

Ågård, A. S., Egerod, I., Tønnesen, E., & Lomborg, K. (2015). From spouse to caregiver and back: A grounded theory study of post-intensive care unit spousal caregiving. *Journal of Advanced Nursing*, *71*(8), 1892–1903. doi:10.1111/jan.12657

Ain, Q. U., Dar, N. Z., Ahmad, A., Munzar, S., & Yousafzai, A. W. (2014). Caregiver stress in stroke survivor: data from a tertiary care hospital—A cross sectional survey. *BioMed Central (BMC) Psychology*, *2*(1), 49–56. doi:10.1186/s40359-014-0049-9

AARP Public Policy Institute. (2015). *Caregiving in the U.S.* Retrieved from https://www.aarp.org/ppi/info-2015/caregiving-in-the-united-states-2015.html

Asociación de Cooperación Bolivia España. (2008). *Situación de familias de migrantes a España en Bolivia.* Madrid, Spain: Author: La Paz, Asociación de Migrantes Bolivia-España.

Beegle, K., Filmer, D., Stokes, A., & Tiererova, L. (2008). *Orphanhood and the living arrangements of children in sub-Saharan Africa* (Policy Research Working Paper WPS4889). Washington, DC: World Bank. Retrieved from http://www-wds.worldbank.org/servlet/WDSContentServer/WDSP/IB/2009/07/24/000112742_20090724110307/Rendered/PDF/WPS4889.pdf

Bengtson, V. L., & Roberts, R. E. L. (1991). Intergenerational solidarity in aging families: An example of formal theory construction. *Journal of Marriage and the Family, 53*(4), 856–870. doi:10.2307/352993

Bevans, M., & Sternberg, E. M. (2012). Caregiving burden, stress, and health effects among family caregivers of adult cancer patients. *JAMA: Journal of the American Medical Association, 307*(4), 398–403. doi:10.1001/jama.2012.29

Brazil, K., Thabane, L., Foster, G., & Bèdard, M. (2009). Gender differences among Canadian spousal caregivers at the end of life. *Health and Social Care in the Community, 17,* 159–166. doi:10.1111/j.1365-2524.2008.00813.x

Cash, B., Hodgkin, S., & Warburton, J. (2016). Practitioners' perspectives on choice for older spousal caregivers in rural areas. *Australian Social Work, 69*(3), 283–296. doi:10.1080/0312407X.2015.1074258

China Development Gateway. (2008). *"Left-behind" rural children numbered at 58 million.* Retrieved from www.chinagate.cn/news/2008-02/28/content_10958410.htm

Coiro, M. J., Bettis, A. H., & Compas, B. E. (2017). College students coping with interpersonal stress: Examining a control-based model of coping. *Journal of American College Health, 65*(3), 177–186. doi:10.1080/07448481.2016.1266641

Croda, E., & Gonzalez-Chapela, J. (2005). How do European older adults use their time? In A. Borsch-Supan, A. Brugiavini, H. Jurges, A. Kapteyn, J. Mackenbach, J. Siegrist, & G. Weber (Eds.), *Health, aging and retirement in Europe: First results from the survey of health, ageing and retirement in Europe,* (pp. 265–271). Manheim, Germany: MEA. Retrieved from www.share-project.org/uploads/tx_sharepublications/CH_5.6.pdf

Cropanzano, R., & Mitchell, M. S. (2005). Social exchange theory: An interdisciplinary review. *Journal of Management, 31*(6), 874–900. doi:10.1177/0149206305279602

Du, P., & Yang, H. (2009). China. In E. B. Palmore, F. Whittington, & S. Kunkel (Eds.), *International handbook on aging: Current research and developments* (3rd ed., pp. 145–157). Westport, CT: Praeger.

Goodhead, A., & McDonald, J. (2007). *Informal caregivers literature review: A report prepared for the National Health Committee.* Wellington, New Zealand: Health Services Research Center. Retrieved from http://nhc.health.govt.nz/system/files/documents/publications/informal-caregivers-literature-review.pdf

Haberkern, K., Schmid, T., & Szydlik, M. (2015). Gender differences in intergenerational care in European welfare states. *Ageing & Society, 35*(2), 298–320. doi:10.1017/S0144686X13000639

HelpAge International. (n.d.). Our values, vision and strategy. Retrieved from https://www.helpage.org

Institute of Medicine. (2014). Elder abuse in Asia: An overview. Retrieved from https://www.ncbi.nlm.nih.gov/books/NBK208577

Kaschowitz, J., & Brandt, M. (2017). Health effects of informal caregiving across Europe: A longitudinal approach. *Social Science & Medicine, 173,* 72–80. doi:10.1016/j.socscimed.2016.11.036

Katz, R., Daatland, S. O., Lowenstein, A., Bazo, M. T., Ancizu, I., Herlofson, K., . . . Prilutzky, D. (2003). Family norms and preferences in intergenerational relations: A comparative perspective. In V. L. Bengtson & A. Lowenstein (Eds.), *Global aging and challenges to families* (pp. 305–326). New York, NY: Aldine De Gruyter.

King, R., Cela, E., Fokkema, T., & Vullnetari, J. (2014). The migration and well-being of the zero generation: Transgenerational care, grandparenting, and loneliness amongst Albanian older people. *Population, Space and Place, 20*(8), 728–738. doi:10.1002/psp.1895

Klaits, F. (2010). *Death in a church of life: Moral passion during Botswana's time of AIDS.* Berkeley, CA: University of California Press.

Kodate, N., & Timonen, V. (2017). Bringing the family in through the back door: The stealthy expansion of family care in Asian and European long-term care policy. *Journal of Cross-Cultural Gerontology, 32*(3), 291–301. doi:10.1007/s10823-017-9325-5

Kumari, C. (2015). Elderly perception of loneliness and ways of resolving it through positive ageing. *Indian Journal of Gerontology, 29*(3), 322–330.

Kuo, C., Cluver, L., Casale, M., & Lane, T. (2014). Cumulative effects of HIV illness and caring for children orphaned by AIDS on anxiety symptoms among adults caring for children in HIV-endemic South Africa. *AIDS Patient Care and STDs, 28*(6), 318–326. doi:10.1089/apc.2013.0225

Leopold, T., Raab, M., & Engelhardt, H. (2014). The transition to parent care: Costs, commitments, and caregiver selection among children. *Journal of Marriage and Family, 76*(2), 300–318. doi:10.1111/jomf.12099

Llanque, S., Savage, L., Rosenburg, N., & Caserta, M. (2016). Concept analysis: Alzheimer's caregiver stress. *Nursing Forum, 51*(1), 21–31. doi:10.1111/nuf.12090

Manderson, L., & Block, E. (2016). Relatedness and care in Southern Africa and beyond. *Social Dynamics, 42(2),* 205–217. doi:10.1080/02533952.2016.1218139

McEwen, B. S. (2005). Stressed or stressed out: What is the difference? *Journal of Psychiatry and Neuroscience, 30*(5), 315–318.

Morgan, T., Williams, L. A., Trussardi, G., & Gott, M. (2016). Gender and family caregiving at the end-of-life in the context of old age: A systematic review. *Palliative Medicine, 30*(7), 616–624. doi:10.1177/0269216315625857

Nadash, P., & Crisp, S. (2005). *Best practices in consumer direction.* Cambridge, MA: Thompson Medstat. Retrieved from https://aspe.hhs.gov/system/files/pdf/177236/CMS-CDBestPractices.pdf

Ogawa, R., Chan, R. K. H., Oishi, A. S., & Wang, L-R. (Eds.). (2018). *Gender, care and migration in East Asia.* Singapore: Springer Nature.

Pfau-Effinger, B., & Rostgaard, T. (2011)., Introduction: Tensions related to care in European welfare states. In B. Pfau-Effinger & T. Rostgaard (Eds.), *Care between work and welfare in European societies* (pp. 1–14). London: Palgrave Macmillan.

Plaza, D., & Below, A. (2014). Social media as a tool for transnational caregiving within the Caribbean diaspora. *Social and Economic Studies, 63,* 25–56.

Queen, T. L., Butner, J., Berg, C. A., & Smith, J. (2017). Activity engagement among older adult spousal caregivers. *The Journals of Gerontology: Series B, 74*(7), 1278–1282. doi:10.1093/geronb/gbx106

Sugiura, K., Ito, M., Kutsumi, M. & Mikami, H. (2009). Gender differences in spousal caregiving in Japan. *Journals of Gerontology Series B: Psychological and Social Sciences, 64B*(1), 147–156. doi:10.1093/geronb/gbn005

United Nations. (n.d.). *Definition of NGOs.* Retrieved from http://www.ngo.org/ngoinfo/define.html

United Nations Children's Fund. (2006). *State of the world's children report 2007: Women and children, the double dividend of gender equality.* New York, NY: Author. Retrieved from http://www.unicef.org/publications/files/The_State_of_the_Worlds__Children__2007_e.pdf

United Nations Open-Ended Working Group on Ageing. (2016). *Coalition of Caregivers and Advocates for the Elderly in Liberia (COCAEL).* Retrieved from https://social.un.org/ageing-working-group/documents/newngos/7session/COCAEL.pdf

United Nations Population Fund. (2012). *Ageing in the twenty-first century: A celebration and a challenge.* New York, NY: Author. Retrieved from http://www.helpage.org/resources/ageing-in-the-21st-century-a-celebration-and-a-challenge

Yi, Z., George, L., Sereny, M., Gu, D., & Vaupel, J. W. (2016). Older parents enjoy better filial piety and care from daughters than sons in China. *American Journal of Medical Research, 3*(1), 244–272. doi:10.22381/AJMR3120169

Zuo, D., Li, S., Mao, W., & Chi, I. (2014). End-of-life family caregiving for older parents in China's rural Anhui Province. *Canadian Journal of Aging, 33,* 448–461. doi:10.1017/S0714980814000373

THE PAIN AND JOY OF CARE

FRANK J. WHITTINGTON

To paraphrase Walt Whitman, the life course is a powerful play and each of us may add a verse or two. If we are lucky, we live long enough to write about our own aging, and, if we are really lucky, about our caregiving experience. Most people write and think about caregiving in the negative. It can be one of life's most difficult, frustrating, and defeating times, but it also can be our most giving, joyous, and uplifting. What I will call "the pain of care" might just as well have been termed "the joy of care." But first I want to illustrate the hard impact none of us is ready for when the role descends on us; later I hope to rearrange the same facts to depict the insights, the deepened relationships, and the utter satisfactions to be gained from the same awful process.

THE STORY

This story has a happy ending: the patient dies. For any story where the beginning and middle are as difficult and sorrowful as this one, death is a welcome conclusion. The American comedian and actor George Burns used to joke that his act had no opening, no finish, and was weak in the middle. Well, this story has a hopeful first act, a tragic second act, and a sad conclusion, tinged with hope and satisfaction. But the patient still dies at the end. And, as I said, that is the good part.

The drama begins, as many others are doing these days, with a man (or it could be a woman) living alone in a care facility. Let us call him "John," though his name could as easily be Juan, or Jan, or Jian, or Samuel, or Mohammed, or Toshiro. However, he is unidentified further for many reasons, and certain facts of the story have been changed here to preserve anonymity. They are fairly typical of many others in their circumstances, no matter the country or the culture, who may see familiar issues and events in the experiences recounted here.

John moved to an assisted living (AL) facility shortly after his wife of 68 years died. In the United States, AL describes a care setting that is not federally regulated, as nursing homes are, but rather provides assistance with one or more ADLs. AL is generally paid for by the person rather than by the government or another third party. John himself was recovering from a serious kidney infection, which was nearly fatal, and needed a good deal of rehabilitation before being ready for AL. Once there, however, he thrived, returning more each day to the high standard of wellness he always had maintained for himself. A lifelong devotee of physical fitness, he took to the exercise program at the AL facility, and his cultivated sociability, sweetness, and wit made him universally liked by all the residents and staff alike. For over a year, despite his 91 years, John benefited from the excellent environment of the facility and improved in both physical and mental status.

A year passes, and John begins his decline. His slight short-term memory loss becomes a bit more pronounced. His difficulty swallowing grows worse, resulting often in choking spells at mealtime. Most troubling to him and his family and friends, his difficulty articulating his thoughts, that is, making his words understandable, becomes quite a problem, interfering with conversation and impairing social relationships. By all accounts, John is slipping, but, with the good support of friends and family, he still attends religious services every Sunday, goes out with the AL group once a week for lunch, returns at least monthly to the home from which he moved to AL in order to "check on things" and pick up the twigs and pull the weeds in his yard. He even traveled halfway across the country to be with his grandchildren at Christmas and made a summer visit back to his old hometown in a distant state to visit his ailing brother, also in AL.

So, John may have been slipping, but he had not slid all the way down that final slope. That event occurred quite suddenly over a 2-week period about a month after his 92nd birthday. One of his children received a call from the AL nurse that John was in distress, often choking on his food and therefore avoiding eating, losing weight, and showing greater signs of dementia. Just that day, she reported, a staff member suspected he had aspirated some food and might be developing pneumonia, so they had "sent him out" to the emergency department (ED) of a nearby hospital for tests. But the ED doctor found no evidence of infection and sent him back to AL. Staff were very concerned that he was moving into the dreaded state called "failure to thrive" that usually marks the beginning of the end of life. They reported sadly that they feared "it wouldn't be long."

Turns out they were correct. John died 3 weeks later, but not before he experienced what can only be described as a massive indignity: He received the best care that Medicare and his own money could buy and modern medical and nursing science could provide. John received wonderful care from the most willing, the most able, and the most compassionate nurses, aides, and physicians one can imagine. Their depth of insight and skill can hardly be described. John and his family felt deeply indebted to them for so many assistances, large and small. Yet, John suffered mightily during his 3-week struggle through the care system—AL to hospital, to nursing home, to hospice—at the end of his life. The rest of this story is a tale of what must be acknowledged as "the pain of care."

THE CARE

As noted, by any standard the care was superior. Any of us would be happy to get it. Let us begin with the nurses, for they are the linchpin of the medical care system in the United States. If they work, the system usually does. John's nurses did the four things one must receive from the nurses on any long-term care case. First, they were watchful, looking for signs of change, indicators of distress or underlying disease. Their constant goal was to prevent something worse from happening, or detect it immediately. Second, they were technically competent. They seemed to know what to do in any situation and when. They used their judgment and professional discretion, seemingly with little hesitation but likely based on the education of experience. The third feature of good long-term care nursing that all John's nurses seemed to possess in abundance was compassion and gentleness. Their normal frustration with a, by now, resistant patient was tightly controlled and channeled toward getting the job done. They appeared to recognize his core character as well as his sweetness and responded in kind during each care task. Finally, John's nurses were honest and direct with both John (though he often could not understand) and his family. They provided what knowledge they had and patiently allowed family members to ask all the mundane questions they wished, along with the many important ones. At the end of this process, the nurses received the family's gold star for excellence.

The aides, also, were models of caring and concern. Theirs was the more personal work, so they had the greater opportunity for personal uplift. Whether bathing, repositioning, feeding, or cleaning, John's aides were model caregivers. Within the limits set by John's various conditions and the care system itself, they performed with a commitment and spirit that is little understood or appreciated outside a care facility. Although AL aides differ somewhat in both skills and tasks from those in the hospital and the nursing home, all are bed and body workers, the front line of health care. They provide the most basic service, those things we normally do for ourselves if we can: bathing, dressing, toileting, eating, and transferring. Doing these tasks for someone else, a stranger, takes a special courage and a humility that few possess. Doing these difficult and often dirty jobs for the least compensation among health care workers should make them the heroes of us all.

The doctor is generally acknowledged as the leader of the health care team, and rightly so. John's doctor provided him with both the technical skill required and the sensitivity we so seldom hear attributed to a physician. As a medical director of both a long-term care facility and a hospice, this physician seemed to know how much the family could hear and tolerate on each visit. He doled out the diminishingly good news, along with the increasingly bad, like an expert angler playing a game fish. With no disrespect to either his technique or the family's dilemma, he reeled them in until they were alongside the harsh reality of their father's condition and could take the last leap into that particular boat on their own. John's internist was, in the word of one insightful care aide, "soft," meaning he was mild, courteous, and nice to nurses and aides. For this, he was universally liked and respected as "a really good doctor." The leadership he provided the health care team in John's case seemed to be based on long experience but also flowed from a personal style as far from arrogance and dogmatism as it is possible to be.

THE PAIN

Having heaped praise on all the caregivers John benefited from in his end story, I must balance the picture drawn with a description of the inherent harshness and utter devastation this process wreaked on both John and his family. In doing so, I mean to highlight the contradictions we labor with and the profound ambivalence—and ignorance—with which we confront the process of dying in our culture. Even the best we can hope for is often the worst experience of our life. Let me describe, if I can, the pain of care, first as John experienced it and then as his family did. In both scenarios, I will focus on both the physical and the emotional pain.

Physical Effects

For many dying persons, the physical pain is paramount. It can be the overwhelming fact, the only reality worth mentioning. Thankfully, John's conditions caused very little actual pain and only occasional discomfort. The physical pain he did experience was caused by the care he received. Remember now: His care was appropriate, as gently administered as humanly possible, and quite minimal, compared with most patients at the end of life. He did not have heart disease, cancer, or arthritis; his liver, kidneys, and digestive system were intact; he did not have surgery; he was not on a respirator; and he did not have a feeding tube. He was taking few medications when he entered the hospital—only two prescribed drugs, one a preventive baby aspirin each day for a heart condition he never developed. I guess it worked.

John was one of the very few, very lucky persons to make this transition with no major, identifiable cause of death. He would, probably inevitably, develop pneumonia, which might kill him. But today we mostly have forgotten the description of this formerly common disease provided by Sir William Osler, famed Canadian physician, a century ago. Pneumonia, he said, was "the old man's friend" because it produced a relatively quick and painless death. Yet, John's pain was real, it caused him great distress, and it was largely unavoidable, given the assumptions we all tend to make in those last days of a person's life.

After John's "failure to thrive" diagnosis in the AL facility, he soon displayed marked difficulty breathing, along with agitation and occasional hallucinations. It might have been an adverse drug reaction since he had been given a prn (as needed) dose of the drug atropine, in the afternoon, to reduce the mucous secretions in his throat that were causing him to cough and breathe with a "gargling" sound. The combination of his agitation and breathing difficulties led to the decision to send him again to the hospital for assessment and, if needed, treatment. The decision to admit him to the hospital was mostly residual: despite the fact that little could be "diagnosed," something clearly was wrong, and he was in no condition to return to AL.

Once in the hospital, routine became master—of both John and of his family. In addition to the discomfort caused by John's minimal physical problems, the following catalog of pains—or their causes—were his daily companions:

- Lying in bed all day/inability to get comfortable
- Being handled for repositioning in bed
- Decubitus ulcer on coccyx
- Inflammation on heels
- Oxygen tubes in nostrils
- Oxygen tubes irritate back of ears
- Needle sticks to draw blood (once a day)
- Breathing treatments (four times a day)
- Vital signs (twice a day)
  - Blood pressure
  - Temperature under arm
  - Oxygen level on finger
- Being waked for tests and treatments
- Being waked at night by staff noise, cleaning sounds
- Unable to control lights
- Unable to regulate temperature or adjust bed linens
- Unable to adjust gown
- Needle stick for IV
- Catheter
- Constipation treated by suppository

Anyone who has spent time in a hospital as either patient or visitor will recognize many of these small and large irritations. Neither did all these sources of pain and discomfort end completely on John's transfer to a skilled care facility under hospice care. While the oxygen tube, catheter, and needle sticks disappeared, and all precautions were taken to eliminate discomfort, the daily personal care itself produced pain and irritation.

The ability to withstand these intrusions or even understand them is made much more difficult by the presence of either dementia or delirium. Communication is faulty at best, and bodily assaults often are misinterpreted as, well, bodily assaults. The physician's creed, *primum non nocere* (first, do no harm), is impossible to live by in a hospital and difficult to achieve, even under hospice care. We might be better warned to do the least harm in the service of at least some good. When it is clear no good can come, the harm should cease.

Psychological Effects

Most people tell interviewers they do not want to die in pain. That seems a reasonable wish based on a real fear. But in advance of the event, most of us cannot imagine the relative importance of the psychological pain associated with the end of life as we often experience it. Again, despite our good intentions, our loving kindness, and the best trained and motivated care staff, both our acute and chronic care facilities are organized to either make us well or make us better by doing something. In addition to the discomfort those acts cause, they rob us of life's normal pleasures and introduce many bad feelings. The list of those emotional impacts is long and disheartening:

- Enforced passivity
- Feelings of vulnerability
- Feelings of powerlessness
- Lack of privacy
- Being handled and bathed by strangers
- Ever-changing cast of caregivers (no continuity of care)
- Inability to understand what is happening
- Deprived of information
- Confusion/institutional delirium
- Social isolation
- Inability to regulate visitors
- Fear of death
- Deprived of knowledge of own dying

Both lists (of sources of physical and psychological pain) could no doubt be expanded with little effort. These are simply the painful issues observed and noted during John's end-of-life experience. As mentioned earlier, John's physical ailments were, by most standards, slight. His distress was far less than many dying people experience; yet his and his family's pain was quite real and awful, a palpable growth beneath the surface of their experience. It could not be understood or dealt with at the time, and its emotional impact endures. None of us can plan to avoid this experience. It is quite likely the kind of end we all will face either for our loved ones or ourselves.

THE JOY OF CARE

On balance, John's long life was a superior one. He loved, he was loved, he lived well, and he contributed much. He died with an admirable number of friends, accomplishments, and legacies. His life was one we all could be thrilled with. At its end, he received the best care available in the United States today, and his family were attentive, informed, and energetic in his defense. Yet neither they nor he could avoid entirely the pain of his exit. John's leave-taking was not the measure of his life, but it was perhaps as good as any of us can hope for. Nevertheless, we will be better prepared if we inform ourselves with knowledge and arm ourselves with resources against that day.

The irony embedded in this story is that the exquisite sensitivity to pleasure that allows us the best of life's enjoyments (physical and psychological), especially the love, intimacy, and appreciation found in our family's embrace and our social network, is the same capacity that condemns us to the harsh pain and sense of loss of all those pleasures at the end. The soon-to-be bereaved are losing a single beloved person; the dying one is losing everyone and everything he or she ever cared about and, probably most crucially, his or her own self. It must be a pain beyond imagining.

Perhaps it cannot be otherwise, but our goal as caregivers can be to eliminate or shorten those discomforts and indignities that are unnecessary and provide whatever emotional cushion we can, while emphasizing and reenacting to the maximum extent possible the care receiver's lifelong pleasures in family, friends, food, and fun. In doing so, caregiving—and perhaps care receiving—can become one of the signal events of life, freighted with meaning, with satisfaction, and, yes, even with joy.

Despite the *pain of care* we all may experience, a well-lived life, supported at the end by an excellent group of hospice workers and family caregivers, can help each of us travel more easily down that final path. We should be well-advised by John's example and that of the philosopher and pacifist Bertrand Russell, who said: "Three passions have governed my life: The longings for love, the search for knowledge, and unbearable pity for the suffering of [humankind]. ... This has been my life; I found it worth living."

Worth living. If each of us can craft for ourselves a life course that includes these three essential elements in abundance—longings for love (and finding it), the search for knowledge, and pity for the suffering of humankind—and if, as life ebbs away, we are as fortunate as John in finding an enlightened and caring living environment, attended by a loving family, not only will our lives be satisfying and rewarding, their end will be as good as it can be.

WORLD RELIGIONS AND AGING

HOLLY NELSON-BECKER | ELEANOR VAN DEN HEUVEL

INTRODUCTION

Religion is both a personal belief system and a sociocultural organization that is part of the social and emotional lives of most of the world's people. Of the estimated 7.7 billion people in the world (Worldometers.info, 2019), our best estimate is that over 85% identify with a religious faith, though many of these are not strictly observant. Most of these adherents are born into their faith: their parents are Hindus, or Presbyterians, or Sunni Muslims, so they learned their religious beliefs and practices from an early age and eventually assumed the same religious identity as their parents. Of course, some people are born into families with no particular religious faith and, therefore, are likely to learn and accept that view as well; about a billion of the world's people are not believers in any particular faith. One can always change views, leaving the faith (or nonfaith) of their parents or even converting to another religion altogether. In addition to the intolerance, conflict, and other negative effects often identified with religion and regardless of which faith one holds, for believers and for communities, religion also appears to offer a number of social and psychological benefits (Nelson-Becker, 2018; Smith, 1994), as the brief vignette in Exhibit 12.1 illustrates.

RELIGION AS A PERSONAL SUPPORT SYSTEM

Religion is often cited by older people as a source of support and reassurance, comfort and consolation. Nearly every religion has sacred texts that hold the wisdom of the tradition, a set of subscribed beliefs, and rituals and practices that can assist followers to grow and learn about themselves and their contribution within the wider society. Beside **intrinsic religion**, a term used by psychologist Gordon

EXHIBIT 12.1

Rediscovering Religion: The Social and Psychological Benefits of Faith

My job as a foot care specialist in Harrow on the Hill in Greater London ... takes me to many different homes and clients. One of the saddest is Sylvia, aged 84. She was a joy to visit while her husband was alive, but in the past 3 years since his death, things have gone downhill. When Sylvia had to give up driving, she became isolated and depressed. Sylvia's daughter-in-law, Janice, was a lifeline, visiting faithfully every week, but now she has moved away to the coast and only keeps in touch by phone. Sylvia is painfully lonely and seems to have lost the will to live.

My foot care visit every 6 weeks has become one that I dread; Sylvia is so unhappy and lonely that I feel depressed myself by the time I leave! Today, however, there was an amazing transformation. Sylvia was happy, chatty, and confident, back to the way she was when I first met her before her husband died. She explained that her new neighbor had arranged to get a lift to church and asked Sylvia if she would like to come along. She decided to go just to get out of the house, but when she got there she felt welcome and included. She remembered how much she enjoyed singing and the peace she felt at church. The following week she was greeted by name and invited to join the lunch club and the weekly knitting-for-cancer group. She was given a number to contact in case she needed any help. The minister came to visit and found out that Sylvia had been a florist, so he asked her to help decorate the church for the Harvest festival. Rediscovering her childhood faith and linking to a local faith community has helped Sylvia see the value and purpose in her life. I am amazed that getting involved in religion has made such a difference to Sylvia. Should I recommend it to more of my clients?

Allport (1950) to address the individual faith journey or individual spirituality, religion also offers **extrinsic** benefit to believers who may sense they form part of something larger than themselves, and they gain social support from spending time together.

Religion can also be used to help people express a shadow side. Some individuals exercise religious beliefs and principles to justify dark actions, terror inflicted on those who do not believe. Since most religious texts are very ancient and sometimes metaphorical, they lend themselves to various interpretations. Religion in certain historical periods and geographical regions has also been a focal point for intense discrimination. Think about great historical conflicts of which you are aware where differences in religious beliefs led to violence, abuse, and death. How many can you name? What about those going on today?

In every religion, there is also variance in terms of what beliefs matter most and how they may be expressed in different groups or cultures. This variance emerged within all the major religions and within denominations. In Islam, a political difference in belief led to two different branches, Sunni and Shia, which is described later in the chapter. Within Christianity, Catholicism emphasizes festival days, such as Our Lady of Guadalupe, as much as Christmas, a major festival across Christian faiths celebrating the birth of the prophet and Messiah, Jesus. Other Christian denominations (Protestants, for example) emphasize and celebrate more intensely the redemptive death of Jesus and his subsequent resurrection. In all religious traditions, some followers adhere strongly to the basic beliefs of their faith, while others may hold those tenets loosely and straddle an imaginary faith boundary, sometimes within and sometimes a bit outside of it. Thus, naming one's religious faith may or may not clearly identify where one is located on a religious or spiritual spectrum.

Historically, particular religious faiths have been sanctioned within certain cultures. This is due largely to origins and geographic dissemination of each particular tradition. The early faith of most people is determined by their birth, though in recent decades there has been much fluctuation in religious adherence, with people changing religious faiths as well as moving toward and away from formal religious affiliation. An older person may have established a varied personal religious history over time. Religious seekers comprise those who are searching for a better "fit" or identity within a religious home, often changing affiliation to a different faith. Religious switching is sometimes known as **conversion**: it involves a major change of religion, such as from Christianity to Judaism. Religious reaffiliation usually refers to changing faiths within a larger group, such as shifting within Christianity from the Baptist denomination to the Presbyterians (Association of Religion Data Archives [ARDA], 2018).

Some individuals also define themselves as spiritual, but not religious. They are not affiliated with any religious organization, yet follow or forge a spiritual path and often continue to believe in God. This group, sometimes termed **the nones**, includes roughly one fifth of all adults, but only 9% of those over age 65 (Pew Research Center, 2012). Similar to Gordon Allport's earlier definition, those who identify as spiritual are concerned with developing an interior life that recognizes what is deemed sacred. There is definitional controversy over the term spiritual or **spirituality** and its relationship to religion.

This chapter discusses five major world religions and their beliefs and practices regarding older adherents and old age generally. The traditions are discussed generally in order of their establishment. Thus, Hinduism is addressed first, followed by Buddhism, Judaism, Christianity, and Islam. Last, the presence of similar beliefs and practices important in the aging experience is assessed across these same religions.

RELIGIOUS COMMITMENT AT OLDER AGES

Recent surveys suggest that changes across the life course may affect the level of religious commitment (Pew Research Center, 2018). Young people are generally less religious than older people but seem to grow more religious as they age, according to recent surveys (Bengtson, Silverstein, Putney, & Harris, 2015). The trajectory of religious attachment tends to be highest during adolescence, declining in young and middle age, and then *increasing* throughout older ages (Pew Research Center, 2018). Generations, too, can vary in religiosity. A swell in religious interest was observed beginning with a 1930s cohort of young adults reassessed at age 75 years and older who reported a 10% increase in religious attendance over time. Earlier cohorts did not always show this same trend, though cohorts following the 1930s group have done so. These data align with Tornstam's (2005) **theory of gerotranscendence**, suggesting individuals focus on religious and spiritual values as they grow older.

In contrast, other theories suggest people living in richer nations are less likely than earlier generations to endorse religion generally. Findings suggest that increasing longevity in a nation can lead to less frequent attendance at religious services (Pew Research Center, 2018). Where people feel vulnerable (as in a poor society), religion provides hope; where people feel more economically secure, they are less likely to rely on religion for support. If a country's economic condition is deteriorating, an opposite trend in religious attendance may appear as young adults attend religious services more frequently as they age. Although few studies exist of religious attitudes before and after national disasters, researchers in New Zealand happened to have surveyed religious affiliation several years before and after a 2011 earthquake. Results revealed a slight increase in religious affiliation following the disaster (Pew Research Center, 2018). In a related example, after Hurricane Katrina in 2006, 67% of those surveyed reported an increase in their religious faith. This seems to imply that historical events and challenges may affect religious faith.

WORLD RELIGIONS AND AGING

Hinduism

BELIEFS AND PRACTICES

Hinduism is about 5,000 to 6,000 years old, and India, where it formed, fosters many diverse faiths. Hinduism is often considered one of the most open, tolerant, and universal of religions, a fusion of several traditions. This religion affirms that there are many paths to God. Although Hinduism is considered a monotheistic religion, it teaches that God manifests in many forms (Chakravarti, 1991). Brahma, Vishnu, and Shiva are expressions of the one God, with Brahma being the Creator God, though Brahma seems to have lost popularity in modern-day India to Vishnu and Shiva. Hinduism is unusual compared to most other religions because it has no single founder.

Religious texts include the Vedas, the Upanishads, and the Bhagavad Gita, part of the Mahabharata. The Vedas date from between 1500 and 800 BCE (Before the Common Era, roughly equivalent to "BC," Before Christ, in Christian tradition; the Common Era ["CE"] begins with the traditional birth of Jesus). The Vedas is a set of orally transmitted Sanskrit texts that are viewed as authoritative scriptures (Melton, 2009). The Upanishads, written a bit later, also provide many primary concepts. The word *Upanishad* means *sitting close to* and is reminiscent of the oral tradition and a teacher teaching his or her seated students. These texts provide a spiritual vision for self-realization, especially through the disciplines of meditation and yoga. The Bhagavad Gita dates from the fifth to second century BCE and narrates the story of Prince Arjuna and his charioteer/guide, Lord Krishna. Conflicted about his duty to fight in war, Arjuna was exhorted by Krishna to fulfill his Kshatriya (warrior) duty. This is considered an allegory of struggles in human life and has served as inspiration for civil rights leaders such as Mahatma Gandhi.

Hindus share beliefs in reincarnation (samsara), nirvana (moksha), and karma, and they often practice forms of yoga (Smith, 1994). How one handles karma in a lifetime determines whether someone will be reborn to a higher or lower level of life, possibly as an animal. **Yoga** is a spiritual path—a way of thinking, a way of conducting oneself, and a philosophical and practical way of living. It consists of four styles or types: *bhakti yoga* (through devotion and/or love), *jnana yoga* (through knowledge), *karma yoga* (through work), and *raja yoga* (through meditative exercises); see Melton (2009). These four forms of yoga appeal to different types of persons and thus are different pathways to God.

In Hinduism, the sacred is acknowledged in nature, a practice dating back to its pagan origins. The river Ganges in India is a holy place and the site of purification rituals at the beginning and end of life. Traditionally, most Hindus were vegetarian out of respect for animal life, and eating beef was strongly prohibited because the cow is held to be sacred. In modern India, however, vegetarianism is losing ground, with fewer than 30% of Indians observing its limitations; of course, given India's 1.2 billion people, that still amounts to about 360 million who avoid eating meat.

Social relationships are important in Hinduism, defined in part by social status. The **caste system** was a social hierarchy that dates back to 2000 BCE. It was strongly identified with Hinduism and has been interpreted with greater or lesser flexibility at different times. The caste was assigned through birth and within each caste are stratifications. The *Brahmins* were the intellectual and spiritual leaders, the priestly class. The *Kshatriyas* were the protectors of society, the politicians, police, and military. The *Vaisyas* were the artisan, farming, or merchant class. The *Shudras* were the maintenance workers or hard laborers. In the lowest stratification of *Shudras*, those who performed menial duties were known as *untouchables*. Within castes there was equality, opportunity, and social insurance. It was assumed that through reincarnation over several lifetimes, people would move up through the castes. Privileges were defined in proportion to responsibility. Positive discrimination or affirmative action policies, known as reservation, offered opportunity in some work sectors to reverse discriminatory practices. The Indian constitution today prohibits discrimination on the basis of the caste system.

HINDUISM AND AGING

Hinduism teaches that respect is offered to older people for their experience and wisdom. Hindu elders acknowledge their age, which is valued, and they are fully involved in reciprocal caregiving in families. Interdependence and interconnectedness form part of dharma, right action. Decision-making for health or mental health is a family process. Older women usually defer to men, especially in a marriage. A husband would have a greater breadth of ritual duties to perform, though a part of this would include offering security to women. Historically, respect was given to women for their roles as mothers, wives, and daughters. When a husband died, a woman's status was lost and she often faced hardship, sometimes choosing to self-immolate on her husband's funeral pyre, a practice known as *sati*. This practice is now banned. On the other hand, female deities as aspects of the divine goddess are worshipped and give status to women. Sacredness is embedded in daily life to the extent that people seek to live in harmony, both individually and communally, with the design of the universe. Meditation, rituals, and use of herbs and oils as in Ayurvedic treatment may form part of a holistic approach to living. As with some other cultures, direct eye contact with older people and others may be seen as disrespectful. For certain purposes, such as asking permission to marry, the supplicants will make appointments with, and touch the feet of, all older family members.

The Hindu religion has a belief system regarding **the four stages of life** (Ashramas) that commence at about age 8 and continue throughout life (Klostermaier, 1999; Mehrotra & Wagner, 2009). Each stage requires certain conduct and expected responses. Women's responsibilities are typically connected to those of the dominant man in their lives and his current stage of Ashrama, whether he is a father, husband, or son. A woman is seen as dependent and protected by the man, so her tasks are to maintain domestic and religious life. This model for aging (developed primarily for males) provides ethical expectations that change over the four different stages: student, householder, retirement, and renunciation.

- The *student stage* begins between ages 8 and 12 and continues for about 12 years. The goal for the student is to be receptive to learning from the teacher and to acquire skills and knowledge necessary for the current and following stages of life. An initiation ceremony is followed by study. The goal is to be able to live an effective life.

- The *householder stage* begins with marriage. The householder develops a career or occupation, raises a family, and contributes to the community. The householder supports people at all of the other life stages. This stage is the height of power and achievement.

- The *retirement stage* may begin with the birth of grandchildren and signals a gradual move from household duties to a more contemplative life. In prior centuries, the retired individual and/or spouse were known as forest dwellers who sought forest solitude for self-discovery (Smith, 1994). Now the older individual centers on deeper questions about life's purposes and seeks meaning amid mystery. The goal is to overcome the senses and dwell with the reality of the natural world, to construct a personal philosophy, and then form that into a way of living.

- The *renunciation stage* is the final life phase, where one grows toward balance and equanimity, mastering any strong feelings. One seeks to unite with the one reality, freeing oneself from the lure of possessions. Through practices such as noninjury to animals, detaching from pursuit of pleasure, and performance of rituals detailed in the Vedas, this unification may occur prior to death. This stage is viewed as the state of serenity, similar to geropsychologist Paul Baltes's (1993) concept of wisdom. Geography previously mattered in the retirement stage, where older people would leave the home and live in the forest or a remote place, but in today's world older people simply become inner-directed. Location no longer matters. Elders are able to clearly differentiate between the finite self and the true or infinite self.

Individuals should be awake and aware at death; saying their mantra surrounded by members of the family is considered ideal. Final rites at death are universal and most deceased individuals are cremated within hours after the body is washed, a shroud placed over it, and flowers piled upon it (Klostermaier, 1999). The eldest son lights the pyre at the cremation grounds, and Vedic hymns are recited. Prayers for safe passage into the next realm are sent. Ritual cleansing and purification of survivors follows. Ceremonies by family members continue for 1 year at given intervals.

One of the most sacred symbols is repetition of the syllable *om*. This represents the wholeness of the universe and the vibratory sound of the universal soul, Brahman. Meditation on the sound *om* is reported to result in enlightenment and immortality. *Ahimsa*, one of the highest ethical precepts of Hinduism (as well as Buddhism), is the pledge of noninjury to life. The practice of vegetarianism originates in *ahimsa*. Common to most Hindu practice is the belief that outward life and suffering are mere illusion, *maya*; recognition of this leads to release from that suffering. In later life, individuals take a larger perspective. Together, these practices represent spiritual disciplines that enhance life.

Buddhism
BELIEFS AND PRACTICES

The life story of the Buddha sets a context for Buddhist principles (Melton, 2009; Seager, 2009). A number of different types or streams of Buddhist practice now exist, developed through varying paths of dissemination over time and nation, yet all are guided by the essential principles from the life of the Enlightened One, the Buddha Siddhartha Gautama. Born a prince around 563 BCE at Lumbini, India, his mother died at his birth. Earlier, she had dreamed that he would be a great leader if he remained in the palace. If he declined his royal role, he would become a Buddha. Gautama grew up in the court and was sequestered from the outside world. At age 17, he married (happily it is reported) and had a child, but he was restricted to life in the palace by his father. However, in 529 BCE (at about age 34), after a series of excursions outside the palace with the help of his charioteer (Melton, 2009), the course of his life was altered. Outside the gates, he observed people living in poverty and illness. He was astonished and felt devastated. He saw a monk, holding a beggar's bowl but radiating peace. He departed from the palace, abandoned his worldly existence, and sought an end to the cycle of suffering and rebirth.

Gautama spent the next 6 years visiting South Asian religious groups and experimenting with asceticism and meditation. He concluded that a malnourished body would not welcome an awakened mind. In 523 BCE, his search came to completion while he was in meditation and contemplation in a state of serenity at the foot of a Bodhi tree located at Sarnath (Melton, 2009). He awakened to the nature of the mind and its delusions, attaining *Bodhi*, or enlightenment, and as a result became known as *Gautama the Buddha* or the *Enlightened One*. After his enlightenment, Buddha began to preach and teach; disciples were drawn to him, and a movement began to grow in northwest India. The Buddha died due to dysentery about 480 BCE at age 80 (Seager, 2009).

The essence of Buddhism lies in the Buddha's teachings. These outline the Dharma, that is, the laws of nature and true living. The Dharma is both profound and simple. Buddhists share a belief in the **Four Noble Truths** and the Noble Eightfold Path. The Four Noble Truths are: (a) all existence involves suffering; (b) the cause of suffering is desire: craving for pleasure, prosperity, and ongoing life; (c) there is a path leading to freedom from suffering; and (d) the eightfold path leads to cessation from desire and suffering.

The **Noble Eightfold Path**, pictured in the eight-spoke wheel—a symbol second only to the seated Buddha as a sign of Buddhist faith—consists of:

- Right understanding
- Right purpose
- Right speech
- Right conduct
- Right livelihood
- Right effort
- Right attention or mindfulness
- Right concentration

The enlightenment of Buddha emerged through his struggle; followers likewise learn that their path to enlightenment is their own responsibility. In his own life, the Buddha had known both luxury and asceticism, but he taught the value of the middle way, the path that avoids excess and ends in moderation. Buddhism is essentially nontheistic and denies the existence of a self. It borrowed heavily from Hinduism and especially the Vedic tradition.

Basic doctrine includes the belief that people have a good nature. **Karma** is the law of moral causation that suggests people earn merit through good deeds and demerits through malicious deeds. Good karma is created through right action, such as giving food and alms to the poor. People are thought to have experienced thousands of lifetimes. To attain human birth is rare and precious. There are no formal dietary restrictions in this nontheistic religion, but Buddhists may be vegetarian out of respect for animals.

The scriptures of Buddhism are the *Tripitaka* (Pali Canon) or Three Baskets. They include the *Vinaya*, the *Sutras*, and the *Abhidhamma*. The *Vinaya* are rules for the monks and information about Buddha's life; the *Sutras* are oral teachings of the Buddha and his disciples; the *Abhidhamma* is composed of seven philosophical discourses of Gautama or his disciples.

Buddhism originated from Hinduism and thus contains certain Hindu principles, although many of these beliefs were revised. Two primary schools of Buddhism that emerged were *Theravada* (Hinayana) and *Mahayana*. Theravada was based on the writing of an early follower of Buddha, Sariputra. His understanding was that a monastic way of life led to nirvana, a state of mind where desire was extinguished. This branch of Buddhism is the majority religion practiced in Southeast Asia, such as Thailand, Cambodia, and Laos and a minority religion elsewhere. *Mahayana* is the largest branch and is practiced in East Asia, including China, Japan, and Korea. It carried a more universal approach that accepted people who were not monks into the faith and promoted salvation for all living beings. *Zen* Buddhism, which emerged from Mahayana Buddhism, teaches understanding the Buddha nature and bringing benefit to other people. Other branches of Buddhism include *Pure Land*, a form of Mahayana that emphasizes chanting the name of Amitabha Buddha, and *Vajrayana* or Tibetan Buddhism, with which the Dalai Lama is associated.

BUDDHISM AND AGING

Recognition of impermanence is a key principle in Buddhism. Changes abound in the aging process, and change is a central feature of most Buddhist practices. People grow old and die, but every breath offers new possibility. Nothing lasts, and acceptance rather than resistance allows one to see reality (what is). In aging, Buddhists let go of some dreams in favor of constructing new ones. On a concrete level, if people choose to downsize or have it imposed on them, they also let go of household stuff and connected memories (Ekerdt & Sergeant, 2006). Mindfulness meditation practice is about letting go, paying attention without judgment to changes in the body and what is happening in the present moment, and doing reflection throughout the course of a day.

Nonviolence is a key principle of Buddhism. To hurt another is to hurt oneself because of the interconnections of all beings. Thich Nhat Hanh (1995) referred to this sense of oneness as *interbeing*. Buddhism teaches that rather than fight the hard parts of aging, acceptance is a better approach. *Ahimsa* is an expression that translates as "do no harm" (Esposito, Fasching, & Lewis, 2012). Violence against the self through negative thoughts toward our aging bodies or diminishing energy can increase suffering. Respecting the process of aging is important, because it decreases the tendency to hurt ourselves when we cannot meet expectations of what we could accomplish at younger ages. Respecting aging also helps older people note the positive aspects of growing older, such as deeper connections with successive generations. Further, although older people may not think or problem-solve as quickly as younger people, they take mental shortcuts that result in access to expert knowledge (Baltes, 1993). This is an integrative problem-solving approach. Reframing experience and demonstrating courage in facing life challenges are key processes that accord with Buddhist principles.

Buddhist practice includes acknowledgment of aging and illness. These concepts align with other Eastern philosophies, such as filial piety and intergenerational responsibility found in Confucianism (Nakasone, 2008). Buddhist teaching (dharma) sets the dilemma between having long life and fear of death. "Youth is the time to learn and to become familiar with the teachings. Then as one grows old ... it is easy to dwell within practice" (Dron-me in Lecso, 1989, p. 64). Finally, the value of spiritual practice is reinforced through the following poem by Nagarjuna: "However, if one practices the spiritual path the mind abides in joy, regardless of one's age. Then when death falls one is like a child gleefully returning to his home" (p. 65). One of the comforting messages of Buddhism for older people is that attention to continual development lessens the perception of problems in old age. Problems will be understood and accepted in context within the greater blessing inherent in longevity. Buddhism, in sum, emphasizes holism and balance.

Judaism

BELIEFS AND PRACTICES

The history of Judaism began with the land, a people, and their story. Referred to as *the people of the book*, the Jewish people arose from a small group of nomads, of whom no one in their eastern Mediterranean region took particular notice. The Jewish people consistently made meaning of the events of their lives in relation to their God. Judaism is a text-based religion, first drawing on the Torah, then the Hebrew Bible, and, finally, rabbinic texts. The Hebrew Bible has served as guide, authority, and inspiration. The history of the Jewish people was guided by their belief in a loving and compassionate God who takes an interest in their lives.

A distinctive contribution of this religion was the belief in monotheism. Rather than a God who was amoral and uncaring, like the god(s) of the Jews' contemporaries, to the Jews, God was a personal and singular entity. Jewish sacred texts are named the Hebrew Bible (Tanakh), which includes the Torah (the law), the Prophets, and the Writings. This is similar to the Old Testament of Christianity with books in a different order, but since the Old Testament implies a new one, that term is not used. The Talmud is a collection of rabbinical commentaries that interpret and apply the Torah.

Four themes emerged in the story of the Jews and their relationship with God: creation, liberation, revelation, and redemption. God is portrayed as all-powerful and a creating force. God covenanted with the Jews, and they sought to understand what it meant to be a chosen people. God's work freed the Jewish people from oppression, gave them ongoing teaching and revelations, and continued with them when they needed to be reclaimed. Obeying the commandments and Jewish law brought God's will into everyday reality. Jews are also required to live out their responsibilities to their neighbors in the Mitzvah, the religious duty to perform acts of kindness, especially to those marginalized in society.

Jewish relationship to society and culture changed in the 18th and 19th centuries, when the role of religion as the core of Jewish experience was challenged. The Jewish way of life was introduced to Western languages, philosophy, and sciences. The Jewish Emancipation, experienced in the 19th and early 20th centuries, meant political enfranchisement for the Jews, resulting in the collapse of traditional Jewish societies. Although many religious groups have faced persecution, the Jews experienced an extreme form in the Holocaust (Shoah) of Nazi Germany (1933–1945). The United Nations established the state of Israel as a home of the Jewish people in 1948, partly for reasons of security for Jews. Holocaust victims still survive in Israel, Europe, and North America, though their number is fast diminishing. New expressions of the Jewish faith developed in the 20th century, including the Reformed, Orthodox, and Conservative forms of Judaism, which now no longer is a unified faith.

For Jewish people, life is grounded in tradition. Those who have seen the Broadway musical play *Fiddler on the Roof* will recall a soulful song ("Tradition") celebrating that powerful communal value in a small Russian village. Ceremonies and rituals are utilized to inculcate ethnic history and script and direct responses to life events such as maturation and death. Celebrations of Sabbath (the weekly day of rest), of coming of age in the bar (male) and bat (female) mitzvahs, the Passover feast (commemorating Jews' deliverance from slavery in Egypt), and the Day of Atonement (Yom Kippur)—a day of repentance and intensive prayer and fasting—all serve to make everyday life holy (Epstein, 2013).

JUDAISM AND AGING

Traditional Jewish texts about old age demonstrate that Judaism values elders, seeing them as a source of knowledge within the community (Sedley, 2012). The Torah proposes that people should rise in the presence of those who are old and the biblical book of Leviticus commands people to honor older persons. The meaning of the term *old* is defined by later commentaries, such as Ecclesiastes and the Psalms, biblical books that acknowledge physical concerns that may emerge with aging. Nevertheless, older people deserve respect: they are seen as leaders, advisors, and guides for the community. Parents are particularly honored and should be cared for throughout old age and frailty. Judaism views old age as a continuation of the path a person has chosen through life; there is no sudden transition to old age. Preparation for late life begins while a person is young.

The rabbis in the Talmud (Avot [Ethics of the Fathers] 5:24) articulated what they saw as the later stages in a person's life (Berkson & Fisch, 2010):

> ... at sixty to be an elder, at seventy for gray hairs, at eighty for special strength (Psalm 90:10), at ninety for decrepitude, and at a hundred a man is as one who has already died and has ceased from the affairs of this world. (as cited in MacKinlay, 2010, p. 89)

Finally, old age is viewed as an opportunity to prepare for death so that older adults can live life without fear. Traditional death rituals include a simple, brief service with a quick burial in the ground. The body is not left alone, but guarded until burial. The body is washed and dressed in a white shroud without embalming. A period of mourning known as *shiva* is held in the home of family members and may last 7 days, though in modern times this has been shortened. The *Kaddish*, a prayer of mourning, is recited daily for 11 months after the death of a loved one.

The Jewish community has a vested interest in developing programs that meet the evolving needs of their older adults. At the forefront of developing community-based programs is a focus on helping older adults age in place and remain connected to their community. With a goal of assisting older people to reach their full potential, a variety of Jewish agencies and programs have been established in most Western countries where Jews live to help older adults meet needs. Often, because of the strong Jewish tradition of communal good works and caring for older people, these have been among the first such programs in many cities.

Christianity
BELIEFS AND PRACTICES

Christianity emerged from Judaism during the first century of the CE in the same eastern Mediterranean territory that the Jews inhabited. Today, Christianity incorporates three main divisions: Roman Catholicism (about 50% of all Christians globally), Orthodox Christianity (about 10%, principally in Russia), and Protestantism (about 40% of Christians, most living in the United States); see VonDras (2017). Each of these branches contains other groups, but Protestantism contains many diverse denominations, holding a range of beliefs that nonetheless subscribe to a belief in Jesus as a prophet and the Son of God.

Like both Judaism and Islam, Christianity is **monotheistic**, but the divine being is seen as a complex unity of relationships (referred to as "the Trinity") between God the Father, God the Son, and God the Holy Spirit. Christianity centers on the life of Jesus, who is considered the Son of God. Jesus was born to Jewish parents in Palestine around 6 BCE, and his life and teaching are recorded in the New Testament of the Christian Bible. After a short, 3-year period of public ministry where many people approached him for healing, his life ended in Jerusalem after a striking series of events. He was about 33 when he was hailed as a king by a large throng of Jews gathered to celebrate the Passover. Due in part to jealousy by Jewish religious leaders, he was arrested by the Roman colonial authorities, tried by the Jewish figurehead king, convicted of sacrilege and provoking insurrection, then sentenced and executed by crucifixion, and buried in a tomb borrowed for this purpose. According to Christian religious texts, he rose from that grave (came back to life) after being dead for 3 days, and this belief became a powerful catalyst for the new religion of Christianity. Much of his teaching was considered countercultural at the time and not well understood. The new religious movement, founded on his teachings and by his disciples, was considered by the Romans to be part of the Jewish nation, but the Jews viewed it as a threat, so early Christians faced great persecution by Jews and (periodically) by Romans before the religion was established. It became more widely disseminated partly with the help of the Roman Emperor Constantine under whose reign (306–337 CE) Christianity moved to a dominant religion, with a set organizational structure and beliefs.

Christians use the Bible, which contains both the Old and New Testaments. The Old Testament contains many of the same books that are in the Hebrew Bible, while the New Testament details Jesus's life and teaching and the period after his death to the late 60s CE when the new church community was being established against intense discrimination and maltreatment. A key belief of Christians is that Jesus was the promised Messiah or Son of God discussed in Hebrew scripture. He taught compassion, service, and the value of inclusion. But important also to Christians is belief in the Holy Spirit, the third manifestation of the trinity God, which remains present with people today, both believers and nonbelievers (Jeffers, Nelson, Barnet, & Brannigan, 2013).

CHRISTIANITY AND AGING

The Christian biblical narrative sees living to old age as a sign of God's blessing; only a very small proportion of the population survived into advanced old age in biblical times, so those who did were generally revered for their wisdom and valued for their advice. Christianity attempts to stand against the dominant Western cultural narrative of burden and dependency in old age by focusing on **three essential truths** drawn from the scriptures. First, older people are reminded of their value as human beings. The innate dignity and value of every human life can be drawn from the Genesis account, where humans are made in the image of God. However, ultimate expression of the value of human beings to God lies in the incarnation: that God should choose, in Jesus, to come to Earth to live and die because of his love for human beings means that each person is infinitely valuable to God. For the Christian, the message of Jesus is that each human being is worth dying for.

The second important truth to consider is the biblical view of suffering. Suffering is an inevitable part of life. Aging brings added physical suffering with reduced strength and body function, where pain and disease become more common. Emotional suffering with bereavement, losses, and difficult changes is often a part of experience. Appreciation of the value of suffering in developing character and moving the older person forward in his or her journey of discipleship is an important countercultural message for aging Christians. Described in the New Testament book of Romans (5:3–5), "... [S]uffering produces endurance, and endurance produces character, and character produces hope, and hope does not disappoint us." The ultimate example of this is seen in the death of Jesus, where his crucifixion is believed to bring freedom and deliverance for the world.

The third essential truth of Christianity is that our lives have a purpose and a meaning; older Christians are not simply marking time waiting to get into heaven. The older Christian understands that each day is not only a gift from God but that it is a day when he or she is called by God to serve. Christians believe that "we are ambassadors for Christ" (2 Corinthians 5:20), regardless of age or ability, and they have a responsibility to make God known through the way that they live. Jesus taught his disciples to pray for God the Father's will to be done on Earth as it is in heaven (Matthew 6:10), so the Christian's life must be directed toward justice, peacemaking, and the reduction of poverty. This challenge does not end when physical or mental weakness in late life prevents active involvement.

Islam
BELIEFS AND PRACTICES

Islam also is a monotheistic religion; it emerged after Judaism and Christianity, but in the same place. The term **Islam** is interpreted as submission to God's will. It is concerned with bringing about peace. Muslims (the term for adherents of Islam) believe in the guidance from Muhammad as a prophet of God. They also believe that prophets of the Hebrew Bible, such as Noah, Abraham, and Moses, and prophets of the New Testament, such as Jesus, were divinely inspired. Beliefs similar to Judaism and Christianity include concepts of heaven, hell, angels, and a Day of Judgment. What is unique to Islam are beings known as *jinn*. The jinn, related to the term *genie*, inhabit the unseen world though they can have a physical manifestation and can be either good or evil.

Muslims believe the Prophet Muhammad (570 CE–632 CE) received revelations subsequently recorded in the **Qur'an** (Westernized spelling: Koran) from the Angel Gabriel. The purpose of these messages was to correct human errors in the Jewish and Christian scriptures (Esposito, 2011). The Qur'an is thus viewed as the direct message from God; oral recitation and chanting of the Qur'an remains a source of inspiration to believers. Whether fully understood or not, Muslims memorize and recite the Qur'an in Arabic as well as praying in Arabic. The Hadith complements the Qur'an by detailing the life of Muhammad. The imam is the religious leader of the community who interprets legal and doctrinal considerations.

The Five Pillars of Islam, or obligations of the faith, frame Muslim life (Esposito, 2011; Gordon, 2002; Lewis, 2009; Smith, 1994). These include the testimony of faith, prayer, giving zakat (support of the needy), fasting during the month of Ramadan, and the pilgrimage to Mecca that occurs, if possible physically and financially, once in a lifetime.

1. *The Testimony or Declaration of Faith:*
   A Muslim bears witness to his or her faith through the public declaration known as the *Shahada* (witness, testimony). Allah is the Arabic name for God, just as Yahweh is the Hebrew name for God used in the Old Testament. To become a Muslim, one need only make this simple proclamation: "There is no God but God, and Muhammad is his messenger" (Gordon, 2002).

2. *Prayer:*
   The second pillar of Islam is prayer (*salat*). Muslims pray (or, perhaps more correctly, worship) five times throughout the day: at daybreak, noon, midafternoon, sunset, and evening. Muhammad established these times in his *hadiths* (sayings). In many Muslim countries, reminders to pray, or *calls to prayer*, echo out across the rooftops from a minaret or tower. Women generally pray at home, but have separate areas designated for them when they pray in the mosque.

3. *Giving Zakat (Support of the Needy):*
   The third pillar of Islam is called the *zakat*, which means *purification*. Like prayer, which is both an individual and communal responsibility, zakat expresses a Muslim's worship of, and thanksgiving to, God by supporting the poor. An annual contribution of 2.5% of an individual's wealth and assets is required, not merely a percentage of annual income. In Islam, the true owner of material goods is not man but God.

4. *Fasting During the Month of Ramadan:*
   The fourth pillar of Islam, the fast of Ramadan, occurs once yearly during the month of Ramadan, the ninth month of the Islamic calendar and the month in which Muhammad received the first revelation of the Qur'an. During this monthlong fast, Muslims whose health permits must from dawn to sunset abstain from food, drink, smoking, and sexual activity. At dusk, the fast is broken with a light meal, the *iftar*, referred to as breakfast. Children and older adults are exempted from the fast.

5. *The Pilgrimage to Mecca:*
   The fifth pillar is the pilgrimage, or *hajj*, to the holy city of Mecca in Saudi Arabia. Mecca is the site of the birthplace of the Prophet Muhammad and the revelations written in the Qur'an. At least once in his or her lifetime, every adult Muslim who is physically and financially able is required to make the sacrifice necessary to make this pilgrimage. The pilgrimage season follows Ramadan. Every year, believers travel from across the world to Mecca to form one community.

As stated earlier, Islam has two major branches, Sunni and Shia. The larger is the Sunni branch, which is dominant in Saudi Arabia, Iraq, Egypt, Pakistan, and Turkey, and whose adherents believe that after the death of Muhammed the Prophet, the most capable person should be elected as leader of the faithful. The Shia, conversely, believe that leadership should continue to be held within the Prophet's family, either appointed by him or through imams (religious leaders) appointed directly by God. Shia is the majority religion in Iran, but also is present as a minority branch in other nations.

ISLAM AND OLDER ADULTS

In the Islamic world, marriage and other aspects of family life are regulated. Family members are strongly interconnected in a system of largely patriarchal authority. Children, parents, grandparents, and sometimes great-grandparents may all live together or visit together often. One rarely finds nursing-care facilities solely for older Muslim people, since expectations are that care of elders is provided in the home. At times, sending parents to a nursing home has been considered elder abuse. Caregiving for parents in later life is viewed as a blessing and an opportunity to grow spiritually (Ibrahim, 2002). Muslims pray for their parents but also are to act with limitless compassion, remembering the time when they were cared for as children. Mothers are especially revered, since they have held the primary tasks of childrearing. When Muslim parents reach older adulthood, they are to be treated with respect, kindness, and selflessness. Serving parents is a duty second to prayer and worship of God. It is considered disgraceful to express impatience if an older person is difficult.

Gender sensibilities also suggest discomfort if intimate care is provided by someone from a different gender in an institutional setting (Al-Heeti, 2007). Further, residential care facilities in Europe and North America make little provision for Islamic religious worship or celebration of holidays. Islamic practice recognizes no stage of life given to renunciation and reflection similar to Hinduism. It is expected that older adults will continue to contribute to society as long as they are able to do so.

As Muslims move toward death, they should lie on their side if possible with their face turned toward Mecca (Rassool, 2000; Ross, 2001). After death, a Muslim is washed, usually by a family member and someone of the same sex, wrapped in a clean white cloth tied at the head and feet, and buried with a brief prescribed prayer, preferably the same day or within 24 hours. The body is not embalmed or cremated. When the body is buried, the head should face toward Mecca in a grave with no casket unless there is a specific reason for it. Mourners each fill the grave with three handfuls of soil. Women are cautioned not to tear clothing, a traditional sign of grief in some cultures, or to engage in loud weeping. Most graves are plain and unadorned.

One of the concerns in modern Islamic society, especially in immigrant communities, is the lack of respect by younger, more modern generations (Khirfan, 2012). Many older Muslims believe that younger people will outgrow this as they age, and this is often the case. However, older Muslims may contribute to a decrease in respect and power if they live in a non–Arabic-speaking country and must rely on the language translation skills of children or grandchildren. Other difficulties faced by immigrant elders include social isolation and inability to drive, so reliance on family to take them to religious functions and social events is common.

DISCUSSION AND CONCLUSION

Different faith traditions attract people with varying needs. Many religions originated in a time and place where they gave great appeal, comfort, or inspiration to a people. Some religions seem to have blended with certain cultures better than others and found greater resonance there. Traditional religions have, to some degree, incorporated traditional notions of gender and gender roles into both their theology and their social ethics, notions we as modern thinkers now regard as sexist, a very modern concept. In modern times, these five major religious faiths often have different local variations as well as room for different sects within the larger tradition. Individual needs or preferences for tradition and familiarity versus those for novelty or openness factor into personal decisions about faith affiliation.

Older adherents of all these world religions have in large part felt that their early religious tradition (or another adopted in later life) has answered deep needs over their life course and answers them still. Table 12.1 presents suggested concepts important in gerontology and identifies how different traditions address these aspects. Belief in an afterlife and/or karma is a distinguishing feature of religious belief. In Hinduism, karma refers to the concept that one's present actions influence what will happen to the person in the future, particularly in a reincarnated form. Models of aging refer to older people held up by the tradition as exemplars, people whose behavior is worthy of emulation. Compassionate action and concerns about Earth and future generations have traction across all religions. Devotional practice refers to collective, individual, or mystical approaches to aging, especially through prayer. Harmony and balance are attributes that some religious traditions hold as being key virtues. Values of releasing attachment, letting go, or surrender in preparation for death have been discussed much in Eastern traditions, much like the disengagement theory in gerontological thought.

This chapter has discussed key concepts of aging related to religious beliefs and practices in five major world religions: Hinduism, Buddhism, Judaism, Christianity, and Islam. Hinduism views aging as a life stage with different tasks from younger ages. Buddhism considers aging as the opportunity to recognize and adjust to the impermanent nature of life. Judaism and Christianity both point to aging as a time to connect or reconnect to God, who provides comfort in suffering. Islam views care of older people as a duty and an opportunity for reciprocal giving. All of these religions identify inevitable challenges of aging, frailty, and dying and try to address these, while maintaining a foundational respect for the aging process and for older people themselves.

TABLE 12.1 Aging-Related Principles of Major Religious Faiths

Concept	Hinduism	Buddhism	Judaism	Christianity	Islam
Belief in afterlife	Yes	Yes, reincarnation	Yes, some sects	Yes	Yes
Belief in karma	Yes	Yes	No	No	No
Compassionate action	Yes, seva, selfless service	Yes, tonglen	Yes, tikkun olan	Yes, servant role	Yes, service to humanity
Concern about the Earth, sacredness of creation	Yes, ahimsa	Yes	Yes	Yes, more recent	Humans are trustees of the Earth, which was created as a place of worship, pure and clean. Whoever plants a tree and diligently looks after it until it matures and bears fruit is rewarded.
Concern for generations to follow	Yes, fulfill role given at birth	Yes, you might be that generation	Yes, ethical will	Yes	Yes, water plants for travelers
Devotional practice: group and individual	Yes, both, puja	Yes	Yes, both	Yes, both	Yes, both. Prayer is the second pillar, group prayer more valued
Forgiveness	Yes, ksanti	Yes, strongly	Yes, repent, forgive, reconcile with God, less humans	Yes, "70 × 7"	Yes, immediate, revenge not allowed
Golden rule (may be worded negatively)	Yes	Yes	Yes	Yes	Yes
Has individual component?	Chant, prayer	Meditation	Kabbalism, prayer	Mysticism, prayer	Sufism, prayer

(continued)

TABLE 12.1 Aging-Related Principles of Major Religious Faiths *(continued)*

Concept	Hinduism	Buddhism	Judaism	Christianity	Islam
Harmony or balance	Accepts many beliefs	Yes	Not specific	Not specific	Yes, but in social justice perspective
Hospitality: welcoming the stranger	Yes	Yes	Yes	Yes	Yes, "Guests are more precious than your father"
Meaning in suffering	Yes, due to samsara—physical attachment—or choice for improved karma	Yes, dukkha in aging, illness, death	Yes	Yes	Yes, divine plan evident in suffering
Models of aging in historic lives	Yes, Gandhi	Yes, Dalai Lama	Yes, Methuselah, Abraham, Sarah, Moses, and others	Yes, some same as Judaism and apostles and more modern day "Desert Mothers and Fathers," mystics	Not explicit. Muhammad died at 62, not considered an aging model
Respect for older people	Yes	Yes	Yes	Yes	Yes
Value in releasing attachments	Yes	Yes	Uncertain	Yes	No

Source: Adapted with permission from Nelson-Becker, H. (2018). *Spirituality, religion, and aging: Illuminations for therapeutic practice.* Thousand Oaks, CA: Sage.

DISCUSSION QUESTIONS

1. On balance, have world religions helped or hurt the position of older people in their societies?

2. In your experience, do religious institutions usually carry out their traditional teachings about older people in everyday life?

3. What are the main differences among the five world religions in how they view aging and older people?

4. What are some significant similarities between your own religion (or a religion you are familiar with) and some of the others?

5. How has the status of women been affected by religious teachings and practices?

KEY WORDS

Caste system
Conversion
Extrinsic religion
Five pillars of Islam
Four Noble Truths of Buddhism
Gerotranscendence
Intrinsic religion

Monotheism
Noble Eightfold Path of Buddhism
Nones
Qur'an (Koran)
Three essential truths of Christianity
Yoga

REFERENCES

Al-heeti, R. (2007). Why nursing homes will not work: Caring for the needs of the aging Muslim American population. *The Elder Law Journal, 15*(1), 205–231.

Allport, G. (1950). *The individual and his religion: A psychological interpretation.* Oxford, UK: Macmillan.

Association of Religion Data Archives. (2018). Religious switching. Retrieved from http://wiki.thearda.com/tcm/concepts/religious-switching

Baltes, P. B. (1993). The aging mind: Potential and limits. *The Gerontologist, 33*(5), 580–594. doi:10.1093/geront/33.5.580

Bengtson, V. L., Silverstein, M., Putney, N. M., & Harris, S. C. (2015). Does religiousness increase with age? Age changes and generational differences over 35 years. *Journal for the Scientific Study of Religion, 54*(2), 363–379. doi:10.1111/jssr.12183

Berkson, W., & Fisch, M. (2010). *Pirke Avot.* Philadelphia, PA: The Jewish Publication Society.

Chakravarti, S. S. (1991). *Hinduism, a way of life.* Delhi: Motilal Banarsidass Publishers.

Epstein, L. J. (2013). *The basic beliefs of Judaism: A twenty-first-century guide to a timeless tradition.* New York, NY: Jason Aronson/Rowman & Littlefield.

Lecso, P. A. (1989). Aging through Buddhist eyes. *Journal of Religion and Aging, 5*(3), 59–66. doi:10.1300/J491v05n03_05

Ekerdt, D. J., & Sergeant, J. F. (2006). Family things: Attending the household disbandment older adults. *Journal of Aging Studies, 20*(3), 193–205. doi:10.1016/j.jaging.2005.10.001

Esposito, J. (2011). *What everyone needs to know about Islam.* New York, NY: Oxford University Press.

Esposito, J. L., Fasching, D. J., & Lewis, T. (2012). *Religions of Asia today.* New York, NY: Oxford University Press.

Gordon, M. (2002). *Islam: Origins, practices, holy texts, sacred persons, sacred places*. New York, NY: Oxford University Press.

Hanh, T. N. (1995). *Living Buddha, living Christ*. New York, NY: Riverhead Books.

Ibrahim, I. A. (2002). How do Muslims treat the elderly? [Online Chapter]. Retrieved from http://www .islam-guide.com/ch3-15.htm

Jeffers, S. L., Nelson, M. E., Barnet, V., & Brannigan, M. C. (2013). *The essential guide to religious traditions and spirituality for health care providers*. London, UK: Radcliffe Publishing.

Khirfan, G. (2012). Muslim elders issues in aging [Online Article]. Retrieved from http://ginakhirfan .blogspot.com/2012/09/muslim-elders-issues-in-aging.html

Lewis, B. (2009). *Islam: The religion and the people*. Upper Saddle River, NJ: Pearson.

Klostermaier, K. (1999). *A short introduction to Hinduism*. Oxford, UK: Oneworld.

MacKinlay, E. (2010). *Ageing and spirituality across faiths and cultures*. London, UK: Jessica Kingsley.

Mehrotra, C. M., & Wagner, L. S. (2009). *Aging and diversity* (2nd ed.). New York, NY: Routledge.

Melton, J. G. (Ed.). (2009). Eastern family, part II: Buddhism, Shinto, Japanese, new religions. In *Melton's encyclopedia of American religions* (8th ed., online). Detroit, MI: Gale.

Nakasone, R. (2008). A brief review of literature of Buddhist writings on spirituality and aging. *Journal of Religion, Spirituality, and Aging, 20*(3), 220–226. doi:10.1080/15528030801988906

Nelson-Becker, H. (2018). *Spirituality, religion, and aging: Illuminations for therapeutic practice*. Thousand Oaks, CA: Sage.

Pew Research Center. (2012). Nones on the rise: One in five adults have no religious affiliation. The Pew Forum on Religion and Public Life. Retrieved from https://www.pewforum.org/2012/10/09/ nones-on-the-rise/

Pew Research Center. (2018). The age gap in religion around the world. The Pew Forum. Retrieved from http://www.pewforum.org/2018/06/13/the-age-gap-in-religion-around-the-world

Rassool, G. H. (2000). The crescent and Islam: healing, nursing and the spiritual dimension. Some considerations towards an understanding of the Islamic perspectives on caring. *Journal of Advanced Nursing, 32*(6), 1476–1484. doi:10.1046/j.1365-2648.2000.01614.x

Ross, H. M. (2001). Islamic tradition at the end of life. *MedSurg Nursing, 10*(2), 83.

Seager, R. H. (2009). *Buddhism in America*. New York, NY: Columbia University Press.

Sedley, R. D. (2012). TAG institute for social development [Website]. Retrieved from http://www .taginstitute.org

Smith, H. (1994). *World religions*. New York, NY: Harper Collins.

Tornstam, L. (2005). *Gerotranscendence: A developmental theory of positive aging*. New York, NY: Springer Publishing Company.

VonDras, D. (2017). *Better health through spiritual practices*. Santa Barbara, CA: Praeger.

Worldometers.info. (2019). World population. Retrieved from www.worldometers.info/world -population

RITUAL SUICIDE AND THE PLACE OF OLDER JAIN WOMEN IN CONTEMPORARY INDIA

ELIZABETH WILSON

India is a nation where fasting has been used effectively for political protest. The legendary fasts of Mahatma Gandhi, leader of the Indian Independence movement, are well-known. Fasting is also a religious ritual for many Hindus. It is common for Hindus to fast for 1 day a week in devotion to a particular deity or to fulfill a vow one has made. But one minority religious group in India uses fasting as a means of ending life, and this practice recently has received a great deal of public scrutiny. The ritual is called santhara or sallekhana, and it is performed as a rite of penance. It is believed that one can reverse the effects of bad deeds done earlier in one's life by refraining from eating, drinking, and ingesting medicines at the end of life. *Santhara* is allowed only when a person is suffering from incurable disease or great disability, or when a person is otherwise nearing the end. It is also permissible in times of famine. In order to carry out the ritual fast of *santhara*, one must receive approval from senior family members and from one's guru or religious teacher.

The ritual fast has been performed for over 1,500 years by members of the Jain religion, which differs from Hinduism. Unlike Hindus, Jains do not believe in gods and view the universe as separated into two categories: life and nonlife. The fasting practice is prevalent in the Jain community, although the numbers are still quite small. It is thought that some 200 to 300 Jains opt for *santhara* each year. Jains are a distinct minority in India. They number 4.5 million out of 1.2 billion Indians, about half of 1 percent. But they are a very wealthy and influential minority; many Jains work in the diamond trade and in banking.

Since 2015, those who opted for *santhara* did so under considerable public scrutiny. The practice has begun to receive attention from human rights activists, who fear that marginalized people are too often coerced into taking their own lives. Feminist activists worry that ritual fasting offers a convenient means of eliminating "leftover" women, especially the indigent, the very old, and those without living offspring. Feminist activists compare the practice of *santhara* in the Jain community to the practice of *sati* (widow immolation) in the Hindu community. *Sati* occurs when a widow enters the funeral pyre of her deceased husband. It was outlawed by the British when India was under colonial rule and became a contested issue in postcolonial India, with some Hindu nationalists arguing that *sati* is an essential Hindu tradition that should not be criminalized. In both rituals, there are questions about whether the woman chooses to die of her own volition or is coerced. In both *santhara* and *sati*, the body of the woman who dies in this ritual manner is venerated, often with elaborate processions and the erection of shrines at the place of death. The family of the deceased woman can benefit from donations made at the shrine, raising questions about the motivation of family members who support these ritual forms of voluntary death.

To give a recent example of the kind of public performance of veneration that can occur when a Jain commits *santhara*, we can look back to the city of Jaipur in 2006. Vimla Devi Bhansali, a terminally ill woman suffering from cancer of the brain and the liver, died after a 13-day fast. Her corpse was dressed up in a red outfit, with a purse placed in her hands and a cotton cloth placed over her mouth in keeping with the Jain practice of covering the mouth to prevent the person from inadvertently inhaling insects. Jains practice nonviolence toward all life forms, and the cotton mask is one way to minimize the harm done to other life forms.

After the death of Bhansali, activist groups were organized and a court action was launched to have the ritual fast to death declared illegal. The effort was spearheaded by a human rights activist named Nikhil Soni, who felt that too many Jains were being coerced into the fast by their families to avoid the financial burden of caring for them. Soni alleged that marginalized people are particularly prone to being bullied into taking their lives in this way. Soni's lawyer filed a public interest litigation with the High Court of Rajasthan (the northwestern Indian state where Bhansali resided) arguing that allowing an older person to suffer without medical assistance, food, and water is inhumane. Other activists who filed briefs before the court mentioned evidence of coercion in other similar cases, such as the case of an older lady who lived in one activist's neighborhood. This lady was known in the neighborhood to be undergoing *santhara*. One evening, however, the activist heard loud screams coming from her home. Those screams were quickly drowned out by the sounds of drums. The lady's death that was being celebrated by local Jains, the activist alleged, was not freely chosen.

Almost a decade after this legal action, no judgment had been reached by the High Court, and Jains continued the practice as before. However, in another case, Badni Devi Daga, an 82-year-old woman also from Rajasthan, began fasting to death in July 2018. Then, 26 days into her fast, on August 10, her family and religious advisors were about to accelerate the process by denying her water, but something stopped them from this step. That day, the Rajasthan High Court ruled that the practice of *santhara* is illegal because it is a form of suicide, which is illegal under Section 309 of the Indian Penal Code. Another statute of the Penal Code mandates that anyone assisting a person to commit suicide also can be prosecuted.

After the Rajasthan High court outlawed *santhara*, thousands of Jains in Rajasthan took to the streets in protest. At the end of August, the Indian Supreme Court stayed the High Court's judgment, making the fast legal in Rajasthan again. The Supreme Court has agreed to take the case, but it will probably be 4 or 5 years before the case comes up in the court docket.

Jainism has recently been granted official status as a minority religion in India. This means that questions about the freedom to practice religion will weigh heavily in the Indian Supreme Court's decision, posing the question of how to balance the human rights of marginalized persons against the claims of a minority religion to practice its traditions freely.

The legal controversy has exposed cracks within the Jain community. Younger Jains often question the place of the fasting ritual in the modern world. They worry that such rituals are not helping what is already one of India's slowest growing religions. One of the practices that is common in the case of *santhara* is that the body of the person who has died is taken on procession and made the object of public display. Such processions are embarrassing to some younger Jains. A related issue that has divided the community is the belief that the dead bodies of those who have died through *santhara* have healing powers. Bodily fluids are sometimes used as massage oils or even ingested by those who need healing.

Given the saintly status that one can obtain in this religion by committing to die by starvation, it is not surprising that outsiders might suspect that some families may push their older family members into committing to die in this way. It could bring honor to a family to have such a saintly person in their midst. Since the majority of those who die by starvation are older women, concerns about coercion are natural. One factor that must be examined in reviewing cases of *santhara* for indications of coercion is the question of mental health. One must be in a healthy frame of mind to be eligible for the ritual fast. There is evidently a good deal of latitude in how Jain authorities interpret evidence of good mental health. In cases where people have been deemed eligible for *santhara*, gender is an important factor. Mental health is often understood in gendered ways. There is not much data on Jain conceptions of mental health, but studies suggest that in a closely related Indian religion, that of Buddhism, premodern texts tend to identify women as more passionate, more emotionally attached to people, and more prone to mental illness if their children or other members of their families die premature deaths. Indian Buddhist texts tend to see women as prone to going crazy from grief at loss of children, especially sons. Indian Buddhist texts also depict insanity as a common outcome for women who through the premature loss of husbands and family members are suddenly made independent when they were used to being part of a collective unit (Berkwitz, 2010). Although these prejudices about women's psyches are in need of examination, such cultural beliefs—if they do exist among contemporary Jain leaders—might actually protect Jain women from being coerced into fasting to death. That is, male leaders might discourage women from taking vows to fast to death because of the belief that women are prone to excessive emotional attachments that, when broken, are more likely to render them mentally ill compared to male counterparts.

As this essay has shown, the Jain community—not to mention the Indian nation—is divided in its views of the practice. Many younger Jains are dubious about it and wish that their religion were free of such controversial practices. Yet, the legal status of the action is not yet clear, and it remains to be seen how popular *santhara* will be in the coming years. Meanwhile, the controversy persists. This ancient practice will no longer go unnoticed in today's India.

REFERENCE

Berkwitz, S. (2010). Madness and gender in Buddhism. In A. M. Pires & L. Namorato (Eds.), *Images of Madness/Imagens da Loucura* (pp. 34–49). Bolivar, MI: From the Scholars Desk.

WORKING WITH THE DIFFICULT STUFF: MEDITATION AND BUDDHIST PERSPECTIVES FOR LIVING, AGING, AND DYING WELL

ADRIENNE CHANG

Has a friend ever advised you that the best way to deal with your problem is to "just let it go?" Did you wonder how, exactly, does one do that? Apart from some problems that may seemingly be buried or ignored, emotional and physical discomfort often arises unexpectedly, commanding our attention. Often, we try to rearrange our outside world to rectify the problem: make a change in our environment, our relationships, our material well-being, and our bodies. We discover, however, that some problems simply cannot be fixed.

UNDERSTANDING AND WORKING WITH SUFFERING

The first teaching of the Buddha in his Four Noble Truths is that within this human experience, there will be *dukkha* or suffering. *Dukkha* can be great or small, physical or emotional. It can range from simple discontentment or boredom, to stress or anxiety, to great pain or anguish (Chang, 2018). *Dukkha* can be found in universal human experiences such as illness, falling in love, growing old, and dying. The Buddha taught that *dukkha* arises from the suffering caused by change, known as impermanence. The law of impermanence states that everything is eventually subject to change. Nothing remains the same. *Dukkha* is felt when we try to hold on to things we cherish but lose over time (e.g., the death of a loved one or the loss of a friendship or marriage). *Dukkha* is also felt when we encounter something that we tried to keep at bay (such as disease or chronic illness). The passage of time brings change. As we age and move through time, we know this to be true.

That suffering of change is further augmented by our *rejection* of negative experiences, which is called the suffering of suffering. While some emotional or physical pain may be out of our control, how we choose to respond is within our control. When we lament our circumstances and ask, "Why me?" or when we continuously ruminate over problems or are aggressive toward ourselves or others because of our problems, this augments suffering. The third type of suffering is the recognition that our desire to hold on to pleasurable experiences is strangely at odds with the workings of the world around us, like the experience of the Greek god Sisyphus, eternally pushing a rock up a hill only to see it roll back down, condemned to pursue an aim that cannot be attained.

When we are able to see and respond to our emotional or physical pain in a healthy and compassionate way, the suffering of our suffering is reduced. That is, while we know we will encounter challenging experiences throughout the entirety of our lives, we have the power to choose how we will *relate* to our negative experiences.

MINDFULNESS MEDITATION

According to Buddhist thought, this push and pull quality of the mind—trying to grasp what we want, trying to push away what we do not want—perpetuates anxiety, stress, and restlessness, an endless cycle. The speed of modern life further burdens the mind. Therefore, many people seek to find moments in their everyday lives to restore mental clarity and peace. The growing appeal of meditation and mindfulness practices in Western society has allowed more individuals to skillfully work with their anxiety, emotional difficulties, and physical pain. Many mindfulness techniques derive from contemplative practices within the Buddhist tradition, practices that help the individual tune into personal experience and develop mental stability. It is not uncommon in many Western countries to find mindfulness practices offered in classrooms, hospitals, and the workplace as a means of working with stress to improve emotional well-being.

Scientific research continues to explore the effects of meditation. Mindfulness meditation practices are known to promote health and help alleviate suffering associated with physical, psychosomatic, and psychological distress (Grossman, Niemann, Schmidt, & Walach, 2004). Research has also begun to show the aging-related specific benefits that meditation practice can bring, not just for older adults but for all individuals as they age, including coping with chronic pain, promoting brain health, and slowing stress-related cellular aging (Epel, Daubenmier, Moskowitz, Folkman, & Blackburn, 2009; Gard, Hölzel, & Lazar, 2014).

What exactly happens during meditation? Normally, one is lost in a chain of thoughts, swinging from one thought to another to another, like a monkey swinging through the trees. As the Buddhist teaching says, beginning meditators must first learn to tame their monkey mind. Mindfulness is a practice for giving attention to what is happening in the present moment. Instead of grasping at every new thought swinging through the mind during meditation practice, the meditator learns to "let go" when lost within the stream of thought and return to the present experience. This technique for developing stability is to place the mind's attention on a sensory object, often the breath and the body. As the attention focuses on the body breathing, the mind learns to come to rest in the present moment. Learning to mindfully stabilize the attention in the present begins to slow the speediness and discursiveness of thoughts. A key feature here is to not want to get rid of thoughts, but to practice a radical "nondoing"—letting the mind settle, like a glass of muddy water clearing by itself when undisturbed.

As we become more aware of our external and internal worlds, we begin to see more clearly the mind's natural movement: sense perceptions, bodily sensations, thoughts, emotions, past memories, future plans, daydreams, and fantasies. We begin to see the rising and dissipation of these mental events: thoughts coming and going and negative emotions and positive emotions coming and going, like drifting clouds in the sky of the mind. Thinking never ceases, but our ability to see and become aware of our mental activities increases. Our awareness deepens. We become more fully present and attentive to our current situation.

Meditators discover how thoughts arise in the mind but remain within a nonjudgmental attitude toward whatever arises. Instead of struggling against everything, cultivating a nonjudgmental attitude allows more room for both the positive and the negative to happen, without selectively shutting out one or the other. We learn to lessen the constant self-evaluation and self-judgment of our experience. We become more attentive to our lives and the people around us. Over time, the meditator develops a deeper awareness of one's mental world, while at the same time developing a more accommodating attitude—a kinder, more compassionate, and gentler attitude—toward facing the difficult experiences of our lives.

WORKING WITH THE CHALLENGES OF AGING

Within the Buddhist tradition, old age, sickness, and death are not only seen as sources of suffering, but also as transformative sources of contemplative inquiry and wisdom. From the Buddhist view, the challenges of growing older, recognizing our finitude, and facing death, as terrifying as they first may seem, serve as poignant reminders of the preciousness of this human life and connect us to the power of our humanity.

As we are bombarded with explicit and implicit ageist messages from society, encouraging us to hide our aging, Buddhist teachings can provide meaningful ways to work with our fears about growing older and see life's transitions as part of a natural unfolding. Meditation practice invites one to gently sit with and recognize feelings of discomfort, uneasiness, and uncertainty, without the need to push them away. American Buddhist nun and author Pema Chödrön (2007) writes, "This willingness to stay open to what scares us weakens our habits of avoidance. It's the way that ego-clinging becomes ventilated and begins to fade" (p. 134). The Buddha taught that suffering is the result of grasping and fixating, particularly clinging to a very fixed, unchangeable notion of the self. As we age and see our bodies and worlds change, we can allow ourselves to be more open and less judgmental toward our experiences.

In addition to mindfulness practices that stabilize the mind, the Buddhist practitioner also may engage in guided contemplations, such as the Four Immeasurable Thoughts, that encourage the practitioner to actively generate attitudes of loving kindness, compassion, sympathetic joy, and equanimity toward both oneself and others. Buddhist practices such as mindfulness meditation or loving kindness contemplations can help us correct how we may be maladaptively relating to our suffering and engender more self-accepting attitudes toward our aging experience.

CARING FOR THE CAREGIVER

Meditation and contemplation help the individual to work not only with his or her own suffering but also when confronting another's suffering. Health care professionals and family caregivers regularly face their patients' or loved ones' pain, discomfort, and fear. Over time, such involvement with these negative emotions can take its toll. Mindfulness practices are becoming increasingly taught to health care professionals and caregivers to foster resiliency and decrease burnout and personal distress. Up to 60% of practicing physicians report symptoms of professional burnout, defined as emotional exhaustion, depersonalization (treating patients as objects), and a low sense of accomplishment (Krasner et al., 2009; Spickard, Gabbe, & Christensen, 2002). Physician burnout has been linked to poorer quality of care, such as increased medical errors, patient dissatisfaction, and decreased ability to express empathy (Shanafelt, Sloan, & Habermann, 2003). Studies show that mindfulness meditation practices integrated into physician well-being programs help physicians to more skillfully work with their own discomfort in witnessing others' suffering and help to lower rates of psychological stress in the practitioners (Beckman et al., 2012; Krasner et al., 2009). By teaching physicians to become more self-aware and attentive to the presence of stress, mindfulness practice helps lessen reactivity to challenging events (Epstein, 1999).

Beyond just professional caregivers, all of us have faced instances when we did not know how to respond appropriately to another's suffering. We may withhold compassion to another out of our own fear or insecurity. Buddhism teaches that paying attention to our own fears can help us feel compassion for others. The 14th Dalai Lama teaches:

> The more we care for the happiness of others, the greater our own sense of well-being becomes. Cultivating a close, warmhearted feeling for others automatically puts the mind at ease. This helps remove whatever

fears or insecurities we may have and gives us the strength to cope with any obstacles we encounter. It is the ultimate source of success in life. (Giles, 2012)

In Buddhist meditation, individuals are often taught the proper physical posture of sitting while meditating. Emphasized is a sense of a "strong back" and a "soft front," that is, to take a physical and symbolic posture that cultivates a "strong back" of equanimity and strength, balanced with the "soft front" of openheartedness and availability to others. Instead of resisting or avoiding the discomfort of difficult situations, developing mindful approaches to working with others encourages us to be more present to other people's suffering, to listen more attentively to their distress, and to act with more empathy and compassion.

REFERENCES

Beckman, H. B., Wendland, M., Mooney, C., Krasner, M. S., Quill, T. E., Suchman, A. L., & Epstein, R. M. (2012). The impact of a program in mindful communication on primary care physicians. *Academic Medicine, 87*(6), 815–819. doi:10.1097/ACM.0b013e318253d3b2

Chang, A. (2018). The gerontology of suffering and its social remediation: A Buddhist perspective. *Journal of Religion, Spirituality & Aging, 31*(4), 400–413. doi:10.1080/15528030.2018.1550733

Chödrön, P. (2007). *The places that scare you: A guide to fearlessness in difficult times.* Boston, MA: Shambhala Publications.

Epel, E., Daubenmier, J., Moskowitz, J. T., Folkman, S., & Blackburn, E. (2009). Can meditation slow rate of cellular aging? Cognitive stress, mindfulness, and telomeres. *Annals of the New York Academy of Sciences, 1172*(1), 34–53. doi:10.1111/j.1749-6632.2009.04414.x

Epstein, R. M. (1999). Mindful practice. *JAMA, 282*(9), 833–839. doi:10.1001/jama.282.9.833

Gard, T., Hölzel, B. K., & Lazar, S. W. (2014). The potential effects of meditation on age-related cognitive decline: A systematic review. *Annals of the New York Academy of Sciences, 1307*(1), 89–103. doi:10.1111/nyas.12348

Giles, C. (2012). Beyond the color line. In C. Giles & W. Miller (Eds.), *The arts of contemplative care: Pioneering voices in Buddhist chaplaincy and pastoral work* (pp. 41–52). Boston, MA: Wisdom Publications.

Grossman, P., Niemann, L., Schmidt, S., & Walach, H. (2004). Mindfulness-based stress reduction and health benefits: A meta-analysis. *Journal of Psychosomatic Research, 57*(1), 35–43. doi:10.1016/S0022-3999(03)00573-7

Krasner, M. S., Epstein, R. M., Beckman, H., Suchman, A. L., Chapman, B., Mooney, C. J., & Quill, T. E. (2009). Association of an educational program in mindful communication with burnout, empathy, and attitudes among primary care physicians. *JAMA, 302*(12), 1284–1293. doi:10.1001/jama.2009.1384

Shanafelt, T. D., Sloan, J. A., & Habermann, T. M. (2003). The well-being of physicians. *The American Journal of Medicine, 114*(6), 513–513. doi:10.1016/S0002-9343(03)00117-7

Spickard, Jr, A., Gabbe, S. G., & Christensen, J. F. (2002). Mid-career burnout in generalist and specialist physicians. *JAMA, 288*(12), 1447–1450. doi:10.1001/jama.288.12.1447

GLOBAL AGING AND GLOBAL LEADERSHIP

If a man takes no thought about what is distant, he will find sorrow near at hand.

—*Confucius*

INTRODUCTION

Several years ago, while considering this quote by Confucius, we read a short article in a satirical publication that poked fun at a universal human tendency (*The Onion*, 2017). You may already know about **ethnocentrism**, the firm belief that one's own culture is superior to all others and, in fact, may be the only "right" way to live. To ridicule such attitudes and beliefs as narrow, uninformed, and socially dysfunctional, the anonymous satirist claimed that a recent survey of over 100 countries found the people in those societies act strangely, dress in wild clothing, eat weird food, and live in ugly buildings. The writer concluded that, compared with us, people in those other countries generally behave in bizarre ways. By pretending to report those ideas as fact, the author actually was saying the opposite, echoing exactly what Confucius had said centuries before. People (or things) who are "distant" are **not** strange and unworthy of our consideration, and dismissing them as such is both ignorant and dangerous. We believe the lesson both writers had in mind for us—whether we are students, citizens, or nations—is that, if we want our plans for tomorrow to succeed, we should adopt the widest possible cultural view because, if we do not, we will regret it and experience sorrow "near at hand."

We have written this book to educate ourselves and our students about how aging is done in those "other countries"—their *ageways*—and to begin to think about, and plan for, the aging world to come and our part in it. We have tried not to make value judgments about any of the "irregular," "crazy," or "bizarre" ways the people in those countries live their lives, think about aging, treat their elders, or behave in late life. We firmly believe all of us can learn something from knowing how other people think and live, especially with respect to a stage of life some of us have yet to reach or certainly to master.

AGING LESSONS FROM ABROAD

Some readers may be quite knowledgeable about what we might call **local aging**—the shape and implications of the aging process for individuals and the impact of an aging population on the society in which they live (Whittington & Kunkel, 2013). If so, they know that aging per se is not scary or depressing although it can have those effects on some people. Many readers probably also know that the processes of aging—physical, psychological, social, cultural, and economic—are a complex web, a puzzle that can stimulate minds and capture attention in ways only the deepest, most fundamental human questions can. Where else but in the field of gerontology can one of the oldest mysteries of our species be addressed: Why do people get old and die? Where else but in gerontology or geriatrics can efforts be made to answer that question and its partner: What can I do about it?

This book focuses on aging as a global phenomenon and attempts to see how our local knowledge plays in Indonesia or Bolivia, to compare what we think we know about our own ageways with what can be learned about the thoughts of other cultures on the subject. At the most basic—and perhaps most obvious—level, our first insight is that *aging is not the same for everyone*; culture, politics, religion, and economic realities, among other factors, shape the internal biological process far more than might be thought. Despite the constraints of limited data about aging in many countries, our inability to access local sources, and the space limitations of this textbook, readers now should be aware of the endless variety of aging experiences in the world. It is hoped, too, that they are now a little more intrigued with that variety and the promise for learning about biology, culture, politics, and society that it offers.

A second major understanding that we hope has emerged from reading this book is that *the life course is a powerful force in all our lives*: what happens to us early in life, and through adulthood, is one of the key influences on how people age *and* how they experience later life. Children who are malnourished, poorly educated, or deprived of fundamental human needs such as security and affection will suffer the effects of those deprivations throughout their lives, and their old age is likely to bear the marks of those early limitations. Evidence of this fact is both plentiful and unequivocal, at least in Western, developed countries. We are just beginning to accumulate the data to show the applicability of the life-course perspective in many regions of the world, however, so we must still approach it as a powerful theory awaiting proof.

A third and final proposition that weaves through the text is: although aging can appear to play out quite differently in diverse people and societies, *all humans experience both body and life changes that are remarkably similar*—in the remotest reaches of the world, in deserts, jungles, urban slums, farmhouses, and castles. Age (or aging) works somewhat mysteriously through the cells and DNA to control human development, that is, what can be done at a given age and how people feel. It is closely related to mechanisms that control the bodily functions and the very life force. Age does not cause people to die, but in a very obvious way it is quite highly correlated with death in all populations in all parts of the world. Age affects also the brain and nervous system and, through them, the very core of individuals' beings, minds, and spirits. Age is also a powerful social timing device that determines when people are protected and when they are expected to fend for themselves; when they receive education and when they are considered to have completed it; and when (or if) they may marry, have children, vote, work, or stop working. The magic of age is that it is both ubiquitous and invisible. Some think about it to the point of obsession but also try (and usually succeed) to ignore it in their daily lives. It works its way so gradually into the bones and muscles and mind that we cannot see and feel it happening; we only experience the result. A common and plaintive late-life question is: When did I become old? The final happy, somewhat reassuring fact is that aging links us inextricably with every other human being; it really does give us all a common life experience that could form the basis for mutual understanding—if we focused on it.

GLOBAL AGING THEMES WORTH REMEMBERING

Throughout this book, we have mentioned several important truths about global aging that bear repeating here.

1. *The world is divided into developed and developing nations.* Development status is more than a simple rich–poor dichotomy. The differences between the haves and the striving to have are sometimes more complex and subtle than we can see, though economic resources are fundamental to this distinction. This obvious fact can escape memory at the worst times, such as when people wish to generalize about the effects on caregiving or retirement. Some things are generalizable, but it is well to remember that economic resources are but one key to health and well-being in late life. While all nations do not have a share in the same bounty as the developed world, all have the advantages of national pride and cultural resilience. In some cases, developing countries may have stronger family and community support systems than those more economically blessed.

2. *Globalization is continuing, and the gap between the haves and many of the have-nots is shrinking.* Through swift scientific and engineering advances in communication, transportation, and medicine, and through increased international migration, the people of the world are becoming less diverse and foreign to

each other. This trend is being fed by personal and population mobility and not a little by the economic interdependence on which the growing number of multinational corporations is dependent. For better or worse, mass popular culture (e.g., the movies, music, personalities, and lifestyles of Western, developed nations) is more accessible and valued throughout the world today than ever before and seems to be growing in popularity, even as the local competition in Latin America, Africa, India, China, South Korea, and Japan, to name a few, seems stronger. Five years ago, as the 8-year U.S. presidency of Barack Obama was nearing its end, some observers were even postulating that a broad, long-term political convergence—toward liberal democracy—was underway. In hindsight, it now seems clear that political convergence was merely a fantasy. What the coming five years will bring—politically or otherwise—remains as murky as ever.

3. *Human health is improving and longevity is increasing.* These facts have been true for some time now and have been demonstrated beyond question. This, in part, is a result of the growth and improvement of modern medical science and the triumph of public health practice. It is, of course, also due to the global dissemination of the principles of healthy lifestyle, which accounts for a substantial share of life expectancy improvements. Finally, our added years are partially due also to past scientific investment and the pursuit of discovery. Most people alive today have benefited from the health explorations and interventions of earlier centuries. Many would not, in fact, have been born if their grandmothers and grandfathers, and their parents also, had not been able to survive childbirth and childhood because scientists discovered the danger of germs and how to kill them and public health professionals so effectively preached the value of disease prevention. It is a provable fact: no grandmother, no you. But since your grandmother survived and lived so long, you now have a chance of beating her record.

We should keep in mind, however, both the limitations of Western medicine (acute care bias at the expense of chronic and palliative care) and the value of culturally appropriate care. As our Dutch colleague Dorly Deeg (personal communication, 2011) has suggested, however, "The question is not who has the best medical model, developed or developing nations, but how can a global society gain by integrating the best of both?"

4. *World and national populations are aging.* These changes are the result of effective population control and better health across the life span for more of the world's people. In turn, the aging of populations means that older people are becoming more visible and more available to all of us. Children are increasingly growing up with living grandparents and great-grandparents, and those relationships can be expected to alter markedly their views of old age. Any stereotypes they may hold of older people as decrepit and out of touch cannot survive a trip to a zoo or a football match with grandma and grandpa. And even family holiday gatherings are very different events when older members are there, mingling with the young and teaching them the family and community traditions.

5. *Public opinion is changing toward older people.* Certainly, ageism is still common in nearly all societies, but it may be—and can be expected to continue—declining as more realistic models of the old are available. This does not mean all aging people are healthy and happy—that would be a stereotype of a different sort. It just means that societies are beginning to see both possibilities for people in later life: health, financial security, and productivity as well as frailty, poverty, and institutionalization. This is beginning to be true (or at least more common) in many, many parts of the world.

6. *The family still is the core and most important social setting for aging.* One of the clear conclusions of the information presented in this book is that family life is necessary to our birth; it sustains and guides us as we mature; it is the cornerstone on which our adult lives are built; and it is our shelter and emotional center in old age. This is true to some extent in nearly all cultures and probably will continue to be. A related core truth is that care of the older population is largely a family affair. Without both nuclear and extended family support—financial, personal, and emotional—old age in any society would be a bleak prospect, indeed.

   Likewise, the tension between independence (autonomy) and family or community control of one's choices in late life remains in all cultures. We offer no predictions, however, on how the balance between these values may change as population aging becomes a larger reality in more countries. Some trends do suggest, however, that the developing world is beginning to mimic the wealthier nations as their families become smaller, more of their women work outside the home, and their governments are forced to take on a greater role in elder care. Yet, established culture dies hard; the value of family care—and family control—will not go away simply because the children (or child) work(s) long hours in a factory or lives far away from the parents. In fact, the burden of government bureaucracy discourages many older people from applying for direct government cash that would increase their ability to choose and pay for their own formal care. They seem to prefer to rely on their families, where fewer choices are available.

7. *Work and productivity are universal human values.* All but the super-rich must work to live, and even many of them continue working far beyond their actual need. Humans seem either genetically or culturally wired to want to produce things, whether products, food, services, ideas, or art. The creative push is both universal and powerful, and it does not seem to diminish much in old age—unless the culture works hard to extinguish it by fostering the stereotype of old age as a time of rest and leisure—and insisting older people conform. That desire to work, to be productive, is probably a good thing, since most of us are required to do it anyway. People might be better off if they would live to work, rather than if they merely work to live. In fact, older people probably are going to be encouraged to work longer, both to reduce pressure on public pension systems and to continue contributing their experience and knowledge to the workforce.

8. *And yet, retirement is becoming more common, even in developing countries.* Despite their apparent need to work, people seem also to have a need for leisure and fun. Once the idea of retirement as a normal life stage becomes culturally accepted, most people seem to adapt to it and even look forward to it. But the habits of a lifetime, rising early to produce something valuable and socially important, can interfere with that adjustment, and the need to be useful sometimes reasserts itself after retirement.

9. *Older adults are becoming more involved in community affairs.* As postretirement health is extended, a growing number of older people seek outlets for their productive urge in community organizations and volunteer efforts. Age Demands Action (ADA) is a perfect example of such a volunteer advocacy group. At least in the United States and many Western nations, tasks that formerly might have been performed by nonworking women (i.e., housewives whose children were in school) are increasingly falling to retirees as younger women have entered the workforce. School and library volunteers, fundraisers for charities, and political activists are all likely to be well above age 60 these days. Some social clubs that formerly depended on older women for membership (e.g., Daughters of the American Revolution, garden clubs) are finding their rolls dwindling as older women move into more socially engaged volunteer roles.

10. *Most national governments—even those of developing countries—are beginning to recognize their growing senior population and enact policies to support them.* Such policies represent a major accomplishment for both advocates and governments. Still, the developed nations are far ahead of the rest of the world due to their greater economic resources. But even a poor country like Kenya recently has established an old-age pension for their older citizens. Still quite small and inadequate to live on, these payments represent a commitment and a down payment on the intergenerational debt that is owed to all our parents and their generation. As nations modernize and populations are exposed to the ways of other richer countries, expectations begin to rise and, with them, demands that government step in where families—too busy working or simply nonexistent—are unable to provide the traditional support.

11. *Older people are actively driving much of the global social change.* In country after country, including many less developed ones, older people are discovering a new, more assertive social (and political) role for themselves. In some cases, the urge for meaningful use of free time leads them into advocacy for themselves and other seniors (e.g., ADA, described earlier). This certainly has been true in the United States, with the rise of AARP (the age-based organization formerly known as the American Association of Retired Persons). With about 38 million members among the age 50-and-older

population, their advocacy messages certainly reach a sizable audience and probably influence them on important policy issues affecting seniors in the United States, such as Social Security, Medicare, and the way health care is delivered and paid for. Many seniors find advocacy for the older population, whether through AARP or otherwise, to be a particularly satisfying way to remain socially active.

12. *A global aging science is emerging, along with a global network of caring professions.* We have called this a "virtual scientific network" because it is largely populated by professionals who do not know each other personally and may never actually meet (Whittington & Kunkel, 2013). This network is emerging through its members' research and its publication in scholarly journals and books that now need not wait to be shipped abroad but can be accessed electronically, purchased, and downloaded to a computer. The globalization of modernity is creating unanticipated marvels of scientific understanding in all parts of the educated world, and that definitely includes the lone scientist working in poor conditions with inadequate tools and support, far from the nearest hospital or modern university. With Internet access—admittedly not yet a universal reality—both Nobel Prize winners and unknown scholars can communicate at the cutting edge of their virtual intellectual community and, if not literally together, can work in concert toward the same solution to a common human problem.

    We are also seeing the emergence of a global, mobile workforce of professional caregivers who will leave their home countries, where few jobs are available and the population so far has not aged into dependence, for better-paid elder care work abroad. Noriko Tsukada (2019) has studied the migration of foreign guest workers to Japan to do the bed and body work of caring for the rapidly aging Japanese society and how those immigrant workers are changing the very culture that must employ them.

13. *In difference is possibility.* As we argued in the introduction to this chapter, much about aging is universal; in many ways, older people are probably more alike than different. Yet cultural differences persist, and we do well to note and study them. However, if our ethnocentrism gets in the way and stereotyping convinces us we know how the stranger thinks and lives, valuable avenues of learning are closed off. We cannot learn what we already think we know. What possibilities await global inquiry? What local solutions are to be found far from home? We can only imagine the answers that may be offered us if we attend to global differences and ask global questions. As we have argued in another forum, "The more we learn about both the global variations and global similarities in ageways—weaknesses and strengths, productivity and waste, elder wisdom and elder despair—the greater will be our chance of aging well" (Whittington & Kunkel, 2013).

GLOBAL EFFORTS AND INTERVENTIONS

Beyond the concerted local efforts of many groups at the community and national levels, a number of international efforts have formed to study, meet, and deliberate about how to build understandings and policies on behalf of the world's older population. Most visible and effective among these are the United Nations (UN) World Health Organization (WHO), the UN World Assembly on Aging, and a London-based nongovernmental organization (NGO), HelpAge International. Sometimes the work of these groups deals generally with beliefs and stereotypes about aging and with the general status of older people; at other times, the focus is on a particular issue or problem limiting the health or welfare of older people globally, such as poverty, disease, or elder abuse.

The Vienna World Assembly

The first such effort, nearly 40 years ago, was a global conference called the World Assembly on Aging held under the auspices of the United Nations in Vienna in 1982. It brought together national government representatives, advocates, researchers, university professors, and older people from around the world. The agenda that emerged from the Vienna World Assembly underscores a theme that ripples through this book: interdependency (UN, 1983). For example, we have emphasized the centrality of family life, especially as we grow older, but we also have tried to make clear that neither individuals nor families can operate in isolation. Just as each individual is embedded in a family, each family is embedded in a community, and communities organize themselves in many ways to provide care for older citizens when it is needed. The Vienna assembly was also important because it was the first step toward global dissemination of important new ideas about aging, and it gave the participants, many of whom had been isolated individual advocates and groups working on behalf of older people, a huge boost in both credibility and confidence as they gained a worldwide network of like-minded colleagues.

The Madrid Plan

Twenty years after the Vienna Assembly, the United Nations convened a Second World Assembly on Aging in 2002. Delegates from more than 160 governments and intergovernmental and nongovernmental organizations came together in Madrid to develop a new plan to respond to the opportunities and challenges presented by global aging in the 21st century (UN Economic and Social Commission on Asia and the Pacific, 2019). Showing how our understanding of aging was evolving and maturing, one principle embraced by those delegates was universal human rights—the notion that adults throughout the world must have the opportunity to age with dignity and security and be accorded all human rights and fundamental freedoms. This was the first time that many governments had publicly supported the idea of linking aging and human rights. The resulting *Political Declaration and Madrid International Plan of Action on Ageing*—subsequently adopted by the United Nations and often called simply the Madrid Plan or MIPAA—is a comprehensive road map calling for changes in attitudes, policies, and practices to ensure that older adults of all nations are active participants in society (UN Economic and Social Commission for Asia and the Pacific, 2019). The ultimate goal was to create a "society for all ages" with the broad aim to "ensure that people everywhere are able to age with security and dignity and to continue to participate in their societies as citizens with full rights" (UN Economic and Social Commission for Asia and the Pacific, 2019, paragraph 10).

The Madrid Plan provides a blueprint for how governments, the international community, and civil society can create a society for all ages by focusing on three priority areas: (a) older persons and development, (b) advancing health and well-being into old age, and (c) ensuring enabling and supportive environments. Across the three major priority areas, the blueprint identifies 18 areas of concern or issues for older adults (see Table 13.1) and makes 239 specific recommendations (UN Economic and Social Commission for Asia and the Pacific, 2019).

The ultimate goal of MIPAA was to ensure the full rights of older people to participate in society with security and dignity. Anyone familiar with human rights in general might question why we even needed the Madrid Plan. After all, the **Universal Declaration of Human Rights** (UDHR), which was adopted by the UN General Assembly in 1948, proclaims: "All human beings are born free and equal in dignity and rights" (article 1). Further:

> Everyone is entitled to all the rights and freedoms set forth in this Declaration, without distinction of any kind, such as race, colour, sex, language, religion, political or other opinion, national or social origin, property, birth or other status. Furthermore, no distinction shall be made on the basis of the political, jurisdictional or international status of the country or territory to which a person belongs, whether it be independent, trust, non-self-governing or under any other limitation of sovereignty. (United Nations General Assembly, 1948, article 2)

Is this not enough to protect older adults? Unfortunately, it is not. Despite its assurances, the UDHR does not specify older people as a protected category; furthermore, the declaration is characterized as "soft" international law, which means that, although it is aspired to, it is not legally binding on any nation. Nonetheless, in the years since the UDHR was adopted, it generally has become customary law (i.e., widely accepted norms and practices that eventually are considered legally binding; Fredvang & Biggs, 2012).

The Madrid Plan, therefore, specifically addresses human rights for older adults. Since adopting the plan, the UN General Assembly has passed resolutions on multiple occasions to reaffirm the plan (UN General Assembly, 2013). In 2009,

TABLE 13.1 Priority Directions and Issues Identified in the International Plan for Action on Aging

Older Persons and Development
Issue 1: Active participation in society and development (2 objectives, 13 actions)
Issue 2: Work and the aging labor force (1 objective, 14 actions)
Issue 3: Rural development, migration, and urbanization (3 objectives, 20 actions)
Issue 4: Access to knowledge, education, and training (2 objectives, 14 actions)
Issue 5: Intergenerational solidarity (1 objective, 7 actions)
Issue 6: Eradication of poverty (1 objective, 8 actions)
Issue 7: Income security, social protection/social security, and poverty prevention (2 objectives, 13 actions)
Issue 8: Emergency situations (2 objectives, 18 actions)

Advancing Health and Well-Being Into Old Age
Issue 1: Health promotion and well-being throughout life (3 objectives, 27 actions)
Issue 2: Universal and equal access to health care services (4 objectives, 22 actions)
Issue 3: Older persons with HIV/AIDS (3 objectives, 9 actions)
Issue 4: Training of care providers and health professionals (1 objective, 3 actions)
Issue 5: Mental health needs of older persons (1 objective, 10 actions)
Issue 6: Older persons and disabilities (1 objective, 10 actions)

Ensuring Enabling and Supportive Environments
Issue 1: Housing and the living environment (3 objectives, 17 actions)
Issue 2: Care and support for caregivers (2 objectives, 14 actions)
Issue 3: Neglect, abuse, and violence (2 objectives, 12 actions)
Issue 4: Images of aging (1 objective, 8 actions)

Source: From United Nations Economic and Social Commission for Asia and the Pacific. (2019). *Political declaration and Madrid international plan of action on ageing.* New York, NY: United Nations. Retrieved from https://www.un.org/development/desa/ageing/madrid-plan-of-action-and-its-implementation.html

the Committee on Economic, Social, and Cultural Rights, an independent group of experts who monitor certain United Nations activities,

> ... highlighted the need to address discrimination against unemployed older persons in finding work, or accessing professional training or retraining, and against older persons living in poverty with unequal access to universal old-age pensions due to their place of residence. (UN Economic and Social Council, 2009, p. 8)

In 2010, United Nations resolution 65/182 established the Open-Ended Working Group on Ageing to advance the principles of the Madrid Plan, "encouraging Governments to mainstream ageing issues into poverty eradication strategies and national development plans. States should reaffirm the role of United Nations focal points on ageing, enhance technical cooperation and expand regional commissions' role on such matters" (UN General Assembly, 2011).

These ongoing endorsements of the Madrid Plan are necessary because large numbers of older adults throughout the world " ... face challenges such as discrimination, poverty and abuse that severely restrict their contribution to society" (Fredvang & Biggs, 2012, p. 5). But this situation appears to be changing. Focus groups with older people who reside in rural and urban areas in 37 countries reveal that older persons' relationships with both their families and communities are characterized by reciprocity or interdependency. Families and communities provide for their older members. But, in turn, many older adults also support themselves, their families, and their communities. Much of this work is done through organized groups of older persons, and their efforts result in economic and social benefits, increased respect from their families and communities, and increasing political power (UN Population Fund & HelpAge International, 2012).

Update of the Madrid Plan

Ten years after the adoption of the Madrid Plan in 2002, the UN Population Fund, in partnership with the NGO HelpAge International (2012), published *Aging in the Twenty-First Century: A Celebration and a Challenge.* This report gave a contemporary snapshot of aging and documented progress that nations had made in implementing and monitoring the Madrid Plan. To summarize, many examples were cited of innovative and successful programs that had been initiated as a result of the Madrid Assembly to address the needs and concerns of older people. It was clear that important progress had been made. However, the report also identified many remaining gaps requiring new policies to improve older people's income, health, safety, security, political rights, and freedom from discrimination. The overriding concern that remained was rapid population aging and how that trend was swiftly changing the political and economic landscape for all other concerns. Perhaps the most instructive contribution of the 21st-century report was its formal statement of the way forward, accompanied by 10 priority actions to maximize the opportunity of aging populations. **These are summarized in Box 13.1.**

We take special notice and commend your attention to recommendation #2, wherein autonomy and independence of older persons are supported as natural products of their economic security. In our view, these values are key elements of the quality of life of all persons, not just the old, and it is reassuring for the United Nations to endorse them so prominently.

Upstream

A story is told among public health professionals of a person walking alongside a deep and swiftly flowing river, when an obviously drowning man is seen being swept along in the current. The person on the riverbank immediately jumps in the water, swims out to the

BOX 13.1

Ten Priority Actions to Maximize the Opportunity of Aging Populations

1. Recognize the inevitability of population aging and the need to adequately prepare all stakeholders (governments, civil society, private sector, communities, and families) for the growing numbers of older persons. This should be done by enhancing understanding, strengthening local capacities, and developing reforms needed to adapt to an aging world.

2. Ensure that all older persons can live with dignity and security, enjoying access to essential health and social services and a minimum income through the implementation of national social protection floors and other social investments that extend the autonomy and independence of older people, prevent impoverishment, and contribute to a more healthy aging.

3. Support communities and families to develop support systems, which ensure that frail older persons receive the long-term care they need and promote active and healthy aging at the local level to facilitate aging in place.

4. Invest in young people by promoting healthy habits and ensuring education and employment opportunities, access to health services, and social service coverage for all workers as the best way to improve the lives of future generations of older persons.

5. Support international and national efforts to develop comparative research on aging and ensure that gender- and culture-sensitive data from this research are available to inform policy making.

6. Mainstream aging into all gender policies and gender into aging policies, taking into account the specific requirements of older women and men.

7. Ensure inclusion of aging and the needs of older persons in all national development policies and programs.

8. Ensure inclusion of aging and the needs of older persons in national humanitarian response, climate change mitigation and adaptation plans, and disaster management and preparedness programs.

9. Ensure that aging issues are adequately reflected in the post-2015 development agenda, including through the development of specific goals and indicators.

10. Develop a new rights-based culture of aging and a new mind-set toward aging and older persons from welfare recipients to active, contributing members of society.

Source: From United Nations Population Fund & HelpAge International. (2012). *Ageing in the twenty-first century: A celebration and a challenge.* New York, NY: Author. Retrieved from http://www.helpage.org/resources/ageing-in-the-21st-century-a-celebration-and-a-challenge

drowning man, supports him and swims with him back to the shore, drags him up on the bank, and begins to administer CPR. Before the hero can proceed, however, another drowning person yells out for help as she also is being carried down the river to what looks like certain death. Again, the hero dives into the raging water, swims into the current, reaches the desperate woman, places her in a lifesaving hold, and swims back to shore, again saving her life. As she is regaining her senses, the hero hears yet another person, apparently a child, struggling to stay afloat in the swollen river and yelling for help. As the lifesaving hero makes ready to dive in for the third time, a stranger standing nearby on the bank remarks, "Why do you struggle to save every drowning person who floats by? Would it not make more sense to go upstream and find out why they are entering the river and put a stop to that?"

The story obviously is meant to illustrate the value of prevention as more efficient than treatment. Prevention is most obviously preferred in health care, where immunization against a disease, for example, is conceded to be a far better (and cheaper) choice than treatment after it strikes. But prevention is also applicable in the case of social problems. Many of the ills that older people face—discrimination in the workplace, neglect or abuse by family members or other caregivers, poor quality health care, political neglect, or simply social disrespect—can be traced to the root cause of **ageism**, often defined as age stereotyping, prejudice, and discrimination. Among the many other global efforts to address the results of a difficult old age, the campaign of the WHO to combat ageism stands out (Officer & de la Fuente-Nunez, 2018). In 2016, the WHO announced it would embark on a long-term effort to establish the extent of aging, to measure it, and to mount a communications campaign to change the image of older people and improve their standing in their communities. Motivated by the understanding that children as young as 4 years old know their culture's age stereotypes, the WHO surveyed over 83,000 people in 57 countries to measure age stereotypes and attitudes to create an evidence base from which to develop effective interventions. Officer and de la Fuente-Nunez (2018, p. 300) report that the WHO is motivated by the vision of nothing less than "a world for all ages" and the ultimate goal to "change the way we think, feel, and act towards age and ageing." Upstream, indeed.

Nongovernmental Organizations

Worldwide, one of the most important community resources supporting older adults and their families is **NGOs**, defined as:

> ... any nonprofit, voluntary citizens' group that is organized on a local, national, or international level to address issues in support of the public good. Task-oriented and driven by people with a common interest, NGOs perform a variety of service and humanitarian functions, bring citizen concerns to governments, advocate and monitor policies, and encourage political participation through provision of information. Some are organized around specific issues, such as human rights, environment, or health. They provide analysis and expertise, serve as early-warning mechanisms, and help monitor and implement international agreements. (UN, n.d.)

NGOs "have become major international players in developing and implementing policies related to the environment, women's rights, and poverty. ... [An important question is] whether civil society organizations, including NGOs, might meaning-fully supplement the family and the state in addressing the needs of growing older populations" (Angel, 2011, p. 557).

NGOs educate older people about their human rights and entitlements and lobby policy makers and service providers for improvements. Working individu-ally and with governmental agencies, NGOs provide education, counseling, and assistance to caregivers in countries with high rates of HIV/AIDS, fight against family violence and especially abuse of older persons, and develop disaster-response strategies that address the specific vulnerabilities of older adults (UN Population Fund & HelpAge International, 2012).

Well-known NGOs with a global mission include the Red Cross, Doctors Without Borders, the United Nations Children's Fund (UNICEF), Oxfam, CARE, and Save the Children. One of the most respected international NGOs working on behalf of older persons is **HelpAge International**. HelpAge was founded in 1983 when five organizations in Canada, Colombia, Kenya, India, and the United Kingdom came together to create a network to support older adults worldwide. Today, through its main office in London and seven regional development cen-ters, HelpAge works in 80 countries and has 140 organizational affiliates across all continents. The mission of HelpAge International

> is to promote the wellbeing and inclusion of older women and men,
> and reduce poverty and discrimination in later life. We work with
> older women and men in low and middle-income countries for better
> services and policies, and for changes in the behaviours and attitudes of
> individuals and societies toward old age. (HelpAge International, 2019)

Among HelpAge International's many activities is ADA, which began in 2007 as a worldwide "grassroots campaign to fight age discrimination and com-bat the perception that older people are not important" (HelpAge International, 2019). Currently, over 290,000 citizens in 60 countries participate in ADA's cam-paign activities, which take place throughout the year, but October 1 is the UN International Day of Older People and a key date for the campaign. On this day, activists of all ages across the world march and lobby their governments on issues affecting older people, such as pensions, health care, and housing. As their fellow citizens see the excitement and accomplishment when older people themselves band together, demonstrating and advocating in their own interest, the stereotype of nursing homes and welfare programs is badly shaken (HelpAge International, 2019).

HelpAge not only works on behalf of older adults; they also work *with* older adults who possess local knowledge that benefits their communities. For example, to identify impending local weather patterns, one international NGO enlists and relies on indigenous Bolivian seniors' observations of the nest-building patterns of birds in the lowlands and on older Kenyans' observation of patterns of the sun, moon, and trees (HelpAge International, 2009). The areas of expertise of some older persons extend beyond what might be considered folk knowledge. A quote by a resident of rural Ethiopia highlights the important role of older adults in their communities: "Socially, older people play leading roles at the community level and are a bridge between the government, NGOs, and the community in all necessary aspects, political and social, and in realizing development interventions" (UN Population Fund & HelpAge International, 2012, p. 142).

BECOMING A GLOBAL LEADER

We conclude this book with a simple suggestion. If thinking globally appeals to you, and if you imagine some form of global work may be in your future, why not aspire to a leadership role? Despite the seeming rush of individuals and organizations to become "global," few will follow through and fewer still will truly succeed. We commend to you these following thoughts about how to become a global leader.

Ángel Cabrera, who formerly was the president of George Mason University but recently moved to Atlanta to become the president of Georgia Institute of Technology ("Georgia Tech"), has studied closely the process of globalization as well as global organizations and the personal characteristics it takes to manage them well. He and his coauthor, Gregory Unruh, have summarized their theories in a fine book, *Being Global: How to Think, Act, and Lead in a Transformed World* (Cabrera & Unruh, 2012). Their views are contained in two broad conclusions: (a) on balance, globalization is good; and (b) a certain type of leader is needed to make globalization work better.

Certainly, they argue, globalization has some negative consequences. Among them are pandemic diseases, terrorism, long-range war and nuclear threats, and the international trade in drugs, guns, and human beings (so-called human trafficking, which is another term for slavery). Scientific advances, modern transportation systems, nearly instantaneous communication, and the global marketplace all have permitted and supported these scourges on all our societies. These activities must be inhibited and their tragic impact limited.

However, globalization is fundamentally about freedom, suggest Cabrera and Unruh—the freedom to travel, to associate, to communicate, to buy and sell, and to learn. They are vastly more optimistic about the positive consequences of opening global markets and new cultural exchanges than they are worried about the negative side of the shift. But they also posit that certain qualities are necessary for leaders to function productively in a global environment. First, they say, leaders must have a *global mind-set*. This means that individuals should value the world outside their own narrow slices of it. Tribal forces—those that command loyalty and obedience only to one's own racial, ethnic, or national group—tend to inhibit and counter globalization. Ethnocentrism (the belief that one's own culture is best) is the enemy of globalization. They admit that suspending judgment of outsiders and learning to tolerate the ambiguity that accompanies any confrontation with difference is hard. They speak of some people having the cognitive architecture to handle it, implying that others may not. The goal of the global mind-set is connection with the rest of the world—its people, its places, and its ways of living. They observe that globally minded people possess a desire for knowledge of the things of the world, the achievement of which increases their intellectual capital. They also believe that persons with a global mind-set are likely to accumulate many friends and contacts around the world, establishing for themselves a global social network, constituting a sort of social capital. Neither intellectual nor social capital is a new concept, but they are handy tools to help us think about what it takes to become a global leader. But, of course, having a global mind-set is not enough if it is not used.

Thus, the second major trait of an effective global leader is *global entrepreneurship*, the ability to see possibilities, make connections, and make things happen. Global entrepreneurship is similar to the local, economic kind, except it is not limited to starting a business and making money. It can encompass almost any endeavor, from working on the ground as a Peace Corps volunteer, to creating or expanding an international nonprofit organization, to studying in another country with a goal of learning a better way of solving problems than one's fellow citizens have devised at home. It may be shocking to realize that the way Americans think about aging, provide for elder care, and utilize their abilities to solve other social problems leaves much to be desired. *Social entrepreneurship* across national borders is in its infancy, especially in the field of aging; but it is on the cutting edge of all that is modern and exciting and *cool*.

But even more *cool* is what Cabrera and Unruh suggest as the third, quite essential, item in the global leader's tool kit: *global citizenship*, which they define as the understanding that all people and all nations are connected and that what is good for one is good for all—and the actions that flow from that understanding. That is, what is good for older Latvians and the caregiving children of aging Kenyans is good also for our older citizens—and for us. They invite a Buddhist way of thinking about social relations and how to live one's life, which, finally, suggests that it is rational to show compassion because it will benefit you and those close to you. Global citizenship, then, is the highly desirable, ultimate expression of global thinking and global entrepreneurship. It is a value-laden approach to global issues, global problems, and globalization itself. These three characteristics of a global person, if it can be called that, will prepare any of us to become effective leaders in an increasingly globalized world.

Returning to the questions we posed at the beginning of this chapter: Why do people get old and die? And what can I do about it? We suggested that gerontology and geriatrics are perfect fields in which to explore the existential mysteries of the life course and, as this book has made clear, how aging is embedded in every society, every community, every family, and every person in the world—including you. Can you imagine a more fundamental or universal or worthwhile set of problems to devote one's life to? ... Just a thought.

DISCUSSION QUESTIONS

1. How relevant is knowledge of local aging in your country to an understanding of global aging?

2. Would you say the countries of the world are becoming more alike or more different with respect to aging?

3. How could the concept of upstream be applied to improving the conditions under which older people live around the world?

4. What could you do now to prepare to become a global leader?

KEY WORDS

Age Demands Action
Ethnocentrism
Global citizenship
Global entrepreneurship
Global mind-set

HelpAge International
Local aging
Nongovernmental organization (NGO)
Universal Declaration of Human Rights

REFERENCES

Angel, R. (2011). Civil society and elder care in posttraditional society. In R. Settersten & J. Angel (Eds.), *Handbook of sociology of aging* (pp. 549–562). New York, NY: Springer Publishing Company.

Cabrera, A., & Unruh, G. (2012). *Being global: How to think, act, and lead in a transformed world*. Cambridge, MA: Harvard Business Review Press.

Deeg, D. (2011). Personal communication.

Fredvang, M., & Biggs, S. (2012). The rights of older persons: Protection and gaps under human rights law. *Social Policy Working Papers, 16*, 1–21.

HelpAge International. (2009). *Witness to climate change: Learning from older people's experience*. London, England: Author. Retrieved from https://www.helpage.org/newsroom/latest-news/older-people-witness-to-climate-change

HelpAge International. (2019). Age demands action. Retrieved from https://www.helpage.org/get-involved/campaign-with-us/ada-global

Officer, A., & de la Fuente-Nunez, V. (2018). A global campaign to combat ageism. *Bulletin of the World Health Organization, 96*(4), 295–296.

The Onion. (2017). Study: Other countries weird. Retrieved from https://www.theonion.com/study-other-countries-weird-1819580226

Tsukada, N. (2019). The need for foreign long-term care workers in Japan. In F. J. Whittington, S. R. Kunkel, & K. de Medeiros (Eds.), *Global aging: Comparative perspectives on aging and the life course*. New York, NY: Springer Publishing Company.

United Nations. (1948). *The universal declaration of human rights*. New York, NY: Author. Retrieved from www.un.org/en/universal-declaration-human-rights/index.html

United Nations. (1983). *Vienna international plan of action on ageing*. New York, NY: Author.

United Nations. (n.d.). *Definition of NGOs*. Retrieved from http://www.ngo.org/ngoinfo/define.html

United Nations Economic and Social Commission for Asia and the Pacific. (2019). *Political declaration and Madrid international plan of action on ageing*. New York, NY: United Nations. Retrieved from https://www.un.org/development/desa/ageing/madrid-plan-of-action-and-its-implementation.html

United Nations Economic and Social Council. (2009). *Committee on Economic, Social and Cultural Rights, forty-second session, Geneva, 4-22 May, 2009. Agenda item 3*, General Comment No. 20.GE 09-43405 E 090709. Retrieved from http://idsn.org/fileadmin/user_folder/pdf/New_files/UN/CESCR _GR20.pdf

United Nations General Assembly. (2011). Resolution adopted on 21 December 2010. Retrieved from https://undocs.org/en/A/RES/65/182

United Nations General Assembly. (2013). *A/RES/67/143.* 67th Session Agenda Item 27 c. February 21, 2013. Retrieved from http://www.un.org/en/ga/67/resolutions.shtml

United Nations Population Fund & HelpAge International. (2012). *Ageing in the twenty-first century: A celebration and a challenge.* New York, NY: Author. Retrieved from http://www.helpage.org/ resources/ageing-in-the-21st-century-a-celebration-and-a-challenge

Whittington, F. J., & Kunkel, S. R. (2013). Think globally, act locally: The maturing of a worldwide science and practice of aging. *Generations, 37*, 6–11.

POPULATION AGING AND VOLUNTARISM IN ROMANIA*

STEPHEN J. CUTLER | TATIANA COJOCARI

Romania has a population of some 20 million persons and a total land area of just over 92,000 square miles—a little larger than the country of Laos or the U.S. state of Michigan, and a little smaller than the nation of Ghana or the U.S. state of Minnesota. Bordered in southeastern Europe by Bulgaria, Serbia, the Black Sea, Ukraine, and Moldova, Romania is a beautiful country, but one beset by many problems. In this essay, we look at one set of challenges faced by Romania (as well as by many of its European neighbors and, indeed, by many other nations throughout the world). We focus on population aging, and we look at implications of this dramatic demographic change for voluntarism. The essay is divided into three parts: (a) we spell out some of the demographic changes currently underway in Romania; (b) we describe the extent to which voluntarism is prevalent in Romania; and (c) we suggest reasons why voluntarism is and has been such a minor part of Romanian life.

THE PERFECT DEMOGRAPHIC STORM

Declining birth rates and increasing death rates have characterized Romanian demography since at least 1990, and these trends are expected to continue into the foreseeable future. The discrepancy between the two—the rate of natural growth—has been showing an increasingly negative figure. In addition, life expectancy at birth has been steadily increasing, from 70 in 1992 to nearly 76 in 2018. Students

*This is an abbreviated, updated, and revised version of an article by Stephen J. Cutler ("Population Ageing and Volunteering in Romania") that originally appeared in *Social Work Review*, *14*, 2015, 5–18.

familiar with demography will know that a third important influence on age structure is migration. It turns out that Romania has seen an excess of out-migration over in-migration, principally in the young adult years and among middle-aged persons.

Taking all of these phenomena together, it is not surprising that Romania is undergoing a period of dramatic population aging. Unless major changes occur in one or more of these prime demographic movers, the median age of the Romanian population (about age 41 currently) will continue to rise, to over 51 years by 2050, just over 30 years from now, and the proportion of the population aged 60 and above (about 23% in 2018) is estimated to be about 40% by 2050. If we focus on the percentage of the population aged 65 and older, the percentage is smaller (31.3%) but still close to a third. Think of a society where just about every third person is aged 65 and above.

These trends are undeniable and underscore the overarching reality already mentioned: although our focus is on Romania, similar conclusions about population aging can be made for many other nations in the world. That is, population aging is a worldwide phenomenon.

VOLUNTARISM IN ROMANIA NOW AND IN THE FUTURE

Voluntarism is "the full range of optional, discretionary activities in which people engage to attain some desired end, for themselves or others, generally through or for an organization" (Cutler, 2015, p. 7). Why do we focus on voluntarism? An increasing truism in the social sciences is that voluntarism is good: It is good for the recipients of volunteer services, it is good for the volunteers, and it is good for the society as a whole. For instance, research has demonstrated time and time again that volunteers have higher levels of well-being (however measured) than their nonvolunteering counterparts (Carr, 2018). The social and psychological benefits of volunteering are so clear that one writer has suggested that volunteering should be considered as an "instrument of health policy" (Stula, 2012, p. 84). And study after study has shown that the overall economic contribution of volunteers to society is substantial (Cutler, Hendricks, & O'Neill, 2011).

Despite the fact that voluntarism is clearly beneficial, in Romania the level of volunteering is much lower than in most European Union (EU) countries. National studies indicate that between 10% and 20% of all Romanian adults volunteer (VOLUM, 2011). In 2016, data from a European Quality of Life Survey on all adults 18 years of age and older put the percentage of Romanians who ever participate in voluntary associations at 17.1%, following only Bulgaria and Hungary. But rates of volunteering among the older population in Romania are even lower. Based on data from the 2016 European Quality of Life Survey, the lowest level of participation among older residents of the EU28 countries is seen in Romania, where only 7.6% of elders ever participate in any type of voluntary association.

Corroborating evidence of a different sort comes from a 2011 Eurobarometer survey in which persons from the EU28 countries were asked to evaluate the contributions of older persons to society as volunteers. Specifically, respondents were asked, "There are many different ways in which people can contribute to society. To what extent do you think people in (OUR COUNTRY) aged 55 and above contribute in the following areas?" When asked about their contributions as volunteers, 25% of older Romanians indicated that persons aged 55 and above did not contribute at all, and another 42% said that older Romanians contributed only a little as volunteers. Compared with older respondents in other EU28 countries, Romania's 25% places it highest among its peer countries in terms of the percentage of older Romanians believing that their age peers did not contribute at all to society as volunteers. Clearly, older Romanians are volunteering to a lesser degree than their EU28 counterparts, and older Romanians are seen—probably correctly—by other older Romanians as not making important societal contributions via their volunteering roles.

We should note that, compared with their older peers, younger Romanians have higher levels of education, are wealthier, are in better health, and are more likely to live in urban areas such as Bucharest. Education, income, health, and residence in urban areas are among the variables that are closely associated with voluntary association participation (Musick & Wilson, 2008). In the future, then, we should expect to see these compositional factors exerting a positive influence by increasing association participation and involvement. But the same may be said for generational differences in other EU nations. Whether compositional changes over time will be sufficient to lift Romania from its bottom position is an open question. More readily answerable is why older Romanians participate in voluntary associations to such a low extent. It is to this topic that we now turn.

WHY IS VOLUNTARY ASSOCIATION PARTICIPATION SO LOW IN ROMANIA?

In Romania, there was no important volunteering culture before 1989, the year of the Romanian revolution (and not coincidentally, the fall of the Berlin Wall). Volunteering was seen by many scholars as an "imported" phenomenon, most often through Western NGOs. The so-called associative or voluntary labor was most often mandatory in the Communist period and closely controlled by the Communist party. These actions created the feeling that public space belonged wholly to the state, and only private space (one's residence) was a place where people had complete freedom for initiative and involvement. Because the Communist regime not only inhibited participation in civic organizations but even discredited the concept of voluntary work, some researchers were led to state that residence in an ex-Communist country has a negative impact on the level of volunteering (Voicu & Voicu, 2009) and that the lower level of volunteering was a characteristic of the Communist "bloc culture." However, other scholars note that the Communist past is unlikely to be an explanation for the rate differentials in volunteering between Romania and other EU countries, because there are now generations of Romanians born and raised in democracy and who have been shielded from the stigma of volunteer work as it was perceived during the Communist era (European Volunteer Centre, 2012).

Another impediment to voluntarism in Romania, correlated somehow with the Communist past of the country, is the weak legislative regulation of volunteering and the lack of coherent public policy initiatives. The first law on volunteering was passed late in 2001. Today, nearly two decades later, the legislative framework regulating volunteering still has not been clearly articulated. For example, there is no clear national definition of volunteering, there is no ethics code for volunteering, and competencies to be gained by volunteering have not been recognized (VOLUM, 2011). Also, volunteering does not appear to be a priority for the Romanian government: there is no minister or any institution responsible for regulating association participation, and no financial resources are allocated to promote and sustain such activities. If programs such as Youth in Action (a program running from 2007 to 2013, which aimed to inspire active citizenship, solidarity, and tolerance and to involve young people in shaping the future of the EU) and Erasmus (a successor program, started in 2014, which also emphasizes youth and nonformal learning) have had a significant impact in raising the interest of young people in volunteering, there are no programs having a similar impact for other age groups, especially for older adults. Moreover, the Volunteering Law 195/2001 refers explicitly and repeatedly to young volunteers, with other age groups being officially marginalized.

In addition, a study conducted by the Civil Society Development Foundation (CSDF, 2010) shows that "over half of the NGO leaders in Romania declare that they have enough volunteers who come to the organization by themselves; 3.3% state that they can't offer involvement opportunities for all who wish to volunteer" (CSDF, 2010, p. 88). These data suggest that public campaigns to increase exposure and recruit volunteers are largely nonexistent, that volunteers themselves seek opportunities to get involved, and that structural weaknesses limit organizations' capacity to absorb the existing volunteering demand.

We would suggest, therefore, that even fewer opportunities exist for older adults, and those that are available are primarily limited to activities in senior clubs, mainly in large cities, and to volunteering activities associated with churches. The poor volunteer infrastructure for older adults at the national level contributes to creating an informal local network for older volunteers, such as taking care of people who are ill, of grandchildren, and so on.

A final important aspect that must not be neglected when we examine the potential for voluntary association participation in Romania has to do with the socioeconomic and sociodemographic characteristics of the country. As the World Bank Active Aging in Romania Report (2014) shows, causal relationships do exist between volunteering and material well-being, education, residential environment, and health among age groups older than 45 years. Specifically, "... [f]inancial hardships, lower levels of education, and residence in rural areas have ... been cited as key impediments to social participation among older adults" (World

Bank, 2014, p. 15). Romania is a country where the older population lives dispro-portionately in rural environments, where access to medical services is limited, where pensions are distributed unequally, and where meeting day-to-day needs and accessing direct material benefits are more important than the intrinsic ben-efits brought by association participation. Further, the high rates of emigration among younger and middle-aged Romanians have created the phenomenon of "children of the grandparents," grandchildren left in their grandparents' care by parents working abroad. This diminishes free time available to older adults that might be used to participate in voluntary activities.

CONCLUSION

Given the very low rate of participation in voluntary associations throughout Romania, especially among elders, probably due in some measure but not entirely to its Communist past, the current contours of population aging do not bode well for reversing the national reluctance to volunteer. Nevertheless, since we now know of the many benefits—economic, emotional, and social—that volunteering can bring to those receiving help, to the volunteers themselves, and to the larger society, it is important that Romania and all countries without a strong ethic of voluntarism make the practice of volunteering a major national priority.

REFERENCES

Carr, D. (2018). Volunteering among older adults: Life course correlates and consequences. *Journal of Gerontology: Social Sciences, 73*, 479–481. doi:10.1093/geronb/gbx179

Civil Society Development Foundation. (2010). Sectorul neguvernamental: Profil, tendine, provocri [Non-governmental sector: Profile, trends, challenges]. Retrieved from http://www.fdsc.ro/library/conferinta vio 7 oct/Romania 2010_Sectorul neguvernamental1.pdf

Cutler, S. J. (2015). Population ageing and volunteering in Romania, *Social Work Review, 14*, 5–18.

Cutler, S. J., Hendricks, J., & O'Neill, G. (2011). Civic engagement. In R. Binstock & L. George (Eds.), *Handbook of aging and the social sciences* (7th ed., pp. 221–233). San Diego, CA: Academic Press.

European Volunteer Centre. (2012, September). Volunteering infrastructure in Europe. Retrieved from https://issuu.com/european_volunteer_centre/docs/volunteering-infrastructure-in-europe/98

Musick, M. A., & Wilson, J. (2008). *Volunteers: A social profile.* Bloomington, IN: Indiana University Press.

Stula, S. (2012). *Active ageing in Europe: Senior citizens and volunteering.* Retrieved from https://www.beobachtungsstelle-gesellschaftspolitik.de/file/?f=bd0bc87060.pdf&name=Expertentreffen_BEO_28.11._2011.pdf

Voicu, B., & Voicu, M. (2009) Volunteers and volunteering in Central and Eastern Europe. *Sociológia, 4*, 539–563.

VOLUM. (2011). Agenda public pentru voluntariat in România, 2012–2020 [Public agenda for volunteering in Romania, 2012–2020]. Retrieved from http://federatiavolum.ro/wp-content/uploads/2016/07/web_agenda_publica_pt_voluntariat_in_romania_A4_210x297_mm_VOLUM.pdf

World Bank. (2014). *Living long. staying active and strong: Promotion of active ageing in Romania.* Washington, DC: World Bank, Human Development Network, Europe and Central Asia Region.

DISASTER PREPAREDNESS FOR OLDER ADULTS

KATHRYN HYER | LINDSAY J. PETERSON

The fire began before sunrise in the rugged foothills of the Sierra Nevada mountains in Northern California, which an area firefighter later would describe as "a matchbox." The tall pines and broad vistas had attracted thousands of retirees to the nearby community of Paradise. That morning, many of them awoke to the sound of embers hitting their rooftops (Cornell, 2018). By the end of that day, 85 people were dead, more than 70 of whom were aged 60 or older.

Jessica Johnson, the administrator of Heritage Paradise nursing home, was driving her children to school at 7:30 that morning when she saw "a huge cloud of smoke" in the distance. The fire was two canyons away, but "just in case," she initiated her disaster plan to evacuate her 66 residents (Connole, 2019). She called to reserve beds for them in a nursing home in Chico, a town 20 miles away. She secured her evacuation transport, including vans with mechanical lifts for seven residents who needed special assistance. Meanwhile, her staff began to prepare the residents. Aides put a change of clothing and essential personal care items in large bags labeled with each resident's name. The nurses created individualized medical records with medication lists and the last time each medication was administered.

The evacuation order came at 8 a.m. The fire was moving quickly. Ms. Johnson decided to evacuate residents who could walk and sit upright in staff members' cars and trucks, which were loaded with equipment, medications, food, water, and the residents' personalized bags. In the gathering smoke, with the sound of helicopters overhead, Ms. Johnson ordered all remaining staff to leave while she and Sonya Meyer, a Heritage corporate executive, remained with the residents needing specialized vans.

Seven hours later, after an excruciatingly slow drive out of Paradise, all residents were safely settled in the Chico nursing home. Paradise had several nursing homes, and all of their residents survived the fire. It was the older adults living independently in the community who died that day. The contrast between the fates of those who lived in residential care and those in the community exemplifies both the progress and the gaps in efforts of the past two decades to protect older adults in disasters.

DISASTERS AND MOBILITY

The terms *emergency*, *disaster*, and *catastrophe* often are used interchangeably to describe a major event requiring planning and response. While, to experts, they signal differences in the scope and impact of the event, all require immediate action at a local level or beyond if the effects are extreme and/or widespread. In this short essay, we use the term *disasters* generically to refer to the broad range of unexpected threats. Disasters also differ by type. Wildfires, earthquakes, and tornadoes can strike with little advance warning. Other natural disasters, such as hurricanes, can be forecast days in advance; however, such forecasts are still subject to uncertainty, particularly concerning the precise location of a hurricane's landfall. A complex disaster is one in which one event follows another, as with the 2011 earthquake in Japan that triggered a tsunami that inundated the Fukushima nuclear power plant, releasing deadly radiation. What all disasters have in common is that they require people to respond quickly when alerted.

To Jessica Johnson, the defining feature of the fire that destroyed Paradise was its speed. Survival for her and her residents required racing against time as the fire advanced. However, all disasters require special preparations for those who are not mobile. This means that in all disasters, the risks are greater for older adults with mobility impairments or other impairments that affect their ability to react. Experience has shown this to be true. Despite representing 15% of the affected population of U.S. coastal areas bordering the Gulf of Mexico, more than 70% of those who died during Hurricane Katrina in 2004 were 60 or older. In Japan, older adults made up more than half of the fatalities from the earthquake and tsunami in 2011, nearly triple their proportion of the population in the affected areas. Disaster preparedness is a matter of urgency worldwide because at the same time that the population is aging, hazardous events are occurring with greater frequency (National Association of Insurance Commissioners, Center for Insurance Policy and Research, 2017).

COMPREHENSIVE PLANNING IN LONG-TERM CARE

Efforts to protect vulnerable older adults in the United States over the past 15 years have focused largely on nursing homes. That is because these facilities are federally regulated. In exchange for their ability to bill Medicare and Medicaid for services they provide to their residents, nursing homes must agree to comply with a broad set of quality-of-care and quality-of-life regulations. Following the Gulf Coast hurricanes of 2004–2008 (e.g., Hurricanes Charley, Katrina, and Ike), the U.S. Centers for Medicare & Medicaid Services established comprehensive new emergency preparedness rules. Widely discussed and publicized over the past several years, the rules were implemented in November 2017 (U.S. Department of Health and Human Services, 2017). They include the following components:

- *Risk assessment and emergency planning.* All facilities must perform a risk assessment that uses an "all hazards" approach prior to establishing an emergency plan. All-hazards planning encourages health care facilities to examine risks systematically for every category of disaster, from the most predictable natural disasters and severe weather events to other threats and potential hazards such as bioterrorism, chemical exposures, and pandemic outbreaks of disease. It requires a facility to plot its geographic proximity to chemical plants, power plants, rivers, and major highways or railroads that can carry toxic materials. An all-hazards approach focuses on capacities and capabilities that are critical to preparedness for a full spectrum of emergencies or disasters.

- *Policies and procedures.* Facilities must implement policies and procedures that assess their risks and support the successful execution of the emergency plan.

- *Communication plan.* Facilities must develop and maintain an emergency preparedness communication plan that complies with both federal and state laws. Patient care must be well coordinated with state and local public health departments and emergency management agencies and systems to protect patient health and safety in the event of a disaster.

- *Training and testing.* Facilities must develop and maintain an emergency preparedness training and testing program. They must offer annual emergency preparedness training so that staff can demonstrate knowledge of emergency procedures. The facility must also conduct drills and exercises to test the emergency plan to identify gaps and areas for improvement.

The new rules represent substantial progress in disaster planning for older adults. When we and our colleagues began studying nursing homes and disaster response after four hurricanes crisscrossed Florida in 2004, we learned that nursing homes knew little about community disaster planning. In a 2004 survey of Florida administrators after the storms, we learned that many administrators did not know their local emergency operations managers. Over the past 15 years, nursing-home administrators and staff have become far more familiar with the language and command structure used by the emergency management offices during emergencies. Administrators are also more likely to participate in their local community preparedness activities and let the responders know of the special needs of their residents when a disaster strikes. The new federal government rules reinforce the need for strong emergency plans that include mock drills to help staff become familiar with best practices.

THE DIFFICULT QUESTION OF EVACUATION

But an important issue—whether nursing-home residents should evacuate or shelter in place—remains a difficult question. The nursing homes in the area of Paradise, California, in the face of obvious and immediate threat to life by a rapidly advancing wildfire, evacuated and were praised for their lifesaving responses. However, our research following Hurricane Katrina revealed that evacuation has its own consequences. The initial research showed that nursing-home administrators wrestled with this decision. Many reported feeling "damned if we do, damned if we don't," citing pressure from emergency managers to leave their facilities despite the toll it would take on residents. They had experienced the stress of loading disabled, frail older adults onto buses not equipped for their needs, then having to travel, possibly for hours, to high school gymnasiums, often without adequate staffing and supplies. They noted that the health and function of many residents worsened in the aftermath (Blanchard & Dosa, 2009).

Our work in a U.S. National Institutes of Health sponsored study evaluated the effect of Hurricanes Katrina (2005), Rita (2005), Gustav (2008), and Ike (2008) on nursing-home residents in Texas, Louisiana, and Mississippi. We found that death rates and hospitalization increased for all nursing-home residents exposed to the hurricanes. We also examined whether facilities evacuated their residents or sheltered in place. The results showed that the very act of evacuation before the storm increased the probability of death within 90 days by 2.7% to 5.3% and increased the risk of hospitalization by 1.8% to 8.3%, independent of all other factors (Dosa et al., 2012).

Why is it potentially more dangerous to evacuate from a hurricane than to shelter in place? We do not have the answer, but experience and research over the past two decades has provided some insights and possible explanations:

1. Hurricanes often deviate from their expected paths after the decision to evacuate must be made. In general, safe evacuations must occur at least 48 to 72 hours before landfall. Unfortunately, hurricanes make last-minute turns and speed up or slow down. Hurricane Irma was expected to be a Category 4, making landfall near Miami, Florida. Many nursing homes evacuated west, only to be evacuated a second time as Irma's path moved westward and threatened the very areas where residents had been moved.

2. The evacuation of frail older adults is a logistical nightmare and requires exquisite planning. Even under the best-developed emergency plans, evacuations create anxiety for both residents and staff, which appears to have serious adverse outcomes. Safe transitions require optimal communication among providers, keen knowledge of the patients, and access to medical records, correct

medications, and appropriate supplies. In emergencies, transitions are seldom ideal, and we have shown the consequences of such forced moves in our hurricane research.

3. Electrical power and generators are essential for residents' safety and well-being. Hurricane Irma devastated Florida's electrical grid; high winds across the state created massive power outages. At the peak of the storm, 70% of the homes and businesses were without power. Without air conditioning, 14 nursing-home residents of the Rehabilitation Center at Hollywood Hills (located in Broward County, just north of Miami) died. The governor and legislature responded to the tragedy by requiring all Florida nursing homes and assisted living facilities to have backup power or generators and fuel for 96 hours of operation.

4. Older adults with dementia represent a particular hardship for evacuating facilities. Without the cognitive ability to follow directions or participate in their own self-care, residents with dementia suffer disproportionately during evacuation.

5. Such common comorbidities as congestive heart failure, chronic obstructive pulmonary disease, and various other cardiovascular diseases require clinicians' knowledge of the resident, careful observation, adequate temperature control (e.g., air conditioning), and adherence to specific medication regimes and dietary needs, as well as needed physical and occupational therapies. Medical record maintenance and medication adherence are critically important.

Permanent residents of nursing homes are an exceptionally vulnerable population. Their physical and cognitive impairments make it impossible for them to live independently. Vulnerable though they are, they do live within a system in which others are responsible for providing the support required to keep them safe in a disaster. More work is needed to understand the complexities of evacuating and sheltering in place; how to choose between those options, depending on the emergency; and how to enable administrators to make the best choice for their residents. Research is needed to track the morbidity and mortality of the nursing-home residents in Paradise to understand the possible consequences of their evacuation. However, their nursing-home caregivers did keep them safe on the day of the fire. This stands in contrast to the events surrounding Hurricane Katrina, in which 70 nursing-home residents died in the flooding that followed the hurricane strike. It suggests that progress has been made to keep the most vulnerable older adults safe in a disaster. Other older adults continue to be at risk, however, primarily those who are less impaired and able to live independently in the community. To some extent, this includes residents of assisted living communities, because in the United States they are regulated on the state level and not subject to the same federal regulations as nursing homes.

VULNERABILITY OF OLDER ADULTS IN THE COMMUNITY

The Los Angeles Times newspaper obtained the names and locations of more than half of the older adults who died in the fire that destroyed Paradise. The oldest was a 99-year-old woman who was found inside her home. An 85-year-old woman died inside a pickup truck less than a mile from her apartment. A 74-year-old man was found under a vehicle less than a quarter mile from his home. The details of their deaths and others illustrate the vulnerability of older adults living on their own when a disaster strikes.

The vast majority of older Americans (96%) live independently: that is, not in care institutions. Most are able to do so only because they receive outside help, much of which is provided informally by family or friends. A national survey found that 15% of adults older than 50 would not be able to evacuate their home without help. Another study found that despite the publication and distribution of preparedness guides, two thirds of adults 50 and older had no emergency plans, had not participated in any preparedness education programs, and did not know about available resources (Shih et al., 2018).

Older adults present problems during disasters because they are more likely to have multiple chronic conditions, declining hearing and vision, and physical and cognitive impairments that heighten their risks in a disaster. Many of the older people who died in the fire that destroyed Paradise were disabled or homebound. Those with poor vision or hearing may not have understood the evacuation calls. Once they did understand, the smoke, falling ash, and poor visibility may have hampered their response.

Older adults with cognitive impairment or Alzheimer's disease face special challenges during disasters. Some may not recognize or respond appropriately to the danger. For others, the chaos and confusion surrounding the disaster may overwhelm them and heighten their anxiety, agitation, or resistance to directions. This complicates the task for the caregivers responsible for their safety, placing both the caregiver and care recipient at risk.

Finally, financial resources often are limited for older adults living on their own, preventing them from stocking up on supplies needed to get them through an event that blocks electrical services and other vital social supports. Older adults without access to transportation are also at great risk in a rapidly advancing event like the Paradise fire.

Many of the disabled elders who survived the fire did so because others helped them before and/or during the event. Providing such assistance is mandatory for nursing homes and for some assisted living facilities, depending on their state regulations. Older adults living independently in the community, however, are mostly on their own in disasters, dependent on family, friends, neighbors, and community groups. Agencies such as the U.S. Centers for Disease Control and Prevention have long recognized this gap and have promoted further research and efforts to build disaster resilience in communities. HelpAge International, a private nonprofit London-based organization that supports services for older people in many countries, has advocated for building resilience in developing countries through planning that employs elders' disaster experience and knowledge. We agree, but also know that much more work is needed to gather that knowledge and coordinate it with the plans and efforts of direct care providers—both formal and informal—and other community organizations, local governments, and agencies, such as public health departments, to prevent tragic losses like those that occurred in Paradise.

REFERENCES

Blanchard, G., & Dosa, D. (2009). A comparison of the nursing home evacuation experiences between Hurricanes Katrina (2005) and Gustav (2008). *Journal of the American Medical Directors Association, 10*(9), 639–643. doi:10.1016/j.jamda.2009.06.010

Connole, P. (2019, November). A story of survival. *Provider Magazine*. Retrieved from http://www.providermagazine.com/archives/2019_Archives/Pages/0119/A-Story-of-Survival.aspx

Cornell, M. (2018, November 13). How catastrophic fires have raged through California. *National Geographic*. Retrieved from https://www.msn.com/en-ca/weather/topstories/how-catastrophic-fires-have-raged-through-california/ar-BBPEuYJ?li=BBnbcA1

Dosa, D., Hyer, K., Thomas, K., Swaminathan, S., Feng, Z., Brown, L., & Mor, V. (2012). To evacuate or shelter in place: Implications of universal hurricane evacuation policies on nursing home residents. *Journal of the American Medical Directors Association, 13*(2), 190.e1–190.e7. doi:10.1016/j.jamda.2011.07.011

National Association of Insurance Commissioners, Center for Insurance Policy and Research. (2017). Natural catastrophe response. Retrieved from https://www.naic.org/cipr_topics/topic_catastrophe.htm

Shih, R., Acosta, J., Chen, E., Carbone, E. G., Xenakis, L., Adamson, D. M., & Chandra, A. (2018). Improving disaster resilience among older adults: Insights from public health departments and aging-in-place efforts. *Rand Health Quarterly, 8*(1), 1–17. doi:10.7249/RR2313

U.S. Department of Health and Human Services. (2017, June 2). Appendix Z, Emergency preparedness final rule interpretive guidelines and survey procedures. Retrieved from https://www.cms.gov/Medicare/Provider-Enrollment-and-Certification/SurveyCertificationGenInfo/Downloads/Survey-and-Cert-Letter-17-29.pdf

INDEX